The Catholic Church Today: Western Europe. Matthew A. Fitzsimons.

A Search For Stability, United States Diplomacy Toward Nicaragua, 1925–1933. William Kamman.

Theory and Practice: History of a Concept from Aristotle to Marx. Nicholas Lobkowicz.

Marx and the Western World. Nicholas Lobkowicz, ed.

Italy After Fascism, A Political History, 1943–1965. Giuseppe Mammarella.

The USSR and the UN's Economic and Social Activities. Harold Karan Jacobson.

Chile and the United States: 1880–1962. Fredrick B. Pike.

The Volunteer Army and Allied Intervention in South Russia 1917–1921. George A. Brinkley.

Catholicism, Nationalism and Democracy in Argentina. John J. Kennedy.

The Russian Revolution and Religion, 1917–1925. Edited and translated by Bolesław Szcześniak.

Soviet Policy Toward the Baltic States, 1918–1940. Albert N. Tarulis.

Introduction to Modern Politics. Ferdinand Hermens.

Freedom and Reform in Latin America. Fredrick B. Pike, ed.

What America Stands For. Stephen D. Kertesz and M. A. Fitzsimons, eds.

Bolshevism: An Introduction to Soviet Communism. Waldemar Gurian.

INTERNATIONAL STUDIES OF THE
COMMITTEE ON INTERNATIONAL RELATIONS
UNIVERSITY OF NOTRE DAME

A Russian European: Paul Miliukov in Russian Politics. Thomas Riha.

Freedom and Authority in the West. George N. Shuster, ed.

Coexistence: Communism and Its Practice in Bologna, 1945–1965. Robert H. Evans.

Argentina's Foreign Policy 1930–1962. Alberto A. Conil Paz and Gustavo E. Ferrari.

Empire by Treaty: Britain and the Middle East in the Twentieth Century. M. A. Fitzsimons.

Peru and the United States: 1900–1962. James C. Carey.

East Central Europe and the World: Developments in the Post-Stalin Era. Stephen D. Kertesz, ed.

Soviet Policy Toward International Control and Atomic Energy. Joseph L. Nogee.

The Fate of East Central Europe. Stephen D. Kertesz, ed.

Christian Democracy in Western Europe, 1820–1953. Michael P. Fogarty.

German Protestants Face the Social Question. William O. Shanahan.

Soviet Imperialism: Its Origins and Tactics. Waldemar Gurian, ed.

The Foreign Policy of the British Labour Government, 1945–1951. M. A. Fitzsimons.

Diplomacy in a Whirlpool: Hungary between Nazi Germany and Soviet Russia. Stephen D. Kertesz.

Theoretical Aspects of International Relations. William T. R. Fox, ed.

Contemporary Catholicism in the United States

Contemporary Catholicism in the United States

Edited by PHILIP GLEASON

CONTRIBUTORS:

Jay J. Coakley · Edward Duff, S.J. · James Finn
Maureen L. Gleason · Philip Gleason · Robert Hassenger
Daniel J. Kane · Aidan Kavanagh, O.S.B. · Richard A. Lamanna
William A. Osborne · Louis J. Putz, C.S.C. · John B. Sheerin, C.S.P.
Thomas J. Stritch · John L. Thomas, S.J. · James J. Vanecko
Walter D. Wagoner · Martin H. Work

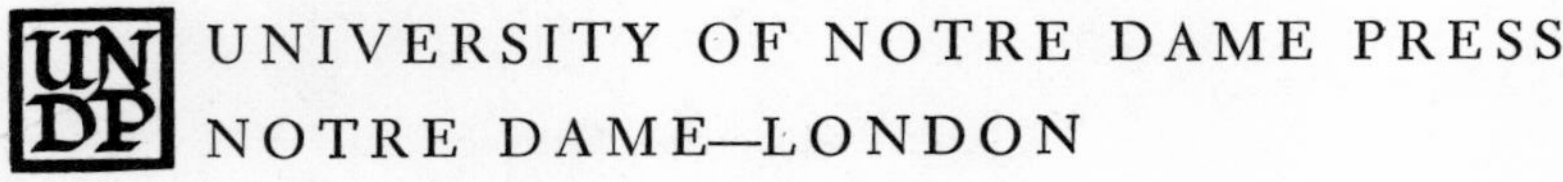
UNIVERSITY OF NOTRE DAME PRESS
NOTRE DAME—LONDON

Notre Dame, Indiana, 46556

Library of Congress Catalog Card Number: 68-58335
Manufactured in the United States of America

To Thomas T. McAvoy, C.S.C.,
Historian of American Catholicism

CONTENTS

INTRODUCTION

American Catholics are conscious today, more than ever before in the past, of belonging to a Pilgrim Church which is passing through a period of change. The fact of change is not new in American Catholicism; from the earliest days of our national life the Church has found itself in novel circumstances to which it has had to make adjustments. But in the past ten years the pace of change has accelerated so rapidly, and its scope has broadened to include so many facets of Catholic life, that the consciousness of change has been forced upon all the members of the Church.

The changes in the liturgy are the most obvious. Even the Catholic who reads nothing but the sports page of his daily paper knows that the Mass is different from what it used to be. He can also hardly avoid observing that the old attitudes of suspicion and hostility toward "outsiders" are in disfavor these days. From the mass media he learns of the more sensational aspects of the new American Catholicism—priests defying their bishops; theologians defying the pope; religious leaving their convents; nuns and seminarians picketing; Catholic coeds demanding the pill; Catholic universities "going secular," being torn by controversies over academic freedom, and so on and on. And the reader of Catholic publications is aware that these spectacular episodes are related to profound shifts in theological thinking, moral attitudes, and the institutional structure and operation of the American Church.

Reactions to these rapid and widespread changes are naturally varied. At one extreme are those who feel the changes have not gone nearly far enough or fast enough; at the other extreme, those who are alarmed or even outraged by what seems to them the abandoning of the faith. No doubt the largest group are those who have mixed feelings, who do not know quite what to think because they cannot form a clear and comprehensive picture of what is happening. This group is sometimes spoken of as being confused. Confusion may not be the most felicitous term to describe their state, but it is certain that the present situation of flux is bewildering and has created a need to review the salient features of the current scene, to identify the major forces at work, and to make a provisional assessment of the state of American Catholicism. The essays that make up this volume are intended to meet that need.

Taking one's bearings in the midst of change is always a problematical business. To attempt a description and evaluation of American Catholicism today may strike some readers as about as unpromising a venture as trying to draw a map of a landslide. The difficulties and limitations of such an effort are undeniable, and all the contributors here are aware of them. But there are also drawbacks to waiting until the dust has settled before looking around to see what has happened. Not the least of them is that the dust does not settle until the action is over. But it is while a process is still in motion that people most need to discover its direction and significance; for such processes in human affairs are shaped by the choices men make. There is, to be sure, a sort of inevitability about profound social changes affecting whole populations and large-scale institutions like the Catholic Church. But such changes are not wholly determined by impersonal "social factors"; they are also affected by what men think is happening, how they react to events, and how they try to influence the course of developments. The understanding men have of the movements in which they are involved, the attitudes they adopt, and the actions they take thus become factors in the outcome of these very movements. For that reason, it seemed worthwhile—even in the buzzing confusion of the present moment—to put together a book which has for its aims to provide some basic information about American Catholicism in transition and to offer interpretations of the causes and significance of the forces at work in the American Church today.

The book is not written from any predetermined or agreed-upon ideological stance *vis-à-vis* the phenomena under consideration. The contributors were chosen on the basis of their competence and their willingness to add another commitment to the obligations of their regular work. Each was asked to focus on contemporary movements in his particular area and to include historical background only to the degree necessary to set recent events in an appropriate perspective; the contemporary period was defined as the years since World War II. The amount of historical background presented in each chapter varies according to the judgment of the author, and so does the general thrust of each writer's assessment of the situation. All of the authors were provided with a skeletal outline of topics to be covered in the volume in an effort to reduce the probability of overlapping treatments. The reader will find, however, that certain events or movements are mentioned under more than one heading. This sort of repetition was not rigorously edited for two reasons. First, it is all but impossible to eliminate it entirely because the same events or movements impinge on more than one dimension of Catholic life and therefore deserve mention in different contexts. Second, the fact that certain subjects appear relevant to different authors serves to highlight their importance for the overall development of American Catholicism.

The chapters are grouped under three general headings according to whether they are broad interpretations of the situation (Part I), whether they focus primarily on Catholicism in interaction with its American environment (Part II), or whether they are principally concerned with one facet or another of the internal life of the American Church and American Catholics as a social group (Part III). I will not attempt to sum up the findings or conclusions of the book as a whole. The reader is left to form his own judgments on those points. However, I would like to draw attention to a few matters touched upon frequently in the book which may deserve further attention.

In the first place, the frequency with which the names of Pope John XXIII and John F. Kennedy recur would seem to confirm the interpretation of those who regard the appearance of "two men named John" as marking a watershed in American Catholic history. At the same time, however, a number of the authors (e.g., Gleason, Osborne, Thomas, Putz, Work and Kane) emphasize that the present ferment in American Catholicism is not traceable exclusively to the Second Vatican Council and cannot be understood as merely the impact in this country of the worldwide *aggiornamento* initiated by Pope John.[1] Dr. Wagoner speaks of a "self-sustaining chain reaction" set in motion by the accumulation of various forces and touched off, as it were, by the "cork popping" effect of the Council. According to this view, new ideas from the Council and European Catholic thinkers reinforced and ac-

[1] In his valuable brief review of "American Catholicism and the *Aggiornamento*" (*Review of Politics*, XXX [July, 1968], 275-91), Thomas T. McAvoy, C.S.C., notes the importance of Pope John and President Kennedy's election and concludes: "*Aggiornamento* has become a word to cover all changes but many of the changes in American Catholicism during the past few years were already in evidence before Pope John XXIII became pope."

celerated indigenous developments that had long been building up below the surface of American Catholicism. The confluence of these two lines of force produced the contemporary maelstrom of change.

If we accept this interpretation as a tentative way of ordering our understanding of the situation and our approach to analyzing it, two broad areas emerge as needing more detailed study—European influences and American influences. Even though American Catholicism is part of a worldwide religious body which has its center in Europe, it is difficult to think of works that systematically examine the channels of communication and influence which link the American Church to European sources of thought and activity. The influence of continental thought on the study of philosophy in American Catholic institutions is alluded to in Chapter 1; other writers touch on European influences in discussing spirituality, biblical studies, catechetics, theological trends, social action movements, and the proddings of Rome on the Negro question (Kavanagh, Putz, Work and Kane, and Lamanna and Coakley). These discussions, however, merely suggest the range of influence. The ties with the Catholic life of Europe are many and intimate, but perhaps American Catholics have become so accustomed to them as to be almost unconscious of their importance and even their existence. If we knew more about how these operated in the past, it might be easier to trace the impact of recent developments.

The important role of religious communities is noted by Kavanagh in discussing schools of spirituality and by Vanecko and Gleason in respect to education. These are hardly more than passing references, but they pinpoint another area badly in need of further study. Religious communities are really distinctive to Catholicism among American religious bodies. Historically they have played a vital part in the development of Catholic life in this country; it is impossible to suppose that they have not been shaped by contact with the American environment. Yet many of them have their roots in Europe and are among the most important institutional links between American and European Catholicism. At the present moment, religious communities are caught at the very center of the cross currents of change—in them intersect the controversies over authority, celibacy, and Christian witness in the modern world. Yet religious communities have been such familiar features of the American Catholic scene that we have neglected to study them—a failure which contributes to our perplexities today. Among other things, such study might give us something concrete to work with in clarifying the much-discussed notion of "community."

A subject that recurs regularly in the historical sections of various chapters is immigration. In Chapter 1, an analytical model derived from study of the assimilation of a Catholic ethnic group furnishes the theoretical perspective from which the examination of contemporary Catholicism is approached. This emphasis on immigration confirms a point many observers have made: that the development of American Catholicism has been profoundly shaped by the processes of immigration and acculturation. In this context, we will add only that in Catholic immigrant groups both European and American influences came together and interacted in ways still too little understood.

The American influences upon Catholicism in the United States are too diverse and complicated to enter upon here. Virtually all the essays deal with the subject either directly or indirectly. Several of them suggest—Lamanna and Coakley making the point explicitly—that Catholics have been influenced by the American environment to a far greater degree than they have influenced it. Without disputing this judgment, which seems both plausible in itself and warranted by the evidence, it might be worthwhile to note that the notion of "Catholic influence" on American society and culture suffers from a certain lack of definition. Catholicism has had a kind of "impact" on American society simply because Catholics are present as constituent elements of the population and the religious fabric of American life. Yet this is not what people ordinarily have in mind when they speak of Catholic influence, or the lack of it. Presumably, they mean a shaping influence on the values, goals, and purposes of the national community or on the attitudes adapted by the American people considered as a whole.

These are the spheres where Catholic influence would be most strategic; it would certainly be desirable to know more about whether there has been any, what it has been, or why there has been so little if that should prove to be the case. But before these questions can be explored fruitfully, it will be necessary to clarify what is meant by Catholic influence. What are the distinctive Catholic values, goals, purposes, or attitudes whose "influence" or "impact" on American life might be identified and measured? Here the problem is analogous to (but more difficult than) the one raised by those who ask: What is it that is distinctively Catholic about a Catholic college or university?

The cultural-influence problem is more difficult than the Catholic-university problem because in the latter instance we are dealing with a specific and well-defined social institution, whereas in the former we are concerned with the whole diffuse area of American social and cultural life.

Kindred difficulties arise even if we confine the discussion to the individual Catholics whose activities have some impact on the national consciousness. In the last few years, for example, several Catholics, or persons of Catholic background, have gained prominence on the American social and cultural scene. Besides the Kennedys, one might list Senator Eugene McCarthy, Michael Harrington, Daniel P. Moynihan, William F. Buckley, Jr., Father James E. Groppi, Marshall McLuhan, and Timothy Leary. Are the activities of all of these persons to be taken as constituting Catholic influence? What is it that is distinctively Catholic in each case? How could it be determined that these men would act differently if they were not Catholic or had not been exposed to Catholic teaching? If this is Catholic influence, what are the criteria for measuring its impact? And finally, what degree of consensus would there be—either among Catholics or among Americans generally—that this sort of Catholic influence is desirable?

No attempt can be made to answer these questions here. Neither are they dealt with directly in the chapters that follow. But they are suggested by reflection on the complexities of the interactions of Catholicism and the American environment. That subject is treated under a number of different headings and from different perspectives. It is the hope of the authors that the essays collected in this volume will contribute to the renewal of American Catholicism by helping all Americans understand better what is happening in the Church and how it is related to our national life.

Philip Gleason

Part I:
General Perspectives

1: THE CRISIS OF AMERICANIZATION

Philip Gleason

Transition is too mild a word for what is going on in the Catholic Church in the United States today. Every day we hear more and more of crises—the crisis in vocations, the crisis of authority, the crisis of faith, and of course the identity crisis. So great is the turbulence of change that hints of uneasiness escape even from those in the forefront of reform. The editor of a journal with the bold title, *Front Line*, remarked not long ago on the danger that the baby might be sent flying out with the bath water, and Michael Novak has pondered the question whether we are witnessing the renewal of Christianity or its slow abandonment. Those of less sanguine temperament might understandably be put in mind of Oliver Wendell Holmes' "wonderful one-hoss shay"; for in describing the vehicle that ran perfectly for a hundred years and then fell apart without warning, Holmes was commenting on the collapse of New England Calvinism a century ago.[1]

The dramatic shifts in American Catholicism can be analyzed from any number of perspectives, each yielding its own insights. To one who has worked in the history of Catholic immigration and learned something of the way immigrant institutions adjusted themselves to the American environment, it seems worthwhile to approach the subject in terms of assimilation or Americanization. This approach does not exhaust the possibilities and it may seem to slight the importance of influences from abroad. But if *aggiornamento* is fundamentally an effort to bring the Church into meaningful contact with the modern world, then for Catholics living in the United States it is surely the

[1] Edward J. Foye, " 'Adjournamento'?" *Front Line*, V (Fall, 1966), 94-96; Michael Novak, "Christianity: Renewed or Slowly Abandoned?" *Daedalus*, XCVI (Winter, 1967), 237-66. J. S. Mattson, "Oliver Wendell Holmes and 'The Deacon's Masterpiece': a Logical Story?" *New England Quarterly*, XLI (Mar., 1968), 104-14, disputes the conventional interpretation as a satire on Calvinism.

modern world in its American form that is of primary importance, and one of our most pressing needs is to understand the relationships between Catholicism and American society and culture.

The expression "crisis of Americanization" may be new, but it is common knowledge that the Church in the United States has been profoundly molded by the processes of immigration and acculturation. Over a decade ago, Will Herberg's *Protestant-Catholic-Jew* stressed the importance of immigration in understanding religious phenomena and underscored the complexity of their mutual interrelationships. More recently, Andrew M. Greeley organized his sociological investigation of American Catholic history around the theme of Americanization.[2] The very familiarity of the cliché, "emergence from the ghetto," bespeaks widespread popular recognition that some sort of assimilation has played a major role in reshaping American Catholicism in the past few years. But while everybody says that the Church has recently come out of its ghetto—or that it should do so without delay—it is not really very clear what it means to emerge from a ghetto. Our first task, therefore, is to try to put some substance into this expression by examining just how the processes of assimilation operated with immigrant groups. Having done this, we can apply the findings in an analysis of the transitions of American Catholicism.

THE AMERICANIZATION MODEL

The terms are often used rather loosely, but in general "assimilation" or "Americanization" are understood as designating the processes by which individuals and identifiable social groups shed the characteristics that mark them as foreign, adopt the cultural norms of American society, become fully integrated into American life, and come to think of themselves simply as Americans.[3] Assimilation, in other words, is a collective name for all the innumerable changes immigrants must make in order to get along in American society—changes in the way

[2] Will Herberg, *Protestant-Catholic-Jew* (rev. ed., New York, 1960); Andrew M. Greeley, *The Catholic Experience* (New York, 1967).

[3] The following discussion of Americanization is derived from my study of the German-American Catholics. See Philip Gleason, *The Conservative Reformers: German-American Catholics and the Social Order* (Notre Dame, Ind., 1968), esp. chaps. I and IX for theoretical discussion.

they act, talk, and think; changes in the pattern of their interaction with others; changes in the conceptions they have of themselves. These changes take place over a long period of time and relatively few persons who immigrate as adults become "fully Americanized." However, it is axiomatic with students of immigration that the American-born children and grandchildren of immigrants—the second and third generations—absorb American ways more completely and are therefore more fully assimilated.

The typical immigrant is not a solitary individual but a member of one or another ethnic, or nationality, group. These groups, made up of persons from the same homeland and sharing the same language and traditions, are held together by a common consciousness of kinship and are given formal structure by a network of institutions such as churches, schools, newspapers, and various kinds of voluntary associations. Assimilation may be thought of as operating on this group level as well as on the individual level. That is, the changes in habits, attitudes, and values among the individual immigrants—especially in the second and later generations—necessarily affect the group of which they constitute the membership and require corresponding adjustments in the institutions which hold the group together and give it form. Assimilation on the level of the organized group takes place more slowly than, and in response to, assimilation on the individual level, but once it has taken place it sets a sort of official seal on the degree of adjustment that has been made.

The "language question," a perennial issue among non-English-speaking groups, provides a good illustration of the relationship between assimilation on these two levels. As more individual immigrants adopt the English language, institutions of the group such as its press and organizations must gradually make room for English or they will eventually wither and die. The linguistic transition often arouses passionate resistance and bitter disagreement, especially between spokesmen for older and younger generations, but when it has been completed, the language shift constitutes an important reformulation of the modality of ethnic loyalty. If an organization of German immigrants, for example, adopts English in its meetings and printed records, the shift amounts to a kind of official group recognition of the legitimacy of a new way of "being German." What had formerly been thought of as essential to the identity and maintenance of the group—use of the mother tongue—is now designated as accidental. Spokesmen for the group then argue that the "German character" endures in spite of the language change and that those of German descent have an obligation to preserve it and to support the institutions created by earlier generations of immigrants.

Such an adjustment is absolutely indispensable because the institutions of the group are doomed to extinction if they do not keep pace with the Americanization of their clientele. But the need to keep pace with Americanization presents enormous difficulties both for discovering what adjustments are needed and for successfully effecting those deemed appropriate. For one thing, it becomes increasingly perplexing to identify the essence of the group's heritage, as language and other concrete attributes of its traditional culture disappear. If assimilation on the individual level proceeds to the point where persons of a certain national descent abandon all their distinctive cultural characteristics, mix indiscriminately with Americans of other backgrounds, and lose all their ethnic consciousness, they are obviously no longer set apart from others in American society by reason of their ethnic heritage. In other words, they are no longer a group of their own. And when the group has been dissipated in this fashion, the institutions which served it can no longer continue on the old basis. They must either go out of business or justify themselves on the basis of some entirely different rationale, making no claims for support in the name of the heritage they formerly embodied and symbolized.

This hypothetically ultimate stage of assimilation is seldom or perhaps never reached, for a lingering sense of ethnic identity is a very persistent phenomenon. A few ethnic organizations may be able to keep going long after the group seems to have disappeared if there remains a remnant of ethnically conscious persons to support them. But let us take the case of a group at an earlier stage in the process of Americanization—a group still clearly recognizable as such, but one whose membership is rapidly becoming assimilated. The institutions serving such a group confront a dilemma: They must accommodate to the changes in their clientele; yet in doing so they must avoid betraying their heritage, for the preservation of that heritage is the fundamental purpose of their existence and the surest ground of their appeal.

A group in these circumstances must tread a narrow and precarious path between the opposing perils of self-isolation and total absorption. Through its institutions, it must find a way of perserving an inherited distinctiveness in American society without rigidly clinging to the past, cutting itself off from society, and becoming irrelevant to the concerns of its more assimilated constituency. On the other hand, the effort to appeal to its more Americanized members by becoming more actively involved in the "mainstream" of society will be self-defeating unless the peculiar heritage and identity of the group is preserved in some new formulation.

The group cannot afford to remain in a ghetto, to use the popular metaphor, but it cannot afford to come out either if emergence from the ghetto will lead to its dispersal, absorption, and disappearance as a group. There is another currently popular expression which could also be legitimately applied to a group caught in this predicament. It is undergoing an identity crisis—a climactic turning point in its development that requires it to resolve the contradiction of being different from what it was in the past, and yet the same. The fact that both of these expressions have become commonplace in the discussion of contemporary American Catholicism suggests that there is a fundamental analogy between what is going on in the Church and the general processes of immigrant assimilation. There are, of course, important differences between the Church and what we usually think of as an ethnic group. It is also true that the foregoing sketch is quite schematic and overlooks a multitude of factors that have conditioned the development of the various ethnic groups in the United States. But treating assimilation in this abstract fashion highlights some of the crucial features of the process and throws the central dilemma it posed for immigrant groups into sharp relief. This brief review, therefore, furnishes a "model" of the process of Americanization which can be fruitfully applied to an analysis of the present ferment in American Catholicism.

ASSIMILATION ON THE INDIVIDUAL LEVEL

In applying the model, let us begin by surveying some recent developments within the American Catholic population. Our interest here is in assimilation on the individual level. What changes have occurred in the life patterns of Catholics that tend to make them less distinctive as Catholics and more like other Americans, in the same way that analogous changes among the members of an immigrant group tended to assimilate them more fully into the national life?

One such change, directly related to immigrant assimilation, is that the Catholic population can no longer be thought of as a foreign population. It would be easy to overestimate the degree of change in this sphere; there are probably more Catholics than we suppose who continue to think of themselves as Irish, Italian, Polish, German, and so on. In the case of Spanish-speaking Catholics, ethnicity is still a major constitutive element in their individual and group identity. Despite the persistence of ethnic consciousness in more or less diluted form, the Catholic population considered as a whole is no longer made up of national "hyphenates"—people whose perception of themselves as Americans was qualified by the awareness that they belonged to distinctive national minorities.

The relationship between ethnicity and religion is complex. Will Herberg argued in the 1950's that religion had become a sort of residual legatee of ethnic feeling, with third- and fourth-generation immigrants identifying themselves more actively with Catholicism or Judaism as a means of retaining a link with their ethnic past. Herberg also emphasized, however, that Catholicism and Judaism now stand alongside Protestantism as equally legitimate forms of American religion.[4] And since their Church is considered one of the "three great faiths" of a society in which religion functions as a chief mode of social identification, Catholics are not set apart by their religion as "outsiders" in the same degree they were in the past.

As their fellow citizens have grown more disposed to regard Catholicism as an acceptably American form of religious expression, many Catholics—especially the best educated and most forward-looking—have become increasingly critical of the strictly ethnic loyalties still cherished in some sectors of the Catholic population. Ethnic cohesiveness and group feeling among Catholics has been associated with resistance to racial integration in cities like Chicago and Milwaukee and has been prominently featured in the press, adding to the conviction on the part of liberal Catholics that the Church must cut itself free from these vestiges of the immigrant past. Recently, Catholics of east-European origin received unfavorable publicity as obstructing open housing, but there were many earlier episodes of conflict between Irish and Negroes, and Irish Catholics are sometimes spoken of as particularly susceptible to racial prejudice.

Before the issue of racial integration drew attention to the unap-

[4] Herberg.

pealing forms that group loyalty could assume among Catholics of other derivations, the Irish were the chief targets for criticism by liberal spokesmen.[5] As Catholic self-criticism mounted in the 1950's, they were blamed for most things critics found objectionable in the American Church—sexual puritanism, separatist tendencies, authoritarianism, anti-intellectualism, liturgical backwardness, and general conservatism. Since they were the most numerous and influential element, the Irish do bear a heavy responsibility for the weaknesses as well as the strengths of American Catholicism, and there can be little doubt that much of the criticism was justified. But it is hardly probable that the negative effects of Irish influence were greater in the mid-twentieth century than at any earlier time. Why then did the critique gain momentum only in the 1950's and 1960's, and why did it sometimes assume a stridency that threatened to make anti-Irishism the anti-Semitism of liberal American Catholics? The explanation would seem to be twofold. First, the criticism underscored the inadequacies of immigrant Catholicism and the need to bring the Church up to date in American society. Second, by singling out the immigrant group with which the Church is most closely identified in the popular mind, the critics—particularly those with Irish names—dramatized their own liberation from the immigrant past and implicitly proclaimed their own Americanization.

Another aspect of the assimilation process closely related to the waning of ethnic loyalties among Catholics is their attainment of social and economic parity with American Protestants. From the onset of mass immigration before the Civil War until the middle of the present century, Catholics were predominantly a low-status, working-class population. Immigrants from Catholic lands in Europe were mostly of peasant background; having little money and lacking the skills suitable to an urbanized industrial society, they came in at the bottom and moved up the status ladder relatively slowly. By 1900 Irish and German Catholics of the "old immigration" were beginning to move into higher status occupations, but the continuation of peasant immigration from southern and eastern Europe through the middle 1920's brought in heavy reinforcements for the working-class Catholic population. The Depression hampered upward mobility in the next decade, but the post-

[5] Criticism of the Irish is reviewed critically in "The Myth of the Irish: A Failure of American Catholic Scholarship," *Herder Correspondence*, III (Nov., 1966), 323-27.

World War II era of prosperity coincided with the maturation of American-born generations even among the more recent Italian and Slavic immigrant groups, and the last quarter-century has witnessed a remarkable improvement in the socioeconomic status of American Catholics.

This notable upgrading of the social status of Catholics has come about so rapidly since World War II that social scientists have only recently become aware of it and its extent. As late as 1955, John J. Kane, a respected Catholic sociologist, concluded on the basis of data published in the late forties and early fifties that "Catholics creep forward rather than stride forward in American society, and the position of American Catholics in the mid-twentieth century is better, but not so much better than it was a century ago."[6] Twelve years later, however, the authors of an article reviewing eighteen national surveys taken between 1943 and 1965 arrived at strikingly different conclusions. Their research corroborates the popular impression that in 1945 "Protestants in the United States ranked well above Catholics in income, occupation and education." But since then, "Catholics have gained dramatically and have surpassed Protestants [but not Jews] in most aspects of status. A lingering critical difference is in the percentages who have been to college. However, this may be only a residue of lower parental status, and even this difference seems to have disappeared among the youngest adults."[7] Greeley and Rossi's *Education of Catholic Americans* confirms these findings and shows that the status edge of Catholics over Protestants still holds when controls are introduced to prevent the Protestant sample from being skewed by including disproportionate numbers of Negroes or country dwellers.[8]

Just as in the case of immigrant groups, the processes operating to make Catholics more like other Americans—more assimilated—are keyed to generational transition as well as to shifts in the economic and educational structure of society. Hence, Catholics born since about 1930 tend to be the most Americanized in their outlook. Those born

[6] John J. Kane, "The Social Structure of American Catholics," *American Catholic Sociological Review*, XVI (Mar., 1955), 23-30.

[7] Norval D. Glenn and Ruth Hyland, "Religious Preference and Worldly Success: Some Evidence from National Surveys," *American Sociological Review*, XXXII (Feb., 1967), 73-85.

[8] Andrew M. Greeley and Peter H. Rossi, *The Education of Catholic Americans* (Chicago, 1966), pp. 28-29.

shortly before then went through the great common experience of World War II alongside Americans of other religious backgrounds, and have taken their places in middle-class occupations more or less indiscriminately with their fellow citizens. The postwar boom of higher education also provided a common experience in which younger Catholics shared much more fully than earlier generations. The influence of the automobile and the mass media in bringing all segments of the population together and furnishing a common fund of experience has likewise tended to make younger Catholics more like other Americans. The generation now entering society as young adults hardly even remembers the period of "Protestant-Catholic tensions" in the early 1950's[9]—to say nothing of the Ku Klux Klan of Al Smith days—but it does remember that John F. Kennedy was a Catholic who became President of the United States. Hence, these young people have little reason to think of themselves as a minority threatened by the society around them, but good reason to believe that they are pretty much the same kind of Americans as everyone else. It is not surprising that they sometimes seem to wonder why older Catholics thought otherwise, that they question the need for separate Catholic schools or societies, or that they ask why Catholics should have different views from other men of good will on such matters as divorce or abortion.

ASSIMILATION ON THE GROUP LEVEL

Changes in the attitudes and beliefs of the more assimilated younger Catholics are bringing about changes in Catholic institutions just as immigrant organizations had to modify their original structures and programs to keep pace with the Americanization of their clientele. Recent developments among Catholic professional associations provide perhaps the clearest illustration of this sort of Americanization at the group level.

Catholic professional associations have performed a function closely analogous to that of ethnic societies. Voluntary associations of immigrants came into being because people sharing a common background and common values saw that they could not fit comfortably into organizations already existing in American society. These ethnic organ-

[9] Cf. John J. Kane, *Catholic-Protestant Conflicts in America* (Chicago, 1955).

izations not only served as congenial settings for sociability and as agencies of mutual support; they also made it possible for those who had a sense of their "peoplehood" (to use Milton M. Gordon's term)[10] to take part as an organized group in the life of the local and national community. Ethnic associations therefore functioned both as institutional symbols of the immigrants' consciousness of their peculiar heritage and character and as organizational vehicles for their participation in American life. But as assimilation eroded the distinctive consciousness of the immigrants and permitted them to mix more freely in the larger society, ethnic organizations were hard put to keep going because the needs that brought them into being were no longer operative.

The case with Catholic professional associations is very similar. They are a new form of Catholic organizational activity. The oldest one of any importance, the National Catholic Educational Association, dates back only to 1904, and an offshoot in the same general area, the National Catholic Guidance Conference, was organized as recently as 1962.[11] Catholic professional associations are clearly a result of the professionalization of nearly all spheres of activity in a highly complex, urban industrial society. Those who set up these organizations were no doubt the first generation of Catholics to be involved in these various spheres of activity after they became professionalized in American society at large. Metaphorically, the founders were the first Catholic "immigrants" to these professional worlds. The organizations they created correspond to ethnic societies in at least three aspects. First, they were designed to improve the performance of activities carried on by, and in the service of, a specific social group. Second, this social group was set apart from other Americans by reason of its heritage, which was regarded as affecting the mode of the group's thinking, the position it should take, and the approach it should follow in whatever professional field was involved. Finally, the associations themselves served as vehicles for Catholics to participate in professional activities and com-

[10] Milton M. Gordon, *Assimilation in American Life* (New York, 1964), pp. 23-24.

[11] Some other professional societies and their dates of founding are: National Conference of Catholic Charities (1910); Catholic Press Association (1911); Catholic Hospital Association (1915); Catholic Historical Association (1919); Catholic Philosophical Association (1926); Catholic Physicians Guild (1927); Catholic Economic Association (1941); Catholic Psychological Association (1946).

municate with others in the field on an organized basis, especially through the publication of a professional journal.

If Catholic professional associations perform functions analogous to those of immigrant societies, the question arises: Will they face the same problems as their membership becomes more Americanized? The answer is that some already have, and others seem to be nearing that stage. There has been criticism for some time of such Catholic "ghetto" societies. The remark of a recent Fordham graduate that he remembers "laughing and crying at the same time" when he first heard of "an outfit called the Catholic Poetry Society of America" is typical of the attitude of Catholic liberals.[12] But it is even more significant that members of these professional organizations are themselves asking whether there is any justification for their perpetuation. Thus the *Linacre Quarterly* recently carried an article entitled, "The Catholic Physician's Guild—Do We Really Need One?" A writer in the *Catholic Library World* for April, 1967, felt constrained to offer a vigorous defense for the existence of the Catholic Library Association. And only five years after the American Catholic Psychological Association began to publish a professional journal it printed an article calling upon the society to go out of business because it "represents a divisive, sectarian, ghetto mentality on the American scene."[13]

Skepticism about the desirability of such societies has been heightened by the postconciliar winds of change, but the example of the identity crisis among Catholic sociologists indicates that the roots of the phenomenon are to be sought in processes indigenous to the American scene. It also furnishes some particularly apt comparisons with the experience of ethnic societies.

The study of sociology in Catholic institutions emerged from a matrix of concern over social problems and reform, and the earliest ventures into the field were by persons primarily interested in social work, social ethics, or moral theology.[14] The prehistory of sociology in

[12] Letter to the editor, *America*, CXVII (Aug. 12, 1967), 141.

[13] *Linacre Quarterly*, XXXIII (Nov., 1966), 332-33; Alphonse F. Trezza, "Like God, CLA is Dead," *Catholic Library World*, XXXVIII (Apr., 1967), 511-13; Daniel C. O'Connell and Linda Onuska, "A Challenge to Catholic Psychology," *Catholic Psychological Record*, V (Spring, 1967), 29-34.

[14] The following discussion draws heavily upon David W. McMorrow, "The Development of Sociology as an Academic Discipline in Catholic Colleges; a Study of the American Catholic Sociological Society," an unpublished senior thesis done for the Department of History, University of Notre Dame, 1967.

non-Catholic universities was generally similar, but it established itself as an autonomous discipline around the turn of the century. Those who founded the American Catholic Sociological Society in 1938 belonged to the first generation of Catholic workers in the field who understood sociology as a subject distinct in itself, separate from philosophy or theology, which had its own proper object and methodology.

But while the first generation of professional Catholic sociologists regarded their discipline as a science, they held that it was "not in the full sense of the word an exact science"[15] because the values espoused by the investigator—his ideological stance or philosophy of life—inevitably colored his approach and the inferences he drew from his data. Sociology as it was carried on by non-Catholics was not fully acceptable because, although it claimed to be clinically neutral and to exclude considerations of value, it was really based on naturalistic assumptions that were viewed as being an integral part of the scientific method itself. In these circumstances Catholic sociologists felt that their position was denied a hearing in the existing professional organizations. They believed that by establishing their own society they could not only work more effectively to improve the teaching of sociology in Catholic schools, but could also provide a forum in which sociological investigations carried on within the framework of Catholic beliefs and values might be brought before the public.

The American Catholic Sociological Society thus began its career thirty years ago with the explicit determination to erect a "Catholic sociology" combining scientific methodology with the value system derived from religion. By the 1950's, however, there was growing dissatisfaction with this approach among the society's members. There was demand for greater scholarly competence—in keeping with the prevailing self-criticism of Catholic intellectual life in those years—and there was also some complaint about the unprofessional management and familial type of control exercised by the group's leaders. Two other factors are of special interest here which illustrate the trends of assimilation and social acceptance at work generally by mid-century. First, more young Catholics entered the society who had been trained in the leading secular graduate schools or in Catholic universities where

[15] Raymond W. Murray, C.S.C., *Introductory Sociology* (New York, 1946), p. 34. Murray is here quoting Ralph A. Gallagher, S.J., the principal founder of the Catholic Sociological Society.

sociology had become a fairly autonomous discipline, pursued in up-to-date fashion. These men had absorbed the viewpoint and approach characteristic of their specialty, and they chafed at what they considered the narrow and self-isolating stance of the organization. Second, the younger men could point out that sociology was no longer dominated by the uncritical acceptance of naturalistic assumptions. There was increasingly wide recognition of the important role played by values in sociological investigation; hence Catholics were not automatically barred from gaining recognition in the profession simply because they operated within a religiously derived value system. Moreover, it was sometimes asserted, the values of Catholics did not differ importantly from those of other scholars in their implications for sociological study. For these reasons, the dissidents felt that a Catholic sociological society on the old basis was no longer justified, and they rejected the notion that there could be such a thing as "Catholic sociology." Rather, sociology had to be pursued as a fully autonomous discipline, with each scholar applying normative criteria worked out from a personal synthesis of his own fundamental philosophical or religious beliefs and his professional knowledge.

By 1961, discontent arising from these sources led to the replacement of Executive Secretary Ralph Gallagher, S.J., who had been the principal founder of the organization and a leading exponent of "Catholic sociology." Those who championed a more autonomous professional approach were then free to reshape the Catholic Sociological Society in keeping with their views. Although some felt it should disband, what actually occurred was a reorientation of its activity and goals. At a meeting in 1963, the members voted to change the name of their organ from *American Catholic Sociological Review* to *Sociological Analysis* and to make it a journal specializing in the sociology of religion. An introductory statement in the first issue of the rechristened journal indicated that the change was the evolutionary result of two developments. First, the realization that Catholic sociologists found their proper professional lodgment in organizations differentiated according to their specialized interests rather than in a society organized on the basis of religion alone. Second, the recognition that the sociology of religion was an area of common concern to many members of the society and thus offered the most satisfactory rationale for its existence as a scholarly association. The name *Sociological Analysis* was chosen to avoid giving the impression that it was "a parochial journal" or one whose pages would present "a distinctly 'Catholic sociology.' "[16]

Catholic sociologists naturally have a sophisticated awareness of the identity crisis through which their organization is passing. It is quite possible that the forces unleashed by the Council will carry the transformation of the society even further, but it should be emphasized that the identity crisis itself took place earlier than, and independent of, Vatican II. So far, the society has weathered the crisis fairly well. By making the study of the sociology of religion its *raison d'être*, it has formulated a new identity which incorporates meaningful links with the past while at the same time justifying its existence on strictly professional grounds. This evolution in the American Catholic Sociological Society is strikingly similar to the experience of certain ethnic societies. It was brought on by the assimilation of the society's individual members in the surrounding American milieu (in this case, the milieu of academic sociology in the United States), and by their gradual loss of the conviction that their heritage entailed an intellectual standpoint different from that of those outside the group. These internal changes, combined with declining external hostility, required the society to find a new rationale—one that maintains some continuity with the organization's distinctive heritage, but at the same time appeals to the interests of its more assimilated members.

This thumbnail history reveals that Americanization involves a basic intellectual reorientation as well as social and institutional shifts. The same fact is demonstrated even more clearly in the case of the American Catholic Philosophical Association. The identity crisis of the philosophers is not as far advanced as that of the sociologists, and it has been more strongly influenced by the general reorientation of Catholic thinking brought on by the Council. Moreover, the teaching of philosophy in Catholic institutions has always been, and continues to be, more intimately related to European currents of thought than is the case with other academic disciplines. (Twenty-five per cent of the Ph.D.'s teaching philosophy in Catholic colleges earned their degrees in Europe, as compared to less than 10 per cent of those teaching in other American schools.) Yet the Catholic philosophers are moving appreciably closer to their counterparts in secular universities in the pluralism that is gaining ground among them. And the existence of an

16 *Sociological Analysis*, XXV (Spring, 1964), 1.

identity crisis is confirmed by the title of the presidential address delivered before their society in 1967: "Who Are We?"

In this address,[17] which is a gem of sympathetic yet incisive criticism, Ernan McMullin points out that the founders of the Catholic Philosophical Association in the 1920's had unbounded confidence that Thomism, the "official philosophy" of the Catholic Church, furnished a solution to problems in every sphere of thought and provided "a corrective to the anarchy and confusion prevailing in the modern intellectual world." That audacious optimism has since been shattered, resulting in what McMullin calls a "massive failure of confidence" on the part of many Catholic philosophers. Although it was a tragic mistake to impose a "philosophy by decree," McMullin argues that because of the special place of the subject in their colleges Catholics still "have a unique opportunity to make philosophy a living and important part of a college curriculum, an opportunity which scarcely exists in any other part of the academic world today."

In looking toward a new rationale for the Catholic Philosophical Association, McMullin makes two points especially pertinent to our interests. First, he notes that in formulating new goals and strategies, Catholic philosophers must keep in mind the characteristics of their "constituency"—the American undergraduate, whose resistance to having a ready-made philosophical system forced upon him is one of the main elements in "the rapid change now going on in the philosophy curriculum of Catholic colleges." Second, McMullin suggests that the goals of the organization might better be attained if Catholics were "to seek allies . . . among other philosophers who are concerned with the implications and demands that Christian faith lays upon the reflective believer in every age." In the future, the Catholic Philosophical Association may well designate itself by the "perhaps philosophically more relevant title, 'Christian.' "

Ideological shifts and redefinitions in self-conception like those traced in these two professional associations may be discerned almost everywhere on the American Catholic scene. Just as the American-born descendants of immigrants tended to depart from traditional patterns and take their ideas and values from their social milieu, Catholics

[17] Ernan McMullin, "Presidential Address; Who Are We?" in *Proceedings of the American Catholic Philosophical Association* (Washington, 1967), pp. 1-16. The quotations in the following paragraphs are taken from this source, as is the information given above about the percentages of doctorates earned in Europe.

today are orienting themselves to new reference groups and taking their values from new sources. This sort of Americanization may take puzzling or paradoxical turns—as when Catholics adopt the current anti-Americanism of the Left—but basically it reflects the acceptance by Catholics of the norms of whatever segment of American society they feel closest to by reason of social and educational background, status aspiration, political preference, or ideological persuasion. The editors of *Commonweal*, for example, were disturbed that non-Catholics whom they respected criticized the magazine's stand on abortion.[18] One of them, Daniel Callahan, had earlier made the point, in connection with the theme of honesty, that as soon as an idea gains currency among Protestants it is very shortly taken up by Catholics. The hidden spring of new currents of thought among both Protestants and Catholics, according to Callahan, is "the contemporary world," which is reshaping the consciousness of modern man.[19]

Although the influence of the world upon the Church is anything but new, the effects of that influence are perhaps more far reaching and deeper now than at any earlier moment in the history of American Catholicism. Institutions that seemed immune to change—such as religious communities—feel the shock waves, and a general crisis of identity leaves Catholics wondering who they are, what makes them what they are, and which way they are going. An examination of the controversy over Catholic intellectual life offers one way of approaching the contemporary crisis of confidence.

THE COURSE OF THE CATHOLIC INTELLECTUALISM DEBATE

It is quite obvious that the Catholic-intellectualism discussion runs parallel to, and was no doubt influenced by, the same sort of discussion

[18] "Abortion and Dialogue," *Commonweal*, LXXXV (Mar. 17, 1967), 667-68. The letter on abortion in the same issue from John S. Holland is also revealing. Among other things, Mr. Holland writes: "If we stick on the unrationalized premise that every foetus has an inalienable right to be born, *the rest of the world will pass us by*" (italics added).

[19] Daniel Callahan, "The Quest for Honesty" *Commonweal*, LXXX (Apr. 24, 1964), 137; and Callahan, *Honesty in the Church* (New York, 1965), pp. 20-21. See also Callahan's discussion, "Theological Stew," *The Critic*, XXVI (June-July, 1968), 10-17.

in American society at large. The evils of anti-intellectualism and "mass culture" were staples of highbrow journalism in the 1950's when the Catholic controversy got under way in earnest. Now that the center of interest has shifted to issues of higher education, there is again a close correlation between the special Catholic concern and the prevailing American preoccupation with the problems of the multiversity, student unrest, the dissenting academy, and so on. But while it was only a subspecies of the larger phenomenon, the intellectualism controversy had a special significance for Catholics and may be understood as the first major phase of the transformation of American Catholicism that is still in progress.

The beginning of the great debate may be dated from the fall of 1955, when John Tracy Ellis' "American Catholics and the Intellectual Life" was published in *Thought*.[20] This thirty-seven page essay, which was reprinted in book form the following year, provoked a greater reaction than any other piece of comparable length in the history of American Catholicism. A collection of readings—*American Catholicism and the Intellectual Ideal*, compiled by Frank L. Christ and Gerard E. Sherry[21]—contains excerpts from forty-six books and articles appearing between 1955 and 1958. But while Ellis' article provided the spark for the explosion of critical writing, Catholics were far from unconcerned before 1955. Christ and Sherry's collection contains treatments of the subject that go back a century; more than two-thirds of their selections appeared before the publication of Ellis' essay. It was only in the 1950's, however, that assimilation had brought the Catholic community to the point where its intellectual status and prestige was a matter of sufficiently wide interest to become the central issue in American Catholic life. A problem that previously seemed pressing to only a minority now occupied the attention of all thinking Catholics.

The controversy eventually took a turn that really was new, but it also included several themes that had already become standard. Three of these—the leadership theme, the prestige theme, and the missionary theme (to give them names)—share the basically apologetical orientation that had dominated earlier discussions. Although writers who stressed these themes no doubt appreciated the intrinsic value of

20 *Thought*, XXX (Autumn, 1955), 351-88.
21 (New York, 1961).

intellectual activity, they focused principally on the role of intellectual work and achievement in advancing the mission and standing of the Church. In emphasizing the instrumental values of education, scholarship, and intellectual accomplishments, these Catholic writers were adopting the same position taken by spokesmen for immigrant groups. For these groups also realized they needed an elite who could provide leadership, and they developed schools, colleges, and various types of scholarship programs to help produce such an elite.[22]

One early example of the leadership theme was quoted by Msgr. Ellis: the plea of Archbishop John Ireland that Catholics strive to become leaders in intellectual circles.[23] Carlton Hayes agreed that "a large and vigorous intellectual class" was needed before Catholics could "influence profoundly the life and thought of America"; the statement of the American hierarchy in 1948 confirmed the point that "our institutions of higher learning are the natural training grounds for Christian leadership"; John J. Cavanaugh's widely quoted question of 1957—"Where are the Catholic Salks, Oppenheimers, Einsteins?"—was taken from an address entitled "American Catholics and Leadership" and illustrates the persistence of the theme in the post-Ellis controversy.[24]

The absence of Catholic leaders was often associated with the question of Catholic prestige—or rather, the lack of it. Ellis opened the main body of his essay with Denis Brogan's remark that "in no Western society is the intellectual prestige of Catholicism lower" than in the United States. The remainder of the essay was devoted to explaining how this situation had come about. Earlier writers had linked the need for scholars with the fact that the Church was "sadly lacking her share of top-ranking names in literature, the arts, and especially in science." A *Commonweal* author said in 1945, "Scientific research on the part of Catholics is the *sine qua non* for the attainment of Catholic status in this highly significant field of human endeavor." And one of the contributions to John A. O'Brien's 1938 volume, *Catholics and*

[22] The interest of immigrant groups in creating leadership elites is discussed in Philip Gleason, "Immigration and American Catholic Intellectual Life," *Review of Politics*, XXVI (Apr., 1964), 161-62.

[23] Christ and Sherry, *American Catholicism and the Intellectual Ideal*, pp. 260-61. Christ and Sherry reprint the main body of Ellis' article, and for the sake of convenience citations will be to their volume.

[24] Christ and Sherry, pp. 73, 140, 227-28.

Scholarship, was unabashedly entitled, "Enhancing Catholic Prestige."[25] Nowhere was the apologetical intent more frankly avowed than in Archbishop John T. McNicholas' preface to this volume. He wrote:

> Catholic Apologetics in our country at the present moment has two aims: first, to show that there is no conflict between science and religion, that Truth is one, and that the Church, . . . welcomes truth in whatever field of research it is found; second, to correct the false judgment which reputed scholars and their prejudiced followers have passed upon Catholicism because of their failure to view culture, philosophy, and science in true perspective.[26]

Implicit in the second aim listed by McNicholas is the belief that there is a Catholic perspective on "culture, philosophy, and science" which secular scholars lack, but which is necessary for the fullness of knowledge and the integrity of truth. This assumption coincides with what I have called the missionary theme. Treatments stressing this theme are usually without the pragmatically apologetical tone of those emphasizing leadership and prestige, but they relate learning to the Church's redemptive mission. Christopher Dawson, for example, whose ideas were discussed with some excitement in the 1950's and made the basis for curricular experiments, argues that the study of Christian culture is not something that benefits only Catholics but something that could serve to unify intellectual discourse in the Western world.[27] Other writers, such as Leo R. Ward, C.S.C., and Justus George Lawler, stress that, while learning is worthwhile in itself and must be sought for its own sake, possession of the Catholic faith provides an added dimension without which the scholar is unable to encompass the full depth and breadth of reality.[28] According to this view, Christian learning or Catholic scholarship is needed to bring adequacy of understanding to the community of intellect. John Courtney Murray, S.J., one of the most eminent spokesmen for this position,

25 Christ and Sherry, pp. 255, 135, 130, 118.

26 John A. O'Brien, ed., *Catholics and Scholarship* (Huntington, Ind. [1938]), Preface.

27 Christopher Dawson, *The Crisis of Western Education* (New York, 1961).

28 Leo R. Ward, *Blueprint for a Catholic University* (St. Louis, 1949); Ward, "Is There a Christian Learning?" *Commonweal*, LVIII (Sept. 25, 1953), 605-07; Justus George Lawler, *The Catholic Dimension in Higher Education* (Westminster, Md., 1959).

put it rather strongly in saying that the role of the Catholic university is "to be the point of departure for a missionary effort out into the thickening secularist intellectual and spiritual milieu."[29] There is a suggestion of the same theme in the closing exhortation of Ellis' article, which takes note of the reawakened national interest in religious and moral values and calls upon Catholics to seize the "unique opportunity" to bring before the intellectual community the riches of "the oldest, wisest, and most sublime tradition of learning that the world has ever known."[30]

The traditional leadership, prestige, and missionary themes persisted in the 1950's, but the discussion soon moved beyond them. The effort to uncover the reasons for the lamentable intellectual record of Catholics and their failure to exert an influence on American culture proportionate to their numbers led to a much more searching critique. When "the real culprit," in Daniel Callahan's words, was identified as "the American Catholic mentality,"[31] it followed that improvements in the intellectual sphere could be achieved only by basic changes in the patterns of Catholic life and thought.

But while the controversy broadened out to include practically all facets of Catholic life, the state of intellectual endeavor and the quality of Catholic schools remained important focal points. It was in the context of debate on these matters that a number of general weaknesses were first subjected to heavy criticism. Thus, in calling attention to the unfortunate effects of formalism, authoritarianism, clericalism, moralism, and defensiveness, Thomas F. O'Dea described these attitudes as "the basic characteristics of the American Catholic milieu which inhibit the development of mature intellectual activity. . . ."[32] On this account, those who committed themselves to a radical reordering of Catholic attitudes and values acquired a vested polemical interest in the finding that Catholics were anti-intellectual and that their schools were inferior. Since the woeful condition of Catholic intellectualism confirmed the need for drastic change, improvements in the intellectual sphere could hardly be admitted before drastic change was

29 Christ and Sherry, pp. 142-43.

30 Christ and Sherry, pp. 277-78.

31 Daniel Callahan, *The Mind of the Catholic Layman* (New York, 1963), p. 98.

32 Thomas F. O'Dea, *American Catholic Dilemma* (paperback ed., New York, 1962), p. 127 ff.

accomplished. This consideration makes more understandable the otherwise puzzling fact that some "self-critics" were quite reluctant to accept research that indicated a noticeable amelioration of Catholic intellectual life. Likewise, the sociological explanation of Catholic inferiority did not commend itself to some, because if immigrant background and lower-class status were primarily responsible, the situation could be expected to correct itself in time and the need for a purposefully executed reconstruction of Catholic life would be lessened.

The reaction to Andrew M. Greeley's investigation of the career plans of Catholic college graduates is very suggestive in this connection.[33] Although the failure of proportionate numbers to enter upon graduate studies had previously been offered as evidence of Catholic intellectual backwardness, Greeley's finding that Catholics were adequately represented in graduate schools in the 1960's was dismissed by some as irrelevant to the question of Catholic anti-intellectualism. Thus, John D. Donovan argued that the subjects of Greeley's study probably lacked the "free-wheeling, critical, creative, and speculative bent of mind that marks the intellectual," being instead merely " 'intelligent' graduates of the collegiate population." And James W. Trent implied that these young people would be "authoritarian, intellectually docile graduate student[s]" who would "contribute little more to the flow of intellectuality and creativity than the ordinary high-school graduate."[34]

These objections highlight a fundamental ambiguity that runs all through the discussion. The nub of the difficulty is: What do terms like "intellectual," "intellectualism," and "anti-intellectualism" really mean? Not only is there no universal agreement on these, but the vagueness of the terminology is such that it is frequently impossible even to specify the points of disagreement. Donovan and Trent seem to think that the term intellectual should be reserved to persons who engage more or less habitually in a certain restricted variety of mental operations. According to this view, the Catholic-intellectualism problem cannot be overcome until there are considerably more Catholics who engage in this sort of mental activity. Greeley, on the other hand,

[33] Cf. Andrew M. Greeley, *Religion and Career* (New York, 1963).

[34] See the articles of Greeley, Donovan and Trent in *Commonweal*, LXXXI (Oct. 2, 1964), 33-42. Cf. also Joseph Scimecca and Roland Damiano, *Crisis at St. John's* (New York, 1967), pp. 105-06, 108; and James W. Trent and Jenette Golds, *Catholics in College* (Chicago, 1967).

accepts the fact that more Catholics are pursuing postgraduate degrees and planning careers in scholarship as evidence of improvement in Catholic intellectual life. His position assumes that graduate work and professorial careers necessarily involve intellectualism, without any need to establish the freewheeling, critical, creative, and speculative qualities of mind that Donovan and Trent would insist on.

While concepts like intellectualism and anti-intellectualism remain nebulous, there has been a significant development since the controversy began in the 1950's. In its early phases, most writers accepted the premise that although Catholics had made a poor showing as scholars and scientists they could do better simply by trying harder; no inherent incompatibility was posited between being Catholic and being an intellectual. As the controversy waxed, however, more and more Catholic attitudes and patterns of thought and life were listed as obstacles to intellectualism. In order to make a real intellectual breakthrough, it appeared that many things traditionally associated with Catholicism would have to be eliminated. This trend culminated in the affirmation that prior commitment to a dogmatic religious position could not be reconciled with "love of intellectuality for its own sake." In other words, true intellectualism was defined in such a way as to exclude religious commitment. Insofar as he was to operate as an intellectual, the Catholic would have to set aside his doctrinal beliefs. The notion that a man might legitimately employ his intellect—as an intellectual—to explicate or defend the Church's position was rejected by Edward Wakin and Joseph F. Scheuer in their book dealing with the "de-Romanization" of American Catholicism. The expression "intellectual apostolate," they wrote, is "a contradiction in terms"; the exhortation to Catholics to take it up "threatens to subvert the intellectual and turn him into a holy panderer for the Catholic Church."[35]

What has happened in the last fifteen years, therefore, is that a campaign which was intended to increase the number of Catholic intellectuals has reached the point of denying that there can be such a thing as a Catholic intellectual. Not everyone who writes on the subject accepts this conclusion; indeed, the conclusion has not even been spelled out in its fullest rigor, although it is logically entailed in the line of reasoning adopted by Wakin and Scheuer. It also corresponds to the progression we have already traced in connection with

[35] Edward Wakin and Joseph F. Scheuer, *The De-Romanization of the American Catholic Church* (New York, 1966), p. 261.

"Catholic sociology" and to the analogous conclusion that there can be no such thing as a Catholic university.

The performance of the Catholic university has always occupied an important place in the controversy. The question of scholarship is intrinsic to the university, and most of the other matters touched on in the debate—the role of the layman, clericalism, paternalism, social divisiveness, and so on—have a bearing on the functioning of Catholic colleges and universities. Moreover, the faculty and students in Catholic institutions of higher education constitute an increasingly large and articulate group with a personal interest in the outcome of the controversy. For all these reasons, which have been dramatized by several spectacular eruptions over academic freedom, the discussion of Catholic intellectual life has tended in the last few years to become a discussion of Catholic higher education.

As the debate has evolved along these lines, Catholic higher education itself has been reshaped by a number of changes. Enrollments have more than doubled since World War II; the social and educational background of students is much higher than in previous generations; lay faculties have grown and have better professional preparation; graduate schools dedicated to research now set the tone in the better institutions; new patterns of administration and policy-making have been introduced looking to the reduction, or elimination, of control by nonacademic religious authorities. These changes have brought about a marked improvement in the academic quality of Catholic higher education. They have also had the effect of making Catholic colleges, and especially universities, more like other American institutions of higher learning. The combined result of improved quality and closer approximation of secular norms has been to raise the question: What is it that is specifically Catholic about Catholic colleges and universities?[36] Bernard Shaw's dictum that a Catholic university is a contradiction in terms has been invoked to the point of tedium; John Cogley, to whom the Catholic university is as outmoded as the Papal States, has rewritten Gertrude Stein in insisting that a university is a university is a university.[37] Contrary to the expectation of many who called for improvements, upgrading the Catholic university has not

36 Cf. Philip Gleason, "American Catholic Higher Education: A Historical Perspective," in *The Shape of Catholic Higher Education*, ed. Robert Hassenger (Chicago, 1967), pp. 15-53.

37 John Cogley, "The Future of An Illusion," *Commonweal*, LXXXVI (June 2, 1967), 310-16.

solved the problem; rather it has uncovered the deeper problem of whether there is any justification for a Catholic university regardless of how good it might be.

If this is an identity crisis, it is equally a crisis of assimilation. In the case of immigrants, it was precisely the identity of the group that was at stake in the process of assimilation. Like the spokesmen for immigrant nationalities, the early writers on Catholic intellectual life took it as a given fact that Catholics were a distinctive group with a distinctive outlook on the world. As such, they needed to train leaders who could expound their position and win recognition for it. Leaders were also needed to explain to the members of the group themselves just what their position was, how it might be applied to the problems of life, and where it should be modified in keeping with changing circumstances. Catholic colleges and universities seemed so obviously the appropriate institutions to perform these functions that no one ever thought of challenging them to justify their existence. Earlier generations of Catholics were critical of the weaknesses of their colleges, but they never really doubted that such institutions had a vitally important role to play.

Now, however, assimilation has brought the Catholic population to the point where it differs only marginally from American society at large. Catholic scholars in various disciplines are discarding the belief that their faith dictates an approach different from that of non-Catholic workers in the same fields. Leading Catholic universities have accepted the model of outstanding secular institutions, pledging their readiness to "pay any price, break any mold" in their pursuit of academic excellence.[38] Only a small minority is demanding the outright secularization of Catholic higher education,[39] but the general trend is clearly in that direction. Those still convinced of the value of Catholic higher education and of the need for Catholic universities find themselves increasingly perplexed at the rising clamor of demands that they

[38] William J. Richardson, S.J., "Pay Any Price? Break Any Mold?" *America,* CXVI (Apr. 29, 1967), 624 ff.

[39] In its draft report on academic freedom, a faculty committee of the University of Dayton was quoted in the press as saying of the Catholic University: "Its purpose is to become secularized; for to be secularized means to come of age, to come into the time and forms of the city of man today." Cf. also Paul J. Reiss, "The Future of the Catholic Liberal Arts College," *Holy Cross Quarterly* (Fall, 1967), pp. 15-23.

explain the grounds of their conviction.[40] In the past, the need for Catholic universities was an *assumption*—an assumption that arose from the consciousness on the part of Catholics that they were "different," a distinctive group whose needs could only be met by institutions that corresponded to their own unique character. Now the assimilation of the Catholic population and the acceptance of secular American norms by Catholic scholars and institutions of higher learning have eroded the social reality which made that assumption seem inevitable and right. Those who still believe that Catholic higher education is needed and valuable can no longer regard their belief as a premise of action whose validity is beyond question. Rather, they are required to bring their assumptions up to the level of conscious analysis, explicate them, and demonstrate their validity to the world.[41]

This sort of task is never easy, for what is at issue is a people's basic understanding of who they are and what it is that makes them what they are. But when the experience of a people forces upon them the consciousness that they no longer are what they once were, yet leaves them uncertain as to their present identity, the task can hardly be avoided. Whether American Catholic intellectuals and educators can accomplish the task successfully is still an open question.

THE AMBIGUITIES OF AMERICANIZATION

The developments we have reviewed correspond closely to the Americanization model sketched earlier. Assimilation on the individual level has not only brought Catholics abreast of their fellow citizens in respect to social and economic status, it has also resulted in a new self-concep-

40 The remarks of Robert A. Nisbet in respect to the cognate demand that the American university articulate an "explicit, verbalized *purpose*" are apropos here. Nisbet writes that "in a large-scale historic institution such as the university, purpose is given, not by rationalist assent, arrived at on the basis of 'dialogue' in conferences, but by continuous historical function, through common, if diversified, effort over long periods of time . . ." See Nisbet, "Crisis in the University?" *The Public Interest*, No. 10 (Winter, 1968), pp. 57-58.

41 Writing of a Protestant college caught in transition from religious to secular orientation, Thomas LeDuc notes: "The very acceptance of an idea operates to make exegesis needless and apology superogatory. Only when its validity is challenged will there appear a body of definition and discussion." LeDuc, *Piety and Intellect at Amherst College, 1865-1912* (New York, 1946), p. vii.

tion for those who have increasingly adopted the attitudes and beliefs prevailing in secular society. These changes in the social composition and outlook of the group require a reshaping of Catholic institutions to bring them into line with the shifting configuration of the clientele whose needs they serve and whose values they symbolize and embody. A number of these institutional and ideological changes were already under way before Vatican II, but the loosening of traditional patterns set in motion by the Council has vastly accelerated the general tendency. All the old beliefs and patterns of action are called into question; all the old institutions must justify themselves afresh and demonstrate their relevance to the new situation.

When an immigrant group reached an analogous stage in the process of assimilation, the challenge faced by its institutions—and by the group as a whole—was to find some middle way between the opposing perils of self-isolation and total absorption. Rigid adherence to traditional attitudes and structures condemned the group and its institutions to slow extinction—but unreservedly embracing the norms and values of the dominant culture was tantamount to admitting that the group stood for no values of its own worth preserving, that it had nothing distinctive to bring to the larger culture, that it was prepared to confess its spiritual destitution and submerge itself in the "mainstream" of society.

This is the kind of Americanization crisis that now confronts the Catholic Church in the United States. Far-reaching changes are needed to bring the Church into line with modern society and culture and to accommodate to the new mentality gaining ground among Catholics. But it is cruelly difficult to make such changes while at the same time preserving an underlying continuity with the past, preventing the loss of identity, and maintaining minimal cohesiveness within the Catholic population. One of the principal problems is simply to form an adequate idea of what is happening, and especially to grasp clearly the dialectical relationship of the demands and dangers of a situation in which the Church must maintain identity without isolation and achieve relevance without absorption. To judge from much contemporary talk, the complexities and ambiguities of this situation are not very well understood; unfortunately, the terms in which the discussion is frequently carried on tend to conceal the problem rather than clarify it.

Consider, for example, the metaphor of "the mainstream." Lionel

Trilling pointed out some years ago that the expression "main currents in American thought" was misleading because it tended toward monism and obscured the fact that culture is a dialectical process involving confrontation and interchange between differing or opposed ideas and values.[42] Nowadays, the Church is being called upon to plunge into "the mainstream" and make itself "relevant." Presumably it would not become especially relevant if it did nothing more than float with the tide. Yet spokesmen for the mainstream policy have little to say about the distinctive additions the Church might make to the mainstream. Nothing that characterized the Church in its "ghetto" days would seem to be acceptable, and one sometimes gets the impression that these writers are exhorting the Church to "get with it" by conforming itself completely to the prevailing currents of American society. There are similar problems with other popular ways of talking. It is far from clear, for example, what "openness" requires, but it might be interpreted to mean that a Church that is "completely open" has no character of its own and must take its substantive content from sources outside itself. And does it not imply something quite similar to say that the only way for the Church to be Catholic with a capital "C" is to be catholic with a small "c"?

According to a writer in *Concilium*, "There is in fact *no* opposition between what is temporal and what is spiritual and eternal."[43] Are we then to conclude that the world in which we find ourselves is sufficient unto itself and that the Church has no unique message to bring to it, no standpoint of its own from which the world can be brought under judgment? If this conclusion were to be accepted, we would have to say that Catholicism emerges from its ghetto with nothing specifically its own to contribute to American society. In that case, the Catholic identity would be nothing but the natural accretion of the history of certain social groups, built up by their common past and sustained by purely temporal institutions that came into being in the ordinary course of human affairs. This sort of Catholic identity would not differ essentially from the Germanness of German immigrants, or the ethnic

42 Lionel Trilling, *The Liberal Imagination* (New York, 1950), p. 9. See also "Prologue: The Myth and the Dialogue," in R. W. B. Lewis, *The American Adam* (Chicago, 1955).

43 Ildefons Lobo, O.S.B., "Toward a Morality Based on the Meaning of History: The Condition and Renewal of Moral Theology," *Concilium*, vol. 25 (New York, 1967), p. 29. Italics added.

identity of any other nationality group. It would amount to nothing more than another kind of tribalism. How ironic it would be if American Catholic reformers, who began with the determination to eradicate the vestiges of ethnic tribalism from their Church, found themselves at the end with nothing to cling to but a new kind of tribalism! Yet Rosemary Ruether suggests this line of reasoning when she writes that "the terms 'Protestant' and 'Roman Catholic' should be regarded as statements of our tribal affinity . . . and not statements of our faith."[44]

Few Catholics would be willing to concede that their Church is a tribal affair. On the contrary, the vast majority of American Catholics, as well as the officially constituted authorities of the Church, would insist that it is precisely at this point that the Americanization model derived from the experience of ethnic groups breaks down. For they would maintain that the identity of Catholics *as Catholics* differs essentially from ethnic identity—that the Catholic identity is of an entirely different order from the culturally generated inheritances that define various ethnic groups. It is of a wholly different order because of something at the core of Catholicism that is *not* purely natural, *not* merely the accretion of the human past. That which specifically defines Catholicism comes to the Church from outside history: It is the transcendant element of divinity which entered decisively into human history through the person of Jesus Christ and has remained present to the world in and through the Church. And precisely because this essential element in the Church is transhistorical and transcultural, Catholicism—and hence the Catholic identity—*can* adapt and maintain itself through manifold historical and cultural changes.

But while the essential dimension of Catholicity is transhistorical and transcultural, the Church must embody itself in time through changing human structures and engage itself in the concerns of persons who live in a variety of shifting social and historical situations, persons whose identity as Catholics becomes closely interwoven with historically conditioned ways of acting and ways of conceiving of themselves. So there inevitably arises a tension—which has always been present in the history of the Church—between what the Church is in its fullest ontological reality and what it becomes in the contingencies of historical existence. Both elements in this polarity are necessary; the dialectical tension between them will remain for as long as the Church

[44] Letter to the editor, *America*, CXVIII (Jan. 6, 1968), 15.

and the world exist. What American Catholics now find themselves grappling with is their own particular form of the classic problem of Christ and culture or the relationship of the Church to the world.[45]

Situating the "crisis of Americanization" in this context places it in the only perspective from which a solution may be adequately approached. But it also raises theological and ecclesiological problems with which I am not competent to deal. I will therefore conclude with one brief comment on the present situation.

American Catholics are concerned about eliminating from the Church the inappropriate cultural forms of the past and making it relevant to modern problems and the modern mentality. Although this concern is necessary and praiseworthy, it also involves two potential perils. Both are related to the inevitable dialectical tension just discussed. On the one hand, Catholics may be tempted to denigrate and despise their own past. But despite the inadequacies of the past, and despite the incongruities between Catholic traditions and structures and the American environment, those now outmoded institutions and cultural forms did embody the Church, making present to the American world the transcendant reality the Church claims to represent. To forget that fact would be to run the risk of losing hold of the conviction that something of surpassing value has been transmitted to us by our past. On the other hand, to strive with blinkered singlemindedness for relevance to the contemporary runs the risk of forgetting that, while the Church must be engaged in the world, it cannot be completely assimilated to the world. Catholicism has come disastrously close to becoming a culture religion in other times and places; for it to become a culture religion now—even in the name of relevance—would be a religious catastrophe and would contribute nothing to the solution of the problems of society.

[45] Cf. the classic study of H. Richard Niebuhr, *Christ and Culture* (New York, 1951).

2: THE CHURCH AS A SOCIAL ORGANIZATION: A SOCIOLOGICAL ANALYSIS

William A. Osborne

In contributing to a volume of this kind, the sociologist is faced with the problem of fitting a variety of data and phenomena into an orderly conceptual scheme. And all too frequently the data is inconsistent if not contradictory. In March, 1965, for example, several hundred priests, sisters, and brothers converged on Selma, Alabama, for the historic confrontation with the police power of the state. While they risked their lives for what they deemed "Christian witness," the local ordinary, Archbishop Thomas Toolen, lamented their presence saying that they "should be home doing God's work." It is, of course, a theological task to resolve this issue of what is really God's work. But the sociologist feels called upon to explain, without trespassing on theology, how such opposites can coexist as members of the same religious body. What holds people together in the same ecclesiastical body when they evaluate substantive moral issues in such divergent ways?

The sociologist's problem is not so very different from that facing the political scientist who must reconcile the membership in the Democratic Party of a Eugene McCarthy and a George Wallace. There are also certain changes which demand explanation: for example, the incongruity between the stand taken by the World Congress of the Laity in October, 1967, on freedom of conscience *vis-à-vis* contraception and the unquestioning acceptance of the Church's traditional teaching which prevailed for centuries. Such a profound theological shift, accomplished in the short span of perhaps two or three years of public debate, suggests a reversal rather than an evolution of teaching. The same period saw a break, perhaps irreparable, in the foundation of filial loyalty that underlay the relationship of bishop and clergy during the course of Church history in the United States as priests challenged bishops, publicly and privately, in countless incidents. If Catholic self-knowledge is to be achieved in an authentic way, such developments require elucidation, particularly from a discipline concerned with institutions and social change.

THE SOCIAL FUNCTIONS OF THEOLOGY

Auguste Comte, often called the founding father of sociology, observed early in the nineteenth century that:

> The vague and variable tendency of theological conceptions impairs their social efficacy by exposing the precepts they supply to perpetual modification by human passions: and this difficulty can be met only by an incessant vigilance on the part of the corresponding spiritual authority. Catholicism had no choice, if the unity of its social function was to be preserved, but to repress the irreconcilable outbreaks of the religious spirit in individual minds by setting up absolute faith as the first duty of the Christian, there was no other basis for moral obligation of other kinds.[1]

If one allows for purity of intent and for the operations of the subconscious mind—or, simply, for the element of mystery in the processes of the mind—it does not seem unreasonable to accept Comte's proposition. Precisely how or when the setting up of "absolute faith as the first duty of the Christian" came about need not concern us. It should suffice to recall the simple pattern of religious behavior woven from this "absolute faith." The solid obligatory core, Sunday observance and frequent Saturday confession, governed religious behavior for millions in every generation. Custodian of all the channels of grace, the Church also offered "extras"—opportunities for spiritual growth through novenas, retreats, triduums, a variety of private devotions, and models of sanctity for every phase and vicissitude of life. For those oriented toward the social order, be it race relations or sports, pious fulfillment was available under Church auspices. Thus a spiritually secure life for a variety of personality types from the contemplative to the activist was available simply by maintaining a state of faith in an infallible Church. Undoubtedly the sense of guilt, triggered by sin and buttressed by fear of eternal damnation, played a critical, but as yet unexplored,

[1] *The Positive Philosophy of Auguste Comte*, trans. Harriet Martineau, 2 vols. (London, 1853), II, 275.

role in keeping the individual "in line" and perhaps in sustaining his faith as well. In any case, "irreconcilable outbreaks of the religious spirit" were, until the 1960's, rare in Catholicism. While it may not be susceptible to empirical proof, Comte's concept of "absolute faith" offers as sound an explanation as any. Certainly the years since the closing of Vatican II prove the converse. Theological pluralism, now rampant in Catholic circles, coexists with "irreconcilable outbreaks of the religious spirit." But before attending to this more recent development it might be better to ask how or why the prior simplistic pattern prevailed. One must assume it had a *raison d'être*. If its theological validity is doubtful (to say the least) then one might hypothesize that such a faith served a social function (purpose) for the Church. Were certain social ends being accomplished by or through the mechanism of absolute faith?

Religion and its institutional forms always exist in some relationship to the containing society and culture. The Christian message finds its expression for the peoples of particular times and places through their respective languages and institutions. Conceivably the Gospel can reach and mold individual lives through its shaping of their language and cultural forms. But if such a Christian-informed society or nation is a possibility, so too is the converse, a national Christianity. That the latter situation has prevailed in the United States is a conclusion reached by many observers. Why this is so is a deeper question. And how American culture has shaped the Catholic Church to its own image is a question for which we must seek answers. Functional analysis,[2] a conceptual tool from sociology, may help us in the search for answers.

When one considers the far-reaching and profound dimensions of the whole of Catholic theology[3] and then examines the variety of cultural expressions historically fashioned in response to it, it becomes evident that a selective process of some obscure sort is involved. The

[2] As used here, the term refers to the contrasting of stated or deliberate goals of a particular activity with those unsought or nondeliberate rewards achieved. A functional analysis of confession, for example, reveals in addition to absolution a mitigation of guilt-induced neurotic behavior. The latter we would label a "latent function" of confession.

[3] Perhaps an apology to theologians is in order for our loose use of the term "theology." In the context of this discussion we are referring to the substance of Catholic belief as held and lived by the laity and clergy alike. Whether it had any authentic theological foundation is another question.

culturally accommodating American Catholic variety, for example, contrasts sharply with that of the thirteenth century, when the culture had been accommodated to the theology. Or we might compare the Jansenist-tinged Irish Catholicism with the loose-reined Latin type. From a vast theological reserve, the national Church appears to construct a more narrowly specified theology which facilitates its adjustment to a particular culture and historical era. The Church is thus enabled to serve not only the manifest needs but also the latent ones of both itself and its members. But further elaboration of this point is needed.

Throughout the historical span of American Catholicism we find an emphasis on saving one's soul, on personal evil (as distinct from institutional or cultural), and on the frequent reception of the sacraments. These elements constituted the cornerstones of the Church's message of salvation. American Catholics whose memory goes back ten or fifteen years will recall the central place this conception of salvation occupied in their lives. Whatever may be said about it from the theological point of view, the crucial point for us is that this understanding of salvation was by some subliminal process abstracted from the vast theological reserve and fashioned into an "absolute faith." If the process by which this was achieved cannot be examined directly, the resultant mentality can be.

One thing seems clear. "The salvation of souls is the supreme law" is not only a recurring episcopal motto but a theme running through the literature, the sermons, and the concerns of American Catholics from the nineteenth century onward. The habit is probably centuries old. The last time in which the Church seems to have had a different and a more integrating outlook on man and society was in the thirteenth century. Then the Church was actively concerned with the just price, with relations between the social classes, with the problems of war and peace. The Church of the High Middle Ages, tangled in nepotism, wealth, and politics, nonetheless seems to have had a more comprehensive vision of the world and man's place in it than it has had at any time since.

Whatever may be its historical origins, the orientation toward personal salvation through the sacramental system has for centuries served a certain "survival" function for the Church, both at large and in this country in particular. This fact very likely accounts for the persistence of this orientation up to the present moment, and suggests that it might be well to spell it out in some detail.

From the point of view of institutional survival and stability in the postfeudal era, the emphasis on personal salvation contributed effectively to the stability and persistence of the Church at a time when socioeconomic forces were demolishing an old social order and building a new one. The commercial revolution, capitalism, budding national states—all were in process of formation when the Catholic Church itself was rent in two by the Protestant Reformation. Even before this the Church had lost a considerable amount of its moral power during the Babylonian Captivity of the papacy and the Great Schism. The defection of Luther and the consequent splintering of the Church delivered the *coup de grâce* to Rome's moral power. Meanwhile, the socioeconomic forces already mentioned continued to shape a new civilization that felt little or no decisive influence coming from the Catholic Church.

Rendered irrelevant to the social order, Catholicism had to shift to safer theological ground if it was to survive and remain functional for its members. Since it could no longer speak with authority to national states, to the bourgeoisie, to capitalists, to incipient democrats (much less command their respect), the Church retreated to the personal dimension. By stressing the personal element in sin, it could maintain a hold on at least those of its members who remained loyal. Such minimal theology, furthermore, served a basic need of the individual in those times of severe stress. Western man undoubtedly suffered during the turmoil accompanying the shift from a feudal to a capitalistic society. The wars of religion and national rivalry, the Industrial Revolution, and later the mass migrations of the nineteenth century demanded a theology that was simple, direct, and reassuring. Buffeted by forces beyond his comprehension or control, the Catholic needed a religion that would promise happiness for a reasonable price: the avoidance of sin and the use of the sacramental system. Considering the burdens he had to bear, a man got a merciful contract from the Church. It was, perhaps, as satisfactory an arrangement as could have been devised, given the circumstances. Certainly today's doctrines on the brotherhood of man, the social implications of the Mystical Body, and the recent definitions of the responsibilities of the laity for the social order, would have made the Church's teaching seem remote, if not futile and irrelevant, to the ordinary believer. In its shattered state, and facing the complexities of capitalism and nationalism, the Church had neither the knowledge nor the power to do battle.

Returning now to the United States of the nineteenth and twentieth centuries, "salvational theology," if we may use the term, again facilitated adjustment of both the Church and its members to a new and often hostile milieu. By keeping the individual's eyes focused on sin as a personal affair and on the sacramental system as the key to salvation, this theology enabled the waves of immigrants to enter the socioeconomic struggles of an amoral and free-swinging capitalistic society on equal terms—religiously speaking, at least. Allowing him to ignore the moral problems of economic life and jingoistic nationalism, the doctrine of personal salvation also satisfied his basic psychological needs: for solace, for identification, for explanations of the unexplainable, for a sense of direction and a sense of holiness. Whatever might happen to him in the economic realm, business success or unemployment, his religion served him well. Salvation was assured; for to repair the occasional lapses into sin, confession and repentance were available. If there were failures in the social order—slavery, lynching, or segregation—they could easily be reconciled, not with Catholic doctrine as such, but with the central concern of all men—salvation. For the slave could save his soul as well as a free man. Socioeconomic conditions were, after all, only temporary in this "vale of tears."

So functional was this theology that it enabled both white and Negro Catholics to adapt to slavery and its sequel, segregated society. As the shackles of *de facto* slavery were refastened on Negroes after the Civil War. there is no evidence that they defected from Christianity. The Protestants among them simply formed their own congregations with their own Negro pastors. The Negro Catholic population likewise found salvation in the segregated parish while managing to grow along the shallow inclines of biological increase. There were no conversions to speak of, for there was never any genuine missionary effort by the Church among colored people.[4] But the point remains that the ostracized Negro who remained a Catholic did so because his theology was functional. It served his need.

[4] This is not a reflection on the heroic quality of the missionary effort that did exist. The "holding action" of the Sisters of the Blessed Sacrament and the Josephite Fathers, among others, was never amply supported, recognized, or rewarded by American Catholics in general.

Meanwhile, as the Catholic population raised its educational goals to the level of college, an intellectual elite grew apace. To this group new theological emphases on the Mystical Body of Christ (and its obvious implications for the race problem) became central. As the civil-rights movement accelerated in the early 1960's, the impatience of the Catholic liberals with the failure of their own ecclesiastical institutions to "clean house" also mounted. Segregated Catholic institutions became incompatible with the doctrine of the Mystical Body of Christ.

But those who held such views were only a minority. Moreover, their theology was alienating them from the larger body of Catholics. In the 1950's it was the race problem. As the 1960's wore on other issues seemed to sharpen the division: Catholic education, liturgical reform, birth control, celibacy, and the problem of peace. Most Catholics continued to be well served by the old absolute faith. For them there simply was no essential religious connection between civil rights or peace in Vietnam and saving one's soul. These "political" problems were just that. But because they were religious or moral problems to the more liberal groups, the latter felt compelled to implicate the Church. Thus began the internal struggle for ecclesiastical reform. It is worth noting that it antedated the Second Vatican Council.

CHURCH REFORM AS A SOCIOLOGICAL PROBLEM

Neither theology nor social science have reached that mature stage in their development as sciences when their findings or theories can be confidently offered as definitive explanations of contemporary religious phenomena. If today's theologian is ambiguous or uncertain as to the nature of the Eucharist or the "People of God,"[5] the sociologist is no less uncertain as to the theory under which to subsume such phenomena as the debate over celibacy or the formation of laymen's associations. Any effort to use sociological theory or concepts as clarifying devices must therefore be regarded as tentative. With this in mind

[5] That theology today is in a state of "befuddlement" is a widely held view. Dr. Albert Outler of the School of Theology of Southern Methodist University made such a statement before an ecumenical meeting in Midlothian, Texas, Nov. 20, 1967.

then, let us focus on the turmoil and confusion that seem to be the salient features of Catholicism since the early 1960's.

If functional analysis has facilitated understanding a religious system or an institution that has been for some two-hundred years integral or harmonious with its containing culture, it does not serve as well when that harmony begins to disintegrate. While this methodological device has allowed us to see the expeditious function of theology[6] in the processes of cultural assimilation and adjustment for millions of Catholic immigrants, it offers little insight when one seeks to understand the debates over celibacy, the priest (well-informed theologically) who "drops out," or in evaluating the results of efforts at diocesan reform.

Still using functional analysis, one can assert that the old theology became dysfunctional for increasing numbers of priests and laity as they swam, for the first time perhaps, in the freedom of scientific inquiry into Scripture. They quickly found out, in other words, that the old Comtean "absolute faith" was unwarranted. If such people abandoned the Church for atheism or agnosticism, then perhaps functional analysis would remain as an effective methodology for explaining the disintegration of a previously ordered system. Fact and theory would harmonize. But since the facts are that such people remain in the Church in the face of a "befuddled" theology, a better methodological approach seems in order. There is no longer *a* theology to analyze.

The first step in formulating another approach would seem to be the recognition of what *is* clear. From the point of view of sociology the labeling of the parish-diocesan structure as a bureaucracy seems to be beyond dispute. The parish-diocesan organization conforms closely enough to Max Weber's classical bureaucratic model. It does possess a well-defined hierarchy of authority, a system of rules covering the rights and duties of its members, a system of procedures for dealing with its tasks, a division of labor based on functional specialization, and a detectable impersonal quality in the interaction of individuals occupying different slots in the hierarchical structure. Granted, there are variations in the fit between each diocese and the model. Even allowing for the dynamic element inherent in all social forms, one can still safely proceed with the Church-as-bureaucracy generalization.

A second, more or less obvious fact is the existence of a significant

[6] We would remind the reader that we continue to take liberties with this term. We use it to connote the *de facto* theology, what the layman believes the Church teaches, as distinct from what the theologian believes.

number of priests, laymen, and members of religious communities, who have in recent years retained their Catholic identity while simultaneously alienating themselves from what they call "the establishment." The methodological problem, therefore, is the reconciling of these two phenomena as constituting the same religious organization—an organization which is explicitly committed to the task of reforming itself.

Working from these two "givens" our procedure is to hypothesize a distinction between what we shall label "religious reform" and "ecclesiastical reform." This distinction, which as we shall see harmoniously explains post-Vatican II developments, suggests first of all that religious reform is of far greater significance and precedes reform in the ecclesiastical or bureaucratic sphere.

This is so because of the very nature of religious reform which, as we define it, means changes in the individual person, in his norms, values, and beliefs. And ultimately in his behavior and ritualistic expression. Such changes, springing from diverse sources in the secular as well as religious universe, seem to have their immediate origins in the mass media—for example, the flood of paperbacks bringing to the individual the unsettling but relevant insights of numerous literary, philosophical, and theological thinkers. The works of Sartre, Camus, Bonhoeffer, Tillich, Barth, and Teilhard de Chardin, to mention only a few, seeped down through the more or less intellectual or professional levels to open sectors of the Catholic populace by way of paperbacks—and through the medium of annual conventions, Newman Club programs, college classrooms, the liberal Catholic press, and, in 1965 and 1966, what might aptly be called "Küng rallies."[7] The conception, therefore, of new meanings for Christianity and its elaboration into altered norms, values, and rituals appears to be the process under way. It moves at its own pace, in an area marginal to the processes or work-a-day world of the parish-diocesan structure. If this then is the nature of religious reform, it constitutes the change which structures must harness or which they must ultimately adapt to.

Ecclesiastical reform, on the other hand, is quite a different matter. Its *de facto* process seem to center largely on such tasks as organizing priests' senates and laymen's associations, creating liturgical commis-

[7] The atmosphere of noisy, joyous enthusiasm which pervaded Catholic audiences, particularly on college campuses, suggests that Hans Küng's message was more a clarion call to relevance than merely a theological discourse.

sions, formulating new codes and policies, and making shifts in personnel. Behind the scenes, conflicting interest groups vie for advantage, and the forces of change clash with officialdom, entrenched behind authority, seniority, accumulated power, and *savoir-faire*. By its nature, change in the realm of the bureaucratic is contrived (rather than spontaneous), slow, and uncertain. As often as not, it seems to result merely in changes of means or procedures, rather than of goals or substance—a weakness peculiar to bureaucracies.

What makes for much confusion is a rather common assumption that both types of change do, or at least should, go hand in hand. In the main body of Catholics one could also assert as a common expectation that "the Church" leads and guides religious change. Our distinction suggests, of course, that it does not—at least "the Church" understood as being the hierarchy does not guide the changes. Those changes are already under way, irreversible, and beyond the control of the official Church. This assertion rests on the assumption that norms, values, and ritual are central or essential to any religion. Change these and perforce the structure must adapt in order to establish equilibrium and become functional.

The task now is to see how adequately this distinction between the two types of reform explains the events of the last few years. Religious reform includes changes in norms. Here the reference is to internalized controls, "absolutes" in the realm of morality which serve as guides to overt behavior. Products of religion or society, they are unassailable by the individual. Hence their violation induces feelings of guilt, shame, or regret.

One of the first norms to change in the 1960's was the stricture on "artificial" means of birth control. This prohibition was a norm which Catholics had internalized for generations with no questions asked. Its effectiveness lay in the sense of guilt which violation induced. Undoubtedly, it resulted in untold defections from Church membership. Yet for those whom the pull of conscience kept in the Church, the terms of that membership were clear. While periodic failures were forgivable by confession, the norm itself could not be challenged. To do so was, in effect, to deny the authority of the Church. Overshadowing the whole problem as it faced Catholic married couples lay the fear of eternal damnation. Until about 1964, Catholic newspapers and journals would rarely allow even discussion of the subject. Rhythm was discussable; other than that, there was nothing to discuss. Sociologically as well as theologically, the norm was intact.

Today only a few intransigents would doubt that the sequence of events following Pope Paul's encyclical "Of Human Life" has all but obliterated the norm. Here a distinction between the norm and the behavior is necessary. Factual or survey research determines the latter, and there are studies indicating widespread practice of artificial contraception by Catholic married couples.[8] Logically and theoretically, however, the norm and the practice are separate; keeping this distinction in mind, one can still assert that the norm is extinct. Its invulnerability has been shattered, and the sanctions have disappeared. In the encyclical and in the controversy that followed, mortal sin and eternal damnation rarely, if ever, came up. These sanctions simply were not invoked. Even in the few years preceding, the subject was rarely preached from the pulpit—a testimony to doubt, or at least reluctance.

True, this particular issue is only one aspect of Catholicism, and it could be argued that it is not even central or fundamental. But readers familiar with the debate know that far more than birth control means was involved. For this stricture rested on the assumption that it derived from the Natural Law of which the Church was the self-appointed guardian. As far as the rank and file of Catholics were concerned, including both priests and lay people, there was more certitude than understanding involved in this teaching of the Church. This certitude not only gave the stricture its effectiveness, but it evidenced a faith that the Church could not possibly be mistaken. The reality of public debate in the years immediately preceding the encyclical undermined this faith and the philosophical system on which it rested. The subsequent attack of over six-hundred American theologians on the papal position represented a *coup de grâce* not only to the rationale for the "Church's teaching" on contraception but for the clarity of faith in infallibility. Catholics therefore are reshaping, by the interactions of their collective behavior, the nature of ecclesiastical authority, and with it the nature of the Church itself.

[8] Cf. Norman B. Ryder and Charles F. Westoff, "Use of Oral Contraception in the United States, 1965," *Science*, CLIII (Sept., 1966), 1199-1205. A Harris poll, (reported in *Newsweek*, Mar. 20, 1967) indicated that one in three Catholics use a birth control pill or mechanical contraceptives.

Another vital norm that can be described as losing its vitality is compulsory Mass attendance. Here again the dearth of "fire and brimstone" sanctions has been remarkable. The sense of guilt and fear a Catholic had to live with when he missed Mass still lingers, but it shows clear evidence of dissolving. Here, however, the need for religious expression and deeply ingrained habits continue to maintain the performance.

On the other hand, the consensus is far less secure among the younger generation of Catholics. To increasing numbers, Mass in the parish, particularly the larger parish, is less meaningful and therefore less obligatory. At the same time, Mass for its own sake attracts few young Catholics. On Catholic-college campuses, Mass of itself draws strikingly small congregations when one considers the sacred meaning attributed to it. True, such verbal attribution might be only perfunctory or "the right thing to say." On the other hand, Mass offered as the culmination of some function or meeting which combines an atmosphere of fellowship or community with religious purpose tends to draw maximum participation. What this phenomenon seems to suggest is that Mass is becoming a function of community or fellowship. In any other situation, it has little appeal. A 1966 survey by Father Fichter of students in Jesuit high schools also confirms the dwindling appeal of the Mass.[9]

Mass attendance as a norm and behavior pattern is one thing. But the Mass is also the central ritual of Catholicism, if not its most distinguishing feature. It is probably no exaggeration to say that with respect to the future of Catholicism "as the Mass goes, so goes the Church." Boas, Malinowski, and a host of other scientific students of religion assert the primacy of ritual. Anthony Wallace, an anthropologist from the University of Pennsylvania, makes the point quite clearly when he says, "Ritual is religion in action; it is the cutting edge of the tool . . . it is ritual which accomplishes what religion sets out to do."[10] What occurs in or around the Mass, therefore, carries far more import for the future of the Catholic religion than what happens to parochial schools or to the chancery. Catholic schools and chanceries are not where "the action" is.

[9] Raymond A. Schroth, "And Get Back a Man," *America*, CXV (Oct. 1, 1966), 382.

[10] Anthony F. C. Wallace, *Religion: An Anthropological View* (New York, 1966), p. 102.

Whatever may be said theologically about the subject, it is a simple matter of observation that over the past few years a limited but real variety has developed in the types of Mass available. Five years ago there was only the low Mass, the high Mass, and the solemn high Mass. Only the motif varied, depending on the occasion—a funeral, a wedding, or a commencement. In the psychological realm, the Mass was the Mass and it was attended principally through a more or less intellectual, bodiless, and silent effort to follow the action at the altar. While the liturgical movement may have changed all this and brought about more participation by the laity, a more profound change has been underway with little or no "ecclesiastical permission." For two or three years a range of Mass types from the very simple to the very elaborate has been evident. At the simple end of the scale is what may be termed the "underground Mass." It is indistinguishable (to the uninitiated observer) from a Protestant *agape* service. It is held in a private home, in the presence of anywhere from a handful to two-score people. The priest wears no vestments, as a form of homily he conducts a discussion with the group. He uses a home-made loaf of bread, a bottle of wine, and a simple chalice. Even before the official changeover, this service was conducted in English, and the participants gave themselves Communion under both species. Appropriate hymns, usually of a folk variety, are sung with marked fervor. Tears of joy are common and expressions of heartfelt gratitude to the priest are even more so. At the other end of the spectrum is Mass concelebrated by a bishop and a number of priests, all fully vested. A choir sings alone or leads the congregation in hymns of a more conventional type. Participation by the congregation varies. Water and wine are in cruets, and the bread is the traditional unleavened white host. Priests and congregation do not mingle before or after. The congregation is too large. In between these two extremes is a variety, with fervor and emotional impact being greatest near the informal end of the spectrum. In the more elaborate type of Mass, the dimension of emotion is usually lacking.

The problem that now arises is that of classifying these varieties of corporate worship which have blossomed in the past few years. It is equally important to identify the kinds of Catholics who attend the various kinds of Masses, and to ascertain their motivations. The evidence seems to suggest, at the very least, that cult formation is in process. Cults have perennially appeared through the history of the

Church at times of distress or turbulent change. Historically, then, cult formation is a phenomenon in keeping with the times. Such an interpretation accommodates quite well the types of religious but nonestablishment personalities who seek fellowship or community-centered worship in the central ritual of their religion. Such cultic types of Catholics are frequently noticed in Newman Clubs, the Cursillo and Better World Movement, the Catholic Worker, Emmaus and Friendship House, the inner-city apostolates, the Los Angeles "underground," and the peace movement. This cultic type looks for a ritual which will provide a more tangible religious experience. Observation of these groups indicates that they experience Mass in a novel and unique way in these esoteric settings. On the other hand, they do not feel the compulsion to attend just any Mass. At least they do not suffer the pangs of fear and guilt if they miss the conventional parish Mass. For them the norm has all but disappeared.

Many from this same minority have meanwhile experienced an *agape* meal or service under Protestant auspices. Significantly this is always a communal one. Catholic college students in the New York metropolitan area, for example, have been identified and interviewed after attending the *agape* service at the Judson Memorial Baptist Church near the New York University campus. The remarkable resemblance between that service and the "Catacomb Mass" of primitive Christianity impresses these students. Whatever theological distinctions they make between the two services is dulled by their feeling of having participated in a Christian community or a genuine religious experience in a Protestant setting. Here, on the fringes of the Catholic and Protestant Churches, are unformed ecumenical groups unwittingly building a bridge between the core rituals of Protestantism and Catholicism.[11] Such groups have also been identified in Chicago and on the West Coast. One particular organizational vehicle seems to have as its latent function the cultivation of this movement—the University Christian Movement, organized on a national scale in 1966.

Other norms and values which at one time were knit into a tight ecclesiastical fabric have come loose. Even before the controversy

[11] Canon John Findlow, the Anglican representative to the Holy See, warned both this own and the Catholic clergy that "the laity are moving ahead on the grass-roots level with ecumenism and toward unity. . . . These laity push aside theological differences . . . they don't attach that much importance to them." *Long Island Catholic,* Nov. 11, 1967.

over *Humanae Vitae,* the norm of unquestioning obedience to the bishop showed strong evidence of erosion. Supporting statistics are hard to come by, but even so the existence of the Association of Brooklyn Clergy, Association of Chicago Priests, the National Association for Pastoral Renewal, the Institute for Freedom in the Church, the "Cardinal's Carpet Club" (Los Angeles)—not to mention the more famous individual cases like Du Bay, Coffield, King, Salandini, *et al.*—point toward a hedging-in of episcopal authority. Until a few years ago this authority was in fact absolute. While it is not the stated purpose of these associations to challenge the authority of the episcopacy directly, their very existence amounts to a *de facto* assumption of power by the lower clergy. And power counterbalances authority.

For the most part these priests have developed an awareness of themselves first and foremost as persons and as Christians. They are orthodox in the sense that they rank their human dignity, problems of justice, and religious reform above the virtue of loyalty to the establishment. They seem inclined to regard the "People of God" as the Church, not exclusive of officialdom, but above it. While such priests have a genuine respect for their bishop as the immediate source of their priestly character, they now have assumed a tactical stance with respect to his staff (they rarely see the bishop in person), and this stance dissipates the power while avoiding too blunt a confrontation with it. Chancery directives and policy they douse with salt and mix with their own common sense and conscience. The norm of obedience is thus being transformed into one which allows for authority, yet brings into play humane and religious values prior to ecclesiastical goals and values. With or without the collaboration of individual bishops, the relationship between priests and their ordinaries is in the process of religious reform.

Shifting now to the realm of values, one can state with some certainty that the high valuation youth formerly placed on the priesthood has sharply declined. The so-called vocation crisis is a case in point. The proportion of seminarians to the Catholic population growth dropped in the decade 1957-67, with downward trend becoming more pronounced since 1965.[12] In Fichter's survey of Jesuit-high school students, one-fourth of the sample thought they would join the Peace

12 See the national statistics given in *Official Catholic Directory* for 1967. Independent research by CARA (Center for Applied Research in the Apostolate) in 1967 confirms the growing shortage of priests.

Corps some day, but only 8 per cent considered it likely that they would give one year of service to the Church.[13]

Also in the offing at this writing is a change in the high value placed on the indissolubility of the marriage bond. Theological writings, particularly by Marc Oraison, on the relationships between sex, love, and marriage, plus fresh attention to statistical surveys on extra-marital sexual behavior—attention which varies directly with increasing interest in sociology—threaten much the same fate for the Catholic view of marriage that befell contraception. The keystone of certitude, linked more or less to a faith in an infallible teaching authority, has been removed.[14] The edifice of norms, values, and beliefs is therefore crumbling. This is not to imply chaos. It does mean a confusing prelude to reconstruction of a new religious system built from more pristine humane and scriptural elements.

THE PROSPECT AHEAD

To summarize, Catholic religious reform consists in the alteration of crucial norms such as those affecting birth control, compulsory Mass attendance, and clerical obedience. It consists furthermore in a diminished valuation of the priesthood, which is symptomatic of the growing dissatisfaction with traditional patterns coupled with uncertainty as to what Catholicism is and is to become.[15] Still another mark of the religious reform is a search for Christian community and fellowship. These developments hold the promise of a more meaningful and vital Christian life. Because they have sprung up and continue to grow outside the parish-diocesan structures they cannot be contained within these. Ecclesiastical reform meanwhile follows the slow, uncertain "law and order" tendencies characteristic of all bureaucratic change. And herein lies the real danger.

[13] See note 9 above.

[14] Most Catholics do not, of course, make accurate theological distinctions about infallibility. Until recent years, what the Church taught was whatever came from the pulpit. "Church teaching" therefore forbade contraception, divorce, impurity, and so on.

[15] This devaluation we believe to be temporary. As new and more relevant priestly roles are delineated and the resulting images projected toward youth, the vocation crisis will resolve itself. It seems realistic to anticipate a revitalization of the priesthood to follow from the ordeal of religious and ecclesiastical reform.

Confronted by these new forms of religious expression, ecclesiastical officials may respond in the wrong modes. They may conceive their role as overseers rather than cultivators, commanders rather than collaborators. They may demand the deference due to rank instead of exploring new avenues to fraternal understanding. Faith in persons, true concern for their welfare, and willingness to experiment are what the situation requires. But apostolic succession still means the "divine right of kings" to many bishops; therein lies the temptation to control the upward development of genuine religious expression and form. Efforts at control run the risk of inducing defection (particularly among the young), confusion among the loyal, and of causing the underground Church to become both larger and more alienated.

Yet such developments seem inevitable, or at least logically derivative from what is already known about religion and about social organizations. The latter, for example, define what is "reasonable" in terms favorable to themselves. Not consciously, of course, but inevitably. Charles Wilson's classic observation, "What is good for General Motors is good for the country," illustrates the point. There is always some truth in such remarks, but they reflect the view from one particular vantage point only. The insidious but crucial element is that they *do* represent the total view, insofar as it can be seen from that perspective. The president of General Motors as a human type fails to allow for what he cannot see and denies existence to what he cannot comprehend. What he sees, is; what he doesn't see, is not. Reality to him is his construct of it; it is to the construct that he reacts. His thinking and his personality in turn evolve from this interplay on the margins of the real world. This theoretical explanation of reality as a social construct and the organic relation of personality to it applies to all human beings, since all are products of some particular culture and some smaller sector thereof.[16]

There is obviously no reason to exempt ecclesiastical administrators from such theoretical analyses. Having lived in bureaucratically structured worlds for many of their adult years they too are likely to have personalities or mind-sets shaped by the interaction with reality-as-conceived. The "organization man" as a bureaucratic type can be found in churches as well as in government or business. This is not to

16 This is not, of course, to deny freedom in thought or behavior to the individual. The theory suggests rather that there are observable patterns of thought and behavior peculiar to classes of people: administrators, workers, etc.

condemn the bureaucrat, but to measure his margin of free and spontaneous response. In a sense, a Father Groppi has more freedom than his archbishop. He does not have a stack of paperwork *demanding* his attention; he does not have a school system to keep an eye on (or dispose of); he has no payroll to meet, no staff to report to him what "is." Nor does he have to spread his time, interest, and commitment to the host of other problems facing the Church in a particular diocese. The individual priest is relatively free to zero-in on the smaller segment of reality that seems to him most crucial to the world or to the Church. Such a view of what "is" lies beyond the range of credibility of a bishop, or at least beyond his range of policy options. By the nature of his position parochial schools, conservative pastors, disgruntled laymen, budgets, peace, poverty, liturgy, the missions, the seminary, *ad infinitum,* all devour his time and mind. His response to the Gospel finds its expression through these responsibilities. Being multiple and varied, they demand the imposition of priorities, a staff of specialists, regulated procedures, delineation of rights and privileges—a system in other words. And the system must be free to proceed under its internally determined rules, which means "law and order" at all costs. On the other hand, truth and justice being the concern of the prophet, the system of its very nature is the prophet's target. Insofar as religious reform includes prophecy, the conflict with the Church-as-organization is inevitable. Insofar as religious reform is a matter of people changing their values, their norms, and their mode of ritualistic expression, the conflict will remain latent. The underground Church by the logic of its frame of reference must stay there until, in one place at a time, ecclesiastical authority can manage to liberate itself from organizational concerns, the demands of national, racial, and class loyalties, and once again look starkly at the demands of the Gospel. As each diocese, parish, religious order reaches this point, the processes of religious and ecclesiastical reform will merge. That time is not yet; the burden of the centuries is too heavy. American Catholics will therefore have to endure the struggle of a "house divided against itself" in the years immediately ahead.

3: THE VIEW FROM WITHOUT: A PROTESTANT EVALUATION

Walter D. Wagoner

Let me preface my remarks by saying that I am a Protestant who has enjoyed more than the normal amount of acquaintance with the Roman Catholic community, both in the United States and Europe. I say this not to claim extraordinary insight, but to underscore three clues to what I have to say: First, the American version of the Roman Catholic Church has distinct features; second, there is a need for constant interlinear translating because, although ecumenical progress is rapid, I still find that we use words differently at many crucial points in the theological dialogue; third, this is, as the editor obviously intended it to be, only one man's impression. It is not based on systematically collected empirical data. It is a case study, if you will, of how American Catholicism "comes through" to an interested and sympathetic observer.

The years since 1961 have witnessed the most rapid and most radical about-face by Christians outside the Roman Catholic Church in the history of the United States. Even those who couldn't care less about either Catholicism or Protestantism know that the "old monolithic mystery" is neither a monolith nor a mystery. In my own life, I can look back on this astounding shift of attitude from a mixture, about evenly divided, of ignorance, awe, and brooding suspicion to a posture of critical acquaintance, awe, and fellow-feeling. It is as important to note that awe remains as it is to reiterate that the new congeniality is not a synonym for indifferentism or for loss of theological discrimination. The differences remain but the overwhelmingly joyful fact is that a Protestant with irenic intentions now feels very much at home in this new companionship. Perhaps for the first time in American church history the Catholic and the Protestant are really "seeing" each other, with masks stripped away and guards down. That basic change is also preface to this article. Before Vatican II the Protestant eye, if it looked closely at all, saw only a St. Patrick's Day parade, the pope on his *sedilia*, priests and nuns (like figures in a Joycean novel) flitting about like black wraiths, a high-school romance nipped in the bud because he or she was "Catholic." Now the eye sees a human unstereotyped Roman Catholic neighbor sharing the confusions, ambiguities, and glories of all Christians.

This dramatic change needs a minimal explanation, if for no other reason than that the non-Catholic often finds himself wondering how it all happened. Three major considerations, at the very least, lie behind these new relationships: first, Vatican II, with its revolutionary ecumenical and ecclesiological pronouncements; second, the powerful, and somewhat ominous, homogenization of religion and American culture, which increases both familiarity and theological superficiality; third, the astringent apprehension by both Protestants and Catholics that they must make common cause, as brother minorities, in a pluralistic world with an increasingly nonreligious style. Thus it is that we now look at each other searching for similarities rather than differences. We define our relationship more in terms of joint possibilities than of mutually exclusive hostilities. "The View from Without" is no longer that of a Protestant peeping from a Trojan Horse so much as it is comparable to regimental commanders, in the same army, sharing binoculars. In conclusion, the fact is that in the United States for the first time in many centuries the "View from Without" is almost the same as the "View from Within."

VIEW ONE: THE PRIMACY OF THE SUPERNATURAL

Supernatural is not the best word to use in many philosophical and theological circles these days, but let me try to define my use of it here. I mean by it that God is a reality, truly believed in as Creator and Sustainer of the universe, with an existence independent of man, that he has a Will best revealed in Jesus Christ, that he is the source of transforming and health-giving Grace. This definition is a Christian one and goes beyond, in a minimal and unsophisticated way here, the sense of the numinous and the awe-filled, although that is included in the definition. I do not use "supernatural" to imply a two-deck universe, or, in the case of the individual Christian, a piety divorced from life. It also should be said, these days, that there are many theological currents which, if carried to an extreme, effectively negate such a use of the word "supernatural" and which blot it out by redefining it completely in immanent and secular terms.

The attentive outsider instinctively realizes that the Roman Catholic Church is before and above all else a theological community living on the edge of the Paschal Mysteries. There is, paradoxically, much which tends on casual first sight to contradict this assertion. It is true that the Roman Catholic Church is a monumental case-study in the church as a real-estate organization, in the church as a web of status-seeking and office-seeking politicians, in the church as a most worldly-appearing juggernaut of religious imperialism. These matters cannot be denied; they are extremely serious dimensions of the church which often alienate outsiders and hobble the mission of the church. One sees all these problems most clearly in Rome itself, where even the most sympathetic non-Catholic is likely to seek fresh air as he staggers away from a complex of edifices and politics which smothers with a baroque hand. Nevertheless, the essential nature of the Roman Catholic community is not to be identified with pomp and circumstance but with a eucharistic community seeking to glorify and to serve the triune God.

As some Catholics have warned, there are undoubtedly too many Catholics who are so impressed by the plenary and material display of the church that one worries lest it be a cover either for a lack of faith or a serious misunderstanding of the nature of the Gospel. Even so, I am absolutely convinced that at its core as a church, as in the heart of each devout Catholic, there is the search for the mind of Christ and the presence of God. This assertion may seem to be the most obvious of any assertion that could be made about any church—to be, indeed, the self-definition of any Christian church. But, unfortunately, the primacy of the supernatural, stated on the letterheads of ecclesiology, is a matter of degree. I would simply testify that if the Roman Catholic Church be judged at its best in practice and by its own self-understanding it is essentially and unqualifiedly a God-seeking community, with a superb beauty fostered by liturgical disciplines, making unique soteriological claims. To miss this would be to miss all.

As part of this view, I would add that the American Catholic theological scene, while it does not yet show as many first-rank theologians as in Europe, is quite clearly on the verge of a theological renaissance. One trouble has been that the American Catholic thinkers have been more engaged in teaching and in administrative chores than they should have been, and perhaps also they have not been encouraged to assert themselves.

For all of the harsh and often deserved criticisms of Roman Catholic theology, it must not be overlooked that we are now seeing a remarkable display of theological life and thought—in the biblical, dogmatic, moral, and ascetical fields. These men (for there are very few women) are noteworthy for two effects: their influence on Protestants as well as in their own community and their avoidance of that kind of theological reductionism which is willing, in the name of being *avant-garde,* to jettison revelation and supernatural categories. Many a Protestant, I am sure, wishes to acknowledge his gratitude to a host of Roman Catholic theologians who have protected the *sui generis* nature of Christian theology without obscurantism and who are, at the same time, acquainted with the best which non-Christian philosophical schools have to offer. Of course, Roman Catholic theologians are, of their own volition and convictions, within basic dogmatic boundaries. While this often poses painful dilemmas for them, it raises equally poignant ones for the Protestant—particularly the question, "How far can one go before getting so far out-of bounds that the distinctively Christian Gospel is lost?"

I notice, with alternating fascination and anxiety, the efforts of some American Catholic theologians to begin to escape (for in this country the influence of Tridentine thought has been especially heavy) medieval thought patterns, particularly with regard to natural law and Thomism, and to come to grips with the great variety of alternative categories and vocabularies which make more sense to modern man. If Roman Catholic theologians can do this—and it is still a big "if"—they are in a fair way to give more balance and direction to the future of Christian theology, ecumenical theology, than any other confession.

The attentive outsider does wonder and does hope that Roman Catholic theology in America will enter into its own. This is not a chauvinistic reaction to the old aphorism that "theology is produced in Germany, packaged in England, and consumed in the United States." It is a legitimate conviction that the lively state of the intellectual community in America—which is to say, a first rate group of critical philosophers and theologians in the type of society which will soon be dominant: automated, cybernetic, with new myths and symbols—ought to provide a magnificent challenge for Christian theologians to reformulate, not basically change, Christian doctrine. If Protestants and Roman Catholics, and, increasingly, Orthodox Christians, can capitalize on this new social milieu some very exciting ecumenical theology ought to emerge. Given the sluggish, conformist, cautious history of American Roman Catholic thought until quite recently, it is, again, a breath-taking sight to see Roman Catholic theologians in the United States struggle to enter into this new inheritance. As so many thinkers have noted, this new era is not only basically ecumenical in its assumptions, but is also no longer satisfied to "do theology" within the categories of the Reformation and Trent.

Parenthetically, I do notice still the tendency within American Catholicism toward theological and ethical over-kill—the scholastic elaboration of all conceivable cases, categories, and rulings.

Reinforcing the strong sense of the supernatural are at least two additional factors. One is the eucharistic emphasis in Catholic worship. Protestant disagreement with certain elements in Catholic sacramentalism and its understanding of the Grace of God (e.g., the *ex opere* assumptions of the sacerdotal priesthood) should not blind the outsider to the nature of a faith which makes sacraments, particularly the eucharist, so normative. This protects an objective view of God, just as it means that the whole Catholic soteriology would become pure nonsense were it not posited on the efficacious Grace of God. Legalism and formalism lurk at every corner for the Catholic, but at its purest the Eucharist and the devotional discipline which it engenders is a sign and signal of the primacy of the supernatural.

Another factor engaging the eye, and undergirding the sense of the supernatural, is the Roman Catholic understanding of the priesthood. There can be no doubt either to outsider or to insider but that the formation of a priestly servant in Christ is the top priority of the seminary both in theory and in practice. Manifestly the priest is conceived to be an *alter Christus,* insofar as that is possible to sinful man. His preparation is directly related to the sacramental mysteries, as intercessor on behalf of the faithful. Many a Catholic priest wishes that his church would give, both in its seminaries and in the style of parish life, more attention to social action, to the techniques of counselling, and to the many competencies of civic leadership; but I have never met or heard of a seminary rector or a parish priest who would in the least hold that the "supernatural" is the opposite of being involved effectively in a professional way in the world.

VIEW TWO: THE RADICAL REFORMULATION OF CATHOLIC-PROTESTANT AGREEMENTS AND DISAGREEMENTS

The polemical extreme has been the norm until quite recently: that is, if a Roman Catholic authority held to this or that position, then most Protestants uncritically discounted or objected to the claim. And vice versa. Invincible ignorance and automatic suspicion peered at each other over the walls. The new ecumenical spirit has gone far to remove such a ridiculous situation. Theological and ecclesiological issues between Catholics and Protestants are now reformulated in more realistic terms. A fair analogy is the way in which former differences between Protestant denominations have been reshaped under the impact of the intra-Protestant ecumenical movement. Thus, for example, it is important to realize that the main theological party lines *cut across* traditional denominational boundaries. The differences which separated Protestants in the eighteenth and nineteenth centuries are hardly visible anymore, and the resolution of those which remain seems more often to require the services of a psychoanalyst than of a theologian.

Both Protestants and Catholics are now keenly aware that what they have in common in Christ *vis à vis* the idolatries of this world is a far stronger bond than their differences. There is a widening agreement about the nature of the Christian community as a servant community. There is heartening progress in biblical studies (which is now that area of seminary education where Protestants and Catholics could exchange classrooms with a minimum of friction). There are in addition: a determined agreement to maximize ecumenical reciprocity and strategy; an emerging consensus that respective insights, personnel, and strategies must be shared; a new and mutual effort underway to share each other's scholarly resources and communities; an extremely busy traffic in both directions as lay people and clergy become acquainted and join in ventures for the public welfare.

In such a heartening milieu the old doctrinal differences are being examined ruthlessly—not with the object of finding new ammunition for church warfare, but to lessen misunderstanding, to define the issues more precisely, and to rank disagreements in some order of priority. And surely there is a growing awareness—as was the case in the early days of the World Council of Churches—that many so-called theological differences are essentially personality clashes, or historical and cultural inheritances, not of the *esse* of Christianity. One notes a remarkable decrease in the old and jaundiced Protestant responses to the place of the Virgin Mary in Roman Catholic ecclesiology, to the nature of Catholic biblical scholarship, to the authority of tradition. Equally apparent is Protestant appreciation for the new vigor in Catholic liturgical life. By and large there is a much greater "outside" awareness that all Catholic positions are not dogmatic and universal; that the Pope speaks *ex cathedra* in faith and morals only on rare occasions; that there is, in short, much more room for intra-Catholic debate and conscientious difference than Protestants once had supposed.

What, then, are the key, top-priority differences? It does not fall within the purview of this article to elaborate on them, to defend them, or to attack them, but simply to indicate what shows up on my viewing-screen. The combination of papal primacy and infallibility is still a matter of grievous difference which the most irenic conversation clarifies more than it dissipates. The other major difference, put in the most general terms (for it is exceedingly difficult to define), is that in some real way the Roman Catholic Church regards itself, in its temporal and manifest dimensions, as an extension of the Kingdom of God, best entered into through its established sacramental system. The soteriological claims which Catholics make seem to most Protestants to be too sweeping. It is not the *extra ecclesiam nulla salus* slogan which is at stake, since liberal Catholics have modified that beyond the keeping, but there is a central Roman Catholic claim which appears to make an ontological reality of the equation: The extension of the Incarnation is the Roman Catholic Church in history, with the primacy of the pope at the apex of a sacramental system of salvation. What is under debate here is the nature of the operation of the Grace of God. Protestants might well be wrong, and Catholics right. But on the two foregoing issues, at least, there is a significant division of opinion which does cut vertically between the two communions. Fortunately, the theological seriousness of the division is now being discussed with a maturity commensurate with the subject matter.

Those are two of the more substantive matters which divide vertically. It is, therefore, one of the most telling signs of the times that on almost all other questions the cleavages between Catholic insiders and Protestant outsiders do not run neatly and vertically, but cut across the two communions. On such issues as liturgy, eucharist, priestly nature of ministry, mariology, preaching, types of religious education, and social pronouncements of the churches both Protestants and Catholics take varying but not mutually exclusive positions. The Protestant certainly discovers, if he enters into prolonged and sophisticated conversation about these matters, that there are very few air-tight definitions which separate out Protestant and Catholic curds and whey.

There is one very interesting, nonsubstantive, nondoctrinal matter which also does not cut vertically between the two churches. A sensitive awareness of this is cause for poignant reflection on what the ecumenical era has wrought in Christian realignment. It is, indeed, the same difference in stance or posture which divides "liberal" from "fundamentalist" Protestants. In religion, as in politics, one finds congeniality with those who, despite differences of policy or belief, have an open, tolerant attitude toward life, combined with a deep sense of the mysterious complexity of the universe. In both religion and politics one finds, on the other hand, persons whose minds are brittle, legalistic, certain to the point of being incapable of dialogue. Their teeth have fastened tight on ideology, their self-identity is so associated with being "right" that any questioning of their views becomes a personal attack. One of the marks of the radical realignment which has been going on between Protestants and Catholics is that the liberal Protestant and the liberal Catholic feel that they have more in common in overall life style and personal affinity than do the liberal Catholic and the fundamentalist Catholic.[1]

One prediction is ventured, for which I can offer no conclusive evidence, only personal observation. The younger clergy particularly and

[1] "Father Schillebeeckx in an article on the Council reprinted in *The Life of the Spirit* revealingly remarked that the conservative's 'thinking and working stems from the self-same faith, the Catholic and Apostolic faith. And yet one sometimes gets the impression that [they] are speaking from a faith apart. One is astonished to find oneself more in sympathy with the thinking of Christian, non-Catholic, observers than with the views of one's own brethren the other side of the dividing-line.' There is no need for astonishment. In a very real sense the conservatives *are* thinking from a faith apart, or more accurately, a belief apart. To put the point another way, many Roman Catholics must find themselves more in agreement with the views of the Anglican (and therefore heretical) Dr. Mascall than with the kind of evangelical Catholicism represented by Dr. Küng. In his turn, Dr. Mascall is religiously nearer the present Cardinal Archbishop of Westminster than he is to his fellow Anglican the Bishop of Woolwich." From, *The Future of Catholic Christianity*, ed. Michael de la Bedoyere (Philadelphia and New York, 1966), p. 66.

many laity, both Catholic and Protestant, have experienced such an intense feeling of common discipleship and Christian unity that the present normal progress of the ecumenical movement seems scandalously slow. This does not mean that there is a debonair disregard for historical identity or for discriminating thought, but there is abroad a more terrible impatience with historical structures than many of us realize.

More so than in Protestantism, for organizational reasons, I suspect that we are witnessing the emergence, one might even say the surfacing, of a second level of Roman Catholicism. The first level is the formal structure and *cultus* which is best known to the public and most acknowledged by practicing Catholics. This is the church, to borrow a military phrase, which operates "by the book." The emerging church, however, seems to care very little for the ponderous ecclesiastical machinery; rather, it is vitally interested in social issues, is far beyond the toe-in-the-water type of ecumenicity, and is quick to criticize established church authority. I take it that while this *sub rosa* church, this "other church," has enjoyed its initial leadership from Europeans, soon its main guidance will come from Americans. Pope Paul's painful dilemma comes from a sensitive awareness of this new, open, ecumenical Catholicism, while all of his own instincts are conservative.

VIEW THREE: CLOUDY WEATHER FOR AUTHORITY

The last remarks lead to an impression which, most certainly, is equally registered on many a Catholic retina: that the old sureties are whirling like dust on the edge of a tornado. It may be more accurate to say that while the faith in Jesus Christ is still present, the interpreters and institutional caretakers of that faith are no longer accepted *ex officio* and at face value. I am not certain as to the most accurate way of describing a very complex set of phenomena, and many Catholics will not see eye to eye with me on this. With only a little oversimplification, it formerly appeared to the outsider that the authority of the Catholic Church was voiced clearly through a *magisterium,* through the several teaching agencies of the Church from the pope to priest. Canon law codified both the major and minor matters of the faith. Popes spoke either *ex cathedra* on basic matters of doctrine or with an almost equal authority in encyclicals. (And this observer is unable to determine just how much authority an encyclical carries.) The proper secretariats and congregations in Rome dispensed, with a fine Italian hand, the last word in disputes. Theologians stayed close to ancient authorities such as St. Thomas. The parish priest was a benevolent oracle with a penumbra of authority derived from his apostolic ordination and the watchful eye of the nearest chancery. To this outsider, at least, there was a neatness and a finality to the entire system which a Protestant minister probably envied as much as he criticized. Little was heard in years gone by of "development of doctrine"; infallible decrees were taken at literal face value and not interpreted, as now, with talk about "essential" teaching as against "the transitory forms." It did appear that with a magnificent assurance the Roman Catholic Church member felt that what Christ had passed on to the Church, via the hierarchy, was known, and well known; that the Church could not err in basic matters; that prudence and obedience, regular Church attendance, and a Catholic education together provided a steady vessel destined for a safe port.

It now *appears* to the outsider that whirl is king. This is, of course, not the case, but the contrast between the present and the immediate past is so enormous, in comparative terms, that what is a normative situation for many non-Roman Christians looks like a revolutionary one for the Roman Catholic. The United States milieu explains part but not all of this confusion and change. One hardly knows where to begin in order to understand this heady scene, but the non-Roman Catholic must give this sight the most careful consideration. To this observer some atomic figure of speech is appropriate: It is as if a critical mass, or a self-sustaining chain reaction, had suddenly been reached by the slow but steady addition of new element piled upon new element. American political democracy, with a heavy ingredient of Protestant individualism, and an *unus inter pares* balance of political power is one powerful factor. Add to that the cork-popping effect of Vatican II on long bottled wine. Then add the rise of a third- and fourth-generation of American Catholics, well-educated and increasingly at home in a pluralistic world. Add also the break-up of the old ghettoes and subcultures. Add the impressive authorities of a technical society. Add the close contact with the Protestant, Anglican, and Orthodox ecumenical movement. Keep adding and adding and adding. Something that Protestants had a great many years to adjust to, Roman

Catholics are now, so it appears, forced to encounter all at once. It is a painful and harrowing situation for the most nimble-footed; it is an excruciatingly difficult time for the Catholic who must adjust not only his individual life-style but do so as a loyal member of Western society's oldest and most unyielding institution, the Roman Catholic Church. Although not an easy time for the Roman Catholic Church, it could be a prelude to one of its finest hours. And it is a situation calling for sympathetic appreciation of Catholic travail on the part of Protestants.

Since the purpose of this article, an ecumenical Baedekker, is to reflect one person's passing view and not to dwell in depth, let me mention several issues in this authority crisis which are of particular and personal interest. I cannot help but see—and would not most Catholics agree?—the emergence of a broader understanding of authority. More, much more, attention is given to the biblical witness, to individual conscience, and to insights from the secular world. The Catholic seems to be moving in that direction, while the Protestant seems to be appropriating more of the Catholic veneration for tradition and the loyalties of a liturgically disciplined community. Catholic theology these days has about it much more sense of involvement—with the secular philosophies, with Protestant theologians, and with the nonreligious man's search for truth. Things do not seem to be so *a priori*, so circumscribed, even though it would be a grievous misreading to think that Roman Catholic theologians do not do theology within the dogmatic boundaries. I, for one, cannot conceive of authority in the old sense being reconstituted or being put back into some massive system of law and order. The outsider need only list a few items of the church's present agenda to appreciate how far gone is the clear and crisp "authority" of yesterday: birth control, parochial schools, papal pronouncements on social and political matters, collegiality, the power of a church council, the effective authority of national and diocesan episcopacies, the plenary authority of the priest, the debate over the meaning of infallibility, the widening use of "development of doctrine," the revision of canon law, the basic changes in seminary education, the new status of the laity. The Roman Catholic who likes his ecclesiology neat, his canon law undefiled, and his churchy world cozy is in for a bad time. Those days are gone forever for all of us, and few tears can be shed. The Protestant who gloats over a long delayed "come-uppance" for that old imperialist, Rome, is equally obsolete and soon forgotten. The outsider's eye should be focused on a larger view and a great possibility: If the Roman Catholic Church, like any church, is faithful to its Lord, and if it does not permit the present transitional stress and strain to be an occasion for "authoritarian backlash" by Catholic principalities and powers, then most likely we will witness a major renaissance of the Roman Catholic Church. In many ways it will be unrecognizable, but its authority will be greater, not less. To an outsider it is hypnotic, painful, and melodramatic to watch this ancient institution struggle with a redefinition of authority in a time of rushing change. Can it do so without internal schism, as *status quo ante* excommunicates the liberal? Can it redefine itself and its authority in an ecumenical fashion while yet being true to what it considers its unique witness? Can it redefine authority and still claim to have a unique witness? It is inconceivable to me that the Roman Catholic Church will not emerge stronger than before. But what will happen to it, here and there, and how it will redefine authority are matters the issue of which the outsider awaits with impatience.

VIEW FOUR: ROMAN CATHOLICISM AS A TIME AND MOTION STUDY

A Protestant who spends much time studying the Roman Catholic Church cannot fail to ponder its strengths and weaknesses simply as an organization quite apart (if that is possible) from its supernatural claims. All organizations of its size in American society are sooner or later studied from the sociological and managerial viewpoint, eliminating any "hands-off" attitude which would imply that church organization is too holy to touch. I hope that what I have to say here is sufficiently free of any disguised Protestant *apologia*.

Since Christians are not docetists, even the most eschatologically or transcendentally oriented church must give sober attention to the personal, political, and social effectiveness of its organizational structure. Is this organization in contemporary America capable of making reasonable progress toward its avowed objectives? This is not to demand perfection or to be that most tiresome of persons, the instant idealist. Nevertheless, all churches have a long way to go as organizations, and we are here concerned with the organizational features of the Roman Catholic Church which catch the eye of an outsider interested in such matters.

Theoretically, the authority-power structure of the Roman Catholic Church is organized vertically, or like a pyramid. This looks nice on a chart, and there are those Catholics who claim that while a representative democracy may be very well and good for a political entity, the very nature of the Church demands a hierarchical structure. That view sees authority coming from Christ to the original apostles (now in some sense represented by the College of Cardinals), out to archbishops, bishops, priests, etc. It is fair, I think, for an outsider to remark that it is nobody's business but the Catholic Church's to decide if it wishes a feudal monarchy as the pattern of church government, or to declare that a hierarchical structure is given by divine fiat. But the problem then becomes one of effectiveness and, secondly, a question of the desirability of organizational blueprints which correspond only slightly to contemporary reality. What this outsider sees emerging is an extremely complicated, subtle, and varied form of church structure. It appears to be more autocephalic than pyramidal; real power often doesn't correspond to official status; most of all, an emerging laity and increasingly assertive clergy simply will not fit the old organization chart. The church is certainly not monolithic. Yet at the present moment in the United States the old feudal organization structure is under backbreaking stress and strain. Sociologically, it is a fascinating question to conjecture just how disparate an organizational structure can be from the prevailing patterns of a culture and still function effectively. Analogies are dangerous, for one must not expect a church any more than a university to conform to A.T.&T. or the Ford Motor Company, but surely the official structure of the Roman Catholic Church is, or appears to be, quite dysfunctional. Let me cite some illustrations.

One example is religious communities and orders. While the Holy See and diocesan chanceries exercise checks and balances on these communities, they are quasi-autonomous, operating without a synoptic and ecumenical strategy. It baffles a Protestant who has just seen Protestantism—by virtue of its centripetal ecumenicity of the last fifty years—begin to slough off so much unjustifiable denominationalism, to comprehend sympathetically why there are so many orders and communities, why they have such a sloppy communication system, why they don't cooperate, merge, or agree here and there to call it quits. Organizationally speaking, it is a very expensive and redundant show. One wonders, frankly, in a Christian church with such a massive mission to perform how there can be even a reasonable marshalling of men and money, of women and money, when these communities so often appear to be going their own way hardly looking to right or left.[2]

Another example is the overclericalization of the organization. This is not an anticlerical remark. It is, rather, an observation which seems beyond cavil that there are too many clergy (including brothers and nuns) in the wrong place. I believe firmly that a strong clergy, well-educated, dedicated, and sophisticated, is an absolute necessity for a strong church in our world. But, to risk an analogy, the Catholic organization chart looks like an army which has too much of its highly trained leadership badly deployed: running schools, hospitals, and tending the machinery of the vast Catholic organizational subculture.

As part of this heavy clericalization, one notes the exceptional power of a bishop. I do not wish an observation to become a judgment, for if the Catholic Church wishes its bishops to have such power, this is its own decision to make. The question raised here, however, is one of the effective mission of the church. Does an organizational system which has to "check it with the chancery" develop the type of creative program and person which the church of Christ ought to have? Or again, can any bishop, however wise, really be responsible for school systems,[3] seminaries, parish life, etc., etc., to the extent that most Catholic bishops are?

A related question is this: To what extent does Roman Catholic polity make for cautious, conformist clergy and laity hiding behind such slogans as "prudence" or "obedience"? The one post in the

[2] The outsider does very much notice, of course, the widespread intramural debate going on within religious communities about their proper function, style of life, *raison d'être*. I would hope that the monastic and contemplative life, both for men and women, would be protected and fostered in three ways: 1) combine and merge; 2) insure some genuinely cloistered and contemplative communities; 3) re-design some orders as highly mobile, flexible, task-forces for the service of urbanized society in a great variety of specialized ways.

[3] Does the Roman Catholic community in the United States really believe that such a vast proportion of its total purse (estimates range from 40 to 75 per cent) should go into the parochial- and collegiate-school system? If so, fine. But if not, it is an extremely compromising organizational item.

Catholic Church most filled with grief and frustration is the episcopacy (when embodied in a conscientious servant of the Church) for who can or ought to be expected to deal with so many complicated issues? Organizationally, our culture would seem to call for a structure which gives more authority and autonomy to more people of competence, especially laity, in a structure with more specialized and differentiated functions. The observer cannot but wonder whether the formal channels, the "printed circuits" of the Roman Catholic Church, are capable of transmitting the energy flow demanded by Vatican II.

The parish structure of the American Catholic constituency is fascinating for an outsider to study. Most Protestants, of course, envy the lack of overlap in the number of parish churches: the fairly well-defined spheres of operation, the commendable focus for local loyalty. I take it, although I am not certain, that new parishes of the Catholic Church are designed according to a synoptic and geographic strategy. At the parish level, most noticeably in the large urban parishes, there does seem to be an unconscionable stacking-up of younger clergy who must wait until well into middle age to have challenging responsibilities. I wish something could be done about that, without falling into the mistake of so many Protestant churches of encouraging through lack of proper supervision too many churches and ministerial personality cults.

I conclude this particular "view" with a prediction. Slowly over the post-Reformation centuries, more and more Protestant churches have reached, or have been forced to, the conclusion that there is no divinely given church polity. There was a day, for example, when a Presbyterian believed that the presbyterian form of church government was "agreeable to the divine will." Much of this earlier and dogmatic attitude was, of course, originally formed in reaction to Roman Catholic polity which Protestants felt was not in accordance with God-given or New Testament-authorized mandates. It now appears the better part of wisdom to change polity from era to era in order that function and mission may be enhanced. My prediction is that something similar will and must happen to the monarchical episcopacy of the Roman Catholic community. An episcopal system with papal primacy can be devised which will be much more flexible, contain much more collegiality, fiscal accountability, and which will dovetail more precisely actual power with officially approved organization form. I see nothing of the *esse* of Catholicism at stake here, and I would further predict that even the Catholic Church for all its grandeur and strength cannot avoid such a transmutation.[4]

VIEW FIVE: TWO REMINDERS FOR PROTESTANTS

The Protestant eye which gazes at the Catholic vision sees many, many bright colors which are missing in the Protestant spectrum. Each viewer reflects his own myopia, naturally, and I do not wish to indict Protestantism in general for what may well be my peculiar blindspots. But one of the bittersweet rewards of continuing acquaintance with the American Catholic community has been the mounting realization that there are two areas of Christian witness, among many, where we Protestants have much to learn. It is a lesson which comes from viewing from afar.

First, the Catholic use of "obedience" should haunt Protestants and thereby disturb our rationalizations. Obedience in Catholic circles, to be sure, has served as a smoke screen for a multitude of unhappy attitudes: caution beyond excuse, prudence beyond reason, obsequiousness out of keeping with Christian freedom. Nevertheless, the American Catholic community, more than it perhaps knows, has fastened here on a basic Christian virtue which is easily lost in entrepreneurial Protestantism. At its best, and in the truest meaning of the word in the Christian vocabulary, obedience demands of each individual Christian, as of any gathering of Christians, a profound regard for the whole commonwealth of Christ. To be "free in Christ" does not imply a rugged *laissez-faire* discipleship; rather, it is held in tension, always, with the needs of the Body of Christ in history as it endeavors to serve the world. I find in the Catholic community a much greater instinct

[4] My friend, Professor Frederick Sontag, of the Claremont Colleges, spent the academic year 1966-67 as Protestant lecturer in theology at San Anselmo in Rome, the international college of the Benedictines. In commenting to me about the relation between Roman Catholic church structure and the Roman Catholic faith, he had this to say: "Can the Roman Catholic church really adopt a pragmatic policy on church organization in order to adapt to current American needs? Isn't the structure of the church in Catholic theology something more sacred and essentially connected to the faith? If this theory about church structure were given up, would it not actually undermine other theological doctrines, even if it did lead to greater efficiency?"

for the health of the whole Body of Christ, a profounder horror of schism, than within most brands of Protestantism. The Catholic witness entails immediately and inescapably, unless one's conscience is outraged (remembering that an outraged conscience can be an excuse for wilfullness), a healthy regard for office and order, together with a compassionate attention to the needs and hopes of all the church.

The dilemma and tension are obvious. From the viewpoint of the individual Christian this virtue of obedience is suspect because of the inevitable corruptions of organization and ecclesiastical due-process. From the viewpoint of the church establishment the virtue of obedience is suspect because it also demands that, in Christ's name, the individual Christian with his precious and peculiar dignity should not be trampled down beneath the tread of church officialdom. But from both viewpoints obedience is necessary if the church, as servant of Christ in the world, is to be effective.

Obedience is to be translated as faithfulness to Christ in community. It is not a synonym for carbon-paper performance, for lack of imagination, or for sycophancy. At this moment in American religious history the Catholic community, to be sure, finds itself in great turmoil as it seeks rightly to balance obedience and authority. At the same moment, Protestantism has not yet recovered—indeed, it is more off balance in its abuse of obedience—that judicious regard for team-play and cooperation.

Second, as a Protestant looking at Roman Catholicism, I am enormously indebted to the devotional and liturgical witness of the American Catholic Church. More accurately, since there is much in both Catholic style and content with which I disagree, I am basically indebted for the centrality of this area of Catholic Christian life and for the faithfulness which surrounds it. Many a parish priest, lamenting what he deems to be the low estate of Catholic devotional practice, may be surprised at this observation of mine, but on a comparative basis, as a matter of emphasis and habit, most Protestants ought to look long and hard at the American Catholic worshipping community. Without elaboration, I would merely point to the centrality of the devotional life in the seminary education of Roman Catholic priests, the eucharistic emphasis in parish life, and the contribution of religious orders. Each of these areas of Catholic life is undergoing the most severe scrutiny and reform by Catholics—mostly with regard to methodology or style, not emphasis or goals. The ecclesiological spectrum of many Protestant churches could well use the added riches and color, the depths, of this Catholic heritage.

Protestants have been skillful at developing the competencies of social action; we have been rigorous about intellectual standards; we have been leaders in clinical and psychological counselling; we know every trick of the trade when it comes to all the electronic gadgets for religious education, and I do not gainsay any of this for a moment. Catholics need to catch up fast in some of these areas. But we are shoddy and debonair, so many of us Protestants, in establishing and staying with the deep rhythms of liturgical practice and devotional habits. We suffer from what the Anglican ascetical theologian, Martin Thornton, terms a "certain light-hearted amateurism" about devotional practice. And here we must learn from Catholics.

Part II:

The Church in the American World

4: AMERICAN CATHOLICS AND ECUMENISM

John B. Sheerin, C.S.P.

To understand the ecumenical hopes, fears, and inhibitions of present-day American Catholicism, it is necessary to know something about Catholic history in the early American setting. The penal legislation and popular hostility from which Catholics as well as Quakers and Baptists suffered under Puritan theocracy was mitigated somewhat as a result of the Revolutionary War. The admirable record of Catholics in the war as well as the wartime alliance with a Catholic country, France, reassured the Protestant majority and prepared the way for toleration. The tiny clusters of Catholics, who had huddled together almost like outlaws in the Colonies, gave a warm welcome to the First Amendment's guarantee of religious liberty. At the time of the 1790 census Catholics numbered about 35,000 in a total population of four million.[1]

They were therefore beginning to breathe more easily at the beginning of the nineteenth century when an unforeseen wave of immigration suddenly brought thousands of Catholic immigrants here. Between 1790 and 1860, about two million Catholic immigrants arrived, the majority of them Irish. A virulent xenophobia, compounded by the cheap-labor competition offered by the immigrants, spread like a plague throughout the States and the foreign-born became the scapegoat for many evils of the time. In 1830 an anti-Catholic paper, *The Protestant,* was launched in New York and in 1842, the American Protestant Association began its campaign to fight popery as "subversive of civil and religious liberty." Out of all this hysteria came the burning of the Charlestown convent in Massachusetts in 1834, the anti-Catholic riots in Philadelphia in 1844, and a prodigious sale of Maria Monk's *Awful Disclosures of the Hotel Dieu Nunnery of Montreal,* a spurious tale of horrors in a convent. Again a war—this

[1] John Tracy Ellis, *American Catholicism* (Chicago, 1956), p. 42.

time the war with Mexico in 1846 in which Catholic generals and chaplains distinguished themselves—took some steam out of the bigotry. The hot war against "popery" became a cold war, but anti-Catholicism never really relaxed its efforts. By 1854 the Know-Nothing Party had come into existence and proceeded to harass Catholics and foreign-born Americans. Typical of the mind-set induced by all of this was Mark Twain. In his *Innocents Abroad* (1869) he confesses: "I have been educated to enmity toward everything that is Catholic, and sometimes in consequence of this, I find it much easier to discover Catholic faults than Catholic merits."[2] There was a lull during the Civil War but afterward the American Protective Association began to declaim against Catholics and continued until the end of the century—the immigrants meanwhile coming to our shores in an almost unending stream, Hungarians, Polish, Italians, and Lithuanians, as well as Irish and German.

Many benevolent Protestants during this century would have welcomed a friendlier atmosphere in Catholic-Protestant relations, but Catholic wounds were deep, and the bishops were understandably reluctant to become involved in interfaith relations. Even at the height of the anti-Catholic violence in the 1840's, an early Protestant ecumenist, John Williamson Nevin of Mercersburg, Pennsylvania, showed supreme respect for the Catholic Church in his writings and sermons, and one can only wish that he had met an ecumenically oriented Catholic bishop.[3] The Protestant Social Gospel, moreover, which rose in the latter part of the nineteenth century, might have served as a bridge, as its social action paralleled that of the Catholic bishops who were busy founding hospitals, orphanages, homes for the aged, and other forms of social-service institutions. However, the Catholic Church had its hands full taking care of the needs of immigrant Catholics and gave scant attention to the Protestant Social Gospel.

Toward the end of the century, signs of interest in Christian unity began to appear. Isaac Hecker, founder of the Paulists, wrote in the *Catholic World* in April, 1888: "There is no reason why a movement towards unity should not set in, under the providence of God in our

[2] Mark Twain, *Innocents Abroad* (New York, 1929), II, 349.

[3] James H. Nichols, ed., *The Mercersburg Theology* (Oxford, 1966), pp. 3-30; James H. Nichols, *Romanticism in American Theology: Nevin and Schaff at Mercersburg* (Chicago, 1961).

day, just as in the sixteenth century the perversity of man brought about disunion and sects."[4] Prelates like Cardinal James Gibbons, Bishop John J. Keane, and Archbishop John Ireland encouraged Catholics to mix freely with Protestants. They took part in the World Parliament of Religions at Chicago in 1893, but some conservative Catholics resented such camaraderie with non-Catholics on the part of their ecclesiastical leaders. They felt that the prelates had encouraged indifference by appearing on the same platform with other clergy, giving the impression that "one religion is as good as another." They forwarded their complaints to Rome. One of the quirks of history is that there was in France at this time a group of Catholics, calling themselves "Americanists," who found American Catholicism praiseworthy precisely because these American bishops had participated in the World Parliament of Religions. These French "Americanists" looked forward to a similar Parliament in Paris in 1900. But in 1895, Pope Leo XIII ruled that Catholics could not participate in interfaith congresses and in 1899 he condemned "Americanism" in his *Testem Benevolentiae,* whereupon Cardinal Gibbons also condemned this "absurd" doctrine but asserted it did not exist in America. In short, the first glimmering signs of Catholic participation in interfaith activities had been extinguished as the nineteenth century came to an end.

ECUMENICAL BEGINNINGS

The ecumenical movement is frequently said to have had its origin in a meeting of Protestant missionaries held at Edinburgh, Scotland, in 1910. The aim of the meeting was to bring about closer cooperation on the mission fields among the various churches; discussion of doctrine was deliberately avoided. The Anglican Bishop Charles H. Brent, however, was unhappy about this attempt to bypass doctrinal and ecclesiastical difficulties, and his efforts led to the convening of the World Conference on Faith and Order at Lausanne, Switzerland, in 1927. This phase of the ecumenical movement paralleled the "Life and Work" phase, designed primarily for collaborative social action. These

[4] Isaac T. Hecker, "The Things That Make for Unity," *Catholic World,* XLVII (Apr., 1888), 109.

two channels merged in 1948 with the beginning of the World Council of Churches (WCC) at Amsterdam, Holland. The new global organization was composed of 148 churches, most of which were Protestant, although a few Eastern Orthodox churches also joined.

In the United States, the growth and development of the ecumenical movement attracted little attention among Roman Catholics. The condemnation of Americanism in 1899 and of Modernism in 1907 had discouraged Catholics from participating in movements that were out of line with the Church's traditional isolationist policy of the preceding four centuries. The official position was that there is only one true Church and that Christian unity could easily be attained by Protestant ecumenists if they would simply submit to the *magisterium* of the Roman Catholic Church. Father Paul James Francis Wattson, founder of the Fathers of the Atonement, Graymoor, New York, began the Church Unity Octave in 1908 to pray for the "return" of all separated Christians to the Holy See. There was no outright Catholic hostility to the ecumenical movement, simply a lack of communication resulting in a cool indifference. If Protestant ministers asked Catholic clergy to speak on the same platform with them, the local chancery's usual response was no, on the ground that it would give the impression that other churches were on an equal footing with Catholicism.

In Europe, however, considerable interest in the ecumenical movement developed among Catholics especially during and after the Second World War. Catholics and Protestants came to know each other and each other's faith through their common sufferings in the concentration camps. The Vatican did not send observers to the World Council meeting in 1948 at Amsterdam, but on December 20, 1949, an "Instruction" was issued by the Holy Office.[5] It showed a positive and somewhat encouraging attitude toward ecumenical work as long as it was carried on within the Catholic Church. That is, it entrusted bishops with the task of fostering interest in ecumenical work, but said very bluntly: "The Catholic Church takes no part in ecumenical conventions and other assemblies of a similar nature." In fact, the tone of the Instruction was favorable to the movement, but the ban on

[5] Cf. the English translation in Bernard Leeming, S.J., *The Churches and the Church* (Westminster, Md., 1960), pp. 282-87.

actual participation in ecumenical assemblies seems to have given the impression to Americans that Rome was hostile. The Instruction provided for the establishment of "reunion-work" centers in each diocese to be staffed by competent priests, but as far as I know no such center was ever begun in the United States. Even though it urged the development of interest in "reunion work" and recommended the joint recitation of the Lord's Prayer with Protestants, the Instruction was interpreted here as a disapproval of ecumenical activity. Thus in 1954, Cardinal Samuel Stritch of Chicago issued a pastoral letter opposing the presence of Catholic observers at the second General Assembly of the World Council at Evanston, Illinois, and forbidding priests even to act as reporters.

Three years later there was an encouraging development. With the approval of a number of American bishops and the Apostolic Delegate, two Roman Catholic observers accepted an invitation to attend the Faith and Order Conference sponsored by the World Council of Churches at Oberlin, Ohio. This Conference was held in the first week of September, 1957. The two observers were Gustave Weigel, S.J. and myself. The World Council officials were most hospitable and interpreted the presence of Catholic observers as a significant step toward Catholic participation in the ecumenical movement. (The only similar development had been the presence of two Catholic priests at the Faith and Order Conference at Lund, Sweden, in 1952, with the approval of the local bishop.) But, the prevailing Catholic attitude toward ecumenism did not noticeably change. The presence of the observers caused scarcely a ripple in the Catholic public's reaction to the ecumenical movement. One can understand, therefore, the impact of Pope John's announcement on January 25, 1959, that he would convene an ecumenical council whose purpose would be the advancement of Christian unity. The American Catholic was at first confused. The daily press gave him the impression that officials of other Christian churches would meet with Catholic dignitaries to discuss terms and conditions of merger. Later it was explained that the pope intended a council for *interior* renewal of the Catholic Church in preparation for Christian unity. At any rate, the American Catholic public was stunned. Much as they loved Pope John, their reflexes were too slow to cope with this sudden new approach to the Protestants and Orthodox, and they were bewildered.

MOVING TOWARD PARTICIPATION

In an article titled, "Inside Roman Catholicism," in the June 8, 1959, issue of the Protestant *Christianity and Crisis,* Father Gustave Weigel asserted that, as of that date, American Catholics knew little of Protestantism and evinced no desire to familiarize themselves with it. The American Catholic, according to Father Weigel, "is totally unprepared for ecumenical dialogue though this is the task that our moment calls for. There is no Catholic hostility to ecumenism. There is just a great ignorance of what it is and why it is important." He admitted that there were a few American ecumenists, but noted that their impact had not been wide or deep. In the same issue of *Christianity and Crisis,* William Clancy agreed with Reinhold Niebuhr that "the relations between Catholics and Protestants in this country are a scandal and an offense against Christian charity."

Surprised and confused, but with implicit confidence in the pope, American Catholics read on June 5, 1960, of his establishment of the Secretariat for Promoting Christian Unity with Cardinal Augustin Bea as its head. On December 2, 1960, Pope John received a courtesy visit from the Archbishop of Canterbury, and in 1960 he sent five Catholic observers to the Third World Council General Assembly at New Delhi, India. One of the observers was an American, Edward Duff, S.J., who had published an excellent work on the social teachings of the WCC.

At the opening of the Second Vatican Council, Pope John spoke to an audience that included observers from other Christian Churches, urging the bishops to take advantage of this Council to prepare for Christian unity. He did not live to hear the bishops give their approval to the Council's decree on ecumenism at the third session, in 1964. Pope Paul promulgated the decree on November 21, 1964, the Council having approved it by a vote of 2137 to 11. Even before the official promulgation, American Catholic enthusiasm for ecumenism had become evident. At the annual meeting of the U.S. Conference for the World Council of Churches in April, 1964, Dr. Roswell Barnes pointed out that the pioneering zest and loyal commitment of World Council enthusiasts was in danger of ennui but that the movement was being reanimated by Roman Catholics "due to the refreshing breezes of renewal blowing through their Church." The enthusiasm increased, of course, with the actual promulgation of the decree. Warren Quanbeck, a Lutheran observer at the Council, wrote in the Lutheran *Dialog* (Summer, 1966) that the new spirit, so welcome to Protestants, was evident in the willingness of the laity to accept liturgical changes, the eagerness of nuns to work out programs of ecumenism, the enthusiasm of seminarians for a new ecumenically oriented biblical theology, the readiness of canon lawyers to revise the Code in line with Council statements, and the eagerness of so many priests and bishops to accept conciliar reforms. During this time, many priests joined ministerial associations. However, the ecumenical movement was slow to reach the grassroots level, the rank and file of the laity. Despite all the ferment of Catholic ecumenical activity, the clergy soon realized what the World Council had long ago discovered—the slowness of most lay people to enter into the movement.

The Council's Decree on Ecumenism states that the Council is gratified to note that the participation of the Catholic faithful in ecumenical work is growing daily and adds: "It commends this work to the bishops everywhere in the world for their diligent promotion and prudent guidance."[6]

In accord with this Council directive, the Conference of American Bishops on November 11, 1964, established the Bishops' Commission for Ecumenical Affairs, with Archbishop Laurence J. Shehan of Baltimore as chairman. The Commission opened its secretariat on January 7, 1965, with Msgr. William W. Baum of the diocese of Kansas City as executive director; on November 15, 1965, Cardinal Shehan was succeeded by Bishop John Carberry, then of Columbus, Ohio. At the meeting of the Conference of Bishops in November, 1966, the name of the Commission was changed to Bishops' Committee for Ecumenical and Interreligious Affairs. At the same time, it was decided that the work of the Committee would be divided among the following special secretariats: 1) a secretariat for Christian unity, 2) a secretariat for Catholic-Jewish relations, 3) a secretariat for relations with non-Christian religions, and 4) a secretariat for secular humanists (nonbelievers). The Rev. John F. Hotchkin of Chicago was named assistant executive director of the committee. The establishment of this body has proved to be the most important ecumenical development in

[6] Thomas F. Stransky, C.S.P., Text of Decree on Ecumenism with Commentary (Glen Rock, N.J., 1965).

American Catholic history, overshadowing all private and unofficial ecumenical activity. In 1967, Rev. Bernard Law succeeded Msgr. Baum as executive director.

THE WORK OF THE BISHOPS' COMMITTEE

As set up at the time of its original establishment the stated aims of the committee were: to act as liaison between the United States hierarchy and the Secretariat for Promoting Christian Unity; to interpret the Decree on Ecumenism and apply it to the United States; to propose guidelines and suggest techniques for fostering ecumenical dialogue; to advise bishops on ecumenical problems and to help them in forming diocesan commissions; to serve as coordinator for the more effective participation of the hierarchy in the ecumenical movement, e.g., by designating, with approval of the ordinary, official observers to ecumenical meetings. Within the new secretariat for Christian unity, special subcommissions were formed for conversations with 1) the Orthodox Church in the U.S., 2) the Protestant Episcopal Church, 3) the Lutheran Churches, 4) the Presbyterian-Reformed Churches, 5) other Christian Churches, 6) the Methodist Church, 7) the National Council of Churches and the U.S. Conference of the World Council of Churches. The Bishops' Committee also appointed the very important Committee for Education on Ecumenism to give an ecumenical orientation to all levels of Catholic education. This group then issued a set of guidelines, beginning with recommendations for seminaries. We shall review the work of the subcommissions in sequence.

1) The subcommission for conversations with the Orthodox had its first discussion meeting in New York with representatives of the Orthodox bishops on September 29, 1966. The joint committee appointed three task forces to prepare projects on a) the diversity of methodology in our separate traditions, b) the problem of Eucharistic intercommunion (the Second Vatican Council urged intercommunion with the Orthodox but the "Guidelines for the Orthodox in Ecumenical Relations" issued by the Conference of Orthodox Bishops in 1966 forbade sacramental intercommunion), and c) the possibility of cooperation in theological education and priestly formation. The next meeting was held in May, 1967; at this time the joint recommen-

dation was that intercommunion between Catholics and Orthodox not be permitted.

2) The joint commission of Catholics and Anglicans met on June 22, 1965, in Washington, D.C. They discussed conditional baptism and decided on "The Eucharist, Sign and Cause of Unity" as the topic for their next meeting, which was held at Kansas City, February 2-4, 1966. There was discussion of the possibility of intercommunion at ecumenical meetings, but it was agreed that there are obstacles even to controlled intercommunion. The third set of meetings took place at Providence, Rhode Island, October 10-12, 1966, on "The Role of the Ordained Minister in the Celebration of the Eucharist." There was an apparent consensus on the relationship between Holy Orders and the celebration of the Eucharist. The topic for the next meeting May 24-26, 1967, at Milwaukee, was the Eucharist as sacrifice.

3) The official Catholic-Lutheran group studied "The Nicene Creed as Dogma of the Church" at their meeting July 6-7, 1965, at Baltimore. They found substantial agreement on the content of the Nicene Creed but not on the source of the authority of the Creed. The next meeting took up the topic, "One Baptism for the Forgiveness of Sin," revealing substantial agreement on the nature, significance, and effects of Baptism. The third meeting discussed "The Eucharist as Sacrifice." There was a high degree of consensus, but it was decided to further discuss the Lord's Supper at a later meeting including topics such as the Real Presence. A steering committee of six Catholics was appointed to confer with Lutheran representatives in planning the observance of the 450th anniversary of the Reformation. After the fifth meeting (September 29-30, 1967, at St. Louis) the committee released a statement to the press which said: "We have found substantial accord in such points as the Eucharist as the Church's sacrifice of praise and self-offering: the sacrificial presence of Jesus Christ in the Lord's Supper: the once-for-all character and full sufficiency of the sacrifice of the Cross."[7] They agreed also on the "real presence."

4) The first Catholic conversations with the Presbyterian-Reformed group took place on July 27, 1965, at Washington, D.C. Some participants asked for theological dialogue on subjects of interest to Catholics and the Reformed tradition while others wanted to discuss collaboration in the social concerns of the day. The theme at the next session

[7] *Lutheran Witness Reporter*, Oct. 15, 1967.

was "The Role of the Holy Spirit in the Renewal and Reform of the Church." This second series of conversations took place November 26-27, 1965, in Philadelphia. At this meeting a project for common prayer and Bible study, designed for use by Catholics and Protestants, was discussed and approved. The group was divided into two sections, one for theological dialogue, the other for worship and mission. The third meeting took place May 12-14, 1966, in New York, where the "theological group" discussed Scripture, Tradition, and the Church while the worship-mission group continued to work on the projected booklet of common prayer and Bible study. At the fourth meeting October 27-30, 1966, in Chicago, the theology section considered "The Development of Doctrine," and chief attention was given to the role of the teaching authority of the Church. The other group discussed the common prayer and Bible study project. It was decided to discuss mixed marriages and the structure and order of the Church at Collegeville, Minnesota, April 27-29, 1967.

5) The subcommission for conversations with other Christian Churches held a meeting with Baptists in De Witt, Michigan, in April, 1967, after an earlier exploratory meeting with Baptist representatives. The two groups found "much wider agreement" than expected in three areas: the relation between believers' baptism and the Sacrament of Confirmation; Christian freedom in relation to Church authority; the role of the congregation in the total life of the Church.

6) The Catholic-Methodist group met in Chicago, June 28, 1966, where participants decided their group would concentrate on the work of the Holy Spirit, including the meaning of the new life in Christ, the experience of salvation, and the nature of the call to perfection and of Christian assurance. The second meeting (at Chicago, December 18-20, 1966) took as its theme "Salvation, Faith, and Good Works." Both groups agreed that this saving faith is not merely intellectual acceptance of divine revelation but is total commitment of the whole man, mind and heart. The topic for the next meeting was the presence of the Holy Spirit in the individual and in the Church.

7) Bishop Carberry and seven others of the Bishops' Committee met with representatives of the National Council of Churches (NCC) in Baltimore on January 25, 1966, in a joint prayer service and all-day conference. The Catholic-National Council Working Group then met in New York, May 25-26, 1966. Among other subjects it discussed mixed marriages, peace, the relation of the Catholic Church to the

National Council as well as to the World Council. In this group were twenty-one leaders of eleven communions plus fifteen Catholic members.

The second meeting was held November 1-2, 1966. It discussed Catholic-National Council relationships, heard reports from task forces on education, mixed marriages, and relations with Jews as well as nonbelievers. The third meeting was held at New York, May 9-10, 1967, and received reports on peace, on the Prayer Vigil for Peace, on Catholic representation on National Council boards (for instance, the program board of the Division of Christian Unity), education, and mixed marriages. The fourth meeting held at New York, October 30-31, 1967, discussed ecumenical planning for clergy training, the Vietnam war, Catholic representation to the National Council of Churches, and ecumenical aspects of the school-aid controversy.

The close relations between Catholics and the National Council have led to rumors of national Catholic membership in the Council. The Archdiocese of Santa Fe was the first Catholic diocese to join a State Council of Churches (1964), and in 1966 several Catholic parishes of greater Tulsa were admitted to the Tulsa Council. Just before the seventh general assembly of the NCC at Miami Beach, Florida (December 4-9, 1966) the general board approved a resolution that "the Roman Catholic Church be recognized as being in agreement with the Preamble to the Constitution of the NCC and that the Roman Catholic Church be added to the list of communions in such agreement."[8] Whereas Roman Catholics previously could act only as observers at NCC meetings, this decision enabled them to become fraternal delegates and be elected to executive staff positions. R. H. Edwin Espy, NCC general secretary, explained, however: "It should be understood that we are not talking here about Roman Catholic membership in the National Council." Yet relations between Catholics and the Council continue to develop. In September, 1966, David J. Bowman, S.J., who had been a consultant to the Department of Faith and Order, NCC, was placed on the executive staff as the department's assistant director; in 1966 the Roman Catholic bishops of Texas appointed a commission to study the possibility of membership of ten dioceses in the Texas Council of Churches. At the fifth meeting of the Roman Catholic-National Council Working Group at New York,

[8] *Direction: Unity,* Dec. 15, 1966.

May 27-28, 1968, the deliberations were given over almost exclusively to the topic of Catholic Church membership in the National Council of Churches. The growing collaboration between Church Women United and the National Council of Catholic Women, and between the NCC Youth and Christian Education Departments and their Catholic counterparts seems to indicate the need of Catholic membership in the NCC.

Some Catholic ecumenists think that close Catholic-NCC ties will tend to obstruct better relations between Catholics and conservative evangelicals. This term describes not a religious body or community but rather a tendency that runs through all the Protestant churches, a conservative tendency hostile to liberal Protestantism and the concern for Church participation in social action that is so abundant in the NCC. However, there seems to be a fresh interest in evangelism on the part of NCC and the World Council, and this may diminish conservative evangelical suspicion of the NCC. At the present time, many conservative evangelicals feel that the Catholic Church is more conservative than liberal Protestantism. But it may be that they underestimate the orthodoxy of many Protestant theologians and overestimate the conservatism of Catholic theology and Scripture study. The fact is, however, that there is a definite trend toward informal ecumenical dialogue on the part of conservative evangelicals.

The Bishops' Committee, while fostering and encouraging the official dialogue groups, was also busy in other ways. It issued "Interim Guidelines for Prayer in Common and *Communicatio in Sacris*" (June 15, 1965), and the following March, "Recommendations for Diocesan Commissions for Ecumenical Affairs." It collaborated with the Bureau of Information (NCWC) in publishing *Direction: Unity*, a bulletin on ecumenical developments (September, 1965); on March 16, 1967, it issued "Guidelines for Catholic-Jewish Relations."[9]

The Bishops' Committee also appointed permanent observers to The Consultation on Church Union (COCU), an ambitious effort to merge some nine Protestant churches in America, including the Methodist Church, the Protestant Episcopal, and the United Presbyterian Church in the United States.

The tendency among Catholic ecumenists is to scrutinize the Con-

[9] "Guidelines for Catholic-Jewish Relations" in *The Dialogue* (National Conference of Christians and Jews, 1967), pp. 2-3.

sultation carefully. They are aware for instance of the "Solemn Declaration" prepared by Rev. J. V. Langmead Casserly in which many noted Episcopalians stated that they would not want to continue with any project such as COCU unless it were clearly understood that nothing is done to which Roman Catholics and the Orthodox might object or which they might regard as a barrier to closer relationships. The Declaration says that "We Anglican Christians" are not "Protestant" and have no place in a "merely pan-Protestant scheme of reunion."[10]

ACADEMIC AND PUBLISHING ACTIVITIES

It is a cardinal principle of ecumenism that we should do all things together except those which conscience commands us to do separately. There is no Catholic or Protestant ecumenism. There is only one ecumenism in which all Christians participate jointly. In the last few years we have witnessed an amazing amount of unified ecumenical activity on the academic level. In colleges and universities we find the University Christian Movement, formed in 1966 to take the place of the National Student Christian Federation. It is an ecumenical organization of Protestant, Anglican, Roman Catholic, and Eastern Orthodox campus groups in which the ecumenical student movement passes from federated status to organic union. It is a colossal enterprise, but it faces serious questions of finance, staff, and organizational form.

There have also been innumerable dialogues and exchanges of scholars between Catholic and Protestant institutions. Yale Divinity School, for instance, appointed Roland Murphy, O. Carm., visiting professor for 1965-66; he was succeeded by Bernard Häring, C.SS.R., for 1966-67. Father George Tavard accepted a post at the Center for Advanced Studies at Wesleyan University, Middletown, Connecticut, in 1966. The first Lutheran ever to enroll at the Pontifical Biblical Institute at Rome was Martin Scharlemann of Concordia Lutheran Seminary in St. Louis. During the week of March 21, 1966, there was a colloquium at the University of Notre Dame to discuss the documents of Vatican II. Here, Second Vatican Council *periti* from all over the world were able to renew acquaintance with Protestant and Orthodox schol-

10 *American Church News,* XXXIV, no. 5, p. 1.

ars whom they had met as observers at the Council. Catholic colleges have joined Protestant seminaries in theological unions. In 1965, the Association of Theological Faculties was formed by four seminaries (the Presbyterian, Catholic, Lutheran, and Interdenominational seminaries) in Dubuque, Iowa. In 1966, Fordham University and Union Theological Seminary in New York agreed to share libraries, exchange professors and accept each other's credits. On December 10, 1967, seven major Protestant and Roman Catholic theological schools in the Boston area announced the establishment of the Boston Theological Institute. The individual schools will continue to grant degrees but the institute will initiate new programs and projects. Since the Vatican Council, Catholic seminarians have been flocking to Protestant seminaries for special courses. In January, 1967, St. John's Abbey, Collegeville, Minnesota, established an Institute for Ecumenical Research, a residential center where ten Protestant, Orthodox, and Jewish scholars will live while doing research. In addition to conversations and conferences on the academic level, dialogue groups have sprung up everywhere. Packard Manse in Roxbury, Massachusetts, has been a center for theological conversation between Roman Catholic and Protestant clergy, and similar dialogues have been held at the Paulist Center in Boston.

There has been a considerable amount of joint Catholic-Protestant publishing, but strangely no mergers of Catholic or Protestant journals or newspapers except the merger of *Direction: Unity* and the National Council of Churches' *Trends*. The newly merged journal began publication on November 1, 1967, as a biweekly called *Unity Trends*, now published by *Our Sunday Visitor* and the NCC and staffed by Catholics and Protestants. The first interreligious weekly, *Community Now*, was launched in August, 1968, to serve the Kansas City metropolitan area. Published by a group including Protestants, Catholics, and Jews, it has no connection with official church bodies. During the Council a number of Protestant writers such as Robert McAfee Brown, Martin Marty, and Jaroslav Pelikan began to write regularly for Catholic newspapers and magazines; they continued to do so after the Council. Michael Novak and Edward Duff, S.J., joined the staff of the Protestant *Christian Century*. The *Journal of Ecumenical Studies* began its first volume, Winter, 1964, with Catholic Leonard Swidler and Protestant Elwyn Smith as coeditors. *Preaching*, published by the Catholic Homiletic Society, has Dr. William Thompson of Eastern Baptist Theological Seminary as an editor. *The Catholic World* has on its masthead the names of Methodist Albert Outler and Presbyterian Paul Ramsey as contributing editors.

A Catholic publishing house, the America Press, the Catholic-oriented Guild Press, and the Protestant Association Press jointly published *Documents of Vatican II* containing all the Second Vatican Council documents along with comments by Protestant and Orthodox observers. The Paulist Press published *Living Room Dialogues,* jointly sponsored by the National Council of Churches and the Confraternity of Christian Doctrine, and written by Rev. William Norgren, an Episcopal priest, and Father William Greenspun, a Paulist. The Paulist Press also published *The Ecumenist,* edited by Gregory Baum, O.S.A., which soon attracted a readership equally divided between 10,000 Catholics and 10,000 Protestants. The Paulist Press likewise issued a series of pamphlets on the Protestant Churches written by Protestant theologians such as Douglas Horton, Robert Nelson, and Robert McAfee Brown.

WORSHIP AND LITURGY

The Vatican Council's decree recommends joint Catholic-Protestant participation in prayer services, and there was enthusiastic participation of Catholic parishioners in a prayer service with Protestant and Orthodox observers at St. Paul's Outside the Walls on December 4, 1965. In earlier years, the prayer formulas used in the Unity Octave called for "return" or submission to Rome. In January, 1965, however, Roman Catholics, Protestants, and Orthodox used the same pamphlet of prayers for services during the week, omitting reference to "return to the Holy See." Since the 1930's, Abbe Paul Couturier had been urging a change in the formula so that all Christians could pray together in good conscience. The modified formula is published by the NCC and the Graymoor Friars, Garrison, New York. A notable unity service was that at Baltimore on January 23, 1965, in which Catholic and Protestant clergy preached, a combined Catholic-Protestant choir sang, and the Scriptures were read. The service opened with a procession of fifty-six Catholic, Protestant, and Orthodox clergymen.

The Decree on Ecumenism says: "There can be no ecumenism worthy of the name without interior conversion." In the area broadly described in the past as "the spiritual life" there has been a remarkable amount of joint Catholic-Protestant activity. For instance, meetings were held at Collegeville, Minnesota, by the Spiritual Life Institute in September, 1965, and men of the stature of Douglas Steere, Quaker observer at the Council, and Godfrey Diekmann, O.S.B., then editor of *Worship*, shared insights into the spiritual life. An Ecumenical Institute on Spirituality was held at a Quaker retreat center, Pendle Hill at Wallingford, Pennsylvania, in September, 1966. The theme was "Prayer and Contemporary Man." The word "retreat" suggests a retreat from the world, yet we find retreats looming large in the ecumenical schedule. Countless retreats for clergymen of different faiths have been conducted at Erlanger, Kentucky. On October 26, 1965, it was announced that the Gustave Weigel Society would be formed for the purpose of sponsoring ecumenical retreats. With Douglas Horton and John Courtney Murray, S.J. as cochairmen, the Society was founded by Robert Balkam and is the first dedicated specifically to conducting ecumenical retreats. It has arranged a variety of them ranging from straight retreats for Protestant clergy to mixed retreats for Catholic and Protestant clergy. The Laos Association in Amherst, Massachusetts, also sponsors ecumenical retreats, including some given by Taize monks.

Catholic and Protestant scholars have also been working together on a common Bible. Walter M. Abbott, S.J., is the representative for the Secretariat of Christian Unity on the project of a common Bible. In 1966 Cardinal Richard Cushing approved the Oxford Annotated Bible with Apocrypha (using the RSV) for nonliturgical use. The text of the version approved was prepared under the auspices of the NCC by a team of Protestant scholars.

The Decree on Ecumenism declares that worship in common is not to be considered as a means to be used indiscriminately for the restoration of unity among Christians. In each case in which it is requested, the decision is usually left to the prudent determination of the local episcopal authority. Catholic theologians generally affirm that since the Eucharist is a symbol of unity, intercommunion now would be inappropriate and should be deferred until the day of perfect unity. Some theologians, however, point out that the Eucharist fosters unity and that intercommunion should therefore be allowed in order to hasten the day of perfect unity. Bernard Cooke, S.J., at the Catholic-Anglican meeting in February, 1966, asked: "Why cannot we in the private and controlled situation that is ours in this conference celebrate together the Eucharist?"[11] Jerome Hamer, O.P., of the Vatican Secretariat for Promoting Christian Unity, delivered a talk at Berkeley, California, on January 24, 1968, in which he discouraged any attempts at intercommunion, saying this development would be premature. His position was adversely criticized by many American ecumenists, Catholic and Protestant.

While Catholics may not actively participate in the official liturgical worship of another Christian Church, they are discovering that liturgy can be a source of unity. The noted Anglican liturgist, Massey Shepherd, observed in a dialogue in Madison, Wisconsin, in 1966, that the greater the degree to which separated Christians can share and participate—if only by their presence—in one another's liturgical traditions, the more readily they will discover how much they are united in worship. The liturgical movement in Protestantism has paralleled Catholicism's in many respects. Both have emphasized the role of the layman, and the Catholic liturgical revival has restored practices long considered specifically Protestant, such as the use of the vernacular. One confusing development is that Protestants are now giving greater attention to the altar, Catholics giving a new attention to the pulpit. This has occasioned the quip that Catholics and Protestants will meet, but pass each other going in different directions.

One of the greatest sources of interfaith friction is mixed marriages. Here is a clear case of *communicatio in sacris,* the Church permitting a non-Catholic to take an active part in a liturgical ceremony. But the general rule is that if a Catholic is being married, the marriage is invalid unless a priest is present. The priest acts as official witness for the Church and presides at the exchange of vows. A new set of regulations issued March 18, 1966, by the Vatican Congregation for the Doctrine of the Faith did not do much to help the ecumenical problem. Under the new rules, the bishop is permitted to dispense from written promises, and the penalty of excommunication for previous marriages before non-Catholic ministers is lifted—but the new law still requires that the marriage be performed before the priest. A minister may give his blessing to the couple after the Catholic rite and offer exhortation from the sanctuary. Other Christian Churches claim that invalidation of marriages before a minister derogates from the

[11] *National Catholic Reporter,* Feb. 9, 1966.

dignity of the minister and shows disrespect for the baptism of the non-Catholic spouse.[12] The Archbishop of Canterbury, on his visit to the Pope in 1966, made it clear that the new regulations did not satisfy the consciences of Anglicans and other non-Roman Christians. A surprising dispensation granted in 1966 may point to relaxation of present legislation: A Protestant minister was allowed to officiate at the wedding of his son in a Roman Catholic church in Oakland, California.

SECULAR ECUMENISM

The ecumenism decree says that all believers, Christians especially, should cooperate in social matters. Such social cooperation should be intensified "in the use of every possible means to relieve the afflictions of our times such as famine and natural disasters, illiteracy and poverty, lack of housing and the unequal distribution of wealth." Through such cooperation Christians come to know each other better.

In recent years Catholics of the United States have participated in common study and effort to solve secular problems. This type of ecumenism is often called "secular ecumenism." Catholics played a large role in the Conference on Religion and Race at Chicago in 1963. A graphic example of secular ecumenism was the participation of priests, nuns, ministers, rabbis, and laity of all faiths in the march on Selma to protest racial injustice. There is, of course, some Catholic opposition to this form of ecumenism on the ground that the Church has no business getting involved in secular matters. Some say that individual lay Catholics may participate, but that priests or nuns should stay close to the church or classroom. In general, there is a close parallel between the position of conservative Catholics and conservative Protestants, both tending to believe that the new forms of social action must not be a major concern of the Church.

In a talk at the Catholic University of America in January, 1966, Avery Dulles, S.J., said: "From many quarters . . . one hears the call for a new ecumenism—one less committed to historical-theological controversies and more in touch with contemporary secular man: one less turned in upon itself, more open to the world and its concerns. The great decisions affecting man's future are being made in the sphere of

[12] *Direction: Unity,* Aug. 31, 1966.

the secular and Christianity does not seem to be there." Some of the younger ecumenists, Catholic and Protestant, are belligerent in asserting that many contemporary ecumenists are theological fuddy-duddys concerned with obsolete controversies. They feel that Catholics and Protestants are laboring under inherited antagonisms, and they call for "relevant ecumenism." Eugene Smith of the World Council of Churches has said that this "rebellious ecumenism may be God's gift to save churchly ecumenism from early ossification."[13]

But there are civic and secular problems on which Catholic prelates have taken strong positions, precipitating bitter controversies and clouding the ecumenical atmosphere. For instance, many Americans have strongly criticized Catholic bishops and Catholic organizations for what they take to be undue influence in regard to abortion legislation and government aid to Catholic education. The suspicion is that certain bishops are trying to impose Catholic moral teaching on the public, or trying to obtain public funds for use in propagating Catholic teaching. Immediately after the Council there seemed to be a tendency on the part of the bishops to withdraw public support of laws unwelcome to the majority, especially when these were considered bad jurisprudence; later, however, they took a firm stand in support of abortion laws and in support of legislation permitting aid to children of Catholic schools. The bitterness that arose over the defeat of the Blumenthal Abortion bill in New York in 1967 was distressing to ecumenists. Obviously there will have to be dialogue in regard to topics that are such likely sources of interfaith friction.

On the whole, since the Council, Catholic ecumenists have not hesitated about "getting our hands dirty together" in civic demonstrations and projects in the slums. When the Inter-Church Board for Metropolitan Affairs was organized in Columbus, Ohio, in 1966, Bishop John J. Carberry explained that its primary purpose was to serve as an instrument through which the Churches could speak with a common voice on community problems.

While the Catholic Church has taken part in the civil-rights movement, many Protestants and Jews have been disappointed that it has played so small a role in the peace movement. It is said that only one Catholic bishop was present at the Interreligious Conference on

[13] Eugene L. Smith, "Ecumenical Developments in W.C.C. Churches," *Christianity Today*, May 27, 1966.

Leaders for Peace attended by 500 religious leaders in Washington in 1966; none was present at the Washington demonstration in February, 1967, although some 2,000 religious leaders took part. Bishop James Shannon of St. Paul participated in the Washington demonstration in February, 1968.

RELATIONS WITH JEWS

Roman Catholic dialogue with Jews in the United States has made slower progress than dialogue with Protestants. One reason for this has been the fact that Orthodox Jews generally are reluctant to engage in dialogue on scriptural or theological subjects but prefer to restrict interfaith dialogue to social questions. Again, the Bishops' Committee ran into problems of protocol in trying to select representative Jewish bodies with whom it might plan dialogue relationships. Immediately after the Council, moreover, some Jews did not relish the thought of participating in the ecumenical movement because they felt the very term had overtones of conversion to Christianity. In fact, certain Christian ecumenists a few years ago did say that Judaism could not logically figure in ecumenism because the ultimate goal of ecumenism was the more effective preaching of the Gospel. Today, however, ecumenism is generally understood in a broad sense, and Jews unquestionably are active ecumenists.

The special Secretariat for Catholic-Jewish Relations, appointed by the Bishops' Committee, issued "Guidelines for Catholic-Jewish Relations" on March 16, 1967,[14] intended especially to give guidance and direction to the numerous diocesan committees for Catholic-Jewish relations established, or to be established, throughout the country.

The guidelines urge that all Catholic-Jewish meetings be carefully planned. Rabbi Marc Tanenbaum has spoken of "an explosion of activity in interfaith circles," but the time has come for more effective coordination of the projects springing up everywhere. In its guidelines, the Secretariat warns that any attempt at proselytization must be avoided. It recommends that whenever feasible services in common be arranged, especially prayers for peace and the welfare of the community. "Such prayers should meet the spiritual sensibilities of both

[14] See note 9.

parties, finding their inspiration in our common faith in God." The guidelines suggest various ways of fostering better Catholic-Jewish relations such as dialogues, open houses, cooperation in social action, scholarly collaboration in research in history, psychology, sociology, the Bible, and examination of prayerbooks and textbooks to expunge offensive anti-Semitic materials. Recommended as themes for discussion are the proper presentation of the Crucifixion narrative and "acknowledgment by Catholic scholars of the living and complex reality of Judaism after Christ and the permanent election of Israel alluded to by St. Paul (Romans 9:29)." This last is a very important subject, as most Catholics seem to take it for granted that the religion of Israel ceased to have any validity after the time of Christ.

It would be impossible to enumerate the multitudinous forms and shapes of Catholic-Jewish activity. According to the *New York Times* (February 20, 1967) the American Jewish Committee and the Union of American Hebrew Congregations together sponsor more than 300 dialogues annually. The Anti-Defamation League cosponsored intergroup conferences on twenty-two Catholic colleges in 1966. The general trend is clear: From the Catholic side, educational institutions are taking the lead in Catholic-Jewish ecumenism. Many Catholic colleges and universities have Jews teaching in their theology and philosophy departments, and scholarly symposiums are frequent, such as those at St. Vincent's Archabbey in Latrobe, Pennsylvania, at Woodstock College in Maryland, and at St. Thomas Aquinas Institute in Dubuque, Iowa. Perhaps one might regret that educational institutions rather than parishes are in the *avant garde*, but after all the students of today are the parishioners of tomorrow.

This does not necessarily mean that the Catholic-Jewish dialogue of the future will be predominantly theological. Undoubtedly, theological dialogue will figure prominently in Catholic-Jewish conversations, but among Catholics there is an increasing interest in secular problems, and secular ecumenism may take priority over theological discussion. This may serve to decrease a certain amount of Orthodox Jewish uneasiness about dialogue. A good example of this type of ecumenism was the Conference on the Religious Conscience held at Boston May 7-8, 1967. Jointly sponsored by the Synagogue Council, the National Council of Churches, and the Bishops' Committee for Ecumenical Affairs, it dealt with the formation of conscience on war and peace, poverty, racial justice, state aid to religious schools, and the conscience-binding force of civil laws. The Conference evoked some criticism in Orthodox Jewish circles and several Jewish groups withdrew. This was because of a misunderstanding: Certain press reports gave segments of the Jewish community the impression that the Conference was to be a theological discussion.

Anti-Semitism is a profound social problem which has loomed large on the agenda of many ecumenical meetings. The volume called *Christian Beliefs and Anti-Semitism* by Charles Y. Glock and Rodney Stark,[15] sponsored by the Anti-Defamation League, has sparked a plethora of discussions all over the country. Certain Catholic experts complained that the work was inadequate in its methodology but few questioned the extent of the anti-Semitism the study revealed. Catholics regret the failure of the Second Vatican Council to make an act of contrition for past treatment of the Jews, since it did make an act of contrition for its sins against the other Christian Churches. Moreover, Catholics are quite honest about the anti-Semitism to be found in St. John Chrysostom and St. Ambrose—even in our liturgy until the time of Pope John. This sense of shame for the Church's part in propagating anti-Semitism has led to projects such as that of St. Louis University which conducted a study of textbooks used in Catholic schools, uncovering some vicious caricatures of Jews.

Knowledge of Christian history not only leads to a sense of contrition but also helps us to understand the Jews. For this reason, history is beginning to find its way into Catholic-Jewish dialogue on anti-Semitism. Coerced conversions, penal laws, pogroms, and persecution have left the Jew with deep psychological wounds. The Jew suffered under the Christian state in the Middle Ages; the modern American Jew's antagonism to religion in the public schools mirrors the Jewish memory of the era when Church and State were united.

One disturbing episode occurred in 1967. When the United Arab Republic threatened the existence of Israel, it was said by certain Jewish leaders that the Christian "establishment" had failed to speak out in support of the Jews' right to exist. This silence, they affirmed, had rendered suspect the ecumenical sincerity of the Christians in Christian-Jewish dialogue. One Jewish group issued a memorandum saying: "It is hard for Jews to understand why the Christian religious

15 Charles Y. Glock and Rodney Stark, *Christian Beliefs and Anti-Semitism* (New York, 1966).

establishment had so much difficulty finding their tongues, particularly since many Christian leaders and denominations have been so outspoken in their opposition to the war in Vietnam." The Jewish attitude seemed to be: "You Christians were silent when the six million were exterminated in Germany and now once again you were silent when it seemed that the Arabs were about to annihilate the Israelis."

However, after a few months had passed, the general impression was that the dialogue would be helped rather than hurt by the affair. Christians would concentrate more carefully on the essential meaning of Jewish peoplehood, and the Jews would make the most of their opportunity in dialogue to explain and clarify the meaning of "Jewish people." For one of the main reasons for Christian silence at the time of the Mideast crisis was that Christian leaders thought of Israel in terms of a political state.

Those Jews who predicted that the Christian silence meant the death of dialogue were back again at dialogue as 1967 ended. The Roman Catholic ecumenists were as ready as ever for dialogue, but aware that the ecumenical euphoria was gone. The Jews felt that men of intellectual integrity could not shut their minds to unfamiliar ideas coming from other children of God. The walls were coming down. The lessons learned from the Christian silence and the plans for future dialogue were discussed by the Secretariat with representatives of the Jewish Reconstructionist Foundation and the Synagogue Council of America on May 14, 1968, at the Commodore Hotel, New York City. Father Edward H. Flannery is executive secretary of the Secretariat. The next day the Secretariat met at the Commodore with members of the American Jewish Committee and the Anti-Defamation League, B'nai B'rith.

OUR SITUATION AND PROSPECTS

If we turn our attention once again to Catholic-Protestant relations in the United States, is it possible to assess the present status of ecumenism and perhaps predict the future? Will the Anglicans follow Bishop Kilmer Myers' recommendation that they acknowledge Pope Paul as leader? Will the Roman Catholic and the Lutheran Churches listen seriously to the proposal made by the National Newman Students Federation and the Lutheran Students Association (September 1,

1967) that the two Churches enter into an organic reunion? To predict the future would be foolhardy. It is easier to attempt a comparative study of the mind-set of the average Catholic and Protestant in 1968. At this moment of history, the typical Catholic still does not understand Protestantism. He feels that unity is to be found ultimately only in "return" to Rome. He is at least subconsciously committed to a predetermined form of unity, one that admits perhaps a degree of contrition for Catholic sins against unity in the past but casts a cool eye on any talk of wide reforms in the Church.

The Protestant, on the other hand, sees no need of "return" to the Catholic Church. He cannot return to the medieval Roman Catholic Church which has vanished. He sees a fundamental unity underlying all the contemporary Christian Churches, based on a brotherhood in baptism, needing to be more fully and visibly manifested because that unity is now buried under the divisions of Christianity. He is ready to follow the leadership of the Spirit in building up this fuller manifestation of unity and is only too happy to read the last paragraph of the Decree on Ecumenism, which begins: "This sacred Council firmly hopes that the initiatives of the sons of the Catholic Church joined with those of the separated brethren will go forward, without obstructing the ways of divine Providence and without prejudging the future inspirations of the Holy Spirit." But he does want to feel sure that it is the Spirit that is leading him, not an ecclesiastical ecumenical bureaucracy, because he is loyal to his own denomination. He would consider it treason to surrender this loyalty unless he were convinced it is the will of God. There was a time when the American Protestant spoke of an invisible Church and perhaps even belittled churches in general as historical accretions; today he sees the visible Church as a Gospel imperative. What is needed is that the American Catholic go beyond the recognition of our basic unity with Protestants through baptism to the recognition of the presence of many other valid Christian elements in Protestant churches. This will lead him to a felt recognition of the fact that God used these Churches as means of salvation for their members, even though he himself believes that the fullness of the means of salvation is to be found in the Catholic Church.

American Protestants are dedicated to the great principles of the Reformation; American Catholics are dedicated to the basic teachings of the Catholic Church. Will the two communions therefore never meet? At the General Board meeting of the National Council of

Churches on June 1, 1967, Dr. John McCaw presented a progress report on Catholic-National Council relationships in the United States.[16] In the report he declared: "It is my conviction that we are approaching, if not actually in, the time of the American Church, and the very center of that Church could well be the Roman Catholic Church." Ecumenists generally would like to see one Christian Church in America but not an American Church. A National Church would be too small to manifest the universal unity of the "*una sancta.*" As St. Paul wrote to the Galatians (3:28): "There is neither Jew nor Greek, there is neither slave nor free, there is neither male nor female; for you are all one in Christ Jesus."[17]

[16] John McCaw, "Progress Report." Unpublished report presented to the General Board of the National Council of Churches, June 1-2, 1967.

[17] Those interested in following ecumenical developments should be acquainted with *Unity Trends,* a biweekly edited by the Department of Faith and Order, National Council of Churches, in consultation with the Catholic Bishops' Committee for Ecumenical Affairs and published by Our Sunday Visitor, Inc. Two other helpful publications are: *The Ecumenist,* a bimonthly published by the Paulist Press, Glen Rock, N.J., and the *Journal of Ecumenical Studies,* a scholarly quarterly published at Temple University in Philadelphia. For further background reading, consult John B. Sheerin, C.S.P., *A Practical Guide to Ecumenism* (Glenrock, N.J.: Paulist Press, 1967); George H. Tavard, *Two Centuries of Ecumenism* (Notre Dame, Ind., 1960); J. Robert Nelson, ed., *Christian Unity in North America* (St. Louis, 1963); and three titles in the "Deus Book" series published by the Paulist Press, Glen Rock, N.J.: Gregory Baum, *The Catholic Quest for Christian Unity* (1962); Gregory Baum, ed., *Ecumenical Theology Today* (1964); and Gregory Baum, ed., *Ecumenical Theology No. 2* (1967).

5: THE CHURCH AND AMERICAN PUBLIC LIFE

Edward Duff, S.J.

A few years ago the Fund for the Republic sponsored a series of scholarly studies on communism and American life under the general editorship of Clinton Rossiter. The author of the volume *Communism and the Churches,* Ralph Lord Roy,[1] spent five years researching the record of an estimated 500,000 clergymen. Among Catholics the only examples of tainted association were two priests, political malcontents from Ireland, who spoke in this country for the Spanish Loyalists. Mindful that some 750,000 Americans were at one time or another members of the Communist Party in the years before the Hitler-Stalin pact, the editor of *Social Order* was moved to inquire whether Catholics escaped being duped by Moscow because they were uninterested in the social and economic evils communism promised to eradicate. But on the other hand, it would be difficult to maintain that Catholics have been overly aligned with the forces of extreme political conservatism. Robert Welch, it is true, boasted that 1 per cent of the nation's priests belonged to the John Birch Society; but when challenged, he offered no evidence to back up his claim.

As has been true of its clergy, American Catholicism in general has felt fully at home in the American political environment. It has shown no disposition to dissent from prevailing institutions or to support radical movements. The Molly Maguires were not thought significant enough for an entry in the *New Catholic Encyclopedia.* Considering the source it is a dubious compliment, but Mark Hanna applauded the Catholic Church as a stabilizing force in American society. The same social reality lies behind Daniel P. Moynihan's remark that it is the Harvard men who are to be checked for security clearance and it is the Fordham graduates who do the checking.

[1] New York, 1960.

This largely uncritical acceptance of the direction of American public policy was in part the result of an avid allegiance to the American promise of liberty and equality for all. Moreover, the Catholic minority recognized its limited capacity to influence national policy dominated by the Protestant ascendancy, and Catholics were eager to be accepted as loyal, first-class citizens. Finally, Catholics generally practiced a religious individualism which separated the business of saving one's soul from the task of reshaping social institutions, the latter presumably a distraction if not a danger and, in any case, supererogatory. Charity, primarily to "our own kind," was preached incessantly, not merely as an obligation of group solidarity but as an imperative of the Gospel. Remaking the nation's laws, redefining its proximate goals in the interest of broader justice, was not considered particularly "religious."

This attitude of social insecurity and spiritual introversion is past; past, too, is the situation of cultural inferiority. The days of overt hostility and covert suspicion have been left behind; Catholics have won acceptance as legitimate contributors to and sharers in the American way of life. The result was predictable, being the working out of the American promise, but its attainment was hastened by the phenomenon of John Fitzgerald Kennedy, the prestige of Popes John and Paul, and the impetus of Vatican II. One can only surmise what forms Catholic participation in public life and national culture will take. It is disturbing that increasing numbers feel that the influence of religion is declining in American life; the strength of this feeling among young people is particularly disturbing. But whatever the general situation of religion in our national life, Catholics have gone beyond the point of explaining that their religion does not conflict with Americanism.[2] Although attained only recently, this state of things is now beyond challenge. When Senator Eugene McCarthy was campaigning in the New Hampshire primary early in 1968, the press wholly failed to take note of his religion; when Senator Robert F. Kennedy announced his

[2] It is not really so long ago that William Clancy wrote: "What does bother me a good deal is the challenge still given us to 'prove' our Americanism, and we hear this challenge even at 'advanced' interfaith gatherings. I, for one, am very tired of explaining that, no, I *really* feel no conflicts between my Americanism and my Catholicism. The day is rapidly coming—I think it has come for me—when American Catholics will refuse to answer such challenges, no matter how well they are meant, and will return them for the insults they are." In *Facing Protestant-Roman Catholic Tensions*, ed. Wayne H. Cowan (New York, 1960), p. 74.

candidacy, no public comment was heard that two Catholics were seeking the Presidency.

COMMITMENT TO THE AMERICAN SYSTEM

From the outset, Catholics unreservedly espoused the American political system. Seven years before the adoption of the First Amendment guaranteeing religious freedom, their spokesman and first bishop, John Carroll, declared: "We have all smarted heretofore under the lash of an established Church and shall be on our guard against every approach toward it." He spoke when his flock had emerged from a crisis menacing its survival. For so hostile was the environment of the Colonies and so repressive the prevailing legislation that the Catholic group, numbering some 25,000, was threatened by extinction on the eve of the American Revolution. The decisive support of officially Catholic France and the demonstrated loyalty of Catholics to the cause of independence changed public opinion considerably. With measured optimism Bishop Carroll could note that: "Thanks to genuine spirit and Christianity, the United States has banished intolerance from its system of government. Freedom and independence, acquired by the united efforts and cemented by the mingled blood of Protestant and Catholic fellow citizens, should be equally enjoyed by all." But intolerance toward Catholics, banished officially, had a long and ugly life; it was, according to Arthur M. Schlesinger, Sr., the oldest American prejudice. And yet the American Catholic community never muted its applause for the political system of the nation, never hesitated in its belief in the American promise.[3]

With its separation of religious affiliation from political allegiance, the American political system was a new thing in history. It is no concern of the government how the citizen worships. Such a self-denying ordinance, incorporated in the First Amendment, is a political statement, not a theological pronouncement, an arrangement to assure civic peace, not an article of a secularist creed. As a political posture it is quite distinct from the position of a *philosophe* like Condorcet, who argued that "Nothing but indifference for religion can bring about a

[3] Cf. John Tracy Ellis, "Church and State: An American Catholic Tradition," *Harper's*, CCVII (Nov., 1953).

durable peace." While refusing to adjudicate the religious claims of the churches, the drafters of our fundamental law had no doubt that religion was essential for public morality and, hence, for civic peace. Promptly on accepting the Conference Committee's report on the First Amendment, the Senate appointed a committee "to wait upon the President of the United States to request that he recommend a day of public thanksgiving and prayer be observed."

Fifty years later a fellow countryman of Condorcet, Alexis de Tocqueville, remarked on the novelty of the situation: "The Americans combine the notions of Christianity and liberty so intimately in their minds that it is impossible to make them conceive the one without the other." Such was not true elsewhere, he noted: "In France I had always seen the spirit of religion and the spirit of freedom marching in opposite directions. But in America I found that they were intimately united and that they reigned in common over the same country."[4] This being the case, De Tocqueville could have predicted that American Catholicism would never be confronted with a *Kulturkampf* or faced with Laws of Exception; the doctrines and ecclesiastical order of the Church of Rome would never come in conflict with the legitimate claims of political authority in the United States nor would true patriotism put a price tag on loyalty to the faith handed down by the Apostles. This is the situation which permits, indeed invites, the unreserved participation of Catholics in the public life of the country. When the Constitution of France's Fifth Republic described the new constitution as a "lay" state, the hierarchy felt obliged to explicate a distinction between *la laicité d'Etat*, an impartiality toward different religious groups, recognizing the pluralism of the nation, and *le laicisme d'Etat*, described as a philosophical doctrine, based on agnosticism and ideological atheism which is to serve as the official inspiration of the State in all its public functions.[5] Such a con-

[4] *Democracy in America*, 2 vols. (New York, 1945), I, 306, 308.

[5] The rationale and methodology of continental Liberalism have been thus described by Professor H. A. Rommen: "The basis for the separation [of Church and State] was not solicitude for the common good, it was not the desire for peace among a plurality of Churches and sects, but rather an adherence to the philosophical tenets of a rationalist liberalism as a kind of civil religion in Rousseau's meaning. Supernatural faith is here simply denied. The Christian rules of morality and the divine law are publicly declared either a myth, irreconcilable with modern science or with the proletarian revolution, or they are said to be only a propaganda instrument of clerical arrogance and of political anti-democratic reaction. Social and

fusion has not been conceivable up to now in the United States. Father John Courtney Murray summed up the point:

> It has been a greatly providential blessing that the American Republic has never put to the Catholic conscience the questions raised, for instance, by the Third French Republic. There has never been a schism within the American Catholic community, as there was among French Catholics, over the right attitude to adopt toward the established policy. There has never been the necessity for nice distinctions between the regime and the legislation; nor has there ever been the need to proclaim a policy of *ralliement*. In America the *ralliement* has been original, spontaneous, universal. It has been a matter of conscience and conviction, because its motive was not expediency in the narrow sense—the need to accept what one is powerless to change. Its motive was the evident coincidence of the principles which inspired the American Republic with the principles that are structural to the Western Christian political tradition.[6]

Quite probably the chief contribution of the Catholic Church to American public life has been its service to this "original, spontaneous, universal" *ralliement*, its active encouragement of immigrants from other political systems to adhere unabashedly to the American proposition, its endorsement of the American dream. This policy has, in fact, been so pronounced, so consistent, and perhaps so undiscriminating as to be the subject of the strictures of a controversial doctoral dissertation which indicts the hierarchy for inculcating a nationalism iden-

---

political life consequently are to be ruled without consideration of Christian and divinely revealed law but exclusively by the immanent rules of political or social or even proletarian science. It can easily be seen that such a 'religion' of indifferentism, even of anti-Christian rationalist scientism, in the new laic religion of the state, when imposed upon the citizen in public universities and schools, in the laws and administrative practices, makes of the state an instrument of rationalist unbelievers of the ruling class to destroy the traditional religion of the still Christian people. The new religion becomes the public religion of the State while the Catholic religion is declared to be exclusively and wholly a private affair of the citizen." Rommen, *The State in Catholic Thought* (St. Louis, 1945) pp. 600-01. Lord Acton similarly observed: "No despotism is more complete than that which is the aim of modern liberals. . . . The liberal doctrine subjects the desire of freedom to the desire of power and the more it demands a share of power, the more it is adverse to exemptions from it." John Emerich Edward Dalberg Acton, *Essays on Freedom and Power*, ed. Gertrude Himmelfarb (Boston, 1948), p. lvii.

[6] *Catholicism in American Culture: Semicentenary Lecture Series, 1953-54* (College of New Rochelle, New Rochelle, N.Y., 1955), p. 22.

tifying the country's goals and actions with God's purposes.[7] No suggestion is made of denominational doctrinal compromises but rather of an overexuberant acceptance of any policy aggrandizing the nation's power.

There is little doubt that our episcopal leadership has been intensely patriotic and has encouraged in its ethnically mixed flock an enthusiastic sense of belonging. "Hyphenated American" was a status to outgrow, betokening as it did a stage of social inferiority. When advocated as explicit ecclesiastical policy, necessary for the preservation of the faith (and the native language), hyphenation was rejected as an intrusion of European influence on the American religious scene. The attempt to perpetuate European language and culture was rejected because it implied a mistrust of the spiritual possibilities of American culture; it impugned the validity of the *ralliement*. In the language of one of the most effective (and emotional) opponents of any attempt of this sort, Archbishop John Ireland, "The Church of America must be, of course, as Catholic as even in Jerusalem and Rome; but as far as her garments assume color from the local atmosphere, she must be American. Let no one dare to paint her brow with a foreign tint or pin to her mantle foreign linings." Such an attitude was not attained automatically, or without minor protests.

Few of the Catholic emigrants to this country had the experience of living under a government of their own choosing; indeed, many had come to these shores not merely from economic necessity but because of hostile regimes. For the Irish, government meant the never legitimatized invader who had added religious persecution to his political oppression; for the German Catholic it frequently meant arrogant Prussian power; for the Slav it was the enemy of his ethnic particularism. To have persuaded this disparate flock that the new and strange political order was beneficent, one to be accepted without reservation, was no small accomplishment of the Catholic Church in America. Writing in 1950, before Vatican II had set straight the Church's position on religious freedom (and, indirectly, on the limitations of government), Henry Steele Commager dismissed speculation on the incongruity of Catholic principles and the American political system:

[7] Published in a trade edition as Dorothy Dohen, *Nationalism and American Catholicism* (New York, 1967).

> Whatever conclusions might be drawn from a scrutiny of Catholic doctrine, the fact was that Catholicism had flourished as a major religion for three quarters of a century without raising serious difficulties except in the imaginations of men and that democratic institutions seemed as sound when the church numbered twenty-four million members as they had been when it counted its communicants by the hundred thousand. It might, indeed, be maintained that the Catholic church was, during this period, one of the most effective of all agencies for democracy and Americanization. Representing as it did a vast cross section of the American people, it could ignore class, section, and race; peculiarly the church of the newcomers, of those who all too often were regarded as aliens, it could give them not only spiritual refuge but social security.[8]

As a conspicuous agent for the acculturation of millions of immigrants, then, the Catholic Church made a signal contribution to American public life.

IMMIGRATION AND ITS PROBLEMS

But if Catholics found American political principles consonant, even congenial, to their religious orientation, their situation supplied limited opportunities to influence public policy. Two Catholics, to be sure, signed the Declaration of Independence. Contemporary American Catholicism, however, does not derive from the miniscule pre-Revolutionary elite of Maryland but from the flood of immigrants that ended in the mid-1920's. These were the dispossessed, the adventurers, the persecuted, the outcasts, even the criminals of Europe; in large measure they were the surplus population of the peasantry, useful only to a new continent where unskilled manpower was essential to a nation under continuous construction. Hampered—except for the Irish—by ignorance of English, they huddled in ethnic enclaves, creating their own protective and self-help associations. Considerable numbers of German-speaking Catholics remained on the land, but most of the immigrants sought work, and homes, in the cities. Exploited, crammed together in teeming tenements near mills and mines and slaughter houses, they were the victims of social disorganization, economic dis-

[8] *The American Mind* (paperback ed., New Haven, Conn., 1959), p. 193.

crimination and their own ignorance and vices. Soon after the Civil War, according to the *Catholic World*, nearly half of those living in New York City were Catholics. The city's death rate was the highest in the world, and its destitution was increasing ten times faster than the growing population. The chief problem, the president of the St. Vincent de Paul Society told headquarters in Paris, was not poverty (since personal industry, according to American folklore, assured economic security here) but intemperance and the consequences of intemperance, the children of broken homes. The Second Plenary Council of Baltimore admitted as much: "It is a melancholy fact and a very humiliating admission for us to make that a very large portion of the idle and vicious youth of our principal cities are the children of Catholic parents."

There was no slackening: Irish and Germans were followed by Catholics from central and eastern Europe and from Italy—2,300,000 arriving from the latter country in the single decade of 1900-1910. Listed as "foreigners," the Catholics of these generations were the poor and the unlettered. Submerged as a socially beleaguered and despised minority in a specifically Protestant culture, American Catholics had more pressing preoccupations than indulging civic concerns. The pastoral problem was appalling. A speaker at the First American Catholic Missionary Congress in 1908 declared that scarcely a million of the six million non-English speaking Catholics were receiving "the blessings of religion."

With neither the ability nor the ambition to attempt much more than to safeguard the faith of the immigrant, American Catholicism erected a whole series of defense mechanisms, beginning with the parochial school, whose role historically has been more apologetic than intellectual. Because of active Protestant proselytizing, and because priests were denied access to inmates of public institutions, additional agencies had to be improvised: clubs for young men, homes for working girls, temperance leagues and fraternal societies, child-care centers and reform schools. Direct action through social-welfare agencies of its own creation was the Church's historic confrontation of American society.

Even the issue of slavery would not be allowed to imperil Catholic unity or the acceptance of the Catholic immigrant as an authentic, patriotic citizen. As the prelates of the border province of Cincinnati explained in a pastoral letter written two weeks after the attack on

Fort Sumter: "While [the Church's] ministers rightfully feel a deep and abiding interest in all that concerns the welfare of the country, they do not think it their province to enter into the political arena." To be sure, the aggressive anti-Catholicism of prominent Abolitionists (as well as the immigrants' fear of the job competition of freed Negroes) were factors in Catholic judgments on Civil War issues. But a determination to maintain the political neutrality of the Church seems best to explain the attitude inculcated by Archbishop John Hughes of New York in 1861: "There is but one rule for a Catholic wherever he is, and that is to do his duty there as citizen." Although seemingly a program of conformism, what is here advocated is a strategy of survival, a strategy emphasized by the same prelate in a speech twenty years earlier: "No matter what sect is assailed, extend to it, in common with your fellow citizens, a protecting hand. If the Jew is oppressed, then stand by the Jew. Thus will all be secured alike in the common enjoyment of the blessings of civil and religious liberty, and the justly obnoxious union of Church and State be most effectually prevented."[9]

IMMIGRANT CATHOLICS AND MACHINE POLITICS

If the immigrant Catholics did little to shape policy in their new land, they were not to be left voteless by the American politician. In Boston between 1850 and 1855, the native vote increased by almost 15 per cent, but the foreign-born vote expanded by almost 200 per cent.[10] These votes went almost automatically to the Democratic Party, whose chief merit was that it was not the instrument of the industrialists and the merchants with interests perforce other than those of the dispossessed. In return for local partisan loyalty there were jobs on the city payroll, understanding when one fell afoul the law, aid in obtaining permits or licenses, and bounteous Christmas baskets for the poor.

[9] The quotation from the Cincinnati bishops' statement is taken from John Tracy Ellis, *American Catholicism* (Chicago, 1956), p. 92; the quotations from Hughes from *Complete Works of the Most Rev. John Hughes*, ed. Lawrence Kehoe, 2 vols. (New York, 1864), II, 157, and I, 269.

[10] This fascinating figure is found in Francis J. Lally, *The Catholic Church in Changing America* (Boston, 1962), p. 30.

There was no ideology here beyond the solidarity of "our kind" and a realization that not much could be expected from the business community and its allies in the Republican Party. As they succeeded one another, each of the Catholic ethnic groups became the beneficiary of the municipal political machine and in time achieved influence in it by delivering the votes from the "Corktowns," the "Little Italys," and the "Warsaws" of American cities. By reason of their priority on the scene, their organizing skills, their flair for colorful speech and, perhaps, their hatred of oppression, the Irish were the first to capture control of the city machines and to present to the nation a gallery of flamboyant popular tribunes, wielding political power with gusto.

Forty years ago George N. Shuster wrote in his book, *The Catholic Spirit in America*: "I honestly believe that most American suspicion of the Catholic from the point of view of the constitutional ideal of government is due to what has happened in large cities like New York and Chicago. The ward and its cabal, the party boss, the graft-riddled police force, the nepotistic judiciary—all these are laid to politicians who are, as a matter of fact, often men with names having something like a Catholic ring."[11] The young professor Shuster was undoubtedly correct in assessing the scandal (often pharasaical) experienced by those shocked by the power tactics of the Catholic city machine. But his judgment would, I suspect, have been found overfastidious by the clients of those same machines which provided them with gestures of concern and a semblance of the welfare state in an era when the nation's public policy on economic justice was in default—and this by a policy decision.

The government which promised equal political rights to all considered it forbidden to interfere with the economic processes which worked cruel inequities between rich and poor. The city machines, admittedly dominated frequently by Catholics, were the protest mechanisms and the welfare agencies of the urban slumdwellers as was Populism for the disadvantaged farmer. Lincoln Steffens, the muckraking journalist, having spotlighted the transgressions of big business, found much to applaud in the political domain of Martin Lomasney, the boss of Boston's West End. Corrupt though they were, the municipal machines supplied jobs, hospitals, parks, and beaches

[11] George N. Shuster, *The Catholic Spirit in America* (New York, 1927), p. 109.

for the poor. They—and the nascent trade union movement—were a challenge and a check to triumphant business interests whose ethos was blessed by the dominant religious forces of the majority.

Moreover, the city machines provided apprenticeship and subsequent support for Catholics who would find places of responsibility in state offices. Conspicuous among such successes was Alfred E. Smith, during whose three terms as governor social legislation was enacted making New York a model of progressive government and Smith the nominee for President in 1928. That his defeat was in part owing to his Catholicism is generally conceded. His alien religion was accentuated by Smith's gaudy dress, his unabashed East Side accent, and his call for repeal of Prohibition, Protestantism's last and self-defeating national moral crusade.

Outstanding administrator though he was, open to ideas of wider state responsibility (he increased the state's contribution to education from nine-million dollars to eighty-two million annually), and independent and far-sighted in attracting talented and dedicated people to public service, Smith's outlook was provincial to a degree that Catholic enthusiasm for him overlooked. Self-educated and shaped by his environment, he was a completely undoctrinaire political practitioner, deficient in experience and, perhaps, interest in national and international problems. He was even unaware of the official (if culture-conditioned) Catholic teaching on the political order. When Charles C. Marshall challenged him, in an open letter to the *Atlantic Monthly*, to explain how he could sincerely subscribe to the principle of separation of Church and State in the light of papal claims to official public recognition of the true Church, Governor Smith expostulated: "So little are these matters of the essence of my faith that I, a devout Catholic since childhood, never heard of them until I read your letter."[12]

It is equally probable that, "devout Catholic since childhood," Smith had never seriously examined the 1919 Bishops' Program of Social Reconstruction, sponsored by the Administrative Committee of the National Catholic War Council and framed by Msgr. John A. Ryan.[13]

[12] Cf. Peter H. Odegard, ed., *Religion and Politics* (New York, 1960).

[13] Cf. John Tracy Ellis, ed., *Documents of American Catholic History* (Milwaukee, 1956), pp. 611-29. For earlier episcopal pronouncements, see Peter Guilday, ed. *The National Pastorals of the American Hierarchy*, 1792-1919 (Westminster, Md., 1954).

A broad examination of the American social scene in the aftermath of World War I, the program called for governmental action on a national level, specifically recommending: 1) minimum-wage legislation; 2) unemployment, sickness, disability, and old-age insurance; 3) minimum age limit for child labor; (4) legal enforcement of the right of labor to organize; 5) continuation of the War Labor Board; 6) a national employment service; 7) public housing for low-income workers; 8) increased wages, even over wartime levels; 9) regulation of public-utility rates and progressive taxes on inheritance, income, and excess profits; 10) participation of labor in management and ownership; 11)control of monopolies, even by government competition. It is to the credit of the episcopal signers of the program (and to their confidence in the competence of Msgr. Ryan in the fields of ethics and economics) that they did not retreat when attacked for endorsing what were called socialistic measures. It is doubtful, however, if the program's call for political responsibility by the Federal government in the areas enumerated had wide support in the American Catholic community at that time.

DEPRESSION DAYS

When on the twentieth anniversary of the 1919 bishops' program a new reprint was issued, Cardinal Mooney in an introduction listed its eleven points and noted that all but one of them had been wholly or partially "translated into fact." What was being signaled, of course, was the result of the Roosevelt revolution, the victory of a coalition in which Catholics certainly played a part. Item ten of the program, calling for labor's participation in ownership and management, while remaining a theoretical *desideratum* for Catholic reformers, was in practice quietly abandoned. It never had active support from the trade union people. National health insurance, also proposed in the 1919 program, was first presented to Congress by Senator Robert F. Wagner of New York in February, 1939, but the bill died in committee. Revived in June, 1943, by Senator Wagner, who was joined by Senator James E. Murray of Montana and Representative John D. Dingell of Michigan —all Catholics—the measure was buffeted about in the halls of Congress over the years, being opposed by (among others) the Daughters of the American Revolution, the National Catholic Hospital Association, and the National Conference of Catholic Charities, until it emerged in truncated and attenuated form as Medicare.

It was the Depression that forced American Catholics to think seriously about national problems. Previously they had been accustomed to thinking of the duties of men in public life in terms of probity, impartiality, and respectability. But in times of crisis, these qualities were not enough, admirable though they might be. Courage, vision, and political inventiveness were required. Catholics were told by the Pope himself (in *Quadragesimo Anno*, 1931) that "Free competition is dead. Economic dictatorship has taken its place. . . . The whole economic life has become hard, cruel, and relentless in a ghastly measure." On the practical level, Catholics knew the reality of acute hardship if not hunger, for whether factory workers, salesmen, or minor managers they were members of the *salariat* rather than the propertied class. Never seriously tempted by socialism because of its anticlerical associations, they were persuaded, nevertheless, of the need of new legislation and of a strong government to protect their interests. Those in the labor movement demanded government protection of the right to organize. With other minority and disadvantaged groups, Catholics flocked to the support of Franklin Roosevelt and were accepted as dependable political allies, if not as major architects of policy.

On the farm problem Catholics demonstrated their inexperience—a phenomenon not unrelated to the absence of any agricultural institution of higher learning under Catholic auspices and to the urban concentration of the Catholic population. The Bishops' 1933 Statement on the Present Crisis deplored by implication the mechanization and scientific management of agriculture and espoused a return of urban families to the land. This impossible solution to the problems of unemployment was described as having "illimitable" possibilities. The 1939 statement on the Church and the Social Order left the farm problem untouched, which was, perhaps, just as well.

The public policies generally supported by Catholics in the 1930's were those which advanced their economic interests, a fact which will surprise only those unacquainted with history and human nature. On two occasions, however, Catholics became obtrusive on the national scene. Father Charles E. Coughlin of Detroit built up a vast audience organized as the Radio League of the Little Flower.[14] Ambi-

[14] Cf. Charles J. Tull, *Father Coughlin and the New Deal* (Syracuse, 1965).

tious to relate the Gospel to the economic crisis, he elaborated a home-made monetary theory which owed much, if unconsciously, to the Populist tradition. Coughlin also castigated a set of familiar devils, notably "the international bankers" who turned out to have Jewish names. Papal encyclicals were freely invoked as supplying ready answers to immediate distress and invoked so decisively and persuasively in a rich, rolling baritone that Protestant rural America came to think of its ancient foe, Rome, as the enemy of its historic oppressor, Wall Street. Intoxicated by his own eloquence and credulous as an astrologer of his fiscal nostrums, Father Coughlin contrived a Union Party to contest the presidential election of 1936, accepting as allies Dr. Townsend's old-age pension movement and the followers of the assassinated Huey Long's Share-the-Wealth program. Father Coughlin's handpicked candidate was Representative William Lemke of North Dakota. Like Lenin he wore a cloth cap. Unlike Lenin he was ineffective, had no viable program, and is not remembered.

The political primitiveness of the Coughlin preaching appealed to the same quality in a large section of the American people for several years. It updated venerable warnings against "foreign entanglements" and "perfidious Albion," deepened the tradition of isolationism, and fostered ethnic prejudices. Coughlin's relentless war on "godless communism" also helped sink a lasting fixation into the American Catholic mind.

Thus, predictably, American Catholics were united in opposing the repeal of the neutrality laws forbidding the export of arms to the republican government of Spain under attack by an army revolt led by General Franco and supported by Hitler and Mussolini. To a degree seldom appreciated, the reaction of the American Church to the Spanish Civil War won it the mistrust of the nation's liberals and intellectuals. Here was ample evidence that the Church, an authoritarian institution, imposed authoritarian attitudes which issued into authoritarian political preferences. That the Soviet Union and its attached international conspiratorial apparatus actively aided (and ultimately robbed) the Spanish government did not daunt the American public (the Soviets were, after all, opposing Hitler). The Spain of the Inquisition and the Black Legend was again stifling freedom—so judged virtually every certified American intellectual, editor, artist, critic, essayist, movie director. In sufficiently influential circles the success of Franco was more harmful to American Catholicism than the scandal of Tammany Hall.

THE POST-WAR ERA AND McCARTHYISM

The editor's introductory chapter to a 1951 symposium, *Protestant Thought in the Twentieth Century,* is entitled "America at the End of the Protestant Era."[15] The Protestant dominance of American culture yielded to a new ideology, "The American Way of Life," an "idolatrous civic religion of Americanism," in the words of Will Herberg, who in his *Protestant-Catholic-Jew*[16] trenchantly argued that the United States has been transformed into a "three-religion country," a situation in which there is a common set of ideals, rituals, and symbols; faith becoming instrumental to promoting "democracy" and civic harmony, and "the three great faiths" viewed as three alternative (though not necessarily equal) expressions of the fundamental commitment which all share by virtue of being Americans.

The Catholic community became more conservative politically as it acquired more to conserve and as it was more accepted socially. In the view of Joseph H. Fichter, S.J., in an earlier Notre Dame symposium, it became undistinguishable in its assimilation:

> Catholics share in the anti-Semitism of the Northeast, in the isolationism of the Midwest, in the prejudice against Mexicans in the Southwest. Catholics acted like Californians when the Japanese-Americans were dispossessed and sent to relocation camps, like Texans when the off-shore oil disputes were discussed and like Ciceronians when Negro families moved into white neighborhoods in Illinois. On this level we are dealing with the moral and social problems on which the American people are confused and on which Catholics demonstrate their achieved Americanization by sharing the confusion.[17]

The Lotusland of the suburbs beckoned to the new class of office managers and junior executives, imposing on the Church a renewed stage of the brick-and-mortar involvement in an effort to provide parish plant, not least parochial schools, for the new neighbors—a stage continuing the attitude of institutional introversion by reason of the funds and

[15] Cf. Arnold Samuel Nash, ed., *Protestant Thought in the Twentieth Century* (New York, 1951).

[16] Revised paperback ed., New York, 1960.

[17] Thomas T. McAvoy, C.S.C., ed., *Roman Catholicism and the American Way of Life* (Notre Dame, Ind., 1960) p. 124.

planning required. Many of these new families—their faith in the country's future unclouded as they lived under twenty-year mortgages—deserted their Democratic allegiance in 1952 and 1956 to vote for Eisenhower, security, and peace of mind.

American Catholicism had arrived and its attitude was less defensive than protective; indeed, it was less protective of its spiritual insights than of its middle-class status. An ambitious if disorganized political charlatan, Senator Joseph R. McCarthy, transposing the billingsgate of ward politics to the national scene, succeeded in disturbing millions and miring public policy in empty controversy. The threat he thundered about came primarily not from any foreign power but from a conspiracy of shadowy people in government whose ideas clearly menaced newly acquired personal wealth. The "communists," it was slyly suggested, were going to take it away from you; while it was emphasized that they opposed religion and traditional morality, their disagreement with the values of free enterprise and the economic security of the individual was underscored as "un-American." It is significant but somewhat surprising that no other Catholic politician trained in the tactics of urban campaigning rose to challenge the McCarthy demagoguery. It would, of course, have called for immense courage in a day when the Soviet Union was pushing westward in Europe, absorbing in its embrace every seventh Catholic in the world; a day when expelled missionaries were explaining that they had not expected communism to triumph in China, a fact that presumably made them experts on how it was triumphing here. The mood of McCarthyism, however, was not concerned with external dangers. In addition to indulging a shabby ambition, it attacked all unfamiliar ideas as alien and, reductively, would have abrogated the welfare role of government. An egregious and costly distraction, it lulled the national conscience until an ex-Catholic, Michael Harrington, in *The Other America*,[18] revealed the existence in a visibly affluent society of forty to fifty million poor lost in our midst. The anticommunist preoccupation delayed action on justice for the Negro, drowned out Labor Secretary James Mitchell's appeals for decent treatment of migrant farm labor, and deterred a forthright assumption of responsibility toward the hungry developing world. For this negative anticommunist mood thoughtful sections of the American public (and perhaps future historians) blame Catholics. Let the record show, however, that when

[18] New York, 1962.

the Senate finally decided to put a stop to McCarthy's antics, six of the eight Catholic senators present voted to censure him.

ROMANTICIZING THE PAST

In his engaging *Reflections on America,* Jacques Maritain notes that "in one sense you [Americans] are freed from the history of your European ancestors, for you have voluntarily cut off your links with this history." European history is "your pre-history." Maritain's point is that we are freed of "all the rotten stuff of past events, past hatreds, past habits, past glories, and past diseases which compose a sort of overwhelming historical heredity."[19] We are said also to be freed of the Marxist myth of historical necessity. The compliment seems excessive. The Confederate flag flying atop the state capitol in George Wallace's Alabama and the boisterous antics of yahoos in Confederate uniforms (thus jeopardizing their right to a United States passport?) at Democratic National Conventions indicate a permanent historical nostalgia or an unreconstructed rancorousness. Nor have foreign ties been forgotten. It is certainly arguable that Irish independence owes as much to American-Irish support as the existence of Israel does to American-Jewish aid. The pressure of ethnic groups was important in shaping American positions in the creation of the successor states to the Austro-Hungarian Empire in the Versailles treaties. The Federal government actively promoted a letter-writing campaign among American-Italians when a communist victory threatened in a postwar Italian election.

Pace Professor Maritain, there has been a covert Catholic—and American Catholic—tendency to romanticize the past; this despite the uninterrupted affirmation by the hierarchy of the superior values of the American system of government. That mentality has been described by Thomas Merton as "the assumption that medieval Christianity was a unique and timeless norm which we must work to reestablish." Christendom was too readily confused with Camelot where, under the aegis of a common faith, conflicts between the spiritual and the worldly were (supposedly) readily reconciled and where justice held sway because men were brothers. Was it this mythology of the Middle Ages, or was it an overliteral loyalty to a

[19] Jacques Maritain, *Reflections on America* (paperback ed., New York, 1964), p. 16.

suggestion of the encyclical *Quadragesimo Anno*, with its concern about the class conflict in European society, that moved the American hierarchy in its 1939 statement on the Church and the Social Order to call for the reestablishment of "some form of guild or vocational groups"? That these guilds would have vast power and fundamentally restructure our political system is clear from the following description: "They are autonomous, embrace whole industries, possess the right of free organization, assembly and vote, and they should dedicate themselves to the common good and, with governmental protection and assistance, function in the establishment of justice and the general welfare in the economic life." Whether such instruments would have power to fix wages and prices, set production quotas, and assign tax priorities, one never learned—or how they would be compatible with antitrust legislation and monopoly control. We are not likely to learn until historians turn to this subject, for the vocational-group approach seems totally forgotten today.

A more serious and damaging devotion to historically conditioned truth was set forth in a standard reference book, *The State and the Church*, by John A. Ryan in collaboration with Moorhouse F. X. Millar, S.J.[20] The book espoused the traditional confessional state as the ideal form of relationship between Church and State. In such an arrangement the State, as the political instrument of society, would profess the Catholic faith and, in consequence, would act to advance Catholicism while discouraging, if not repressing, false religions.[21] When the doctrine was invoked against Governor Smith in 1928,

[20] New York, 1922.

[21] What the doctrine demanded may be surmised from quotations which Paul Blanshard stitched together from three consecutive pages of the Ryan-Millar book: "If these [religious practices] are carried on within the family, or in such an inconspicuous manner as to be neither an occasion of scandal nor of perversion of the faithful, they may properly be tolerated by the State. . . . Quite distinct from the performance of false religious worship and preaching to the members of the erring sect is the propagation of false doctrine among Catholics. This could become a source of injury, a positive menace, to the religious welfare of true believers. Against such an evil, they may have a right of protection by the Catholic State. . . . If there is only one true religion and if its possession is most important good for states as well as individuals, then the public profession, protection and promotion of this religion and the legal prohibition of all direct assaults upon it, becomes one of the most obvious and fundamental duties of the State." Blanshard, *American Freedom and Catholic Power* (Boston, 1949), p. 71. The composite quotation is from Ryan-Millar, pp. 35, 35-36, 37.

Msgr. Ryan sought refuge in the expediential distinction of *thesis-hypothesis,* writing to the *New York World:* "While all this is very true in logic and in theory, the event of its practical realization in any state or country is so remote in time and in probability that no practical man will let it disturb his equanimity or affect his attitude toward those who differ from him in religious faith."

The same intransigent stand, repeating the Church's reaction to continental Liberalism and especially the Italian *Risorgimento,* was expounded in a series of articles in the pages of the *American Ecclesiastical Review* in the early 1950's, in which one argument for the religious function of the State was derived from the liturgy of the anointing of a king in medieval times. These assertions of the rights of the one true Church were ritualistically accompanied by the assurance that in the United States, at least, such rights would not be imposed even should Catholics become a majority. The explanation wouldn't wash. When in 1959 an enterprising Catholic publisher invited a small group of non-Catholics to set down their impressions of American Catholicism, one of them, Professor Stringfellow Barr, declared: "It is simply a brutal fact that American non-Catholics are afraid of the Catholic Church, and its behavior in certain other countries has not reassured them. Fear is a bad basis for good communications and breeds a kind of cold war."[22] It was ironic: American Catholicism had felt no compulsion to answer the papal appeal for volunteers to defend embattled Rome in 1870, but felt an obligation to defend indiscriminately the *Syllabus Errorum* of 1864 even after the Lateran Treaty.

More operative than any nostalgia for a culturally conditioned past in influencing the attitudes of American Catholics towards public policy was a scepticism about the efficacy of political means to improve the human condition and a confidence in our spiritual armor to meet life's problems. Long reliance on paternalistic measures in dealing with the Negro and apparent unawareness of the clear issues of justice involved would be a case in point. Politics, to be sure, was counted on to protect public morality, serve the institutional needs of the Church, and advance the economic interest of the group. But "the world" was not taken seriously because it was destined to "pass away." Moreover, the compromises inherent in the political process were deemed spiri-

[22] Philip Scharper, ed., *American Catholics: A Protestant-Jewish View* (New York, 1959), p. 18.

tually debilitating. One could boast of clean hands but, as Péguy noted, at the price of having no hands. Most of this spirit was unconscious; its rhetoric, a product of spiritual writers and pulpit orators given to ascribing most remediable ills to God's (presumed) permissive will.

The Church in Europe in the nineteenth century found itself outside (and opposed to) the great movements of social change and opted for (or was forced into) a policy of reproach, rejection, and retreat. By reason of the intellectual colonialism dominating seminary training, this policy impregnated ascetical and theological thinking in this country as well. In part, too, it resulted from the earlier enforced isolation of American Catholics from the mainstream of society and their dependence on the corporal and spiritual works of mercy. In any case, not least on issues of national public policy, pre-Vatican II American Catholicism was embarrassingly vulnerable to the biting charge of William Stringfellow that "Christianity is concerned with religion and not with life."

KENNEDY AND THE COUNCIL

The fact of John Fitzgerald Kennedy and the teaching of the Second Vatican Council, it has often been observed, have had an effect of seismic proportions on American Catholicism. With the tremors still continuing, the future shape of the once familiar terrain—not least as it will influence Catholic attitudes on public policy—is not yet clearly visible.

The success and the charism of Kennedy made Catholics feel taller. An authentic war hero, a Pulitzer Prize winner, an Overseer of Harvard; young, buoyant, intelligent, handsome, modest yet of mordant wit; unafraid of power yet conscious of its responsibilities, grave and gay in turn, answer to the aspirations of the young and the undisillusioned—here indeed was a legitimate folk hero (soon to be a legend), a flattering symbol of the fondest hopes of a religious minority delighted with the world's affectionate approval of its favorite son. Roger B. Taney and Edward D. White had been Chief Justices of the Supreme Court, but now a Catholic was President of the United States and the political leader of the free world. But John Kennedy's significance was much larger than this. His was the layman's free assumption of responsibility for the direction of history. In his inaugural address the citizenry was reminded in the final sentence that "here on earth God's work must truly be our own."[23] Life was not a "vale of tears," nor an opportunity to acquire pension rights to heaven, but an eligibility for service to country and world "with a good conscience our only reward." Here, too, was the layman's clear assertion that the political order was his particular province because specifically secular, an area of engagement with its own rules because of its particular functions. At the time—the pre-Council era—some were disconcerted by the Kennedy disavowal: "I do not speak for the Catholic Church on issues of public policy—and no one in that Church speaks for me." Accountable to God in the confessional for his sins and to his fellow citizens at the polls for his public performance, with neither embarrassment over his denominational loyalty nor confusion of civic duty and ecclesiastical allegiance—such was the convincing commitment of John Kennedy that introduced a new era in American Catholicism.

The teachings of Vatican II reinforced the credibility of the Kennedy political posture. It authenticated his opposition (as expressed to the Ministerial Association of Greater Houston) "to the state being used by any religious group, Catholic or Protestant, to compel, prohibit, or persecute the free exercise of any other religion," a position that had enjoyed the uninterrupted support of the American hierarchy. For in a special declaration, the Vatican Council not only reproved any coercion of religious freedom and espoused its free exercise both personally and in association with others—and this as a human right—but the Council also placed responsibility for the protection of this right upon "the people as a whole, upon social groups, upon government, and upon the Church and other religious communities, in virtue of the duty of all toward the common welfare and in the manner proper to each."

On a more important level the Council in its Pastoral Constitution on the Church in the Modern World offered a new orientation toward human progress and a new mandate of Christian involvement. In its specifically theological discussion, the document protested that: "Christ, to be sure, gave his Church no proper mission in the political, economic or social order. The purpose which He set before her is a religious one" (#42). But such a mission does not authorize the

[23] The Kennedy quotations are from Edward J. Richter and Berton Dulce, *Religion and the Presidency* (New York, 1962).

Church's members to abstain from the sweaty realm of the secular: "They are mistaken who, knowing that we have here no abiding city but seek one which is to come, think that they may therefore shirk their earthly responsibilities. For they are forgetting that by faith itself they are more than ever obliged to measure up to those duties, each according to his proper vocation. . . . Therefore, let there be no false opposition between professional and social activities on the one part and religious life on the other. The Christian who neglects his temporal duties neglects his duties toward his neighbor and even God and jeopardizes his eternal salvation" (#43).

Evidence that the bishops of the Council had come to understand the nature and workings of contemporary society may be sensed in their insistence that "secular duties and activities belong properly although not exclusively to laymen." Moreover, in the exercise of his proper function in the secular realm—including that of devising and supporting correct public policy—the layman is to act as an adult: "Let not the layman imagine that his pastors are always such experts that to every problem which arises, however complicated, they can readily give him a concrete solution, or even that such is their mission. Rather, enlightened by Christian wisdom and giving close attention to the teaching authority of the Church, let the layman take on his own responsibility" (#43). John Kennedy had anticipated this disclaimer of clerical competence. "I believe in an America," he said at Houston, "where no public official either requests or accepts instruction from the pope, the National Council of Churches, or any other ecclesiastical source. . . . I do not accept the right of, as I said, any ecclesiastical official to tell me what I should do in the sphere of my public responsibility as an elected official. . . ." Similarly and subsequently, persuaded that the state's jurisdiction is over public order not private sin, a lay Catholic professor at the Jesuit university in Boston circulated a petition which proved useful in the repeal of the Massachusetts statute which made the sale or use of contraceptives a crime. Believing that good law must accommodate itself to the moral convictions of the people, Catholics testified in favor of the liberalization of New York State's adultery-only divorce statute, despite the pressure of the bishops to retain a measure the effectuation of which was attended by widespread, suborned perjury. Catholics similarly testified before a Senate committee as to the legitimacy of the Federal government making birth control information available at home and abroad, while the Archbishop of Washington and the Apostolic Delegate were damning the government's action.

UNFINISHED BUSINESS

In estimating the postconciliar attitudes of American Catholics on issues of public policy, it is essential to keep in mind the increasing difficulty of drawing conclusions, clear and viable in the legal order, from transcendental truths of the religious order. This difficulty the Pastoral Constitution on the Church in the Modern World acknowledges:

> Often enough the Christian view of things will suggest some specific solution in certain circumstances. Yet it happens rather frequently, and legitimately so, that with equal sincerity some of the faithful will disagree with others on a given matter. Even against the intentions of their proponents, however, solutions proposed on one side or another may be easily confused by many people with the gospel message. Hence it is necessary for people to remember that no one is allowed in the aforementioned situations to appropriate the Church's authority for his opinion. They should always try to enlighten one another through honest discussion, preserving mutual charity and caring above all for the common good (#42).

Neither the unilateral opinion of even the national hierarchy nor the narrow institutional needs of the Church can, therefore, be controlling in these matters. Nor is an assertedly Catholic view controlling, for the same Council document observes in its chapter on political life: "Christians should recognize that various legitimate though conflicting views can be held concerning the regulation of temporal affairs. They should respect their fellow citizens when they propose such views honorably even by group action" (#75).

One basic reason for this diversity in the choice of political means, even when there is agreement on social goals, was once explained by Reinhold Niebuhr:

> The lack of a clear spiritual witness to the truth in Christ is aggravated by certain modern developments, among them the increasing complexity of moral problems and the increasing dominance of the group or collective over the life of the individual. The complexity of ethical problems makes an evangelical impulse to seek the good

of the neighbor subordinate to the complicated questions about which of my neighbors has first claim upon us or what technical means are best suited to fulfill their need. The Enlightenment was wrong in expecting virtue to flow inevitably from rational enlightenment. But that does not change the fact that religiously inspired good will, without intelligent analysis of the factors in a moral situation and of the proper means to gain desirable ends, is unavailing.[24]

Granted, then, the impossibility of contriving a Catholic party line on issues of public policy, and grateful that a kind history has spared American Catholicism the need of elaborating specific political instruments and of upholding traditional political positions in defense of its existence (as happened in Europe),[25] are there discoverable general political preferences, or at least orientations, dictated by the theological vision and special situation of the Church in this country? I think that there are. To be sure, the relation of these Catholic insights to the political process will be general rather than specific and indirect rather than direct, legal specification being left to the political prudence of the national community.[26]

Nothing is more repugnant to the universalism of Christianity than racism and national egoism, twin manifestations of a single moral evil —pride, the root sin. Since God has made of all men a single race to dwell upon the earth and since in Christ there is neither Jew nor gentile, male nor female, Greek nor barbarian, slave nor free man, the institutionalized injustices imposed on people of color in the United

[24] *Christian Century*, LXX (July 22, 1953), 841.

[25] "Catholic social action organizations date from the era when Church and state were in active conflict. Their primary goal was to support the interests of the Church in what seemed like a life-and-death struggle." William Bosworth, *Catholicism and Crisis in Modern France* (Princeton, N.J., 1962), p. 156.

[26] An appreciation of the complexity of decision-making in foreign policy emerges from the description by former Atomic Energy Commissioner Thomas E. Murray of what would be involved in tracing "the making of a basic nuclear policy decision." The inquirer "would have to go through a tortuous maze of governmental agencies that initiate or suggest policies, draft position papers on proposed policies, advise, dilute, compromise and modify policy proposals. He would probably get lost or give up before he had completed his quest through the State Department, the Department of Defense, the Joint Committee, the National Security Council, the Operations Coordinating Board, the President's special staff assistants on scientific affairs, disarmament and other matters, and the Atomic Energy Commission itself. I have never embarked on such a quest." Murray, *Nuclear Policy for War and Peace* (Cleveland, 1960), p. 202.

States is abhorrent to the Christian conception of the dignity and destiny of the person. Moreover, since more than 70 per cent of the American people live in cities where 85 per cent of Catholics are concentrated, any realistic effort to change the caste status of the Negro must have the active support of the Catholic citizenry. The moral obtuseness of the Church in the past explains the ignorant if unsurprising protest of the band of bigots in New Orleans: "Since *when* has segregation become a sin?" Behind us is a history of spiritual schizophrenia that mounted a campaign to convert and baptize Negroes while tolerating conditions in which they could save their souls only by heroic virtue. These attitudes were personified by Chief Justice Taney who would refuse to preempt the place of a Negro in the confessional line at Holy Trinity Church in Washington, and who yet could decree him in law to be not a person but a thing.

In the past two decades much progress has been made, which is described elsewhere in this volume. But the embarrassing fact is that the Catholic community is not deeply persuaded of the oppression encumbering the Negro, is not prepared to make the substantial sacrifices needed to achieve a tolerable measure of civic peace (not to speak of human decency and moral right), and lacks the political will to implement its theological vision of the fraternal city. Arrived at middle-class respectability, American Catholics prefer to believe that the Negro, through virtue and personal effort, should raise himself from his disadvantaged plight and, like other ethnic minorities, forge for himself a proper place in the mainstream of American society. There is no recognition here of the psychic destructiveness of centuries of slavery and systematic oppression, no awareness that in the United States color demarcates not a social class, but a *caste* whose lot is fixed by folklore sanctions almost as absolute as Hindu fatalism. Somehow the fuse connecting revealed truth and relevant action has been removed. The bewilderment and contradictory counsel following the riots in the nation's cities make it plain that no simple solution of the Negro's alienation is available. What is clear, however, is that any program failing to recognize his essential dignity will only increase his rancor. What also seems probable is that no national policy can succeed that does not have the genuine support of Catholics, given their concentration in urban centers.

The solidarity of mankind as celebrated by humanitarians is given a deeper dimension in the Christian vision of a universal redemption and a transhistorical destiny of all men, thus creating new bonds of brotherhood. One would suppose, therefore, that Catholics would be foremost in efforts toward building an effective international political order. Such has not been notably true of American Catholics, nervous perhaps that their national allegiance be suspect. Bishop John Wright has remarked caustically: "Any super-duper patriotic organization that wants the United Nations kicked out of New York will always find a large number of Catholic cranks going around collecting signatures. You can always get loads of Catholics to write in to the magazines asking what the Foreign Policy Association is doing. These little things, you know, are a kind of sick-in-the-head patriotism—not patriotism at all but mere nervous indigestion." To ask whether American Catholics will change their previous political preferences here is to ask whether Vatican II will influence more than our liturgical practices, whether its teaching on international cooperation and work for peace will ultimately have as much appeal as the Mass in the vernacular.

On one point of international life American Catholics would seem to have a special responsibility: to actively advocate sharing the nation's increasing affluence with the poor nations growing poorer each year. An inevitable part of the process includes the transfer of capital. So far, American Catholics have been deficient in recognizing the moral imperatives in this issue of public policy; certainly they have expended much less effort propagandizing for foreign aid than in suppressing indecent literature. It was an English Catholic, Barbara Ward, who reminded us that our foreign aid in 1965 amounted to about 10 per cent of our annual *increase* in wealth. Since then, our country's contribution has become proportionately and absolutely less. Conceivably the priest and the levite who passed the man robbed and left at the roadside did not consider it a "religious" matter to aid him. Or perhaps they were hurrying on to committee meetings of their congregations.

Their own congregations, in the sense of the institutional interests of the Church, have absorbed a considerable amount of the political activity of American Catholics, particularly since the financial burden of the parochial-school system (and indeed of Catholic higher education) became painful. From an original position of rebuffing state aid as compromising educational freedom, through a protest against discrimination should a Federal subsidy of schools be made available, we have come to press for whatever state aid is legally possible. Will such pressure, certainly legitimate in a democracy, continue? To ask the question is to ask about the shape of American Catholicism in the future. Despite questions about the religious efficacy of the parochial schools and doubts about the wisdom of concentrating the Church's effort on the child (and only on every other Catholic child at that), the eagerness of young parents to have their children in a Catholic school seems unabated. Increasingly they feel aggrieved at the double taxation involved. With lay boards becoming more a part of the parochial-school system, there may well be a more vocal call for public aid. Less predictable would be the reaction of such boards to the charge that the parochial school is promoting not merely religious divisiveness but *de facto* racial segregation.

A significantly larger role for the laity will surely characterize American Catholicism in the future and thus will inevitably condition its attitude on questions of public policy. But even more decisive will be the character and values of American society in the future. The moralistic mission of the Protestant churches to maintain official recognition of Christian symbols in public life has been largely abandoned. For a time American Catholicism acted as if it had inherited a mandate to make the government enforce the moral code of nineteenth-century cultural Protestantism. Today there is less crusading, more permissiveness, or perhaps more restraint in the public expectations of American Catholics. Indeed, they often seem unreflectingly to assent to the idea expressed by Dean Acheson: "Religion is a private affair. At least that is what the First Amendment says."

It would be unhistorical to assume that the current comfortable coexistence of Catholicism and American culture is so permanent that conflict on issues of public policy is forever ruled out. Pope John XXIII made "prophets of doom" unfashionable; one cannot overlook, however, a shift during the past decade in our Constitutional assumptions on the relation of religion to American society. An article by the perceptive Peter F. Drucker in 1956 (therefore after the McCollum decision) will be useful here.[27] He notes that the First Amendment forbids the favoring of any one religious denomination but holds that

[27] Peter F. Drucker, "Organized Religion and the American Creed," *Review of Politics*, XVIII (July, 1956). Reprinted in *The Image of Man*, eds. M. A. Fitzsimons, Thomas T. McAvoy, C.S.C., and Frank O'Malley (Notre Dame, Ind., 1959), pp. 355-57.

"at the same time the State must always sponsor, protect, and favor religious life in general. The United States is indeed a 'secular' state as far as any one denomination is concerned. But it is at the same time a 'religious' commonwealth as concerns its general belief in the necessity of a truly religious basis of citizenship." Moreover, "religion," whose free exercise is protected, is, he insists, what would be recognized as such by Billy Graham, Cardinal Alfredo Ottaviani and Comrade Nikita S. Khrushchev. For, Professor Drucker continues, "To be a 'religion' a creed must be supernatural. It must be based on an acknowledgement of a power above man. . . . Secondly, a religion must seek its kingdom in the other world. A creed, however infallible it claims to be, is not a religion—as the Constitution and the American tradition understand the term—if it aims at establishing its kingdom in this world."

Professor Drucker's reading of the First Amendment proved overly optimistic. Subsequent Supreme Court decisions have fixed the face of our political institutions in a frown against association with any and all religious structures, seemingly suspecting them of political imperialism. Moreover, admittedly nontheistic beliefs and private ethical ideologies have been accepted as qualifying for protection under the religious-freedom clause. With a widespread erosion of belief in traditional theological assertions, are we witnessing here the emergence of a majoritarian humanism as the basis of our culture, a syncretistic, democratic, normless Shintoism as the inspiration and sanction of our laws? Does such a trend, if it is a trend, portend future conflict for American Catholics on issues of public policy? For Catholicism is not a private affair, nor can its consequences, adequately understood, be restricted to individual behavior. With no program of political proposals, with no promise of political competence among its members, Catholicism does nevertheless dictate general orientations concerning the meaning of existence and the proper functions of community life; these in turn have meaning for judging the direction in which society is moving and for suggesting priorities in public policy.

In their satisfaction at being generally accepted today, American Catholics might well reflect that their present opportunities augment their responsibilities in the political order. They might also ponder the observation of Christopher Dawson as he surveyed contemporary American society: "In the past our civilization—and, indeed, every civilization that is known to history—has recognized the existence of a moral order which is derived not from conflicting individual interests or from the collective will of the State but from a higher spiritual order. This great and ancient truth, as Edmund Burke wrote, is the ultimate foundation of human society and no society which denies it or loses sight of it, can endure."[28] The cherishing and implementation in the political order of that "great and ancient truth" might turn out to be the heritage and burden of American Catholicism.

[28] Christopher Dawson, *America and the Secularization of Modern Culture* (Houston, Tex., 1960), p. 31.

6: AMERICAN CATHOLICS AND SOCIAL MOVEMENTS

James Finn

As we approach the end of the 1960's, what is the response of the American Catholic to national problems of economic development, labor and poverty, to the heavy responsibility in matters of war, peace, and international affairs? How does he relate the conditions of American life to the lives of other peoples around the world?

It is always difficult to answer such questions adequately, but it has become even more so since the end of World War II as the problems themselves have become even more complex—so complex that even their definition often escapes precision. Many of the difficulties flow from the vast changes America has undergone since 1945, others from the equally significant changes that have taken place within American Catholicism. For instance, it gradually became clear after 1945 that the war had sensibly altered the international structure of power and had elevated the United States to a position of preeminence which it would apparently occupy indefinitely. The war had also altered domestic arrangements. It had, to offer one example, allowed unionism to consolidate its strength, enabling workers, through collective bargaining, to move from the status of hired help to something closer to partners. The ongoing changes within Catholicism internationally, most visibly marked by the papacy of John XXIII and Vatican Council II, unquestionably affect the way Catholics, both clergy and laymen, engage the world. Within America, the election of John F. Kennedy to the Presidency in 1960 both symbolized and ratified the changed status of Catholics in our society, the actual change having been the work of many decades. Although the potential importance of American Catholics in relation both to the United States and to the world community has altered remarkably since 1945, it has been by a process of evolution and rapid change, not disjunction or revolution.

AMERICAN CATHOLICS AND LABOR

The history of Catholics and social reform, particularly in regard to labor, is both well-known and honored. The first decisive step to assure that the Church in America would not be sundered from the working class was made by Cardinal Gibbons in 1887 when, against opposition, he successfully argued in Rome against the condemnation of the United States Knights of Labor. Retrospective judgment supports his contention that such a condemnation would have been dangerous as well as unjust. Subsequently, as Will Herberg attests, "the path which Gibbons thus blazed was followed by the Church, despite many changes and uncertainties. The Catholic Church has remained, by and large, pro-labor and has shown a deep concern for retaining the allegiance of its working people."[1] In the early years of this century it helped form an alternative to socialist programs through the efforts of such leaders as Father John A. Ryan and Father Peter E. Dietz and organizations such as the German Catholic Central-Verein. From these early years John Ryan was to emerge as the strongest single influence on the shaping of Catholic social thought. When in 1919 the bishops of the National Catholic War Council[2] wished to adopt a program for social action, they issued under the names of the Council a statement previously drawn up by Ryan. The Bishops' Program of Social Reconstruction, as it came to be known, was almost immediately denounced by the president of the National Association of Manufacturers as "partisan, pro-labor union, socialistic propaganda."[3] While most of the proposals look quite tame at this distance, having been substantially adopted under the Roosevelt Administration, they met continuing and deep opposition until their long delayed acceptance. The thirties saw the founding of the Association of Catholic Trade Unionists (ACTU), the Catholic Worker movement, and the effec-

[1] Will Herberg, *Protestant, Catholic, Jew* (New York, 1960), p. 156.

[2] The National Catholic War Council (NCWC), formed during World War I, proved so effective an instrument for the Catholic bishops of this country that it continued its existence after the war. With appropriate changes it became in 1923 the National Catholic Welfare Conference and is presently the United States Catholic Conference.

[3] Quoted by John Tracy Ellis ed., *Documents of American Catholic History* (Milwaukee, 1956), p. 611.

tive leadership of priests who attempted to relate the condition of the American social order to the principles enunciated by Pius XI in his encyclical *Quadragesimo Anno* (1931). During the years of the Depression and the New Deal these activities—which included the formation of labor schools, picketing, organizing union campaigns, and publishing labor papers—fed into some of the best efforts of the labor movement.

By the end of World War II most of the proximate goals of these efforts had been realized. Those Catholics who were active in the postwar unions struggled to fend off communist control, racketeering, and union bossism. ("I run the union just like a business. We deal in one commodity—labor," said Dave Beck, president of the International Brotherhood of Teamsters.) Much of this work was arduous, and the accomplishments of a number of "waterfront priests" such as John M. Corridan, S.J., were justly acknowledged. But union success, general prosperity, and the increasing complexity of socioeconomic relations brought apathy to many union members. It was not like the thirties, when it appeared to many, according to Charles Owen Rice, a long-time labor priest, that "the world was simple and justice seemed easy to find." Although one can still point to Catholics who are prominent in unions, and although labor-management relations are still of national importance, the labor schools, associations, and meetings all have seen a decline in interest.

One indication of the shift in attitude toward the labor movement is that not too long ago in a sermon at a Labor Day Mass, Msgr. George G. Higgins, director of the Social Action Department of the then NCWC, felt compelled to defend organized labor against many of its former allies. Admitting that "it is true that the American labor movement has no sensationally stirring plans or exciting programs," Msgr. Higgins nevertheless asserted that it "is doing a job and is a credit to the nation as a whole." But he also added that neither labor nor industry has a good record in race relations and that both need to unite with government to cope with the "problem of widespread unemployment and degrading poverty in the midst of bounteous plenty."[4] In pointing out labor's faults of omission in race relations and a general failure to cope with the problem of poverty, he directed attention to profound national problems which are the seedbed for many others.

[4] Sept. 7, 1964. The entire sermon appears in *Catholic Mind* LXII (Nov., 1964), 47-54.

RURAL LIFE AND FARM LABOR

Because American Catholics have been and are an urban people, official Church recognition of the demands of rural life has only slowly developed. The National Catholic Rural Life Conference (NCRLC), founded in the 1920's, continues to maintain that the home in the country is the natural habitat for the family and that it is the family farm, the farm on which the decisions and most of the work are the responsibility of a single family, that has made our agriculture great. But both the increasing productivity of American agriculture (less than 5 per cent of the population can produce more food than they can sell at a profit to the remaining 95 per cent) and government policies that reward large growers at the expense of the small, make the position of the family farm more difficult to maintain. While the farmer with much land and advanced agricultural methods and equipment has a substantial income, the small farmer does not. This explains why, although agricultural production is high, 43 per cent of farm families are poor. The pool of cheap, unorganized labor that results from this situation perpetuates the depressed conditions of the farm worker, particularly the migratory laborer.

Partly because successes among this group are so rare, the recent accomplishments of the California workers led by Cesar Chavez attracted much attention. Described by Msgr. William Quinn of the Bishops' Committee for the Spanish-Speaking as "the greatest labor leader to come along in a generation" and "perhaps the most important Catholic in California," Chavez refused attractive jobs in order to build up slowly and arduously the National Farm Workers Association (NFWA). *La Huelga* (The Strike), which he has successfully led, represents a great step in the attempt to transform the reactionary sweatshop ethos of agricultural workers into something more nearly approximating that of industrial workers. It has been supported by SNCC, CORE, other civil-rights groups, and the churches, notably those in the California Migrant Ministry. (Most Catholic churches in the area, however, are timid, for it is estimated that 75 per cent of the growers are Catholic and it is reported that they threaten the churches with financial reprisal.)

On their march from Delano to the state capital in 1966, the workers distributed a moving statement of justice and dignity long denied and now demanded. Among other things they asserted: "We seek, and have, the support of the Church in what we do. At the head of the Pilgrimage we carry *la Virgen de la Guadalupe* because she is ours, all ours, patroness of the Mexican people. We also carry the Sacred Cross and the Star of David because we are not sectarians, and because we ask the help and prayers of all religions. All men are brothers, sons of the same God; that is why we say to all men of good will in the words of Pope Leo XIII: 'Everyone's first duty is to protect the workers from the greed of speculators who use human beings as instruments to provide themselves with money. . . .'"[5]

NFWA has won some victories, but the long-term outcome is not yet clear. Until it is, farm workers across the country will remain untouched by the social-welfare legislation that has been passed in the last several decades. The limited victories of the NFWA suggest that with inspired and intelligent leadership the social teachings of the Church continue to provide sound support for workers in their struggle against gross exploitation, and that Catholicism can be a deeply unifying and cohesive element in that struggle. But this should lead no one to think that Catholics generally have concerned themselves with the problems of rural labor, or that such union activity, however necessary and however effective, will substantially alter the massive problems of widespread poverty amid national abundance. It is, unfortunately, even necessary to question the long-range value of the bitterly contested and hard-won victories of the organized farm workers, for modern technology may yet eliminate their present jobs.

The activities of the Washington office of NCRLC point to the extent of these problems. Under the able leadership of Msgr. Luigi Ligutti and his successor, James L. Vizzard, S.J., the Washington office has since 1955 engaged itself with a variety of public issues including foreign aid and trade, food for peace, the Peace Corps and Volunteers in Service to America, soil and water conservation, the food-stamp plan, cooperatives and credit unions, and even international peace. Its tools have been publications, speeches, liaison with other organizations, congressional testimony. At its best the Washington office of the NCRLC has functioned as a lobbyist for the poor. But the support it has been given by the Catholic community, including the hierarchy, has been meager. If one were to accept as an index of the

[5] "The Plan of Delano," *Catholic Mind*, LXIV (June, 1966), 21.

Church's concern for the poor only the attention it has given to the impoverished farm worker, the judgment would be dispiriting. The best that might be said is that the problems of the agricultural worker would have received scant attention from the Church because relatively few Catholics are involved. This implies, of course, that one could then with justification expect to see the efforts of the Church more manifest in the nation's cities. That expectation would not be wholly fulfilled.

CATHOLICS AND URBAN PROBLEMS

Three of the massive social ills that afflict our society—poverty, racism, and urban blight—coalesced in the riots that became a familiar feature in American life in the late sixties. If it can be said that the Church neglected rural problems because these affected few Catholics, the same explanation cannot hold for the problems of urban life. As Archbishop John F. Dearden of Detroit said in the summer of 1967 after massive rioting in that city: "The Negro-White confrontation in American cities is in great part a Negro-Catholic confrontation. This is true because so small a percentage of Negroes are Catholic. It is true also because Catholics traditionally have been heavily concentrated in urban areas." He went on to say that "if Catholics were truly committed to social justice, the record of our legislatures, both at state and Federal levels, would be quite different."[6]

The problems which converged in the urban riots are of massive proportions and can be met only by the combined resources of our entire society. But Archbishop Dearden's harsh judgment is accurate: American Catholics have yet to show consistent dedication to social justice. In the fight against racism, the Church—again with notable exceptions—is moving with the rest of the nation in its slow, unsteady advance. And in terms of affecting the political and economic structures of our society in order to remedy inequities, the Church has been a negligible influence.

As a Church of immigrants its early efforts were directed to the establishment of various Church-directed welfare agencies. With the

[6] The quotations are from the text of an address "Challenge to Change in the Urban Church" published in *The Catholic Messenger* (Davenport, Ia.), Sept. 14, 1967.

gradual social elevation of the Catholic community many of these were dismantled, and those that remain are fated to become less significant. The change involved here has been an accommodation to, and an acceptance of, the general conditions and values of American life. In her autobiography, Dorothy Day describes the response she encountered in establishing a Catholic Worker House of Hospitality in the thirties:

> It was cold and damp and so unbelievably poverty-stricken that little children coming to see who were the young people meeting there exclaimed that this could not be a *Catholic* place; it was too poor. . . . We were not taking the position of the great mass of Catholics, who were quite content with the present in this world. They were quite willing to give to the poor, but they did not feel called upon to work for the things of this life for others which they themselves esteemed so lightly. Our insistence on worker-ownership, on the right of private property, on the need to de-proletarize the worker, all points which had been emphasized by the popes in their social encyclicals, made many Catholics think we were communists in disguise, wolves in sheeps' clothing.[7]

What Dorothy Day wrote here about her experience in the late thirties would serve as a text for Catholic attitudes in the fifties and, to a lesser degree, in the sixties. American Catholics, particularly those who have attained a relatively comfortable place in our society, have been relatively content with the conditions of that society. This is not too surprising. Although Catholics played a significant role in the early accomplishments of American labor, Edward Duff, S.J., the editor of *Social Order*, could ask in 1962 if this represented "anything more than a sociological solidarity between American Catholicism and the trade union membership."[8] Without dismissing these earlier accomplishments one can acknowledge that as that sociological solidarity weakened and as the union membership counted for less, the contribution of Catholics to social action, both practical and theoretical, declined.

A judgment of what this means in terms of Catholic influence in determining the course of our future society depends to a great degree

[7] Dorothy Day, *The Long Loneliness* (New York, 1959), p. 183.

[8] Edward Duff, S.J., "Catholic Social Action in the American Environment," *Social Order*, XII (Sept., 1962), 308.

upon how one evaluates the trade union movement. For example, Daniel Patrick Moynihan, then Assistant Secretary of Labor and addressing a conference early in 1965, stressed quite accurately that it is not possible to solve problems of the American poor in isolation from other problems—specifically, our unfinished social insurance system, our unbalanced and incomplete wage system, our problems of fluctuating unemployment. He added that there is not yet a consensus that these fundamental political issues *should* be resolved. But, he went on to say, "the only force in American society—or any other industrial society that I know of—that is capable of providing the mass citizen support for solving these fundamental problems, and for sustaining such efforts over long periods of time, is the trade union movement. The trade union movement was the original antipoverty movement in this nation, and it remains incomparably the most significant one."[9] If Moynihan is correct in his assessment, the failure of Catholics to contribute significantly to the future course of the movement would be a significant failure.

The yet unfinished decade of the sixties has complicated the overall judgment that might reasonably flow from the previous comments, and again the reasons must be sought within both the civil community and the American Catholic community. A relatively complacent society was morally shocked and stirred when an initially small group of young Negroes led an intensely idealistic assault on racist practices in the South in the early sixties. That assault grew, developed, and then splintered into many overlapping and conflicting efforts to combat racism. But those early acts tapped a vein of moral energy on which we continue to draw. In the early sixties there also appeared a small book of controlled outrage that disclosed to Americans who knew they lived in an affluent society that there was an "invisible" sector of that society, "the other America," made up of forty- or more-million poor. The time for this kind of disclosure was ripe, and *The Other America* is generally credited with opening the Administration's "war on poverty." (Not wholly incidentally, Michael Harrington, its author, developed much of his initial interest in the problem of poverty as a staff member of the Catholic Worker House in New York.)

The national ferment aroused by the civil-rights movement and the war on poverty coincided with a general ferment within the Church

[9] Daniel Patrick Moynihan in an address to the Conference on Poverty in America at the University of California, Berkeley, Feb. 26-28, 1965.

most publicly signaled by the innovating reign of John XXIII and Vatican Council II. Many Catholics felt that they had been given strong and additional warrants to commit their best efforts to the secular society and to a war on the worst evils of that society. Their efforts took many forms and merely to mention some of them is to make clear the difficulties of reaching a fair, summarizing judgment at this time.

The actions of Father James E. Groppi are probably a fair example of the most dramatic activities in which a small number of the clergy have been involved. An advisor to the Milwaukee NAACP Youth Council, Father Groppi interprets Christian service in immediate, practical terms. "I'm obligated to minister to the needs of the people I serve, and if those people need freedom from discrimination, segregation, and exploitation, then that defines my pastoral responsibility." And, he has said, the Church should not be overconcerned with white sensitivity but should be concerned with "the poverty-stricken people in the black ghetto." If white people leave the Church because it is involved in the fight for civil rights, "they shouldn't have been there in the first place."

Given the expression of such sentiments and the abrasive actions which follow from them, it is not surprising that Father Groppi has aroused hostility and criticism from civic and religious leaders. But he is not alone in his fierce dedication to the pursuit of social justice through disruptive public acts. His counterparts exist in cities throughout the nation, and they are supported by a new brand of activist laymen.

There are also less visible manifestations of renewed interest in problems of social justice. The Catholic Adult Education Center (CAEC) of Chicago, for example, has an ongoing program that includes a John A. Ryan Forum and inner-city research that is, among other things, conducting a survey of the work done by religious communities of sisters in the inner city. The Center is also affiliated with the decades-old Catholic Council on Working Life and the relatively recent *New City* magazine. The programs of the Chicago Center frequently serve as pilot projects for the growing Chicago adult education groups across the country, now numbering more than fifty. Vaile Scott, director of CAEC, has said that "since the Council, there has been a general recognition among Church leaders that something must be done to educate the laity in the new spirit of the Church."

There are, in addition, a small number of Catholics who combine in their attack on urban problems a broad theoretical approach with practical, professional experience. Dennis Clark, to offer one example, has written articles and books that attempt to relate both secular studies and encyclicals on industrial life to "cities in crisis," the title of one of his books. He has also served as a specialist in urban problems for the city of Philadelphia. And one could add to the small list of active theorists such men as Father Henry Browne in New York and Msgr. John Egan in Chicago.

The efforts of these various groups and individuals are a sign that a small but growing number of Catholics is struggling to understand and combat some of the most destructive social evils of our society. Whether their number will grow, whether they will have sustained effect, whether they will develop theories adequate to their present commitment and action, are all uncertain quantities at this moment. But to the degree that the answer to these questions becomes even a qualified "yes," American Catholics will have moved beyond the descriptive strictures of Dorothy Day and Edward Duff, S.J.

THE PROBLEM OF WAR

The general ferment and uncertainty that is evident in Catholic attitudes toward domestic conditions is equally evident in Catholic attitudes toward questions of international affairs generally and questions of war and peace specifically. A favorable judgment on the state of Catholic thinking about modern war would be that it is fluid, free from past formalistic constraints, open to new insights and new convictions. A critical judgment would be that Catholic thinking is in a confused state, only slightly less confused than it has been for the last several decades.

In this century Catholics have not generally been noted for their presence in efforts to limit wars nor for their attachment to peace groups. In addition to the popes and national hierarchies one can mention some outstanding Catholic scholars who have addressed themselves to the problems of establishing international peace, justice, and order, but their influence has not been determining. Today, however, the institutional Church is looked to for moral guidance in these areas, and significant numbers of Catholics are now prominent and active in peace movements and even pacifist groups. Since America is today the world's most powerful nation and since its military strategy is based on a highly sophisticated nuclear-weapons system, the attitude American Catholics adopt when confronted with the problems of modern warfare is of some moment.

On the question of war, the titanic struggle of 1939-1945 left the ethical thinking of the churches in America, both Catholic and Protestant, in almost total disarray. Although it has constantly been breached in practice, the mainstream of Christian teaching about war has attempted to place moral limits both on the ends or goals which justify war and on the means employed once war is initiated. In traditional "just-war" theory, war is seen as an extension of political activity, not disjunctive with it. And as an extension of political activity, it should be subject to political and moral scrutiny and judgment. The traditional practice of Americans, however, is as peace-loving people to abhor war and try to avoid it, but once engaged in it to throw off all restraints. It is fair to say that by the end of World War II the American people and their leaders accepted the idea that war is now total, that the purpose of war is to drive through to military victory, and that victory includes the unconditional surrender of the enemy—all of which is controverted by traditional Christian thought. The few lonely voices that protested the fire-bombings of Hamburg, Dresden, and Tokyo were too faint to have any effect. Not until atomic bombs were dropped on Hiroshima and Nagasaki were religious sensibilities shocked into public questioning of what was by that time accepted military policy. Acknowledging the failure of any significant segment of the Church to question the fire-bombings, the late John Courtney Murray, S.J., commented: "I think it is true to say that the traditional doctrine [of the just war] was irrelevant during World War II. This is no argument against the traditional doctrine. . . . But there is a place for an indictment of all of us who failed to make the traditional document relevant."[10]

From our present perspective, the way in which the religious and intellectual communities initially reacted to the problem of atomic weapons seems woefully inadequate. Far from attempting to make the

[10] Quoted by Robert C. Batchelder in *The Irreversible Decision, 1939-1950* (New York, 1961), pp. 216-17. Originally in "Remarks on the Moral Problem of War," *Theological Studies*, XX (Mar. 1959), 54. Mr. Batchelder's book is recommended for its political and moral analysis of the decisions which led to the first use of the atomic bombs.

traditional doctrine relevant, they joined with the many others—statesmen, scientists, educators—who developed with varying degrees of sophistication the syllogism that since all future wars would be atomic and therefore total, and since total wars were immoral, no future war could be a moral or justified war. The rationalist thought the bomb would force men to give up the irrational enterprise of war: it would be "world peace or world destruction." The Christian pacifist said the choice must now be made between the way of total war and the way of Jesus. And those who tried to uphold traditional teachings failed to face the contradiction of an analysis that said it was immoral to drop atomic bombs on cities but that military necessity might require it.

The struggle to emerge from this state of confusion was, for Catholics, slow and arduous. In 1960 the editor of a book of essays by Catholic writers on morality and modern warfare was able to introduce them, quite accurately, with this comment:

> That the publication of this symposium on morality and warfare has the character of a pioneer effort fifteen years after Hiroshima indicates something of the failure of the Christian community to come to terms with that event. The moral confusion that this failure evidences may be but part of the general state of shock the public has invoked as a psychological defense against the horrors of modern warfare. Many desire neither to hear about these realities nor to think about them.[11]

To some extent this statement still stands, but progress has been made. In this country a small group of Catholics has, through conferences, informal meetings, and relatively specialized publications, advanced the state of the moral question concerning the nuclear-weapons system. Pope John's encyclical *Pacem in Terris* initiated widespread discussion about questions of war and peace not only—and maybe not even primarily—among Catholics. In the Constitution on the Church in the Modern World, the Vatican Council laid down some guidelines which will remain helpful for years. This was accomplished not by resolving but by presenting the central dilemma: The great nations depend for their ultimate self-defense upon an extremely powerful, highly sophisticated nuclear-weapons system; the effectiveness of this system as a deterrent rests upon the belief of any potential

[11] William J. Nagle, ed., *Morality and Modern Warfare* (Baltimore, 1960), p. 3.

aggressor that these nuclear weapons will be used; if these weapons were aimed only at military targets they would inflict widespread destruction even on the civilian community, but in fact they are not restricted to military targets.

In one of his annual appearances before a joint committee, former Secretary of Defense Robert S. McNamara presented a detailed anlysis of what was entailed. For example, in his report for the 1968 defense budget he explained the concept of "Assured Destruction" thus:

> In the case of the Soviet Union, the destruction of, say, one-fifth to one-fourth of its population and one-half to one-third of its industrial capacity would mean its elimination as a world power for many years. Such a level of destruction would certainly represent intolerable punishment to any industrialized nation and thus serve as an effective deterrent to the deliberate initiation of a nuclear attack on the United States or its Allies.[12]

Most simply put, the problem is that the military defense of the United States rests upon the threat to inflict damage so extensive that traditional Christian teaching would condemn it as immoral. From this dilemma some people have reasoned to the conclusion that if the deterrent truly is necessary to an adequate defense, defense against aggression is no longer morally justified. Morally responsible action will move toward unilateral disarmament and the preparation of what follows from that. While this argument has been developed at greater length and with deep conviction by Catholics in other countries, only a small group of intelligent, informed American Catholics support it. The majority of concerned Catholics are either still burdened with the profound moral dilemma, or have resolved it, at least partially, in another fashion. For if one is concerned with the devastation likely to be wrought by nuclear war and intends to avoid it, one must ask if unilateral disarmament would make it more or less likely. A number of Catholic theorists judge that it would be more likely and conclude, therefore, that the United States must maintain the deterrent system while working toward a more stable international order. And, they

[12] Statement before a Joint Session of the Senate Armed Services Committee and the Senate Subcommittee on Department of Defense Appropriations on the Fiscal Year 1968-72 Defense Program and 1968 Defense Budget. (Washington Printing Office, 1967), p. 39.

argue, if Vatican Council II did not urge this position it allowed it as an option.[13]

It is not surprising that the most intensive work in this area, where the problems are profound and complex and authoritative analyses are scarce, has been done by professional laymen. (It gradually became clear, for example, from the ease with which people could support opposing views on nuclear war by quotations from Pius XII that his reservations had little political relevance.) There are indications that those in charge of Catholic education in colleges and seminaries are beginning to respond to the problem, but the amount of interest is not yet encouraging.

Since 1945 all military actions in which the United States has engaged have been conducted under the umbrella of the nuclear deterrent. With one exception these have been limited operations which did not threaten the use of nuclear weapons. That exception—the Cuban missile crisis of 1962—is generally regarded as an aberration not likely to be repeated. If this general understanding is accurate, if the major powers have determined that nuclear war is not a rational enterprise, the conflicts in which the United States will be involved will be limited wars, some of which are likely to resemble the ongoing war in Vietnam. That is, they will be guerrilla or counter-insurgency wars which will escape easy description, in which nationalism and communism will be evident, in which the vast military might of the United States will be at a discount, and in which torture, terrorism, and high civilian casualties will be expected.

AMERICAN CATHOLICS AND VIETNAM

The war in Vietnam is an immediate crisis for the United States, demanding and divisive. But the way in which it is finally resolved will have reverberations far beyond Southeast Asia and far beyond the present decade. The way in which the Churches react to this crisis is, therefore, of long-range as well as present importance. And the reaction of the Catholic community shows that thoughtful and articulate

[13] The best brief presentation of this view now available is William V. O'Brien, *Nuclear War, Deterrence and Morality* (New York, 1967), Dr. O'Brien examines modern warfare in the context of traditional Catholic teaching and recent authoritative statements.

Catholics are struggling to come to a new assessment of their politico-moral responsibilities.

In September of 1966 a Gallup poll indicated that Catholic support for the Administration's Vietnam policy significantly exceeded Protestant and Jewish support. This corresponds to a general expectation that, for a number of historically discernible reasons, American Catholics would be more hesitant to criticize Administration policy during a time of war than would those from other religious traditions. And there is much additional evidence that supports the difference indicated by the poll. While official Protestant and Jewish organizations sharply questioned the justice and morality of the Vietnam conflict and the morality of the means used to prosecute the war, and while a number of prominent ministers and rabbis publicly condemned the war as unjust, their Catholic counterparts were initially silent or subdued, speaking out neither for nor against the war. When the editors of the *National Catholic Reporter*, early in 1966, wrote to 225 Catholic bishops asking them to comment on the goals and conduct of the war, on the silence of Catholic spokesmen, and on the rights of the person who conscientiously objected to participation in the war, they received only six replies, of which only three were for publication. None of the three opposed Administration policy in Vietnam. It was correctly pointed out at the time that American bishops might not wish to respond to questionnaires generally or to the *National Catholic Reporter* particularly, but it was also pointed out they did not create their own opportunities to respond to such urgent questions.

When, in November of 1966, the National Conference of Catholic Bishops did issue a pastoral statement on "Peace and Vietnam," it acknowledged the honest differences that existed among citizens of all faiths in assessing the moral issues of the conflict and followed this with the carefully limited statement that "while we do not claim to be able to resolve these issues authoritatively, in the light of the facts as they are known to us, it is reasonable to argue that our presence in Vietnam is justified." But the bishops also said that "no one is free to evade his personal responsibility by leaving it entirely to others to make moral judgments."

The way in which moral leadership is being exercised within the Catholic community on the question of Vietnam is, therefore, noticeably different from the way it is exercised within the other religious communities, depending less upon the institution of the Catholic

Church in America than upon (first) those who have established their authority through experience, study, or personal *charisma* and (second) upon the documents of the Vatican Council and the statements of John XXIII and Paul VI. But while Catholics remain divided over the moral issues involved in Vietnam, their criticism has increased in volume and intensity as the violence of the conflict has mounted. Within Catholicism as within the country as a whole the dissenters are a minority, but they include some of the most informed, articulate, and influential Catholics in the United States. The most committed of these were early members of activist groups such as the national interfaith organization known as Clergy and Laymen Concerned About Vietnam. Lonely figures at first, they gained allies as the war continued.

For example, in the fall of 1967 four bishops (Archbishop Paul J. Hallinan of Atlanta, Bishop Victor J. Reed of Oklahoma City-Tulsa, Auxiliary Bishop John J. Dougherty of Newark, and Auxiliary Bishop James P. Shannon of St. Paul-Minneapolis) endorsed Negotiation Now, a national program which called simultaneously for a halt to United States bombing in Vietnam and immediate negotiations among all concerned parties. Bishop John J. Wright of Pittsburgh endorsed the program with reservations, Archbishop James P. Davis of Santa Fe made a separate statement similar to that of Negotiation Now, and Bishop Fulton J. Sheen of Rochester called for immediate United States withdrawal, a position which the other bishops had specifically rejected.

The public stance of these men made evident what common sense would have suggested: Members of the national hierarchy no more agreed on the justice of war in Vietnam than did other members of the Church. Important as their open declaration was, it was probably less significant than the accompanying change that took place in many Catholic publications. After evident struggle many judged editorially that, to quote one title, "The War in Vietnam is Immoral." Among these are journals such as *Commonweal*, *National Catholic Reporter*, *Catholic World*, *Critic*, *U.S. Catholic*, and *St. Louis Review*. These journals did not, of course, persuade all of their readers. For example, when William V. Shannon in his regular column for *Commonweal* outlined the reasons why he supported Administration policy in Vietnam he received strong support from a number of his readers.

Regrettably, even in some of the superior Catholic journals, the struggle to arrive at a sound politico-moral judgment on the war had thin intellectual support. One of these journals stated that "It is now clear that the war can no longer be considered merely a political issue. Rather, it is a moral question which American citizens as individuals must resolve for themselves." In less crude form this unfortunate tendency to sever politics from morality, to speak as if they exist in separate compartments and are open to separate consideration, was evident in other statements prepared by usually thoughtful Catholics. They quite properly insisted upon the need to make moral judgments and upon the right of the individual conscience, but they sometimes failed to acknowledge that a moral problem in the political arena must be resolved by political means and that, as a member of a political community, the individual has not only undeniable rights but also restricting obligations.

One national Catholic organization that has done much admirable work sent out a large mailing of an appeal that was entitled "Politics or Peace?" suggesting, apparently, that peace was obtainable only if we gave up political activities. The inadequate and disappointing contribution which Catholics have made to the national political debate during a time of crisis is a fair indication of the thought and attention they had devoted to international affairs before that crisis. Like much of the rest of the country they were unprepared to consider the significant issues in a developed and principled manner.

Again the interest shown in Catholic organizations specifically designed to cope with problems of international affairs provides some objective measurement. The Catholic Association for International Peace (CAIP) developed out of the Social Action Department of NCWC in the 1920's. It is self-described as being interested in "educating all Catholics as to their obligations of justice and charity in the cause of international peace. It is the *only* organization in the United States that offers the opportunity to benefit by and take part in Catholic thinking on vital questions—questions affecting the immediate and ultimate peace of the world." The CAIP sponsors annual conferences, issues policy statements at times of particular political crises, publishes a newsletter and occasional material. Because it depends almost entirely on volunteer efforts, its course over the years has been uneven. In spite of the evident importance of its undertaking and the hard work of a number of interested individuals, it has not succeeded in attracting widespread support—moral, intellectual, or financial. Even during the late sixties, when religious groups had become more publicly involved in public questions and the war in Vietnam had overshadowed domestic problems, the CAIP attracted little new membership.

One of the Catholic organizations that did show a noticeable and surprising growth during this same period is the Catholic Peace Fellowship, which is affiliated with the Fellowship of Reconciliation. Initiated in 1964, its primary purpose is "the introduction of the various traditions of the Church in regard to war and peace to our fellow Catholics." Not specifically pacifist, it has a number of pacifist sponsors and has strong pacifist sympathies. Among the services which it provides is counseling to those interested in conscientious objection. A number of years ago this service would have been little in demand. Gordon Zahn, a Catholic sociologist who has made studies of conscientious objectors, has said that there was one American Catholic conscientious objector in World War I and approximately two hundred in World War II.[14] At the present time the religious denomination which has shown the greatest percentage increase in conscientious objectors is the Roman Catholic. Though still a small number, it is indicative of a widespread willingness among Catholics to review traditional attitudes.

Although there have always been Catholic pacifists, the pacifist tradition has not, in modern times, been highly honored in Catholicism. The traditional attitude has been that most sharply expressed by Pope Pius XII in his Christmas message of 1956. At that time he said:

> If, therefore, a body representative of the people and a government—both having been chosen by free elections—in a moment of extreme danger decide, by legitimate instruments of internal and external policy, on defensive precautions, and carry out the plans which they consider necessary, they do not act immorally; so that a Catholic citizen cannot invoke his own conscience in order to refuse to serve and fulfill those duties the law imposes. On this matter We feel that We are in perfect harmony with Our Predecessors Leo XIII and Benedict XV, who never denied that obligation. . . .[15]

But the combined impact of modern weapons systems, with their terrifying destructive power, and the reign of John XXIII has engendered among Catholics new thinking and new reactions to questions

[14] In James Finn, *Protest: Pacifism and Politics* (New York, 1968), p. 69.
[15] Harry W. Flannery, ed., *Pattern for Peace* (Westminster, Md., 1962), p. 283.

of war—and the conscientious objector. This was confirmed by the Church Fathers during the Second Vatican Council and ratified in the Constitution on the Church in the Modern World, which says that "it seems right that laws make humane provisions for the case of those who for reasons of conscience refuse to bear arms, provided, however, that they agree to serve the human community in some other way."

With this statement, Catholic CO's had for the first time an undisputably official Church statement to which they could turn to justify their position. Catholics who are drawn to the Catholic Peace Fellowship, the American Pax Association, and the Catholic Worker are intent upon exploring the changes represented by that statement.[16]

LARGER INTERNATIONAL RESPONSIBILITIES

However important the problem of modern weapons and modern war, they are but part—and not the larger part—of questions of justice between nations. Pope Paul's encyclical *Populorum Progressio* stresses that peace is not the mere avoidance of war but depends upon the development of peoples. There are a number of American Catholic specialists who do not question the seriousness of the problems analyzed in *Populorum Progressio* but who do question the basis of the optimism which pervades that encyclical. The problems of the development of peoples and the development of new economic measures are, they say, more intractable than the encyclical suggests. The critics point out that the Food and Agricultural Organization of the United Nations announced, in the middle of its "Development Decade," that the developing countries were more poorly nourished in 1965 than they had been before World War II, and that trend is increasing rather than the reverse. The critics also point out that the United States, with 6 per cent of the world's population and over 50 per cent of its wealth, is reducing its foreign-aid programs. Though but two examples (but others could readily be added) they are important, for there is no international agreement on how to remedy or overcome the great and increasing discrepancy between the economic fortunes of the

[16] Citing this statement in their pastoral letter of Nov. 15, 1968, the American bishops endorsed selective conscientious objection—Ed.

modern industrialized countries and those of the developing countries.

Because of the enormous strength and wealth of the United States, the policies which it develops will be of crucial importance. To return to our initial question, what is the response of the American Catholic to our heavy national responsibilities in matters of war, peace, and international affairs as we look forward to a new decade? The answer must necessarily be inconclusive. There are encouraging signs. There is, undoubtedly, a greater interest, a greater sense of involvement, obligation, and responsibility evident in the Catholic community. It is apparent in the seminaries, particularly among the younger men, and in universities where, in an increasing number of instances, changing curricula reflect the change in interests. It is also reflected in the work of groups such as the Catholic Adult Education Center, which has a small but vigorous World Peace Center; in the fledgling Commission on Justice and Peace, headed by Bishop John Dougherty; and in the recently established Association for International Development, directed by James Lamb.

The signs of interest and activity are plentiful. They indicate that there is, among many Catholics, an increasing willingness and ability to engage great national and international problems. What has yet to be tested is the depth and perseverance of their interest.

7: THE CATHOLIC CHURCH AND THE NEGRO

Richard A. Lamanna and *Jay J. Coakley*

The problem of the legal and social status of the Negro people has placed a severe strain on the American political system and posed a great challenge to the belief of Americans in freedom and equality. Although we have spent more time, more debate, more bitterness, and more blood on this issue than on any other in our history, Negroes are still behind the majority of citizens in measures of social and economic well-being, and we still lack a consensus on the proper role of the Negro in American society. This chapter will examine the role played by the Catholic church and individual American Catholics in the long and unfinished struggle to achieve justice and equality in a multiracial society. Our subject, in other words, is the Catholic role in what Gunnar Myrdal has aptly called the "American Dilemma."

THE EARLY BACKGROUND

When American Negro slavery developed in the seventeenth and eighteenth centuries, Catholics were a numerically and culturally insignificant minority in the British colonies. Some of them did, however, own slaves. Data allowing comparisons between Catholic and non-Catholic slaveholders is scanty, but it seems clear that in general the practices of Catholics conformed to local norms and community expectations. Their behavior was influenced by the interplay of individual attitudes, economic considerations, the immediate social situation (including perceived community and reference group expectations), and the general cultural context of the recently formed New World colonies. In Maryland and Louisiana, where the Catholic population was relatively large, public opinion and the pattern of slavemaster relationships were more consistent with traditional Catholic doctrine. The Catholic slaveholders in these areas usually took it upon themselves to see that the slaves received religious instruction, were baptized, and attended church regularly. In Maryland, for example, the interest Catholics took in the Negroes frequently elicited the accusation from the Protestants that the "papists" were in league with the slaves and were plotting against the government of the colony. In the French settlement of Louisiana the religious status of slaves was, until 1803, legally fixed in the provisions of the *Code Noir*. The code stipulated that slaveholders were to bring their slaves to church, see to their instruction and baptism, and allow them time for rest and worship on Sundays and religious feast days. But even in these regions the treatment of slaves by Catholic slaveholders did not involve a radical departure from the general colonial pattern. In short, while Catholicism may have played a crucial role in the differential development of slavery in the Spanish and Portuguese colonies,[1] it appears that the Church and individual Catholics in the North American colonies tended to adapt to and reflect local conditions rather than to shape them.

The relationship of Catholics to the abolitionist movement was also heavily influenced by a number of historical circumstances.[2] The emergence of the movement in the 1830's came at a time when the Church was still struggling to cope with internal problems and trying to establish a stable institutional structure in the United States. Beginning about 1820, much of the time and energy of the hierarchy and clergy was devoted to caring for the heavy influx of Irish immigrants into the cities of the Northeast. Ecclesiastical leaders, many of whom were immigrants themselves, had to perform their administrative duties and guide Catholic Americans amid increasing hostility toward their Church. Consequently they refrained from making any formal statements concerning the slavery issue which might invite additional animosities, or endanger the unity of the Church in the United States by causing regional splits within the Catholic population.[3] Madeleine

[1] Stanley M. Elkins, *Slavery: A Problem in American Institutional and Intellectual Life* (New York, 1963), pp. 68-71.

[2] Madeleine Hooke Rice, *American Catholic Opinion in the Slavery Controversy* (New York, 1944), pp. 62-84.

[3] The experience of Bishop John England of Charleston, S.C., who had shown concern for Negroes in his diocese, indicates the depth of these feelings. He was forced to close his Negro school, opened in 1835, after a year because of the threats of anti-Abolitionist mobs.

Hooke Rice, in a detailed discussion of Catholic opinion and the slavery controversy, points out that while the Church did not issue a formal statement regarding slavery, the majority of its membership adhered to the belief that evils in the slave system made eventual emancipation desirable, but that "such emancipation should come gradually and with due regard for the welfare of the society and the protection of the property rights of the owners."[4] This view was not unlike that of most moderate Americans at the time. In general, Catholics felt that the tactics of the abolitionists were unnecessarily extreme and ran counter to the best interests of the country as a whole. While the conservatism and the silence of the Church in the slavery controversy has led to the widespread belief that Catholics were proslavery in sentiment, it did serve to prevent the regional schism experienced by a number of the other religious bodies in the United States.

It has been estimated that not more than 5 per cent of the nearly 4.5 million Negroes in the United States were Catholic at the time of emancipation. The fact that a large number of these left the Church after the bonds tying them to their Catholic masters had been severed has led to the conclusion that in spite of "the fact that in many instances Catholic masters watched over the religious interest of their slaves, the majority of Catholic slaves were Catholic in little more than name."[5] The movement of freed Negroes away from the Church was at least in part a result of the fact that the Catholics of the late nineteenth century, like the Protestants, accepted the color line and organized the institutional structure of the Church around it. Attempts to halt the movement were limited because the Church in the South was weak (Catholics constituted less than 4 per cent of the southern population) and lacked both money and priests—especially priests trained in missionary work. The few priests located in the South were concentrated in the urban areas and had little contact with the predominantly rural Negro population. Negroes left the Church to join other social organizations or to form their own religious groups. This postwar formation of separate Negro religious bodies, while encouraged by the prejudice and discrimination of whites, was also the result of

[4] Rice, p. 155.

[5] John T. Gillard, S.S.J., *The Catholic Church and the American Negro* (Baltimore, 1929), p. 260. Gillard also reported that in one section of Louisiana an estimated 65,000 Negroes left the Catholic religion in the years immediately following the Civil War.

Negroes' desire to be part of an organization they themselves could control and one that would specifically serve their needs and interests, which were quite different from those of the white population.[6] In cases where Negroes remained Catholic, the relationship between them and the Church was characterized by white paternalism and segregation. When separate facilities and services could not be provided, Negroes were tolerated rather than welcomed in the white churches. They were confined to crowded pews in the rear of the church and were not allowed to participate in any of the social functions of the congregation.

The same circumstances which caused Negroes to leave the Church after the Civil War also limited the effectiveness of missionaries trying to convert them. In the South, the color line prevented missionaries from coordinating their efforts with the Catholic Church in the general community. While the Church in the South was not committed to a formal policy of segregation, Gillard reports that the missionaries could not "with safety ignore present racial anticipation and consequent demands for separation."[7] Resistance from the white community was coupled with resistance from the Negro community. Conversion to Catholicism often meant that the Negro would have to withdraw from the social life of his own community, which usually revolved around membership in one of the Protestant sects or churches. And as William A. Osborne points out: "For the Negro, dark skin itself was a heavy enough burden without taking on the added one of membership in a maligned Church."[8] In the North, the Negro usually met indifference from the Church and hostility from Catholics. The Church in northern cities was highly ethnic in character. During the era of slavery, competition between free Negroes and Irish Catholics provoked frequent outbreaks of violence and created animosities which negated the possibility of any large-scale conversion of Negroes to Catholicism. After emancipation, the problems presented by millions of Catholics

[6] It is interesting to note how slow the Catholic Church was in adapting its organizational forms to this reality. The first Negro Catholic Church edifice in the United States, a chapel for the Oblate Sisters in Baltimore, was built in 1836. Not until 1864 did the first Negro church, St. Francis Xavier in Baltimore, under the care of the Jesuits, appear. P. E. Hogan and J. B. Tennelly, "Negroes in the U.S. (Apostolate to)," *New Catholic Encyclopedia*, vol. 3 (New York, 1967), 310-14.

[7] Gillard, p. 69.

[8] *The Segregated Covenant: Race Relations and American Catholics* (New York, 1967), p. 29.

pouring into the northern cities of the United States from different cultural backgrounds required the constant attention of the clergy. While a few Catholics—such as Archbishop John Ireland of St. Paul and John Boyle O'Reilly, an Irish-Catholic leader in Boston—recognized that the Church was neglecting the Negro and spoke out firmly against the evils of prejudice and discrimination, little was done to remedy the situation.

The Church's first formal declaration regarding Negroes in the United States came immediately following the Civil War. At the Second Plenary Council of Baltimore in 1866, the American hierarchy implored that priests "consecrate their thoughts, their time, and themselves wholly and entirely, if possible, to the service of the colored people."[9] Archbishop Martin J. Spalding of Baltimore, one of the leading spokesmen for the Church at that time, pointed out to the American clergy: "Four millions of these unfortunates are thrown on our charity, and they silently but eloquently appeal to us for help. It is a golden opportunity for reaping a harvest of souls which neglected may not return. . . ."[10] Nine decrees on the Negro apostolate were enacted by the Council, among which was one accepting the principle of segregation in those regions where it was in vogue. The extent of this acceptance is reflected in the action of Peter Richard Kenrick, Archbishop of St. Louis, who gave the St. Louis Jesuits permission to open a church for Negroes but on condition that no sacraments were ever to be administered in the church to whites.[11]

Shortly after the decrees of the Second Plenary Council were approved by Rome, Father (later Cardinal) Herbert Vaughan, in response to a request by Pope Pius IX, brought his newly founded English missionary order—St. Joseph's Foreign Missionary Society of Mill Hill—to the United States to work among the Negroes. By 1892 the Mill Hill missionaries had charge of eight churches in Baltimore, Washington, Charleston, and Louisville, and had established a major and a minor seminary. In 1893 the American branch of this order was made independent, named St. Joseph's Society of the Sacred Heart (Josephite Fathers), and was committed to work solely for the Negroes in America.

[9] Gillard, p. 36.

[10] John Tracy Ellis, *The Catholic Church and the Negro* (Pamphlet, Huntington, Ind. [n.d.]), p. 4.

[11] Ellis, p. 5.

In addition to the Josephites, priests and religious orders such as the Jesuits and the Sulpicians and two orders of Negro nuns—the Oblate Sisters of Providence founded in 1829 by four Negro refugees from San Domingo, and the Sisters of the Holy Family founded in 1842 by Josephine Alicot—engaged in Negro missionary work; their accomplishments, however, were few, and little significant progress was made. Consequently at the Third Plenary Council in 1884 the American bishops, recognizing that the Church in the South was unable to achieve the goals and ideals proposed eighteen years earlier, formed the Commission for Catholic Missions among the Colored People and Indians, and ordered that a special annual collection be taken to finance its work. If the results of this yearly collection are an indication of the commitment of American Catholics to the Negro missions, it would seem to have been almost nonexistent. The collection provided missions with only minimal assistance; some received as little as $100 annually while others received nothing.

The greatest individual contribution to this missionary effort came from Katherine Drexel of Philadelphia. She devoted her family fortune and her life to the missions by founding the Blessed Sacrament Sisters for Indians and Colored People (1891). This order still conducts Xavier University in New Orleans, established as the first Catholic institution of higher learning for Negroes on September 27, 1915. It remains the only one of its kind in the United States and now enrolls more than 1,400 students in its college and graduate departments.

In 1906 efforts were again renewed when Cardinal Gibbons, at the request of Pope Pius X, met with the archbishops of the United States to initiate a more effective means of financing Negro missions in the South. The meeting resulted in the organization of the Catholic Board for Mission Work among the Colored People in 1907. The Board functioned solely as a fund raising organization but, like similar efforts in the past, failed to win the financial support of American Catholics.

This period also witnessed the emergence of separate lay organizations. In 1889 the first major national organization of Negro Catholics—the Congress of Colored Catholics—met in Washington, D.C., to discuss the needs of the Negro and devise ways of bettering religious and social conditions. The group met annually until 1894. In 1909 in Mobile, Alabama, four Josephite priests and three Negro laymen organized the Knights of Peter Claver—a black Knights of Columbus which today has over 17,000 members in some 200 councils and courts in the United States.

WORLD WAR I AND AFTER

With the outbreak of World War I, a reversal in the tide of European immigration, and a severe labor shortage in northern industries, thousands of Negroes saw their chance to escape the miserable conditions in the South and began to migrate northward. These experienced a general improvement in employment, income, and standard of living. But the formalized patterns of discrimination and Jim Crow laws of the South were replaced with informal discrimination and *de facto* segregation in the North. While white Catholics have frequently demonstrated that they are not immune from being prejudiced or engaging in discriminatory behavior, Osborne reports that "the record of priests and bishops, as far as access to parish churches was concerned, has been generally good, even though the Negro press occasionally reported a number of incidents in which it was clear that membership in some churches was denied nonwhites."[12]

In a pastoral letter of 1919 the American bishops clarified the Church's stand on intergroup relations by stating that "In the eyes of the Church there is no distinction of race or of nation; there are human souls, and these have all alike been purchased at the same great price, the blood of Jesus Christ."[13] This position received further support in 1929 when Cardinal Patrick Hayes of New York said that segregation "does not represent the attitude nor the spirit of the Catholic Church."[14]

In 1928, the first official national census of Negro Catholics was taken.[15] At the time there were 203,986 Negro Catholics (less than 2 per cent of the total Negro population) in the United States; 54 per cent of them were registered in exclusively Negro congregations. Over half (55 per cent) of all Negro Catholics were in the southern states,

[12] Osborne, p. 33.

[13] Charles Dollen, *Civil Rights: A Source Book* (Boston, 1964), p. 15.

[14] Cited in Osborne, p. 33.

[15] See Gillard, pp. 47-78, for the details on the methods of data collection and the results.

another 20 per cent were in the border states, and 25 per cent were in northern states. The pattern of separate parishes was especially strong in the border states (81 per cent of resident Negro Catholics in separate parishes) and the southern states (59 per cent) where three-fourths of all Negro Catholics resided. However, even in the northern states about 23 per cent of the Negro Catholics were registered in all-Negro congregations.

The settlement pattern of the Negro migrants in northern cities and the need for some type of group affiliation to provide emotional and status reinforcement led to the formation of a large number of separate "Negro churches." While these separate parishes provided organizations Negroes could consider their own and priests who devoted full time to their interests and needs, they also served as barriers to communication between white and Negro Catholics and tended to reinforce the social distance between them. Prior to 1930, when Negroes moved into an urban neighborhood surrounding a parish, it was common practice for the bishop of the diocese to turn control of the parish over to a religious order. A negative consequence of this practice was that, for all practical purposes, the Negro parish was isolated from the rest of the diocese as well as from the diocesan clergy.

While Negro-white relationships in the Church may have been characterized by a good deal of segregation and white paternalism, Negroes have by no means been totally passive. Their response to paternalism and discrimination began to take organized form in Maryland in 1917 when Dr. Thomas W. Turner, a Negro Catholic professor at Howard University, and a small group of his friends founded the Committee Against the Extension of Race Prejudice in the Church. Through written appeals to the American hierarchy, Dr. Turner and his group urged eliminating discrimination in churches, church services and social functions, schools and seminaries. In 1925, under the guidance of Abraham J. Emerick, S.J., and Dr. Turner, the Committee expanded and changed its name to the Federated Colored Catholics of America. Negro Catholics were encouraged to join and to form similar groups throughout the country so that Catholic practice in racial matters could be brought more into line with the principles enunciated by the Church's official spokesmen. Although the federation claimed a membership of more than 100,000 Negroes, met annually, held rallies in a number of large cities, and received the endorsement of many bishops and clergymen, it accomplished little more than to demonstrate to a number of Negroes that parity—even within an institution such as the Church—was a difficult goal to achieve.

The federation was not the only group interested in interracial justice during the 1920's. In 1927 John LaFarge, S.J., a champion of Negro rights until his death in 1961, founded the Catholic Laymen's Union—a small group of Negro Catholic business- and professional men in the New York City area. The members of the Union constituted the elite of the Negro Catholics in the New York area; membership was by invitation only and each participant had to be a responsible and respected individual in his parish and community. The group emphasized the spiritual development of the members, engaged in frequent discussions of religious issues, and initiated a social-action program to educate both white Catholics and those in the Negro community about the implications of Catholic principles for Negro-white relations. In the early 1930's Catholic young persons became increasingly aware of the problems facing the Negro when the national Catholic Student Mission Crusade, under the leadership of the late John T. Gillard, S.S.J., endorsed and promoted the cause of Negro rights. These years also saw the growth of the clergy's interest in interracial justice. In 1933 a number of priests met in Newark to work for "a more sympathetic attitude toward the colored people and toward work for the colored among the rest of the clergy and the Catholic people of the United States"; they organized the Clergy Conference on Negro Welfare, which was the first formal attempt to involve the clergy in the field of Negro rights. Soon there was a similar group in the Midwest and two others in the South. Their primary goal—making their fellow priests and nuns aware of the fact that the Church had for too long neglected the Negro—was pursued through letters, pamphlets, coverage in the mass-communications media, and lectures at Catholic high schools and colleges.

Through the years Father LaFarge had been working closely with major Catholic organizations concerned with Negro rights both within the institutional framework of the Church and in American society in general. He firmly believed that these organizations would never significantly improve race relations as long as whites and Negroes continued working in separate groups and aimed merely at making Catholics "aware" of prejudice and discrimination. Rather, lasting and meaningful progress depended, first, on the merging of both white and Negro forces into a combined interracial front and, second, on the expansion of aims to include influencing policy changes and bringing about attitudinal changes. It was largely through Father LaFarge's influence that on Pentecost Sunday, 1934, at an interracial meeting of 800 people, convened by the Catholic Laymen's Union in New York's Town Hall, white and Negro leaders joined and unanimously endorsed the formation of the Catholic Interracial Council (CIC). Speaking at the meeting, James J. Hoey, the Council's first president, said that the CIC represented a "joint cooperation venture by both white and colored leaders for the promotion of a consistently Christian attitude in race relations." The Council obtained ecclesiastical approval from New York's Cardinal Patrick Hayes; an organizing committee was selected; George K. Hunton, a Brooklyn lawyer, was appointed executive secretary; and Father LaFarge was named chaplain. The meeting decided that the CIC's primary task was educational and that it should work to involve Catholics in the interracial movement, to close the gap between American principles and practice in regard to race, and to bring the Catholic Church to the Negroes of this country.

The CIC began its operations with the combined resources of the Federation of Colored Catholics, the Laymen's Union, and the Clergy Conference. In September, 1934, the Council took over the publication of the *Interracial Review,* a monthly magazine originally founded in St. Louis by William M. Markoe, S.J., and circulated by the Federation of Colored Catholics. The *Review* served as the CIC's official organ and was also used as a means of developing the interests of others sympathetic to the interracial movement. Its editorials and articles dealt with a variety of topics, ranging from papal teachings on interracial justice to the latest press releases related to the Negro community or Negro-white relations.

One of the notable accomplishments of the Council was to establish friendly relations with Negro newspapers which, at that time, were extremely negative in their approach to all things Catholic and often misinterpreted or presented a distorted picture of Catholic affairs and issues. Harold Ley, in commending the Council on its work in this area, wrote:

> High on the list of accomplishments of the Council is its success in transforming the attitude of the secular Negro press toward the Roman Catholic Church. To change the attitude of that press, which largely dominates Negro thought, from hostility to warm apprecia-

tion of the Catholic Church in a decade, represents a notable achievement.[16]

Cooperation has created mutual feelings of confidence and helped responsible coverage of news in both the *Review* and Negro publications. Of equal importance has been the Council's influence on the Catholic press, which rather than misinterpreting or distorting Negro news simply did not report it. Lines of communication with editors of Catholic papers were established and relevant press releases were channeled from the Council through the National Catholic Welfare Conference News Service to Catholic newspapers around the country.

Between 1934 and the early 1960's the CIC received recognition for a number of its civil-rights activities and programs. From the beginning the CIC was close to the mainstream of civil-rights activity—participating in most of the major events of the period. An indication of the way its efforts were received in the Negro community is the fact that in 1942 Father La Farge was the only white speaker at a Madison Square Garden rally launching the drive for the Fair Employment Practices Commission. In 1954, George Hunton, CIC executive secretary, was elected to the board of directors of the National Association for the Advancement of Colored People.

By the time of CIC's twenty-fifth anniversary in 1959 there were thirty-five local and regional Councils in major cities of both the North and South. These councils were autonomous groups and were responsible to the bishop of their respective dioceses. While specific programs have varied from city to city, they have all retained their general orientation toward converting Catholic principles into behavior.

The 1930's also saw the emergence of several other groups that were concerned with the welfare of the Negro.[17] In 1933 in New York Dorothy Day and Peter Maurin founded the Catholic Worker, a group of young Catholic men and women who devoted themselves to full-time social work in the Worker's Houses of Hospitality. Its philosophical affinity to agrarianism, anarchism, and pacificism has limited its appeal and influence in the larger society, although it still functions as an impressive radical Christian witness.

16 Harold E. Ley, "Catholicism and the Negro," *Christian Century*, LXI (Dec. 20, 1944), 1476-79.

17 See Thomas Harte, *Catholic Organizations Promoting Negro-White Race Relations In The United States* (Washington, 1947).

The settlement-house approach was also adopted by the Friendship House movement organized in the United States in 1938 by the Russian emigree, the Baroness Catherine de Hueck. Staff members adopted a life of poverty and lived and worked among the poor in Negro slums in five American cities. Their orientation was pragmatic, romantic, and apolitical. The monthly publication of the movement, the *Friendship House News,* later called the *Catholic Interracialist,* was circulated among a number of priests, religious, and laymen all over the country (at one time as many as 6,000 a month).

In both cases, the greatest impact was on the white volunteers and only indirectly on the larger societal patterns or the condition of the Negro. The Friendship House movement has all but disappeared from the scene and the Catholic Worker has become almost totally absorbed by the issue of peace.

In November of 1939 the American Church received another gentle prod from Rome, in the words of Pius XII:

> We confess that we feel a special paternal affection . . . for the Negro people dwelling among you; for in the field of religion and education we know that they need special care and comfort and are very deserving of it. We therefore invoke an abundance of heavenly blessings and we pray fruitful success for those whose generous zeal is devoted to their welfare.[18]

Five months prior to this message, a meeting of the Second National Catholic Social Action Congress was held in Cleveland. Here a group of southern clergy and laymen organized the Catholic Committee of the South. One of the primary aims of the committee, which remained active only until 1951, was the betterment of race relations in the South. As early as its 1949 convention the committee went on record as advocating the integration of southern schools. Every year at conventions held in various southern cities the committee presented an award to an individual who had made a significant contribution to the progress of the South.

With the large influx of Negroes into the Northern cities during World War II the American hierarchy found it necessary to again remind Catholics of Church teachings about accepting all men as brothers in Christ. Pastoral letters written by the bishops in both 1942 and 1943 called for respect for the rights of the minority groups in the

[18] *Sertum Laetitiae,* partially reprinted in Dollen, p. 76.

United States "especially for our colored fellow citizens." Well aware of the racial tensions that existed in many urban areas, the bishops declared that it was "the duty of every good citizen to do everything in his power to relieve them." Catholics were reminded of the numerous contributions of the Negroes to the development of the United States and were urged to see that Negroes were accorded all their constitutional rights, which implied "not only political equality, but also fair economic and educational opportunities, a just share in public welfare projects, good housing without exploitation, and a full chance for the social advancement of their race."

The concern of the bishops, however, did not extend much beyond the written word; no efforts were made to initiate any programs that could have provided rural Negro migrants the assistance they so desperately needed to help them adjust to an urban way of life. While the few Catholic organizations dedicated to the cause of Negro rights frequently received the vocal support of the hierarchy, they never received its financial support. Little could be done on budgets which depended solely on contributions from a few concerned Catholics. Many members of these organizations became discouraged and lost interest. The enthusiastic spirit which had prevailed within the Catholic interracial movement during the 1930's and early 1940's began to fade in the late 1940's and the early 1950's. Why this happened is difficult to say, but the fact remains that the Church neglected an opportunity to give of itself to a socially and economically deprived segment of the population.

Prior to 1940, the fact that approximately 70 per cent of the Negro population was concentrated in the South (80 per cent in 1910) greatly limited the extent of its contact with the Church, which has never been an influential force in the southern states. Between 1940 and 1960, however, the Negro population outside the deep South more than doubled, rising from nearly four million to over nine million. This increase occurred mostly in the twelve largest metropolitan areas of the North and West—all strongholds of the Catholic Church in America—which according to most recent statistics now house over 30 per cent of the total United States Negro population. Opportunities for bringing the Church to the Negro were many; only a handful of priests and a small number of the laity made any effort to take advantage of them.

Moreover, the organizations dedicated to promoting the welfare of the Negro were at best on the fringe of institutional power. Tolerated in most cases, encouraged in some, they were never forcefully supported or influential in Church decision making. In fact, it can be said that they never enjoyed the full confidence and support of the hierarchy. They were concerned with what was for most a peripheral problem at a time when the attention and resources of the Church were being absorbed by Americanization of the immigrant and the rapid expansion of the Catholic educational system.

In summary, then, the early period of our history was marked by a rather reluctant response of American Catholics to the needs of the Negro and the prodding of Rome. Moreover, the effort, such as it was, was largely missionary in character. As we approach the contemporary scene the emphasis shifts to broader secular concerns, with a growing amount of the initiative coming from within the American Church—from both laymen and clergy.

RECENT DEVELOPMENTS: POLICY STATEMENTS AND PRACTICAL ACTION

The trends that began during the 1930's and 1940's have come into their own during the past two decades. The postwar years have been a period of drastic change in race relations in the United States, and the Church has not only been swept along by these general changes but has played an increasingly active role in bringing them about.

There has been a steady stream of official pronouncements reiterating traditional Christian teachings on justice and charity as they apply to Negro-white relations. Something of a turning point was reached in 1958 when the American bishops at their annual meeting in Washington, D.C., issued a pastoral letter on Discrimination and the Christian Conscience. The bishops lamented the fact that "in recent years . . . [the interracial movement had] slowed if not halted in some areas." They reminded American Catholics that the "heart of the race question is moral and religious" and emphatically declared that adherence to policies of racial segregation could not "be reconciled with the Christian view of our fellow man." The letter continued:

> Our Christian faith is of its nature universal. It knows not the distinction of race, color, or nationhood. . . . Every man has an equal right to life, to justice before the law, to marry and rear a family

> under human conditions, and to an equitable opportunity to use the goods of this earth for his needs and those of his family. . . . No one who truly loves God's children will deny [Negro citizens] this opportunity.

The bishops concluded with a plea for the study of existing problems and a plan of action characterized, not by "a gradualism that is merely a cloak for inaction," or "rash impetuosity that would sacrifice the achievements of decades in ill-timed and ill-considered ventures," but by "the quiet and persevering courage [that] has always been the mark of a true follower of Christ."

Pope John XXIII in his encyclical *Pacem in Terris* not only condemned discrimination but declared: "Truth requires the elimination of every trace of racism." He went further and began to elaborate a theology of intergroup relations:

> There are, in many lands, groupings of people of more or less different racial backgrounds. However, the elements which characterize an ethnic group must not be transformed into a watertight compartment in which human beings are prevented from communicating with their fellow men of other ethnic groups. That would contrast with our contemporary situation, in which the distances separating peoples have been almost wiped out. Nor can one overlook the fact that, even though human beings differ from one another by virtue of their ethnic peculiarities, they all possess certain essential common elements and are inclined by nature to meet each other in the world of spiritual values, whose progressive assimiliation opens to them the possibility of perfection without limits. They have the right and duty, therefore, to live in communion with one another.

Vatican II, in the Pastoral Constitution on the Church in the Modern World, also addressed itself to the problem in no uncertain terms:

> The basic equality of all [men] must receive increasingly greater recognition. . . . With respect to the fundamental rights of the person, every type of discrimination, whether social or cultural, whether based on sex, race, color, social condition, language or religion, is to be overcome and eradicated as contrary to God's intent.

Most recently, a "Pastoral Statement on Race Relations and Poverty" adopted November, 1966, by the National Conference of Catholic Bishops, says:

> We affirm once again, as we did in our statement of 1958 and our letter of 1963, and on many occasions in the pronouncements of Vatican Council II, that discrimination based on race, language, religion or national origins is contrary to right reason and to Christian teaching. We are all the children of God. We share the same rights before God and man. All men of good will desire that the doors of opportunity be opened equally to all who are their brothers under one eternal Father.

They also spelled out a detailed program of social action.

These official pronouncements and a score of others, coupled with the effective action of a few churchmen like Archbishop Joseph F. Rummel of New Orleans, Cardinal Albert G. Meyer of Chicago, Cardinal Patrick A. O'Boyle of Washington, D.C., Cardinal Joseph E. Ritter of St. Louis, Archbishop Robert E. Lucey of San Antonio, and Bishop Vincent S. Waters of Raleigh, N.C., in desegregating their churches and schools and putting the full authority of their offices behind the effort to achieve interracial justice, helped to drastically change the image and stance of Catholics on this issue. Also important in this respect was the service of religious like the late Bishop Francis J. Haas on the President's Fair Employment Practices Commission and Theodore M. Hesburgh, C.S.C., on the Federal Civil-Rights Commission. Because of the visibility of priests, they tended to have greater impact than their actual numbers would justify. Even so, it is remarkable to what extent the leadership in this area came from the clerical ranks. Catholic laymen tended to follow rather than lead—and while it has become fashionable to note the failure of the hierarchy to take more vigorous action, it is rarely noted that on this issue laymen have not met the challenge nearly as well as the clergy.

Typical of the reaction of non-Catholic observers to these efforts is that of the historian Thomas F. Gossett:

> In recent years, the Catholic church has taken a strong position in favor of racial equality. The acceptance of Negro students in Catholic colleges and universities has been cordial and widespread. In the Deep South, even when they were a relatively small minority and when there was strong community opposition, the Catholics have shown courage and foresight in their widespread willingness to integrate their schools. Though there are many critics among the Catholics who maintain that the church has been too cautious on racial matters, their record in comparison with that of Protestants is very good indeed. Even severe Protestant critics of Catholics have recog-

nized that their record in the field of race relations has been an enviable one.[19]

The change in outlook was not always a smooth one, nor was it uniform throughout the Church. From Philadelphia to Los Angeles and Selma to Chicago, there developed at both the local and the diocesan level various forms of conflict on this issue. In some places not only are laymen divided, but there are sharp differences among the clergy, especially regarding tactics and style. Direct action, civil disobedience, and especially attempts to integrate residential neighborhoods have caused the greatest difficulty among the conservative members of the Church.

Nevertheless, the trend is clear. The moral imperative to achieve racial justice has been clearly enunciated. Discrimination within the Church and its related institutions has been sharply reduced. The problem is being given serious and continued attention. There has developed a broad concern for the fate and welfare of the Negro as citizen and person, independent of any interest in him as a potential convert. Finally, there is a growing recognition of the need to use the influence and authority of the Church in cooperation with other groups to actively seek change in the larger society.

These last two points should perhaps be elaborated. In 1960 a revitalization movement occurred when more than sixty Catholic Interracial Councils and similar groups federated themselves under a newly founded nationwide organization, the National Catholic Conference for Interracial Justice (NCCIJ). The federation represented an attempt on the part of interracial groups to move from an amateur, volunteer basis to professional operations and a united and organized program of action headed by permanent staff members. William Osborne aptly describes the significance of this new organization for the direction and tenor of the Catholic interracial movement:

> For many years the local councils performed a valuable function in spreading "the Catholic viewpoint on race" within the Church and in the community at large. Today they are becoming conscious that the "race problem" will not yield to principle alone, however sound and however often reasserted; that it requires involvement—and above all, professional competence—in such fields as housing, education, equal employment opportunities and urban renewal.[20]

[19] Gossett, *Race: The History of an Idea in America* (New York, 1965), p. 449.
[20] Osborne, pp. 40-41.

Conference headquarters were established in Chicago with a field office in New Orleans added in 1962. The structure of the NCCIJ is similar to that of the old Catholic Interracial Council, with local groups remaining autonomous and conducting programs shaped to meet local needs and solve unique local problems. The offices in Chicago and New Orleans are the sources of publications, program aids, and professional assistance. The extent to which such material and assistance can be provided is determined by NCCIJ's budget, which depends solely on the contribution of member organizations, donations, and foundation grants.

While the organization does represent a fresh start and a new generation of laymen capable of representing the Catholic community in the kind of coalition politics that have come to characterize the civil-rights movement, there is still some question as to whether it is really all that different from its predecessor, the Catholic Interracial Council movement. To many observers, it appears to be largely a public-relations office with a vague educational function and a dedicated but ineffective staff. Certainly, compared to the major Jewish defense groups its resources are meager, its staff amateurish, and its research and service activities negligible.[21] But NCCIJ has broken some new ground that is worthy of note.

In 1963, NCCIJ was partly responsible for the formation of the National Conference on Religion and Race, the first interfaith organization to become involved in the civil-rights movement. At the first meeting of this new group in January of 1963 the 700 religious leaders in attendance endorsed the organization of local interfaith groups in ten cities across the country in an attempt to bring Protestants, Catholics, and Jews together in prayer and action for the cause of human equality and dignity. Later that year, NCCIJ organized Catholic participation in the March for Jobs and Freedom which took place in Washington, D.C., on August 28. The mobilization of Catholic participation in the march from Selma to Montgomery in March, 1965, was also largely attributable to NCCIJ, especially to the advance work of its executive secretary, Mathew Ahmann, and his four staff

[21] In 1966, for example, the Anti-Defamation League of B'nai B'rith had a budget of $4.2 million, published six national periodicals, maintained twenty-eight regional offices and a professional staff of 300, and supported several major research programs. The effect on NCCIJ of the resignation of its respected executive secretary, Mathew Ahmann, cannot be gauged at this point.

members, who were responsible for obtaining ecclesiastical approval for the active participation of priests and religious in the march. On the local level the member councils and groups of NCCIJ have organized such activities as interracial home visits, leadership training in Negro communities, and programs for tutoring underprivileged Negro children and providing them with recreational opportunities.

The actual position of the Church regarding the extent to which laymen and clergy should become involved in the civil-rights movement has remained ambivalent throughout the 1960's. The call for constructive programs of action in the 1958 letter of the American bishops was restated in their 1963 letter, which points out that "respect for personal rights is not only a matter of individual moral duty; it is also a matter for civic action." A clarification of "civic action" is made when the bishops state that Catholics should do what is possible to remove racial barriers in their own area of work, in their neighborhoods, and in their community. "We must act," they continue, "through various lay organizations of the Church, as well as with civic groups of every type." This seems to be a rather clear statement of the Church's position. However, ambivalence arises on the diocesan level and within religious orders when official Church personnel must still, as Osborne points out, "run the gauntlet of permissions and approvals before they can figuratively speaking, go to Selma."[22] Approval at this level has been slow in coming, with bishops and religious superiors tending towards conservatism because of "organizational considerations" and fear of the negative consequences which may result when priests and nuns march, carry picket signs, and engage in acts of civil disobedience.

The eruption of racial violence in recent summers has demonstrated to a number of American bishops that the racial issue is something that cannot be ignored; it has brought the Church on the local level face to face with contemporary urban problems and has forced many hesitant diocesan authorities to confront the issues. While some dioceses have lagged behind others in the formulation of constructive human-relations and community-relations programs, a number of efforts are being made on the local level. The Diocese of Cleveland, NCCIJ, and the American Council for Nationalities Service have organized Project Bridge, a program which is attempting to work through white nationality groups to develop intergroup awareness and lines of com-

[22] Osborne, p. 244.

munication between white and Negro communities in the Cleveland area. Project Equality, initiated by NCCIJ and organized in approximately twenty dioceses as well as in some Protestant and Jewish communities, has been an effective means of influencing a number of business concerns to adopt fair employment practices by consolidating Church purchasing power to buy only from companies which follow a policy of nondiscrimination. This program also serves to encourage Catholic parishes, hospitals, and schools to make jobs available for Negroes and other minority group members. In early 1968, NCCIJ received a grant of $522,200 from the Ford Foundation to expand Project Equality with a view to making its organization and influence nationwide. While it is not yet possible to measure the effect of Project Equality on employment patterns, its realistic methods are calculated to get results.

Recent research on Catholic education which shows that students in Catholic schools are neither more nor less tolerant of Negroes than Catholics attending public schools has led several dioceses to consider various educational programs to reduce the negative attitudes that do exist among a number of the students.[23]

For the most part, diocesan programs are insufficiently staffed and financed and too narrow in scope to become an influential force in fields such as housing, employment, and urban renewal. A notable exception, however, has been Detroit's Archdiocesan Department of Community Relations, which has initiated a comprehensive program dealing with urban problems. The program's success is largely due to the support and encouragement it has received from Archbishop John F. Dearden. A recent statement by the Archbishop clearly indicates what Christian involvement in the "urban crisis" means to him:

> The Church must understand the urban community. And this understanding must be built up by direct contact with the people involved, by the use of experts in areas of study and research, and by identification with the people who constitute the total urban community. This search for understanding is quickened by the spirit of Christ, searching out truth in Charity.[24]

[23] These studies will be discussed in more detail in the following section of this paper.

[24] John F. Dearden, "Challenge to Change in the Urban Church," in *The Church and the Urban Racial Crisis*, eds. Mathew Ahmann and Margaret Roache (Techny, Ill., 1967), p. 42.

On the national level the United States Catholic Conference (formerly National Catholic Welfare Conference) has functioned as the official agency dealing with today's urban problems. Its Social Action Department, however, has not been provided with the finances or the staff to do effective work; its annual budget amounts to forty thousand dollars, seventy-five times smaller than the three million-dollar annual program administered by a similar department in the Protestant Episcopal Church, a religious body one-tenth the size of the American Catholic Church.[25]

The Church has been deeply affected by the changes in major urban areas during the post-World War II years. As the older Catholic immigrant groups experienced a high degree of upward mobility, many of them joined other economically successful Americans in their exodus from the inner city to the more desirable residential areas on the periphery of the city and beyond. With them they took much of the inner city's clerical and religious manpower, as well as a good deal of its financial resources. The neighborhoods they vacated were quickly filled by the incoming Negroes—most of whom were not Catholic. The impact of these changes is indicated by the Social Action Department's 1968 report that over 200 Catholic schools located in the ghettoes have closed their doors in the last two years. The needs of the newcomers to these areas are great, but the scarcity of resources within the old parishes and the lack of support from other sources have impeded the development of effective parish programs. Perhaps even more important than the lack of material resources is the lack of ideas and adequately trained personnel. There is still great confusion and uncertainty about the appropriate role of an inner-city priest and the techniques and approaches that would be most effective in serving the needs of the new population.

One encouraging development was the establishment in 1965 of the Center for Applied Research in the Apostolate to investigate problems of the inner city and provide guidelines for effective action. A good start in this direction was the Conference on Inner-City Research held in 1965, at which a distinguished group of social scientists discussed the problems and research needs of the inner-city apostolate.[26]

[25] Mathew Ahmann, "Strategies for the Future," in Ahmann and Roache, p. 235.

[26] The papers given at this meeting have been published in *The Church In The Changing City*, ed. Louis J. Luzbetak, S.V.D. (Techny, Ill., 1966).

Recently there has been a growing amount of criticism and dissatisfaction with present efforts within the Church. For example, in the fall of 1967, during the period of national soul-searching that followed the most destructive civil disorders in our recent history, Pedro Arrupe, S.J., General of the Society of Jesus, in a special letter to American Jesuits declared:

> Our record of service to the American Negro has fallen far short of what it should have been. . . . There have been great pioneers like Fathers John LaFarge and John Markoe . . . but unfortunately our apostolate to the Negro in the United States has depended chiefly upon individual initiative and very little upon a corporate effort of the Society. . . . The Society of Jesus has not committed its manpower and other resources to that apostolate in any degree commensurate with the need of the Negro to share in our services. . . . It would be wholesome practice for each of us, individually and as members of Jesuit communities, to examine our consciences and to inquire why so little of our effort in the past has been expended in work for and with the Negro. . . .[27]

He went on to spell out a ten-point action program for the Society.

In February, 1968, at a meeting in Chicago to establish a national federation of priests' associations and senates, the seven black priests working in the Chicago archdiocese issued a statement deploring, among other things, the traditional "enlightened paternalism" of the Church in its relations with Negroes; the lack of leadership from the Catholic Church in the drive to fulfill Negro aspirations; the "suspicious disdain" within the Church toward the militant elements in the black communities. They proceeded to outline ten proposals, which they contended "are only minimal steps toward erasing the present image of the Catholic Church in the black community, the image of a white Church unrelated to the needs of the black community for identity and power."[28]

On April 18, 1968, fifty-eight Negro priests, including the only Negro American bishop, Auxiliary Bishop Harold R. Perry, S.V.D., of New Orleans, at a meeting of the Catholic Clergy Conference on the Interracial Apostolate formed a Black Catholic Clergy Caucus. The caucus issued a statement which read in part:

[27] *Catholic Mind,* LXVI (Jan., 1968), 20-21.

[28] "Statement of the Black Priests of the Archdiocese of Chicago, April, 1968," pp. 1-4.

> The Catholic church in the United States is primarily a white racist institution. . . . Because of its past implicit and active support of prevailing attitudes and institutions of America, the Catholic church is rapidly dying in the Black community. . . . And unless the church, by an immediate, effective and total reversing of its present practices, rejects and denounces *all* forms of racism within its ranks and institutions and in the society of which she is a part, she will become unacceptable in the Black community.

This sweeping and unsubstantiated indictment, as well as the more temperate and carefully written earlier statement by the Chicago priests, is significant for a number of reasons. First, it provides additional evidence of the deep resentment Negro Americans feel over the discrimination, real and imagined, they experience in American society. Second, it shows how poor communication can be even among people strongly united on ultimate questions. Third, the demands for recognition of their distinctive cultural identity, a separate voice in church affairs, and a certain amount of organizational autonomy are not unlike those made by earlier immigrant groups when they were being assimilated into the American Church and American society. Finally, it shows that Black Catholics, like white Catholics, are subject to influences in American society other than their religious faith. It is perhaps as natural today for Negro Catholics to be influenced by the black-power philosophy as for earlier generations of white Catholics to be influenced by the values and attitudes then dominant in American society.

NEGRO CATHOLICS IN THE AMERICAN CHURCH

The size of the Negro Catholic population has nearly tripled in the last twenty-five years. Before World War II Negro Catholics numbered fewer than 300,000 and annual conversions did not exceed 4,000. In 1967 there were 783,720 Negro Catholics; converts for 1966 numbered 13,614.[29] *The Negro Almanac* asserts that "there is good cause

[29] These and the following figures on the size and distribution of the Negro Catholic population are derived from the annual reports of the Commission for Catholic Missions Among The Colored People and the Indians as reported in *National Catholic Almanac*, ed. Felician A. Foy, O. F. M. (Paterson, N.J.). The reports are based on data supplied by the ordinaries of the dioceses.

to believe that the Catholic Church is today the third or fourth largest religious organization among American Negroes (exceeded only by the two Baptist conventions and the African Methodist Episcopal denomination)."[30]

An American Negro priesthood was late in getting a start and has developed slowly.[31] The first three priests were the remarkable Healy brothers, sons of an Irish father and a mulatto mother: James Augustine, ordained (1854) in Paris for the diocese of Boston and consecrated bishop of Portland, Maine in 1875; Alexander Sherwood, ordained in Rome for Boston (1858); Patrick Francis, ordained a Jesuit in Belgium (1864) and later President of Georgetown University (1874-1882). The first Negro ordained in the United States was Charles Randolph Uncles, a Mill Hill father, who was ordained in Baltimore (1891). It was not until 1910 that the first American-trained diocesan priest, Stephen L. Theobold, was ordained in St. Paul by Archbishop John Ireland. A significant advance occurred in 1920 when the Society of the Divine Word started St. Augustine's Seminary in Bay St. Louis, Mississippi, to train Negro candidates for their community. Their first candidate, Maurice Rousseve, was ordained in 1934. By 1968, sixty-one of the 171 Negro-American priests belonged to the Divine Word order. Moreover, two of them had become bishops—Bishop Harold R. Perry of New Orleans and Bishop Joseph Bowers of Accra, Ghana.

While some of the lag in the development of Negro priests may be attributed to the poorer educational opportunities available to Negroes and the consequent lack of academic preparation, it is largely the result of overt discrimination and the lack of encouragement. Father Rollins E. Lambert, the first Negro ordained as a priest of the Archdiocese of Chicago (1949) and the archdiocese's first Negro pastor (1968), points out that prior to 1940 only one male religious order and one diocesan seminary would accept Negro candidates for the priesthood.[32] This discrimination has all but ended, and the doors

[30] Harry A. Ploski and Roscoe C. Brown, Jr., eds., *The Negro Almanac* (New York, 1967), p. 796.

[31] The following discussion is based on Hogan and Tinnelly, p. 312 (see note 6).

[32] Rollins E. Lambert, "The Negro and the Catholic Church," *Roman Catholicism and the American Way of Life*, ed. Thomas T. McAvoy, C.S.C. (Notre Dame, Ind., 1960), pp. 156-64.

FIGURE I

GROWTH OF CATHOLICISM AMONG NEGROES, 1890–1960

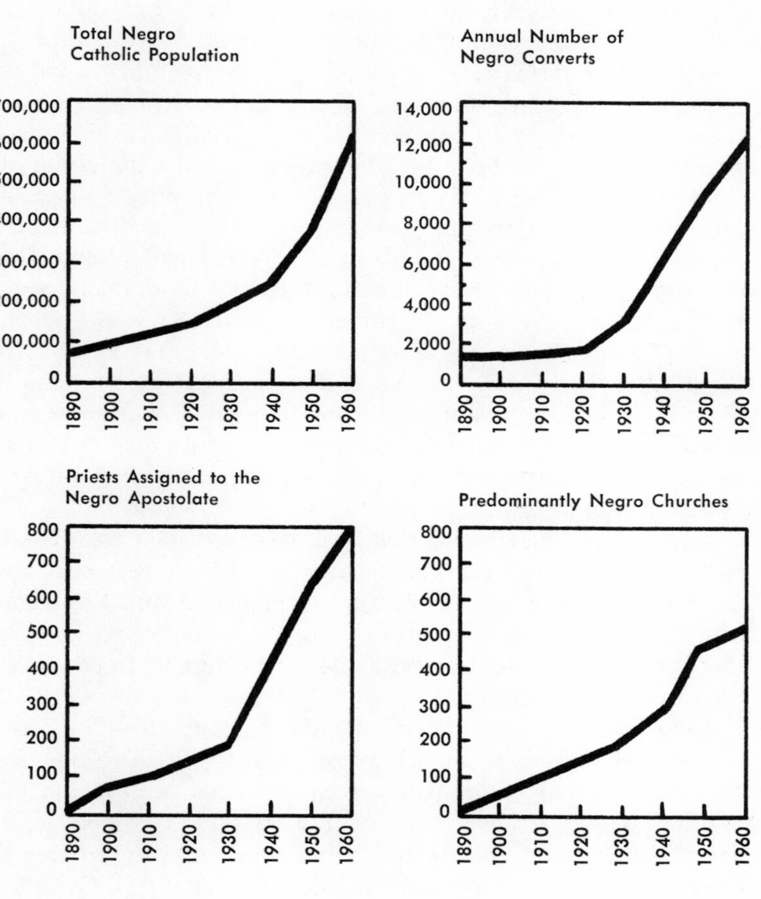

Source:

Reports of the Secretary to the Commission for Catholic Missions
Among the Colored People and the Indians

of seminaries are now open to Negroes, although it is said a number still do not encourage Negro vocations.

The changed policy is reflected in the growth of the Negro priesthood. In 1935 there were only six Negro priests in the United States; in 1944 there were thirty-eight; in 1957, sixty-two; in 1961, 120; and in 1968, 171.

Figure I dramatically shows the growth of the Negro Catholic population, also the accelerating rate of growth in recent years. It is impossible to tell from this data whether the growth in churches and priests followed or preceded the rise in membership and number of conversions. In any case, there can be little doubt that the achievements of this apostolate have been very impressive. In 1890 only one out of eighty Negroes was a Catholic; only twenty-seven priests were engaged primarily in ministering to Negroes; twenty-four small churches had been provided for them, and about eighty-five small schools. In 1967 one out of twenty-five Negroes was a Catholic; more than 800 priests were in charge of over 500 Negro congregations, each with its church and 345 with schools. About 12 per cent of all converts were Negro, slightly less than one would expect if recruitment were random from the non-Catholic population, but considering the tradition of separate Negro denominations and the prevalence of white prejudice, it seems significant that Catholicism has been nearly as successful with Negroes as with whites in this respect.

Figure II, however, shows that Negroes constitute a relatively small part of the total Catholic population and are underrepresented in the ranks of the clergy (diocesan and religious) and the hierarchy. Moreover, the number of priests committed to the Negro apostolate is short of what one would expect based on the number to be served and the success of past efforts.

Table I provides a detailed picture of the size and distribution of the Negro Catholic population by region. A study of these figures indicates that this population is highly concentrated, both regionally and in terms of dioceses. Over 42 per cent of all Negro Catholics are in the South—almost half of these are in two dioceses: Lafayette and New Orleans in the state of Louisiana. One-fifth of all Negro Catholics are in the Northeast (40 per cent of these in the New York archdiocese); another one-fifth are in the Midwest (30 per cent of these in the Chicago archdiocese).

FIGURE II

RACIAL COMPOSITION OF THE CHURCH IN THE U.S., 1967

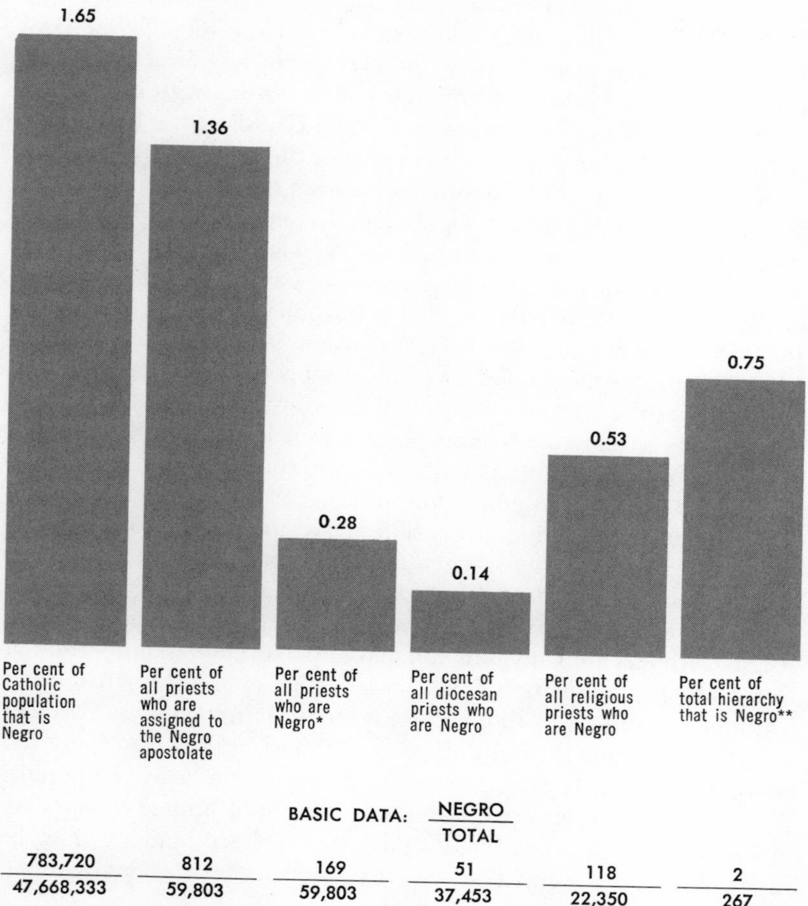

BASIC DATA: NEGRO / TOTAL

783,720 / 47,668,333	812 / 59,803	169 / 59,803	51 / 37,453	118 / 22,350	2 / 267

* Negro total includes three chaplains in Armed Forces and twenty-two foreign missionaries.

** Includes one bishop serving in Africa.

Source:

Catholic Directory, 1968; 1968 National Catholic Almanac, pp. 557–58

Although the report indicates there are sixty-seven dioceses and archdioceses with Negro Catholics, in fact this population is highly concentrated in a few places. The twelve dioceses with 25,000 or more Negro Catholics account for almost three quarters of the total.[33] The New York City area (including both the New York archdiocese and the Brooklyn diocese) is the largest single concentration, with over 91,000 Negro Catholics (12 per cent of the total). Louisiana has the highest state total, with over 168,000 (21 per cent of the total).

In no region except the South do Negroes constitute a substantial part of the total Catholic population. In only fifteen dioceses do Negroes make up 5 per cent or more of the Catholic population, and all of these are in the South or border states.[34] Comparing the percentage of the total population that is Catholic and the percentage of the Catholic population that is Negro gives us a perfect inverse correlation—the greater the proportion of the total population that is Catholic, the lower the Negro proportion of the Catholic population. What this suggests is that most Negroes become acquainted with the Church, and compose a substantial part of it, in those regions where the Church is weakest in numbers and influence. This pattern is probably the result of the differing proportion of Negroes in the total population, rather than of the differential effort made by the Church in these regions; nevertheless, it is important in understanding the Catholic response to the problem of race relations. In the South, where Negro Catholics are numerous and make up a substantial proportion of the Catholic population, the social climate is restrictive, and Catholicism, itself a weak minority, is relatively impotent as an agent of change. Outside the South, Negro Catholics are too scarce and too concentrated in a few localities to fully engage the Catholic population. While social concern obviously should not be limited to one's fellow religionists, it seems highly probable that acceptance would be easier, traditional prejudices weakened, and the institutional Church

[33] Lafayette, La. (78,284), Washington, D.C. (66,731), New Orleans, La. (64,000), New York, N.Y. (62,678), Galveston-Houston (63,500), Chicago (45,000), Philadelphia (41,383), Los Angeles (40,000), Detroit (30,000), Brooklyn (28,500), Baltimore (27,600), St. Louis (25,633).

[34] Galveston-Houston (20.5%), Lafayette (19.7), Washington (17.4), Mobile-Birmingham (14.5), Savannah (11.3), Charleston (10.4), Alexandria, La. (10.4), New Orleans (10.2), Natchez-Jackson (10.1), Baton Rouge (8.9), Raleigh (7.6), Oklahoma City-Tulsa (6.2), Baltimore (5.8), Kansas City-St. Joseph, Mo. (5.4), St. Louis (5.0).

less accommodating to the status quo, if Negroes constituted a greater force within the Catholic population.

Adult Negro conversions tend to be highly concentrated in the most urban areas, especially outside the South. Ten dioceses, each with 500 or more conversions, accounted for almost two thirds of all conversions. All ten were large metropolitan centers, and only three were in the South.[35] However, because of the high rates of migration from the South in recent years, it is difficult to say where the initial contact was made and the groundwork laid.

Commenting on what he has termed an "unprecedented movement of Negroes toward Catholicism," Dr. Joseph R. Washington, a Negro Protestant minister, writes:

> Catholics are willing to seek members among the majority of Negroes who have turned away from the Church or who have never been concerned with its life, and the Roman Catholic Church is not unreceptive to the Negro who no longer finds his needs met in Negro communions and is unwelcome in mainstream Protestantism.[36]

Similar comments by E. Franklin Frazier, the late well-known Negro sociologist, indicate that many Negroes have looked favorably on the Church because of its doctrine of universal acceptance and its advocacy of racial equality.[37] Washington also observes that:

> The Roman Catholic educational system and patterns of worship, even in segregated Southern churches, have impressed Negroes with a sense of belonging to the universal church so profoundly that there is a deep sense of identification with the Church among Negro Catholics; they do not think of themselves as Negro Catholics but as Catholics. This is in contrast to Negro Protestants, who have no sense of identification with the Church or Protestantism or faith, but consider themselves Negro Baptists, Methodists, Congregationalists, Presbyterians, or Episcopalians.[38]

[35] New York (1209), Washington, D.C. (1116), Chicago (1107), Mobile-Birmingham (1104), Philadelphia (1032), Detroit (1012), St. Louis (662), Los Angeles (618), New Orleans (537), Brooklyn (500).

[36] Joseph R. Washington, Jr. *Black Religion: The Negro and Christianity in the United States* (Boston, 1964), p. 243.

[37] E. Franklin Frazier, *The Negro in the United States* (rev. ed., New York, 1957), p. 363. Gunnar Myrdal, *An American Dilemma* (New York, 1944), pp. 870, 1411, also makes this point.

[38] Washington, p. 246.

TABLE I

SELECTED CHARACTERISTICS OF DIOCESES REPORTING NEGRO MEMBERS BY REGION, 1967*

Characteristic	Totals	Northeast	Midwest	West	South	Southwest
Total population	144,858,728	27,713,760	33,820,933	24,018,292	46,439,563	12,866,180
Per cent Catholic	21.2	40.8	26.4	18.7	8.8	15.0
Per cent of Catholic population that is Negro	2.5	1.4	1.6	1.7	8.1	3.8
Distribution of Negro Catholic population	783,720	156,046	145,543	77,810	331,123	73,198
Per cent	100.0	19.9	18.6	9.9	42.3	9.3
Per cent distribution of priests assigned to Negro apostolate	100.0 (812)	10.7	30.3	4.1	48.8	6.1
Per cent distribution of Negro priests in the U.S.**	100.0 (146)	20.6	27.4	8.9	39.0	4.1
Per cent distribution of adult Negro baptisms	100.0 (13,614)	23.4	27.9	6.0	38.9	3.8

* Dioceses Reporting: Northeast: Buffalo, New York, Brooklyn, Pittsburgh, Philadelphia, Erie, Newark, Camden, Trenton, Boston; Midwest: Belleville, Chicago, Indianapolis, Evansville, Gary, Kansas City, Wichita, Detroit, Lansing, St. Paul-Minneapolis, St. Louis, Kansas City-St. Joseph, Omaha, Cincinnati, Columbus, Toledo, Cleveland, Milwaukee; West: Los Angeles, Monterey-Fresno, Oakland, Sacramento, San Diego, San Francisco, Reno, Portland, Seattle; South: Little Rock, Washington, D.C.,

Wilmington, Mobile-Birmingham, Miami, St. Augustine, Atlanta, Savannah, Louisville, Covington, Owensboro, New Orleans, Alexandria, Baton Rouge, Lafayette, Baltimore, Natchez-Jackson, Charleston, Raleigh, Nashville, Richmond; Southwest: Tucson, San Antonio, Amarillo, Austin, Corpus Christi, Dallas-Ft. Worth, Galveston-Houston, Oklahoma City-Tulsa.

** Compiled from a mailing list provided by NCCIJ. This total does not include three Negro priests who are chaplains in the Armed Forces and twenty-two who are missionaries abroad. It does, however, include fifteen priests who belong to dioceses not listed above, that is, from which other data was not obtained.

Source: *Official Catholic Directory*, 1968; 1968 *National Catholic Almanac*, pp. 557–58.

TABLE II

WHITE CATHOLIC, PROTESTANT, AND JEWISH RESPONSES TO TWO QUESTIONS CONCERNING ATTITUDES TOWARD NEGROES (GALLUP, 1961)

Question	All Regions			Non-Southern Regions		Non-Southern Metropolitan Areas*	
	Prot.	Cath.	Jew	Prot.	Cath.	Prot.	Cath.
Think Negroes in the U.S. have more power than they should have	24.4	23.2	7.4**	19.2	21.3	22.8	23.8
Would vote for a generally well qualified Negro candidate for President	39.1*	60.0	85.0**	48.7*	59.8	47.7	56.4

* Protestant-Catholic difference significant at the .05 level or beyond.

** Both Protestant-Jewish and Catholic-Jewish differences significant at the .05 level or beyond.

Source: Leonard Broom and Norval D. Glenn, "Religious Differences in Reported Attitudes and Behavior," *Sociological Analysis*, XXVII (1966), 187–209.

Although one cannot say with any great confidence what impression Catholicism has made on the Negro community as a whole, it seems clear that the impact of the Church and its institutions in some cases extends far beyond actual communicants. For example, the impact of Xavier University in New Orleans on the larger community is considerable. One-third of its 1,400 students (10 per cent Caucasian) are non-Catholics; a 1965 survey showed that Xavier graduates accounted for 40 per cent of the teachers, 75 per cent of the principals and almost all of the guidance counselors in previously all-Negro schools of New Orleans. Xavier also produced the first Negro teachers on all-white faculties and the first white teachers on all-Negro faculties in the local schools.[39]

Many Negro Americans, on the other hand, have not had sufficient contact with the Catholic Church to formulate any clearcut attitudes. In the absence of detailed data it is difficult to determine the extent to which any such attitudes have developed, or whether the attitudes that do exist tend to be favorable or unfavorable. Some information was gathered in a poll taken by *Newsweek* magazine and published under the title, *The Negro Revolution in America.* This book shows that 58 per cent of the "rank and file" Negro population feel that Catholic priests have been "helpful" in the struggle for civil rights.[40] Only "Kennedy Administration" and "U.S. Supreme Court" ranked higher than priests; and priests ranked above both Jews (considered "helpful" by 44 per cent of the Negroes) or white churches in general (by 24 per cent). When a sample of Negro leaders was asked to assess the contributions of priests, the general response pattern persisted. Seventy-four per cent felt that priests had been helpful, Jews were named by 73 per cent, and white churches by 36 per cent. These data suggest that priests, a highly visible segment of the Catholic Church, have generally made a favorable impression on the Negro community.

It is ironic that at this time of greatest involvement and popularity among Negroes, as reflected in conversions and general attitudes, the Church is subjected to sharp criticism from within its ranks. Although one student of the subject noted that the tide toward an inclusive

[39] John Egerton, "Two Way Bridge to Girt Town," *Southern Education Report,* III (June, 1968), 27.

[40] William Brink and Louis Harris, *The Negro Revolution in America* (New York, 1964), p. 232.

communion is an unmistakable trend of the Church, ". . . a trend which is impressive beyond the fact that its organizational structure [hierarchical authority] provides for this action,"[41] the recently held Black Catholic Clergy Caucus called for "an immediate, effective and total reversing of its present practices. . . ."

Washington had observed four years previously:

> Catholics have not taken seriously the full inclusion of Negroes on every level, and have tended to be concerned about social problems which have captured the imagination of the Negro. In the long run, Negroes will not be satisfied with an approach which tends to do things for instead of with them. A deliberate and sustained effort to accept Negroes in strategic places will be necessary if they are to be recruited for the mission of the church.[42]

The Caucus demanded "that there be Black priests in decision-making positions on the diocesan level and above all in the Black community," and "that within the framework of the United States Catholic Conference, a Black-directed department be set up to deal with the Church's role in the struggle of black people for freedom." The demands seemed, at least in part, to grow out of the well-publicized activities of Negro participants in other religious and secular conferences and conventions, as well as the changed mood of the Negro community.[43] Statements that have emanated from these meetings have often been characterized by a strident language and a belligerent tone that seems oddly out of character for religiously committed persons.

In the case of the Catholic clergy, there is little question that the prejudice and paternalism of the past have created some serious prob-

[41] Washington, p. 244.

[42] Washington, p. 247.

[43] Gary Marx, in a national study of Negro attitudes, discovered that those individuals in largely white denominations (Episcopalian, Presbyterian, and Catholic) appear somewhat higher in militancy than those in Negro denominations, in spite of the greater civil-rights activism of the latter. Moreover, this was true even when social class was held constant. The proportion militant varied from 15 per cent among members of sects and cults to 43 per cent among Episcopalians. Thirty-six per cent of the Negro Catholics were militant. These findings raise some interesting questions regarding the long run effects of black control and autonomy. Gary T. Marx, *Protest and Prejudice: A Study of Belief in the Black Community* (New York, 1967), pp. 98-99.

lems.[44] But given the shortage of qualified black personnel after a century of neglect and discrimination, it is unlikely that these problems can be corrected by *fiat* or overnight. After all, when only 171 of the nation's 59,000 priests are Negroes, obviously it will be a long time before the work of the Negro apostolate can be taken over by black priests, or before black priests can be expected to play a more decisive role in the life of the Church. This is not to deny that changes are in order—but given the limited resources, the immediate changes can have only limited impact. For example, not long after the black priests' call for a larger role, a national meeting was held in St. Louis by Catholic clergymen and laymen concerned with the updating of the Church.[45] Only one Negro was in attendance, although efforts had been made to involve more. This sort of thing does not result from exclusion or lack of black interest, but from the fact that there is such a limited pool of people from which to draw.

THE ATTITUDES OF WHITE CATHOLICS TOWARD NEGROES

One of the major factors shaping the relationship between the Church and the Negro today is the attitude of white Catholics. While the teachings of the Church provide no theological basis for negative racial attitudes, experience and recent research clearly indicate that white Catholics are not immune from harboring such attitudes.[46] By itself, this fact is significant because it demonstrates that a considerable number of American Catholics have either failed to internalize some of the

[44] This phenomenon is by no means limited to the experience of the Negro. Other groups, Italians, Poles, Spanish-speaking, have had trouble developing their own clergy and getting what they consider to be a fair share of the important posts in the Church.

[45] The group assembled Apr. 25-27 under the title of the National Committee of Catholic Concerns.

[46] For discussion of Catholic racial attitudes see: Gerhard Lenski, *The Religious Factor* (New York, 1963), 164; Andrew M. Greeley and Peter H. Rossi, *The Education of Catholic Americans* (Chicago, 1966); Paul B. Sheatsley, "White Attitudes Toward the Negro" in *The Negro American*, eds. T. Parsons and K. Clark (Boston, 1966), pp. 303-24; and Leonard Broom and Norval D. Glenn, "Religious Differences in Reported Attitudes and Behavior," *Sociological Analysis*, XXVII (1966), 187-209.

social teachings of their faith or have compartmentalized them in such a way that they do not extend across racial lines. The extent to which white Catholics hold negative attitudes toward Negroes and the reasons for these attitudes are, of course, difficult to determine. It is possible, however, to compare the attitudes of Catholics to those of Protestants and Jews on a number of questions relevant to determining whether Catholics are more or less hostile than other Americans toward the Negro.

Until the early 1960's, data on the attitudes of Catholics and comparative data on other religious groups were generally lacking. The few studies of Catholics that had been done were usually inconclusive and, because of sampling inadequacies, did not permit any generalizations to be made. The methodological problems resulting from the use of biased samples have plagued not only studies of Catholics, but most studies of other religious groups. The first nationwide data providing a relatively sound basis for a comparison of the racial attitudes of Protestants, Catholics, and Jews are reported in a 1961 Gallup Poll.[47] The results (Table II) showed that Jewish respondents manifested a significantly higher degree of racial tolerance than either Protestants or Catholics; this difference persists even when compared to Christians living outside the South.[48] The responses to the first question indicate that the differences between Catholic and Protestant attitudes toward the Negroes, both nationwide and among nonsouthern respondents, are negligible. One out of four Christians (one out of five outside the South) felt that Negroes had more power than they should have.

The responses to the second question, however, indicate that Protestants are significantly less likely to "vote for a generally well qualified Negro candidate for President" than are Catholics. This difference should be viewed in light of the fact that in the year immediately preceding the poll Catholics had witnessed the election of John F. Kennedy and were highly sensitive to the candidacy of minority-group members. Nevertheless, two out of five white Catholics, regardless of region, indicated they would not vote for a generally well-qualified Negro candidate for President.

The data from a 1963 National Opinion Research Center survey of a national sample of white Americans also permits a comparison of

47 Broom and Glenn.

48 Part of this difference may be attributed to differences in social class and level of education which were not controlled.

Catholic, Protestant, and Jewish attitudes.[49] The mean scores on a Guttman Scale of Pro-Integration attitudes showed that among northern whites, Jewish respondents were more favorably inclined toward racial integration (scale score: 6.44 out of a possible 8.00) than either Catholics or Protestants; Catholics were somewhat more integrationist than Protestants (scale scores: 5.18 and 4.75 respectively). In the South, the Catholic-Protestant difference was even greater (3.41 and 2.38 respectively) than in the North.

The data from the 1963-64 NORC study directed by Greeley and Rossi also indicates there is relatively little difference between non-southern Protestants and Catholics in their attitudes toward Negroes.[50] A comparison of scores received on a five-item "racism index" shows that 27 per cent of the respondents in a representative sample of American Catholics scored high on the index (i.e., four or five responses indicative of negative attitudes toward Negroes), while 29 per cent of a Protestant sample, comparable to the Catholics in both age and regional distribution, were reported to have high scores.

While four out of five of all Catholics, regardless of where they received their education, and the same ratio of Protestants agreed "there is an obligation to work toward the end of racial segregation," roughly two out of five persons in these same categories indicated they would strongly disapprove if a Negro family moved next door to them. There seems to be, then, general acceptance of the principles involved, coupled with strong objections from a sizable minority to application on the personal level.

The data from these national surveys indicates that while negative racial attitudes exist in each of the three major religious groups, Catholic attitudes are more frequently negative than those of Jews, but tend to be less negative than those of Protestants in the South; in areas where most Catholics reside, however, their attitudes are neither better nor worse than those of Protestants. Significant segments of the white Catholic population harbor attitudes toward the Negro that are in sharp conflict with the teachings of their Church.

Some people have actually suggested that religion is itself a factor in the development of these prejudicial attitudes. Or, the argument runs, if prejudice does not spring from religion itself, persons prone to

49 Sheatsley, pp. 310-12.

50 Greeley and Rossi, p. 252 (Table A-2.18).

prejudice are the sort most likely to be attracted to conventional religion. Unfortunately, the precise relationship between racial intolerance and religiosity has eluded clear definition. One difficulty lies in isolating the effects of religiosity from the effects of other variables presumed to be related to racial attitudes. Another problem is operationalizing the concept so that it validly measures true personal commitment to religious ideals and values. The fact that religiosity is understood and measured differently by different denominations is an added difficulty—one that makes it almost impossible to compare two different groups in terms of the relationship of religiosity to the attitudes of individuals.

The most notable efforts to understand the seemingly contradictory coexistence of church membership, religious beliefs, and racial intolerance have been made by Gordon Allport and Robin M. Williams, Jr.[51] Allport suggested that there are two major types of religious beliefs: extrinsic and intrinsic. An individual holding extrinsic religious beliefs maintains church membership for conventional reasons and sees his attachment to a religious group as necessary for social acceptance within the community. An individual with intrinsic beliefs, on the other hand, maintains membership and participates within his church for internal and personal reasons involving a belief in and a full commitment to the ideals held up by the church itself. Allport hypothesized that the former was positively associated and the latter negatively associated with racial intolerance. Williams qualified and extended Allport's hypothesis by suggesting that the relationship between religious participation and racial intolerance is curvilinear; that is, both highly active, regular churchgoers and the entirely inactive nonchurchgoers exhibit a higher degree of tolerance than the infrequent churchgoers, whose religious behavior suggests "conventional religiosity." It is the "respectable conformity" of the infrequent churchgoer that accompanies the acceptance of conventionalized patterns of prejudice and discrimination within American communities. On the other hand, those who reject the conventional community patterns—either by displaying a firm commitment to a set of religious principles or by not attending church at all—are less likely to be intolerant.

While the applicability of the curvilinear hypothesis to American

[51] Gordon W. Allport, *The Nature of Prejudice* (Reading, Mass., 1954), 444-57, and Robin M. Williams, Jr., *Strangers Next Door: Ethnic Relations In American Communities* (Englewood Cliffs, N.J., 1964), pp. 57-65.

Catholics is not yet known, Allport's hypothesized relationship between religious beliefs and negative racial attitudes has been partially tested.[52] Using data collected by the Greeley and Rossi study, James Vanecko has constructed an informative table (Table III) illustrating the association between twelve dimensions of religious behavior and negative attitudes toward Negroes. Three of the dimensions have a strong *negative* association with intolerance:[53] 1) adherence to ethical norms (indicated by a high agreement with eleven statements of the ethical position of the Church); 2) acceptance of doctrinal orthodoxy (indicated by a high agreement with five statements regarding official Church doctrine); 3) religious knowledge (indicated by the number of correct answers to six questions on Catholic doctrine). Vanecko points out that all three of these dimensions of religious behavior go beyond mere conventional participation in the Church and closely resemble Allport's concept of intrinsic religious beliefs; they are "ideally conformist and modally deviant." These findings suggest that the Catholics least likely to be intolerant are those who know what the Church teaches, accept these teachings, and apply them to situations demanding ethical decisions. If these three indexes can be taken as a measure of personal religiosity, the data tends to support the contention that a commitment to Catholicism is negatively associated with racial intolerance.

The data does not permit a direct operationalization of Allport's concept of extrinsic religious beliefs, but it highlights the dimensions of American Catholic religious behavior most likely to be associated with racial intolerance. The strongest *positive* associations with intolerance are found with three dimensions in particular: 1) instrumentalism (i.e., religion is viewed primarily as serving personal interests); 2) religious extremism (indicated by high agreement with extreme and erroneous statements regarding Church doctrine); 3) Manicheism (indicated by agreement with statements portraying the world as basically evil). As Vanecko points out, these are all deviant forms of religious behavior that are neither ideal nor modal. This suggests that the hypothesized positive association between intolerance and con-

[52] See James J. Vanecko, "Religious Behavior and Prejudice: Some Dimensions and Specifications of the Relationship," *Review of Religious Research*, VIII (1966), 27-37.

[53] The items for each of these three dimensions of religious behavior are listed in Greeley and Rossi, Appendix #2, 237-60.

TABLE III

THE RELIGIOUS BEHAVIOR OF CATHOLICS AND NEGATIVE RACIAL ATTITUDES

Those Scoring High on the Index of:*	Per cent High on Negative Racial Attitudes %	N
Church as teacher	21	(75)
Devotional practices	32	(283)
Instrumentalism	37	(252)
Adherence to ethical norms	16	(822)
Acceptance of doctrinal orthodoxy	15	(435)
Religious knowledge	14	(190)
Religiosity of parents	31	(267)
Acceptance of social teachings	31	(338)
Catholic education	29	(320)
Religious extremism	39	(425)
Jansenism	25	(114)
Manicheism	41	(306)
Total Sample	27	(1,878)

* Indexes of religious behavior were divided in such a way that those scoring high would be in a minority of the sample. In some cases this produced a quite small group due to the skewed distribution of the index.

Source: James J. Vanecko, "Religious Behavior and Prejudice: Some Dimensions and Specifications of the Relationship," *Review of Religious Research,* VIII (1966), 27–37.

TABLE IV

ATTITUDES OF CATHOLIC ELEMENTARY AND SECONDARY SCHOOL STUDENTS IN ONE SOUTHERN AND TWELVE NON-SOUTHERN DIOCESES, 1966*

Question	Response	Deep South diocese %	Twelve Non-Southern dioceses %
It makes no difference to me whether I receive Holy Communion from a white or colored priest.	Disagree	13.0	4.2
	Agree	77.4	91.2
	Uncertain	9.6	4.6
Totals		100.0(N=1320)	100.0(N=13,060)
Manual labor and unskilled jobs seem to fit the Negro mental and physical ability better than more skilled or responsible work.	Agree	36.7	20.5
	Disagree	51.5	68.5
	Uncertain	11.8	11.0
Totals		100.0(N=1315)	100.0(N=13,087)
It would bother me to sit next to or near a person of another race (e.g.: a Negro, a white person) in school.	Agree	30.7	14.5
	Disagree	58.2	77.8
	Uncertain	11.1	7.7
Totals		100.0(N=1313)	100.0(N=13,027)

* Source: *Catholic Schools in Action:* The Notre Dame Study of Catholic Elementary and Secondary Schools in the United States, ed. Reginald A. Neuwien (Notre Dame, Ind., 1966).

ventional religious practices may need to be qualified to include unconventional components of religious beliefs which, similar to negative racial attitudes, are inconsistent with Church teachings.

More comprehensive studies are needed to discover just which Catholics are most likely to be intolerant. The findings of Neuwien and others, in a study of Catholic elementary and secondary schools, indicate that there was little variation in attitudes concerning the mentality of Negroes and interracial contacts among Catholic students in dioceses outside the Deep South[54] (Table IV). It is interesting to note that tolerance is greatest for a Negro in a sacramental role sanctioned by the Church (distribution of the Host). Nine out of ten students outside the South and over three out of four in the South indicate the race of the priest would make no difference to them. Resistance increases when equal status contacts are involved (school integration), although substantial majorities in both the South and other regions do not object. The traditional stereotype of the mentally inferior Negro seems to persist to a remarkable degree. Almost 37 per cent of the southern students and 21 per cent of the nonsouthern indicated agreement with this view. Students in the "Deep South diocese" are roughly twice as likely to have unfavorable attitudes toward Negroes as the students from the twelve nonsouthern dioceses. This is further evidence that Catholics tend to reflect the attitudes of those around them, interpreting racial situations in terms of the normative standards of the community rather than solely in terms of the teachings of the Church.

Two other factors that might conceivably be related to the racial attitudes of Catholics are parental religiosity and the amount of Catholic education received. Surprisingly, the available data seems to indicate that neither of these factors is of major importance. A cluster analysis testing the interdependence of the twelve dimensions of religious behavior listed in Table III showed only moderate relationships between the religiosity of parents and Catholic education with the three dimensions indicative of personal religiosity. This led Vanecko to suggest that "religious commitment is not merely a function of adult-child socialization."[55] Similarly, the role played by parental and family religiosity and Catholic education in promoting racial intoler-

[54] See Reginald A. Neuwien, ed., *Catholic Schools in Action* (Notre Dame, Ind., 1966), p. 201.

[55] Vanecko, "Types of Religious Behavior and Levels of Prejudice," *Sociological Analysis,* XXVIII (Fall, 1967), 117.

ance does not seem to be significant. Neuwien notes that children from highly religious families are slightly more apt to reject racially biased statements than children from families of medium or low religiosity, but the differences are small and somewhat inconclusive.[56]

A discussion by Greeley and Rossi of the effects of Catholic education on racial attitudes points to the fact that Catholic-school Catholics are neither more nor less tolerant than those not attending Catholic schools. It is the total amount of education, rather than how much of it is Catholic, which appears to be most important as far as racial attitudes are concerned. While denying that a Catholic education fosters racial intolerance, Greeley and Rossi suggest that the reason why Catholic schools have not been successful in cultivating more Christian racial attitudes is not "that education for racial justice was tried and found wanting, but that it was found hard and not tried."[57] There is reason to believe that this situation may be changing. When controls were introduced for both the respondents' age and the amount of Catholic education, it was discovered that fewer Catholics in their twenties scored high on the "racism index" than those in older-age categories; likewise, the effects of an "all-Catholic" education were more pronounced in this age category than in any of the others. This is the generation reared in the post-World War II years; their differential attitudes perhaps reflect the changing stance of the institutional Church, as well as the secular trend toward greater tolerance among all Americans.

The lessening of intolerance among younger Catholics must also be considered in light of the socioeconomic and ethnic status of the Catholic population. The Catholic Church unlike most Protestant denominations maintains a heterogeneous membership which spans the range of class positions and ethnic composition.[58] While in the past the Catholic population has experienced relatively slow rates of upward social mobility, improvement has been rapid in recent years and Catholics are now distributed throughout the class structure proportionally. Accompanying socioeconomic improvement has been an

[56] Neuwien, p. 197.

[57] Greeley and Rossi, p. 114 (also 121-25).

[58] For a discussion of class and ethnic heterogeneity among Catholics see Harold J. Abramson and C. Edward Noll, "Religion, Ethnicity, and Social Change," *Review of Religious Research*, VIII (1966), 11-26.

TABLE V

PER CENT FAVORABLE ATTITUDES TOWARD NEGROES BY ETHNIC HOMOGENEITY AND SOCIAL CLASS OF RESPONDENT, 1963–64

Social Class	Ethnic Homogeneity*		
	Homogeneous (1 group)	Mixed (2 groups)	Diverse (3 or 4 groups)
Lower	43 (203)	50 (139)	46 (54)
Middle	42 (155)	54 (130)	57 (51)
Upper	48 (88)	52 (99)	67 (64)

* The terminology used here differs from that used in the original. The three groups here are based on the *number* of different nationality groups represented by the fathers and mothers of the respondents and their spouses. The *Homogeneous* are those whose four parents all belong to the same nationality group; *Mixed,* those whose fathers and mothers are reported as representing two different ethnic origins; and *Diverse* are those whose four parents are identified as belonging to three or four different ethnic groups.

Source: Adapted from Harold J. Abramson and C. Edward Noll, "Religion, Ethnicity, and Social Change," *Review of Religious Research,* VIII (1966), 11–26.

increase of interethnic marriages, resulting in a decrease of ethnic cohesiveness among Catholics.

The effects of these two trends on racial attitudes have been investigated by Abramson and Noll in an analysis of the NORC data.[59] A segment of their data, contained in Table V, suggests that an interesting phenomenon is likely to occur among Catholics as class position is improved and ethnic cohesiveness declines. The data indicates that when social class is held constant, the respondents of homogeneous

[59] Abramson and Noll, pp. 22-23.

ethnic background are consistently the least favorable in their attitude toward Negroes. On the other hand, when ethnic homogeneity is held constant, lower-class respondents tend to be the least favorable. While each of these variables makes an independent contribution to the explanation of attitudes toward the Negro, the effect of each is to an important extent conditioned by the other. In other words, ethnic diversity results in greater tolerance if one also happens to have achieved higher social status, and higher social status has its greatest effect on increasing tolerance among those respondents with the most diverse ethnic backgrounds. When the two variables act in concert the effect is quite significant. Only 43 per cent of lower-class, ethnically homogeneous respondents had favorable attitudes toward Negroes, whereas 67 per cent of the upper-class respondents with diverse ethnic backgrounds did—an increase in the proportion favorable of over 50 per cent.

There are promising implications in these results and others which suggest that recency of immigration (Irish and Germans more favorable to Negroes than Italians or Poles) is an important factor explaining differential attitudes among Catholics. As the newer immigrants become more assimilated and Catholics continue to marry outside of their nationality backgrounds and continue to experience economic gains leading to upward social mobility, racial attitudes may be expected to become more tolerant and more consistent with Church teachings. The unanswered question is whether these changes will occur or be recognized quickly enough to satisfy the growing impatience of the black community.

THE FUTURE

Historically, the Church's response to the race problem involved attempts at the resolution of at least three sometimes conflicting forces. First, the moral imperative to acknowledge and respect the essential dignity of all men was an ever present factor. Whether by reason of the general ethical thrust of the Judeo-Christian tradition, the prophetic activities of individual members of the Church, or the prodding of Rome, Catholics were never allowed to forget the incongruities of the racial situation in America. On the other hand, their weak status as a minority group dictated a policy of accommodating to the status quo and seeking to win acceptance from dominant elements of the population. Finally, in the process of becoming American the Church and its members assumed both the vices and the virtues of the American way of life. No human institution can completely detach itself from the cultural milieu in which it must operate, and the Church proved itself all too human in this respect.

Nevertheless, religion can under some circumstances assume a more active role in promoting change and resisting the encroachments of other parts of the social system. Our review has shown that in recent years the Church has aligned itself with the larger society's more progressive elements seeking change in race relations and has begun to purge itself of practices and attitudes inconsistent with its basic beliefs. Some segments of the Church have moved faster than others—some have hardly moved at all. The response from the laity has been especially mixed. Having gained acceptance in the larger society, a degree of affluence, and most importantly self-confidence, the Church is now in a position to exercise more leadership and act more boldly in putting into practice what it has been preaching for so long. In spite of recent advances, the potential for constructive action has nowhere been realized, and it must be admitted that the continuing lack of unanimity within the Church remains a serious restraint.

In the years to come, the Church will be challenged on at least two levels: 1) its impact on the general welfare of Negroes through its contribution to major social problems confronting our cities and their residents; 2) its ability to attract and retain Negro members and to totally integrate them into its life. The Church's success in responding to these challenges will depend on a number of factors of which three seem especially worthy of note.

The most fundamental problem is: What is the role of the Church in the inner city and what should be its relationship to the large numbers of non-Catholics residing there? Much will depend upon the answers given to these questions. Present practice seems to vary from the extreme of the traditional aggressive proselyters with their emphasis on personal salvation and spiritual needs to the exclusion of all else, to the more *avant-garde* social actionists who preoccupy themselves organizing and leading what are essentially secular activities (e.g., protest marches, credit unions, welfare unions, recreational programs, etc.) and resent any suggestion that they may harbor an ulterior motive like the attraction of Negro converts. In the first case, conversion becomes the all important goal—often to such an extent that baptism is frequently made the price of admission to the parochial school. While this approach was fairly successful in the past, it now seems seriously out of tune with the post-Vatican II Church. At the other extreme, the commitment to ecumenism and service to the most needy is so strong that the social activists sometimes even resent the Church's continuing to serve nonghetto people and maintaining the "Catholic" character of inner-city churches and schools. What these priests sometimes forget is that the clerical role is primarily an expressive role related to human emotional needs, and not an adaptive role related to adjustment to or manipulation of the environment.[60] It is significant that the fastest growing religious groups in the inner city are the otherworldly Pentecostals. Needless to say, most persons working in the Negro apostolate fall somewhere in between these two extremes. However, it is apparent to many observers that the Church cannot move with any degree of effectiveness until these fundamental questions are resolved.

The second major determinant of success is the ability to assemble qualified personnel and carry out the planning necessary to develop sound programs. Past efforts have been plagued by the widespread assumption that commitment and social concern are adequate substitutes for professional competence. The lack of a corps of trained experts and the absence of a tradition of employing professional advice make it doubtful whether anything useful would result from "crash" programs conceived and launched by the people who now have decision-making power. Moreover, the urgency of the situation has created increasing pressure for action and an impatience with research and the study of fundamental problems.[61]

Finally, much will depend on the ability to mobilize the white community to make the sacrifices necessary to cope with this problem. There are signs of an awakening and a growing sensitivity. There are also signs that some recent efforts are backfiring. At a time when the clergy is becoming increasingly involved in social issues, a growing proportion (57 per cent in 1968, up from 35 per cent in 1957) of lay Catholics think the Churches should keep out of political and social

[60] For an insightful discussion of this point see, Sigmund Dragastin, O.F.M., "What's Happened to the Priest's Prestige?" *America*, CXVIII (Feb. 24, 1968), 254-57.

[61] Note the discussion related to this question in Luzbetak, pp. 20-21.

matters.[62] Unfortunately, too many young priests assume that being Christian means strongly condemning "white racism" and making guilt-provoking accusations. This latter-day version of the hell-and-damnation sermon seems likely to be as counter-productive as its predecessor in generating truly Christian attitudes and behavior. Regrettably, an effective means of communicating the Christian message on race to people ill-disposed to hear it remains unknown. Those who try to outshout the black militants are likely to find that they alienate far more people than they attract. Few clergymen have built up the "capital" of respect and esteem that would enable them to effectively influence their flock on unpopular questions. It may be that the ability to influence on the question of race depends more on how other aspects of the priestly role are played than on what one explicitly says and does about race as such. A program to overcome racial antipathies and create a real sense of Christian community must really be part of a total institutional renewal including a rethinking of the role of the priest and the function of religion in urban industrial society.

62 "53% in Gallup Poll Want Churches to Keep Silent on Social Issues," *New York Times*, Apr. 12, 1968.

Part III:

The American Church

8: SPIRITUALITY IN THE AMERICAN CHURCH: AN EVALUATIVE ESSAY

Aidan Kavanagh, O.S.B.

The phenomenon known as spirituality is a complex one constantly shifting, however slightly, from one generation to another. It is thus notoriously difficult to define clearly, much less to treat adequately within the scope of a short essay. Yet at least a brief and pragmatic description of it will be necessary before one can proceed historically to examine its presence in the Roman Catholic community in this country.

By spirituality I mean primarily that awareness any religious society has of itself—that is, of its own living relationship with the continuum of faith-objects in which it believes.[1] This awareness is so subjective that it can be ascertained only discretely as it is polarized into the various patterns by which the religious society responds to stimuli, either internal or external. The scholar will describe a given religious society's spirituality by induction from analysis of the ways it reacts to stresses endemic to its own peculiar faith- and time- and space-conditioned existence. Any other method of procedure will result in an ideological projection of what the religious society's spirituality *should* be. Such a method would restrict itself *a priori* to the continuum of faith-objects the society ought to believe in: the society itself would be dealt with only ideally, and in the subjunctive mood. This does not mean that such a method is without value. When employed competently it results in the finest forms of catechesis—the purpose of

[1] For more extensive discussions of a definition of spirituality see for example L. Bouyer, *The Spirituality of the New Testament and the Fathers*, trans. Mary P. Ryan (London, 1963) pp. vii-xi; H. Urs von Balthasar, "The Gospel as Norm and Test of All Spirituality in the Church," *Spirituality in Church and World*, ed. C. Duquoc, Concilium Series, vol. 9 (New York, 1965) pp. 7-23; M. de Certeau, "Culture and Spiritual Experience," *Spirituality in the Secular City*, ed. C. Duquoc, Concilium Series, vol. 19 (New York, 1966) pp. 3-31.

which is to lead the religious society to an ever more adequate spirituality. This is not the method to be employed here, however. My purpose is to describe what in fact the spirituality of the Roman Catholic religious community in the United States has been, is, and gives evidence of becoming in the future. One must first inquire what patterns of response to the stress stimuli peculiar to the American Catholic community can be isolated for purposes of analysis. Several such patterns might be named, but for the purposes of this essay primacy will be given to that of formal religious practice itself: worship.

THE FUNCTION OF WORSHIP

I focus on this aspect first of all because of the function worship has in religious societies generally. In such societies the phenomenon of worship simultaneously articulates and resumes the society's whole awareness of itself *vis-à-vis* the epoch in which it lives. Indeed, the ritual patterns in which worship is actualized perform the same function in any human society, religious or not. Thus, when cult is said to be the basis of culture, the statement is not necessarily theological: rather, it is a psycho-anthropological affirmation of the human propensity for transforming the raw stuff of experience and behavior into formal patterns of action and reaction known as rituals.[2] Human societies do this connaturally in order to "objectify" themselves in a manner that can be experienced and participated in by each member of the society. The result is that the society itself is reinforced through the individual members' simultaneously expanded senses of social reciprocity, historical perspective, and cosmic cohesion. Seen in this perspective, ritual patterns polarize much more than just religious sentiment or piety.[3] And since this is true, a critical examination of ritual patterns in a given religious society such as the American Cath-

[2] See the remarks on this phenomenon made in an architectural context by Frank E. Brown, *Roman Architecture* (New York, 1965) p. 9.

[3] Not only ritual patterns but also those correlative ones of myth accomplish the same object on the secular as well as the religious levels. See M. McLuhan and Q. Fiore, *The Medium is the Massage* (New York, 1967) pp. 113-14, especially; also, this matter is treated at length in the works of Mircea Eliade and in the series of papers entitled "Ritual Behaviour of Animals and Men," *The Philosophical Transactions of the Royal Society of London*, Series B, no. 772, vol. 251 (1966), 249-526.

olic Church should bring into motion that whole complex of attitudes constituting the religious society's "spirituality."

There is a second, more specific reason why patterns of formal religious worship are primary to this essay. It is that the post-medieval Catholicism in which the American Church was born and has grown up exhibits an absorption with cult that is uniquely Western. It may be described as a syndrome that has tended to make the religious experience center in a sacral, numinous divine presence realized almost exclusively within the perimeters of formal cultic activity. To this activity, carried on by a validly ordained clerical priesthood,[4] the rest of the community was seen to be subordinated as passive recipients of the cult act's results. The syndrome has affected not only the spirit and forms of worship in the Western Church:[5] it has penetrated every aspect of the Catholic community's life and structure.

Yet one should emphasize that it is not so much the presence of the syndrome as the degree of its intensity and its peculiar results that make it unique in the post-medieval Western Church. All societies, no matter how secularized they may seem, articulate their individual awareness of themselves in culto-symbolic forms (not necessarily "sacral" in a religious sense) that may range all the way from sacrificial banquets, as in Christianity, down to almost incoherent systems of incantational sloganeering, as in Nazi Germany or Red China. There can be little doubt that a cohesive society vigorously responsive to threat, whether real or imagined, results when a high degree of experiential effectiveness is packed into the culto-symbolic forms by which that society articulates its own self-awareness. Here one may begin to detect something of the ambivalent potential for good or evil such

[4] The growth of a theology of validity in priestly ordination, together with an almost total restriction to the ministry of a numinous cultic agency in the Church, is a matter whose history needs yet to be written. The *reductio ad absurdum* of this tendency may be seen in the bizarre underground traffic in "valid" ordinations recounted by H. R. T. Brandreth in *Episcopi Vagantes and the Anglican Church*, 2nd ed. (London, 1961), and more recently by Peter Anson in *Bishops At Large* (London, 1964).

[5] For example, what might be called a spirituality of valid eucharistic consecration that came to form a central part in various schools of clerical formation in the Western Church. Such an attitude assumed the priest's private low Mass as the norm and reinforced it in turn. The active agency of the community of believing but unordained laity in such an act was occluded in the process, as indeed was the structure of the act itself apart from the very words of consecration.

forms possess. Value judgments on them cannot be made simply on the basis of their being experientially effective. Such judgments must take into consideration how far their effectiveness does or does not inhibit examination of their content and purpose as well. This examination is both critical and reflective—which is to say *humane* in the fullest sense. Lack of it does not inhibit the power of the form to produce a society vigorously responsive to threat: On the contrary, the sheer power of the form, especially when it exists in a threatened society, tends to suppress critical examination of its content and purpose. The more traumatic the threat, the more total will be the suppression of the humane factor; the more totally the humane factor recedes, the more wholly mechanical and totalitarian become both the culto-symbolic forms and the society they articulate. Critique of the forms thus amounts to an attack on the society they are helping to affirm and produce. The more under stress the society feels itself to be, the more rigid its culto-symbolic forms become.[6] The process through which this happens is multiform and usually of such long-term duration that its presence is imperceptible except to the prophet, the outsider and the historian. Due precisely to the tacit acceptance of the process by most of those within a given society, they slip into a sort of aphasia in its regard, unable either to name it or bring it under critical scrutiny.

WORSHIP AND "SCHOOLS OF SPIRITUALITY"

In broad-stroke outline this appears to be something of the matrix of reciprocities within which a society evolves an awareness of itself, whether for better or for worse. I have suggested that such an awareness in specifically religious societies is what is meant by the term spirituality. Spirituality is a more or less conscious articulation—through many media, but especially in that of formal worship—of the society's living relationship with the continuum of faith-objects in which it believes.

Two observations seem consequent upon this. The first is that the

[6] Thus, the groups in a society that work closest to the point at which such culto-symbolic forms are generated—groups such as the political, military, and religious establishments—tend to be most resistive to change in the forms themselves. This rather implicit factor may account for the conservative and even reactionary character of such interests in the social status quo.

articulation of such awareness through the symbolic forms of ritual worship is more *experiential* than rationally discursive. Even so, while such symbolic forms may possess a definite priority in both effecting and reflecting the spirituality of a given religious society, their data must be rendered less ambiguous by subsequent reference to the society's more discursive statements found in its creeds of belief and codes of behavior.[7] This means that adequate exegesis of the forms of ritual worship cannot restrict itself merely to the forms themselves apart from their social context in the largest sense. The second observation is that spirituality runs far deeper than what is meant by modern authors when they speak of "schools of spirituality," such as the monastic, Ignatian, Franciscan, Spanish, etc. These appear to constitute no more than eddies, themselves constantly changing, in the temper of religious milieux: Their very plurality has made study of them a recent and highly complex discipline. At the same time, their modern proliferation has tended to obscure the more fundamental meaning of spirituality so far advanced in this essay.[8] Despite these factors, however, the distinct ideological structures of such "schools of spirituality" yield invaluable data concerning the awareness post-medieval Catholicism, especially in this country, has of itself.

One may question whether so seemingly remote a thing as a school of spirituality can in fact influence the whole awareness a religious society has of itself, particularly in view of the role that formal patterns of worship have in the process. How do these disparate elements enmesh? The answer is to be found, it seems to me, in the remarkable tendency schools of spirituality have for assuming concrete sociological existence—mainly in the foundation of religious orders. A given "spirituality" becomes not only an actual, institutionalized way of life for an elite group of people: it simultaneously becomes a political force

[7] This seems to be the manner in which the classic statement *legem credendi lex statuat supplicandi* ("the law of worship should be constitutive of the law of belief") must be understood. It is absurd to suppose that worship and belief are separable acts: even more absurd is a subordination of worship to "the law of belief" simply as a tableauesque representation of credal statements. See A. Tegels' comments on this matter in his "Chronicle," *Worship*, XLI (1967) 562, and my own in "The Theology of Easter: Themes in Cultic Data," *Worship*, XLII (1968) 194-204, especially 199-200.

[8] See F. Vandenbroucke, "Spirituality and Spiritualities," *Spirituality in Church and World*, ed. C. Duquoc, Concilium Series, vol. 9 (New York, 1965) pp. 45-60.

in the life of the Church at large. To the extent that this happens, the "spirituality" of such a group is in a position to influence the way the whole community lives. For example, the renascence of monastic observance in the West during the ninth and tenth centuries was one factor that laid much of the foundation for the sweeping redefinition of ecclesiastical polity in the reforms of Pope Gregory VII (1021-1085). The Gregorian Reform in turn enunciated the new world-view that was the nucleus of the medieval European social and cultural synthesis—a synthesis that lasted until its disintegration under the pressures of Renaissance and Reformation in the sixteenth century.

The Gregorian Reform, with all it initiated, both sprang from and perpetuated a school of spirituality that was monastic in character. Executive in all this was the system of intrinsic structure, piety, and forms of worship centered in Cluny and, later, in the houses of the Cistercian reform. Medieval European spirituality thus imbibed a certain ethos that was distinctly different from what had gone before. In terms of worship patterns specifically, forms that had been emerging even prior to the tenth century became definitive and were further elaborated under monastic influence.[9] The ideal of celibacy, deriving from an increasing identification of minister with sacral function, was translated into canonical requirement for all clergy from the subdiaconate onward.[10] The Divine Office assumed a monastic length and format that removed it utterly beyond parochial use and the ability of most secular clergy. As for the Mass, it absorbed many of the *apologia* forms (such as the *Confiteor*) from monastic use.[11] The proliferation of private celebrations in large monasteries increasingly populated by priests led to the low Mass rite becoming usual—especially as a point of departure in eucharistic theology. And choral celebration led to the Mass becoming a culturally stunning performance, often in spectacular proportions, done by specialists and witnessed passively by a lay audience.

Such patterns of worship are cited here only as examples of how

9 For the enormous prestige of monastic liturgical observance and, hence, piety during the tenth and eleventh centuries, see J. A. Jungmann, *The Mass of the Roman Rite*, trans. F. Brunner (New York, 1950) I, 96-99, 203-05, 301. See also C. J. Peifer, "Monastic Renewal in Historical Perspective," *American Benedictine Review*, XIX (1968) 1-23.

10 By Lateran Council I (1123), canon 3.

11 See Jungmann, I, 301 ff.

they are *caused* by an institutionalized school of spirituality. Yet it must be emphasized that these patterns are also *causative:* they enforce and expand the school that gave rise to them. It may be observed in general that the effect of these medieval patterns of worship was to link imperceptibly the majority of Christians to the tradition of ecclesial worship in an attenuated manner at best.

This attenuated relationship eventually came to be sustained by forms of popular devotions, especially those in veneration of the reserved Sacrament and of the saints. Points of cultic focus were thus being provided (especially from the twelfth century) for a burgeoning subjectivism that was already present in the west, and the groundwork was being laid for the often hyperbolic piety that was to become so notable a feature of Western Catholicism by the time of the Reformation. The act of worship in its objective or "liturgical" sense was in fact becoming a highly clerical affair, while the surrogate of such worship as found in popular devotionalism was at the same time becoming an individual, private, and lay affair. Popular devotions attained a degree of greater influence at the grassroots level because of their immediacy and vigorous imagery. The act of formal worship, on the other hand, tended to recede both in its sense of immediacy and in its imagery. The result of these developments was, quite simply, a disintegration of the previously close relationship of check and balance that had obtained in earlier centuries between cult and piety—a rupture that became so deeply entrenched in Catholicism after the Reformation that it was considered to be in some way "normal."[12]

RESULTS OF THE DISINTEGRATION ON SPIRITUALITY

Three observations may be made concerning this rupture and its importance for understanding the spirituality in the American Church. First, the sort of Christian formation—or, more technically, the *catechesis*—produced by popular devotionalism may have been attenuated

[12] See F. Vandenbroucke, "Aux origines du malaise liturgique," *Les Questions Liturgiques et Paroissiales,* XL (1959), 252-70; B. Luykx, "Adaptation de la liturgie en pays de mission," *Eglise Vivante,* XII (1960), 33-45. For a much larger study of the Western roots of this syndrome, see J. A. Jungmann, *The Place of Christ in Liturgical Prayer,* trans. A. Peeler from the second German edition of 1962 (Staten Island, 1965).

when viewed against the criteria of what had gone before: it was nonetheless vigorous and personally immediate to those whom it formed. It supplied something for those who were less than expert to fill the vacuum that had developed separating the people from the late medieval forms of the Latin liturgy. One might even say that the natural creativity of religious societies in producing ritual patterns expressive of their own awareness of themselves shifted in the Western Church from the area of official worship to that of popular devotions. From the private sector there emerged certain ritual patterns better able to project and inculcate Western Christianity's own historically conditioned awareness of itself, for better or for worse.

A second observation appears to be immediately related to the first. It is that this shift inevitably qualified the structural forms of the Catholic community. If, as seems the case, the shift was envigorated by what I have called a subjective and hyperbolic piety emerging from below over the course of several centuries, then one must expect all this to have affected both new structural forms as they developed and old forms as they received new interpretations. This seems the sort of context within which, for example, the presbyterate came to assume an almost exclusively cultic character. This also seems the sort of context against which the reformers of the fifteenth and sixteenth centuries protested; yet, paradoxically, far from shaking itself free of this context, classic Protestantism rather included it as an assumption in one form as Counter-Reformation Catholicism did in another. It is possible, therefore, to view classic Protestantism and the sort of Catholicism that emerged after the sixteenth century as sharing *au fond* in a single religious world-view that had become endemic in Western culture by the time medieval social structures had collapsed. The Protestant and Catholic sides of the Western religious world-view thus came to find themselves moving more and more together, despite their continuing differences on matters that can only be called secondary and of detail. It is significant that this unification of the two has been forced rather more from without than from within. The pragmatic evolution of social structures to replace those of the Middle Ages proceeded along secular and revolutionary lines, as often as not against the opposition of Protestantism and Catholicism combined. Not only have the two confessional patterns increasingly come to share a united front in the face of secular pressures: The two have more recently begun to be aware that a new, vigorous, and quite competitive kind of religious experience is emerging from among secular systems. The immanent and terrestrial eschatologism promising an earthly heaven produced by human means that is explicit in communism and implicit in capitalism has ruptured the facile Western Christian view of the secular as unreligious or nonsacral—rather to the consternation of those within both confessional religious bodies.[13]

The third observation arises from the foregoing. It is that the medieval and post-medieval forms of ritual activity in Protestantism and Catholicism alike—whether rigidly cultic in an objective sense or popularly devotional in a subjective sense—have broken down. The purely sacral is no longer seen to be the exclusive product of a clerically directed activity that takes place in a church; the vigorous imagery of popular devotions has been overshadowed by the impact of television, and the subjectivism of those same devotions has been made to seem selfish and hypocritical with the intensification of social concern. This means that the familiar patterns by which Western Christian groups have conventionally objectified themselves, thus attaining a certain sense of socio-religious cohesion, no longer function adequately. The result is an identity crisis of major proportions in such groups—in short, a crisis in *spirituality*. The ability of the individual members for experiencing and participating in their religious society is thus hampered or made increasingly ambiguous, if not frustrated altogether.

Nowhere in Roman Catholicism is this so clearly evidenced as in those institutionalized schools of spirituality, the religious orders. The problem is especially acute in orders that were founded in the eighteenth and nineteenth centuries around a particular form of devotionalism. What amounts to the discrediting of a given devotion—through a shift in worship patterns toward more objective and classic dimensions such as has been set in motion by the last Council—has in fact removed the point of intrinsic social focus of many religious orders. A definite identity crisis has been produced in all of them, and in some its degree has already reached the proportions of social dissolution.

[13] This accounts in large degree, I think, for the sensation caused among Christians across classic denominational lines by Harvey Cox's *The Secular City* (New York, 1965). Raising some of the same points earlier was J. Danielou in *The Lord of History*, trans. N. Abercrombie (Chicago, 1958) pp. 72-95, especially, in which an apologetic and defensive note is sounded.

Their survival will depend upon the extent to which they can reassert patterns that secure objectification of the given society and participation in it on the part of its members.

In American Catholicism this phenomenon is of serious consequence for the institutional Church. It would be difficult to overstate the role religious orders have come to play in the financial, educational, and pastoral efforts mounted by the Church in this country during the last two centuries. So central has this role come to be that one can say the orders represent in microcosm the state of the American Catholic community, and they are usually the first to exhibit stresses that are developing within the community at large. Their present crisis of spirituality—that is, of identity, continuity, and cohesion—may thus be regarded as a compound prognosis of the state of Catholic spirituality in America.

CATHOLIC SPIRITUALITY AND AMERICAN SOCIETY

This prognosis yields data that seem to be not wholly negative. It suggests that Catholic spirituality in this country is in a state of crisis that may be positively salutary. It also suggests that the painful aspects of the crisis, while real, may be strains that are necessary in any process of growth toward greater maturity. It suggests, finally, that the crisis is larger in its extent than its presence in the post-conciliar Catholic community would seem to indicate. Not only do the problems of identity cross the confessional lines that Christians draw among themselves, but they can be detected throughout Western society itself. The technological revolutions in transportation, automation, cybernetics, and above all in communications have forced all social groups in Western society into an inescapable unity that is rapidly reaching a critical mass. Social structures that formerly not only permitted but required separateness within nations as well as between them have begun to dissolve. With this dissolution there is inevitably a loss of identity, continuity, and cohesion: the psychic and social results are fear, uncertainty, and defensiveness on the part of those who no longer can be sure where there individual lives focus. The conventional cultic patterns by which they were able to objectify themselves socially, and thus experience and participate in their society to obtain a sense of cohesion, are either being called into question or gone entirely. The crisis calls for new patterns that creatively reflect and project the new dimensions of the society's awareness of itself—dimensions formerly closed to the society by the presence of moribund rigidities. In this sense the crisis is salutary. Should such new patterns not be forthcoming, however, the crisis will deepen into social disintegration through a revolutionary process that could become negative in the extreme.

If this is true, then cultic patterns must be regarded as matters that go beyond ecclesiastical ceremonial and exclusively religious concern. These patterns come to exist from social motives: Where such patterns are in question, or in instances where their effectiveness has become attenuated, their host society's ability to objectify itself is at issue. Cultic patterns of formal worship in a religious society are thus indirectly reflective of the broader social state within which the religious group finds itself.

The Roman Catholic religious community in this country has until recent years steadfastly conceived of itself as existing in a hostile environment. In this, the defensive Counter-Reformation reaction to religious threat has served as a platform upon which a response to other threats could be mounted—threats such as the attack of political revolutions and intellectual advances upon the Catholic world-view. Added to these, the early experience of immigrant groups in this country served to join the faith with ethnic solidarity, a combination that produced a tightly inward-directed and defensive Catholicism which placed a high premium on patterns that would above all secure religious identity and cohesion. Those in the history of the American Church who stand in contrast to this tendency (men such as Isaac Hecker, John Ireland, John Lancaster Spalding and John Gilmary Shea) seem to prove the point by their exceptionalness, as do the reactions their positions evoked from ecclesiastical authorities at home and abroad.[14]

The various immigrant groups brought with them both specific patterns of religious observance and their own clergy—the latter already formed by those patterns in the old country. Popular devotions such as those centering on the reserved Sacrament and on veneration of saints, as well as structures of organization such as special sodalities

[14] The examples range from the celebrated condemnation of "Americanism" by Leo XIII in the encyclical *Testem Benevolentiae* of Jan. 22, 1899, to Pius XII's letter of congratulations for the American hierarchy on its sesquicentennial, *Sertum Laetitiae*, Nov. 1, 1939, with its continued cautions concerning the dangers for the Church in American society.

and institutionalized schools of piety, served to foster ethno-religious identity. At the center of the immigrant enclave stood the pastor, who increasingly became the group's director not only in religious but also in secular, even political, matters. De Tocqueville's observations concerning the largely pre-immigration American Church of the early 1830's stood in need of revision by the end of the century:

> . . . the American clergy stand aloof from secular affairs. . . . I have seen no country in which Christianity is clothed with fewer forms, figures, and observances than in the United States, or where it presents more distinct, simple, and general notions to the mind. . . . There are no Roman Catholic priests who show less taste for the minute individual observances, for extraordinary or peculiar means of salvation, or cling more to the spirit and less to the letter of the law than the Roman Catholic priests of the United States. Nowhere is the doctrine of the church which prohibits the worship reserved to God alone from being offered to the saints more clearly inculcated or generally followed. . . .[15]

The whole complex of organization, clergy, religious orders and devotions revolved about the act of formal worship at Sunday Mass. If nothing else, this was the central social event and main means of communication for immigrant groups well into the present century. The two systems of national parishes and the parochial schools, furthermore, bolstered the ethno-religious group. Even after the first began to fade before the powerful forces of Americanization, and after the second more recently began to break down under the same pressures, as the ethnic group blurred into third and fourth generations the patterns of worship at Sunday Mass and in religious devotionalism remained static. Embracing a strong sense of numinous effect, the sacral character of these socio-cultic patterns was heightened the more because in derivation, structure, and symbolic language they were so alien to the daily fabric of the lives of those who participated in them. In this the patterns had a high degree of experiential effectiveness for their users, and thus they became more cohesive in their socio-religious results and even more resistive to change.

[15] In *De la démocratie en Amerique,* cited in John Tracy Ellis, *Documents of American Catholic History,* 2nd ed. (Chicago, 1967) I, 235. The number of Catholics is estimated to have been 318,000 in 1830, the year before de Tocqueville arrived in America: the figure had more than doubled a decade later due to the influx of immigrants.

It can be noted at this point that the absorption with cult in the post-medieval Church generally, and in the American Church especially, is not an incomprehensible phenomenon for all the justifiable criticism that may be laid against it. If the cultic absorption accomplished nothing else, it produced a vigorous and simple point of focus to support an equally vigorous and simple awareness of itself, a spirituality, on the part of the religious society in which it functioned. That spirituality, moreover, was remarkably efficient at least in its externalism, as Bishop John Lancaster Spalding noted indirectly in his comments on the intellectual weakness in the American Church in 1884:

> The fact that the growth of the Church here, like that of the country itself, is chiefly external, a growth in wealth and numbers, makes it more necessary that we bring the most strenuous efforts to improve the gifts of the soul. The whole tendency of our social life insures the increase of churches, convents, schools, hospitals, and asylums; our advance in population and in wealth will be counted from decade to decade by millions, and our worship will approach more and more to the pomp and splendor of the full ritual; but this very growth makes such demands upon our energies, that we are in danger of forgetting higher things. . . .[16]

While almost everything Spalding mentioned went on changing—population, facilities, income, ecclesiastical personnel, and the process of indigenization—the Catholic community's spirituality and the cultic patterns giving it foundation remained virtually the same.

A salient factor responsible for this was the system of education for the clergy. Remarkable for its success in correcting the general lack of clerical education prior to the sixteenth century, by the turn of the twentieth century the Tridentine seminary system had become less educational and more ideological in function. This was especially so in the United States, where "seminary theology" was mostly apologetic, geared to polemic in defense of the faith of the masses, derived from European manuals, and inhibited by various papal condemnations of largely non-American intellectual movements such as continental rationalism, evolutionism, Modernism, and the like. The result was that American clergy found themselves seriously cut off not only from the

[16] From a sermon preached at the Third Plenary Council of Baltimore, Nov. 16, 1884, and which in a sense can be said to have launched the Catholic University of America: cited in Ellis, II, 416-17.

literature produced by their own culture but also from the very sources of their own religious tradition as well. The movements toward *re-sourcement* studies of the Bible, the early fathers of the Church, and of the liturgy were slow in becoming established in this country, especially in Catholic seminaries. The priest more often than not found himself almost exclusively the administrator of facilities, finances, and of cultic patterns learned by rote according to what could be called at best a juridical methodology. In this latter capacity his intimate association with the divinely numinous core of the cultic complex placed him above ordinary criticism, beyond the need for ordinary learning and the context of ordinary social relationships. The same can be said for other ecclesiastical personnel who are not clergy in the technical sense but who share in the same role, especially in the area of education of the young. The ideological formation and life-patterns of all these persons have come to be intimately associated with the cultic patterns and their concomitant spirituality in the Catholic community: for this reason, the lives and formation of such persons have become almost as resistant to change as the cultic patterns themselves.

FACTORS OF CHANGE IN CONVENTIONAL PATTERNS

Perhaps no other single factor has been as responsible for the diminution of that strongly centripetal and externally efficient sense of identity in the American Catholic community as the movement for reform of cultic patterns in the liturgy. The liturgical movement may be said to date from the time of the Renaissance, and it pursued for the most part a course of scholarly historical research until the end of the nineteenth century. But because of the external stresses of the industrial and social revolutions in Europe during that century, the movement became vigorously pastoral after 1900. The immediate cause of this was, quite simply, the growing alienation of the working classes from the Church—a critical problem that conventional structures and attitudes in the Church seemed unable to deal with effectively (this despite the social encyclicals of Pope Leo XIII).

From its beginning, the pastoral phase of the liturgical movement was conceived in strongly social terms. Its founders—men such as Lambert Beauduin in Belgium and Virgil Michel in the United States—were less esthetes and historians than they were practical theologians who concentrated on the realities of Christian living in contemporary society. No suggestion they made was greeted with greater reserve than that of the primacy of the social dimension of Christian worship over its subjective, rigidly static, and numinous character—aspects that were hitherto generally assumed to have priority. Thus Michel described the spirituality consequent on the principles of the liturgical movement as nothing other than the true spirituality of the Christian community restored and reemphasized. In 1939 he wrote that this ". . . is eminently the view of that religion whose liturgy is at once the perfection of the individual and the *union of the individual in a common fellowship*, and whose liturgy is not the spasmodic exercise of isolated acts of worship but the spiritual source and inspiration of a life that is lived every minute of the day."[17]

Not only was the theme of worship's social relevance fostered by the movement a new element, but the approach contained a much deeper implicit critique of a whole set of conventional assumptions that had imperceptibly created the sort of Catholicism that reacted with truculence, if not outright hostility, to the movement in general. More faithful to tradition than to conventions, the leaders of the movement regarded the conventional assumptions as inadequate at best or diseased at worst. Their diagnosis of the malaise centered on the gradual sundering of Christ from the world, a process that stemmed from a growing emphasis on his divine nature and prerogatives throughout the medieval era. The image of Christ in popular theology and piety thus came to be over-divinized and extra-worldly: the connection between him and men came to be grace viewed as an altogether extrinsic factor, not as an ontological sharing in the same life—viewed as a gift of God above to those here below who qualified for it by satisfying certain moral, legal, and ritual requirements. In short, the classic New Testament and patristic concept of God present incarnately and corporately among men in the world shifted, under historical and cultural pressures, to one of a God present to men from outside the world and often in spite of it. Man was thus really alone in the world except for periodic inruptions of the divinity, especially through

[17] "Liturgy and Modern Thought," *Orate Fratres*, XII (1939), 209, italics mine. For Michel's position and involvement in social movements see Paul B. Marx, *Virgil Michel and the Liturgical Movement* (Collegeville, Minn., 1957) pp. 176-210 and 298-337.

the instrumentality of formal worship. The results of this could be called a social anxiety neurosis in Western Christianity's world-view that both manifested and alleviated itself in patterns of obsessive compulsion which frequently took ritual forms. The extrinsic understanding of worship consequent on this, which largely formed generations of clergy and congregations, was what the pastoral phase of the liturgical movement had to overcome.

It began to do so with the slow elaboration of a more ample and, therefore, corrective theological theory of worship derived from the newly reopened sectors of biblical, patristic, and liturgical studies—an elaboration carried on in the face of sporadic cautions from ecclesiastical authorities even while these same authorities were coming to accept the main points of the theory.[18] What the Second Vatican Council finally did, in its Constitution on the Sacred Liturgy (1963), was mainly to give official sanction to the corrective theory as it had been elaborated until then and to initiate massive changes in cultic patterns such a correction entailed. Yet the administration of these changes in theory and in detail, together with the reactions to them on the parochial level, have been largely carried out on the basis of those conventional assumptions that antedated not only the Council but the pastoral phase of the liturgical movement itself. The method of carrying out cultic changes by authoritative decree, and the rigid retention of the same emphases on the numinous in ceremonial details (such as those surrounding the act of sacramental communion received only on the tongue and while kneeling) together have caused conflicting tensions in the evolution both of new worship patterns and the spirituality they are geared to produce in the community at large. Massive shifts in cultic patterns cannot be expected to produce immediately and of themselves an evolution in community awareness that will secure that greater sense of social identity, cohesion, and adequate response to stress. Here the conventional Catholic confidence in the power of ritual to "effect what it signifies" is surely misplaced. Without concomitant re-formation of the attitudes and assumptions of the whole community through really creative programs of education, the social role of new cultic patterns will be maimed to a great

[18] Viz. Pius XII's encyclicals, *Mystici Corporis* (1943), *Mediator Dei* (1947), and *Humani Generis* (1950).

extent, and their presence can degenerate into as much an irritant to unity as a cause of it.

CONCLUSIONS

On this uncertain note it is necessary to end. It has been my concern to profile the spirituality of the American Catholic community from some analysis of the ways in which it has reacted to stresses endemic to its own peculiar faith- and time- and space-conditioned existence. In the course of this it has perhaps become more clear how complex a full analysis would be, how much more needs to be done before the American Church can be adequately aware of itself, how polymorphic are the structures that are responsible for such an awareness, and how filled with promise a revitalization of structures and their resultant sense of awareness may be for the future.

What is definite for the present is that this future remains ambiguous. Unless more creativity is forthcoming in replacing previous outmoded cultic patterns, and unless this creativity is patient enough to innovate without breaking totally the community's necessary sense of continuity with its past, then one has a right to be pessimistic about the future.[19] It will not be enough simply to discredit those forms that maintained a Christian spirituality of a defensive, subjective, individualistic, ideological, and romantic kind: for better or worse, this sort of spirituality, based on this sort of cultic pattern, is all that many Catholic Christians know. Far from being a reason for inaction, however, this matter is a challenge to the wisdom and vigor of all those who claim to love Christ not only in the Church but among all men everywhere. The fact remains that cultic patterns, in the very broad sense in which I have tried to define them, are communication media that reach down into the depths of the psyche and thus make social intercourse possible, if richly ambiguous, precisely on matters of ultimate concern. These patterns, moreover, catalyze a host of other social structures—such as those of authority, of education, and of the arts—

19 I have tried to suggest schematically something of what is involved in such a process in "How Rite Develops: Some Laws Intrinsic to Liturgical Evolution," *Worship*, XLI (1967), 334-47.

to the same end. In this view it is a gross oversimplification of the task at hand to suggest that such patterns and structures as these are irrelevant in times like ours when social dissolution seems upon us. Indeed, it would seem that the ossification of these patterns and structures may be as much responsible for the state of things as any other set of factors.

My own suspicion is that if these patterns are to be revitalized anywhere in the world it will have to be done first in the United States. This is so because the United States is today what other countries will be only in the future—a technological society verging on a degree of dehumanized massiveness that could become the ultimate degradation of man. The dissolution of the Christian community into mere retreats of ineffective discontent would, I think, do little more than hasten so baleful a state. The effective and vigorous cohesion of the Christian community in the face of such threat must be of concern not only for the survival of the churches but for the life of mankind itself.

9: THE AMERICAN CATHOLIC FAMILY

John L. Thomas, S.J.

If we rely on external evidence, it appears that American families are becoming increasingly alike in size, structure, and in the general pattern of activities throughout the life cycle. Some differences related to various regional, social class, ethnic, and "racial" traits obviously persist, but the overall trend toward uniformity is unmistakable. In part, this reflects the adjustments required by an industrialized urban environment. American families live in a technologically advanced, rapidly developing, open-class society. They are spatially and socially mobile, enjoy relative affluence, and are highly receptive to the uniformities promoted by mass communications. Since they must adjust to similar social environments, it is not surprising to discover that they adopt somewhat similar family patterns.

Families have always been alike, of course, in the sense that they share certain universal features derived from the biological nature of the human species. These universal givens are related to the complementary reproductive endowments of men and women, as well as to the comparatively long period of dependency characteristic of the human infant. Wherever the family exists, it serves to regulate sexual behavior for purposes of reproduction and to provide for the organic social development of offspring. In spite of these universal "givens," individual families and family systems may differ widely. Man can devise a variety of ways to fulfill his sexual and parental needs. The approved family system in any given society will depend on how people define these needs, on the relative personal and social value they attribute to them, on the institutionalized means or concrete, normative patterns of relationships they establish to assure their satisfactory fulfillment, and on the natural, social, and cultural resources available in the environment.

Because American society is religiously pluralist—containing groups holding fairly diverse views of man's nature and destiny and consequently of the religious and moral aspects of marriage—it does not have a clearly defined, universally accepted family system. The term "American family" is a broadly descriptive label covering a wide variety of family types. To be sure, the roughly forty-million domestic units to which the term applies share a number of similar traits, but they also display considerable diversity in their beliefs, values, and attitudes relating to sex, love, marriage, and parenthood. This does not mean that Americans have developed no distinguishing national characteristics relating to marriage and the family. In contrast to many of their contemporaries in other industrialized Western nations, the American people apparently regard marriage and the family as almost indispensable components of the good life. Thus a greater proportion of Americans tend to enter marriage, they marry on the average at younger ages, and they marry oftener!

Since our major concern here is with American Catholic families, we must make it clear at the outset on what grounds we can regard them as an identifiable, distinctive subgroup meriting separate consideration. Obviously, it is not on the assumption that for some reason Catholic families have remained apart from American society and consequently confront a different social environment. Together with other American families, they have faced and continue to face the challenge of adjusting to rapid and extensive change. They differ from other families to the extent that they must work out their adjustments in terms of a different framework of family values and norms related to their religious beliefs. In other words, in spite of the similarities with their contemporaries, American Catholic families constitute an identifiable subgroup because they share distinctive religious beliefs that largely determine their basic marriage and family values. Most of these values are easily identified, for Catholics believe that the Church has authority to teach in such matters, and the marriage teaching promulgated and sanctioned by the Church over the centuries leaves no essential aspects undefined.

This is not to say that Catholic families ever have been, or presently are, all alike. Change is endemic in every society; and the process of adjusting to change, particularly in regard to the family, is always a two-way street. For example, changes such as industrialization and urbanization not only affect the way families make a living, where they live, and how they rear their offspring, but they also bring about a restructuring of marital, parental, and kinship relationships; this in turn leads to a reappraisal of the meanings, values, and normative standards formerly associated with these relationships. Thus families living in industrialized urban environments tend to stress the basic equality of the partners, conjugal companionship, and responsible parenthood; those in agricultural societies are more likely to emphasize family solidarity, the domestic role of woman, and the authority of the father as head of the family enterprise.

These different emphases, associated with different ways of defining the status and role of family members, are the result of the family's attempt to adjust to the different social environments within which it must operate; from this it is evident that diverse social or cultural conditions can predispose people with the same basic religious beliefs to develop and accentuate different aspects of these beliefs in the practical order. We can take it as a general principle, therefore, that the practical implications of any system of religious beliefs will depend not only on the intrinsic content of its doctrinal teaching but also on the cultural and social settings within which these implications are developed. Religiously derived marriage and family values remain abstract concepts until they are embodied in concrete social relationships designed to insure their attainment. This process of actualizing family values is always conditioned both by the inherent demands of the situation and the way these values are interpreted in a given society and at a given historical period.

Consequently we may expect Catholic families around the world, even within the United States, to display a range of differences. So we cannot really speak of *the* Catholic family. The beliefs, values, and behavioral patterns associated with Catholic families during different historical periods or in different social settings represent only more or less adequate "cultural approximations" of the Catholic ideal. The Church's teaching on marriage and the family is not situational, but it is conditioned by and related to a specific historical and cultural setting in regard to its interpretation, practical implications, and concrete implementation. This quality of historical and cultural relatedness acquires special significance today when Catholic families must work out adjustments to extensive and rapid changes. Under such conditions it is just as erroneous to identify past cultural approximations with the Christian ideal as it is to regard this ideal as no longer relevant. American Catholics share with all their contemporaries the challenge of change. But as members of a pluralist society in which there is little agreement on basic family values and in which conflicting or contradictory norms of conduct enjoy apparently equal public approbation, they face the added task of adopting only those values and practices that are consonant with their religious beliefs.

THE HISTORICAL DIMENSION

In order to understand the present position of Catholic families in American society it will be helpful to take a brief look at the history of American families in general.[1] Three major factors merit special attention: the original domestic background of those who settled the country; the influence of the environment and the adjustments it required; rapid industrialization, resulting in the family's transition from a rural to an industrialized urban setting. When considering these factors we should keep in mind that although basic needs, ideals, and life goals may remain relatively stable, their personal and social implications, as well as their implementation in concrete relationships, undergo constant modification from different cultural emphases and changing circumstances. The family unit, although fundamental, is only one of the institutions through which man satisfies his elemental needs. It affects and is affected by all his other goals and relationships.

The early settlers in America were representatives of European societies which under the influence of the Renaissance, nationalism, and the Reformation were gradually breaking away from the medieval ideal of a unified Christianity. The colonists held marriage in high esteem; except for the Catholic settlers of Maryland, however, they denied its sacramental character and placed the marriage contract under the jurisdiction of civil authorities. Family organization was patriarchal in form, with wife and children expected to obey the head of the family as a religious duty. With the rapid westward movement of settlers after the War of Independence this family system began to change. Frontier conditions required youth to be trained for early

[1] See Arthur W. Calhoun, *A Social History of the American Family*, 3 vols. (New York, 1945); Willystine Goodsell, *A History of Marriage and the Family* (New York, 1934); John L. Thomas, *The American Catholic Family* (Englewood Cliffs, N.J., 1956); and Carle C. Zimmerman, *Family and Civilization* (New York, 1947).

independence and aggressive individualism, while the important domestic roles fulfilled by women upgraded their status toward closer equality with men. This neglect of tradition and continued shift toward a more democratic domestic pattern constitutes one of the dominant traits of the American family experience.

Thus although the early legal norms regulating domestic relations followed English family law—with the exception that full divorce could be granted even by civil officials—this patriarchal pattern came under heavy attack during the nineteenth century because of changes in the economic and social status of women. The final result of over half a century of agitation and reform was legally embodied in the various "Married Women's Acts," which most states had enacted by the time of the Civil War. Henceforth married women were allowed to own and control their property and earnings, make wills with no more restrictions than on their husbands, and share equal guardianship of their children. During the same period many states passed omnibus divorce clauses, which, besides for certain specified "causes," allowed divorce to be granted "for any other reason which the court shall deem necessary." In general, Americans have traditionally regarded the family as a highly personal concern and consequently feel that legislation dealing with its establishment, maintenance, and dissolution should be minimal. There are no Federal laws relating directly to marriage and the family, and though the individual states have accumulated a large assortment of legal enactments, these are far from uniformly enforced.

The primarily Anglo-Saxon, Protestant view of the family was basic in the initial shaping and later orientation of the American family system; yet the observation of historian Oscar Handlin that immigrants *are* American history is also highly relevant, particularly for an understanding of American Catholic families. The Catholic Church in America has grown primarily through immigration. Around the time of the Revolution there were some Catholics in America—perhaps 35,000 of them scattered throughout the Colonies. The Louisiana Purchase and the annexations following the Mexican War added several hundred thousand, mostly of French and Spanish extraction. But the major growth of the Catholic population resulted from the heavy flood of immigrants coming at first from Ireland and Germany after 1830, and later, from southern and central Europe and the Americas, chiefly after 1880.

Several consequences of immigrant history are relevant for an understanding of contemporary Catholic families. In addition to being put on the defensive as foreigners and Catholics, the majority of the immigrants, with the exception of the Irish, encountered a language barrier that slowed down their economic, social, and political integration, intensified their dissimilarity with the dominant group, motivated them to settle in relatively closed communities clustered around their national churches, and created painful parental problems as their children moved more quickly toward acculturation.

At the same time, most entered the country through the ports of the East; from necessity—for they were generally poor—and from choice—for they wished to be near their compatriots—they tended to settle not far from the point of debarkation, or in the rapidly industrializing centers around the Great Lakes. Even today, over 70 per cent are clustered in or around major cities in the area north of the Ohio river and east of the Mississippi valley region. This concentration made possible the construction of a church and school system without parallel, and undoubtedly mitigated some of the hardships of transition to a strange cultural system; it also slowed down the pace of acculturation and fostered national rivalry within the Church.

Moreover, since the majority of Catholic immigrants were relatively unskilled, or possessed skills not highly useful in an industrialized society, they started their lives in America at the bottom of the socioeconomic ladder. Using the ample economic and educational opportunities available in our open-class society, their second- and third-generation descendants gradually achieved middle-class status. This group now constitute the bulk of American Catholics. They tend to be socially mobile and, following the national pattern of the past few decades, are moving away from their original concentrations in urban centers out to the suburbs or to various rapidly developing regions throughout the country. Thus, although the Church in America has drawn its strength primarily from the working classes and has so identified with their interests that they have preserved the faith even under difficult conditions, the now substantial increase of a well-educated laity rightly calls into question many administrative ecclesiastical structures and forms of authority.

The rapid industrialization of the American economy after the Civil War has been another major influence shaping the American family system. For the most part the family's transition from a rural to an industrialized urban environment proceeded unnoticed, though the resultant changes were considerable. There was a gradual weakening of the extended kinship bonds that formerly had supported the individual family unit; as social and spatial mobility, individualism, and early economic independence increased, the relatively isolated nuclear or conjugal family type came to be regarded as an ideal. Yet, this limitation of formal kinship rights and obligations, with the contraction of meaningful familial relationships to the individual conjugal unit, by intensifying the emotional load and other burdens of the restricted family circle tended to render it less stable and to require the assistance of society in caring for its dependent, sick, or aged members. Our high divorce rate and extensive social legislation clearly reflect these changes.

The rural and immigrant family systems were characteristically patriarchal in structure and highly prolific. The transition to an industrialized urban environment was associated with a gradual modification of the statuses and roles of family members as well as of traditional attitudes regarding family size. Since the major portion of the husband's time, energy, and interest was focused on his job away from home the scope of the couple's shared activities was narrowed, while the primary responsibility for the socialization of the children devolved upon the wife. Furthermore, children not only ceased to be an economic asset, or at least a minimal parental charge, but became a considerable financial and emotional burden. For example, in addition to the rising cost of better health care, lengthened period of formal education and consequent increased parental supervision, an extended period of child bearing restricted the mother's chances of adding to the family's income with a job outside the home.

To summarize the present situation: Although Americans are heterogeneous in national backgrounds, recency of immigration, social class, regional environment, and religious beliefs, they are beginning to share a number of views and attitudes relating to marriage and the family. Mate selection should be free, marriage should be based on love, the marital bond should be permanent though legal provision should be made for separation or divorce, parenthood should be responsible and therefore somewhat restricted, newlyweds should establish a household apart from their parents, grown children should be self-supporting, and kinship solidarity should be founded on affection rather than formally defined obligations. Some residual ethnic and regional differences still persist in the form of distinctive family customs, marital- and parental-role patterns, or national prejudices. Discrimination and exploitation continue to deprive a sizable number of Americans of the social and economic bases necessary for stable family life, as in the case of lower-class Negroes, migrant workers, and others; apart from these, the trend toward conformity is evident.

MINORITY PATTERNS AND PROBLEMS

As we have noted, external similarities may conceal sharp differences in beliefs and values. Members of the Catholic minority in particular cherish a distinctive set of beliefs regarding the meaning of life, the sacramental quality of the marital bond, the purposes of the marriage vocation, and the normative values relevant to the use of sex. Since they constitute an identifiable cultural subgroup and must consequently rely chiefly on their own resources to actualize their distinctive marriage and family values, we may safely predict that they will encounter some distinctive problems as they continue to move toward fuller integration with American society.

Stated briefly, a minority can retain its religious identity either by isolating itself from the alien influences of the dominant culture, as some groups such as the Amish have done, or by selective integration. American Catholics have always opted for the latter, but until the last few decades the majority of them remained relatively isolated, because of their ethnic and regional urban concentration, immigrant and culturally alien origins, and related socioeconomic status. This incidental form of isolation is rapidly decreasing, with the result that Catholics are beginning to experience the full impact of the secular environment.

Under the conditions of pluralism and rapid change, modern Catholic couples can be expected to retain their distinctive family values only on condition that they clearly understand the religious foundations of these values, are adequately motivated, and enjoy some measure of group support from their coreligionists. Because selective integration requires careful discernment in adopting behavioral patterns and practices consonant with religious values, the religious formation of minority-group members must give priority to the development of critical acumen and discriminating moral judgment. This clearly calls for a considerable change in the Church's traditional system of religious indoctrination, which up to now has been concerned primarily with only the routinized transmission of basic doctrine, ritual etiquette, and a more or less standardized series of moral imperatives.[2]

Keeping in mind their historical background, religious minority status, and relatively high mobility, what are the major problems that Catholic families now face? In general, evidence that the modern American family's adjustment to its industrialized urban environment is not proceeding satisfactorily appears in the approximately half-million marriages annually broken by divorce or separation, in the apparently steady increase in all types of juvenile delinquency, and in the indications of widespread premarital and extramarital sexual promiscuity. Catholic families are necessarily exposed to all the social factors generating these difficulties, but they are bound to experience their impact somewhat differently than others, because they cherish a distinctive set of marriage and family values. In this regard we may assume that since the Catholic family is designed to promote the happiness and development of the couple and the adequate socialization of their children as these basic functions are defined by the Church, anything that inhibits or impedes their satisfactory fulfillment will constitute a source of disorganization.

MIXED MARRIAGES

What features of contemporary society are most relevant in this regard? Let us begin with one of the more obvious. Out-group marriages pose a perennial threat to the survival of any cultural or religious minority.[3] The intimate bond of unity between spouses that marriage establishes readily transcends differences in religious beliefs and values; thus it may lead to compromise, rejection, the conversion of one of the partners, or loss of faith on the part of both. Moreover, because marriage is normally procreative, mixed marriages may inhibit the religious formation of offspring. For these reasons such marital unions are opposed by all religious minorities who take their distinctive be-

[2] Thomas, pp. 327-82.
[3] Thomas, pp. 138-69.

liefs seriously. The Catholic position on mixed marriages is clearly stated in the Code of Canon Law and in various encyclicals. Although the current ecumenical movement has generated considerable opposition to some features of this legislation, centuries of experience, together with all modern research findings, leave no grounds for reasonable doubt concerning the dangers to the faith normally involved in mixed marriages.

There are a number of reasons why this problem must be regarded as acute for American Catholics. Their continued social and residential mobility increases their opportunities for meeting those who do not share their beliefs. Contemporary dating patterns make it possible for Catholics to become emotionally involved with non-Catholics even though valid marriage is out of the question or would prove extremely hazardous. On such relevant moral issues as the right use of sex, the indissolubility of a valid marriage bond, and the sacramental quality of marriage, Catholics maintain doctrinal teaching clearly at variance with the beliefs of the majority in American society; the gap between the Catholic position and dominant cultural values in this regard is steadily increasing. Finally, although religious leaders of all denominations have expressed strong opposition to mixed marriages, both Catholic and non-Catholic young people appear little concerned with the dangers involved in such unions.

When discussing mixed marriages from the Catholic viewpoint, we must distinguish between valid and invalid unions. Valid mixed marriages require a dispensation, promises regarding the religious formation of offspring, and celebration in the presence of a priest and two witnesses. On the other hand, invalid mixed marriages are unions entered into without the Church's permission. At present, the valid mixed-marriage rate runs a little over 30 per cent. Since a mixed marriage involves only one Catholic partner, this means that about eighteen out of every one-hundred Catholics enters a valid mixed marriage. Because invalid marriages are not recorded as such by either ecclesiastical or civil authorities, we have only indirect evidence regarding their rate. According to reliable research, their rate runs roughly similar to the rate of valid mixed marriages, though some of these initially invalid unions may eventually be validated by the Church. In other words, it appears that about thirty out of every one-hundred Catholics initially enters some type of mixed marriage.

A number of studies show that mixed marriages tend to be much more unstable than marriages in which the spouses share similar religious beliefs. This need not mean that quarrels over religion or over the religious education of the children constitute the major source of the difficulty. Such quarrels undoubtedly occur in some cases, but it appears that tensions more frequently result from in-law pressures, divided church loyalties, differences in moral values and aspirations, and above all from lack of communication and sharing of spiritual outlooks, feelings, and practices. Moreover, research shows that about 45 per cent of the Catholic partners involved in valid mixed marriages either sever all connections with the Church or attend services very sporadically; while approximately 40 per cent of all children born to such unions are either unbaptized, or baptized as Protestants, or baptized as Catholics but receive no formal instruction in the faith.

It seems safe to predict that the rates of both valid and invalid mixed marriages will continue to increase. Not only are many of the formerly inhibiting factors such as ethnic solidarity, high urban concentration, and lower social-class status of Catholics gradually disappearing, but there is some indication that young persons today are not strongly disposed to accept religious restraints in what they regard as matters of personal decision. Even those who identify themselves as Christians, or at least as earnest seekers after truth, are little inclined to acknowledge the need for legal codes or formal authoritative structures. Further changes in the Canon Law affecting mixed marriages will probably be forthcoming, yet the major problems these marriages involve are not legal, but distressingly human. The intimacy normally associated with marital companionship and parenthood is not easily reconciled with marked differences in beliefs, values, and practices acquired through long years of learning and conditioning. This observation applies to all marriages, though its special relevance for mixed marriages should be clear.

DIVORCE AND FAMILY INSTABILITY

Another feature of contemporary society that is bound to affect Catholic families increasingly in the future is the widespread acceptance of divorce and separation as solutions for marriage problems. The shift to a nuclear-type family has placed a heavy strain on marital unity, for the restricted family circle now remains the only acceptable social vehicle for the expression of affection and for emotional interaction that is potentially explosive. Add to this the popular notion that each individual has the right to seek complete personal fulfillment regardless of previous commitments, present responsibilities, or future consequences; the toleration of early cross-sex relationships, leading to precocious emotional involvement, sexual experience, and premarital pregnancy; the limitation of family size and consequent shortening of the period during which women must be preoccupied with the immediate needs associated with bearing and rearing children; the increased freedom of married women to enter the work force, enjoy wider social contacts, and achieve greater independence; the extensive acceptance of contraceptive techniques that effectively separate sexual relations from procreation and which, together with family limitation, give rise to a new awareness of women's capacity to enjoy sexual relations; add all these and it should be evident that the maintenance of marital fidelity and stability will constitute an increasingly difficult challenge.

Unfortunately, national statistics on the current rate of marital instability among Catholics are not available. Studies based on the admittedly selective caseloads of marriage counseling centers, domestic-relations courts, and chancery offices suggest that Catholic couples probably differ very little in this regard from their contemporaries of similar educational and socioeconomic status, though they are more likely to choose separation or desertion rather than divorce when serious marital difficulties arise. This latter probably reflects the Church's teaching regarding the indissolubility of marriage, yet it does not affect the basic finding that a considerable number of Catholic couples are currently experiencing serious instability and breakdown.

Religious leaders as a whole have been slow to recognize the real dimensions of this problem and the consequent need for competent therapeutic action. Most dioceses lack adequate counseling facilities. Contrary to popular belief, competency in marriage counseling requires much more knowledge and supervised clinical training than the usual seminary courses in pastoral theology can provide. With few exceptions, the Catholic school system has revealed little critical concern with the quality of its religious instruction in regard to sex, marriage, and the family. It has rather generally been assumed that teachers require no special preparation for dealing with these subjects, with the result that the sisters or busy young clerics who usually conduct such courses have tended either to give them short shrift or to emphasize the negative elements in the Church's teaching. Although a vigorous pre-Cana movement has been developed in some major cities during the past several decades, such conferences can provide no adequate remedy for basic deficiencies in the educational system, for they are designed to deal with only immediate marriage preparation.

Moreover, many of the factors associated with marital instability are also the sources of new parental problems. Not only have travel and communication notably increased the number and variety of extra-familial influences affecting children today, but changes affecting the structure of the family have tended to weaken parental control. Except during early childhood, the expanding activities associated with the school, youth organizations, and the peer group claim a large share of young people's time and interest, with the result that many no longer regard their limited family circle at home as the primary source of recreation and emotional support but look rather to their age-group associates for approval, acceptance, and for normative standards.

This tendency is increased by the fact that our technologically advanced society requires the majority of youth to undergo progressively longer periods of formal study and training, during which they are supported by their parents, treated more or less as irresponsible adolescents, subjected to goals and norms devised by an older generation, and excluded from responsible participation in the adult community. Under these circumstances, young people tend to form their own subculture or separate world; their confused parents, feeling that they have few precedents to guide them and sensing that their growing children regard them as outdated or overly conservative, become increasingly reluctant to impose or even express forcefully their own preferences and values.

This parental loss of nerve stems from several sources. Recent changes within both the Church and society have left the entire conventional framework of beliefs, values, standards of conduct, and behavioral patterns in a state of flux. Under such conditions, little can be counted on to endure from generation to generation, and everything seems open to revision or obsolescence. Because they are aware that they cannot anticipate the kind of world their children will confront as adults, modern parents are far from sure that their own past experience offers any reliable precedents for guidance. Their parental self-assurance has been further undermined by their exposure to a puzzling series of conflicting, though purportedly scientific, child-rearing theories and fads. Proceeding on the assumption that the "authoritarian" pattern of the past was harmful, the currently "in" theory encourages parents to be permissive—yet they are not told how they can reconcile permissiveness with serious concern for the development of their children. As a consequence, some do little or nothing in the way of constructive guidance; others content themselves with supplying protection, nurture, and affection while anxiously hoping for the best.

At the same time, the widespread social acceptance of premature and relatively unsupervised cross-sex associations among youth, together with the disintegration of traditional sexual codes and the consequent exploitation of sex in advertising, literature, and entertainment, finds most parents either unprepared or unwilling to deal with the inevitable problems confronting their children during the prolonged period between puberty and marriage. Apparently because of the puritanical aberrations from Christian conceptions of modesty and chastity that took hold in Western culture several centuries ago, most parents—mothers in particular—seem incapable of understanding the obvious biological, psychological, and social implications of sexual development in their growing children—perhaps even in themselves. Anxious to foster popularity and future success, they assiduously promote their children's precocious, unchaperoned, couple-centered social life; at the same time, aware of the increasing need for formal education, they urge serious study, strict observance of premarital chastity, and later marriages, as if healthy adolescents were insensitive to normal human drives and emotional involvements. Small wonder that some troubled teenagers regard their parents and elders with a mixture of pity and contempt.

FERTILITY AND FAMILY LIMITATION

The family problems we have been discussing constitute a serious challenge to the survival of the Catholic minority, for they affect the adequate transmission of its distinctive religious beliefs, values, and practices. Yet their present significance for the average Catholic couple is completely overshadowed by concern with the issue of birth control. Problems related to the regulation of family size are far from new in the Western world, but a number of recent developments in science and theology have forced these problems into the forefront of popular awareness and discussion for the first time. The discovery of an effective oral anovulent "pill" may be regarded as the immediate precipitating factor stimulating Catholic theological concern. But a whole series of cultural and social changes, beginning around the end of the sixteenth century, have radically modified modern man's understanding of and approach to procreation and made inevitable a thorough reappraisal of the Church's traditional teaching on marriage, sex, and family limitation. Since contraceptive birth control is generally assumed to be one of the key issues involved, it may prove helpful to review the relevant historical facts in the situation.

The fertility of the American people from the time of the first permanent settlements to the early nineteenth century was among the world's highest.[4] During this period of more than two centuries, women of completed fertility are estimated to have had an average of eight children. After the first decade of the nineteenth century, however, the fertility history of the United States may be characterized as one of relatively rapid transition from large families to small. Thus from 1810 to 1940 the decennial censuses show a virtually uninterrupted decline in the ratio of young children under five to 1,000 white women twenty to forty-four years old (from 1,358 to 419, or 939 points). The bulk of this decline occurred in the nineteenth century (about 29 per cent before 1840 and 70 per cent before 1900) and was the result of falling birth rates among both urban and rural families.

The annual number of births increased, however, elevenfold between 1800 (about 280,000) and 1921 (about 3.1 million), because increases in the number of women of childbearing age more than offset the effect of the declining birth rate per woman. There was a gradual decline after the twenties to a low of 2.3 million in 1933; then followed a slow increase to 1940 (2.6 million); a sharp but fluctuating increase

[4] See Ronald Freedman, Pascal K. Whelpton and Arthur A. Campbell, *Family Planning, Sterility and Population Growth* (New York, 1959); Wilson H. Grabill, Clyde V. Kiser and Pascal K. Whelpton, *The Fertility of American Women* (New York, 1958); Charles F. Westoff, Robert G. Potter, Jr., and Philip C. Sagi, *The Third Child* (Princeton, N.J., 1963); Charles F. Westoff, Robert G. Potter, Jr., Philip C. Sagi and Elliot G. Mishler, *Family Growth in Metropolitan America* (Princeton, N.J., 1961); Pascal K. Whelpton, Arthur A. Campbell and John E. Patterson, *Fertility and Family Planning in the United States* (Princeton N.J., 1966); Pascal K. Whelpton and Clyde V. Kiser, eds., *Social and Psychological Factors Affecting Fertility*, vols. I-V (New York, 1946-58).

during the war years; record increases after 1945, reaching an annual average of somewhat over four million during the last ten years. Although the crude birth rate has gone down by more than one quarter since 1957, this does not in itself indicate a decline in fertility. The number of women available for childbearing during this period was relatively smaller (women born during the late twenties and Depression years); above all, there appears to have been a large transformation of the time pattern of childbearing, from a progressively earlier pattern in the previous decade to a progressively later pattern since 1960. This may presage an eventual drop in completed fertility; it probably does, but prediction in this regard is hazardous.

We have no adequate information on the fertility history of American Catholics and consequently cannot document the changes that may have occurred. Judging from numerous studies relating to desired family size, as well as reports on actual reproductive performance, we may safely conclude that among practicing-Catholic couples fertility is higher than among Protestants, Jews, and others; while all couples in all religious groups have apparently adjusted their reproductive patterns in the same direction to similar environmental changes, this reaction is less marked among Catholics than others. Thus, although they still marry considerably later than non-Catholics, they follow the current trend of marrying earlier than in the past; the majority desire family size below normal biological potential but significantly larger than other couples; compared class by class, with the exception of couples at the lowest socioeconomic levels, they tend to have larger completed families than others.

To what extent is the progressive lowering of the birth rate the result of positive intervention? There is no reliable information on the rate of abortion, though there is some evidence to suggest that it is relatively high in most urban centers and is probably coming to be used as a second line of defense in case of contraceptive failure. The current rate of surgical sterilization is also unknown. It is doubtful whether the rate is high among men, but a 1955 study, based on a scientific probability sample of all white married women between the ages of eighteen and thirty-nine inclusive, found that 6 per cent of the Catholics and 12 per cent of the Protestants interviewed were definitely sterile as the result of an operation.[5] These findings are only sugges-

[5] Ronald Freedman *et al.*

tive, for we are not informed what proportion of these operations were performed for the sole purpose of avoiding pregnancy.

Judging from the findings of a number of excellent national studies,[6] it seems that with the exception of the 10 per cent in the lower socioeconomic class the great majority of fertile non-Catholic couples now employ some form of contraceptive birth control either for spacing pregnancies or limiting family size. A fair percentage of Catholic couples are apparently following this general trend. Thus, although the proportion of all Catholic women attempting to regulate their fertility exclusively by the use of periodic continence changed very little between 1955 and 1965 (from 27 per cent to 25 per cent), the proportion who at one time or another during this period had used a method not in conformity with traditional Church doctrine increased from 30 per cent to 53 per cent. Stated in other terms, the proportion of married Catholic women aged eighteen to thirty-nine using no method of birth control declined from 43 per cent in 1955 to 22 per cent in 1965. Recent research shows a relatively widespread acceptance of the "pill," particularly among better educated young Protestant and Catholic couples, but it is too early to judge whether this indicates only a change in preferred means or a further reduction in completed family size.

To grasp the full implication of family limitation for Catholic couples we must understand the function that contraceptive birth control currently fulfills in the American social system. Early marriage, low infant and maternal mortality rates, increasing costs of child rearing, the relative isolation of the modern nuclear type family, the tendency to "bunch" or restrict pregnancies to the early years of marriage, and changing attitudes regarding the significance of marital relations, feminine roles, and parental responsibilities have made some form of family regulation inevitable. In the development of this situation the practice of contraceptive birth control functioned both as cause and solution; that is, given some need for family regulation, once contraceptive practice gained widespread social acceptance and use all the institutions and practices associated with sex and parenthood were adjusted and adapted to it. The practice became institutionalized—"geared" into the total social system as an integral part of its structure.

[6] In addition to the references given above on family planning, see William T. Liu, ed., *Family and Fertility* (Notre Dame, Ind., 1967).

Henceforth, "social equlibrium," the balance between institutionalized practices and accepted social goals, became established and maintained in terms of it. If it were removed or made morally unavailable, the whole social system would be thrown off balance.

This is precisely the situation in which Catholic couples find themselves in contemporary society. Because traditional Church doctrine prohibits them from attempting to maintain social equilibrium by employing contraceptives in the planning of their families, they tend to be thrown out of balance with the dominant culture and its institutional patterns. Given little practical assistance in working out their equilibrium in terms of their distinctive moral values—for even the permitted practice of rhythm was generally discouraged and is presently available on a relatively scientific basis only in limited areas—they are bound to feel frustrated and penalized because of their religious beliefs. At best, they experience considerable strain in striving to maintain their social position and provide for their growing families in an industrialized urban environment. As they move toward fuller conformity with dominant cultural trends relating to early marriage, family size, and the expanding goals of an affluent society while at the same time rejecting contraceptive practice, they find themselves caught in a series of contradictory needs and requirements.

PLURALISM AND THE CHALLENGES OF CHANGE

Considered in the wider cultural context of religious-minority survival, the problem of family planning may be regarded as a paradigm of the kinds of difficulties American Catholic couples can expect to encounter under present conditions of pluralism and change. Pluralism denotes the existence of marked differences in basic beliefs and values; change affects our social system at all levels: beliefs and values, institutions, and patterns of conduct. Although informed Catholics are aware that their religiously derived values relating to sex, marriage, and the family are not fully shared by the majority, they tend to overlook the fact that these values have definite social requirements or functional exigencies. These requirements include the entire complex of appropriate social conditions, relevant attitudes, motivations, and cross-sex relationships that both embody these values and foster their attainment in the practical order.

If Catholic couples fail to take cognizance of these requirements, they are bound to experience frustration and stress in trying to achieve their distinctive values, for the American social system within which they must live is by definition geared to the implementation and attainment of different values. Such failure acquires special significance in our rapidly changing society, for the entire web of relationships constituting the social framework of mutual expectancies and interactions within which couples develop and strive for fulfillment is constantly being modified. In making the necessary adjustment and adaptation it is not always easy to perceive what the long-range consequences may be. In other words, Catholic couples must be aware that they may not thoughtlessly "follow the crowd" if they wish to preserve their distinctive values.

If developing and maintaining integrated programs of action were the only challenge facing Catholics, one might assume that appropriate changes in religious education, together with more active promotion of current family movements such as Cana and CFM (Christian Family Movement), would probably supply all the help needed. But the problem of family planning and the other problems we have discussed present a much more crucial challenge, for they call into question some significant elements of traditional Church teaching relating to sex and marriage. Until very recently, it was rather generally assumed that the Church's teaching on the purposes of marriage and the right use of sex was substantially unchangeable. Through cumulative effort down through the ages moral theologians and canon lawyers had worked out the solutions to all possible contingencies, with the result that Catholic couples knew clearly what was expected of them in their marriage vocation, while religious teachers felt sure that the beliefs, values, and norms they transmitted to the faithful of each generation were solidly founded on revelation, tradition, and authoritative pronouncements.

During the past few years the climate of opinion in this regard has changed radically. For example, an analysis of current discussions regarding the morality of birth control shows that the entire context of moral discourse—that is, the entire conceptual framework of beliefs, attitudes, and reasonings within which such moral problems were formerly defined and resolved—has been profoundly affected by several major forces currently operative in both Western society and the Church. Indeed, some of the family difficulties we have discussed are already beginning to be regarded as problematical, in the sense that significant moral elements in our traditional frame of reference are now being questioned. This implies that we can gain some insight into the future of the American Catholic family only if we understand the relevant forces shaping contemporary moral trends.

One of the most significant of these forces is the ongoing confrontation between the traditional Judeo-Christian ethos or way of looking at man, nature, and society and the rapidly emerging rationalist, scientific, "secular" (no transcendental referents) ethos fostered implicitly or explicitly by modern man "come of age," to use Bonhoeffer's phrase. The significance of this confrontation stems from the fact that although the emerging secular ethos leads to the abandonment of the traditional beliefs and credibilities underpinning society's institutions and normative standards and supplying its moral energy, it provides no alternative unitary system of common beliefs to replace it. Modern industrial society's twin goals of efficient production and technological exploration, with their associated requirements of increasing organization and specialization, not only provide no criteria for the optimal or the ethically permissible, but no set of ideas or ideals presenting a convincing world-image with which modern man "come of age," and modern youth in particular, can identify.

The result is unthinking accommodation to the demands of the current "establishment" on the part of many; a retreat to a kind of wishful utopian humanism on the part of some; the assumption of a no-illusions-and-no-commitments stance on the part of a growing minority. All are more or less deeply conditioned by the preceding "enlightened" generation that systematically made light of all settled convictions and substituted a pragmatic philosophy of impulse release for the doctrines of self-denial and self-discipline traditionally designed to assure co-operation in the attainment of common goals. In short, doctrines of renunciatory control governing releases from impulse were replaced by doctrines of impulse release enjoining uninhibited self-expression. This has led to questioning all contemporary forms of authority, as well as to a type of hedonism expressed in a demand for unlimited and unpostponed sentient or sensory, rather than creative, experience.

The second force reflects the post-Vatican II confrontation between two mentalities within the Church; that is, between a mentality based on the classical, relatively static, scholastic view of man, nature, and truth and a mentality that takes a more dynamic, developmental view of these realities because it is based on a more adequate understanding of man's place in both sacred and secular history and on an increasing awareness of the cultural limitations inherent in all human approaches to truth. To grasp the full import of this clash of mentalities within the Church we must view it against the broader cultural backdrop mentioned above, for it is occurring at the very time that members of the Catholic minority, through extensive spatial and social mobility, are moving toward full participation in American society and consequent complex exposure to dominant cultural trends. In other words, the current controversy within the Church is so significant because it calls in question many past formulations of beliefs, moral directives, and ecclesiastical structures just as Catholic couples are beginning to experience the full impact of their increasingly secularized environment.

This is not meant to imply that we regard present theological developments as either untimely or unfruitful, though we must admit that they are tardy. With a keener awareness of the historical dimensions of man's quest for religious understanding, as well as of the necessarily culture-bound limitations of all formal conceptualizations of religious beliefs, should come a deeper recognition of the pedagogical character of God's continuing dialogue with his people, and more particularly, of the dynamic quality of the operations of the Holy Spirit in promoting the progressive enlightenment of the faithful through time. This development constitutes a positive theological enrichment; yet it must be admitted that to the extent that it calls in question the adequacy and absolute certainty formerly attributed to past doctrinal pronouncements, it runs counter to what Catholic couples have uniformly been taught. Unless this point is fully understood, it is bound to remain a source of serious confusion.

Moreover, when controversy involves a confrontation of two distinct mentalities, whether these are the Judeo-Christian and secular ethos in the Western world or the classically static and the historical-minded dynamic approaches within the Church, little real dialogue is possible. Because the parties to the controversy do not share a common universe of discourse, although they may use the same terms they tend to talk past each other. For example, words such as "freedom," "fulfillment," "commitment," "authority," "law," and "love" are frequently used as self-evident terms, yet their meaning depends on the total frame of reference within which they are used. Thus, in spite of the spate of books, articles, and discussions on religion that followed Vatican II, the overall result, considered from the viewpoint of the average Christian, appears to be confusion. In particular, Catholic couples raised in a system of religious indoctrination geared to foster the faithful acceptance of an authoritatively defined creed, cult, and code are puzzled by the variety of opinions and views expressed or tolerated by those whom they were taught to regard as religious leaders; furthermore, they are urged to make important moral decisions for which very little in their previous religious training has prepared them.

Viewed against this backdrop of opposing mentalities within the Church and society, it is predictable that Pope Paul's recent restatement of the Church's traditional stand concerning the morality of contraceptive birth control will be regarded as a reassuring clarification by some and a troublesome anachronism by others. Future historians will probably note that the statement was irrelevant, the "last hurrah" of a school of thought that has persistently refused to develop an integrated Christian view of human sexuality. A review of the development of family limitation in the Western world during the past two centuries indicates clearly that once the need to regulate family size becomes obvious and religious leaders fail to provide feasible directives the majority of concerned couples simply take matters into their own hands and have recourse to whatever means are available at the time. Although this fact may be dismissed as little more than the result of human weakness, it may also be regarded as a clear indication of the failure of religious thinkers to provide an interpretation of sex, love, and marriage consonant with the Gospel and the current human condition.

Considered from the viewpoint of the Church as the People of God, the recent papal statement raises a number of basic questions that extend far beyond the immediate problem of contraceptive birth control. The crucial issue it brings to the forefront of Christian awareness is the nature, form, and extent of authoritative teaching within the Church. During the past 150 years there has been a concerted effort to emphasize the supremacy of the pope and the various organizational structures included under the term "Holy See." Vatican II attempted to counterbalance this trend by reintegrating the bishops into the teaching structure of the Church under the rubric of "collegiality," but the effort obviously failed.

In its preparation, content, and promulgation the recent papal statement not only makes nonsense of collegiality, but ignores the inspiration of the Holy Spirit among the People of God as expressed in the thinking of the vast majority of professional theologians and married couples. Although this important statement was without precedent in being issued during the normally inactive summer-vacations period, when seminaries are closed and scholars dispersed, the major lines of clerical reaction in this country became rapidly discernible. The hierarchy submitted with various shades of enthusiasm; a relatively large contingent of clerical teachers and theologians reacted negatively; a good number of the active clergy appeared dismayed and further demoralized; a fair segment preferred not to discuss the matter for the time being; a few did not hesitate to remark, "I told you so!"

For the most part these mixed clerical reactions were to be expected, and some of their negative aspects may even prove to be ephemeral. In any case, it appears that the statement will not be officially challenged in theory. What about practice? Here teaching authority encounters a new climate of opinion. In contemporary society the problem of family regulation intimately affects a large proportion of the faithful. It involves a number of not easily postponable normal human wants. According to the Council Fathers of Vatican II, long continued sexual abstinence when necessitated by the need to limit family size may jeopardize the major purposes of marriage. For almost a decade the basic issues have been widely discussed and the Church's traditional stand has been seriously questioned. Each individual's personal responsibility for commitment, involvement, and decision has been widely stressed. Under these conditions it seems safe to predict that a fair number of clergy and laity will insist on the right to form their own consciences in this regard. Yet such a solution involves a contradiction, for it leaves unresolved the basic issue regarding the nature, form and extent of the Church's teaching authority; as presently defined, this teaching authority as vested in the pope constitutes an essential component in the formation of a Christian's conscience. All things considered the immediate future is bound to be profoundly disturbing.

We will not hazard an estimate of the long-range consequences for the American Catholic family in this, hopefully, transitional period of confusion and uncertainty. Although many adult Catholics may question various aspects of the present ecclesiastical establishment, the majority will probably persevere in the faith of their childhood. But what of the coming generation? What beliefs and values should parents transmit to their children? What normative standards relating to religious practice and sexual conduct should they enforce? What position should they take in regard to mixed marriage, divorce, and remarriage?

Rather than attempt to guess at the future, let us restate the challenge. Granted that the family functions as the primary communicator of a religious minority's distinctive beliefs, values and practices, and that parents teach primarily by the ideals and convictions they model and reflect in their attitudes and actions, what happens when parents are no longer clear about the distinctiveness of their beliefs or no longer convinced that preserving this distinctiveness is worth the costs under conditions of pluralism?

10: RELIGIOUS EDUCATION AND SEMINARY STUDIES: SOME RECENT TRENDS

Louis J. Putz, C.S.C.

Everything in the Church seems to be turning topsy-turvy these days, and catechetics, religious education, and seminary studies are no exceptions. No clear-cut pattern has yet emerged from the general ferment, but certain new trends are discernible. Or perhaps it would be more accurate to call them new impulses—gusts of thought and energy which move across the scene like fresh breezes and set all the rigging aflutter but lack the strength and steadiness to permit free sailing. This is somewhat the situation in which religious education finds itself today: No longer becalmed, it is not yet sure of its new course.

In recent years religious education has been dominated by the task of presenting the basic message of salvation history to students in Catholic elementary and secondary schools—and even in colleges. A great variety of new manuals were devised, used for a while, and then replaced by others as the effort to meet this task continued. We have gone through a whole series of different strategies, none of which quite met the expectations that had been aroused. Along with many another professor of "religion," I can recall teaching the catechism in college classes twenty-five years ago. Then we switched to a fairly extensive religion course based largely on theology manuals. This in turn was dropped in favor of almost exclusive study of Scripture. But we were still failing to get the message across, so to arouse student interest we adopted a problem-centered approach. Here, however, so much depended on the individual ability of the teacher that the new method left many people more frustrated than ever.

In the search for the most effective approach, the task of the Catholic religious educator became greater than ever, because we finally realized that fewer than half of those who need instruction are being reached by the Catholic schools. Now, with the Catholic school system over-extended and in disarray, the effort to reach the public-school youngster takes the highest priority. It should always have been so. But this kind of catechetical work received very little emphasis as long as the goal was to bring every Catholic child into a Catholic school. With the overcrowded buildings, shortage of teachers, and financial problems of the last few years, even the most stubborn have been forced to acknowledge the inescapable limitations of Catholic schools. We simply have to go where the people are. This means seeking out the public-school students. It also means adult education to assist parents in providing religious instruction at home. The necessity for new departures in all these directions is widely recognized by Catholic-school officials. As a spokesman for the National Catholic Educational Association put it: "An approach that in practice treats Catholic schools as the only medium of Catholic education not only fails to deal with present-day realities but in effect locks the educational program of the Church into an inefficient pattern of increasing neglect of those whom Catholic education should serve."[1]

Many of the factors at work in Catholic education are also making themselves felt in seminary studies. The Second Vatican Council, the new liturgy, and the striking upsurge in social concern among young people all require that we rethink and restructure seminary programs. For one thing, theology and philosophy have to be brought together rather than studied in tightly sealed-off compartments. The work of St. Thomas himself is a marvelous example of how theology can flourish in confronting all the speculative problems of an age. The example unhappily has not been followed in the theological and philosophical manuals that have traditionally furnished the seminarian's staple intellectual fare. The writers of these works adverted to modern thinkers only to discredit them from a biased defensive position. The whole enterprise was apologetical; there was no real effort to enter into the minds of modern philosophers and theologians and understand what they were saying about the needs of contemporary man. Small wonder that seminary studies had drifted dangerously out of touch with the world of today.

In addition to a livelier awareness of contemporary philosophical and theological currents, there is a growing emphasis on the seminarian's

[1] Russell Shaw, "Breaking Down the Walls in Catholic Education," *America*, CXVIII (Jan. 20, 1968), 72-73.

formation for pastoral work. Implied here is the need to learn more about people, individually and collectively; for if a man is ignorant of how people think and act, he cannot effectively present to them the message of salvation no matter how deeply he may understand and treasure it himself. Hence subjects like psychology, anthropology, and sociology are taking on new importance in the seminaries.

So also are Scripture studies and patristics. We thought we knew Scripture and Tradition in the past; actually we lacked a deep understanding of the message conveyed by the Bible and the Fathers. As greater historical and archeological learning enriches our insight into the real meaning of the authors of Scripture we are less inclined to use their words as proof texts, or to try bending them to fit our traditional theological formulations. And history also contributes to a fuller understanding of how theological positions and dogmatic formulas change and develop through time. Far from being disconcerting, the historical approach to doctrine and theology opens up fascinating vistas for research and invites us to discover or create that particular expression of our faith that accords with the thought and temper of our own age.

The historical approach is rather difficult to reconcile with a theological mentality that was only too familiar in the past, the mentality which held that Catholics already had the final answers to all the questions that really matter; the know-it-all mentality which regarded the theology absorbed in the seminary as unchangingly true, adequate, and sufficient for a lifetime. This point of view is now definitely out of step with the times and rapidly being left behind, but we must inquire what system produced the cocksure cleric with all the answers and the ever vigilant theologian who reported to Rome the slightest deviation from received opinion.

CHARACTERISTICS OF THE OLD SYSTEM

The modern historical approach to truth contrasts sharply with the static, conceptualist mode characteristic of the era we are now leaving behind. According to the conceptualist understanding, truth existed independently of the knowing subject; the act of knowing consisted in the discovery, appropriation, and assimilation by the human mind of this ready-made, objective truth. In the area of theology and faith, the surest source of truth was the *magisterium* of the Church. The truth to be accepted by the believer and taught by the religious educator was derived from the Church's *magisterium*, which was regarded as being embodied in theology manuals that were approved by the proper authorities and backed up ultimately by the Holy Office, the guardian of orthodoxy and truth. The notion that openness to reality is necessary to arrive at truth, or that the searcher for truth himself has a part to play in its development, was completely foreign to the old mentality. Development in theology could take place only in the sense that the same truth, while remaining unchanged, might be applied differently in different times and places, with perhaps an incidental touching-up of previous formulations.

This kind of rigidly static conception of theological verities killed all curiosity and spontaneity—and all possibility of genuine theological research. It made the Holy Office in Rome the source and arbiter of orthodoxy; the theologian who departed from the officially approved dogmatic or moral teachings was immediately suspect. Even the slightest divergence from doctrine traditionally conceived was enough to raise the specter of Modernism, the heresy condemned in 1907 by Pope St. Pius X.

Obviously, this closed mentality ruled out the investigation of theological controversies which made modern Protestant research interesting and exciting. Catholic theologians talked only to themselves, and were very careful about how they did that. Having lost touch with modern developments, their work became less relevant even to Catholics; for Catholics, after all, do live in the twentieth century and have to confront contemporary problems—with or without help from their theologians. It is quite understandable that the Council fathers had such a difficult time at Vatican II trying to draw up the Constitution on the Church and the Modern World. We simply have not had a theology of the modern world. The failure to have reflected on the problems posed by our own times accounts for the inadequacies of the Council's decree on communications, one of the weakest documents produced at Vatican II.

Charles Davis comments on some of these points in his controversial book, *A Question of Conscience*:

> An hierarchical teaching authority rests upon a view of truth as static, just as hierarchical orders in general presuppose a view of society as static. The deposit of faith is regarded as an unchanging

timeless body of truth, capable of being definitely formulated in authoritative statements imposed as irrevocable. Christian tradition in what concerns its essential preservation and transmission is taken out of the hands of the community as whole and given to a special class empowered to decide any controversial question. Any role assigned to the community must, despite the increasing stress upon such a role, be kept essentially subordinate to the hierarchy and is controlled by it. This removes the Christian tradition from the context of open questioning by the community of believers. . . .[2]

Although Charles Davis may not be an altogether satisfactory guide or authority on the subject of the hierarchical system in the Church, there is an important kernel of truth in what he says about the effects on doctrinal development when faith "is taken out of the hands of the community as a whole and given to a special class empowered to decide any controversial question." This results, all too easily, in a fortress mentality, a fondness for sniffing out error rather than searching for truth. One cannot but regret the inhibitions the old attitude laid on theological speculation. And it is even more sad to recall the treatment accorded genuine pioneers in Catholic theology before Vatican II: men like Yves Congar, Henri de Lubac, Karl Rahner, and Pierre Teilhard de Chardin who were disciplined, or under a cloud, because they dared to express some new ideas. But as the mention of these names reminds us, new ideas were stirring in the years before the Council.

PRECONCILIAR BREAKTHROUGHS

Long before Vatican II sent tremors through the Catholic world, certain significant developments had taken place in the American Church which prepared the way for renewal. Interest in the racial apostolate and the problems of the cities did not make headlines, but there was a steady growth through such agencies as the Friendship House movement and Catholic Interracial Councils, discussed in other chapters of this book. These activities brought together Catholics and those of other faiths interested in the same problems, and generated fruitful religious dialogue. The appeals of Pope John XXIII for Catholics in the United States to devote themselves to the apostolate to Latin

[2] Charles Davis, *A Question of Conscience* (New York, 1967), p. 242.

America stimulated greater interest in that area; new energies were mobilized through the annual meetings of the Catholic Inter-American Cooperation Program (CICOP). Even earlier, Catholic labor schools and the Association of Catholic Trade Unionists (ACTU) focussed attention on the problems of labor and on the social encyclicals. American Catholics were still mightily preoccupied with building churches and schools, but a number of twentieth-century churchmen like Bishop Francis J. Haas and priests associated with the Social Action Department of the NCWC—notably John A. Ryan, Raymond A. McGowan, and George G. Higgins—devoted themselves to contemporary social problems. So did a number of other priests closer to the rank and file, such as Charles Owen Rice of Pittsburgh, Raymond Clancy, the longtime chaplain of ACTU, and Clement Kern, the apostle of Detroit's skid row. Numerous lay people were also involved in the same kind of work, especially under the inspiring leadership of Peter Maurin, Dorothy Day, and their Catholic Worker movement. There were few spectacular achievements, to be sure, but these people were a constant affliction to the comfortable and a thorn in the side of triumphalist Catholicism.

The liturgical movement had a larger following and perhaps greater acceptance among members of the hierarchy. Under the leadership of the Benedictine Virgil Michel and his successor, Godfrey Diekmann, at St. John's Abbey in Minnesota—and with assists from priests like Martin Hellriegel, H. A. Reinhold, and Michael A. Mathis, C.S.C.—the liturgists prepared an elite for the radical changes that took place with surprising speed after the Council. There was no widespread demand for changes from the average man in the pew, but enough interest had been awakened by the annual liturgical conferences to create a climate favorable to the acceptance of reforms. The movement had also developed centers of publication, especially the Liturgical Press at St. John's Abbey, that were ready to bring out the revised office books and vernacular materials for congregational use when the reforms went into effect. The magazine *Worship*—founded by Virgil Michel in 1926 and then called *Orate Fratres*—was likewise on hand to serve as a forum for scholarly discussions of theological and liturgical questions.

The gradual growth of an apostolically minded laity went hand in hand with the liturgical movement and the development of social consciousness among American Catholics. The specialized Catholic Action movements discussed in chapter fourteen, particularly the Christian Family Movement, were precursors of the People of God concept which was to be the central theme of the Second Vatican Council. The educated and aware lay people involved in these movements wanted a proper role of their own in the work of the Church, rather than merely the status of helpers of the clergy. Even now we are without the sort of structures which would enable the layman to take his proper place in the Church and permit easy communication between the bishops and the People of God, but the spadework done by lay organizations in the pre-Vatican II decades points the way to a realistic approach to the task. The contrast between the strongly clericalized character of the Church along the Atlantic seaboard and the much more flexible structures of the Midwest (especially in the Archdiocese of Chicago, where the lay movements were most active) suggests the extent to which these movements may shape the social structures of the Church.

But changing traditional patterns is a slow business, and for a long time the influences tending toward change move below the surface. When shifts do become visible, the first impression the observer gets may be one of confusion; for while the old ways no longer seem satisfactory, it is not always immediately clear which new approaches will replace them. It will be helpful to keep this consideration in mind as we turn to a closer look at the area of religious education.

RELIGION COURSES AND THEOLOGICAL STIRRINGS

For a very long time, our faithful stand-by in religious education was the Baltimore Catechism. First published in the year following the Third Plenary Council of Baltimore in 1884 and revised in 1941, it was the indispensable piece of equipment both at home and at school for generations of American Catholics.[3] Besides being the cornerstone

[3] For a sketch of the origin and revision of the Baltimore Catechism see Francis J. Connell, C.SS.R., "Catechism Revision," in *The Confraternity Comes of Age; A Historical Symposium* (Paterson, N.J., 1956), pp. 189-201. Cf. also Josef Andreas Jungmann, *Handing on the Faith: A Manual of Catechetics*, trans. A. N. Fuerst (New York, 1959), pp. 35-36.

of religious education, the Baltimore Catechism also served in effect as the Bible for the great majority of American Catholics. For although Pope Leo XIII encouraged reading of the Bible in his *Providentissimus Deus* (1893), few Catholics developed the habit; nor were they systematically exhorted to do so. The passages of Scripture read at Mass and often commented on by the priest in his sermon constituted their acquaintance with the word of God. The average Catholic was certainly more familiar with the Catechism, which was his basic religion textbook from the primary grades on up, than with the Bible.

After World War II, when interest in religious education quickened, more elaborate materials came into use. High-school teachers of religion, who were almost desperate with the old methods, turned enthusiastically to the Quest for Happiness books, a four-volume series edited by Clarence E. Elwell and others.[4] Another series that appeared in the 1950's, the Christian Life books of Sister Jane Marie Murray, O.P., was published by the apostolate-oriented Fides Publishers Association and reflected some of the emphases described in the preceding section.[5]

Teaching religion in the colleges has naturally been closely related to theological trends in the United States. The revival of Thomism in the twentieth century made itself strongly felt, especially through the influence of the four-volume *Companion to the Summa* of Walter Farrell, O.P.[6] This work, adopted in many colleges in the 1940's, was described in the preface as not about the *Summa Theologica* of St. Thomas, but as "the *Summa* itself reduced to popular language." The Dominicans, who were particularly devoted to Thomism, had few colleges themselves but priests from that order served as teachers of theology in about seventy other colleges, and a hundred Catholic institutions adopted a series of theology textbooks published by the Priory Press of the Dominicans in Dubuque, Iowa.[7] Between 1952 and 1955, another influential teaching order, the Jesuits, published a four-volume series under the general title, *Theology: a Course for College*

[4] C. E. Elwell *et al.*, *Our Quest for Happiness; the Story of Divine Love*, 4 vols. (Chicago, 1945-46).

[5] Sister Jane Marie Murray, *The Christian Life Series*, 4 vols. (Chicago, 1957-58).

[6] Walter Farrell, A *Companion to the Summa*, 4 vols. (New York, 1938-42).

[7] For the Dominican approach see Reginald Masterson, O.P., ed., *Theology in the Catholic College* (Dubuque, 1961).

Students.[8] At almost the same time, the University of Notre Dame Press put out the University Religion Series—four textbooks by Holy Cross priests for use in college theology courses.[9]

These works, which were essentially seminary theology manuals adapted for the use of lay students, held their own strongly through the 1950's. But further changes were already making themselves felt. For one thing, priests were losing the virtual monopoly they had heretofore enjoyed in teaching religion. The Religious Education Department established at the Catholic University of America in 1936 and brought to a high level of distinction under Father Gerard S. Sloyan did much to give the subject a professional academic orientation and to open it up to sisters and lay people as well as priests. The Graduate School of Theology at St. Mary's College (Notre Dame, Indiana) was established in 1944 and accepted lay women as well as sisters who wished to prepare themselves as teachers of theology. Summer schools in theology followed in most of the major Catholic institutions, and the popularity of books like Frank Sheed's *Theology and Sanity* (1946) demonstrated that a layman could write theology that other laymen were interested in reading.

At the same time as awareness of the liturgical movement was growing, there were the stirrings of new interest in biblical research, and we began to hear about "salvation history." And with the renewal led by Pope John the field of religious education opened out in ecumenical and secular directions. For the first time the rank and file of Catholic religious educators acquainted themselves with the vast literature, previously untouched by Catholics, issuing from Protestant sources. Very few theologians had kept professionally abreast of Protestant thought. Only a handful of men, like the Jesuits Gustave Weigel and John Courtney Murray, had ventured into this foreign territory. Today no one who seriously contemplates religious teaching would think

[8] The Jesuit series was developed from a freshman theology course sketched out by John Courtney Murray, S.J., in the early 1940's. See the "Acknowledgment" in John J. Fernan, S.J., *Christ as Prophet and King* (Syracuse, 1952). Cf. also the remarks of Gerard S. Sloyan in Josef Andreas Jungmann, S.J., *The Good News Yesterday and Today*, trans. W. A. Huesman, S.J., ed. J. Hofinger, S.J. (New York and Chicago, 1962), p. 218.

[9] These works, all published at Notre Dame, Ind., are: Joseph H. Cavanaugh, C.S.C., *Evidence for Our Faith* (1949); Charles E. Sheedy, C.S.C. *The Christian Virtues* (1949); Theodore M. Hesburgh, C.S.C., *God and the World of Man* (1950); and Albert Schlitzer, C.S.C., *Redemptive Incarnation* (1953).

of doing so without some study of Paul Tillich, Karl Barth, Rudolph Bultmann, Reinhold Niebuhr, Oscar Cullmann, Martin Buber, and so on.

The dialogue has now begun and it augurs well for the future of both Catholic theology and religious education in the United States. In the recent past, the best religious thought has come from German universities where Catholic and Protestant faculties of theology exist side by side. The University of Tübingen, for example, can point to men of the stature of Bultmann among Protestants, and Karl Adam and Hans Küng among Catholics. Karl Barth himself testifies that of all theologians, Küng is the one who has best understood Barth's theory of justification. And it can hardly be doubted that one of the principal reasons men like Rahner, Congar, de Lubac and Edward Schillebeeckx were able to make such great contributions to the Vatican Council was that they had studied deeply the theological and biblical research of Protestant scholars.

The writings of European theologians, both Catholic and Protestant, have found an enthusiastic reading audience in this country in the years since *aggioramento* got under way. These men have also spoken widely and taken part in numerous conferences on American Catholic campuses. This sort of interchange has improved the theological climate significantly; for one thing, it stimulated Catholic writers to explore new approaches, since they found that their Protestant confreres were in no way impressed by the seminary-manual type of theology that used to be the order of the day.

Catholic theologians, biblical scholars, and religious philosophers are also finding their way to Protestant and secular institutions. Not long ago *America* magazine featured reports on such Catholic scholars on non-Catholic campuses.[10] Temple University's program in religious studies, for example, has drawn Father Sloyan from Catholic University and Leonard Swidler (formerly of Duquesne University), coeditor of the *Journal of Ecumenical Studies*. A similar cross-fertilization of personnel is taking place on Catholic theological faculties. Both an Orthodox priest and a Jewish rabbi have recently taught at Notre Dame, and the theology faculty will add a Mennonite theologian in

[10] "Catholic Professors on the Secular Campus," *America*, CXV (Sept. 24, 1966), 318-23. This report consists of statements by two lay scholars, Michael Novak and Barry Ulanov, and four priests: Roland Murphy, O. Carm., Joseph Fichter, S.J., Robert McNally, S.J., and David Stanley, S.J.

1968-69. In addition, the university will administer two large-scale ecumenical institutes in theology and religious studies which are now in the process of being established, one on its own campus and another in Jerusalem. I can personally recall only ten years ago being denied permission to invite a Protestant minister to speak before the Advent Symposium sponsored by the National Federation of Catholic College Students. What a change in a decade's time!

Ecumenical collaboration is perhaps most advanced right now in the field of biblical studies. Biblical research has been a Protestant monopoly for a century, and the usual Catholic reaction ranged from strong suspicion of heretical tendencies to outright condemnation. Today, however, the notion that "demythologizing" Scripture is necessary is widely accepted among Catholic biblical students. This sort of freedom for Catholic scholars is of recent date. Had it not been for the intervention of Cardinal Augustin Bea, the head of the Biblical Commission in Rome who enjoyed the confidence of Pope Pius XII, the whole of modern biblical scholarship might well have been condemned in the encyclical *Humani Generis* of 1950. At the same time, we should note that collaboration between Catholic and Protestant biblical scholars was going on long before Vatican II. Such was the case at the renowned center for biblical studies at Jerusalem founded by the Dominican priest, Marie Joseph Lagrange, in 1890; and men of the stature of W. F. Albright and Roland de Vaux, O.P., found confessional differences no barrier to their shared concerns as scholars. The effort to understand the word of God that was their common heritage helped to bring together Christians from various denominational traditions; hence, biblical scholars anticipated in practice the ecumenical collaboration that has become a general prescription since the Council.

CATECHETICS

Ecumenical and biblical emphases have emerged strongly since World War II among American Catholics interested in religious education. The ecumenical dimension is illustrated in Catholic participation since the late 1940's in the activities of the Religious Education Association, an organization established by American Protestant groups in 1903. A general catechetical revival, strongly influenced by new kerygmatic and salvation-history approaches worked out by biblical scholars, made itself felt both in Europe and the United States around the time of the Second World War. In the following two decades these became the dominant themes.

The Confraternity of Christian Doctrine (CCD) is the principal official organization within the American Church charged with the task of religious education.[11] Pope St. Pius X is considered the patron of this organization, which he ordered established in every parish early in this century. A few years later, parochial organization of the CCD was made obligatory under canon law, and was further specified by Pope Pius XI in 1935. Although it had its beginnings in this country around World War I, the CCD became a national movement only in the 1930's. By 1935 it had been placed under the guidance of a committee of the hierarchy and made a bureau of the NCWC; in the same year it sponsored the first national catechetical congress held in the United States. Archbishop Edwin V. O'Hara, ordinary of the diocese of Kansas City, Missouri (1939-56), was the outstanding leader of the CCD and chairman of the episcopal committee until his death in 1956. Under his leadership the main effort of the CCD was directed toward reaching Catholic children not in parochial schools and providing them with religious instruction on weekends and in vacation schools. The Baltimore Catechism was the mainstay of instruction in the early phases of the CCD's work, but it also sponsored the publication of the Confraternity translation of the Bible in 1941, the sale of which (one-million copies of the New Testament by 1945) astonished the editors.

Although the biblical orientation had not yet taken root in the CCD at that time, the favorable reception of the Confraternity translation pointed the way toward developments that were to become more popular in he 1950's and 1960's. The background of the new catechetical approach was European. German-speaking scholars took an early interest in catechetics, with Munich and Innsbruck as especially important centers of research and writing. In the early 1940's, a group of Belgian Jesuits established the International Center for Studies in Religious Education, first at Louvain and then at Brussels. This center, better known as Lumen Vitae, always stressed the international aspects

[11] For the development of the CCD see *The Confraternity Comes of Age*. Jungmann, *Handing on the Faith*, pp. 1-78, gives "The History of Catechesis" from apostolic times to the present. See pp. 34-35, 40-49, for developments in the U.S.

of the need for catechetical renewal. Its activities were very important in diffusing and popularizing the message of catechetical reform in the United States. The Belgian center's journal, *Lumen Vitae*, which began publication in 1946, appears in an English-language edition; the book *Faith and Commitment*, edited by Mark J. Link, S.J., of Loyola University in Chicago, made available in convenient form more than a score of articles which were published in *Lumen Vitae* in the 1950's and '60's.[12] The Religious Education Department at the Catholic University likewise transmitted the findings and methods of European catechists to this country. Summer-school programs elsewhere contributed to the effort. At Notre Dame, for example, the liturgist Father Mathis brought in scholars like the Jesuits Josef A. Jungmann and Johannes Hofinger during the summer; the Notre Dame Press also published Hofinger's *The Art of Teaching Christian Doctrine* and a separate Contemporary Catechetics Series, of which ten volumes have so far appeared.[13] Various orders of teaching sisters also devoted themselves to the work. For example, the Sisters Servants of the Immaculate Heart of Mary of Monroe, Michigan, have been very active; their work, carried on in conjunction with the University of Detroit, is modelled on the Lumen Vitae approach. By 1964 the catechetical movement had gained sufficient momentum that a high level quarterly devoted to religious education, the *Living Light*, began publication under the auspices of the National Center of the Confraternity of Christian Doctrine in Washington. The executive editor of this journal, incidentally, is Mary Perkins Ryan, a prominent critic of the traditional approach to religious education through the Catholic schools.

The "catechetical revolution" of which all of these activities were a part owed much to the work in the 1930's of Josef A. Jungmann, S.J. As Father Sloyan puts it, Jungmann showed that "the [Christian]

[12] Mark J. Link, S.J., ed., *Faith and Commitment* (Chicago, 1964).

[13] Johannes Hofinger, S.J., *The Art of Teaching Christian Doctrine* (Notre Dame, Ind., 1957; rev. ed., 1962). Hofinger has described this book as "the first manual in English for priests and catechists which gave a detailed account of the kerygmatic approach to Christian doctrine, together with a systematic exposition of the Christian message." See Hofinger, "The Place of the Good News in Modern Catechetics," in Jungmann, *The Good News Yesterday and Today*, p. 181. The volumes in the Notre Dame catechetics series are short inexpensive paperbacks by European (mostly German) catechists.

message and its mode of coming to us, both in history and in mystery, always determine the basic method of its presentation."[14] Traditional American Catholic religious instruction, based on the Baltimore Catechism, did not accord at all with this dictum, for what it did was abstract the conceptual substance of faith from its biblical and historical matrix and present it in schematic form, organized along the lines of creed, code, and cult. Inevitably, the emphasis came to be placed on systematic intellectual mastery of this body of doctrine. This catechetical method was quite in keeping with the rigid conceptualist mentality of American Catholic theology and philosophy which prevailed until very recent times. Conversely, the new catechetical approach was linked to the biblical and historical emphases which have been gaining ground so rapidly in recent years. The new approach stressed salvation history—the story of God's dealings with man in the Old Testament and the proclamation of Good News of salvation by Jesus Christ. The aim of religious education was not so much to give the student merely an intellectual grasp of certain doctrines, but to enable him to understand and assimilate in a more integral and personal way the meaning of the story of God's saving action in history and to form him as a member of the Christian community.

The formation of members of the Christian community was also a principal aim of those interested in liturgical renewal, hence the new catechetics, the biblical renewal, and dedication to liturgical reform all went hand in hand. These new perspectives and approaches tremendously enriched and improved religious education, and it is understandable if those involved in the catechetical revolution sometimes seemed to feel that all the basic difficulties had been surmounted and that only a more thorough prosecution of what they were already doing was required for complete success. We can now see that things are not that simple. In part, the problems spring from the degree of acceptance the salvation-history approach has won. For this reason the catechetical renewal finds itself today at a sort of dead center in spite of—or perhaps even because of—the successes it has attained.

[14] Gerard S. Sloyan in *New Catholic Encyclopedia*, 15 vols. (New York, 1967), III, 225. Jungmann, *The Good News Yesterday and Today* is an abridged translation of Jungmann's classic work of 1936, *Die Frohbotschaft und Unsere Glaubensverkündigung*, along with four evaluative essays on its importance, of which the most pertinent here is Father Sloyan's contribution, "The Good News and the Catechetical Scene in the United States," pp. 211-28.

Two interlinked problems can be noted. The first is the need on the part of catechists to overcome an antitheological bias. The bias developed naturally enough since the old-fashioned catechetical approach was part and parcel of the old theology; indeed, the Baltimore Catechism was a pocket version of the whole traditional theological system. Reform-minded religious educators developed a generalized distaste for theological speculation because it seemed "that catechetics began to make advances [only] when it separated itself from an encrusted theological system and began to speak in simple terms of God's plan of salvation presented in Scripture and liturgy."[15] Although this attitude may have been understandable and even justifiable in the earlier phases of the movement in this country, it is a decided handicap to further progress now. Theology has been renewed too, and the catechetical movement has a very real need of the guidance that a renewed theology can give it.

The religious educator's need for a deeper appreciation of contemporary theology is related to a weakness of the salvation-history approach which has become more noticeable in the past few years. The problem is that salvation history tends to focus on the past, whereas the student who lives in the present is preoccupied with the issues of our own time—with the relevance of God and faith to the contemporary questions of freedom, authenticity, and human dignity and value. It is true, of course, that salvation history is presented as something which is still going on in our own time, something in which the Christian community and humankind at large are still involved. Nonetheless, revelation—the official record, as it were, of God's transactions with man in human history—is held to have been completed with the last book of the New Testament.

The difficulties in applying in the present what has been assimilated from a story essentially completed ages ago have been pointed out by Brother Gabriel Moran, F.S.C., an outstanding American catechist and student of the theology of revelation. In an article addressed to religious educators and entitled "The Time for a Theology," Brother Gabriel writes:

> The Christian student is thus encouraged to live in the present except that his mind must be pointed backward to where all the

[15] Brother Gabriel Moran, F.S.C., "The Time for a Theology," *The Living Light*, III (Summer, 1966), 7-8.

> revealed truths are. This is an unhappy situation for the Christian, but it is hardest of all upon schools and religion classes whose function, one would suppose, is to raise the level of understanding in order to set men free. Schools cannot exercise their function unless they are allowed to focus on the real world of men and events and thus discover the truth in the world through the application of human intelligence. Unfortunately, the conception of revelation which is presupposed throughout catechetics prevents just such an openness to the present event. No one is more aware of this than the students. They know that whatever questioning and open discussion may be allowed in class the answers have already been given. By the end of the class the cards must be laid upon the table.[16]

As the title of Brother Gabriel's article indicates, a rapprochement between catechetics and contemporary theology, with its attention to secularity, relevance, and incarnational themes, offers one promising way of dealing with this problem. Another is what the Lumen Vitae center designates by the term pre-catechetics. The idea here is that religious educators must adapt their methods to the conditions of those whom they wish to reach. We live in an age in which society itself, the social environment, does not predispose people to a favorable reception of the Christian message. A sense of sin and of man's need for salvation, a feeling of awe before nature, a keen awareness of man's finitude and the limitations of his knowledge and powers, a spiritual longing which is instinctively felt to be beyond hope of human fulfillment—all of these things which operated in the past to prepare the ground for reception of the Christian message are largely absent from the world of the twentieth century. In these circumstances the religious educator cannot proceed directly to the presentation of the Christian message. Many of those whom he would address simply do not see how the message he would impart corresponds to any need they feel in themselves. Hence the religious educator must take people as he finds them, attending first to the questions of value and meaning which are alive in their own minds, and showing how these matters—as well as the unformulated aspirations and spiritual hunger of modern man—are related to the Good News of salvation. Only after having done this work of pre-evangelization can he move toward the fuller exposition of the Christian message through salvation history or whatever other method may fit the circumstances.

[16] Moran, pp. 10-11. See also the same author's "Catechetics for the Real World," *America*, CXV (July 16, 1966), 57-59.

Work along these lines is only beginning; the same is also true with respect to the forging of new ties between catechetics and theology. Progress in the area of religious education has been very notable in this country in the past couple of decades, but it is clear that much still remains to be done.

SEMINARY STUDIES: A MAJOR REVAMPING UNDERWAY

The kind of intellectual formation provided by seminaries has certainly been partially responsible for the malaise existing in the Church today. The old formation failed to keep up with the times and tied us to a system that had become an intellectual prison. Much that is going on in seminaries today is altogether to be approved and will help us break out of the intellectual stagnation that had been allowed to collect around us.

One of the areas in need of immediate attention is the classical manner (from the seminary point of view) of teaching philosophy as a preparation for theology. The seminary philosophy course has not deserved the name of philosophy, being instead instruction in the terminology to be used in theology, a species of apologetical training. In an excellent essay on "Philosophy in the Seminary Curriculum," Robert O. Johann, S.J., discusses the matter in the context of the Thomistic revival. The passages deserves quotation at length:

> Writing on the Thomistic revival instituted by Pope Leo XIII, Roger Aubert makes the following comments about the initial effects of this restoration on the teaching of philosophy in Roman Catholic seminaries. He states that while the introduction of Thomism was undoubtedly an improvement over the previously dominant Cartesianism and general eclecticism, and also had the merit of giving the young clerics a taste for a coherent philosophical synthesis, it was nevertheless accompanied by certain drawbacks. First of all, Thomism was overly developed in the function of theology and was conceived too simply as a Christian apologia for it to equip the student to meet the strictly philosophic thinking of the period. Secondly, it tended to abuse the argument from authority and limit its concern to finding in St. Thomas (or, more usually, in his later commentators) an explicit answer to all questions. Finally, it relied too much on verbal formulas and encouraged the idea that all one needs in order to settle complex questions once and for all is to utter the appropriate cliche.

What is interesting about Aubert's evaluation is that many would say it applies equally well to the teaching of philosophy in American seminaries today. One has only to pick up a current popular periodical to find a layman criticising present-day seminary education or a bishop complaining that too much time is spent in the seminary "memorizing . . . classical theses, syllogisms, deductions, and solutions of problems which have long since ceased to occupy the minds of men," whereas the "truly difficult job of finding solutions for problems that agitate the minds of men today is left to the seminarian himself"; or seminarians and seminary professors themselves wondering out loud whether the verbalism of the seminary curriculum and its isolation from modern currents of thought have not made it wholly irrelevant to the modern world.

But, however interesting the parallel between Aubert's analysis and the latest American criticisms, it is not too surprising. For, although much additional attention has been given by the Holy See to the intellectual formation of seminarians since the momentous *Aeterni Patris* of Pope Leo, the philosophy curriculum in the seminary has by and large followed the course he charted. The succession of papal documents on the subject has had the effect not of changing but rather of developing and institutionalizing the original Leonine impetus in ecclesiastical faculties throughout the world. Thus the prescribed conception of philosophy is that of a "coherent, logical system, a Scholastic and speculative whole, founded on the sure methods and principles of St. Thomas." What the student is supposed to acquire is first of all "a solid body of doctrine," and only after this is "the step to be made to judgments on other philosophical systems." Moreover, "it is not sufficient to set forth philosophical doctrines in eloquent and enthusiastic discourse; with what might well be termed an intransigent forcefulness, [the Holy See] prescribes the Scholastic method, and for the presentation of arguments and the discussion of difficulties syllogistic form."[17]

Those familiar with seminary education will not dispute the accuracy of Father Johann's description of how philosophy has been taught. Few would deny that the system has critical shortcomings. For, while the average candidate for the priesthood will not go on to become a professional philosopher, he does need to have a grounding in philosophy—a philosophical position that he himself understands because

[17] Robert O. Johann, S.J., "Philosophy in the Seminary Curriculum," in J. M. Lee and L. J. Putz, C.S.C., eds., *Seminary Education in a Time of Change* (Notre Dame, Ind., 1965), pp. 451-52.

it has been formed in contact with problems and currents of thought that are meaningful today. If the priest is to be a relevant member of society he must be able to justify to himself and to those around him his response to the word of God and to the Church's mission. And unless he can do this with an informed understanding of history and current problems, he will serve to discredit not only his priesthood but the Church in general. The failure of seminary philosophy to prepare men adequately in this regard has contributed to the seeming irrelevancy of the clerical mind, and thus to the present crisis of priestly vocations.

More important still, the philosophy and theology courses need to coalesce and form a more integrated whole. They should mutually penetrate one another; philosophy should not be thought of as merely a preparation for theology, as the "handmaid of theology" (*Ancilla Theologiae*), to use the scholastic terminology. Neither philosophy nor theology is a perfected, or already completed, body of knowledge waiting simply to be mastered by anyone willing to apply himself assiduously to a textbook. Rather, both are disciplines that can absorb a lifetime of study and reflection; both should be taught in such a way that the student is left with a desire to continue his search for meaning and truth, a desire to probe ever more deeply the mysteries of man's existence and destiny. To quote Father Johann once more:

> The function of philosophy . . . cannot be adequately understood if it is seen merely as a matter of supplying categories and principles for the theologian to work with. For the priest cannot be an effective minister of the Word unless, besides a comprehensive and scientific grasp of the Word itself, he brings to his work also a profound understanding of the problems and difficulties involved in its responsible acceptance. In other words, not only Revelation, but the people to whom it is directed, as well as the concrete situation in which they find themselves must be thoroughly understood. This understanding must not merely be in the light of faith, since the very belief of these people is just what is at stake, but precisely in terms of experience. Such an understanding however, of the experiential situation in which the Word is supposed to take root comes only from philosophical reflection.[18]

[18] Lee and Putz, pp. 475-76. For essays on a closely related problem see J. Barry McGannon, S.J., Bernard J. Cooke, S. J., and George P. Klubertanz, S.J., eds., *Christian Wisdom and Christian Formation: Theology, Philosophy, and the Catholic College Student* (New York, 1964).

It is, after all, only common sense that communicating divine truth requires that the Word is not known only in itself, but also in the light of man's present situation and sensibilities. The recipients' ways of knowing and receiving are varied and demand to be studied according to the various circumstances of each specific time and place. Too often the message of divine truth does not register on the modern mind when presented in the categories worked out in the past. Even the meaning of the terms themselves changes over the centuries, and it is problematical whether we know precisely what the Scholastics had in mind when they developed the philosophic and theological formulas that gave intellectual articulation to the faith centuries ago. In any case, these formulas are no longer compelling, now that we find ourselves living in a different world and thinking in new ways.

But theology still needs philosophy—and other studies as well. It needs them in order to penetrate revealed truths with new insights and discover in them new dimensions. The enriched understanding of man given to us by anthropology, for example, should surely be of interest to the theologian who ponders the mysteries of God's love for men. As Maurice Nedoncelle has said, the theologian "turns to philosophy as to a spectacle; he wants to read in it spiritual adventures different from his own, adventures that can teach him things he does not even suspect. Perhaps in reflecting on this material he will understand revelation better. His mental attitude is not different from the one he adopts toward exegesis and historians."[19]

The present world is replete with knowledge and experiential data that may be used to find new perspectives in theology and, thus, new approaches in the preparation of seminarians (although, admittedly, the procedures whereby these materials may best be incorporated into seminary education have not yet been worked out in detail). The tragic death of Dr. Martin Luther King, Jr., and of Senator Robert F. Kennedy, for example, must cause us to ponder afresh the mystery of Calvary and its significance for humankind. A better informed understanding of motherhood should provide insights into certain aspects of Mariology. The new interest in symbolism and the role of intention in communication through symbols suggests new approaches to sacramental theology, which in the past minimized the importance of in-

[19] Maurice Nedoncelle, "Philosophy, Handmaid of Theology," *Concilium*, vol. 6 (New York, 1965), p. 99.

tention and concentrated heavily on the *ex opere operato* efficacy of the sacraments. The fact that we know so much more about human relations than earlier generations ought to shed some new light on the relations of the Persons of the Trinity—the relationship of Father and Son, or consideration of the Holy Spirit as the feminine principle within the Trinity.[20] The manifestations of man's creativeness and of his strivings for unity and fulfillment all offer new data upon which the theologian can draw. The materials are there; we have only to reach out for them, and assist our seminarians in reaching out, to bring about a reawakening and renewal of theological formation.

The materials that have been most fully exploited to date are really the oldest materials we have—the Scriptures. The influence of scriptural studies on the catechetical movement was noted earlier; their impact has been equally great in the seminary. But while the Scriptures are the oldest materials of Christians, it has been the willingness of scholars to apply new techniques and the insights provided by new disciplines like anthropology that has revolutionized our understanding of the Bible. Seminary studies in other disciplines have not yet caught up to scriptural men in this respect, but even the scriptural renewal among Catholics in this country lagged behind Europe.

Building on the work of Protestant scholars of the nineteenth century and later and stimulated by the pioneering efforts of Father Lagrange and the Biblical School in Jerusalem, American Catholic scriptural scholarship really began to enter its modern phase in the 1930's. The Catholic Biblical Association of America was founded in 1936, largely as a result of the encouragement and patronage of Bishop Edwin O'Hara who was seeking the collaboration of biblical scholars in providing a revised New Testament for use by CCD workers. A close and lasting relationship developed between the Biblical Association, Bishop O'Hara, and the Confraternity.[21] The first major task to which the Association devoted itself was the revision of the Rheims-Challoner New Testament; the finished work was published as the Confraternity New Testament in 1941. Three years earlier the As-

[20] Cf. Willi Moll, *The Christian Image of Woman: A Threefold Response of Love* (Notre Dame, Ind., 1967).

[21] In 1955 the *Catholic Biblical Quarterly* dedicated a special issue in honor of Archbishop O'Hara. Cf. esp. Stephen J. Hartdegen, O.F.M., "Sinite Parvulos Venire," *Catholic Biblical Quarterly*, XVII (Apr., 1955), 121-31 [pp. 1-11 of the special issue].

sociation had begun publication of the *Catholic Biblical Quarterly*, a scholarly journal which has attained high standing in the field. Since then progress in biblical studies has been on a steady increase. The American Church has made significant contributions to the field through the work of John L. McKenzie, S.J., Bruce Vawter, C.M., Roland E. Murphy, O. Carm., Barnabas Ahern, C.P., Carroll Stuhlmueller, C.P., and Thomas Barrosse, C.S.C., to name but a few of the most active scholars. Now almost every Catholic seminary has a scriptural scholar on its faculty. A Canadian, Roderick A. F. McKenzie, S.J., is presently the head of the Biblical Commission in Rome.

It bears repeating that the new scriptural emphasis has done much to foster ecumenism and create a climate more conducive to cooperation and friendship between Catholics and Protestants. Even on the pedestrian level of those who try merely to absorb the findings of the biblical scholars, Catholic priests find themselves brought closer to churchmen of other faiths as we approach our common task of trying to understand more deeply the riches of God's revelation. This is quite an improvement over the polemical atmosphere of the past, when seminarians were trained to refute the errors of Protestantism, using biblical texts somewhat as darts to shoot at the enemy. In discussing the place of theology in the seminary curriculum, one of our leading scriptural scholars, Father John L. McKenzie, took note of the need to break away from the polemicism of the past. "The modern priest," he said, "must be trained in dialogue, not disputation; and those who like neither the word nor what it designates must accustom themselves to live with it. Dialogue is here to stay."[22]

One of the areas in which those responsible for Catholic seminaries can profit from dialogue with Protestants is pastoral theology. The theological schools of Princeton and Duke universities have done pioneering work in pastoral theology, and there is much to be learned from programs offered by the Menninger Institute of Topeka, Kansas. What are to Catholics almost wholly new fields have been opened up in pastoral counselling and pastoral group work, and we have need of the longer experience which Protestants can share with us in these areas.

The broadening of the spectrum of studies which seminaries should

[22] John L. McKenzie, S.J., "Theology in the Seminary Curriculum" in Lee and Putz, p. 417.

offer will require certain modifications both in respect to what the seminarian is expected to master and in respect to the locus in which the seminary carries on its educational task. As Father McKenzie observes, "More and more seminaries will probably come to accept the 'double-track' curriculum in one way or another, by which is meant an honors or a degree program, and a general or pastoral program." The reason for this, McKenzie continues, "It is quite unrealistic to treat all seminarians as equally endowed, equally capable of theological understanding, and destined to be trained as universal parts which will fit into any place in the machine."[23] And in order to diversify their programs and offer more opportunities for specialization in keeping with the individual capabilities of seminarians, it makes sense for seminaries to abandon their old isolation and move closer to universities, which provide a far greater range of specialized instruction carried on at a higher academic level than most seminaries can attain even within a more limited range. The trend of Catholic seminaries moving closer to, or affiliating with, universities is already well established. St. Louis University has a cluster of religious-order seminaries around it; the Jesuits moved from West Baden, Indiana, to the Chicago area and will probably affiliate themselves with a university there; the Holy Cross theologate is moving to the University of Notre Dame; the famous Jesuit seminary at Woodstock will relocate in the vicinity of Union Theological and Columbia in New York. A consortium of Catholic and Protestant seminaries is developing in the Boston area, and a similar consortium on the graduate level already exists among Catholics, Episcopalians, Lutherans, and Presbyterians in Berkeley, California.

It is to be hoped that one of the results of closer relations between the seminary and the university will be to instill among seminarians an appreciation of the fact that the priest's education is not finished when he leaves the classroom. As is the case with most professions, the education of the priest must be a continuing process; there will certainly be a continuing need to understand and adapt to new situations. Unfortunately, the old seminary failed badly in this regard. Perhaps this was its most serious shortcoming. Again, Father McKenzie has some highly pointed remarks: "The unwillingness of the clergy to accept development in theology, exegesis, liturgy, the function of the layman

[23] McKenzie, p. 415.

in the Church, and other sensitive contemporary questions is only a little less than scandalous. Somehow seminaries have left their graduates with the impression that they will never have to unlearn anything old or learn anything new."[24]

The performance of priests is now being scrutinized more critically than ever before by American Catholics—and, indeed, by priests themselves. It is impossible to say with any certainty just how much this period of trial for the priesthood owes to the inadequacies of earlier clerical formation and how much it is the result of larger social changes presently making themselves felt in the religious sphere. What is clear is that a fundamental reexamination is in process and that a restructuring of the institution of the priesthood is in the offing. A whole new approach to the world is needed if the clergy are to lead the Church in discovering its mission in the modern world. Unless the reexamination issues in a renewal of the priesthood, the task of leading the Church in the near future will necessarily fall entirely upon lay people. The situation is fraught with both danger and hope. If the tasks and trials of the period of transition are accepted with confidence, courage, and faith, then we can look forward with hope. And there are certain developments that give strong grounds for hope. One is the creation of priests' associations, both diocesan and national. It is encouraging that these men are not waiting for guidance from higher authority, but are banding together to mobilize their collective talents and experience in searching for the most effective ways for American priests to serve both the Church and the world today. Another encouraging sign is the ferment in seminaries themselves and among seminarians who are demanding new approaches and new structures.

THE NEED FOR NEW STRUCTURES

The seminarian of today is not the docile, obedient, bashful type that rectors were accustomed to dealing with in the past.[25] The present-day seminarian is a product of the twentieth century and reflects a culture and value system quite different from those of previous generations.

[24] McKenzie, p. 415.

[25] I have developed some of the following points more fully in "A Plea for New Seminary Structures," *U.S. Catholic*, XXXIV (June, 1968), 17-20.

There is less concern for the traditional means of salvation—the Mass and the sacraments—and virtually none for devotional practices of a nonliturgical nature such as visits to the Blessed Sacrament, the rosary, or benediction. The value of the whole traditional framework of the religious life and the philosophical and theological systems which underlay it are called into question. This spirit of radical questioning has given rise to the fear on the part of some that we are witnessing a crisis of faith among seminarians. Anxiety and even alarm have been generated, not merely by the falling-off of vocations, but by the lack of obedience and respect for venerable institutions of the Church among those who remain in the seminary. While we cannot pretend to analyze the whole situation, or prescribe remedies, it will be helpful to list some of the characteristics of this new breed of seminarian.

1. Perhaps the most obvious characteristic is the critical spirit of the present generation. Its members want to know the whys and wherefores of existing practices and structures; they are eager to learn and to understand, but only on the condition that what they are taught makes sense to them. The mere fact that something worked well in the past is not regarded as sufficient warrant for its preservation. Young people have seen too much change and progress in science and other spheres for that. Nothing is to be accepted on an *a priori* basis; everything must be tested and validated anew. Why, they ask, is it so important to attend daily Mass? Why are the Divine Office and daily meditation required in the seminary? The world is crying out for help, and it seems a waste of time to sit for hours in the chapel where there are none of one's fellow men to be encountered or to be served.

2. The new generation is extremely sensitive to questions of freedom. Contemporary young people grow up in an age that has made freedom and self-determination absolute values in the personal, social, and political spheres. The Council formally affirmed that religious freedom is a right of man. The seminarian is intensely jealous of his freedom; limitations on his right to self-determination or restrictions on the scope of his decision-making he regards as infringements of his personal dignity. Like the American Negro, he wants "freedom now!"

3. Accompanying skepticism about the traditional and the stress on freedom, there is a strong antiinstitutional bias. Every institution is put to the test; if it does not produce good fruit it will be cut down without mercy. Especially repugnant are institutions that tend to depersonalize, that absorb human beings, that pigeonhole men without

leaving room for personal decision. Personalistic values take the highest priority.

4. Young people are repelled by anything that smacks of complacency, routine, repetition, or even security. They are dedicated to experimentation, to working for something they can put their hearts into. Static ways of doing things, magic formulas, dull automatic functions are not for them. What they want is spontaneity and creativeness. Their guitar music is the expression of their own feelings; it comes from them, and hence it is preferred to the chants and hymns of the past even though the latter may be musically superior.

5. They have a deep appreciation for people as people—for their feelings, their aspirations, their opinions. And they want others to treat them with the same sort of consideration. They react vigorously if their motives are impugned. They prefer to be invited rather than commanded; to be asked rather than ordered. They like the term "communication" better than "obedience." They do not wish to be assigned to any apostolate without having already chosen it themselves by free, personal commitment.

6. It is a generation with profound respect for human values. Authenticity is perhaps the word that expresses it best. Our seminarians shy away from dichotomies: natural-supernatural, sacred-profane, Church-world. Rather they seek the incarnational: unity of religion and life. In effect, they prefer to find Christ in their neighbor rather than in the sacraments.

7. They are a generation oriented toward the future; for the past they have no love. They belong to the space age; they are confident, optimistic, and intolerant of obstacles to progress. They yearn to stretch out into the unknown, to live for the future alone. The present they accept only with an eye for what it is to become.

These characteristics do not define the phenomenon, but they are marks of the contemporary generation of which seminarians are a part and with which they identify themselves. All of this they feel and live to the roots of their being. They are impatient with those who do not feel with them or understand them. Such persons are not "with it," young people say. And those who are not with it don't count; they are simply "tuned out"; they can exert no formative influence on young people.

Obviously, the old form of seminary education was not designed with this mentality in mind, and it simply will not serve the purpose of forming priests from this generation of young men. If anything, the traditional approach and practices are more likely to turn away from the priesthood those who are most desirous of serving Christ. The seminary through which my generation passed formed men to be docile and obedient to higher authority, to be respectful of tradition, and to be submissive to venerable institutions. This formation was achieved by requiring a life of conformity to rules and discipline. The old method was not all bad, by any means, but the modern seminarian will not "buy it." The pattern of the past is totally foreign to the mentality of our present free-wheeling generation. Should we be surprised, then, at the current unrest in our seminaries?

The more pertinent question is, of course: What is to be done? Merely relaxing the rules of the old system does not offer much promise for at least two reasons. First, it means that no new principled approach replaces the old, thus leaving a sort of vacuum of purpose and method as the old is progressively weakened. Second, and more important, mere relaxation of the old fails to confront the problem that, even in its modified and diluted form, the traditional method is predicated on values that are no longer accepted by young people. Authoritarianism and regimentation are regarded by them as un-American; nor do they look upon submissiveness and unquestioned obedience as admirable modes of conduct on the part of those subject to authority. Even the notion that some should be "subject to authority" is distasteful. These now discredited values were more closely associated with the seminary than with any other institution of Catholic life, with the possible exception of religious communities. A root-and-branch reform is clearly needed—one that will build upon the values of the young, make room for their personal creativeness, and mobilize their deep spiritual commitment. We do not yet know how this is to be done, but at least the need is clearly recognized. The bishops of the United States have established a committee to study the whole area of the priesthood and to make recommendations for new methods and styles of seminary formation. Much rides on the outcome of this effort. The Church's need for leadership was never greater; if adequate leadership can be found its prospects were never brighter.

11: THE AMERICAN CATHOLIC EDUCATIONAL ENTERPRISE

James J. Vanecko and *Maureen L. Gleason*

One aspect of the universal Church peculiar to its American configuration is the vast network of schools maintained by Catholics without assistance from the State and quite separate from the public school system. Confessional schools are not uncommon in other countries, but a system of privately financed religious schools on the scale of the Catholic schools of the United States exists nowhere else in the world. And although other religious bodies maintain schools in the United States, none of them supports an educational enterprise that approaches the Catholic system in size and scope.

There are almost 14,000 Catholic educational institutions in this country, of which some 10,500 are elementary schools and about 2,300 are high schools.[1] Their total enrollment is more than 5.7 million. Approximately one elementary-school pupil out of eight in the United States is being educated in a Catholic school. The comparable proportion for high-school students is one out of twelve. Catholic schools are to be found in all 156 dioceses in the country, but they are concentrated in heavily urbanized regions where the Catholic population has historically clustered. Half the Catholics in the United States live in twenty dioceses; these few dioceses account for 40 per cent of the Catholic schools and 53 per cent of the students in such schools. Analysis of the figures for attendance at nonpublic schools confirms the urban concentration of Catholics and indicates the quantitative significance of their educational undertaking. In 1960 three quarters of the nonpublic schools and 90 per cent of their student population

[1] These figures and the following discussion are based on the statistics given by the *Official Catholic Directory* for 1968 and on "fact sheets" on Catholic education prepared by the National Catholic Education Association in the fall of 1967 and the spring of 1968.

were Catholic. In the ten largest metropolitan areas one out of four elementary students was attending a nonpublic school; in the twenty areas next largest in size, the figure was 19 per cent. In individual cities the figures ran as high as 69 per cent (Dubuque) and 55 per cent (Green Bay).[2]

In recent years Catholic schools have been following the Catholic population in its move from the city to the suburbs. Figures for the Illinois counties in which Chicago and its suburbs are located are suggestive of the trend. Between 1930 and 1960, the percentage of children aged five to fourteen in nonpublic schools rose from 24 per cent to 28 per cent. This moderate overall increase masks the significant changes that are revealed when the statistics are broken down for different areas. Thus, in the same period the percentage of children in nonpublic schools *decreased* slightly in the inner city (from 28 per cent to 26 per cent), while it almost doubled on the outer fringe (from 22 per cent to 40 per cent) and increased by seven points (17 per cent to 24 per cent) in the suburbs.[3] It should be added that many of the students in Catholic schools in the inner city were themselves not Catholics.

Although they are numerous, Catholic schools are of course greatly outnumbered by public schools. And especially at the secondary level, the individual units in the Catholic system are often smaller than their public-school counterparts. A recent comprehensive study found that in October, 1962, half the Catholic high schools in the country had enrollments of fewer than three hundred; in 47 per cent of the Catholic high schools the senior class numbered fewer than thirty-nine pupils.[4]

Some 207,000 priests, sisters, brothers, and lay persons teach full time in Catholic educational institutions from the grade school to university level. In former times sisters—and to a lesser degree, brothers and priests—were thought of as *the* Catholic-school teachers. This is changing rapidly. The growth of enrollments naturally caused an ex-

[2] Robert J. Havighurst, "Social Functions of Catholic Education," a position paper prepared for the Washington Symposium on Catholic Education, Nov. 5-10, 1967. Professor Havighurst's figures are from the 1960 census.

[3] James W. Sanders, "Catholic Elementary-School Enrollment: Chicago, 1925-65," *Elementary School Journal*, LXVIII (Nov., 1967), pp. 88-96. The lack of comparable studies for other cities prevents drawing firm conclusions about the representative character of these statistics.

[4] Reginald A. Neuwien, ed., *Catholic Schools in Action* (Notre Dame, Ind., 1966), pp. 53, 55.

pansion of the teaching ranks, but between 1950 and 1961 the number of lay teachers increased twenty-three times faster than the number of religious teachers on the elementary level and four times faster on the secondary level. If we include Catholic higher education, about 40 per cent of those teaching in Catholic institutions are lay persons, and in some dioceses the figure is as high as 60 per cent. In 1959 there were three sister-teachers for every lay teacher; now the trend toward lay teachers is so pronounced that some have estimated they will outnumber nuns two to one by 1970.[5]

This vast number of students, teachers, and institutions is commonly called the Catholic educational *system*. Through much of the history of Catholic education in the United States it was a gross misnomer to call the aggregation of unrelated units a system, and even today there is so little unity of organization, administration, or policy that use of the term is questionable. For one thing, there are several distinct varieties of Catholic schools. Any school which has been "canonically authorized and recognized" by the bishop of the territory in which it exists is designated as a Catholic school. By far the most common type is the parochial school: In the early 1960's more than 10,000 of the nation's 16,000 or so parishes operated schools. In such schools, nearly all of which are elementary-level institutions, the pastor acts as the agent for the bishop in managing the school and, most importantly, in dispensing parish funds for its operation and maintenance. But while the pastor is officially in charge of the school, its academic administration and operation is usually turned over to a teaching community of religious. The superior of the religious community appoints the principal of the school; hence the principal is subject to two independent authorities, the pastor and the religious superior.

Another important type of Catholic school is the private institution fully under the jurisdiction of the religious order. Although relatively few in numbers—1,250 schools with just under half a million students—these private institutions are important because the majority are high schools. Independent of the parish, these schools operate without any need to accommodate to a pastor's wishes (also without direct support from parish funds). But in most dioceses, there is a superintendent of schools who represents the bishop and is charged with the

[5] George N. Shuster, *Catholic Education in a Changing World* (New York, 1967), pp. 56-57; Anna F. Friedlander, *The Shared Time Strategy* (St. Louis, 1966), p. 19.

overall coordination of educational policy and administration. Another kind of control and supervision is the school board, diocesan or parochial. Such bodies have multiplied rapidly in the past decade and add a new element of complication to the picture. But before considering the contemporary situation further it will be helpful to glance at the historical development of the Catholic education in the United States, for its organizational pattern and many other features have assumed their present form as a result of a long growth.

THE HISTORICAL BACKGROUND

Little scholarly work has been done on the history of Catholic education in the United States.[6] The story is really not very well known or understood, and any brief statement such as the one that follows is subject not only to qualification but to considerable revision. But the historical dimension is too important to be dismissed entirely, and a few general points seem reasonably clear.

The first is that Catholic education in the United States cannot be understood unless it is seen in the context of American history. More specifically, it cannot be understood without taking into account the crucial role of education in American society and the historical commitment of the American people to making education available to all citizens. The fundamental reason why the American Catholic educational system has no counterpart elsewhere in the Catholic world is that Catholicism developed here in a social system that placed unprecedented value upon equality and upon opening the doors of educational opportunity to all the people. The fact that Catholic schools expanded in keeping with the expansion of American public education, although on a smaller scale, reflects the influence of the American environment and is eloquent testimony to the Americanization of Catholicism.

While the stress on education in American society caused Catholics to pay special attention to schools, the particular form taken by the

[6] The standard work is James A. Burns and Bernard J. Kohlbrenner, *A History of Catholic Education in the United States* (New York, 1937). Neil G. McCluskey, S.J., ed., *Catholic Education in America: A Documentary History* (New York, 1964) is an excellent collection of documents with a very useful historical introduction by the editor.

national educational system also influenced the forms and development of education among Catholics. Since Catholics existed as a minority, they could not be indifferent to the larger pattern and their schools were necessarily shaped by the need to accommodate to the majority system. But the general educational system of the country did not spring up suddenly in its present form at the birth of the republic. As it evolved into its present shape through the course of time and as new elements appeared in the national system, corresponding elements were introduced into the Catholic system. High schools offer the best illustration. Free public secondary schools grew rapidly in the late nineteenth century, and Catholic educators followed suit around 1900 by laying much greater emphasis on the development of Catholic high schools. The work of accrediting agencies at the turn of the century in establishing and enforcing uniform educational standards is another example of a development which exterted an influence on Catholic schools.

The shifting character of the general educational scene in the nineteenth century meant that some things which seem perfectly obvious to us today were not nearly as well defined for earlier generations of educators. Again, high schools provide a good illustration. It is often said—and in a sense it is quite true—that Catholic colleges in the nineteenth century were really high schools. But it is also true that in those days there was a great deal of ambiguity about what we would now call the secondary, collegiate, and university (or graduate) levels of education. In other words, it did not become clear what high schools really are, or how collegiate education is distinguished from secondary education, until the institution of the high school was widely introduced and thought of as occupying a distinct place between the elementary school and the college. Part of our task in trying to understand the development of Catholic education, then, is to reflect upon the situation of men who were feeling their way along in a movement whose precise directions were yet obscure.

But while the American environment shaped the development of Catholic schools, and while the complexities of the American educational system account in part for the difficulties in understanding the pattern of their growth, there were also distinctive features in the Catholic tradition. For example, the problem of differentiating the secondary and collegiate levels of instruction was more troublesome for Catholics because their colleges in the nineteenth century were based on a continental European rather than an English institutional model. Like the German *gymnasium* or French *lycée,* Catholic colleges started out with a six- or seven-year program that combined studies on the secondary and collegiate levels. It was only by a slow process of adjustment that Catholic institutions brought themselves into line with the prevailing American pattern of four years of secondary work followed by four years of collegiate studies in a separate school.[7]

Another distinctive feature of Catholic education was that the teaching force was composed almost exclusively of priests, brothers, and most importantly nuns. This means that the history of Catholic education is inextricably interwoven with the histories of the teaching orders, some of which (particularly the Jesuits) had a specific tradition which influenced their approach to the task. The sheer numbers and bewildering variety of religious communities engaged in the work of education add another element of complication to the story. The standard history of Catholic education in the United States lists seventy-one teaching orders of sisters which began their work here between the years 1833 and 1913. By 1930 there were more than 200 religious communities involved in Catholic-school work; today there are more than 500.[8]

The vast and organizationally pluralistic enterprise which absorbed the energies of all these religious teachers evolved slowly both in the policy commitment which brought it into being and in the administrative procedures that sought to impose some order upon it. The pastoral statements of the hierarchy and the fact that early bishops like John Carroll sponsored the establishment of seminaries, academies, and colleges show that they were aware of the importance of Catholic schools from a very early date. Denominational sponsorship of schools was the prevailing American pattern in the late-eighteenth and early-nineteenth centuries. Since they were a religious minority that was suspected if not despised by other Americans, Catholics were unwilling to entrust their children to schools dominated by the religiously hostile majority. And so as "common" or public elementary schools were more widely introduced from the 1830's onward, more parishes began

[7] Cf. Philip Gleason, "American Catholic Higher Education: A Historical Perspective," in *The Shape of Catholic Higher Education,* ed. Robert Hassenger (Chicago, 1967), p. 33 ff.

[8] Burns and Kohlbrenner, pp. 121-23, 127; NCEA figures for spring, 1968.

to establish primary schools to provide the basic education that was becoming increasingly necessary for civic and social advancement.

But the full-scale commitment to a separate and privately supported system of schools was reached very gradually. The controversies that arose in New York in 1840 and on a wider front in the 1850's over attempts by Catholics to get tax funds for their schools played an important role in this development. These battles, often very bitter, confirmed the belief of many Catholics in the hostility of the majority and convinced them they would have to go it alone in securing a religiously acceptable education for their children. Even so, the policy of requiring a school in every parish, except where extraordinary circumstances prevented it, was not formally adopted for the American Church as a whole until the Third Plenary Council of Baltimore in 1884. Parochial schools were widely established by that time, and in a sense the Council merely made official what was already being done. But recent research indicates that many churchmen were not enthusiastic about the requirement. In fact, the series of steps culminating in the Council's decree was initiated not by a bishop but by a layman, James A. McMaster, the ultramontane editor of the *New York Freeman's Journal*.[9]

In the half-century following the Third Plenary Council the percentage of churches with parochial schools increased by twenty points (from 40 to 60 per cent). This fell far short of the goal of placing every Catholic child in a Catholic school; only about half the eligible Catholic children were in parochial schools in 1962.[10] But the expansion created an imperative need for more unified administration of the schools. Except for an abortive effort in Philadelphia in the 1850's, there was no machinery for overall direction of the Catholic schools even on a diocesan basis until the 1870's. In 1879 a system of diocesan supervision was introduced in Fort Wayne, Indiana. Three years later this plan was adopted in the ecclesiastical province of Cincinnati, and a decree of the Third Plenary Council extended a version of it to the rest of the country.[11] After that various arrangements for diocesan

[9] Thomas T. McAvoy, C.S.C., "Public Schools vs. Catholic Schools and James McMaster," *Review of Politics*, XXVIII (Jan., 1966), 19-46. See also Marie Carolyn Klinkhamer, O.P., "Historical Reason for Inception of Parochial School System," *Catholic Educational Review*, LII (1954), 73-94.

[10] Burns and Kohlbrenner, pp. 144-45; Shuster, p. 55.

[11] Burns and Kohlbrenner, pp. 184-86.

boards or superintendents came into being, but with many local variations. By providing a national forum for exchanges of information and views, the Catholic Educational Association (established in 1904) contributed to the improvement of Catholic schools both in respect to administration and instruction, although it had no authority to set or enforce policy.

Because Catholics were overwhelmingly an immigrant people whose religious faith was interwoven with linguistic and cultural elements of their heritage, the factor of ethnicity was also involved in their educational efforts. Loyalty to language and culture reinforced loyalty to religion, and among such groups as the Germans, the Poles, and the French Canadians of New England, the parochial schools served to pass on to American-born generations the whole undifferentiated religious-linguistic-cultural complex. But Irish Catholics, who were without a distinctive language of their own, were also very loyal to Catholic schools. Statistics gathered by the Immigration Commission in 1908 showed that Irish children were much more likely to be in Catholic schools than Italian youngsters, and the recent study by Greeley and Rossi reveals that ethnic background is still a factor that enters into the choice between Catholic and public schools.[12]

The highly inflammable issues of nationality and language were often present in controversies about Catholic education, with the critics charging that Catholic schools were being used to perpetuate foreign ism and were thus retarding the Americanization of young people. These disputes occurred among Catholics as well, and they concerned much more than questions of language. Precisely because the school is such a crucially important institution in American society, disagreements concerning education have a very high ideological content—they impinge directly on what America is and what policies and practices are to be followed in shaping it. For this reason, it is understand-

[12] The Immigration Commission found that whereas Irish children constituted 4.8 per cent of the public-school population of thirty-seven cities surveyed, they made up 26.9 per cent of the population of parochial schools in twenty-four cities included in the study. Comparable figures for Italian children were 6.4 per cent of the public-school population and 7 per cent of the parochial-school population. See *Reports of the Immigration Commission*, Vol. 29 (Washington, 1911), p. 151. See also Andrew M. Greeley and Peter H. Rossi, *The Education of Catholic Americans* (Chicago, 1966), pp. 36-41, 89-95.

able that perhaps the most striking feature of the history of American Catholic education has been its perennially controversial character. From 1840 on, hardly a decade had gone by without Catholics being exercised over "the school question" in one form or another. Our own age is no exception.

SOME ASPECTS OF THE PRESENT CONTROVERSY

Since the end of World War II Catholic schools have been argued about in popular magazines and learned journals, at the sessions of various organizations, and at informal gatherings in every suburb, university community, and rectory in the country. The effectiveness, structure, academic quality, and social consequences of Catholic schools have been criticized and the justification for their very existence has been challenged. Since the days of Paul Blanshard's books and the "divisiveness" issue around 1950, criticism of the Catholic schools has been carried on almost exclusively by Catholics. The condition of Catholic education was a central theme in the great "Catholic intellectualism" debate initiated by John Tracy Ellis and carried further by such writers as Gustave Weigel, S.J., and Thomas F. O'Dea. Perhaps the best known critic of the Catholic schools as such is Mary Perkins Ryan, who castigates them for failures in the specific area of religious education in her book *Are Parochial Schools the Answer?*[13]

Among those interested in Catholic education all of this criticism has stimulated a demand to know more about what is actually happening in the schools. At the same time, educators and sociologists have grown increasingly interested in Catholic schools as fertile areas for investigation, and a number of studies of their operation, effectiveness, and impact have appeared. The two most extensive are the Notre Dame study, sponsored by the Carnegie Corporation, which gathered statistics on the Catholic school system in 1962-63 and conducted an intensive inquiry into the schools of thirteen dioceses, and the Greeley-

[13] John Tracy Ellis, "American Catholics and the Intellectual Life," *Thought*, XXX (Autumn, 1955), 351-88; Gustave Weigel, S.J., "American Catholic Intellectualism—a Theologian's Reflections," *Review of Politics*, XIX (July, 1957), 275-307; Thomas F. O'Dea, *American Catholic Dilemma* (paperback ed., New York, 1962); Mary Perkins Ryan, *Are Parochial Schools the Answer?* (New York, 1964).

Rossi report, also supported by Carnegie funds, which was based on a national sample survey of Catholic adults conducted in 1963-64 by the National Opinion Research Center (NORC) at the University of Chicago.[14] The latter's purpose was to assess the effects of Catholic education, but both studies served to establish some factual and statistical bases for a discussion of the issues raised by the critics.

One of the major criticisms of the Catholic schools deals with their alleged academic inferiority. To determine the relative quality of two schools or school systems is one of the thorniest problems in social science. There is little agreement on what characteristics of the physical facilities, teachers' abilities, social organization, or service provided by a school are the most important determinants of its quality. In fact, there is no universal consensus on whether there actually are such characteristics, leaving aside the question of how to measure them. Some would argue that the student body is the most important factor, and that the performance of a school cannot be judged without taking into account the unique requirements of its own student body. If this is true, then even measurements based on standardized achievement tests have to be examined with careful control over the initial I.Q. level of the students, their parents' educational and occupational background, and parental interest and involvement in their children's education.

The Notre Dame study, *Catholic Schools in Action*, does present a broad review of the various factors involved in assessing the relative qualities of school systems directly. Unfortunately, the data provided here on facilities, teacher training, services, and the organization of Catholic schools is not shown in comparison with public schools; hence one cannot say how well Catholic schools compare with their non-Catholic counterparts in these respects. However, this study compares standard achievement-test scores for the Catholic schools with national means. In the forty-one Catholic schools included in this aspect of the investigation, 80 per cent of the high school seniors were achieving at or above the expected level for their grade and individual intelligence scores. This finding would seem to indicate that the quality gap between public and Catholic schools is nonexistent. But other

14 Reginald A. Neuwien, ed., *Catholic Schools in Action* (Notre Dame, Ind., 1966); Andrew M. Greeley and Peter H. Rossi, *The Education of Catholic Americans* (Chicago, 1966).

TABLE I

TYPE OF EDUCATION AND OCCUPATIONAL AND EDUCATIONAL ACHIEVEMENTS OF CATHOLICS

Achievement	Type of Education		
	All Catholic	Some Catholic	No Catholic
Mean occupational prestige score	5.0	4.6	4.1[a]
Per cent who attended college	26%	21%	18%[a]
N	345	699	796

[a] Significantly different from "All Catholic."
Source: Adapted from Andrew M. Greeley and Peter H. Rossi, *The Education of Catholic Americans* (Chicago, 1966), p. 140.

investigations suggest the need for caution,[15] and given the peculiarities of standardized tests and the problems of comparison alluded to already, it will be helpful to approach the question of academic quality from another perspective as well.

The Greeley-Rossi volume, entitled *The Education of Catholic Americans*, provides this other perspective. By looking at the adult population and comparing those who went to Catholic schools with those who did not, we can get a reading on the long-range effects of Catholic education. The most relevant evidence on academic quality given by the Greeley-Rossi report concerns the subsequent achievement of those who went to Catholic schools: Were they more or less likely to achieve than Catholics who did not attend Catholic schools? Two measures of achievement are included in Table I—the educational attainment of the respondents and their occupational attainment; that is, whether or not they are in high-status occupations.

The evidence here is contrary to the results one would expect on

[15] Neuwien, pp. 73-79. A recent review of research in this area concludes that "the burden of proof is clearly with those who claim the educational inferiority of Catholic elementary schools, [but] there is simply not enough evidence on which to base any general conclusion about Catholic high schools." Michael O'Neill, "How Good Are Catholic Schools?" *NCEA Bulletin*, LXIV (Feb., 1968), 11-17.

the basis of the criticisms made of Catholic schools. Catholics who went to Catholic schools are more likely to have gone on to college—26 per cent of those who had all their education in Catholic schools as opposed to 18 per cent of those who had none of their education in Catholic schools. The same is true for occupational achievement. Using the Duncan Index of occupational prestige, which is based on the income of the occupation and the education it requires, occupations are ranked in ten groups. The mean occupational-prestige score for those having all their education in Catholic schools is 5.0, as opposed to 4.1 for those who had none of their education in Catholic schools. The higher score for the former group holds up even when one controls factors that might affect the scores, such as parental occupation, education, and income, generation since immigration, sex, and size of hometown.

Both the Notre Dame and the Greeley-Rossi studies indicate, therefore, that viewed in terms of their graduates Catholic schools are doing at least as good a job as their public-school counterparts. It is *not* clear that the schools are the only force involved in producing this effect, but at least it would seem that they are not preventing their graduates from passing tests of accomplishment prescribed by this society and from partaking of the material rewards that follow from attaining this level of accomplishment.

Another argument leveled against Catholic schools is that they are divisive, that they retard in their students a ready identification with the rest of society and reinforce an intolerant attitude toward minority groups. The Greeley and Rossi study attempted to get at this matter by examining responses to a number of questions. Table II, taken from their data, shows the per cent expressing tolerant attitudes toward other groups.

With the exception of the statement that Jews have too much power in the United States, there are no significant differences between those who went to Catholic schools and those who did not. The item about Jews shows those having attended Catholic schools as being more tolerant than those who did not. If one assumes that the Catholic schools should be teaching the ethic of tolerance markedly better than other schools, then they are not doing their job. But the divisiveness argument implies that Catholic schools tend to make those who attend them more *intolerant* than products of the public schools, and this is clearly not the case. It is possible that instructionally

TABLE II

SCHOOL ATTENDANCE AND PER CENT EXPRESSING TOLERANT ATTITUDES TOWARD OTHER GROUPS

Item and Response	School Attendance		
	All Catholic	Some Catholic	No Catholic
Jews have too much power in the United States (disagree strongly)	45	42	37[a]
Jewish businessmen are about as honest as other businessmen (agree strongly)	41	41	38
Negroes shouldn't push themselves where they are not wanted (disagree)	37	38	38
White people have a right to live in an all-white neighborhood if they want to, and Negroes should respect this right (disagree)	24	26	26
I would strongly disapprove if a Negro moved next door to me (disagree strongly)	24	22	22
Negroes would be satisfied if it were not for a few people who stir up trouble (disagree)	21	21	18
Most Protestants are inclined to discriminate against Catholics (disagree)	70	73	67
Protestants don't really take their religion seriously compared to Catholics (disagree)	34	38	33
N	345	699	796

[a] Significantly different from "All Catholic."

Source: Adapted from Andrew M. Greeley and Peter H. Rossi, *The Education of Catholic Americans* (Chicago, 1966), p. 123.

the Catholic schools do teach tolerance but that the effect of the social environment of the schools may be to induce intolerance; thus the two influences may cancel out each other and produce a zero effect. In any case, the Catholic schools do not seem to have had the negative effects which their critics postulate. Other evidence available in the Greeley-Rossi volume leads to the same conclusion.

A third objection raised by the critics is more difficult to evaluate. The criticism has to do with the ineffectiveness of the schools in instilling religious commitment in their students. What "real" religious commitment is seems to be an unanswerable question, and unless this commitment can be identified and defined, it is obviously impossible to determine with certainty whether Catholic schools are helping or hindering its development. Without claiming to have settled the matter definitively, Greeley and Rossi suggest six different areas of religious behavior in respect to which one can examine the effects of the Catholic schools.[16]

1. Are Catholics who went to Catholic schools more likely to be engaged in approved formal religious behavior? Do they go to Mass, receive Communion, and go to Confession more frequently?
2. Are the Catholic-educated more inclined to acknowledge the teaching authority of the Church and to recognize the right of religious leaders to indicate the appropriate stand for Catholics in controversial issues?
3. Are the doctrinal and ethical attitudes of those who went to Catholic schools more orthodox?
4. Do they have a more accurate knowledge of the formal teachings of their religion?
5. Are they more inclined to participate in the organizational activities of the Catholic Church?
6. Are they more dedicated in their practice of the virtue of charity?

There is far from universal agreement about the importance of these six dimensions of religious behavior and whether they comprise all of the important dimensions. It is also a matter of debate how these dimensions are to be measured. However, the foregoing questions do

[16] Greeley and Rossi, p. 55 and chaps. 3 and 4, *passim*.

cover a broad spectrum of religious behavior and some parts of the spectrum are canonically defined as central to Catholic religious commitment.

Table III presents measures of five of the dimensions of religious behavior derived from the Greeley and Rossi study. An index was developed for each of these dimensions from several questionnaire items. This table gives the percentages of those scoring high on these indexes for each of the three categories of educational background we have been using.

This table is a summary of a great deal of detailed information and its implications are quite clear. Those who received their education exclusively in Catholic schools scored significantly higher in religious commitment (as measured by the indexes adopted) than those who received only part or none of their education in such schools. If par-

TABLE III

RELIGIOUS BEHAVIOR AND PER CENT ATTENDING EACH SCHOOL CATEGORY

Religious Behavior	School Attendance		
	All Catholic	Some Catholic	No Catholic
High on sacramental index[c]	37	24[a]	14[b]
High on accepting Church as teacher[d]	46	35[a]	31[a]
High in doctrinal orthodoxy[e]	33	24[a]	17[b]
High in ethical orthodoxy[f]	35	28	23[a]
High on religious knowledge index[g]	36	22[a]	13[b]
N	345	699	796

[a] Significantly different from "All Catholic."
[b] Significantly different from "All Catholic" and "Some Catholic."
[c] Mass every week, Communion several times a month.
[d] Accepting Church's teaching authority in four or more areas.
[e] Four or more orthodox responses to questionnaire items.
[f] Eight or more orthodox answers to questionnaire items.
[g] Three or more correct answers to questionnaire items.
Source: Adapted from Andrew M. Greeley and Peter H. Rossi, *The Education of Catholic Americans* (Chicago, 1966), p. 81.

ticipation in formal ritual, acceptance of the Church as teacher, acceptance of doctrine, acceptance of the ethical teachings of the Church, and the development of religious knowledge are the kinds of religious commitment that one thinks the schools are meant to instill, then it would seem that they have been a success. But there are further complications that must be considered in interpreting these results.

First, some have argued that while the schools should encourage sacramental participation, ethical and doctrinal orthodoxy, and religious knowledge, they should also produce more critical Catholics—which would mean less acceptance of the Church as teacher than is indicated by the results shown here. Whatever the merit of this line of thinking, it was not the view which organized the Catholic school system. Hence it is not a strong argument against the schools to point out that they do not produce an effect which it was not their intention to produce. The fact that the schools have achieved, to a limited degree, that which they set out to achieve would seem to indicate that if new goals were set, those goals might also be achieved. New goals, however, have not yet been established.

The second complication has to do with whether or not the dimensions covered in Table III are related to the sixth question listed earlier: Are those who went to Catholic schools more dedicated in their practice of the virtue of Christian charity? While most people would agree that this is the most important question, there is also doubt that it can be measured with the tools of social science. We have seen in Table II that those who went to Catholic schools are not notably more tolerant than those who did not. This might be interpreted as indicating a lack of impact on the part of the schools in respect to the practice of charity. The Greeley-Rossi study also approached this matter from another direction by seeking to discover whether Catholic schools were producing more people who went out of their way to help others. A very simple test was used: Respondents were asked whether they had helped anyone recently and if anyone had talked to them about personal problems. Table IV gives the percentages answering "yes" to each of these questions for each educational category. The results show clearly that Catholic schools are not producing any more "Good Samaritans" than public schools. Catholic schools seem to have made no difference in respect to this extremely critical dimension of religious commitment.

The final complication is that these tables tell us only that there is

TABLE IV
MEASURES OF CHARITY, BY SCHOOL ATTENDANCE
(PER CENT ATTENDING EACH TYPE)

Questionnaire Item (response in parenthesis)	School Attendance		
	All Catholic	Some Catholic	No Catholic
Have you spent any time in the past few months helping someone who needed help? (yes)	52	57	56
Has anyone talked to you about his personal problems in the last few months? (yes)	48	50	41[a]
N	345	699	796

[a] Significantly different from "All Catholic" and "Some Catholic."
Source: Adapted from Andrew M. Greeley and Peter H. Rossi, *The Education of Catholic Americans* (Chicago, 1966), p. 67.

a positive association between Catholic schools and the first five dimensions of religious behavior. They do not establish with certainty that the Catholic education received by these adults when they were children is the reason for the association. Space does not permit a full discussion of all the other factors that enter into the picture, but one which was found to be critical in the NORC study should be noted briefly: the religious commitment of the respondent's parents or the religious atmosphere of the home in which he was reared. Many critics of Catholic schools maintain that the family, not the school, plays the key role in religious formation. The Greeley-Rossi study confirmed the reinforcing effect of a strong religious home life, for it showed that Catholic schooling had a greater impact on those whose parents were more deeply religious. But it also showed that Catholic schooling has a positive independent effect of its own in influencing religious behavior as measured by the indexes adopted in the study. Even when the respondents are broken down according to the religious background of their homes (i.e., those whose parents were designated as more fervent or less fervent), the influence of the Catholic school upon its graduates is still discernible in their religious commitment.

CONTINUING SUPPORT FOR CATHOLIC SCHOOLS?

These pioneering studies from Notre Dame and NORC provided much information necessary for evaluating the criticisms of Catholic education. But they also showed that much more information is needed and stimulated the demand for more exhaustive and sophisticated studies of the Catholic schools. Moreover, they highlighted the need for a detailed and continuously updated statistical picture of the operation of these schools. For the whole atmosphere has changed and events are moving rapidly. Those who wish to see further changes are, on the whole, well informed concerning the schools and are often quite positive about what they want to see done. Catholic school authorities, if one can judge by the bishops' statements and the tone of the papers delivered at conventions of the National Catholic Educational Association (NCEA), have abandoned much of the defensiveness of the late 1950's and are more open to change.

This does not mean, however, that they are likely to follow the urgings of those who believe the entire Catholic school system should be scrapped in favor of a totally different approach to religious education. It is true that after reaching a peak in the academic year 1963-64, and showing insignificant decreases in the next two years, Catholic elementary school enrollments dropped 5.5 per cent in the fall of 1966. This decline continued in 1967; high-school enrollments, which had risen slightly in 1966, also fell off in the 1967-68 school year. These decreases may signal the beginnings of a general weakening of support for Catholic schools, but there are a number of other factors that should be taken into account. By the mid-1960's, a decade and a half of unprecedented expansion had brought the Catholic schools to a saturation point. They were overcrowded; there were too few nuns to handle the students; increasing reliance on lay teachers added significantly to the financial burden. Reassessment and readjustments were obviously called for. Among the readjustments that followed were strict limitation of class size, the elimination of whole grades, consolidations, and the closing of some rural schools so as to make the best use of scarce resources. All of these actions contributed to the decreases noted in the most recent period.[17]

It is clear from the figures given earlier that Catholic schools are still a vast enterprise involving millions of individuals and large numbers of semiautonomous units; consequently, they are not likely to be disbanded very soon. Nor is there any organized campaign calling for the abandonment of the schools. Those with final authority over Catholic schools are certainly not contemplating any such course. A recent statement by the National Conference of Catholic Bishops affirms that "Catholic elementary and secondary schools are an indispensable component of the Church's total commitment to education in the United States." The official statement drawn up by the Washington Symposium on the Future of Catholic Education (a gathering of 120 persons representing various fields of knowledge and interested organizations, convened by the NCEA in November, 1967) includes the assertion that "the Church will always maintain an institutional base for educational service. . . ." The statement concludes, "It would be premature to urge immediate massive redeployment of Catholic educational resources into new patterns of Christian education." Even Mary Perkins Ryan, who disagrees with the position taken by the Symposium, concedes that this stand probably reflects the views of the majority of the participants.[18]

The NORC study found no trend toward diminished commitment to the Catholic schools among those interviewed in 1963-64. On the contrary, the children of the respondents in this national sample of Catholic adults were more likely to have received, or to be receiving, Catholic schooling than was the case with the respondents themselves. The difference between the two was slight, however. Among the respondents, 57 per cent received all or part of their education in Catholic schools; for the children of the respondents, the corresponding

[17] *National Catholic Reporter* (Kansas City), Feb. 8, 1967, and May 28, 1968. The *Official Catholic Directory* for 1968 shows an overall decline of almost 219,000 in elementary and secondary enrollments between 1966-67 and 1967-68. For statistics on consolidations of Catholic schools see *School & Society*, XCVI (Jan. 6, 1968), 4.

[18] The Bishops' statement is quoted in *NCEA Bulletin*, LXIV (Feb., 1968), 17; *National Catholic Reporter*, Feb. 21, 1968, gives the statement of the Washington Symposium.

figure was 66 per cent.[19] Although this would indicate at least a weak trend in the direction of stronger support for Catholic schools, it might be argued that the change from commitment to the separate school system will make itself felt only when the children of the most recent generation of Catholic adults reach school age. But this hypothesis runs counter to Greeley and Rossi's finding that higher socioeconomic status correlates positively with the tendency to patronize the Catholic schools. The younger Catholics are the ones with the highest socioeconomic status, and it is precisely this group which has provided the strongest supporters of Catholic schools.

The explanations given by NORC respondents whose children were not attending Catholic schools do not suggest any basic alienation from the system. In 52 per cent of the cases, the reason given for not sending children to a Catholic elementary school was simply that none was available, or that it was too far away. The complaints that Catholic schools were too expensive and too overcrowded accounted for another 38 per cent of the responses from those whose children were in public schools. Only 5 per cent said that they did not send their children to Catholic schools because there was too much religion in them; and only 2 per cent objected that the schools were too narrow in outlook.

Equally interesting are the reasons given by parents who were sending their children to Catholic schools. The basic reason for the existence of Catholic schools is to provide religious instruction, and almost three-quarters of the respondents (73 per cent) gave this as the motivation for sending their children to such schools. Aside from this consideration, the most frequently given reasons were that discipline is better in Catholic schools (38 per cent) and that they give a better education than public schools (31 per cent).

Thus there is a decided contrast between what the intellectual critics think of Catholic schools and the views of the great mass of Catholic parents as revealed in the NORC study. It seems evident that many more Catholics would send their children to Catholic schools if such institutions were conveniently available. And the major complaints of those who could but do not patronize these schools is not that they are poor in quality or concentrate too much on religion, but that they cost too much and are too crowded. On the positive side, those who

[19] Greeley and Rossi, pp. 25, 203, and chap. IX, *passim*.

do patronize Catholic schools count on their providing religious instruction, discipline, and a good overall education. On the basis of this evidence, we can conclude that the demand for Catholic education is not waning and that an expansion of the system would be welcomed. But the demand is not sufficiently strong to call forth a system that would put every Catholic child into a Catholic school, and it is probably not strong enough to increase the percentage attending Catholic schools very significantly.

CURRENT TRENDS AND PROBLEMS

While it is virtually certain that Catholic schools will be around for a good many years to come, it is almost as certain that the system will not continue in precisely its present form. Too many proposals for change are being widely circulated and passionately promoted. What is even more significant is that many changes are already under way either as general developments or in experimental situations. Diocesan school systems all over the country are studying themselves with a view to change. And to assist them there are recently established institutions such as Notre Dame's Office of Educational Research and Boston College's Catholic Educational Research Center. While it is impossible to predict what the future holds, we may take note of certain trends and of some basic problems in respect to the structure and administration of the schools, their religious impact, and their role in society.

One of the most obvious developments is a movement away from the exclusive identification of Catholic education with Catholic schools. The Washington Symposium emphasized the need for a unified approach by the schools, the Confraternity of Christian Doctrine (CCD), and adult education agencies, in order to provide for the religious formation of *all* Catholics. Nearly all current writing on Catholic education stresses the same point.[20] According to the pre-

[20] *National Catholic Reporter*, Feb. 21, 1968, and Russell Shaw, "Breaking Down the Walls in Catholic Education," *America*, CXVIII (Jan. 20, 1968), 72-75. James Michael Lee, "Catholic Education: The Winds of Change," *Ave Maria*, CVII (Apr. 13, 1968), 7-9, 29-31, touches upon many of the points discussed in the following paragraphs.

scriptions of these writers, diocesan school boards should be reoriented into true boards of education, with more comprehensive authority to plan and allocate available resources, aiming at the religious education of the whole Catholic population within their jurisdiction. A team effort is urged upon all who teach Catholics, whether in the schools, in the home, through the CCD, or through other organized groups. Too little has been done along these lines to permit evaluation, but a redirection of approach is clearly under way.

Another development still in its early stages is the increased involvement of laymen in every phase of the Catholic educational enterprise. As we noted earlier, the proportion of lay teachers in the schools has already increased dramatically. The Notre Dame study showed, however, that in 1962-63 the median academic preparation of lay teachers was much less than that of nuns or brothers in the schools.[21] The situation has probably improved since then, but as a group the lay teachers still rank much lower than their public-school counterparts in professional preparation. This inadequacy may have something to do with the fact that only an infinitestimal fraction of lay teachers is entrusted with administrative responsibilities. Even more important, of course, is the traditional relationship between the religious orders and the schools. In any case, the Notre Dame study found only forty-nine out of 31,742 lay teachers in elementary schools and thirty-five out of 10,801 in the high schools who were in administrative positions.[22] But before well-prepared lay teachers can be attracted, salaries will have to become more competitive with the public system and possibilities for professional advancement opened up. There is evidence of progress in the area of salaries. The South Bend-Fort Wayne diocese recently adopted a salary scale which exceeds that of the South Bend public system on the lower levels, and every week brings an announcement of substantial increases elsewhere. It remains to be seen whether the financial resources will be found to retain the professional staff attracted by improved salaries and benefits.

Another sphere of lay activity is Catholic school boards, the numbers of which have increased very rapidly in the last half-dozen years. According to one authority, the late Msgr. O'Neil C. D'Amour, one-third of the Catholic elementary schools in the United States have boards

[21] Neuwien, pp. 85-87.
[22] Neuwien, p. 104.

on which laymen are represented; 130 dioceses have school boards, ninety of which include laymen.[23] There is tremendous variation, however, in the role played by these boards in educational policy and administration. Of thirty-five boards surveyed by the magazine *U.S. Catholic* in April, 1967, only twelve appeared to have real jurisdiction over policy-making. Some of those that do were described in papers delivered to the NCEA convention in 1967, and it seems likely that the boards will assume a more important role in the future.[24] Some spokesmen argue that laymen must assume complete responsibility for the schools, separating them from the parishes and incorporating them as autonomous entities. Another suggestion heard frequently is that regional Catholic school boards should be set up, perhaps coextensive with the public-school districts in the same locality.

All of these new developments have financial implications for Catholic education. If the lay staffs are to grow and if salaries are to be competitive with the public system more money must be found; both of these movements seem inevitable if Catholic schools are to be maintained at all. There are many suggestions as to how the problem may be met, none of which promises to be the sole solution. The most comprehensive proposals come from those who, like James Michael Lee, call for concentration on certain levels of education and the dropping of others.[25] The difficulty here is that even the experts disagree on what the schools can do most effectively, and whether it is best done at the pre-school, elementary, or secondary level. The *U.S. Catholic* survey revealed no consensus among superintendents as to which if any grades should be dropped. As a result, although grades (usually primary) have been dropped by various dioceses (e.g., Cincinnati and Louisville), or by individual schools, such decisions are usually dictated by immediate financial considerations.

The trend toward more unified control of the Catholic schools could mean financial savings through shared facilities, more rational accounting and purchasing procedures, and joint administration of funds.

[23] *National Catholic Reporter*, Sept. 27, 1967. According to NCEA figures for spring 1968, there are 2,100 parochial school boards today.

[24] See the papers of Ellen Casey, Robert Mooney, and Aloysius Lacki reproduced in *NCEA Bulletin*, LXIV (Aug., 1967). Cf. "Here's What Is Happening to Catholic Schools in the U.S.A.," *U.S. Catholic*, XXXII (Apr., 1967), 6-18.

[25] See James Michael Lee, ed., *Catholic Education in the Western World* (Notre Dame, Ind., 1967), p. 307.

Experts in educational economics, who have begun to take an interest in the problems of Catholic schools, emphasize the desirability of a budget that meets needs in the order of priority on a fiscal-year basis. In an area where traditionally only the pastor knew what was going on —a situation which still prevails in many places—these procedures seem utopian. But the views of the financial experts were featured in the Washington Symposium, and there is no doubt that the trend is in this direction.

Inseparable from improvements in financial administration are substantive questions about how the money should be spent. If, for example, all Catholics and not just the children in Catholic schools are to be adequately included in programs of religious education, a reallocation of financial resources is obviously required. It has been estimated that in the average parish with a Catholic school, 95 per cent of the educational funds are expended in educating 42 per cent of the children, leaving only one dollar in twenty for the CCD and other such programs.[26] Although these estimates often overlook some of the hidden costs of the CCD, the disproportion between what is spent in the schools and what is spent anywhere else is very great. Moreover, the concentration on Catholic schools means that most of the money is being spent on the education of a group that is relatively highly "advantaged"—white children of middle-class background. This is quite natural in view of the improved status of the Catholic population and the costs of attending Catholics schools, but it is nevertheless disturbing to many observers concerned with social and racial problems.

The relationship of Catholic schools to urban racial problems is a complicated matter. According to a paper prepared by the Research Institute for Catholic Education in New York state, parochial schools act as a "holding" force, slowing down the out-movement of whites in a changing neighborhood.[27] Nearly half of the 13,000 students in Catholic schools in Washington, D.C., are Negroes, and these schools are relatively well-integrated compared to the city's public schools. And the Archdiocese of Chicago operates ninety-two schools in the inner

[26] Cf. Sister Mary Peter Traxler, "High School Responsibility and Human Rights," *NCEA Bulletin*, LXIV (Aug., 1967), 122.

[27] Cited in James C. Donahue, "De Facto Segregation—Its Impact on Schools," *Catholic Educator*, XXXVIII (Feb., 1968), 42. See also Sanders, "Catholic Elementary-School Enrollment," *loc cit.*

city; more than half of their students are non-Catholics.[28] All of this might be viewed positively. But many of the Catholic schools that have closed in recent years were in the inner cities, and the middle-class Catholics who have been the financial mainstay of the schools have increasingly joined the flight to the suburbs. These developments, along with the worsening urban racial situation, have stimulated much soul searching by those who believe the Church must not abandon those in need.

Some suggestions call for drastic change. A letter writer in the *National Catholic Reporter* (September 27, 1967), for example, proposed that the Church eliminate parochial schools and direct the money instead to inner-city community-action programs, to the development of a free, integrated, high quality, secondary school system, and to special education classes for the disadvantaged, designed to supplement and enrich the offerings of the public schools. Many others would like to see the Church do more along these lines, but do not like to contemplate abandoning the parochial school.[29] However, it is doubtful that the financial support freely given to the parochial school would be equally available for this kind of alternative program. The prospects are better for more limited programs aiming at the same general ends. City-suburban bussing of children, which is often suggested, is to be instituted on a small scale in the fall of 1968 in the Archdiocese of Chicago. Perhaps the best hope lies in special home-and-school programs for economically depressed areas conducted in cooperation with public schools, for which Federal funds may be available.

But the fact remains that even to maintain the Catholic schools at their present level more money is needed. Structural and procedural changes are little better than marginally useful in resolving the financial plight. The major problem is to find new sources of funds. More

[28] Havighurst; Traxler, "High School Responsibility," *loc. cit.* p. 123.

[29] Msgr. Donahue's recent suggestion for a reordering of priorities which would place the Catholic schools below educational assistance to disadvantaged ghetto youth, and below religious education of the CCD variety, brought much criticism from Catholic school administrators. See James C. Donahue, "New Priorities in Catholic Education," *America*, CXVIII (Apr. 13, 1968), 476-79, and the reaction reported in the *Catholic Messenger* (Davenport, Ia.,), May 9, 1968. U. S. Commissioner of Education Harold Howe II has also challenged Catholic educators to assume new responsibilities in the area of urban education. See the report of his speech before the NCEA convention in Apr., 1968, in the *Catholic Messenger*, Apr. 25, 1968.

equitable assessment of the whole Catholic community would be helpful; while this is often suggested, there are few clearly defined and workable proposals. Endowments or grants from Catholic sources, from businesses, or from the community as a whole are another possibility. Perhaps with this in mind, Catholic school administrators have begun to develop an interest in improving their public relations. Thus the *U. S. Catholic* report discusses the findings of the Wallach survey which dealt with the Catholic school's "image" in the community at large.

Discussion of the need for money inevitably gets around to government as a source, particularly the Federal government. Here Catholic opinion ranges all the way from those who oppose Federal aid flatly to those who support the position of the Citizens for Educational Freedom. The CEF argues that the right to "freedom of choice" in education requires the government to assist those who want church-affiliated schools for their children. As a matter of fact, the Federal government is already providing some financial assistance to Catholic schools. Title I of the Elementary and Secondary Education Act of 1965 makes funds available to both public and private schools which are educating substantial numbers of disadvantaged students. Catholic schools can get textbooks, library books, and audio-visual materials on loan through Title II of the same legislation; Title III supports co-operative Catholic-public school innovative efforts through educational centers and services. Some states also provide supplementary services to Catholic schools; shared time programs (in which Catholic-school pupils use public school facilities for certain subjects) exist in thirty-five states. In 1965, the NCEA reported that 251 Catholic elementary and high schools were involved in some sort of shared-time arrangements. Many of these programs are of very limited scope, however, affecting a relative handful of students in home economics and shop classes. Very few experimental programs are exploring the wider possibilities of dual enrollment.[30]

Some groups favoring strict separation of Church and State oppose even the limited government aid now being received by Catholic schools, and it is conceivable that the courts might rule against it if the issue comes before them. But two words mentioned above may point the way toward more hopeful developments—innovation and

[30] Cf. Friedlander, *The Shared Time Strategy.*

cooperation. All of American education is in turmoil today. The problems faced by public schools are also overwhelming, particularly in large cities. In a study of the two school systems in a typical northern city, Richard P. Boardman came to the conclusion that dysfunctional elements prevented a constructive relationship and that, without cooperation and exchange of ideas between them, the education of all school children was unfavorably affected.[31] Although the main responsibility for education in American society will remain with the public school, a Catholic school system constantly seeking to improve itself and to find those areas where it could meet special needs could make a unique contribution by undertaking bold and imaginative educational programs. But before any such possibility can be realized at least three things are necessary: Catholic schools must be willing to break with tradition and accept new functions and goals; stronger cooperative links between Catholic schools and public schools must be forged; more funds must be made available both from private and public sources.

It seems unlikely that our educational system will undergo any such drastic reorganization as that recommended in the Friedman-Jencks plan, whereby parents could use governmental tuition grants at schools of their own choice—schools operated by industry, foundations, and churches, as well as by units of local government, all competing to offer the best education.[32] But there is no question that changes of some sort will be made; no question that all kinds of educational experiments and new departures will seek to realize the promise of a better life for all American children. If Catholic education in the United States is to live, it must be part of these efforts. The research, the self-studies, and the many experimental programs are a good beginning—a beginning that demands to be continued and expanded. The educational tasks facing our society are enormous; the energies of all the groups making up the society will be needed to meet them. Several times in their history, Catholic schools have been called upon to meet new challenges. By doing so today they will not only contribute to the great common task of the American people, they will also assure for themselves a future as exciting and as honorable as their past.

[31] Boardman's study is cited in Donahue, "De Facto Segregation," *loc. cit.*

[32] Cf. Christopher Jencks, "Is the Public School Obsolete?" *The Public Interest*, No. 2, Winter, 1966, pp. 18-27.

12: THE STRUCTURE OF CATHOLIC HIGHER EDUCATION

Robert Hassenger

One need not be a cliché-monger to assert that Catholic higher education is in transition. It is, with a vengeance. Not without considerable misgivings, therefore, I address myself to the "structure" of this effervescent phenomenon. Several years ago I attempted to assay its "shape," or broad outlines. In the present essay, I am attempting to present a rather different perspective on the Catholic colleges and universities, drawing on both my own work and four recently published volumes.[1]

College and university[2] enrollments are growing four times faster than the general population. There was an increase of 6.2 per cent in full-time student enrollment in the fall of 1967. Although freshman enrollment was up 2.3 per cent (compared to a decrease of .9 per cent in 1966-67), there were 5,000 fewer eighteen-year-olds in the country in 1967 than in 1965 (reflecting the peak birth year of 1947); thus, larger percentage increases occurred for the junior and senior classes than for freshmen or sophomores.[3] Still, there were 18,250 more

[1] Andrew M. Greeley, with the assistance of William Van Cleve and Grace Ann Carroll, *The Changing Catholic College* (Chicago, 1968); Joseph Scimecca and Roland Damiano, *Crisis at St. John's* (New York, 1967); George N. Shuster, *Catholic Education in a Changing World* (New York, 1967); James W. Trent and Jenette Golds, *Catholics in College* (Chicago, 1967).

[2] To avoid the constant use of the phrase "colleges and universities," I shall use "colleges" to refer to higher educational institutions generally, unless otherwise noted. I sometimes also use "school" to refer to colleges and universities, to avoid repetition.

[3] All statistics are from Garland G. Parker, "Statistics of Attendance in American Universities and Colleges, 1967-68," *School and Society*, XCVI (Jan. 6, 1968), 9-24.

freshmen in accredited colleges in 1967-68 than in 1966-67.[4] Teachers' colleges showed the largest percentage gains for full-time students, as enrollment increased by nearly 10 per cent; large public universities were up 7.5 per cent; about two-fifths of the full-time students in American higher education were in eighty large public institutions. Large private universities reported a 3.3 per cent increase in full-time students; about 13 per cent of the full-time people are found in these institutions. Arts and sciences colleges showed a gain of 4.7 per cent, but this was lower than in the three preceding years. Fewer than 30 per cent of the full-time students are now found in private universities and colleges. Two decades ago, a majority of students were enrolled in such institutions. Probably about half of this number are in Church-related schools, and about 40 per cent of these (or approximately 6 per cent of the total), in colleges sponsored by the Catholic Church.[5]

THE INSTITUTIONS

A question long asked by scholars concerned with Catholic higher education is the exact number of Catholic colleges and universities. Of the 817 schools reported in the Danforth Commission Study, 339 were affiliated with the Catholic Church.[6] But the Committee on Higher Education of the National Catholic Educational Association reports 457 Catholic institutions of higher learning.[7] Two hundred of these are conducted primarily for clergy and religious, 257 for lay men and women.

It is difficult to find reliable statistics on the distribution of Catholics on Catholic and other campuses, but apparently somewhat less than

[4] The percentage of women was rising faster than that of men, reflecting the increased draft calls.

[5] Loyola of Chicago is now the largest (12,651), after the decline in enrollment at St. John's (11,677 students in 1967-68) following the shameful incidents there. The other largest Catholic universities include Marquette (11,488), Fordham (10,449), and Dayton (10,131). For comparison, here are some of the 1967-68 enrollments at several other well-known Catholic schools: Notre Dame, 7,716; Georgetown, 7,480; Holy Cross, 2,353; Manhattanville, 1,402; Newton, 830.

[6] Manning M. Pattillo, Jr. and Donald M. Mackenzie, *Church-Sponsored Higher Education in the United States* (Washington, 1966).

[7] Charles E. Ford and Edgar L. Roy, Jr., *The Renewal of Catholic Higher Education* (Washington, 1966). This research is referred to as "the NCEA (National Catholic Educational Association) Study" in this chapter.

a third of the Catholics in college, or about 430,000 in 1967, were found in Church-sponsored institutions. Between 9 and 12 per cent of the bachelor's degrees are awarded each year by Catholic institutions; over 90 per cent of these are to Catholics. This proportion will probably decrease considerably as efforts are made to diversify enrollments and as a largely assimilated population becomes less intent on a Catholic college education. The best guess is that by 1985 only about one-sixth of the Catholics in college will be in Catholic institutions.

Some of the colleges are very small: More than a third of the Catholic institutions covered in the NCEA-sponsored study had fewer than 100 fulltime students. Only a handful had more than 2,000. The statistically typical Catholic college was for women, with between 300 and 750 students. In 1965, the U.S. Office of Education listed 136 four-year Catholic women's colleges and more than forty junior colleges. Taken together, five out of six Catholic schools are sex-segregated, nearly half of the colleges admitting women only, an additional third taking men exclusively. But the few large coeducational universities enroll so many that considerably more than one in six students is in a coeducational setting. Very few of the formerly male, Jesuit universities are without women on the undergraduate level (and all admit them to graduate and professional schools, where these exist).

There are vast differences in quality within Catholic higher education. Many of the small colleges were without regional accreditation when Ford and Roy did their study. Yet that same year there were forty National Merit Scholars enrolled at Notre Dame, thirty-four at Georgetown, eighteen at St. Louis, twelve at Marquette, and eight at Holy Cross, to take only the leaders; Boston College, Rosary, Catholic University, and Fordham were also attracting an increasing number. When the choice of colleges by NMSC students is compared to the number of places available in freshman classes, Notre Dame and Georgetown are overchosen by men, Georgetown and Catholic University by women. Notre Dame is eighteenth among all American colleges for men in choice by NMSC scholars.[8]

[8] Robert C. Nichols, "College Preferences of Eleventh Grade Students," *National Merit Scholarship Research Reports*, 2 (#9), 1966. It should also be noted, however, that Catholic men were only about half as likely as non-Catholics to win NMSC awards between 1956 and 1959. See E. D. Farwell, H. Warren and T. R. McConnell, "Student Personality Characteristics Associated with Types of Colleges and Fields of Study," *College and University*, XXXVII (1962), 229-41.

Two other indexes of quality are Phi Beta Kappa affiliation and the number of national fellowships awarded to a school's students. At this writing, six Catholic colleges and universities are ΦBK affiliates: Catholic University, Fordham, Georgetown, Notre Dame, St. Louis, and the College of St. Catherine. Notre Dame has the best record for national fellowships; between 1952 and 1966, its seniors received 122 Woodrow Wilsons, twenty-three Danforths, nine Root-Tildens, and six Rhodes scholarships. But Fordham was highest for Wilsons received in 1968 with eleven, compared to eight at Boston College and Notre Dame, six at St. Louis, and five at Marquette.

Such traditional measures of college quality have been supplemented by more recent attempts to assess the overall atmosphere or "climate" of an institution. Elsewhere I have examined the results of the research on Catholic colleges, using such devices as the College and University Environment Survey,[9] and will not repeat the discussion here. The findings can be summarized by saying that, while strong group ties are found on most Catholic campuses, particularly at women's colleges, there is at the same time a high degree of organization and structure of the curriculum and even of student extracurricular life. Basic student freedoms were often not preserved, and there was considerable regulation of students' lives. Academically, the colleges seemed characterized by a rather anti-intellectual vocationalism, with relatively little interest in liberalizing courses and experiences. Passports to suburbia were being purchased. These characteristics were more typically found in large urban universities than in small liberal-arts colleges, and of the latter, several women's colleges (Manhattanville and Newton, to name two) were highest in intellectuality and social concern. The pragmatic, utilitarian orientations of many in the largest and best known Catholic universities may be in large part because of the up-and-out objectives of students from the more recently arrived ethnic groups who commute to such institutions. And this brings us to the question: Who *are* the students in Catholic colleges and universities?

UNDERGRADUATES

The most useful studies of Catholics in college have been done by the National Opinion Research Center (NORC) at the University of Chi-

[9] Robert Hassenger and Robert F. Weiss, S.J., "The Catholic College Climate," *School Review*, LXXIV (Winter, 1966), 419-45.

cago. These have been mainly the work of Andrew M. Greeley,[10] who has summarized his general findings in a recent book. I shall draw from these here.[11]

After noting that "half the adult Catholic population are either immigrants or the children of immigrants," Greeley goes on to cite NORC data which show that students in Catholic colleges differ very little from their Protestant counterparts (although both differ from American Jewish collegians). He or she (about two-fifths are girls, which is close to the proportion for Protestants) is just as likely to have come from a family where both parents were college-attenders and whose income was over $7,500 annually. [12] By comparison, Catholics in non-Catholic institutions were less likely to be girls (fewer than a third were), or to come from families with as high an educational or economic level. They were also more likely to be married before graduation (another indirect indication of somewhat lower socio-economic origins).

Nearly nine of ten Catholics in the NORC sample of Catholic college-attenders came from north of the Mason-Dixon line and east of the Mississippi, compared to only two-thirds of the Catholics in non-Catholic colleges. Not surprisingly, they are also likely to come from larger metropolitan areas. The most heavily represented ethnic group was the Irish (almost two-fifths), although this is undoubtedly a decline from earlier years, as the more recently arrived groups catch up.

The writer has uncovered some interesting data on the economic and educational backgrounds of students at two neighboring Catholic colleges for men and women, both located in somewhat remote rural districts. About four-fifths of the students in each school are from the state in which the colleges are located, even though about 90 per cent at each institution are residents. Two-thirds come from cities under

[10] See Andrew M. Greeley, *Religion and Career* (New York, 1963); A. M. Greeley and Peter H. Rossi, *The Education of Catholic Americans* (Chicago, 1966); and Seymour Warkov and A. M. Greeley, "Parochial School Origins and Educational Achievement," *American Sociological Review*, XXXI (1966), 406-14.

[11] The next two paragraphs are a close paraphrase of Greeley's *The Changing Catholic College*, pp. 23, 33-35.

[12] Others have suggested that Greeley reported data selectively, in taking the $7,500 figure, and go on to present other evidence that, if one looks at the comparisons for $10,000 and over, he finds 32 per cent of the Jews, 24 per cent of the Protestants, and only 18 per cent of the Catholics there (Norval D. Glenn and Ruth Hyland, "Religious Preference and Worldly Success: Some Evidence from National Surveys," *American Sociological Review*, XXXII [1967], 73-85).

50,000, about half of these from towns under 5,000 or farms. Only one-quarter are from metropolitan areas of 100,000 or more (at the women's college these students are more likely to transfer). About a quarter of the girls' fathers are farmers and another quarter are self-employed, probably in the small towns which service farmers. Thus, their educational level is not high, although one-quarter make more than $11,000 annually, and about 14 per cent more than $15,000. The men's fathers are rather better educated: 26 per cent of the 1967 class had fathers who graduated from college (compared to 19 per cent for the women); 13 per cent of the men's mothers had graduated, compared to 10 per cent for the women. In each of the colleges, however, there has been a rather alarming decline in social-class levels since the early 1960's (alarming in the sense that each school needs middle-class students to survive, since they must raise tuition). Among those entering in 1967, 15 per cent of the men's fathers were professionals, whereas nearly one-third had been in the 1964 freshman class. Their average income in 1967 was $9,000. At the neighboring women's college, the educational levels of parents has fallen since 1965, when 18 per cent of the mothers and 22 per cent of the fathers had graduated from college. For at least one of the schools, students with modest economic backgrounds were costing them money in an additional way: 61 per cent of the freshmen received some form of financial aid, and the college simply cannot afford to maintain this level without greatly increased endowments. And yet, located in a rather isolated setting, the school must offer inducements to some good students to get them to enroll and remain. There is a 60 per cent drop-out rate at the women's college; more than half of these occur after one year. Three-fourths of the drop-outs are in the upper half of their high-school classes. Girls from urban areas are more likely to leave than those from small towns and rural areas. At the same time, there was a lower freshman enrollment in 1967 than five years before. Clearly, such colleges are in real trouble.

An interesting—if overdrawn—portrait of a quite different kind of undergraduate student, the commuter to a large metropolitan Catholic university, can be found in an otherwise uninteresting book on New York's St. John's.[13] Typically the first in his family to attend college,

[13] Scimecca and Damiano have done a surprisingly sloppy book for a major publishing firm to claim, both in its production and in the approach taken by two aspiring sociologists. Much of the data they (selectively) adduce to bolster their "case" is a decade out of date.

the St. John's undergraduate is likely to come from a working-class or lower middle-class family living in Brooklyn or Queens and is interested only in acquiring the credentials that will allow him to get his feet on the bottom rung of the upward-mobility ladder. He tended to be, in the middle 1960's, relatively uninterested in the academic freedom issues at stake in the St. John's strike, more worried that his own grades and credits might be in jeopardy. Many came from second- or third-generation immigrant families, with strong emphases on order and discipline. The Catholic high schools these students attended often only reinforced this style. Their social and political attitudes underwent little change during their St. John's years: The "status politics" which bred a superpatriotic conservatism among their parents was reflected in the overwhelming victory of William Buckley in the campus mock mayoral election. But with the assimilation of the Catholic immigrant groups —often using the education or engineering degrees obtained by commuting to the St. Johns of the major cities—such patterns may largely disappear. Increased tuition costs will also likely mean an increasingly upper-middle-class clientele.

With such patterns in the backgrounds of many in Catholic colleges it is not surprising that the available data shows relatively little effectiveness in the schools' attempts to lastingly affect their students. I have elsewhere attempted an exhaustive summary of the available research on Catholic-college impact (to 1965)[14] and will present only the briefest digest of my conclusions here, supplemented by reference to the recent Greeley and Trent volumes.

One reason for the separate existence of church-sponsored colleges and universities is the difference they are intended to make in the lives of people who attend them. Although others disagree, it seems to me reasonable to expect colleges to have a significant impact on their students; a forthcoming monograph presents considerable evidence that significant changes do occur for certain students within certain educational contexts.[15]

[14] In Robert Hassenger, ed., *The Shape of Catholic Higher Education,* (Chicago, 1967), chap. V. This summary follows a similar digest, which appears in my chapter, "Catholic Higher Education," in *Catholics, U.S.A.: Perspectives from Behavioral Science,* eds. N. J. Pallone and W. T. Liu (New York, 1968).

[15] R. Hassenger, "A Rationale for Changing Student Values," *Educational Record,* XLVIII (1967), 61-67; and Hassenger, "Freedom and the Quality of Student Life," in *Academic Freedom and the Catholic University,* eds. E. Manier

Although the data reported in Greeley is rather different, there has been a pattern of association between Catholic-college attendance and what might be called "conservative" social and political attitudes. But the recent NORC study indicates that, if anything, Catholic-college graduates tend to be liberal Democrats and are lower in anti-Semitism and anticivil-libertarianism than Catholics who went to non-Catholic colleges, so perhaps the earlier findings were a reflection of ethnicity and social class.

Catholic-college students have also appeared to be more religious than their secular-college counterparts. Whether the criterion was church attendance, self-described religiousness, or indexes of religious knowledge and understanding, Catholic-college products have consistently come out ahead. But in the past knowledge and attitudes have been little reflected in religious commitment, at least as measurable. The greatest impact of the schools and colleges has seemed to be less on social consciousness than on doctrinal and ethical matters and those which had, in Greeley and Rossi's words, "crucial symbolic importance for American Catholicism—church attendance, sexual morality, and organizational 'loyalty' (to the papacy and to the teaching authority of the Church.)" More recent data shows that dramatic changes in at least some matters, such as birth control, have taken place since the early 1960's.[16] There is an increasing pool of data on the effects of the colleges on the personalities of Catholic students. Earlier research consistently found that Catholics were higher in measured authoritarianism, dogmatism, and general conservatism than those on secular campuses, with Catholics in Catholic schools higher than Catholics on non-Catholic campuses. More recent investigations provide mixed results. Stern and Trent found a general constraint and restrictiveness in the Catholic schools in their samples; in the Trent research, seniors in the five Pacific Coast Catholic colleges

---

and J. Houck (Notre Dame, Ind., 1967), pp. 145-61. The monograph referred to is *The Impacts of Colleges on Their Students*, by Kenneth Feldman and Theodore Newcomb, available in preliminary form as a Report to the Carnegie Foundation for the Advancement of Teaching.

[16] C. F. Westoff and N. B. Ryder, for example, found that a majority of married Catholic women aged 18-39 were not conforming to Catholic doctrine on birth control in 1965 ("Methods of Fertility Control in the United States: 1955-65," *Studies in Family Planning*, XVII [Feb., 1967], 1-5).

studied looked little different from freshmen, despite the general movement toward a freer expression of impulses and the concern with intellectual and esthetic matters found for non-Catholics in the sample.[17] But other studies suggest that at least some Catholic collegians are no higher in dogmatism than their non-Catholic peers and that changes do take place on some Catholic campuses.[18] Or those with particular characteristics may be influenced by membership in one campus subculture, but not another. There are no investigations with which the writer is familiar that control for differential backgrounds, student traits, and college exposures. Until we have them, it is difficult to know just how effective Catholic colleges are.

There are some indications that church-affiliated colleges do not change their students as much as they reinforce the formation which has occurred in the home and to some extent in elementary and secondary school.[19] To date, the colleges seem to have been most successful, to quote the NORC research, at "inculcating precisely those norms already reasonably well accepted among American Catholics . . . attendance at Mass, sexual morality, acceptance of authority." It is questionable whether separate Catholic colleges and universities have been needed to achieve these unimpressive results. The same kind of reinforcement effects for Catholics on secular campuses who are active

[17] George G. Stern, "Psychological Characteristics of Denominational Colleges," paper read at the 1965 Meetings of the American Catholic Psychological Association, Chicago; Trent and Golds.

[18] See, for example, Barbara Long, "Catholic-Protestant Differences in Acceptance of Others," *Sociology and Social Research*, XLIX (1965), 166-71; and R. Hassenger, "Catholic College Impact on Religious Orientations," *Sociological Analysis*, XXVII (1966), 67-79, where it was found that authoritarianism and dogmatism decreased significantly during the first two years students spent in a Catholic women's college, with corresponding increases on scales assessing social maturity and concern with civil liberties. Even in Trent data can be found showing the greater growth by Catholic than non-Catholic National Merit Scholars (Trent and Golds, Table 19, p. 115), and references to the research of Peterson showing the greatly increased activism of Catholic collegians. Throughout much of his book, Trent generalizes too widely from a handful of colleges on the West Coast, most in California.

[19] Greeley and Rossi found that the Catholic schools were effective reinforcers of the religious training received in highly religious homes, but had little effect on those from less religious backgrounds. Catholic colleges seemed to make a difference only for those who had attended Catholic grade and high schools.

members of Catholic campus organizations, such as Newman Centers or student parishes, have been found by Menard.[20] Since this is where at least four-fifths of the Catholic collegians will be within twenty years, there may be good reason for many colleges to seriously consider abandoning their separate efforts, to become cluster colleges affiliated with major universities. This is not to say that Catholic colleges cannot be restructured to have significant effects on their students. But this will depend in large measure on the kinds of socializing experiences available on the Catholic campus—the distinctiveness of the programs, the structuring of the curriculum and of student life, the *charisma* of priests and professors, the kinds of students attracted, and —most important—the resources available. Schools which do seem to have an unmistakable effect on their students are those which have allocated considerable resources to just this end. If Catholic schools fail to exert the influence many feel they should have, it may well be because of an inability to provide the necessary funds which have gone to bolster graduate programs.

GRADUATE EDUCATION

Although post-baccalaureate programs seem to be attracting an increasingly larger proportion of the available money, Catholic graduate education has not, even recently, been impressive.[21] Although nearly thirty Catholic institutions award either the Master's or Ph.D., only twenty graduate *departments* were ranked in the recent Cartter survey, with but three of these considered really good.[22] Not a single social-science department in a Catholic graduate school was ranked.

This unflattering appraisal is reflected in the meager research money flowing into Catholic graduate programs. In 1962, no Catholic univer-

[20] Lawrence Menard ("Effects of the Newman Club on the Religious Commitment of Its Members," paper read at the 1966 meetings of the American Catholic Sociological Society, Miami) found that such students in five New York City colleges underwent less decrease in traditional belief and practice than Catholic nonmembers. Some attrition from traditional Catholicism occurred, but it was less for Newman participants than nonparticipants (and, of the members, less for women than for men).

[21] This section has been taken in large part from my contribution to Liu-Pallone.

[22] Allan M. Cartter, *An Assessment of Quality in Graduate Education* (Washington, 1966).

sity ranked among the top seventy-five recipients of federal research money, and three of the four in the first 100 had medical schools, which obtained the largest share of these funds.[23] Nor has the situation improved much since, judging from the data available through the National Science Foundation. Only 147 of 5,996 National Defense Education Act fellowships were allocated to Catholic universities in 1966-67, less than 3 per cent of the total. But this is not surprising, considering the fact that Catholic schools award only about 3 per cent of the nation's doctorates.[24]

The Greeley data indicate that Catholics now go to graduate school in proportion to their numbers in the population and that they persist to the Ph.D., although Trent presents rather different findings. Jencks and Riesman estimate that, even if all the doctoral candidates in Catholic universities were themselves Catholics—and an actual count would probably show that about 75-80 per cent are—only a third of the Catholic Ph.D. candidates would be accounted for, indicating that about two-thirds are seeking degrees in non-Catholic graduate departments.

One of the reasons for this is undoubtedly that the professionally oriented faculty in Catholic colleges often feel obliged to suggest that their best students go to the ranking graduate departments. These have not been in Catholic universities. The graduate departments in

[23] From C. Jencks and D. Riesman, *The Academic Revolution* (New York, 1968), chap. IX, who cite the House Committee on Education and Labor, *The Federal Government and Education* (Washington, 1963). The very medical departments which are among a school's best are also a considerable financial drain on the institution. Too many struggling Catholic colleges in the past sought instant university standing by buying up nearly bankrupt dentistry, medical, pharmacy, and law schools. These provide no services today that state-supported facilities do not, although they do allow fund-raisers in urban Jesuit institutions to appeal to civic pride and pragmatism, telling the local or state citizenry that "half the lawyers in ——— are the products of . . ." Marquette has recently amended its Medical School's charter and by-laws, severing all legal ties between the university and the medical school, which has been sustaining heavy operating deficits for some time. The Marquette School of Medicine, as it is now called, will cooperate with county and other local health officials, as a multi-institutional medical center.

[24] Compared to 11 per cent of all B.A.'s, 8 per cent of the M.A.'s, and 7 per cent of the professional degrees (National Catholic Welfare Conference, *Summary of Catholic Education*, 1963; U.S. Office of Education, *Digest of Educational Statistics*, 1965). Only Catholic University, Notre Dame, Fordham, and St. Louis are among the top fifty producers of Ph.D.'s.

the best of the Catholic universities seem to pull students from the less visible Catholic liberal-arts colleges, such as St. Ambrose, Rockhurst, St. Thomas, or the Marymounts, and from second-level Catholic universities (e.g., Fairfield, Detroit). Perhaps Fordham, St. Louis, and Notre Dame are attractive to those who have spent four years in less exciting college climates—but the best of the Fordham, St. Louis, and Notre Dame undergraduates head for Berkeley, Chicago, and Harvard. (And often come back with shiny Ph.D.'s to Fordham, St. Louis, and Notre Dame to send their best students to Berkeley, Chicago, and Harvard.) There are, of course, people who suggest throwing out all but a small number of doctoral programs in Catholic higher education and concentrating on top-quality sequences in a handful of universities. Unfortunately this is not likely to happen, for at least six pragmatic reasons.

First, graduate-school attendance has never been higher. The number of people taking the Graduate Record Examination for admission to graduate school—not counting exams for professional schools, nor the GRE's taken at many schools as part of their institutional testing programs—jumped from 57,922 in 1962-63 to 81,768 in 1963-64, and 106,100 in 1964-65. No doubt many take the examinations without actually enrolling. But some of those who take the exams as part of the institutional testing programs have their scores forwarded to graduate schools, and a few graduate programs do not require the GRE, preferring such measures as the Miller Analogies Test. With this fantastic jump in the graduate-school attendance, which may be expected to resume after the current Selective Service crisis, it would be unrealistic to expect Catholic colleges and second-rate universities with higher aspirations not to start even more graduate programs.

Second, those universities with fairly good programs have their sights set on higher things. Whatever "excellence" is, it seems to be currently denoted by foundation grants and research projects, which go to institutions with the men who prefer to concentrate on training graduate students. There are indications that this situation is at least partly dysfunctional for the overall educational picture, as the Berkeley rebels would be the first to insist.[25] Nevertheless, it is the name of the game as presently played, and it would be naive in the extreme to ex-

[25] One of the dangers in rating graduate schools, as in the Cartter Report and its predecessors, is that institutions and departments on the edge of that kind of excellence are constrained to follow the "tried-and-true" path to this exalted state and become fearful of innovative programs.

pect those Catholic university presidents who have this kind of "excellence" within their grasp to pull out of the race now.

Third, some suggest that those schools which confine their efforts to undergraduates will become, in effect, prep schools for the universities.

Fourth, there is the eminently pragmatic consideration of the need to staff the myriad second-rate Catholic colleges and universities. The vast majority of these, alas, will not amalgamate, coordinate, or disappear, whatever the recommendations of the planners, and faculty will probably continue to come predominantly from Catholic universities.

Fifth, graduate students provide cheap help for teaching huge freshman classes in financially strapped schools. A university like St. John's on Long Island needs graduate programs not only for its ambitions to intellectual respectability, but to staff the many course sections required by its penchant for bigness.

Sixth, despite the changing patterns of control in Catholic higher education, religious orders will be heavily involved for the foreseeable future, and many members with more pastoral than intellectual concerns will prefer the less rigorous, second-rate doctoral programs. In addition, it will probably be less expensive for orders to send the majority of their people to Catholic schools, where there are usually rebates on tuition.

After reviewing this uninspiring list of reasons why Catholic institutions will continue to maintain graduate programs, one cannot resist entering the hope that they will be cut back in most Catholic universities and that the availability of government and foundation grants will not determine the shape graduate education takes. It would be unfortunate indeed if the Catholic colleges within a few major universities which are presently considerably superior to the graduate schools in the same institutions—at least in the students they attract—should suffer because graduate sequences are begun higglety-pigglety. Some of the graduate schools seem to be building social-science departments, particularly, in a helter-skelter manner, depending upon what kinds of research funds are available, following a "main chance" kind of curricular philosophy. It would be tragic if the best of the undergraduate programs were weakened in this mad scramble for top-twenty membership.

To be sure, Catholic universities should strengthen their doctoral sequences—especially in the woefully weak area of the social sciences.

But they must resign themselves to the impossibility of providing programs in every conceivable area, and map out some kind of strategy whereby the best men in an area concentrate in one institution, avoiding needless duplication and the overextension of resources. While such duplication is no monopoly of Catholic graduate education, institutions with limited resources must be especially prudent and give up trying to compete in every graduate discipline. They have something to learn from the seven English universities formed in the 1960's: Each of the institutions is building in certain areas only, having abandoned the notion that each school has to offer every academic discipline.[26] Among the developments which may contribute to more rational planning is the Consortium of Universities in Washington,

[26] The small Catholic colleges also need to study Sussex, York, Warwick, and the like. Many of these will not be able to be microcosms of the world of learning, offering the traditional liberal-arts education. Some may have to specialize, capitalizing on their resources and traditions. Colleges cannot go on offering art and music courses which cost them $95 a credit, when students pay only $35. It may be that a large number of colleges will become affiliated in a loose network, something like the Associate Colleges of the Midwest, or Central States College Association. But there will have to be considerably more traffic between the schools than is presently found in such associations. Students of the 1980's and 1990's are likely to be more mobile, intending to sample three or four colleges during their undergraduate years. The Catholic schools will want to capitalize on this, entering into alliances with a variety of institutions (Catholic or not), each planning to keep students only one or two years, as they move into the broad concentrations on which they will focus. A student might begin at Loyola-Mundelein in Chicago, one of twenty-odd colleges emphasizing the social sciences. With computer consoles, films and tapes doing the information-imparting, instructors will be freed for much more individual attention to students. From such encounters, a student will decide that his interests are more likely to be met by a concentration in city planning, say, than in the sociology of education. Sophomore year he will go to Boston College or Boston University, or perhaps to a coeducational Albertus Magnus in New Haven for a liberal-arts approach to the city: what it has been in history, its sociology, even its theology. After two years there, he may finish at Fordham's Lincoln Center, or Los Angeles' Loyola-Marymount, or return to Chicago. Or he might take a year at the Catholic University in Santiago. Another student may begin at Newton, where she decides on art history rather than literature. Because she is particularly interested in liturgical art, she spends the following summer, fall, and second summer at St. John's-St. Benedict's in Minnesota (which operates on a March-November calendar, having decided in the 1970's to capitalize on the fine summer weather, and close down during the Minnesota winters). She spends the next year at Lincoln Center, and her senior year in Florence.

with five participating institutions: American, Georgetown, George Washington, Howard, and Catholic Universities. If this and similar ventures are emphasized and the Catholic graduate schools thrive, one of the reasons will be the increasing professionalism of the faculty.

FACULTY AND ADMINISTRATION

There is no need here to repeat the "Where Are the Catholic Scholars?" debate which is discussed in another chapter of this book. It seems clear, however, that until relatively recently little first-rate scholarly work was being done in Catholic universities.[27] But the dominance of teaching-oriented, character-building nonprofessionals on the Catholic campuses, found by Donovan in the early 1960's, seems to be disappearing.[28] Greeley reports that the Catholic in his sample now nearing completion of his doctoral work intends "to write a book, to become important in his field, to publish a magazine article, to make an important contribution to science or technology, to have literary works published, to produce original works of art or music, to become famous or eminent, to be financially and occupationally successful" to the same extent as does the Protestant graduate student.[29] These future professors are much more likely than their Catholic college mentors to be the sons of college-educated men and to have professional fathers.[30] They are also more likely to come from homes with more democratic family structures, which Donovan found to be closely related to a research orientation.

[27] For empirical evidence of this, see John H. Smith, "The Greater Glory: Scholarship and the Catholic University," in *Toward New Dimensions in Catholic Higher Education,* ed. L. C. Vaccaro (Arlington, Va., 1967), pp. 37-55.

[28] John Donovan, *The Academic Man in the Catholic College* (New York, 1964).

[29] *The Changing Catholic College,* pp. 43-45. It may be argued that these data only indicate hopes, but it is to the point to show the data also tell us that these Catholic graduate students are just as likely to have passed their comprehensives, to have an A average, and to have a dissertation topic approved or a committee picked as are Protestant students.

[30] See Gleason's comparison of data from Greeley and Donovan, showing that 44 per cent of the 1961 Catholic collegians had college-educated fathers, compared to 13 per cent in the Donovan sample; one-half had professional or managerial fathers, compared to one-third of Donovan's professors' fathers ("American Catholic Higher Education: A Historical Perspective," in Hassenger, *Shape,* p. 20).

In addition, Catholic universities are now moving toward establishing the conditions which make it easier to attract good men. Notre Dame hopes to move to a standard six-hour teaching load by 1970, and several schools now rate A- or B in the AAUP salary scale.[31] If fringe benefits and academic citizenship have been slower in coming, every indication is that these, too, are close at hand.

In early 1967, a flurry of announcements heralded long overdue changes in the boards of control at a number of Catholic colleges and universities. Although laymen had been represented on some boards of trustees for some time, and although many Catholic schools and the religious orders administering them have been separately incorporated,[32] only a score or so had appointed laymen by 1940. But between a third and one-half of the Catholic colleges and universities had laymen on their boards by 1967, according to McGrath and Dupont. Most likely to have lay representation were schools sponsored by a diocese or by an order of religious brothers (which—I do not think it cynical to say—probably had more need for such help).

Many institutions had been considering such changes for some time, and they would undoubtedly have moved in this direction as a natural outcome of their own evolutionary processes. But some of the would-be laggards were probably prompted to action by the research of John J. McGrath, which seemed to offer definitive legal evidence that

> Charitable and educational institutions chartered as corporations under American law are not *owned* by the sponsoring body. The legal title to the real and personal property is vested in the corporation. It

[31] The 466 full-time faculty at Notre Dame had the highest average total compensation and salaries in 1967-68, $12,870 and $11,788, respectively, to regain their lead in Catholic higher education, held by Boston College in 1966-67; B.C.'s figures in 1967-68 were $12,321 and $11,273, for 333 full-time faculty members. The other leading Catholic universities were (number of reported full-time faculty in parentheses): Santa Clara (146), Marquette (307), Catholic University (387), Loyola of Los Angeles (84), Detroit (219), and Fordham (331). (Some schools escalate their averages by reporting for only some of their faculty; compare Marquette's, C.U.'s, Detroit's, and Fordham's 1966-67 and 1967-68 figures, for example.) Sources: AAUP *Bulletin*, LIII (Summer, 1967), 136-95 and LIV (Summer, 1968), 182-241.

[32] Earl J. McGrath and Gerald E. Dupont report that at least six Catholic schools had lay representation on their boards even before the turn of the century ("The Future Governance of Catholic Higher Education in the United States," Institute of Higher Education, Columbia University, 1967). Some communities

> is the corporation that cares for the sick or grants academic degrees. It is the corporation that buys and sells and borrows money. If anyone *owns* the assets of the charitable or educational institution, it is the general public. Failure to appreciate this fact has led to the mistaken idea that the property of the institution is the property of the sponsoring body.[33]

McGrath further pointed out that a religious or sectarian body cannot transform such a corporation with its clearly defined rights and powers into assets for the sponsoring body, and urged that great care be taken to separate the finances of the institution from those of the religious community. Even the food and lodging of community members should be financed under the same contracts as other university personnel. Not only does this clarify the contributions made by the order to the university; it also

> gives the individual religious faculty member a greater sense both of obligation and of accomplishment as well as an added incentive to pursue his professional career as effectively as possible; and it solves the serious problem of the essential differences which used to exist between the appointment of religious to faculty or administrative positions as contrasted with the procedures we follow in the case of laymen . . . religious are no longer appointed to positions in the university by an outside authority.[34]

The matter of clearly delineating college and religious community should not be underestimated. After presenting evidence in *The Changing Catholic College* that the administrative style of the president was the single most important factor in distinguishing "rapid growth" from "medium growth" Catholic institutions, Greeley went on to discuss the crucial character of the relationship between a college and the order historically sponsoring the school and the danger in picking men for administrative posts according to criteria which would be appropriate for the religious community, but dysfunctional for an edu-

with hospitals seem to have been motivated to separately incorporate because they feared losing a great deal in a malpractice suit, and incorporated their colleges at the same time. (Sometimes one wishes it were possible to bring malpractice suits against higher educational institutions.)

[33] John J. McGrath, *Catholic Institutions in the United States: Canonical and Civil Law Status* (Washington, 1968), p. 33.

[34] Letter to the writer from President Paul C. Reinert, S.J., describing the changes at St. Louis University, Feb. 8, 1968. "Jesuit" appears in the original letter where I have written "religious."

cational institution. Such a man might be appointed in spite of his lack of interest in the position; Greeley estimated that "perhaps 40 to 50 per cent of the presidents, vice-presidents, and deans that we interviewed sincerely wanted to get out of their jobs," and suggested that "somewhere between three-fifths and two-thirds of the college presidents interviewed would fall into the category of being good men from the religious order's viewpoint but not from the educational institution's viewpoint." The difficulties and inequities bred by such a situation have been many. The most obvious has been the frustration of the lay faculty. Donovan found almost four-fifths of the lay professors in his sample indicating that "lay-religious" problems were the chief sources of frustration in their academic lives, compared to less than one-fifth among the religious faculty. Almost half the lay academicians felt they were "second-class citizens," "necessary evils," and "without any significant voice." It is a good bet that the lay faculty at St. John's so considered themselves. Scimecca and Damiano report that an analysis of the 1964-65 catalogue revealed that 34 per cent of the Vincentians there were full professors, compared to but 9 per cent of the lay men and women. Thirteen per cent of each group were associate professors, but the Vincentians had proportionately more assistant professors, 47 per cent to 34 per cent. Only 6 per cent of the Vincentians were instructors, and nearly half (42 per cent) of the laymen. Only two of the Vincentians had a Ph.D. from a non-Catholic university, and twenty-nine had all their degrees from Catholic institutions, twelve of these from Vincentian schools exclusively. It is not surprising that many of these men had little understanding of how things should be done in a real university. But not all clerics are the enemy.

Whatever the situation in the not-too-distant past, today's layman in the major Catholic university may be more free and have fewer problems than his clerical counterpart. For one thing, there is a feeling among some religious that they are professionally inferior to their lay colleagues who may have been trained in more prestigious graduate schools. For another, a religious faculty member is likely to be overworked, expected "to teach twelve hours of class during the regular year as well as in summer session, hear confessions and say Mass on the weekend, moderate a Sodality, prefect a corridor of a residence hall, give nuns' retreats, teach a special course for a contemplative community, and serve as assistant sexton in the college chapel." This, despite his Chicago or Princeton degree. Third, the cleric in some places has no contract and no tenure and can be moved across the country if the "needs of the order"—which can mean a variety of things—require it. Fourth, the priest-professor typically lives in a residence hall and is much less able to get off by himself for serious thinking and reading. And there is the whole area of order politics, of which a layman knows too little to do more than simply mention here.

It goes without saying, however, that religious communities have made immeasurable contributions to Catholic education on all levels. They have the principal resource of countless institutions. Those outside Catholic higher education often are unaware of how meager is the direct financial assistance provided to colleges by the Church. Pattillo and Mackenzie found that less than half of the 339 Catholic schools in their sample received educational or general income from Church sources, while about 12 per cent received less than a tenth of their income from religious orders. What support is available nearly always is in the form of contributed services. Data available in this volume indicates how large is this contribution: Three-fifths of the Catholic schools reported more than 10 per cent of their educational and general income could be attributed to this indirect type of support.[35]

There are other aspects to the relationship of the college to a religious community. Often such arrangements are the colleges' great weaknesses as well as strengths. At a place like St. John's in Collegeville, Minnesota, there is even a physical interpenetration of the College and the Benedictine community, with the latter paying for the physical expansion of the school and contributing 80 per cent of their salaries back to the college. In another institution, a community of sisters which sponsors (and, until recently, was 90 per cent of the faculty) a women's college is in effect picking up the very high interest for a short-term loan taken to build a magnificent building. Although it is not clear to the sister-president whether she is expected to eventually pay the community back, it seems apparent that this is most unlikely, given the present financial status of the college. Nor is she as subject to pressure as one who is more dependent on her record as president: She cannot really be fired in the same way. She may be removed as president, of course, but as a religious she will always have

[35] The religious comprising half of even a small faculty may bring contributed services of a half-million dollars annually. It would take considerably more endowment than most such schools have to bring in this amount at 5 per cent interest.

a home and plenty to eat. (Many suggest that such comforts prevent the achievement which being "hungry" seems to facilitate. Training in "humility" probably exacerbates this, although obviously not in some cases.)

It is such ambiguous situations that Reinert expects to be changed by the new organizational patterns at St. Louis and Notre Dame—and this will serve to protect the religious communities. For example, it was noted above that the St. John's Benedictines retain 20 per cent of their salaries for community expenses. St. John's is better endowed than most Catholic colleges, yet they could use 89 per cent of these Benedictine salaries, in 1968, to make up an existing deficit. But if the order does not hold the line at 80, they will undoubtedly find that they are contributing 95 and then perhaps 103 per cent of their salaries, as soaring educational costs begin to draw funds from other Benedictine activities such as the Liturgical Press. These dangers will disappear when St. John's reorganizes its board of control.

It would be naive to expect the presence of laymen on trustee boards to automatically solve all a college's problems. There is today a certain "antiauthoritarian romanticism," as David Riesman put it,[36] that seems to characterize the discussions of many young priests and laymen who appear to believe that the problems of Catholic higher education would disappear if only the universities could be completely laicized. Of course they would not. For one thing, the lay trustees are more likely to be chosen from among businessmen and industrialists than from among educators and social critics, and the former may be even more likely than religious who attended graduate school to "see the Catholic colleges as turning out patriotic, sports-loving, smooth but unsophisticated young men and piously protected, 'feminine' young women."[37] Then, too, the distinctive sense of purpose which some religious seem to have (a *charisma* stemming partly from a belief in a special grace for leaders, partly from the attribution of certain powers to them by a subservient laity in the past) has forced change and contributed greatly to the vast improvements which have characterized several leading Catholic universities, but may well be dissipated in a radical democratization that creates departmental or divisional baronies. As Greeley

[36] In his Foreword to *The Shape of Catholic Higher Education.*

[37] Riesman. Should this happen, the Catholic colleges will be faced with some of the same problems as universities in states where contractors and tycoons dominate the state boards of regents.

and Jencks and Riesman point out, the great leaps forward of several Catholic schools have been due in large measure to charismatic leaders, and institutions on the make cannot afford to spend their energies on internal pacification programs. With decentralization, mediocrity can protect and perpetuate itself.

There is one undue restriction which still is found in even the reorganized St. Louis and Notre Dame: the stipulation that the university president must come from the ranks of the religious order.[38] There are undoubtedly many members of the Jesuits and Holy Cross who would meet the criteria for Greeley's charismatic leader. But such a requirement is bound to limit the school's possibilities, if only by the law of averages. It may be that these stipulations are the outcomes of political maneuverings, as a *quid pro quo* to community members less persuaded of the need for reorganization, and that the requirements will disappear five or ten years hence. What is significant are the changes which have already occurred and that Orders like the Jesuits and Holy Cross reason that it is better to hold a smaller place at a St. Louis or Notre Dame by competence than a much larger place by inheritance. But it would be unrealistic to expect such changes to assure survival.

THE FUTURE

How viable are the Catholic institutions of higher learning? Most will undoubtedly continue to exist. The real questions they face are two: How successful will they be in their quest for upward mobility? What about them will be distinctively Catholic, or even Christian?

Barring changes in state and Federal policies, monetary resources will continue to be in short supply. So might another basic resource: clients. Early in this chapter it was suggested that an increasingly smaller proportion of the Catholics in college will be enrolled in Catholic institutions in the years to come. There are several reasons for this. For one, it is not at all clear that Catholics will continue to support their colleges as in the past. Founded to defend the faith of their student-clients, Catholic colleges and universities no longer are called

[38] At each university the board-of-trustees chairman must be a layman, and the preponderance of board members are lay. The statutes at each place can be altered only by two-thirds votes of the boards of control, slightly more than the number of laymen on either board.

upon by an embattled, defensive minority to perform this function. As they have made it in the larger society, Catholics—like other Americans—appear to be more interested in providing their sons and daughters with the kind of education which will equip them for competition in the status race. And to young Americans who have been exposed to the effects of McLuhan's electronic revolution, colleges resembling their Catholic high schools look less and less attractive.

Further, with the mushrooming of public education, it becomes not only cheaper to commute to the large public urban institutions like CUNY and the University of Illinois at Chicago, but even less expensive to go away to a state institution than to commute to a Catholic college. As Jencks and Riesman point out, growth in college enrollment during the past generation has been due in large part to the greater number from less educated and less affluent families. Irish and German Catholics who sent their sons to Notre Dame and Georgetown in the 1940's and 1950's are more inclined now to look to Princeton, Stanford, and Northwestern, while Catholic colleges have lately been attracting more Italian and Polish students—the sons and grandsons of those in the "second wave" of immigration in the early years of the present century. Commuter colleges particularly have drawn them. But these are the institutions which will have most difficulty competing with the new public colleges and junior colleges, especially since larger proportions of lay faculty have meant increased tuition charges, and these hit commuting students proportionately harder. In addition, as the Catholic colleges become more like their secular counterparts, there are fewer reasons to pay twice as much for the same education.

Given these developments, many expect Catholic colleges to become institutions attracting predominantly upper-middle class students, particularly if public funds do not become available to provide scholarships to less advantaged youngsters. More and more of these may come from the most recently arrived ethnic groups, however, as third- and fourth-generation Italian- and Polish-Americans reach the affluence levels of the Irish and German Catholics who preceded them. Or perhaps not, if the lack of interest in Catholic primary and secondary education that Greeley and Rossi found among Italians is manifested on the college level. But whichever ethnic groups are represented, it is almost certain that the heavy Irish concentration of the past will greatly diminish. Data can be found in Greeley (1968) showing that nearly half of the Irish Catholics in the early 1960's were in Catholic colleges, compared to less than a quarter of the non-Irish Catholics. But as tuitions increase, both the Irish and the other Catholic groups will be less eager to pay Ivy League rates for educations in less posh settings, the more so if the Catholic colleges seem to be providing essentially the same curricular offerings, and if an education including Catholic theology and philosophy is no longer considered essential in the post-Vatican II world. Both the predominantly working-class, commuter schools, then, and the traditionally middle-class colleges may be hard put to survive by the late 1970's.[39]

Some are already in trouble. The data from Ford and Roy indicates that fewer than one-half of the schools in their sample had met their predicted freshman enrollments in 1966-67. This comes at the same time that the heavy interest payments accompanying tremendous physical expansion are soaking up all available funds. College costs tripled between 1955 and 1965, and Neil McCluskey reports that the United States Office of Education estimates a student in a private college in 1975 will be paying an average of $4,294 for each year of his education, compared to $3,102 in 1965 and $1,875 in 1955.[40] The federal government has made available an increasing amount of money for long-term, low-interest loans, but banks seem less interested in handling loans at these lower rates.

Some Catholic colleges tried guaranteed-tuition plans to attract students from money conscious lower-middle or working-class families but have had to abandon these in the face of soaring costs. There are Catholic college administrators who seem to believe that if only they could attract more students they could somehow survive. Institutions such as New York's St. John's and the University of Dayton have grown from 6,000 to 12,000 and from fewer than 3,000 to approximately 10,000, respectively, between 1946 and 1965. (One often finds at such schools quite lavish student facilities, compared to even the leading

[39] Some schools may follow the evolution of Chicago's Mundelein College, overwhelmingly Irish in the 1930's, with Italian and Polish girls attending in such numbers in the 1960's that, by 1963, the largest ethnic segment was Polish. But as the college restructured its program and mission, and acquired additional dormitory space to accommodate more out-of-Chicago students, it underwent further evolution, changing back from a primarily commuter, working-class school, to a heavily resident, middle-class college (see "Portrait of a Catholic Women's College," in Hassenger, *Shape*).

[40] Neil G. McCluskey, S.J., "Ferment in the Catholic University World," *Religious Education*, LXII (Jan.-Feb., 1968), 12-20.

Catholic universities; with very poor endowments, they have had to depend almost entirely on student fees, while the better heeled Notre Dames and Fordhams have preferred to spend their money on new science or library facilities.) What such administrators seem not to grasp is that, when colleges are assuming more and more of the cost of education (it is the rare good college where tuition covers more than half of the instructional costs), a college can fall further and further behind the more students it attracts. A larger student enrollment can, of course, mean more resources for proportionately less expense. There is a relatively fixed cost to some things. To staff, say, a registrar's office for a college of 2,000 probably costs only a fraction more than for a college of 1,000. Book stores and cafeterias will probably return more proportionately with 2,000 than 1,000 students. But there are plateaus, beyond which are diminishing returns. One finance officer told the writer that he sees plateaus at his institution as 1,200 and 1,800. If more students that 1,200 are enrolled, the college should think in terms of 1,800 rather than, say, 1,500, because it is then that it will get the greatest return for the least proportional expenditure.

Even with such relatively sophisticated planning, there are many Catholic colleges and universities which will not have the resources to survive as four-year colleges. There is just too much competition. It is instructive to cite here the Jesuit administrator quoted by McCluskey in a recent paper:

> Recently I sat as a member of the Board of Review for the North Central Association. Our task was to evaluate the resources of institutions seeking accreditation for new doctoral programs. Frankly, the experience was shattering! The new state universities (the teachers' colleges of ten years ago) have resources in many areas far beyond those we hope to have. A private institution (I have always considered it second-rate) could point to three gifts from trustees of the institutions. These three gifts were well over twice the total of our first five-years priority campaign.[41]

The resources may well exist in a Catholic community now largely indistinguishable from other Americans in socioeconomic terms. But whether these will be channeled into Catholic higher education—and if so, whether into the more than 300 colleges and universities—is an-

[41] Cited in Neil G. McCluskey, S.J., "The New Catholic College," *America*, CXVI (1967), 414-17.

other question. The handful of universities that have charged ahead in the past two decades will probably continue to prosper, and one or two may become great. But their secular counterparts will not be standing still, and if it is encouraging to realize that the College Board Scores of 1967 Notre Dame freshmen are not unlike those in many Ivy League colleges in 1957, it is frustrating to realize that the gap separating these institutions is still immense. Many second-rate Catholic colleges will die, not with a bang but a whimper. As more and more American Catholics begin to question the wisdom of a separate system of higher education—and more to the point, begin to shop elsewhere—the majority may go under, or so drastically alter their character as to be unrecognizable.

In an attempt to stave off such a fate increasing numbers of Catholic colleges are talking about closer cooperation. There seems to be the feeling at these institutions that their long-run survival depends on the elimination of duplicated facilities and programs, and there is talk of either "merger," "affiliation," or "coordination" in a number of places. St. Thomas (men) and St. Catherine (women) in Minnesota have exchanged students since 1957. Thomas More College within Fordham University (Bronx Campus) enrolls women although the remainder of the undergraduate student body is entirely male.[42] Marymount in Los Angeles has moved to the campus of Loyola; Ursuline and Bellarmine in Louisville consider themselves "coordinate colleges," and St. John's in Collegeville will merge with St. Benedict's, four miles away. St. Mary's and Notre Dame send students to each other's campus; in the spring of 1968, 120 Notre Dame students were enrolled in 168 courses at St. Mary's, with 263 ladies making the trip the other way to take 423 Notre Dame courses. There is every indication that such cooperative ventures will continue and perhaps be expanded. For example, there has been talk of building another women's college or two on Notre Dame's perimeter which would serve—as would a changed St. Mary's—as cluster colleges for women around the university, sharing classes and facilities. This is more likely than that Notre Dame will itself become coeducational, particularly in light of the recent decisions of Yale and Vassar to remain apart and the resistance of a large number of St. Mary's faculty to what they fear will be absorp-

[42] The College at Lincoln Center will be coeducational, however, and 1967 applications from women were running ahead of those from men by three to one.

tion by Notre Dame.[43] Such people are concerned, quite legitimately, about what will become of the bottom half of a faculty to whom the college has some moral obligations. Often such people would be qualified to teach lower-division courses—more so than the increasing numbers of graduate students who are pushed into instruction as institutions on the make begin to garner more research funds, which means reduced teaching loads—but this would mean giving up "their" courses and teaching freshmen and sophomores (who may, of course, be brighter and more sophisticated than the upperclassmen they have been teaching). If such problems can be solved, it is likely that we shall see even more articulation, and some amalgamation, in the years ahead.

But for the schools that do survive, the second question mentioned above will have to be faced: What about them will be distinctively Catholic or even Christian? One of the key statutes of the reorganized Notre Dame reads:

> The essential character of the University as a Catholic institution of higher learning shall at all times be maintained, it being the stated intention and desire of the present Fellows of the University that the University shall retain in perpetuity its identity as such an institution.

Few people pretend to know the exact nature of the "Catholic university" in the late 1960's. The Notre Dame statutes specify that the intellectual life of the University "should at all times be enlivened and sustained by a devotion to the twin disciplines of theology and philosophy," which are "viewed as being central to the University's existence and function." Similar language is used by the president, in his Introduction to the new Notre Dame Faculty Manual, effective September, 1967. In the section on academic freedom, the faculty member is reminded of his responsibility not to "maintain a position contrary to the basic aims of this Institution as outlined in the Introduction."

[43] A good number of the St. Mary's faculty would be qualified to teach in a university, but prefer either a small liberal-arts college, an all-female school, or both. And there are of course some who would not make acceptable university faculty. There is also a glaring discrepancy in the salary schedules at the two schools, with Notre Dame's B-plus/A-minus rating in the 1967-68 salary schedule of the American Association of University Professors, compared to St. Mary's D rating.

In a later section defining criteria for dismissal from the university, one matter is "continual serious disrespect or disregard for the Catholic character of this institution." And what is "Catholic character"? Assuming this can be answered, how does one square Catholic with university? The president of now laicized Webster College, Jacqueline Grennan, has stated that "the very nature of *higher* education is opposed to juridical control by the Church."[44] Yet both the document released over the signatures of some twenty-six representatives of the International Federation of Catholic Universities, and the section on higher education of the document produced by the participants in the 1967 Conference on the Future of Catholic Education, suggested that, within a Catholic university, "Catholicism is perceptibly present and effectively operative," although this remains at a fairly high level of abstraction.[45]

Jencks and Riesman observe that while they have not themselves heard a satisfactory answer to the classical question, "What is a Catholic University?" the only answer may be that a Catholic college or university should help its students explore the question "What does it mean to be a Catholic?" in an informed and disciplined way. A number of people have attempted to provide partial answers.[46] The query is outside the competence of the sociologist (although I have dealt

[44] *National Catholic Reporter*, Jan. 18, 1967 (her italics). It was widely noted that Jacqueline Grennan—formerly Sister Jacqueline, S.L.—has been dispensed from her vows to return to secular life. For the time being, she has stayed on as Webster's president. Miss Grennan's thinking is shared by a number of people. For two, see John Cogley, "The Future of an Illusion," *Commonweal*, LXXXVI (June 2, 1967), 310-16, and Paul Sherry, "Church or College: Either, but not Both," *The Christian Century*, XXXIV (Oct. 4, 1967), 1247-50.

[45] "The Idea of the Catholic University," drawn up at Land O' Lakes, Wis., July 23, 1967; "Statement of the Washington Symposium on Catholic Education, November, 1967," released Feb. 1968, and appearing in its entirety in *National Catholic Reporter*, Feb. 21, 1968. It is noteworthy that the Land O' Lakes document also stated that the Catholic university "should carry on a continual examination of all aspects and all activities of the Church and should objectively evaluate them."

[46] See, e.g., Frederick Crosson, "Personal Commitment as the Basis of Free Inquiry," in Manier and Houck, pp. 87-102; William J. Richardson, S.J., "Pay Any Price? Break Any Mold?" *America*, CXVI (Apr. 29, 1967), 624-42; Shuster, *Catholic Education in a Changing World* (New York, 1968); John E. Walsh, C.S.C., "The University and the Church," in Manier and Houck, pp. 103-18.

with some aspects of the question, and can refer the reader to these contributions).[47] It does seem obvious that if Catholic institutions of higher learning are to be considered real universities, scholars there must have all the freedom available to their colleagues in other groves of academe. It should be clear that Catholic colleges and universities do not represent the teaching authority of the Church. Nor are they likely to aspire to this role, particularly after the academic freedom controversies of St. John's, Dayton, and Catholic University.

The tendency of those contributing heavily to colleges and universities to claim their right to some kind of "seal of approval" is what makes many Catholic educators resist financial support from the bishops, as a Catholic college president recently urged.[48] While there are admittedly dangers inherent in the increasing proportion of financial aid which is likely to come from outside sources, including the Federal government, Catholic educators who believe that the affirmation of a Catholic university's independence from the teaching Church was long overdue are understandably reluctant to seek help from the bishops. It is absolutely necessary to insist on the university's autonomy; it must not be subject to pressure from outside interest groups. For a Catholic university, one such group is the institutional Church. But even if something is believed to be, in fact *known* to be, contrary to present Catholic teaching, any investigations must be by one's academic peers, with all the procedures of due process observed. If this is not assured, and if the local bishop, or apostolic delegate, or any other Church official can interfere with what occurs within a university, then it will make little difference whether deeds to Catholic schools are in the hands of lay trustees. In such a case, it would be difficult to disagree with Jacqueline Grennan: Higher education would, if not by its very nature then in the practical order, be opposed to Church control.[49]

Speaking for myself, I do not think it has to be. Catholic colleges

[47] See Hassenger, *Shape*, pp. 295-334, esp. p. 318 ff, and Hassenger in Manier and Houck, pp. 145-61.

[48] John P. Leary, S.J., "The Bishops and the Catholic College," *Ave Maria*, CVII (Feb. 10, 1968), 6-9.

[49] At the same time, it should be clear here, as McCluskey recently insisted (*Religious Education*, LXII ([Jan.-Feb., 1968], 17): "Juridical control and sponsorship are not the same thing. . . . If Miss Grennan means that any other kind of group may sponsor a college except an ecclesiastical group, then I am in disagreement and I fail to see where this discrimination grows out of the nature of the collegiate institution."

and universities exist[50] to provide opportunities for faculty and students who share certain commitments and wish to explore certain questions, to come together for mutual influence and learning. The Catholic colleges and universities will provide environments which attract, among others, those who want to discover what it means to be a Catholic Christian, and who seek to do so in a free yet informed way. They will want to begin or extend and deepen their own religious commitments. But these environments will not demand that such commitments be made by all, nor that such questions be asked by all. These are matters of individual choice and conviction.

The principal means of individual growth is the influence of people on each other; while seeking to develop high quality graduate and professional programs, Catholic higher education should provide sufficiently for maximal personal development by students. This means students must have the freedom to make mistakes and the opportunities to learn from them.

By fostering academic excellence, Catholic colleges and universities will attract talented and creative people. By fostering an atmosphere where ultimate questions are asked and a diversity of standpoints presented, the colleges and universities will attract those with a high level of personal commitment and promote the dialogue between the Church and the contemporary world; by providing opportunities to deepen and extend one's Catholic Christianity, the institutions will attract both those who will seek excellent training as theologians and those who will seek to influence society in other capacities, but who will want the best possible education in their religious heritage. Thus the college and university are not only focal points for the Church's thinking, but also settings where the commitment and competence to serve the world are promoted.

50 What follows is from my draft of the section on higher education for the Statement of the Washington Symposium. I should add that not all of this statement appeared in the symposium's final document, but it represents my best thinking for now of what the Catholic university ought to be.

13: COMMUNICATIONS AND THE CHURCH

Thomas J. Stritch

Communication is central to the Church: it is her mission to "teach the whole world" the "good news" of the "Word made Flesh." The Son of God is Himself the "Logos," the Word that is communicated. Moreover, despite the wordless Carthusians and the cloistered Carmelites, the Church is essentially social, "the communion of saints," "the People of God." To be social is to be involved in communication.

The heart of communication within the Church is the liturgy, its public worship. At the risk of vast oversimplification, the present experimentation with the liturgy can be seen as the first real attempt to make the liturgy reach the whole of the People of God. No doubt the early Church did, but the whole was not great, and as soon as it became great a gulf began to divide the masses with their popular devotions from the religious with their official prayer. One has only to look at a medieval church to see this: The choir was for the religious, and only they really participated fully in the services. The people milled around in the nave and transepts, from which one could not even get a good look at the high altar. Only the art and the sermons were "mass communications."

Although the Counter-Reformation made some effort to include a greater number of people in liturgical celebrations, the ordinary faithful still inclined more toward popular devotions than toward the official liturgy. Not until the time of Pope St. Pius X was there a real attempt to enlarge the observance of the liturgy, but the currents he fostered still made the choir, the servers, and the minor religious surrogates for all the people, even though increasing literacy developed wider participation through the use of missals. Not until Vatican II did the doors to the sanctuary burst open and the people surge in.

Their doing so raises once again the difficult liturgical question: How much tradition, how much high art, how much pop, how much vulgarity? Even though they can't join in, and only dimly understand it, is a congregation better off for hearing a choir do the plainchant well, or sing Vittoria, rather than themselves singing "Lord Accept the Gifts We Offer"? Does it matter that the longed-for vernacular used at Mass is mostly bad English? Will the people respond to good art? Doesn't participation result in breakdown? One hears surprisingly little about these questions today; authority, celibacy, birth control drown them out.

In all this history there is a constant in mass communication: the sermon. "The poor have the Gospel preached to them," says Scripture, and that is the main communication of the historical Church. Even today the best known religious leaders in the United States, Bishop Fulton J. Sheen and Billy Graham, are fundamentally preachers, and the new liturgy retains the homily as an essential feature. The very word "homily," however, plays down the rhetorical approach, and experiments with the dialogue homily suggest something very different from preaching, which, *pace* Sheen and Graham, seems waning. The parish mission is almost dead and the old-fashioned retreat, nearly all preaching, is slowly being displaced by group discussions, films with religious implications, Cursillos, Pentecostal meetings, and the like.

Such are the fruits of what Marshall McLuhan calls "the new tribalism." McLuhan says that the new electronic media create a group psychology similar to that of oral-aural societies—that is, societies whose principal form of communication is word of mouth, not print. This theory suggests there is some truth in that reading of history which ascribes the success of the Protestant Reformation to the invention of printing. The evidence is that Protestants did adopt the new medium of print very successfully, for some purposes, while the Counter-Reformation was by comparison geared more to preaching and "tribal" endeavors by the religious orders, old and new. However, this is not true of worship. Having divested themselves of the "tribal" Mass, most Protestants turned to preaching as their central act of worship, while Catholic worship clung to the silent mystery of the Mass, made more silent and more mysterious by their valiant loyalty, until Vatican II, to its Latin form.

In some ways this history—the continuity of preaching among both Catholics and Protestants—contradicts McLuhan's thesis, unless he means that the preaching of, say, Cardinal Newman is first written and only then *spoken*, and that Peter the Hermit at one end of the spectrum and the dialogue-homily at the other are only spoken, not written at all. All this is part of the fascinating history of rhetoric;[1] and spoken rhetoric did indeed decline as print came on. Yet preaching persists, even though congregations everywhere, Catholic and Protestant alike, complain that it's bad.

AUDIENCE AND IMPACT

Among American Catholics one seldom hears what seems to me the basic point about contemporary sermonizing: the difficulty of doing it at all. Our churches must have family congregations; there is no other way. In the past city parishes reserved different Sunday Masses for specific groups: at eight o'clock for the children, at eleven o'clock a high Mass for those who liked music, etc. But with today's automobile congregations this is impossible. The result is congregations too diversified to be reached by one message. How can one devise a sermon appealing to teen-agers, professional men, housewives, conservative oldsters, radical youngsters, laborers, academicians—the whole parish spectrum? All can join in the *Gloria* and the *Pater Noster;* most have to tune out the sermon. Some communication from the pulpit is no doubt necessary, but it can hardly be the old-fashioned fifteen- to thirty-minute sermon.

This stubborn fact, the difficulty of communication to a wide variety of people, explains why mass media have to settle for the least common denominator among their audiences. Most good sermons have to settle for that, too. And what makes them good is what makes the mass media popular: brevity, variety, cheerfulness, timeliness. The younger clergy know this almost instinctively, but many of their elders are still preaching twenty-minute exhortations whose rhetoric is as corny as it is obsolete.

If it will not work with parish congregations, it certainly will not work with the larger audiences of press and broadcasting. Most people assume big audiences mean big effects. Because mass communications do affect attitudes about cereals and soap, most people assume they affect, almost equally, beliefs about important matters. Research shows almost the exact contrary to be true. Long before Marshall McLuhan

[1] See Walter J. Ong, S.J., *Ramus, Method, and the Decay of Dialogue* (Cambridge, Mass., 1958).

coined his famous phrase, communications research found that the medium is indeed the message, in the sense that serious messages in the mass media rarely reach their targets, and even more rarely in the way they are meant to. The famous formula of Bernard Berelson in 1948—"Some types of *communication* on some kinds of *issues* brought to the attention of some kinds of *people* under some kinds of *conditions* have some kinds of effects"—has never been seriously challenged.[2]

Television, the most massive mass media, is largely concerned with trivia; when it tries a higher level, it swiftly ceases to be mass.[3] The great mass-circulation newspapers of the free world are on the same level: gaudy, sensational, vulgar, aiming at the least common denominator among readers. Radio was the same; so were films in their heyday. But more important is the ineffectiveness of the mass media when they do try to make dents in strongly held beliefs about important matters. On channels of communication attuned to trivia and chatter, the important messages simply do not register. Generally speaking, if one wants to affect American foreign policy, *Foreign Affairs* is a more influential medium in the long-run than *Reader's Digest*; an article in *Public Interest* is likely to have more influence on the fate of the guaranteed annual income than one in the *New York Daily News*. The readers of these smaller-circulation journals are tuned in to the message; swayed one way or another, they act as opinion leaders likely to spread their convictions to others, and the public mind is gradually reached through the familiar ever widening circles. But the readers (and viewers) of the big-circulation journals (and stations) just are not attentive. To return to McLuhan: Of course the medium is the message if there isn't any other.

To judge from their pronouncements and their practice, most American Catholics either don't know or don't believe the foregoing. By and large, theirs is a message communication. In fact, the most striking thing about Catholic communication in the United States is the implacable insistence on *content*. Rarely is anything written for atmo-

[2] For the best account I know of the actual effect of mass communications, as opposed to the naive assumptions concerning them, see Berelson's article, "The Great Debate on Cultural Democracy," in *Values in America*, ed. Donald N. Barrett (Notre Dame, Ind., 1961).

[3] Check the current ratings of "Meet the Press," or the Leonard Bernstein show.

sphere or humor. Even writers with a genuine light touch get to the solemn pronouncement eventually, bravely choking down the smile; even the juvenile and family magazines get in the exhortation lick before they're done; the broadcasts are usually cathedral-solemn. There are plenty of good writers among Catholic journalists, but they tend to write at the top of their voices, to echo Bernard Shaw's complaint about Hall Caine. This is almost the hallmark of the American Catholic communicator. It comes insistently from the pulpit, from the magazines both high and low, and from radio and TV programs. All this earnestness reflects an admirable seriousness of purpose, but it suggests that weakness which is the obverse: lack of balance, taking oneself too seriously, even an occasional touch of the fanatic. And this, of course, leads to the absurdities which too often have hurt the Church's communications: ignorant, foolish, or obvious statements dished up as solemn wisdom.

CATHOLIC EDUCATION AND CATHOLIC COMMUNICATION

It is tempting to blame this state of affairs on Catholic education, notoriously indifferent to the arts, including communication arts, and as firmly committed to moralizing as the pulpiteers. However, the temptation may be only that. For one thing, moralizing is a trait shared by all Americans, if more noticeably by Catholics in their public communication.[4] Furthermore, there is no clear relationship between Catholic higher education and Catholic communication. Most Catholic writers have been educated in Catholic colleges,[5] but they are stamped more by their profession than by their education; indeed, their profession often seems to require a repudiation of their education to a greater degree than obtains among their fellow intellectuals, the scholars and teachers. The writers are a coterie, an establishment. In an article imitative of Richard Rovere's famous piece about the American

[4] "The American," said H. L. Mencken, "save in moments of conscious and swiftly lamented deviltry, casts up all ponderable values, including the value even of beauty, in terms of right and wrong." Quoted in Editors of Fortune, *The Permanent Revolution* (New York, 1951), p. 68.

[5] See John R. Talevich, "A Survey of the Educational and Professional Backgrounds of the Editorial Staffs of Some Catholic Magazines" (unpublished master's thesis, Marquette University Graduate School of Journalism).

establishment, John Leo identifies most of them, priests, nuns, and laymen who write for and edit the intellectual Catholic magazines, publish intellectual books, and write columns. Not all of them are "in"; Leo identifies the "outs," too. But the ins have great fellow-feeling for one another. Together they make and mar reputations, help establish trends. Here, in the little magazines, with an intense and influential audience, are opinions changed and modified—not in the big-circulation journals. Leo's description of this group of writers reminds one of the New York group so acutely described by Norman Podhoretz, editor of the Jewish intellectual magazine *Commentary*, in his recent autobiography.[6]

Earlier, Msgr. S. J. Adamo had also identified some of these Catholic writers and went on to characterize them as a coterie, who write with "little courtesy and less modesty."[7] It is true that by-line Catholic journalism often seems to be a carry-over from college undergraduate journalism, devoured by suspicion, arrogance, and defiance. Nevertheless, this group of journalists does represent a powerful intellectual force within the Church and, taken as a group, they have much going for them. They are intelligent, eager, hard-working, accomplished, high-minded, idealistic, tenacious. If they seem not yet wise, it may be because they lack roots. They don't seem to come from anywhere—not even Kansas City, let alone Atlanta or Spokane or Oklahoma City. Nor do they come from this or that university—there is no stamp of Fordham or Villanova or Marquette here or there. They weave in and out of the universities less than their compeers in specialized secular journalism.

This may be the fault of Catholic universities, which lack the resources for such interchange. At least two Catholic writers, Donald McDonald and Michael Novak, have found haven for study in secular institutions, but not in Catholic ones. John Deedy, now managing editor of *Commonweal*, then editor of the *Pittsburgh Catholic*, feeling the need for this sort of thing, several years ago suggested seminars in theology at Catholic universities similar to those held by the Amer-

[6] John Leo, "The Catholic Establishment," *The Critic*, XXV (Dec., 1966-Jan., 1967); Richard Rovere, *The American Establishment* (New York, 1962); and Norman Podhoretz, *Making It* (New York, 1967).

[7] S. J. Adamo, "Dilemma in the Catholic Press," *America*, CXIII (Aug. 14, 1965).

ican Press Institute at Columbia for secular journalists.[8] This, or something similar to the Niemann Fellowships at Harvard for secular journalists, might be a useful adjunct to the undergraduate programs in journalism offered at some Catholic colleges and universities. Many offer a course or two, but only the following are listed in the *Editor & Publisher Yearbook* as having undergraduate-major programs: Creighton, Detroit, Duquesne, Fordham, Marquette, Notre Dame, St. Bonaventure, St. Joseph's (Rensselaer, Indiana), Seattle. All these have turned out good students who work in Catholic journalism, but the market is obviously larger than the supply, and no school has made a distinctive mark.

Marquette has made the best bid. It has the only separate College of Journalism and the only Graduate School of Journalism, which has done excellent work for Catholic journalism. It sponsors the Institute of the Catholic Press, which has been a valuable forum for the exchange of ideas among Catholic journalists, and the Catholic School Press Association, which has done good work in raising the standards of Catholic high-school journalism. Lack of resources has kept its work from the highest fruition, but an admiring critic might add that it has perhaps steered a little too close to practical journalism and a little too far from more basic scholarship. Nonetheless, its contribution has been unique and valuable.

The future of university training in journalism is everywhere in doubt. Undergraduate journalism is more and more devoted to developing group consciousness among students rather than to furnishing a kind of laboratory for secular journalism. However, since most good students now go on to graduate schools, there is little need for technical undergraduate training. It is not likely, therefore, that schools and departments of journalism will directly influence Catholic journalism in the future any more than they have in the past.

Compared to the hopes of the past, this is a gloomy view. Just after World War II, idealistic veterans flooded the university journalism schools and rejuvenated them. Most of the best Catholic journalists now writing came from this flood. Their idealism had been seasoned by their war experience; their intellectual energy, pent-up during that experience, remade Catholic journalism and gave it the professionalism

[8] John Deedy, "The Missing Dimension," *America*, CIV (Feb. 4, 1961).

and critical sense which makes it today so much better than it has ever been, better certainly than since 1900. John Deedy believes there are few young people coming along to replace this now forty-fivish crop.[9]

Like schools of business, schools of journalism never really caught on as academic disciplines; surprising, perhaps, in view of their importance in our culture, but unsurprising in view of the steady and self-perpetuating conventionalism of most university faculties. Now that "journalism" is being replaced by the broader term "communications," and especially now that the Ford Foundation has announced it will devote a major share of its resources to educational television, perhaps there will be a drift toward its acceptance.

For everybody concedes the importance of communications; every failure, from Watts to broken marriages, is blamed on the lack of communications; the "dialogue" is meant to supply them. Moreover, technical marvels have misled even experts into thinking that heart speaks to heart when transistor speaks to transistor. This is, as noted earlier, a bemusement to the student of how communication actually does work. When Maine was linked to Texas by telegraph, Thoreau inquired prophetically: "But what if Maine has nothing to say to Texas?" Today those who believe that literacy and even style will follow hard upon satellite transmitters are answering again, "But Maine *must* have something to say to Texas."

And so Maine does, but not much. Most communication is the harmonious murmur of assent, "the warmth and intimacy of the contemplated me" as another perceptive New Englander, William James, said. The hum of the telegraph wires, in 1860 and 1968, is mostly people reassuring one another, exactly like the hum rising above the Tuesday Bridge Club or Henry's Tavern. What Maine tells Texas is what Texas already knows and believes, and what the Catholic Press tells Catholics is mostly what they are prepared to believe. This does some good, certainly; everybody needs to be reassured. Plainly, the note of assent was more widespread ten years ago than it is now, but as Michael Greene notes in a recent essay, the new dissent reflects the confusion and cross-purposes within the Church; the press did not create it, and perhaps does not reflect as much of it as there is.[10] Yet

[9] Deedy.

[10] Michael Greene, "The Catholic Press," in *Catholics, U.S.A.: Perspectives from Behavioral Science*, ed. N. J. Pallone and W. T. Liu (New York, 1968).

the main tension in the Catholic diocesan press is over what can and can't be printed, and what should and shouldn't be.

THE CATHOLIC PRESS AND ITS PROBLEMS

In part this tension reflects the professionalism of Catholic journalists. The professional journalist is schooled in dissent. The principal arena for his dissent, however, is democratic politics. In the Church the analogue is bishops and their chanceries. The journalists complain they are not permitted to cover the chancery and the individual parish as they would a city-council meeting. But there is a difference between the two sets of readers. Most citizens want to know about the goings-on in the city council; I am not convinced that most Catholics want to read about the bickerings in their parishes.

Let me put it this way: As the harmonious chorus of assent, the Catholic press fulfills a necessary and useful function; as the equally necessary and even more useful recorder of dissent, it is insecure, unstable, and unsettled. Most Catholics do not want city-hall and police-court journalism in their press; most Catholic journalists want that above all. Without it, they are in their view demeaned to writing and editing a bishop's house organ.[11] Two cases illustrate this tension.

The first is that of the *National Catholic Reporter*, published at Kansas City, Missouri. Now in its fifth year, it has had a profoundly influential impact on Catholic journalism. It is the outstanding voice of dissent within the Church, publishing article after article, and letter after letter about the articles, on the most controversial issues in the Church. *NCR* has a newspaper format; it looks like a diocesan weekly. But it doesn't sound like one. This is no house organ of the hierarchy. It is far closer to being their *bête-noir*. It plays up things they would rather play down: news of official slips and mistakes, statements of those opposing authority, opinions contrary to official policy.

The *NCR* is far from a mass medium. Its 75,000 circulation reaches an audience 77 per cent college-educated with an average family income of $13,000. Sixty per cent of these have postgraduate degrees,

[11] There is ample documentation for this point. A good starting place is the Catholic Press issue of *Commonweal*, LXXVII (Feb. 15, 1963). A briefer account is "The Self-Criticism of the American Catholic Press," *Herder Correspondence*, IV (Jan. 1967).

which suggests a professional audience—to which may be added the avid readership of the liberal clergy and religious. A significant index to this elite audience is that in a survey conducted by the paper 78 per cent said they liked the editorials. In a mass medium only 6 per cent even read them.

NCR, then, despite its news format belongs with the intellectual weeklies—the *New Republic, Commonweal, Christian Century*—both for its elite audience and its coterie tone. Much of what it publishes could not withstand the pressures a mass audience would generate in opposition. It has made its way by the brilliance of the group which founded and sustains it, some of them professional journalists, some Kansas City Catholic businessmen. Why this happened in Kansas City is hard to say, except that its atmosphere has for many years seemed hospitable to Catholic liberalism. The *NCR* is run by a board of trustees about half of whom are Catholic publicists. The bishop of Kansas City did not sponsor its founding, but did permit the use of the facilities of the diocesan paper as a launching pad and contributed to the pre-publication expenses. Recently he has publicly disclaimed any connection with the paper, but he has not troubled it otherwise.*

What is the future of *NCR*? Will it displace the official diocesan weeklies as the ordinary reading matter of educated Catholics? Will it attract national advertising? Will it spread wider its news net, a conspicuous weakness in view of its format? Time, and the paper's ability to attract new young talent, will tell.

The second case which illustrates the tension between the official Church and its press differs essentially from the case of the *NCR* because it is an official publication. The *Delmarva Dialog*, the official organ of the diocese of Wilmington, Delaware, is also a new paper, less than five years old. To found it the bishop brought in John O'Connor from the diocesan paper of San Francisco. O'Connor did a brilliant technical job, won prizes from over the spectrum of the Catholic press for his work, became a semiofficial spokesman for the

* Since this was written the bishop of Kansas City has publicly denounced the *NCR* as a spreader of heresy and asked the editors to remove the word "Catholic" from their name. This the board of directors declined to do. Predictably most of the more professional Catholic press regretted the bishop's action. Incidents like this—almost certain to give *NCR* at least a temporary boost—and things like the debate over *Humanae Vitae* may make the Catholic press more dissent-minded than the tone of this section suggests.

professional journalist's point of view in the diocesan press, and was elected president of the Catholic Press Association. Although tame by comparison with *NCR*, and largely focused on local news and issues, O'Connor's views were far too liberal for the bishop and for much of the diocese, both lay and clerical. He was forced out of his post in the autumn of 1967 after a prolonged and weighty struggle with the bishop.

The case of the *Dialog* sharply points up the pertinent issues. It was subsidized by the bishop (to the extent of $500,000); how much control does this give the bishop? Theoretically the paper was run by an independent board, but when the board supported O'Connor, the bishop merely asked for some resignations.

But the really difficult questions are those of readership acceptance and editorial freedom. Without independent surveys, it is hard to know just how much acceptance the paper had or had a chance to get in the future. Certainly O'Connor had a great deal of support, and some of it came from opinion leaders in the area, non-Catholic as well as Catholic. The paper also met much opposition. Who is to chart its course? The bishop never interfered with O'Connor's editorial independence; indeed, he resorted to the unusual step of taking a full-page advertisement in the paper to state his case. That case seems to come down to this: Granting editorial independence, when can the editor be fired? O'Connor's supporters include most of John Leo's coterie and the overwhelming majority of his compeers—other lay editors of Catholic publications (and, at a guess, most of the clerical ones too). If one takes the view that an official paper is a house organ, they are, of course, wrong. And if one takes the view that it is free, under the "Freedom of the Press" concept, then it is hard to justify the subsidy, without which O'Connor could not have operated.

The O'Connor case is having an already perceptible effect on diocesan papers. *Delmarva Dialog* continues publication, but it is tepid after the warmth and brilliance of the O'Connor regime. Other liberal editors are bound to settle for the dull rather than risk the daring. Personal journalism is likely to dim. Dale Francis, the widely read columnist of the mass-circulation *Our Sunday Visitor*, has left it to publish a new right-wing paper called *Twin Circle*, a counter-balance to *National Catholic Reporter*. Without him, *Our Sunday Visitor*, in a partially new format, seems dimmer. The other mass-circulated weekly, the *Register*, also seems a little less personal and a little duller than it was in the days of its vigor. Both *Our Sunday Visitor* and the *Register* furnish copy to smaller diocesan papers, but their heyday is gone. The present tendency is to make more papers more and more diocesan.

Nearly all the diocesan newspapers in the country are subsidized one way or another by the diocese. Sometimes parishes are taxed for the subscriptions, sometimes the drives for subscriptions are pressured by hard-to-refuse school children or religious, sometimes the diocese picks up the deficit. Only two or three diocesan papers are on their own. But even those which are and carry the designation of "official," have an uneasy relationship with bishop and chancery, repugnant to professional journalism.

Nearly five-million copies of these papers reach Catholics every week. John Deedy says this means a readership of only 10 per cent of American Catholics,[12] but I think it rather more. And certainly the press is more important than this fraction would indicate. There is no doubt in my mind that the Catholic press as a whole is indispensable to the American Catholic Church. As Father John Reedy, editor of *Ave Maria*, puts it: "Without the Catholic press the community life of the Church in our nation would be shattered. There are official communications which can be distributed through correspondence, bulletins, and newsletters. But the continuing flow of information, significant and trivial, which gives bishops, priests, and laymen their awareness of the community which is the Church comes from our Catholic publications."[13]

MAGAZINE AND BOOK PUBLISHING

The magazine press is barely touched by these tensions. Editors are freer, their relations with their publishers and owners more clearly defined and usually more personal, and life is rather more bracing in the magazine uplands. Most Catholic magazines are subsidized by religious orders (like the Jesuits' *America*), a specific press or enterprise (like the Thomas More Association's *Critic*) or, less frequently, by an organization set up just for the purpose (like the *Catholic Digest*).

[12] Deedy.

[13] John Reedy, C.S.C., "The Purposes and Policies of the Catholic Press Association," *The Catholic Journalist*, XVII (Apr., 1966).

Given the forced-draft circulation, most diocesan papers probably make money; hardly a magazine does. Many of them are part of a money-raising complex, and hence are public-relations expenses; many are public relations for the religious communities that publish them. It is, indeed, an interesting question why so many religious communities subsidize magazines. Some years ago, when a distinguished Catholic editor and fund raiser tried to merge some magazines in the hope of improving both them and their identical apostolates, he met a resounding defeat. The communities just did not want to give up their publications. With some a tradition plays a part, but most are not that old.

In any case, the top magazines are better than the diocesan press. They are better written, better edited, have better art and make-up. Their total circulation of 21.5 million for 335 publications is also better than the ratio of the diocesan press (126 papers with 4.8 million circulation, according to the Catholic Press Directory for 1966-67). But there are all kinds of magazines. A few titles may indicate the variety: *Catholic School Journal, Homiletic and Pastoral Review, Catholic Historical Review, Friar, Catholic Boy, Benedictine Review, Catholic Charities, Liturgical Arts, Catholic Traveler*. The Catholic Press Association divides them into the following categories for the annual awards: General Interest, Opinion and Public Affairs, Professional and Specialized, Mission, Youth, Devotional, and Trade; but it adds a miscellaneous category.

So varied a lot makes generalization difficult. Occasionally magazines do a good job of in-depth reporting—the best report of the academic freedom controversy at the University of Dayton was done by *Ave Maria*. However, this is exceptional: As Professor Edward Walsh, Journalism Chairman at Fordham, noted in his comment on the Catholic Press Association's Magazine Awards for 1966, "The essay is still the curse of Catholic journalism. Again and again it is used as a substitute for reporting. . . . Reliance on it—and the almost total exclusion of genuine reporting—continues to be a serious flaw."

Professor Walsh's stricture reflects the most serious flaw in all Catholic journalism: lack of resources, and these spread too thin. This, in turn, leads to another characteristic in the syndrome: lack of professionalism, itself compounded by the number of religious thrust into journalism (or money-raising or public relations or broadcasting) without training, or at least enough education and taste to make experience swiftly meaningful. Some laymen, irritated not only by the lack of professionalism among the religious but by their lack of respect for it, would like to bar religious from editorial positions, but there are two good reasons why this is not likely to happen: the sheer number of them and the fact that some are really good. But those who are really good do not prevail. Again and again through the years the old cries re-echo: We have too many magazines and papers; let's kill some and merge some, and so use our total resources better. (One hears the same cries about Catholic education.) But who commits suicide?

Perhaps the columnists—Francis, Cogley, Greeley, Kennedy, and many another—are in one sense a bad influence on the Catholic press as a whole. They carry on the tradition of personal journalism of the nineteenth century, developed by Orestes Brownson, James McMaster, Maurice Francis Egan, John Boyle O'Reilly, Father Isaac Hecker, Father Daniel Hudson, and others. This encourages the younger men and women to think in terms of editorials, comment, and exhortation instead of reporting. Catholic journalism has largely ignored the *Time*-inspired team journalism, with its emphasis on dramatic fact backed by research. One excellent attempt, *Jubilee*, met with an ill-deserved eventual failure; lately it has been acquired by the publishing firm of Herder and Herder and is making another try. *Jubilee* had a powerful influence for good on Catholic magazine photography everywhere, just as *Life* did in the secular field. Other magazines like *Sign* also helped to make photography the area of greatest improvement in Catholic magazines of the past twenty years. In other areas development lags—in criticism, for example. With a few notable exceptions—like Msgr. John S. Kennedy on books, James Arnold on films, and the excellent *Critic* magazine on almost everything—Catholic magazine criticism is sophomoric.

What is the future of these 300-odd magazines? The general interest ones are fading, just as in the secular field: The *Messenger of the Sacred Heart* is gone, *Sign* and *Extension* are in a sharp decline. Every year six to ten magazines die, and fewer than this are born. Yet so long as most magazines are tied to some other activity, it is likely that they will last as long as the activity does. The mission magazines, for example, are geared to missionary activity. They change as the missions change: before World War II the focus was on the Far East, now it is on Africa; in just the same way the mission magazines have changed.

Like the missions, as activities become more centralized magazines will be fewer, but they will be there as necessary adjuncts to the activity—whether it be food services or the life of the mind.

For magazines are largely the communication of special groups. Like liberals and conservatives, lawyers and doctors, alumni and prison wardens, religious groups need their magazines. But it is not into magazines, I believe, that the best energy of Catholic intellectualism goes: It goes into books. If this is true, it is a curious exception to the general trend of American intellectual life, which seems to me article-minded rather than book-minded. The Catholic intellectual writes a better book than he does an article, I think; in any case, American "Catholic" books for the last twenty years make a more impressive display than they did for the twenty years between 1920 and 1940—much more so than the same comparison for magazines would show. And this is true not only for specifically Catholic publishing houses, but also for the Catholic lists developed by secular publishers, notably Doubleday. Moreover, the paperback revolution, which has everywhere revolutionized both reading and higher education, has had more reverberations among Catholics than it has elsewhere, simply because there was more for it to do. Catholic college courses in philosophy and theology, which used to be geared to Thomist handbooks, now find in paperbacks a range and a depth quite unknown to the previous generation.

CENSORSHIP AND THE CINEMA

Books on faith and morals are required by the law of the Church to be submitted for approval before publication to the bishop of the diocese in which they are written. This law has caused little disturbance in the United States in recent years and, indeed, might be abrogated by the time this is printed. Generally speaking, when it has been applied (as it was to the distinguished Jesuit theologian, John Courtney Murray) it is the long arm of Rome and not that of the local superior. Most American religious, especially those who publish, detest Rome's long arm and join in the current drive to amputate it, or at least to narrow its reach. Neither this prior censorship, nor the post-publication censorship by the much maligned Index of Forbidden Books, has had much operative force in this country. The Church may uphold her right to censor, but the thorny difficulty of applying it in the past has made most bishops and theologians chary of condemnation.[14] The present mood may be described as one of wide permissiveness. Even the National Office for Decent Literature is quiet in most places. This was set up by the U.S. bishops in 1938 to bring pressure on publishers and booksellers to prevent the sale of lascivious literature. Spurred on by it, some pastors and bishops organized committees to persuade booksellers to keep obscenity off their shelves and had some success with neighborhood drugstores. Court decisions against their goals prevented greater effectiveness, along with some unfortunate judgments about what is lascivious.

It is hard to blame a Church group for condemning obscenity and making efforts to check it. Surely religion has a legitimate concern in public morality. The question is: Does religion also have the positive duty of encouraging good art? Censorship can lead to a purely negative mentality, a litany of don'ts which inhibit do's. The observer who has watched the Catholic Church condemn may well ask: What has the Church done to encourage good art? Wherever Catholics are he sees ugly architecture and uglier decoration. Although he can find good Catholic art and artists in the United States he has to look hard for them; it is not right in front of him, as it is with Lutheran architecture and Jewish literature. When he relates this to official negativism, he is entitled to feel that the Church is simply against art of all kinds. The Catholic sensitive to art has at least the history of Christian art to comfort him, but in some ways he is worse off: The prayers he says in Church, the hymns he sings there, under a roof which is more often than not plastered with pretentious fake art, give him little esthetic substance. Yet he remembers Veronese's dog as well as *Baby Doll;* he knows that the artist's vision and the censor's frown usually clash.

The most dramatic (because the most effective) case of Catholic censorship was the Legion of Decency, which censored films. The film art offers an interesting example of the positive-negative dualism within the Church regarding popular art. For some reason the art of the film

[14] A fairly recent, but preconciliar, explication of the Church's position is Harold C. Gardiner, S.J., *Catholic Viewpoint on Censorship* (paperback ed., New York, 1961).

seems congenial to the Catholic spirit. The superb achivements of the Italian film makers of the last twenty years are in sharp contrast, for example, to the meretricious Italian church art of the same period. And perhaps their relations with the Church can suggest something about the Church, at least in Italy. Federico Fellini is steeped in the Catholicism of his boyhood, but as an adult he cannot resist at least one violently anticlerical touch per film. Roberto Rossellini is notoriously not in the Church, yet he made one of the finest religious films of all time, *The Little Flowers of St. Francis*. By far the finest biblical film I have ever seen, *The Gospel According to St. Matthew*, was made by an avowed Marxist, Pier Pasolini. Indeed, the religious sense of certain great film makers, as contrasted with novelists and dramatists, is an intriguing aspect of contemporary art. Think of Bergman, of Bresson, of Bunuel, of Cloche; remember, too, occasional religious films of Ford, of Lean, and of many others. Since the same religious sense is in much modern music, the parallel suggests a closer relationship between music and film than is ordinarily made.

In pluralistic America, the case is different. Film making here early attracted a great many Catholic actors, directors, writers, producers, and financiers. Many of these came from the stage—a profession crowded with Catholics in the early 1900's—but many more came straight to films. They gave to their films no specifically Catholic flavor that I discern. The official Church paid small attention to the art of the movies, as did the Catholic press. A sampling of Catholic magazines and newspapers between 1924 and 1934 reveals the usual stories about Catholics prominent in films and specifically Catholic themes and happenings in films, but scarcely any recognition of their art or social power.

On the negative side there were a growing number of pronouncements by bishops and preachers against films for the corruption of morals. Certainly there was ample provocation for these.[15] The protests culminated in the founding of the Legion of Decency in 1934. The Legion, whose headquarters was in New York, engaged housewives (members of the National Federation of Catholic Alumnae who volunteered for the job) to rate films as morally objectionable, or not, or partially so, for adults and children. Once a year in church Cath-

[15] See Raymond Moley, *The Hays Office* (Indianapolis, 1945).

olics were asked to pledge their support of the Legion, and the rating lists were given wide publicity in churches, schools, and the press.

So far this was a Church matter. What made the Legion more than that was its effectiveness in boycotting films it rated objectionable. Theaters which regularly showed such films were also boycotted. Faced with this loss of revenue, the film industry put teeth into a self-censoring code it had adopted three years before, and got a Catholic, Joseph P. Breen, to administer it. The code's seal of approval meant something then. Theaters wouldn't show films without it. Breen's job was widely applauded in the Catholic press, and both code and Legion were operative until television undercut the film audience after World War II. The independent producers who then dominated Hollywood repeatedly challenged or ignored the code, which still remains as a somewhat moribund function of the Motion Picture Producers' Association. It has recently been revised by that office under the direction of its current president, Jack Valenti.

The success of the Legion of Decency gave rise to the first papal pronouncement on film (or any popular art, as far as I know): the encyclical *Vigilanti Cura* of Pius XI (1936). Here the Pope presented a film esthetic as well as a pronouncement on it as a social medium. But it was not until after World War II that a tide of Catholic feeling changed the whole picture in the Church.

From the beginning the Legion had faced opposition even within the Church. Now criticism of the negativism and its methods began to mount, helped along, I believe, by the tastelessness of the Christopher movement, an apostolate of Catholic action within the professions, especially communications. *Commonweal* magazine especially distinguished itself by the good sense of its criticism of the Legion, but many others joined in. Gradually the Legion shifted; in 1965 it changed its name to "The National Catholic Office for Motion Pictures," and is now stimulating a more positive approach to films by encouraging study groups and publishing defenses of its new system of rating.

This turn has been greatly helped by the enlightened leadership of Patrick Sullivan, S.J. He is one of many influences: the writings of Moira Walsh, Donald Costello, and Edward Fischer; especially two seminal books, one by Fischer, *The Screen Arts* (Sheed and Ward, 1961), the other by William F. Lynch, S.J., *The Image Industries* (Sheed and Ward, 1959). Fischer at Notre Dame and John Culkin,

S.J., of Fordham, have led the way in the schools; their students, especially the high-school teachers, have spread good standards for the film art throughout the country.

Fischer has also made an influential film series on film appreciation, produced and distributed by The Hour of St. Francis Productions, and has pioneered in writing and producing documentaries on a university campus, a vogue which students everywhere are eagerly picking up. The writings of Sister Bede Sullivan and Paul Carrico, C.S.C., have been seminal. All in all, the rise of interest in film among Catholics in the last ten years has been phenomenal. Parishes use them for Lent and Advent, schools use them to teach theology, study groups pioneered by the excellent Adult Education Center of the Archdiocese of Chicago use them everywhere. There are two recent books listing films for religious education, one by Father Patrick McCaffery, and the other by William Kuhns.[16] The encouragement by the Vatican II Decree on Mass Media Communications has helped.

All this is a far cry from the negativism of the 1930's. In part it is surely a revulsion against it. All art is the expression of honest human emotion, and the film is its most popular modern medium. If what is going on in the Church now reflects joy, not fear of the emotional life, and a sense of the fusion of art and apostolate, it is surely the most hopeful development in Catholic communications.

RADIO AND TELEVISION

The American Church has historically been little concerned with radio and television. Quite a few Catholic universities were among those who early received radio broadcasting licenses[17] and occasional services were broadcast in the 1920's, but the general attitude of the Church was hands off, reinforced by the embarrassment of Father Coughlin's success in the early 1930's.[18] More important, I believe, was the fear that broadcasting the Mass would lead to a loss in Sunday

[16] Patrick J. McCaffrey, *A Guide to Short Films for Religious Education Programs* (Notre Dame, Ind., 1967); William Kuhns, *Short Films in Religious Education* (Dayton, O., 1967).

[17] Erik Barnouw, *A Tower in Babel* (New York, 1966), p. 32n.

[18] See Charles J. Tull, *Father Coughlin and the New Deal* (Syracuse, 1965).

congregations; the Catholic press made the point repeatedly that listening to a broadcast does not fulfill the Sunday obligation of attending Mass. Richard Walsh, director of communications for the National Council of Catholic Men, says that his organization was given the task of producing the Catholic Hour for network radio because the hierarchy did not wish to take direct responsibility for any trouble arising from the broadcasts.[19]

This contrasts sharply with contemporary attitudes. Most diocesan staffs today list, along with the Superintendent of Schools, a "Diocesan Director of Broadcasting," about a dozen of whom work full-time. They belong to the Catholic Broadcasting Association, founded in 1958. They produce some local programs, but generally they assist local stations with their religious programming and help produce the Catholic ones. Their very presence bespeaks willing cooperation with broadcasting.

The Catholic Hour, established for radio in 1930, at present produces sixty television programs besides 110 radio programs for the three major networks. It also runs a film-rental library. Other network radio and television programs are produced monthly by religious orders and placed with various cooperative stations throughout the country.

Perhaps the most significant new activity in television, however, is the development of closed-circuit educational networks for the school systems of some dioceses. New York, Brooklyn, and Rockville Center in New York, Miami and St. Augustine in Florida, Baltimore, Detroit, and Los Angeles have led the way; others are sure to follow.

How effective is this broadcasting? One of the troubles with it is the lack of a research check. Certainly it shares with the press a too facile assumption that it will be heard and, being heard, be effective. What Roy Danish, director of the Television Information Office, told the Catholic Communications Convention of 1966 in San Francisco is too often ignored: "[Religious broadcasters who bought certain radio time] disregarded this salient fact: Any mass communication, whether in print, by sound, or through television, will *select* [his italics] its viewers and it cannot be expected, except in the most unusual circumstances, to reach or attract everyone or even most people." Danish goes on to talk about the necessity for quality and professionalism in program making, once the audience has been identified.

[19] R. J. Walsh, "Media of Social Communication II—Church Use of," *New Catholic Encyclopedia,* IX, 559 *et seq.*

COMMUNICATION AND THE ARTS

This affects much Catholic communication, so often mediocre or perfunctory. The best in quality and the most effective in impact of Catholic communication through the arts is the Graduate School of Drama at the Catholic University. Its director, Gilbert Hartke, O.P., assembled a staff of extraordinary merit—Jean and Walter Kerr, Leo Brady, and Josephine Callan among them. Its graduates go everywhere to remake the theater in Catholic schools and colleges, and its excellent travelling company tours the country to show how to stage great plays stylishly and inexpensively. In the thirty or so years of its existence it has been the chief instrument in upgrading the theater in Catholic education to its present high standards.

There have been other good efforts. In music, the work of the Manhattanville College of the Sacred Heart (now removed to Purchase, New York) in teaching choir directors plainchant has been outstanding; *Liturgical Arts* magazine had done a similar work for church decoration.

With varying influence and success, the Marquette Graduate School of Journalism, the Catholic University Graduate School of Drama, and the Pius X School of Music at Manhattanville College of the Sacred Heart have been the kind of centers the American Church needs more of. There have been good Catholic artists of recent times—J. F. Powers and Flannery O'Connor in fiction, Rico LeBrun and William Congdon in painting, Paul Creston and Vincent Persichetti in music, just as there has been in one place or another good instruction in all the arts. One thinks of Notre Dame's tradition of the teaching of writing; the work of Sister Thomasita and Sister Corita in art; of the journalism of Edward Rice, Robert Burns, Donald Thorman, Edward Skillin, and many other editors; of the poetry of Henry Rago, John Logan, John Frederick Nims, Robert Fitzgerald, John Fandel, and Ernest Sandeen. But these have been fitful gleams here and there; they have not suffused the Church with their ideals of communication. Seminary education especially has been indifferent to the arts.

I believe that the arts are the key to the whole body of communication within the Church. Not the studio arts, not the arts of fiction and sculpture and composing music, but wide feeling for these among Catholics. The difference in atmosphere between cultivated Catholics and cultivated Protestants and Jews is not, in my observation, a difference of intelligence or specialized scholarship; the difference is made out of love and understanding of the arts. Among so many Catholics, Matisse, Verdi and Brecht are almost unknown and mostly uncultivated. Yet I sense especially among the young a deep hunger for understanding the arts.

The arts are of key importance, I think, because Catholics seem especially prone to believe that good communication is a matter of techniques. They want to learn broadcasting, not writing; layout, not design; they believe that play-writing and sportswriting and writing commercials and making speeches and movies are all separate activities involving separate techniques. This is, of course, true on the surface. But there is an underlying unity to all these, a unity provided by taste, discernment, and judgment. And that unity comes at bottom from esthetic experience. Each art has its separate techniques, too, and it is the work of a lifetime to master even one set of them. Yet all the arts are one in that all communicate honest human feeling; all are one in that their disciplines refine and ennoble the human spirit; all are one in that they provide, as I believe with Suzanne Langer, "images of the forms of feeling" of culture.

What besets mass communications most is, of course, vulgarity; that is its natural vice, just as snobbishness is the natural vice of the esthete. Between the two, it is easy to choose vulgarity as the more attractive. But just as the esthete's danger is that he can get too far from life in his worship of art, so the vulgarian's is that he can ignore or reject art. Mass communications will never suffer from a too-refined estheticism, but I do not see how its tendency to vulgarity can be redeemed except through constant reference to those arts which are its more stylish and more permanent kin.

Bad taste, as Walter Kerr once remarked, is not one of the seven deadly sins.[20] Perhaps because of this Catholics don't hesitate to commit it. Let one example suffice. In our generous turn to ecumenism we have found much in common with Protestants not previously realized, and we are now acknowledging this with gladness. But there is one thing which we have ignored (Catholics with taste have always known how good this thing was): their good translations of Scripture

[20] Walter Kerr, "Catholics and Hollywood," *Commonweal*, LVII (Dec. 19, 1952).

and well-composed public prayers and hymns. Only occasionally do we borrow the hymns. With a few notable exceptions—such as the Jerusalem Bible and the new translation of the Canon of the Mass—we hear the word of God in English that is revoltingly bad, and we say our prayers in language nearly as dreadful as the sentimental modern Italian devotions from which they are copied. Billy Graham does better. If one is going to touch the masses, at least let the performance have a professional snap.

Let's rest on that word "professional." Too many Catholic authorities assume that a communicator can be made by the *fiat* of religious authority. They would hardly turn to an amateur for a brain operation, but they have no hesitation in turning to one to be the editor of a paper or direct the public relations for an important event. Admittedly, training in communications does not have the clarity and sense of direction that training for brain surgery has, but in this country only the Church fails to seek professional public-relations counsel.

In whatever atmosphere, we are going to keep right on communicating as long as there is a Church. For we are bound by Christ's command to communicate our Good News, his Gospel.

14: THE AMERICAN CATHOLIC LAYMAN AND HIS ORGANIZATIONS

Martin H. Work and *Daniel J. Kane*

Nicolas Berdyaev has written that the pace of modern history is "catastrophic." Catholic lay people in the United States today might well agree with that judgment. In 1962 Donald J. Thorman portrayed "the emerging layman" as standing on the threshold of a "new and exciting era." In 1967, however, he wrote that "in terms of changes of attitude and approaches to Catholicism" the intervening period was more "like five centuries" than five years. Thorman speaks now not of the emerging layman but of "today's layman: an uncertain Catholic."[1]

The emerging layman of 1962, believing himself to be coming "into his own" in the Church, looked forward to the Second Vatican Council with great expectations. The post-World War II era had been a period of growth in leadership, responsibility, and recognition in the Church; laymen regarded the Council as both a climax and a new point of departure in these developments. But by 1967 some of the most liberal and forward-looking elements had become disillusioned. One leading spokesman for this view, Michael Novak, wrote that "the glow of Vatican II has almost entirely waned—its promise has been squandered by an inept institutional structure nearly impervious to serious change." The result, Novak added, was that "the prospects for reform in the institutional Church leave many of us bored."[2]

Others dissatisfied with the older structures undertook to work through a new organization—the National Association of Laymen—

[1] Donald J. Thorman, "Today's Layman: an Uncertain Catholic," *America*, CXVI (Jan. 14, 1967), 39.

[2] Michael Novak, "The Revolution of 1976," *Commonweal*, LXXXVI (July 14, 1967), 441.

apart from the official institutional Church. And as the American delegation prepared for the Third World Congress of the Lay Apostolate being held in Rome in the fall of 1967, John Leo was writing that "the institutional Church as we know it is breaking up" and "the convulsions within Catholicism are just beginning."[3] For the growing number of laymen who have responded to the summons to more active participation through parochial school boards, parish councils, and similar structures, voices such as those of Novak and Leo constitute a sudden and urgent challenge. So do the views expressed by many others who argue that the Christian finds his proper work in the "real world," with its problems of race, poverty, and war, rather than in strictly Church-related activities.

"Catastrophic" may be too dramatic a word to describe the transitions affecting American Catholic laymen; nevertheless, many are presently harried, confused, and even alarmed at the pace of events. They may have "emerged," but they are troubled as they study their life amid the crises confronting the postconciliar Church—the crises of faith, of doctrine, of authority, of the Church as institution, and the crisis concerning the existence of God Himself. But in the midst of this turmoil, increasing numbers of lay leaders feel that to falter, to stand numbed before the problems, to yield to the "prophets of doom" would be to desert what can truly be called the providential task of today's layman: working with consummate skill and consuming love—and patience—for the renewal of the Church and society. For such laymen, renewal must come from within the Church. But being "within" the Church provides for a wide latitude in approaches to renewal. There is only one limitation—one does not destroy in order to recreate.

The layman's long struggle to achieve recognition as a mature, responsible member of the Church cannot be fully recounted in this brief chapter. But there are certain historical aspects of the story which should be better known if American Catholics of today are to understand the development of the movement of which they are the heirs. And an understanding of this history will be equally beneficial whether the layman seeks an individual witness in today's world or works within organized Church structures.

[3] John Leo in *New York Times Book Review*, July 30, 1967.

LAY BEGINNINGS AND EARLY GROWTH

John Tracy Ellis has said that "the impressive Catholic laity of today must not be thought a new thing on the American scene; rather they are a product of between 300 and 400 years of growth in the soil of this Republic."[4] The roots of this Catholic growth were planted by Spanish, French, and English settlers of the New World and nurtured in subsequent eras by Catholics of many other national origins. The same year that saw the birth of the new Federal government also witnessed the establishment of the new Church, which in 1789 received its first bishop, John Carroll, and organized its first diocese, Baltimore. Bishop Carroll could look to thirty priests to serve the needs of about 30,000 laity (out of a total population of about four million).

Early in the nineteenth century a crisis occurred in the American Church, the aftereffects of which remained into our own time. The crisis, known as "trusteeism," pitted laymen (and some priests) against bishops in matters dealing with the appointment of pastors and the management of parishes. The bishops were victorious in the struggle with the lay trustees, but as Archbishop Robert Dwyer has said, their victory "resulted in a situation where the part of the laity in this co-operative effort which is the work of the Church was reduced almost to a minimum."[5] In the mid-twentieth century, Catholic voices were still calling on the American Church to rid itself of the "ghost" of trusteeism and its unwarranted fears of the new lay apostolic efforts.

The worst of the trusteeism problems were barely surmounted when the great era of immigration began. The role of the layman in this period was one of response "in physical energy, sacrificial generosity, and raw courage" to the task of providing a Catholic life for the immigrants and helping them preserve their faith. Suspect in American society as "foreign" and without leadership status in his Church, the layman still helped that Church deepen its roots in American life and prevail over forces of bigotry and intolerance prevalent in that era. A different breed of Catholics inhabits the American Church in 1968 but

[4] John Tracy Ellis, Commencement Address at Carroll College, Helena, Montana, May 27, 1962.

[5] Robert Dwyer, "The American Laity," *Commonweal*, LX (Aug. 27, 1954), 503.

as Msgr. Ellis has said, without the Catholics of the last century, laymen as well as bishops and clergy, "many of us would not so much as own the faith today and for that alone they are entitled to an enduring remembrance."[6]

Concommitant with the growth of the Church through immigration, as Daniel Callahan interprets the era, was the growth of episcopal power to such an extent that "any real possibility of either lay or clerical initiative was effectively uprooted, not to be replanted for many generations."[7] Near the end of the nineteenth century there were two national meetings of the laity. The Lay Congress of Baltimore in 1889 and the Columbian Catholic Congress at Chicago in 1893 were hopeful signs of new lay initiatives. Organized by lay leaders, well attended by delegates (1,500 at Baltimore, 2,500 at Chicago), with talks and papers that indicated the concern of laymen not only for institutional problems of the Church but for the layman's role in temporal society, these two efforts were not sustained. The laymen could not secure the necessary episcopal support to continue the work and the fires of lay enthusiasm were soon banked.

It was not until after World War I and the establishment of the National Catholic Welfare Conference that American Catholic lay leadership organized and became active in significant measure. An earlier venture was the American Federation of Catholic Societies, which was organized in 1901 and claimed a peak membership of some three million. The Federation was very loosely put together, however, and it never won the effective support of the hierarchy. But its affiliated societies included a number of Catholic fraternals and other worthwhile societies such as the German Catholic Central-Verein. It concerned itself with social problems and lent its support to new ventures like the layman's retreat movement and the National Catholic Educational Association.

THE NCWC

In 1908 the twelve-million Catholics in the United States were declared by Rome to be no longer living in mission country. The American

[6] John Tracy Ellis, "American Catholicism in 1960: an Historical Perspective," *American Benedictine Review*, XI (Mar.-June, 1960), 1-20.

[7] Daniel Callahan, *The Mind of the Catholic Layman* (New York, 1963), p. 44.

Church had come of age. Further evidence of the new maturity came in 1917 when the hierarchy organized the National Catholic War Council to coordinate the works of charity and war relief called for during World War I. When the war ended, the bishops voted to continue the Council and extend its work under the title, the National Catholic Welfare Council (renamed National Catholic Welfare Conference in 1923 and United States Catholic Conference in 1966). The Conference—usually called NCWC—was "a common agency under the authority of the bishops to promote the welfare of Catholics and unify, coordinate, and organize the Catholic people of the United States in works of education, social welfare, immigrant aid, and other activities." Among the departments established was one for lay organizations, and with it came the birth of the National Council of Catholic Men (NCCM) and the National Council of Catholic Women (NCCW). In other subsections of the NCWC, such as press, legal, and other departments and bureaus added in subsequent years, individual laymen and women were also to function. The formation of the NCWC was a pioneer work in the Church, a work which many years later was to serve as a model for the episcopal conferences called for by the Second Vatican Council.

The formation of NCCM and NCCW signaled the serious intention of the American bishops to develop, train, and support a more dynamic lay movement in the United States. These organizations were the precursors of the specialized apostolic groups which we shall discuss in another part of this chapter and they laid the groundwork for structures permitting the layman's voice to be heard in the Church.

In 1919 the Bishops' Program for Social Reconstruction was issued. The influence of this prophetic call for social justice and welfare was reflected in the activities of the NCCM and the NCCW. The Councils also concerned themselves with the internal problems of the Church and provided a valuable training ground for the formation of lay leaders and a forum for the consideration of problems affecting lay people. NCCW was particularly noteworthy in that it gave Catholic women the chance to function within their own apostolic organization and to make the voice of Catholic women heard on the issues confronting Church and society, a voice seldom heard in the American Church up to that time.

In one particular area, communication, the NCCM did pioneer work. In 1930 it originated the "Catholic Hour" on the NBC radio network, an apostolic work which still continues. In 1951 NCCM began producing television programs for the national television networks. NCCM's thrust in communications led into further pioneer work in developing "structures for dialogue." Its parish opinion surveys, National Consultants program, and its research orientation constitute an important response to the Vatican Council's call for "family dialogue."

ACTIVITIES OF THE INTER-WAR YEARS

A more traditional type of Catholic organization, the Holy Name Society, continued to enlist the support of laymen after World War I. This venerable parish-centered society provided Catholic men with a local rallying point for parochial action. Its spiritual and social programs and annual public demonstrations afforded Catholics the opportunity to give public witness to their faith. Similarly, a variety of Catholic benevolent and fraternal organizations maintained their programs of welfare and spiritual activities. And Catholic men continued to find a vehicle for the practical exercise of Christian charity through the Society of St. Vincent de Paul.

The 1928 presidential campaign was a traumatic experience for many Catholics. Believing themselves completely a part of American society, proud of their growth in numbers and loyalty as Americans, they were shocked at the virulence of the anti-Catholicism of the Smith-Hoover campaign. Thirty years later John Cogley was to recall that Al Smith's defeat gave him his "first doubts about the power of prayer and the power of the American idea as well" when the Sister told his class that none of them "should ever hope to be President of the United States."[8] But perhaps the 1928 campaign also had some positive effects in causing a reevaluation of Church-State relations, in focusing attention on problems of religious bigotry and discrimination, and in stimulating Catholics to reexamine the nature of their contributions to American society.

Certain other developments of the 1920's and 1930's foreshadowed the dramatic emergence of the layman which was to take place in the next generation. A growing number of young people were graduating

[8] John Cogley, "American Catholic Panorama," in *American Catholic Horizons*, ed. Eugene K. Culhane, S. J. (New York, 1966), p. 269.

from Catholic secondary schools and colleges. The *Commonweal*, which was to become a major organ to lay thought, was founded in 1924; the Social Action Department of NCWC conducted institutes and conferences on industrial relations and the social teachings of the Church; Catholic journals made a modest beginning in the self-examination of Catholic cultural and intellectual life.

Reflecting the many writings of Pope Pius XI on the subject, the NCWC's emphasis on "Catholic Action" was another important development of this period. By summoning the Catholic laity "to participation in the apostolate of the hierarchy," the bishops gave their endorsement to lay work and increasing numbers of men and women were attracted to this "official" form of collaboration and cooperation. Their role in the Church began to appear more attractive, more responsible, and more meaningful. In the 1930's some American lay leaders were being introduced to the work of their confreres in Europe, thus initiating the international collaboration that was to be pursued so fruitfully after World War II.

There was also some dissent from majority Catholic opinion on such controverted subjects of the 1930's as communism and the Spanish Civil War. A few Catholic activists and journalists criticized the sterility of an anticommunism which was not equally concerned with the grave problems of society; *Commonweal* and *Catholic Worker* took issue with the almost unanimous Catholic support of Franco in the Spanish conflict. This public opposition to well established and widely propagated Catholic positions gave the country a foretaste of the divergence of opinion which was to become more frequent after 1945.

NEW APOSTOLIC EFFORTS IN THE 1930's

The age of the Depression also saw the beginnings of certain works of the lay apostolate which are still active. The unrest and misery of the thirties and the climate of social experimentation generated by the New Deal constituted the background for the work of Dorothy Day and Peter Maurin, the founder and propagandist, respectively, of the Catholic Worker movement. From a House of Hospitality in the Lower East Side of New York the movement spread to Boston, Philadelphia, Chicago, Baltimore, St. Louis, Detroit, and other industrial centers. Castigating Catholic indifference to the social crisis in the United States and Europe, denying the morality of modern warfare, and urging a new economic system to replace what they believed to be a decadent capitalism, Miss Day and Mr. Maurin posed a disturbing challenge to the consciences of American Catholics.

The Catholic Worker centers, or "houses," have a two-fold purpose. They are refuges for the poor and unemployed, centers where the love of Christ is manifested through the volunteers who staff the houses. In addition, they are intended to serve as centers for the discussion of crucial moral, economic, social, and political problems. The great mass of American Catholics was completely unaware of the existence of these Houses of Hospitality, but through the publication of the *Catholic Worker* and by word of mouth, thousands of lay men and women were drawn to the centers, not merely to feed the poor but to feed on the exciting intellectual fare offered by the gentle Miss Day and the philosophers, theologians, sociologists, and radical activists who constituted the faculty of these unusual adult-education centers. Here many of the lay leaders of the 1940's and 1950's were first introduced to Catholic social action, to the liturgical movement, to the writings of European social thinkers. Here these same lay persons made their commitments—commitments, for the most part, to other aspects of Catholic action besides the Catholic Worker, but which were stimulated by Dorothy Day and Peter Maurin.

A Catholic response to the troubled agricultural situation of the twenties and thirties was the National Catholic Rural Life Conference. In its beginnings this organization comprised a small band of clerics and a few laymen who came from the rural areas of the nation where Catholics were a distinct minority. Seeking to hold Catholics "on the land," to improve working and living conditions for poor and migrant farm families, to modernize the farm operation, and to seek legislation which would alleviate the inequities of the farmer's economic life, the Conference was a force nationally and, by the mid-1940's, internationally. Under the dynamic and creative direction of its executive secretary, Msgr. Luigi G. Ligutti, the Conference took its cause to the urban centers of academic, economic, and political influence, and its voice also influenced Protestant rural leaders. The Rural Life Conference was founded in 1923 by Father (later Archbishop) Edwin V. O'Hara, who also was to be a pioneer in establishing the Confraternity of Christian

Doctrine in the United States. Through its institutes for pastors, teachers, and farmers, its annual conventions, and its publication, *Land and Home,* the Conference introduced many Catholic lay men and women to the credit union and the cooperative, to the growing liturgical apostolate, and to the beginnings of ecumenical work with Protestant rural-life groups. The Rural Life Conference was also a pioneer among Catholic lay groups in developing an awareness of the international dimension of the problems with which it was concerned.

Europe was a major source of inspiration for new departures in action after World War I. American priests studying abroad in the 1930's became acquainted with new forms of apostolic work and brought their methods and mystiques back to the United States. Chief among these groups were the Young Christian Workers (YCW) and Young Christian Students (YCS). Founded by the Belgian priest Joseph Cardijn (who died as Cardinal Cardijn in 1967), these movements aimed to "Christianize the milieux" of workers and students and to train them in responsible leadership. The "apostles" to these milieux were the workers and students themselves. Msgr. Reynold Hillenbrand in Chicago and Louis J. Putz, C.S.C., at the University of Notre Dame pioneered in adapting these approaches to the American scene. From the Chicago-South Bend nucleus the YCW and YCS soon spread to other parts of the country, carrying with them a leavening effect that stimulated the social consciousness of a generation of young Catholics.

The Grail, an international movement of women founded in Holland after World War I, is another example of a specialized lay movement that came to the United States from abroad. Dr. Lydwine Van Kersbergen and Miss Joan Overboss established the first Grail center at Libertyville, Illinois, in 1941, and the permanent national headquarters at Grailville (Loveland, Ohio) in 1944. The movement brought a fresh impetus to Catholic laywomen's activities; its center at Grailville became a place of study and discussion of the liturgy, social and interracial action, and ecumenical and cultural programs. Very early in its history, the American Grail initiated lay missionary work which was also to become a concern for other apostolic groups in the 1950's. The Grail's emphasis on woman's role in the Church and in society was an important contribution in the 1940's; along with groups such as the NCCW it presaged the increased participation of women in organized lay work.

An outstanding laywoman of the period was Catherine de Hueck, who began her interracial work in Canada and in 1938 initiated the Friendship House movement in the United States by opening a center in a Harlem apartment. Dedicated to the apostolate of interracial justice, Friendship House resembled the Catholic Worker movement in its emphasis on sharing the life of the poor and on voluntary poverty and personal witness-bearing. Demanding an unequivocal commitment to evangelical charity, the Friendship House approach appealed to the imagination and apostolic yearning of young men and women, many of them college students, who willingly gave of their services during holidays and vacations. The lecture tours of Catherine de Hueck, an exiled Russian baroness, made the movement better known and challenged the Catholic conscience on racial discrimination and segregation. An even earlier response to the race problem had been Catholic Interracial Council founded in 1934 by George Hunton and John LaFarge, S.J. This organization, whose work is discussed elsewhere in this book, spread from its original beginnings in New York and, along with the Friendship Houses, expressed the concern of at least some Catholics for the social and economic welfare as well as the spiritual well-being of Negroes.

Another organization growing directly out of the social and economic problems of the times was the Association of Catholic Trade Unionists (ACTU). Founded in 1937, the ACTU eventually had chapters in fifteen industrial cities. Classes were organized in the social teaching of the Church, labor, law, public speaking, parliamentary procedures, and so on. The Association sponsored public forums, Labor Day Masses, evenings and days of recollection for working men, and the publication of several lively labor papers. The ACTU was more pragmatically oriented than was the Catholic Worker group, which had a strong utopian tendency and which regarded modern industry and technology with hostility. Closely related to the ACTU in approach were the Catholic Labor Alliance of Chicago, the labor schools which the Jesuits were particularly active in organizing, and diocesan ventures into the labor field in Hartford, Connecticut, and Brooklyn, New York. All of these efforts reflected the same general aim: to preserve the American worker in the Church; to check communist penetration of labor unions; to agitate for a social order based on the principles of the encyclicals; to create a spirituality relevant to the needs and outlook of working people.

ISSUES AND ACTIVITIES OF THE WORLD WAR II ERA

Taken together, these movements represented growth in the area of Catholic lay activities; they also represented a departure in method and spirit from the more traditional forms of Catholic organizational life. In their specific spheres of activity and in the ferment which they collectively stirred up, these new movements made a permanent and valuable contribution to the age of lay action in which we find ourselves today.

As these groups continued their work, however, it became clear that disagreement existed on a fundamental issue. The problem centered on just how the layman was to confront the modern age. Was he to accept the modern industrial, technological, and scientific world in an unqualified way, aligning himself with the tendencies inherent in it? Should he attempt to reshape the modern world while working within it? Or should he reject twentieth-century society and strive through withdrawn communal groups to create a more desirable alternative to it? These questions were debated in the pages of the *Catholic Worker*, in *Integrity* (a journal founded in 1946 by Carol Jackson and Ed Willock), in the correspondence columns of the Catholic press, and in the meetings of specialized lay organizations. Strong arguments were made from all points of view. The two journals named above were among the most extreme in their rejection of modern society. The evils of mechanization were deplored and rural life enthusiasts sometimes spoke of a "green revolution" that would bring modern man "back to the land." But the apostolic groups in Chicago led by Msgr. Hillenbrand and such laymen as Ed Marciniak, John Cogley, and James O'Gara called for involvement in the urban industrial environment where the great majority of Catholics actually lived and where most of the great problems of modern life had to be confronted.

The debate was of course never settled, and some aspects of it may appear merely quaint in these days of inner-city work and Christian secularity. But the tension between acceptance of society and withdrawal from it is a perennial feature of Christian history, and there are ambiguities in contemporary American Catholic thinking on these points that deserve closer examination than they are now being given.

Another issue that divided apostolic lay people in the days around World War II was the distinction between "Catholic Action" and

"Catholic action." Insofar as there was a substantive point involved in this orthographic battle, it centered on the question of which Catholics and which Catholic organizations were "officially" participating in the apostolate of the hierarchy. In part this controversy, which now seems so remote and inconsequential, represented a struggle for recognition by the newer specialized lay groups as opposed to the more traditional forms of apostolic work such as the Sodality, or the Holy Name Society.

But there was a deeper issue. The specialized movements conceived their apostolates in large and inclusive terms. They saw themselves as called into existence by the Church and given a mandate by the bishops to develop and follow a way of Christian lay life aimed directly at the penetration of the social order, seeking to renew that order through social justice and social charity. This was true "Catholic Action." By way of contrast, "Catholic action" was understood as being less directly related to the work of the Church, not as concerned with social problems, often being merely "activity by Catholics," limited in scope and depth. Those associated with YCW, YCS, and the Christian Family Movement (CFM) claimed to be the real practitioners of Catholic Action. The leaders of the Catholic Worker, the Legion of Mary, the Grail, and the rural and interracial conferences were less concerned over what their work was called, but they too were drawn into the controversy. So also was the Sodality movement, which, under Daniel Lord, S.J., had carried its vision of the apostolate to young people in Summer Schools of Catholic Action all over the United States. And the American founder of the Confraternity of Christian Doctrine, Bishop Edwin V. O'Hara of Kansas City, Missouri, took his case directly to Rome, where he was told that the CCD was, indeed, Catholic Action.

A good deal of time and energy was dissipated in this semantic squabble; nevertheless, much constructive work was done in the forties and fifties. One noteworthy emphasis was on youth. The Catholic Youth Organization (CYO) grew into a national movement attracting hundreds of thousands of boys and girls and thousands of adult lay leaders. Veterans of World War II who entered Catholic colleges likewise lent a new impetus to the National Federation of Catholic College Students (NFCCS); their more mature leadership added to the seriousness and effectiveness of this organization. In 1940 the Youth Department of NCWC was established, and its National Council of

Catholic Youth developed programs with a fourfold emphasis: social, cultural, intellectual, and spiritual.

Still another development in the same general area was the new look imparted to Newman Clubs on the campuses of state colleges and universities. As the Catholic enrollments in these schools rose, the obligations laid upon Newman Clubs increased correspondingly. In the late 1950's and early 1960's, Newman dropped "club" from its title and became the Newman Apostolate, stressing extensive apostolic, cultural, spiritual, and intellectual programs. Both NFCCS and Newman contributed to the lay missionary movement which emerged in the late 1950's. College students and graduates were moved to give a certain period of service to the Church in other nations, especially in Latin America. There they contributed their talents in catechetical work, health services, community development, and education.

The year 1943 was a landmark in the area of Catholic family life, for it was then that John Delaney, S.J., held the first Cana Conference, in New York City. These sessions of reflection and discussion by married couples on the problems of family life were soon taken up in Chicago, St. Louis, and other cities. By 1947, former members of the YCS and YCW—now married and wishing to continue their Catholic action as couples—began the Christian Family Movement. This unique American contribution to lay apostolic work has since been extended to many other nations. Using the same small-group, or "cell," technique of the specialized movements, as well as their "observe, judge, act" method of operation, the CFM very soon became a major group in the lay apostolate under the leadership of Mr. and Mrs. Patrick Crowley at Chicago.

Cana, CFM, and other forms of the marriage and family apostolate soon appeared in different parts of the nation. The Family Life Bureau of NCWC, diocesan family-life bureaus, and family-life institutes of Catholic colleges and universities aided in the expansion of this particularly important work. One of the early services of the new movement was the Pre-Cana Conference, or marriage preparation course for engaged couples, with most of the courses being given by couples and professional laymen (doctors, lawyers, etc.). Pre-Cana Conferences are now an accepted method of marriage preparation in all dioceses of the United States.

The interest and concern for interracial work aroused by the formation of Catholic Interracial Councils in the 1930's continued to increase. These groups had an educational influence within the Church since they helped to put "interracial justice" on the agendas of other Catholic lay organizations and movements. From 1945 to 1960 their number increased, resulting in the latter year in the formation of the National Catholic Conference for Interracial Justice. Besides acting and speaking in its own right, the NCCIJ now services the needs of over 150 diocesan human-relations and interracial commissions.

The American Catholic responses to the social encyclicals since the time of Pope Leo XIII have taken a variety of forms and have been integrated into the action programs of many lay groups. In 1956 leaders of these social-action groups and allied lay organizations formed the National Catholic Social Action Conference. NCSAC meets annually and provides an opportunity for the exchange of ideas and of concrete proposals for social action. Unfortunately, the lack of funds has limited the work which the group has been able to undertake, but its meetings have stimulated action on the individual level. The National Christian (originally Catholic) Conference of Employers and Managers is another recent initiative in the area of social and economic questions, and it ministers to a group whose viewpoint and needs had been previously overlooked by Catholic organizations.

MOVING TOWARD THE PRESENT

In the 1950's, the increased interest in lay apostolic work was capitalized on by the National Councils of Catholic Men and Women in a two-fold manner: by their program services for their parochial affiliates and by the increased opportunities they afforded their national leaders for more responsible witness within the Church. Though many parish societies were still using old methods of operation and concerned themselves with trivial issues, NCCM and NCCW aided others to more meaningful programs in areas of education, international relations, social and interracial action, rural life, liturgy, and family life. Because they federated thousands of parochial, diocesan, and national groups and had to program for large numbers of men and women of varied educational and social background, NCCM and NCCW could not be so highly specialized as were CFM, YCW, the Grail, and others. But the national federations of men and women did reach many thousands of "ordinary" Catholics. These activities also created a cadre of diocesan and national officers who were capable of assuming responsibility for representing the American layman in various national and international assignments. In 1951 and 1957, for example, such men and women from the American lay groups were among the leading delegates to the First and Second World Congresses of the Lay Apostolate in Rome. For the Third World Congress held in October, 1967, the Holy See named Martin H. Work, executive director of NCCM, a member of the world committee of laymen which planned the Congress and its program.

All of the modern lay American groups have had the valuable assistance and cooperation of the liturgical, scriptural, and catechetical movements to assist them in the spiritual formation of their individual members and to guide their program efforts in these particular areas of action.

The liturgical movement in the United States has its roots in the 1920's and especially in the pioneer efforts of the late Virgil Michel, O.S.B., who in 1926 founded the liturgical journal, *Orate Fratres* (now *Worship*) at St. John's Abbey, Collegeville, Minnesota. National Liturgical Weeks held since 1940 have drawn many laymen to this "primary apostolate" as a means of finding greater participation in the life of the Church. In 1960 a layman, John Mannion, became executive secretary of the Liturgical Conference. Not only individual Catholics but all the major lay organizations have felt the influence of the liturgical movement and were prepared by it for the sweeping liturgical changes which took place in the pontificates of Pope Pius XII, John XXIII, and Paul VI.

The "public washing of our linen" which took place following John Tracy Ellis' now famous critique, "American Catholics and the Intellectual Life,"[9] was largely the work of laymen who were themselves products of the system under scrutiny. The debate itself certainly gave evidence of the maturation of a sophisticated and well-educated lay elite, but critics still faulted the Church, pointing among other things to the relatively minor role played by intellectual groups such as Pax Romana and the Catholic Commission on Intellectual and Cultural Affairs. According to Msgr. Ellis, when the National Council of Catholic Men in 1961 gave awards to four Catholics for intellectual ex-

[9] John Tracy Ellis, "American Catholics and the Intellectual Life," *Thought*, XXX (Autumn, 1955), 351-88.

cellence it was the first such public recognition ever given by a national Catholic organization solely for intellectual achievement!

No doubt a greater number of Catholic lay people have been troubled by the difficulties facing the Catholic parochial and high schools. As economic and personnel problems mounted, laymen concerned themselves with programs aimed at recruiting lay teachers for the schools, with efforts to educate the total Catholic community on the needs of its own schools, and with programs aimed at influencing public opinion on the Catholic schools. Lay leaders represented the case of Catholic schools before Congress and before the educational associations. A welcome by-product of these programs has been the new relationships established in many American communities between Catholics and public-school officials and administrators. Catholic concern for their own school system has led many to an equal concern for the total educational effort in their communities.

Other Catholic laymen gave themselves to the dialogue within the Church which was sparked by Mary Perkins Ryan's book, *Are Parochial Schools the Answer?* While granting the necessity of a parochial school system in the past and praising its achievements, these laymen question the future of the system, its relevance in a pluralistic society, and the economic ability of Catholics to support it in the face of a public system increasingly strengthened by state and Federal financial aid.

Many thoughtful Catholics now suggest alternatives to a full-scale school system—catechetical centers, for example, where children who attend public schools may receive religious instruction. Still another approach is that taken by the Citizens for Educational Freedom, an organization in which Catholics have joined forces with Protestants and Jews to work for tax aid for pupils who attend religious schools. On every hand, the fact is confirmed that lay people are going to demand a greater voice in the future education of their children.

In 1960 with the election of its first Catholic President, the nation gave evidence of the progress made toward an authentic pluralism in American society. A side effect of Kennedy's victory was to stimulate Catholic laymen and women in their effort to achieve first-class citizenship in the Church. Many others were inspired by the spirit of Kennedy's "New Frontier" to move out more confidently into areas of public discussion and service and to witness to Christ through such new programs as the Peace Corps, poverty projects, community development, etc. Pope John XXIII had already fired the imaginations of such lay men and women with his encyclical *Mater et Magistra* and with his bold call for an Ecumenical Council.

The exciting pluralism and change of the American scene were matched by corresponding pluralism and change within the Church. On the great issues of the day there were still liberal and conservative positions, but the general tide was moving towards ecumenism, greater freedom, concern for the poor and for minority groups, increased awareness of international responsibilities and of the role of the laity in the life of the Church. The tide was moving slowly but it was discernible to a growing number of committed men and women who were now seeking apostolic fulfillment not only in officially approved Catholic lay organizations but wherever opportunities presented themselves for involvement and action. What the modern popes from Leo XIII to Paul VI unleashed with their increasing exhortations to the laity "to be" as well as "to do" in the Church will surely be a major area of study for Church historians in decades to come. In the 1960's the manner in which American Catholic lay men and women were responding to the challenge was already a historic page in American Church history.

Under Pope John XXIII the ecumenical movement in the Catholic Church received inspired impetus, and the major lay apostolic groups responded quickly. Protestant speakers began appearing on Catholic platforms and there was an exchange of ideas among the Catholic and Protestant professionals in intergroup and interracial work, as well as among those from the national level of religious organizations and federations. Because pluralism in the American religious scene includes Jews as well as Christians, the words "and interreligious" were added to "ecumenical." Interreligious cooperation among Catholics, Protestants, and Jews is only beginning, but it has scored solid gains in such areas as race relations. One notable event was the 1963 National Conference on Religion and Race, held in Chicago, under the cosponsorship of groups of the three religions. Another was the religious support of the historic civil-rights march in Washington, D.C., in August of 1963, and the interreligious cooperation and lobbying for Federal civil-rights legislation since that time. Although officially the Church in this period was moving cautiously, individual Catholic laymen and lay groups were extending their ecumenical and interreligious contacts and were looking hopefully to the Vatican II Council for further advances.

THE COUNCIL AND AFTER

Laymen's hopes were raised in anticipation of the Council, but the scope provided for their participation in the preparations for it were negligible. Few efforts were made by the American hierarchy to seek out lay opinion in advance of the Council sessions, although in a few instances—as in the Archdiocese of Cincinnati—lay groups communicated their views to their bishops. A great breakthrough occurred when lay auditors were added at the sessions in St. Peter's. The Americans named as auditors were Martin Work, James Norris of the Catholic Relief Services, and Mrs. Joseph McCarthy, then president of the NCCW. Their advice was sought especially by the Council commissions preparing the documents on the lay apostolate and on the Church in the modern world. As the content of conciliar discussions and documents became available in the United States lay organizations began programs of study. In 1963, after the first session, Pope John issued his encyclical *Pacem in Terris* which joined the encyclicals of Pius XII on the Mystical Body and the liturgy as well as John's earlier *Mater et Magistra* as major material for study and discussion groups. At the grassroots level these study groups were becoming an increasingly effective means of continuing education for the American laity.

There were other immediate results of Vatican II. The earlier lay movements did not attract great numbers of Catholics, but since the Council there has been a quantitative increase and, many would argue, a qualitative advance in lay work. Of particular note is the intensified lay interest in the parish as a center of apostolic activity—activity designed not merely to strengthen the parish but also to reach out into the community at large. Voluntary lay missionary work through such agencies as PAVLA (Papal Volunteers for Latin America), the Grail, and many others received added impetus from the Council as did the whole broad field of religious education. The University of San Francisco had already pioneered in the formation of a group of laymen, schooled in theology and professionally competent in catechetics, who were employed by parishes to conduct adult classes. The Council also had a quickening effect on the National Catholic Laymen's Retreat Movement and on such professional groups as the National Council of Catholic Nurses and the Catholic Broadcasters Association, as well as on the Knights of Columbus and other fraternals which launched new ecumenical and social-action programs. Serra International, the lay group dedicated to securing and strengthening priestly vocations, likewise drew new vigor from the Council; the vocation crisis challenges them to develop bold new approaches.

"Relevance" became the "in" word of the 1960's. In search of relevance, the major lay movements initiated self-studies and renewal programs or brought in management consultant firms to review their operation and organization. Various types of self-appraisal are still going on, but certain overall changes in lay activity have begun to emerge clearly. Among the most important new features are: an emphasis on freedom among the People of God; a willingness to shed outmoded forms associated with the institutional Church; an awareness of the need to purify the apostolic motivation of activity, along with a new openness to the values of the secular world; a greater sensitivity to social problems in both the domestic and international spheres.

Many able lay people have found a theater for their talents and dedication in the Catholic press, whose recent blossoming is treated elsewhere in this volume. Catholic women have also been active on other fronts. In 1965 the NCCW, under the leadership of its executive director, Miss Margaret Mealey, joined its Protestant, Jewish, and Negro counterparts to form WICS (Women in Community Service), a national ecumenical and interracial effort to recruit and screen young women for the Women's Job Corps. While activities of this sort symbolize a new degree of civic involvement by Catholic lay women, the earlier efforts of such groups as the International Federation of Catholic Alumnae, CFM, the Catholic Daughters of America, and many others all helped prepare the way for today's move into the mainstream. Within the Church itself, women are still second-class citizens of a masculine world. A few hopeful signs point toward improvements to come; for example, the presence of women as auditors at the Council and their increasing presence on various kinds of parish and diocesan commissions and boards.

The various parish and diocesan commissions are structures called forth by the Council's summons to renewal. Laymen have been named to nearly all of the new bodies created on both the parochial and diocesan levels. There are also laymen serving as executive directors of statewide Catholic Conferences (the state counterparts of the United States Catholic Conference), as directors of diocesan bureaus of information, and as trustees of Catholic institutions of higher education. A few have penetrated into chancery offices where they act as advisers on financial matters and other needs.

In 1967 Pope Paul named two Americans to two new international structures called for by Vatican II—Martin H. Work to the twelve-member Council of the Laity, and James Norris to the Commission on Justice and Peace. As the Council of the Laity began its work in Rome advising the pope on lay matters, the National Councils of Catholic Men, Women, and Youth were authorized by the American hierarchy to recommend a new national pattern for lay involvement. Undoubtedly, the Vatican Council of the Laity will be an influence in drawing up this national plan.

Accompanying the increased "participation of the laity in the apostolate of the hierarchy," certain tensions have developed between laity and hierarchy. These tensions seem to be deepening at present, as we become more conscious of the fundamental nature of the issues confronting the Church. In a time of crisis and sweeping change it is not surprising that some bishops regard the criticism and demands emanating from certain quarters of the lay world with a good deal of uneasiness and even alarm. But as lay people see it, all they are asking for is full freedom, a voice in decision-making, and recognition as adult Christians capable of significant work in the Church and the world. In the nineteenth century, when the great American Catholic publicist, Orestes A. Brownson, demanded the same things in the name of the laity, he too was often heard with suspicion and irritation. Today Brownson would find himself part of a much larger company. And conservative Catholics, as well as liberals, contribute to the tensions between laity and hierarchy, particularly with conservative resistance to liturgical changes, suspicion of the social and economic teaching of papal encyclicals, and fears of the ecumenical movement.

Among the best known lay voices being raised today are those of Mathew Ahmann, Brent Bozell, William Buckley, Daniel Callahan, Dennis Clark, John Cogley, Joseph Cunneen, Dorothy Day, Dale Francis, Dan Herr, Robert Hoyt, John Leo, Gary MacEoin, Michael Novak, James O'Gara, Rosemary Ruether, Mary Perkins Ryan, Philip

Scharper, Donald Thorman, and Garry Wills. Nearly all of these persons stand outside the sphere of the organized Catholic lay activity. Admittedly they do not speak for the great majority of Catholics, but their papers, lectures, columns, journals of opinion, and books do reflect the honest concerns of a growing number of leaders in both lay and clerical ranks. Their presence, with that of other lay voices of prophecy and criticism, is unmistakable—and sometimes uncomfortable—evidence of the growth of the layman in the American Church. The response of Church authorities to these voices and to the issues to which they address themselves—authority, freedom of conscience, birth control, celibacy, academic freedom, war and peace, poverty, and the secular order—will be a factor in determining the future position and progress of the layman within the Church and, indeed, the future of the Church itself. Lay spokesmen, on the other hand, must stand prepared to be judged on their competence and knowledge, their spirit of charity, and their own desire to see truth advanced.

One of the most sensitive issues between lay liberals and the bishops concerns the implementation of the decrees of Vatican II, particularly the speed with which conciliar changes are put into effect. This issue also divides laymen from each other. Some find cause for hope in the more active participation of laymen in established Church structures. But to the more liberal, or radical wing, this is a trifling achievement. They want total *aggiornamento*—and quickly. They want the Church to really get out where the action is in the secular city. Self-satisfaction, complacency, and hostility to prophetic criticism are obviously the major temptations for the former group of laymen, while the latter may be tempted to sneer at present gains and even, in their frustration, to abandon all efforts to work within the institutional Church. In the present context of questioning, criticism, and rejection of the institutional Church, it is altogether possible that sizeable numbers of discontented lay people will detach themselves entirely. Such a prospect understandably arouses grave apprehensions on the part of those in authority; these apprehensions may in turn add to the climate of mutual suspicion and thus aggravate the tension between lay liberals and ecclesiastical authorities.

Such apprehensions at lay restiveness seem to have moved the pope to issue a grave warning to the 3,000 delegates to the Third World Congress of the Lay Apostolate in the fall of 1967. Pope Paul greeted these dedicated and loyal lay leaders as "a father, brother, and friend" and recalled their immense responsibilities in the mission of the Church, but then in uncompromising language he warned them "not to set up two parallel hierarchies, turning aside from tradition and becoming their own interpreters of God's Word." It was an "absurdity" for lay people to think they could "emancipate themselves from the Church's *magisterium*," the Pope continued; nor should they attempt "to act without the hierarchy or against it."

This sermon left many of the American delegates baffled. But not for long. They plunged back into the eight-day program divided into eighty work groups on sixteen different subjects related to the theme of "God's People on Man's Journey." Neither the discussions nor the resolutions seemed dampened by the Pope's message. The United States delegation, led by NCCM's president, N. A. Giambalvo, discussed and approved a wide variety of resolutions that ultimately were passed by all delegates. Among these were statements on racism, world development, the rights of women, and freedom of the press. It was in the omnibus resolution on world development that the controversial statement on family planning was included. This resolution called for a clear statement on "fundamental spiritual and moral values," leaving the "choice of means" to parents "acting in accordance with their Christian faith." The press described this resolution as "defiance" of the Pope; to the lay delegates, it was simply testimony to the need as they saw it.

However this particular episode may be interpreted, the distinguishing mark of this Third Congress of the Laity, especially in contrast to the previous ones in 1951 and 1957, was that it reflected the mood of the postconciliar Church. The change was symbolized by the fact that this time laymen spoke *to* the Church, rather than the reverse. The whole Congress was characterized by overwhelming concern for the Christian's mission in the secular world and by a great desire for dialogue in the Church between all the People of God, and for democratic procedures allowing an authentic lay voice to be heard all the way from the local parish to the newly constituted Council of the Laity in Rome. The fears of some that the Congress would prove to be a meeting of anticlericalists and anti-institutionalists were not realized. But neither were the misgivings of those in the opposite camp that it would be a "safe" gathering devoted to conservative institutionalism.

The United States delegation was a cross section of the American laity and lay movements, ranging from the pioneering personalist,

Dorothy Day, to representatives of most of the "official" Catholic organizations. Whether or not this group was adequately "representative" of the new laity in this country might be debated, but it did furnish a number of leaders for various aspects of the work. The excellent statement on racism was drawn up principally by Rawson Wood, president of the NCCIJ, and Thomas Melady of the Africa Institute Service. Even in the general sessions, the United States had a share in leadership since Mrs. John Shields, president of the NCCW, was one of the five presidents of the Congress and was selected to deliver its message to the Synod of Bishops meeting in Rome at the same time.

A few years ago, one might have concluded a survey of American Catholic lay action by recalling the appealing vision of a new springtime in the Church. Somehow or other we forgot that spring is the season of equinoctial storms and, in some areas, of violent tornadoes. The last couple of years have reminded us of those facts and tempered what was, perhaps, a too innocent optimism. But while recent experience has had a chastening effect, it would be unchristian to lose hold of the confidence that the Holy Spirit is working mighty things in our days. After a long winter, we are now in the season when the encrusted earth is broken open, but not without travail. The seed being planted and the new shoots that begin to appear will, in due time, grow and ripen and make an abundant harvest.

CONTRIBUTORS

PHILIP GLEASON is Associate Professor of History at the University of Notre Dame and author of *The Conservative Reformers: German-American Catholics and the Social Order.*

WILLIAM A. OSBORNE is Professor of Sociology at St. John's University, Jamaica, New York, and author of *The Segregated Covenant: Race Relations and American Catholics.*

WALTER D. WAGONER is Director of the Boston Theological Institute, Cambridge, Massachusetts, and author of *The Seminary: Protestant and Catholic.*

JOHN B. SHEERIN, C.S.P., is editor of *Catholic World* and author of A *Practical Guide to Ecumenism.*

EDWARD DUFF, S.J., is Associate Professor of Political Science at the College of the Holy Cross, Worcester, Massachusetts. He was formerly associate editor of *America* and editor of *Social Order*, and is the author of *The Social Thought of the World Council of Churches.*

JAMES FINN is editor of *Worldview*, published by the Council on Religion and International Affairs, and author of *Protest: Pacificism and Politics.*

RICHARD A. LAMANNA is Associate Professor of Sociology at the University of Notre Dame and the author of a forthcoming volume, *The Negro Teacher and School Desegregation.*

JAY J. COAKLEY is working for a doctoral degree in sociology at the University of Notre Dame under a National Defense Education Act Fellowship.

AIDAN KAVANAGH, O.S.B., an associate editor and frequent contributor to *Worship*, is Director of the Graduate Program in Liturgical Studies at the University of Notre Dame.

JOHN L. THOMAS, S.J., is Research Associate at the Cambridge Center for Social Studies, Cambridge, Massachusetts, and author of *The American Catholic Family.*

LOUIS J. PUTZ, C.S.C., Superior of Moreau Seminary, Notre Dame, Indiana, is also Chairman of the Board of Directors of Fides Publishers, Inc., and coeditor of *Seminary Education in a Time of Change.*

JAMES J. VANECKO is a member of the Department of Sociology at the University of Illinois at Chicago Circle and a Senior Study Director at the National Opinion Research Center.

MAUREEN L. GLEASON, presently a housewife, was formerly a reference librarian in the area of social sciences at the University of Notre Dame.

ROBERT HASSENGER is Director of the Office for Educational Research at the University of Notre Dame and editor of *The Shape of Catholic Higher Education*.

THOMAS J. STRITCH is Chairman of the Department of Communication Arts at the University of Notre Dame.

MARTIN H. WORK is Executive Director of the National Council of Catholic Men, Washington, D.C.

DANIEL J. KANE is Assistant Executive Secretary of the Council of Catholic Men of the Archdiocese of Cincinnati, Ohio.

INDEX

C0-BEG-153

GARLAND PUBLICATIONS IN AMERICAN AND ENGLISH LITERATURE

Editor
Stephen Orgel
Stanford University

GARLAND PUBLISHING, INC.

Dickens in America

Twain, Howells, James, and Norris

Joseph Gardner

GARLAND PUBLISHING, INC.
NEW YORK & LONDON 1988

Library of Congress Cataloging-in-Publication Data

Gardner, Joseph.
Dickens in America : Twain, Howells, James, and Norris / Joseph Gardner.
p. cm. — (Garland publications in American and English literature)
Originally published as the author's thesis (Ph.D. — University of California, Berkeley, 1969)
Bibliography : p.
ISBN 0-8240-0183-4
1. American fiction—19th century—History and criticism. 2. Dickens, Charles, 1812-1870—Influence. 3. Dickens, Charles, 1812-1870—Appreciation—United States. 4. American fiction—English influences. 5. Twain, Mark, 1835-1910—Knowledge—Literature. 6. Howells, William Dean, 1837-1920—Knowledge—Literature. 7. James, Henry, 1843-1916—Knowledge—Literature. 8. Norris, Frank, 1870-1902—Knowledge—Literature. I. Title. II. Series.
PS377.G37 1988
813'.4'09—dc 19 88-16286

Printed on acid-free, 250-year-life paper
Manufactured in the United States of America

PREFACE

I would like to acknowledge the people who have helped me in this effort. My greatest debt is to Professor Henry Nash Smith. My spelling has been to him as the boils were to Job, i.e., not the only thing he had to be patient with. Professor U. C. Knoepflmacher read the final draft with a care above and beyond the call of duty. Professor Ada Nisbet has been more than kind to a complete stranger; Professor Howard Baetzhold has shared his detailed knowledge of Mark Twain's relations with Dickens and England; Mr. Graham Storey has answered freely questions about Dickens's unpublished correspondence. My debt to Frederick Anderson can, I think, only be understood by those who have been happy enough to enter his domain. William Fischer, Fred See, William Messenger, and Thomas Blues have lent books and insights with equal generosity. Final typing was made possible by a grant from the Kentucky Research Foundation. If knowledge of the professional perfection of Mrs. Frances McGowan, Research Librarian of the Margaret King Library,

University of Kentucky, were to become widespread, Lexington would indeed become the Athens of the South.

I wish to thank my daughter, without whose help the typescript for chapter five would never have been used for coloring paper; and, finally, I understand now why acknowledgments always end with bouquets for the writer's wife. My own has typed, proof-read, and brewed an ocean of coffee; best of all, she has, for three years, remained blissfully indifferent to things Dickensian.

TABLE OF CONTENTS

CHAPTER I

DICKENS IN AMERICA: "THE GREAT ACTUALITY OF THE CURRENT IMAGINATION"

> Onlie to point out and nakedlie to joyne tcgither their sentences, with no farder declaring the maner and way, how the one doth folow the other, were but a colde helpe, to the encrease of lerning.
>
> --Roger Ascham

> ...with a novel (unlike a poem) the study of influence seems to be an elaborate exercise in walking upon eggs.
>
> --George Ford

Early in the morning of Friday, 22 April 1842, Charles and Catherine Dickens, accompanied by their American secretary, George W. Putnam, left the Neill House in Columbus, Ohio, to travel by stage to Sandusky, where they were to catch the steamship _Constitution_ for Buffalo and Niagara Falls. Since the regularly scheduled Columbus to Sandusky stages did not run on Fridays, Dickens had hired an "extra" to carry his small party; the opportunity to be, for once in America, alone seemed well worth the forty dollar expense. Armed with a picnic basket filled with cold meats, fruit, and wine, the three set out on what was to prove a remarkable journey. "It is impossible to convey an adequate idea of the kind of road over which we travelled," Dickens wrote to John Forster in a letter he was later to incorporate, virtually word for word, into chapter xiv of American Notes:

> I can only say that it was, at best, but a track through the wild forest, and among the swamps, bogs, and morasses of the withered bush. A great portion of it was what is called a "corduroy road": which is made by throwing round logs or whole trees into a swamp, and leaving them to settle there. Good Heaven! if you only felt one of the least of the jolts with which the coach falls from log to log! It is like nothing but going up a steep flight of stairs in an omnibus. Now the coach flung us in a heap on its floor, and now crushed our heads against its roof. Now one side of it was deep in the mire, and we were holding on to the other. Now it was lying on the horses' tails, and now again on its own back. But it never, never, was in any position, attitude, or kind of motion to which we are accustomed in coaches; or made the smallest approach to our experience of the proceedings of any sort of vehicle that goes on wheels.[1]

One wonders if at any point during the raucous, sixty-two mile journey Dickens was reminded of another passenger on another stage, of his own Mr. Pickwick in frantic pursuit of the run-away Alfred Jingle:

> "Ah! we *are* moving now," said the old gentleman [Mr. Wardle] exultingly. They were indeed, as was

> sufficiently testified to Mr. Pickwick, by his constant collisions either with the hard wood-work of the chaise, or the body of his companion.
>
> "Hold up!" said the stout old Mr. Wardle, as Mr. Pickwick dived head foremost into his capacious waistcoat. ...
>
> Mr. Pickwick had just drawn in his head, and Mr. Wardle, exhausted with shouting, had done the same, when a tremendous jolt threw th › forward against the front of the vehicle. There was a sudden bump--a loud crash--away rolled a wheel, and over went the chaise.
>
> After a very few seconds of bewilderment and confusion, in which nothing but the plunging of horses and breaking of glass, could be made out, Mr. Pickwick felt himself violently pulled out from among the ruins of the chaise; and as soon as he had gained his feet and extricated his head from the skirts of his greatcoat, which materially impeded the usefulness of his spectacles, the full disaster of the case met his view.[2]

In the passage from American Notes the focus is upon the antics of the coach; in the scene from Pickwick Papers it is upon the pratfalls suffered by the passengers. In a third passage, attention is directed toward both coach and riders:

> Our senator went stumbling along, making moral reflections as continuously as under the circumstances could be expected,--the carriage proceeding along much as follows,--bump! bump! slush! down in the mud!--the senator, woman and child, reversing their positions so suddenly as to come, without any very accurate adjustment, against the windows of the down-hill side. Carriage sticks fast, while Cudjoe on the outside is heard making a great muster among the horses. After various ineffectual pullings and twitchings, just as the senator is losing all patience, the carriage suddenly rights itself with a bounce,--two front wheels go down into another abyss, and senator, woman, and child, all tumble promiscuously

> on to the front seat,--senator's hat is jammed over his eyes and nose quite unceremoniously, and he considers himself fairly extinguished;--child cries, and Cudjoe on the outside delivers animated addresses to the horses, who are kicking, and floundering, and straining, under repeated cracks of the whip. Carriage springs up, with another bounce,--down go the hind wheels,--senator, woman, and child, fly over on to the back seat, his elbows encountering her bonnet, and both her feet being jammed into his hat, which flies off in the concussion. ...
>
> At last, with a square plunge, which puts all on to their feet and then down into their seats with incredible quickness, the carriage stops,--and, after much outside commotion, Cudjoe appears at the door.
>
> 'Please, sir, it's powerful bad spot, this yer. I don't know how we's to get clar out. I'm a thinkin' we'll have to be a gettin' rails.'
>
> The senator despairingly steps out, picking gingerly for some firm foothold; down goes one foot an immeasurable depth,--he tries to pull it up, loses his balance, and tumbles over into the mud, and is fished out, in a very despairing condition, by Cudjoe.

But this, of course, is not by Dickens. It is taken from chapter ix of Harriet Beecher Stowe's Uncle Tom's Cabin and describes the flight of Eliza and the kindly, if politically timorous, Senator Bird from the slave hunters, Loker and Marks. The setting is a corduroy road, through a swamp, in Ohio. The point to my rather obvious trick is that Mrs. Stowe was an American, had lived for several years in Ohio, and had undoubtedly travelled over corduroy. Yet when she comes to explore, novelistically, the comic possibilities of a journey over such a road in such a setting, her imagination works not upon her own experience but upon her memory of Dickens. To read the three passages together is to agree with Dickens himself, who wrote to his friends the Watsons, "She (I mean Mrs. Stowe) is a leetle unscrupulous in the appropriatin' way. I seem to see a writer with whom I am very intimate (and whom nobody can possibly admire more than myself) peeping very often through the thinness of the paper."[3]

Mrs. Stowe's case is by no means unique or even particularly unusual. It is merely one example out of thousands of Dickens's suzerainty over American fiction in the nineteenth century. For three generations of Americans Dickens was, as Henry James put it, "the great actuality of the current imagination."[4] James's friend, William Dean Howells, was to recall that for their contemporaries Dickens was more "real" than "reality" itself: one judged experience by his novels rather than his novels by experience. "People talked and lived as well as read Dickens."[5] In a remarkable passage in <u>Notes of a Son and Brother</u> James describes the spiritual as well as physical presence of Dickens for a young American novelist:

> There has been since his extinction no corresponding case--as to the relation between benefactor and beneficiary, or debtor and creditor; no other debt in our time has been piled so high, for those carrying it, as the long, the purely "Victorian" pressure of that obligation. It was the pressure, the feeling, that

> made it--as it made the feeling, and no operation of feeling on any such ground has within my observation so much as attempted to emulate it. So that on the evening I speak of at Shady Hill it was as a slim and shaken vessel of the feeling that one stood there--of the feeling in the first place diffused, public, and universal, and in the second place all unfathomably, undemonstrably, unassistedly and, as it were, unrewardedly, proper to one's self as an already groping and fumbling, already dreaming and yearning dabbler in the mystery, the creative, that of comedy, tragedy, evocation, representation, erect and concrete before us there as in a sublimity of mastership. I saw the master--nothing could be more evident--in the light of an intense emotion, and I trembled, I remember, in every limb, while at the same time, by a blest fortune, emotion produced no luminous blur, but left him shining indeed, only shining with august particulars.[6]

One detects here, of course, certain echoes of the genteel cult of "ideality"; but one is also aware that it is an "ideality" that serves not as a substitute for emotion but as its correlative; it is an "ideality" that does not ignore "august particulars." To the more direct mind and style of Samuel Langhorne Clemens the practical results of the kind of "public" emotion James describes were clear: "There were a great many people in America at that time who were ambitiously and undisguisedly imitating Dickens."[7]

Despite kaleidoscopic changes in critical standards the mass popularity of Dickens during the American nineteenth century was immutable. In 1842 American Notes sold 50,000 copies in three days in New York City alone.[8]

In 1864, in the heart of Confederate gloom and deprivation, a Mobile, Alabama, press continued to print Dickens's stories--on wall-paper.[9] And at the turn of the century David Copperfield was still the one novel most in demand at American public libraries and Dickens the most sought after novelist.[10] Thus in an age that labelled Cooper "the American Scott" and Emerson "the American Carlyle," it was inevitable that search would soon be begun for "the American Boz." But unlike the American Scott and the American Carlyle, the American Boz turned out to be, despite a plethora of candidates, an elusive entity. For example, although the Pickwick "rocket" did not begin to ascend in the United States until late in the year of 1838, in that same year a Philadelphia publisher brought out the first specimen of what was to be a tidal-wave of American Dickens pseudepigrapha, Pickwick Abroad, or The Tour in France,[11] and shortly thereafter a New York litterateur began work on the novel that was to establish him for all posterity as "the American Dickens." The author was Cornelius Matthews and the novel was entitled The Career of Puffer Hopkins. I know of only one other twentieth-century American ever to have read it; there is, perhaps, no greater proof of that great spirit's dedication to scholarship and American literature than that he persevered to the last page.[12] But if Matthews failed, others were eager to enter the lists, and the search continued right up to 1900, when a popular and influential American journal was still willing to give prominent attention to an article by a now-forgotten critic, James Ford, entitled "The Chance for an American Dickens."[13]

One source of the sense of urgency in the quest lies in a peculiar paradox of American literary history. The immense popularity of Dickens in America coincided with two other well-known, if elusive, phenomena: "literary nationalism" and the persistent concern with the idea of "the Great American Novel." Curiously, the three became fused in the critical mind of the century. In an address on "Novels and Novelists: Charles Dickens," originally delivered before the Boston Mercantile Library Association in December, 1844, E. P. Whipple made the point clear. Whipple, one of the most astute, interesting, and unjustly neglected critics of the day, begins by asserting the primacy of the novel as genre. "The novel, indeed," he observes:

> is one of the most effective, if not most perfect forms of communication, through which a comprehensive mind can communicate itself to the world, exhibiting, as it may, through sentiment, incident, and character, a complete philosophy of life, and admitting a dramatic and narrative expression of the abstract principles of ethics, metaphysics, and theology.

Thus the ideal novelist must be at once poet, philosopher, and man of the world:

> Understanding man as well as men, the elements of human nature as well as the laws of their combinations, he should possess the most extensive practical knowledge of society, the most universal sympathies with his kind, and a nature shrewd and impassioned, observant and creative, with large faculties harmoniously balanced.[14]

Observing that, naturally, such a novelist has never existed, Whipple then launches upon a capsule history of fiction, pointing out those areas in which this or that novelist has succeeded and where failed of the ideal. Arriving finally at the advent of The Pickwick Papers, Whipple brings his themes together. Dickens "as a novelist and prose poet, is to be classed in the front rank of the noble company to which he belongs," coming closest of any mere mortal to the high ideal Whipple has posited.[15] The evidences he adduces need not be gone into here; in general they repeat in cogent form assertions about Dickens's art that echo throughout American criticism during the century. More interesting is the grand peroration with which the lecture ends. Whipple's assertions (and their rhetorical flavor) are so central to the spirit of the age that they demand quotation at length:

> In closing these desultory remarks on Dickens, and the department of literature of which he is the greatest living representative, it may not be irrelevant to express a regret that we have not a

class of novels illustrative of American life and character, which does some justice to both. Novelists we have in perilous abundance, as Egypt had locusts; some of them unexcelled in the art of preparing a dish of fiction by a liberal admixture of the horrible and sentimental; and some few who display talents and accomplishments of a higher order; but a series of national novels, illustrative of the national life, the production of men penetrated with an American spirit without being Americanisms, we can hardly plume ourselves upon possessing. ...That Sam Slick, Nimrod Wildfire, and the Ethiopian Minstrels, do not comprehend the whole wealth and raciness of life as it is in the North, the South, and the West, might easily be demonstrated if a man of power would undertake the task. But one would almost suppose, from hearing the usual despairing criticism of the day, that in the United States the national novel was an impossible creation. Are there, then, no materials here for the romantic and heroic,--nothing over which poetry can lovingly hover,--nothing of sorrow for pathos to convert into beauty,--no fresh individualities of disposition over which humor, born of pathos, can pour its floods of genial mirth,--no sweet household ties, no domestic affections, no high thoughts, no great passions, no sorrow, sin, and death? Has our past no story to tell? Is there nothing of glory in the present, nothing of hope in the future? In no country, indeed, is there a broader field open to the delineator of character and manners than in our own land. Look at our society, the only society where the whole people are alive,--alive with intelligence and passion,--every man's individual life mingling with the life of the nation,--avarice, cruelty, pride, folly, ignorance, in a ceaseless contest with great virtues and noble aims, and thoughts that reach upward to the ideal. In the noise and tumult of that tremendous struggle, a man of genius not blinded by its dust or deafened by its din, at once an actor in life and a spectator of it, might discover the materials of the deepest tragedy and the finest and broadest humor; might hear, amid the roar and confusion, the "still sad music of humanity"; might see, through all the rancor and madness of partisan warfare, the slow evolution of right principles; might send his soul along that tide of impetuous passion in which

> novelties are struggling with prejudices, without being overwhelmed in its foaming flood; and in the comprehensive grasp of his intellect might include all classes, all sects, all professions, making them stand out on his luminous page in the clear light of reality, doing justice to all by allowing each his own costume and language, compelling Falsehood to give itself the lie, and Pride to stand abased before its own image, and guided in all his pictures of life and character by a spirit at once tolerant, just, generous, humane, and national.[16]

The implication must have been to the dullest merchant nodding in the back row: to write the national novel, imitate Dickens.

Whipple's lecture was an immense success. It became a stand-by on his lecture tours, was published in the North American Review, October, 1849, and subsequently resuméed and pirated in newspapers and journals all over the country. It was reprinted in a volume of Whipple's Lectures on Subjects Connected with Literature and Life the following spring; by 1866 the Lectures were in their sixth edition. Nor did its imperative disappear. Fifty-six years later Ford's essay had as its point the conviction that the Great American Novel (still to be written), would, of necessity, be produced by the American Boz (still to be born).

These are facts well-known to students of American fiction. Yet the degree to which they have become clichés of literary history makes it all the more remarkable that no systematic study of Dickens's role as a shaper of the American novel has been written. The present work attempts such a study treating four major writers, Mark Twain, William Dean Howells, Henry James, and Frank Norris, all of whom flourished, roughly, in the thirty years from Dickens's death to the turn of the century. Three chapters (one, three and six) describe my subjects' readings in and comments on Dickens's works and attempt, briefly, to place those responses in the context both of the contemporary critical climate and of the writers' individual personalities. The other four discuss the nature and quality of their imaginative response to Dickens as measured in their own writings. All of these chapters have a similar structure. They are divided into two main parts, the first a broad survey of Dickensian elements in the author's work as a whole, considered either chronologically or thematically, and the second a detailed discussion of Dickens's presence in one, from this point of view representative, novel.

A word about a fundamental assumption underlying the study is in order. The words of Roger Ascham prefixed to this introduction sound a clear warning to all who would explore relationships between authors. Unfortunately, many scholars (not all of them French or German) have failed to follow his advice and, as a result, so-called "source studies" have come, with few exceptions, to be associated only with narrowness, dryness, and ultimate futility. I am only tangentially concerned with "sources" in the traditional sense, and my title is not "Dickens's Influence on...." I am, however, deeply concerned with "mutual interpretation." The term comes from Mark Spilka, whose Dickens and Kafka well illustrates both the merits and the liabilities of the approach. Spilka writes:

> A comparison that stops with parallels is, I believe, sterile; but a comparison which leads to mutual readings of specific texts, and to the illumination of related worlds, is critically rewarding. A fund of insights becomes available which might escape direct approach; and, through mutual reinforcement, a common vision emerges which supports the continuity of art and culture.[17]

I concur wholeheartedly. Hence I intend only as a preliminary to make a case for direct historical "influences." My primary endeavor is to compare the four American novelists in question with Dickens in order to demonstrate similarities in their visions, their attitudes, their modes of experience, their ideas of what life is and what the novel should be. The evidences of direct "influences," such as they are, are all to the good, but the force of my argument does not depend upon them; and while I wish to be as precise as possible, they need not be exaggerated. Put differently--

less belligerently, perhaps--the study is not intended to be a mere catalog of passages that indicate direct imitation of Dickens by my American subjects, but rather to be a study of those elements in their works that suggest what the wisest of them called a "conscious sympathy with Dickens," that imply that at one point or other in their lives "Dickens had been a revelation" to them.[18]

Such an approach may lead to some discomforts, especially since I have had to assume the reader's fairly extensive familiarity with all five novelists and because I have frequently been forced to borrow an awkward structural device from "The Reeve's Tale": "Now pley, Aleyn, for I wol speke of John." But it is not a device that readers of nineteenth-century fiction are unacquainted with, and I do believe that the advantages of the method outweigh the disadvantages. Mutual interpretation can be a double-edged sword, for approached from its perspective, Dickens becomes a way of seeing American fiction, and the Americans under discussion become an index of the man they all called "Master." Thus I hope my audience may include partisans and students of each.

Notes to Chapter I

[1]John Forster, The Life of Charles Dickens, 2 vols. (London and New York, 1927), I, 244.

[2]Works, Gadshill Edition, ed. Andrew Lang [and B. W. Matz], 38 vols. (London, 1897-1908), I, pp. 138-40. Subsequent references to all Dickens's works, with one exception, will be keyed to this "the most complete standard edition." (Ada Nisbet, "Charles Dickens," in Victorian Fiction: A Guide to Research, ed. Lionel Stevenson [Cambridge, Mass., 1964], p. 53.) In order that the reader may have easy access to any other edition, citations, to be included in the text, will include chapter numbers as well as volume and page. (Thus: I, ix, 138-40.) The one exception is Oliver Twist, which will be cited from the excellent and long overdue "Clarendon Edition," ed. Kathleen Tillotson (Oxford, 1966). This is the first volume to appear in what will be a fully edited edition with definitive texts supplemented by variant readings and full critical apparatuses.

[3]The Letters of Charles Dickens, ed. Walter Dexter et. al., 3 vols. (Bloomsbury, 1938), II, 431.

[4]The Autobiography of Henry James, ed. F. W. Dupee (New York, 1956), p. 70.

[5]"The Editor's Easy Chair," Harper's Monthly, CV (July, 1902), 311.

[6]Autobiography, pp. 388-89.

[7]Mark Twain in Eruption, ed. Bernard DeVoto (New York, 1940), p. 267.

[8]James D. Hart, The Popular Book (Berkeley and Los Angeles, 1961), p. 103.

[9]W. G. Wilkens, First and Early American Editions of Dickens (Cedar Rapids, 1910), pp. 38-39.

[10]Arthur A. Adrian, "David Copperfield: A Century of Critical and Popular Acclaim," MLQ, XI (1950), 330.

[11]Wilkens, First and Early American Editions, p. 47.

[12] Perry Miller, The Raven and the Whale, (New York, 1956), pp. 93-94.

[13] Munsey's Magazine, XXIII, 281-85.

[14] Lectures on Subjects Connected with Literature and Life (Boston, 1866), pp. 44-45.

[15] P. 59.

[16] Pp. 80-83.

[17] (Bloomington, 1963), p. 23.

[18] Partial Portraits (London and New York, 1888), p. 222. The phrases and their implications to James himself are discussed in chapter vi.

CHAPTER II

MARK TWAIN: A PERSONAL CASE

"What is...difficult to understand is his lack of appreciation for Dickens."[1] William Lyon Phelps's belief that Mark Twain had been one of the rarest of nineteenth-century creatures, a writer who had had no interest in Dickens and who had avoided his influence, was shared by most Mark Twain critics for many years. Although those who, like Minnie M. Brashear, sided with Bernard DeVoto in the Brooks-DeVoto controversy often pointed out that Clemens had been frequently exposed to Dickens's works, the consensus was stated by Stephen Leacock when he remarked that while Mark Twain and Dickens are undoubtedly the two greatest humorists of the nineteenth century, "there is no record, and no internal evidence, to show that either was influenced by the work of the other."[2] Recently there have been signs of a shift in critical opinion concerning Mark Twain's relationship to Dickens. Walter Blair has shown the indisputable influence of A Tale of Two Cities on Mark Twain's masterpiece.[3] Ada Nisbet's survey of Dickens research calls for further study of the "promising subject" of Clemens's indebtedness to Dickens, and in a recent review Ellen Moers has suggested at least one direction such a study might take.[4]

Yet to review what has been written about Mark Twain's relationship to Dickens can be a confusing and discouraging experience. One authority, for example, maintains that "most of Mark Twain's reading of Dickens took place during the years before 1870, and that he was not afterwards too enthusiastic...about any of the books, with the one exception...of _A Tale of Two Cities_";[5] while another informs us that "the curious fact is that Twain, until his marriage and removal to Hartford, was not particularly a devotee of Dickens," but that after 1870 Dickens became "a household institution" in the home at Nook Farm.[6] A third writer solemnly assures us that there is no evidence Clemens had read _Martin Chuzzlewit_ before 1873, when the very sources he cites to support his statement show, beyond doubt, that Clemens indeed had read the book, and probably more than once.[7]

Much of this confusion must, of course, be laid at the door of Clemens himself. No one could contradict himself so rapidly and so blithely as he. Thus he is reported to have said on one occasion that although his brother, Orion, had often urged him to read Dickens, he had never been able to do it, and to have remarked, on another, that he had "always been a great admirer of Dickens."[8] Clemens presents, therefore, a peculiar personal case for any study of Dickens's influence in America. As a later chapter will show, he was not the only writer of his day to deny any enthusiasm for, or even knowledge of, Dickens's fiction. But his motives were, for the most part, emphatically his own; and it is difficult, if not impossible, to work him into any pattern larger than the history of his own consciousness. In his relationship to Dickens, as in so many other respects, he stands alone and must be treated in isolation. Later chapters may, by implication, serve to make this isolation a little less absolute, but what follows will, I hope, justify the special consideration granted him here.

I.

Accompanying, and perhaps contributing to, the confusions concerning Mark Twain's attitudes towards Dickens is an uncertainty over what works Clemens actually read. In research prepared for presentation elsewhere I have shown that his knowledge of Dickens's writings was much more extensive than either he allowed or his commentators have realized. By surveying his published works and private papers I have been able to establish that, without doubt, he read The Pickwick Papers, Barnaby Rudge, American Notes, Martin Chuzzlewit, Dombey and Son, Bleak House, Little Dorrit, A Tale of Two Cities, and Our Mutual Friend. Moreover, if there is no definite proof, there is a near certainty that he also read Oliver Twist, The Old Curiosity Shop, Pictures from Italy, David Copperfield, A Child's History of England, The Uncommercial Traveller, Great Expectations, and Edwin Drood. This leaves only Nicholas Nickleby, Sketches by Boz, and Hard Times to escape his attention.[9] All in all it is an impressive list of titles and indicates, at the least, that the history of his relationship to Dickens is worthy of detailed investigation. The first priority would seem to be the establishing of some sort of pattern in his readings and attitudes. For Clemens was given to vast fluctuations in his opinions and tastes.

His working a reference to Little Dorrit into his first published sketch and the memories his Keokuk neighbors held of seeing him wander about town with a volume of

Dickens under his arm indicate his enthusiasm for Dickens in his print shop days, as does the pleasure he took in discussing his reading with his St. Louis friend J. H. Burrough.[10] Dickens was one of Burrough's favorite authors. Years later Clemens was still full of praise for his friend's "fine literary appreciations" and his "sound and competent literary judgment."[11] His enthusiasm continued throughout his Mississippi and Washoe years and is nowhere better expressed than by the boisterous description of Dombey and Son in a letter to Wm. Clagget written in February, 1862--although a remark about the trial episode in Pickwick Papers published in the Territorial Enterprise shows that even in the early sixties his fervor was not entirely uncooled by his critical faculties.[12]

It is likely that, for reasons discussed below, Clemens began to gain in critical restraint vis-a-vis Dickens when he encountered the undiscriminating cult of Boz that Bret Harte was leading as high priest in San Francisco. He was, however, still willing to grant Dickens status as a master. One of his excursions into the gold fields took him to a small log cabin at Jackass Gulch, whose replica stands today to lure tourists off the main road through the Mother Lode. The modern tourist notes only the cabin's boring similarity to every other abandoned log cabin in the country; Mark Twain was surprised by the contrast between its crude architecture and the remarkable library it sheltered: "Miner's cabin in Jackass: No planking on the floor; old bunks, pans, and traps of all kinds--Byron, Shakesphere, Bacon, Dickens, and every kind of only first class Literature."[13]

Clemens's career made several tangential brushes with Dickens's (their biographies are remarkably similar; they both had the same English stage manager; Charles Dickens, Jr. was once a house-guest in Hartford; in Australia Clemens admired a showing of paintings by a man he perhaps significantly identifies as "Dickens's son-in-law" rather than as Wilkie Collins's brother). But he saw him in person only once when, on December 31, 1867, he heard him read in Steinway Hall, in New York.[14] Ellen Moers lets her desire to make a point get the better of her accuracy when she says Clemens "sat literally at the feet of Dickens." Actually the point is much more subtle; Dickens was literally at the feet of Mark Twain. Clemens sat in Jervis Langdon's private box, well above the stage and so far back he had difficulty hearing.

After settling in Hartford, Clemens continued to consider Dickens "first class Literature," although he undoubtedly read him with a much calmer eye than he had earlier. But he did continue to read, and Stone is quite right in asserting that Dickens was a "household institution" on Farmington Avenue. Livy's biographers tell us that Dickens was one of her favorite authors, and while they supply no evidence, there is no reason to doubt them.[15] Katy Leary, the family's life-long maid, recalled that Clemens used to read Dickens aloud after dinner, and that once, when the rest of the family was reading Dickens privately, Livy made her read him too.[16] From London, 1873, Clemens writes of his pleasure in learning that his promoter, George Dolby, had also managed Dickens and sends home long anecdotes of Dickens's adventures on the platform, while assuring Livy that he is making the best of his opportunity to track down fine English editions of Dickens and Thackeray for the family library.[17] The Howells letters show that Dickens was a favorite topic for dinner table conversation. Clara Clemens, at age nine, thought he ranked with Mark Twain and Christopher Columbus as one of history's six great men.[18]

Even in the eighties and nineties, when his critical assessment of Dickens was at its lowest, Clemens occasionally returned to the novels, and the family continued reading Dickens together until the Hartford home broke up forever.[19] They all admired the Dickens tableaux at the local "Carnival of Authors" in 1884; Livy went back to see them again the next year.[20]

In 1886 Clemens began his Wednesday morning reading class for a select audience of Connecticut lady-folk. The ubiquitous Katy Leary describes it as follows:

> One winter they had a reading class of Dickens. Mr. Clemens used to read every Wednesday morning to a lot of ladies that come there. ...Oh, lots of ladies in Hartford come. They'd all come--all that was invited. They'd go up to the Billiard Room and sit there while Mr. Clemens read to them--read aloud from Dickens. He read about an hour or so every Wednesday morning, and they was all so delighted--they'd go away laughing and telling what a lovely time they'd had.[21]

Mark Twain would have been charmed by the paragraph; it is precisely the kind of uneducated "literature" he prized so highly and waxed so tedious over. The scene as Katy describes it reminds us of Mr. Pickwick trapped by a swarm of cackling little-old-ladies in the Card Room at Bath, although, unlike Pickwick, Clemens enjoyed every minute of his ordeal. But it was primarily Browning, not Dickens, who was the object of study in these Wednesday morning sessions.

One might have hoped Katy would know the difference. However, her mistake does indicate something of the importance of Dickens in the Hartford household. Clemens says the readings continued for forty-two weeks;[22] forty-two weeks of unrelieved Browning seems an excessive dissipation for even so enthusiastic a Browningite as Clemens. Moreover, his professional experience on the platform had taught him the importance of variety in any performance. A reproduction of the agenda for an 1886 class shows that two Uncle Remus stories and Bram Stoker's "Scotch Christening" anecdote worked their ways into that day's curriculum.[23] So Katy may not have been entirely wrong.

If Clemens's reading of Dickens slowed and faltered in the nineties, the scattered references in the last notebooks show that it began to regain its momentum in his final decade. Significantly, these references are primarily to Dombey and Son. If they are not quite so exclamatory as the letter to Clagget, they nevertheless indicate that a book he enjoyed in his youth was still capable of giving him pleasure in his old age, that in one sense the child was father of the man.[24]

II.

> "I don't know anything about anything...and never did. My brother used to try to get me to read Dickens, long ago. I couldn't do it--I was ashamed; but I couldn't do it. Yes I have read the Tale of Two Cities, and could do it again. I have read it a good many times; but I never could stand Meredith and most of the other celebrities."[25]

Huck Finn's insight into his creator, "he told the truth, mainly," is as applicable to this casual remark to Paine as it is to The Adventures of Tom Sawyer. As a statement of biographical fact the remark is patently false. As a statement about the man Samuel Clemens it embodies several important truths. On one level it exposes his well-known stubbornness, his tendency to refuse to do something simply because someone else asked him to do it. He was particularly prepared to believe he had been unable to follow someone else's suggestion if that someone else was Orion. Although Clemens thoroughly enjoyed playing God-Almighty with his elder brother, he was quick to squelch anything that might suggest a reversal of their roles.

On another level, the statement reminds us that even at the height of his fame, Clemens never overcame that peculiar kind of intellectual insecurity (and its concomitant aggressiveness) which often characterizes self-educated men. Unsure of his own knowledge, extensive thought it was, he found it easiest to disclaim all learning whatsoever. Hard, cold facts, the kind which can be securely mastered by an absorbing and energetic mind, these he felt at home with and liked to parade almost as show-pieces. His frequent displays of expertise in astronomy and geology are cases in point, as is his almost awesome admiration of Samuel Moffett's photographic memory and the pride he felt in thinking he had been instrumental in establishing a man with such remarkable talents in a highly successful career.[26] But the kind of knowledge that requires some functioning of the critical sense, a sense which he, like other autodidacts before and after him, somehow saw as the exclusive property of formal, genteel education, almost always brought forth the disclaimer, and with the disclaimer a thinly veiled hostility toward the "celebrities." In the same conversation with Paine he says that he always felt himself about as well equipped for Jane Austen as a barkeep is for heaven; in _Following the Equator_ he cannot criticize _The Vicar of Wakefield_ without becoming violent.[27] His tedious fondness for what he called "literature," the semi-literature, unself-conscious cuteness and sentimentality he found in Susy's biography and a cowboy's letter to Helen

Keller, allowed him to pontificate like the "real" critics and celebrities without taking too many chances. He liked to brag about his reading; a letter to Mrs. Fairbanks's daughter, Mollie, begins with the coy complaint that he has not had much opportunity to read then proceeds to rattle off some dozen titles, including such multi-volumed works as Carlyle's French Revolution and Motley's Dutch Republic.[28] Even in the remark to Paine he manages both to avoid being caught out by anyone who knew his fondness for A Tale of Two Cities and to let it slip that he had indeed read some Dickens and read it more often than have most people, including those regarded as "celebrities." But he could never live with his knowledge.

In addition to Samuel Clemens, the self-taught man, the remark also expresses a side of Mark Twain, the writer, speaking in understandable self-defense against the claims of a potentially dangerous rival. Clemens, the private citizen, could enjoy garnering and passing on anecdotes of greatness from George Dolby, could indulge in harmless self-aggrandizement by pointing out, whenever opportunity arose, that he had had the same promoter as Dickens, and could want to see Dickens encased in blue morocco on his family's shelves. But for Mark Twain, the writer, to be associated with Dickens was something else indeed. The Mark Twain described by the more radical followers of Bernard DeVoto in the DeVoto-Brooks controversy of the thirties and forties and the Mark Twain beatified by the schoolteachers and lawyers of the Mark Twain Society, this ultra-indigenous untutored genius, this white-washer of fences and writer of funny books (with a hidden message) <u>cum</u> prospector <u>via</u> steamboat pilot, was ultimately the creation of Mark Twain himself. Although he came at the last to chafe justifiably at what would now be called his "image"--his pleasure in wearing his Oxford Doctor of Literature robes has generally been recognized as much more than a merely childlike delight in "dressing up"--he clung to that "image" as "the native humorist who is really funny" to the very end. As shown by the myriad clippings he saved, the newspaper reporters assigned to cover his public appearances had two stocks in trade. They transcribed his lectures, and they compared his platform style to Dickens's. The reviews of <u>The Gilded Age</u> that Byrant Morey French exhumes prove that Col. Sellers's debt to Mr. Micawber was as obvious to Mark Twain's contemporaries as it is to us. Clemens tended to see such comparisons as a kind of threat and felt called upon to dissociate himself from Dickens as much as possible.

One stratagem was to raise himself up by putting Charles Dickens down. From 1852 to 1867 Clemens had been an enthusiastic reader of Dickens. In 1868 in a dispatch to Alta California reporting Dickens's performance in Steinway Hall he made his first public statement about the English novelist. The dispatch is not quite what we might expect, knowing Clemens's reaction to the novels:

> ...His pictures are hardly handsome and he, like everybody else, is less handsome than his pictures. That fashion he has of brushing his hair and goatee so resolutely forward gives a comical Scotch-terrier look about the face which is rather heightened than otherwise by his portentous dignity and gravity. But that queer old head took on a sort of beauty, bye and bye, and a fascinating interest, as I thought of the wonderful mechanism within it, the complex but exquisitely adjusted machinery that could create men and women and put the breath of life into them and alter all their ways and actions, elevate them, degrade them, murder them, marry them, conduct them through good and evil, through joy and sorrow, on their long march from the cradle to the grave, and never make a mistake! I almost imagined I could see the wheels and pulleys work. This was Dickens--Dickens. There was no question about that, and yet it was not right easy to realize it. Somehow, this puissant god seemed to be only a man, after all. How the great do tumble from their high pedestals when we see them in common flesh, and know that they eat pork and cabbage and act like other men! ...He read David Copperfield. He is a bad reader in one sense--because he does not enunciate his words sharply and distinctly--he does not cut the syllables cleanly, and therefore many and many of them fell dead before they reached our part of the house. (I say "our" because I am proud to observe that there was a beautiful young lady with me--a highly respectable young white woman.) I was a good deal disappointed in Mr. Dickens's readings. I will go further and say, a great deal

> disappointed. ...Mr. Dickens's reading is rather monotonous, as a general thing; his voice is husky; his pathos is only the beautiful pathos of his language--there is no heart, no feeling in it--it is glittering frostwork; his rich humor cannot fail to tickle an audience into ecstasies save when he reads to himself. And what a bright intelligent audience he had! He ought to have made them laugh or cry, or shout at his own good will or pleasure--but he did not. They were very much tamer than they should have been.
>
> He pronounced Steerforth "St'yawfuth." This will suggest to you that he is a little Englishy in his speech. ...Every passage Mr. Dickens read...was rendered with a degree of ability far below what his reading reputation led us to expect.[29]

The dispatch is interesting in several ways. It illustrates some of the issues raised in preceding paragraphs. It also expresses another of Mark Twain's well-known impulses, the impulse to attack overtly or covertly established renown whenever and wherever he encountered it, the impulse he succumbed to in the celebrated Whittier birthday speech and flirted with dangerously in his speech "The Babies" at the Grant banquet in 1879. It certainly suggests a young man boosting himself at the expense of his elders. The display of expertise in matters of enunciation, the jokes about "the highly respectable young white woman" and the "bright intelligent audience," the tenderfoot's criticism of Dickens for not speaking American, all say 'look at me' to a newspaper audience which, conveniently, had not witnessed the performance. Significantly, Mark

Twain does not say 'the reading was poor'; rather he says "I was a good deal disappointed." The terms of the hostility must be carefully distinguished if we are to read the review as one artist commenting, for his own ends, on another's craft. Mark Twain praises Dickens the novelist in exalted terms but belittles Dickens the platform performer. The reason would seem to be that Mark Twain feels himself a competitor in the second of these roles but not in the first. At this point in his career he had not yet thought of writing novels himself, but he was actively engaged in the attempt to establish a national reputation for himself as lecturer.

Other correlary but not conflicting explanations are also available to account for Clemens's low opinion of the reading itself. He acknowledges that he was rather far from the stage and had difficulty hearing. Most accounts of Dickens's readings speak of his loud and dramatic voice; Mark Twain's remarks about his huskiness and his reading to himself suggest that he was having a difficult night. He was at the time a very sick man. Exhausted by a wretchedly uncomfortable train ride from Boston to New York in over-heated, foul-smelling cars which jolted and tossed the whole way, he came down on Christmas Day with a severe cold which aggravated the heart condition he had suffered since the preceding spring. On the 26th he had to force himself to give a performance and was the next morning advised by his doctor to cancel his engagements for several days, but refused.[30] His performance on New Year's Eve could not have been among his best.

In addition to being unaware of Dickens's illness, Clemens greatly underestimated the difficulties of the peculiar kind of performance Dickens originated. He seems to have thought one merely had to stand before an audience, pick up a book, and read. He tried this naively simple process when he first introduced readings into his own lectures; the results were so ghastly that his estimation of Dickens's art rose considerably.[31]

Whatever its causes, Clemens's sense of disappointment in the reading was not lasting. In an essay on "Platform Reading" dictated thirty-nine years later, he recalls 'holding hands' with Livy and the dramatic lighting effects he had mentioned in 1868, but his evaluation of the reading itself is quite different from what it had been earlier:

> He read with great force and animation in the lively passages, and with stirring effect. It will be understood that he not merely read but also acted. His reading of the storm scene in which Steerforth

> lost his life was so vivid, and so full of energetic action, that his house was carried off its feet, so to speak.[32]

Moreover, it is necessary to note again what has in the past been overlooked, that it is Dickens's readings and not his writings that are attacked. Indeed, the writings, even their pathos, receive considerable praise, although the nature of the praise is more interesting than the fact of it. The latter is what we might have expected; the former is something else again.

In *Mark Twain: The Development of a Writer* Henry Nash Smith carefully traces the profound tension running throughout the whole corpus of Mark Twain's work between two opposing sets of values, those Smith labels "vernacular" (a kind of 'horse sense' which attempts to see things 'as they actually are' and distrusts stereotyped attitudes divorced from actual experience) on the one hand and those he calls "genteel" (a quasi Hartleyan-Kamesian associationism which finds an attenuated value in 'ideality' and 'propriety') on the other. Mark Twain never completely resolved the tension. It came to one of its first crises during the courtship of Livy and the writing of *Innocents Abroad*, the period into which the *Alta* dispatch falls; we should not be surprised to see this tension making itself apparent in Mark Twain's pronouncements on Dickens.

Both ways of viewing the world find expression in the dispatch. The voice speaking in the sentence beginning "But that queer old head" is the genteel "Mr. Twain"; the style is unmistakable: the excessive alliteration, the carefully matched phrases, the periodic structure, the clichés, and the elaborate rhythmic patterns all point to a Mark Twain robed in his best Sunday-go-to-Transcendental-meeting outfit. Moreover, the epistemology of the sentence is decidedly genteel. What is important to the speaker is not the actual man standing before him, but the wealth of associations which cluster around the name of Dickens. (Mark Twain repeats it, "This was Dickens--Dickens," in an almost conjuring way--as if the attempt to capture the appropriate set of emotions required a conscious effort of will.) However, Mark Twain cannot maintain this outrush of ideality for long, and a vernacular voice soon pops through to undercut it. To call Dickens's mind a "complex but exquisitely adjusted machinery" is genteel enough, but to add "I almost imagined I could see the wheels and pulleys work" is to reify the metaphor in a highly irreverent, specifically vernacular way. It is this second voice, with its emphasis on actuality, that wins out in the paragraph; what is important to it is that the man seen is, in reality, less than handsome and eats pork and cabbage like everyone else. Ultimately the attack is not on Dickens but on the genteel cult that lionized him.

Phelps, who believed Mark Twain failed to appreciate Dickens, explained his supposed dislike by saying Clemens too much believed what he was told and was, therefore, a victim of the nineteenth-century opinion which praised Thackeray at the expense of Dickens who, after all, was "not quite a gentleman."[33] Phelps's hypothesis made sense in Phelps's day, but profiting from the proliferation of Mark Twain research since 1935 and from the liberal policies of Clemens's present executors, we can see all the evidence pointing to an opposite conclusion. While I am convinced that despite his many disclaimers Clemens read almost all Thackeray's major works, he nowhere expresses any special fondness for them, and they seem to have made only a slight impression on his mind.[34] What hostility there is in Mark Twain's public pronouncements on Dickens is motivated not so much by his having been taught to prefer Thackeray, but rather to a significant degree by his profound distaste for the way in which his friends idolized "Boz."

The idolization must have seemed inescapable. The enthusiasm for Dickens which he had encountered in Orion in Hannibal and Keokuk was expanded by Clagett and others of his friends in Virginia City; in San Francisco it was the order of the day. In the East Livy expressed the proper genteel worship of Dickens, and "Boz" was one of the penates in the neighboring houses at Nook Farm. Although Howells was forced to maintain a strategic fastidiousness about Dickens in his public criticisms, he delighted in him on the sly, and Clemens even had to listen to Elinor Howells chatter away at the dinner table about the way "Boz" liked his mutton cooked. We can hardly wonder at Clemens's impatience.

Mark Twain's repugnance toward genteel worship of "Boz" which finds covert expression in the vernacular voice of the _Alta_ dispatch is brought out into the open in the "Memorandum" entitled "The Approaching Epidemic" he sent to _The Galaxy_ on the occasion of Dickens's death:

> One calamity to which the death of Mr. Dickens dooms this country has not awakened the concern to which its gravity entitles it. We refer to the fact that the nation is to be lectured to death and read to death, all next winter by Tom, Dick, and Harry, with poor lamented Dickens for a pretext. All the vagabonds who can spell will afflict the people with "readings" from Pickwick and Copperfield, and all the insignificants who have been ennobled by the notice of the great novelist or transfigured by his

> smile will make a marketable commodity of it now, and turn the sacred reminiscence to the practical use of procuring bread and butter. The lecture rostrums will fairly swarm with fortunates. Already the signs of it are perceptible. Behold how the unclean creatures are wending toward the dead lion and gathering to the feast.

The "Memorandum" goes on to ridicule people like the man who will claim fame for having "once rode in an omnibus with Charles Dickens" and lectures like "Heart Treasures of Precious Moments with Literature's Departed Monarch" which will be delivered by "Miss Susan Amelia Tryphenia McSpadden who still wears, and will always wear, a glove on the hand made sacred by the clasp of Dickens. Only death shall remove it."[35]

Mark Twain's predictions were not inaccurate. A New Yorker named Winter put on public display a brandy glass which had touched the lips of Dickens, and a tidal wave of Dickens readers and lecturers flooded the platforms in the early seventies.[36] Later Clemens recalled how Kate Field won "a wide spasmodic notoriety" by her "frenzy of praise--praise which approached idolatry" of Boz at a time when "the country was itself in a frenzy of enthusiasm about Dickens." Significantly, although Miss Field turned out audiences sufficient to insure her an annual income of $10,000, Clemens thought her lectures "house-emptiers."[37]

Mark Twain's contempt for the kind of praise "which approached idolatry" and his delight in seeing the idolators discomfited can also be seen in one of his favorite anecdotes. For over thirty years Clemens made it a practice to fill either the first or the last pages of a new notebook with mnemonic signals of jokes and anecdotes he found particularly pleasing. Some flourish for a few years then disappear; many, like "long dog" and "rake handle" (both obviously ribald) may never be fully deciphered, but references to "Robinson--Dickens" run a steady course from the early eighties to sometime after 1905 and are explained by a letter Clemens wrote to Frederic Kitton that Kitton preserves in his volume Charles Dickens by Pen and Pencil. Kitton, collecting the reminiscences of American authors who had met Dickens in 1867, assumed Mark Twain to be one of them and wrote requesting an account of what he thought would be a memorable interview. Because Kitton's book is somewhat rare and because Clemens tells his story extremely well, I quote his reply in full:

> I would be glad to be numbered among the contributors, but I have not the wherewithal to get admission.
>
> Pity that Henry C. Robinson, who plays billiards at my house every Friday night and runs for Governor of the state in the 'off years,' isn't a literary notoriety--for he saw Dickens, saw him away back, when he came over here the first time--in

> '42. When the news flashed over the country in '67 that Mr. Dickens was coming again, there was a vast meeting at Cooper Institute in New York to concert measures to welcome him. Enthusiasm ran high, the speeches were full of fire; any man who could say he had seen Dickens in the flesh was an envied person, and was sure of a grateful hearing, and got it, too, every time. Finally somebody sang out:--
>
> "Gentlemen, I see Robinson of Hartford, over yonder! [Hurrah, 'rah! 'rah! from the audience.] You know him for the most eloquent man in New England ['rah! 'rah!], a man who can picture a scene in words that will live and burn forever in a memory--and I am told _he_ has seen Dickens! [Fetch him out! Robinson! Robinson! way for Robinson!]
>
> In the intense and expectant hush that follows an author's preliminary clearing of his throat, Robinson said impressively:--
>
> "The meeting was brief, and yet, fleeting as it was, I can never forget it. It was a beautiful day; one of those days which soothe the spirit, which make the heart happy, which endear existence to man, and man to his kind. I was passing the City Hotel, in my ancient town of Hartford, when suddenly I stopped, as one that is paralyzed: for there, in the great bay-window, alone--and meetly solitary in a greatness which could be no otherwise than companionless--sat one whom all the universe knew--Dickens! Eagerly I pressed my face against the pane, and in one moment was lost, absorbed, enchanted. Presently I saw his eyes begin to open: was he going to speak to me?--to me? I verily held my breath. And--gentlemen--he _did_ speak to me!"
>
> [Immense applause--thunders of applause--in the midst of which it was noticed that Robinson was blandly walking off the platform. Voices--"Hold on, hold on!--what the nation did he say?"]
>
> "Well, he only said, 'Go 'way, little boy, go 'way!'"[38]

One of the things the genteel idolators who crowded Cooper Institute to hurrah Henry Robinson and who flocked to hear the Kate Fields and Susan Amelia Tryphenia McSpaddens lecture admired most in Dickens was his pathos and sentimentality. To attempt a full definition of Mark Twain's attitude toward pathos and sentimentality in fiction requires some courage. It is perhaps safest to say he despised them in almost everyone's writings except his own. To his friend Will Bowen he called sentimentality "mental and moral masturbation,"[39] and his attack on Goldsmith, mentioned earlier, is angry to the point of rant. Yet in a letter to a Mrs. Beardsley he defends his own bathetic story "A Horse's Tale" with all the self-righteous piety of a Quaker City pilgrim. "I know it is a pity to wring the poor human heart, and it grieves me to do it; but it is the only way to move some people to reflect." Further on in the letter he explains that, painful though it may be, "'The Horse's Tale' has a righteous purpose."[40] To us it seems obvious that Clemens should have realized that this principle which justified pathos when it serves a righteous purpose could be applied to the works of Dickens and his American imitators as readily as to his own, but his celebrated attacks on Bret Harte show that he did not.

He first mentions Harte as "a deliberate imitator of Dickens" in a letter to Howells, November 23, 1875.[41] The letter is moderately restrained in tone, but his attitude toward imitation was extreme. When Orion sent him the manuscript of a novel which blatantly drew upon Jules Verne, he wrote to his mother, "To imitate an author, even in a sketch, is not an elevated thing to do; to imitate him to the extent of an entire book is such an offense against good morals, good taste, and good manners--I might say even decency--that I should very much hate to see the family name [put?] to such a production."[42] Clemens's feelings toward Harte may have influenced this denunciation of Orion; at any rate, whatever moderation he displayed in 1875 has disappeared by 1906:

> This was the very Bret Harte whose pathetics, imitated from Dickens, used to be a godsend to the farmers of two hemispheres on account of the freshets of tears they compelled....
>
> In the San Francisco days Bret Harte was by no means ashamed when he was praised as being a successful imitator of Dickens, he was proud of it. I heard him say, myself, that he thought he was the best imitator of Dickens in America, a remark which indicates a fact, to wit: that there were a great many people in America at that time who were ambitiously and undisguisedly imitating Dickens. His long novel, Gabriel Conroy, is as much like Dickens as if Dickens has written it himself.[43]

Although the attack is clearly on Harte, this passage has often been taken as exemplifying Clemens's attitude in his later years toward Dickens. It certainly tells us something about his attitude toward Dickens's pathetics, but it is not so simple a statement as it is often taken to be.

For one thing we need to remember that the implied criticism of Dickens is tainted by the personal animosity hurled at Harte. Clemens never cooled in friendship toward another San Francisco companion, Ralph Keeler, and throughout his life delighted in Keeler's sole novel Gloverson and his Silent Partners, a production every bit as full of Dickens as Gabriel Conroy. Additionally, the marginalia in Clemens's copies of Harte's tales preserved in the Mark Twain Papers show that in the late seventies or early eighties his major criticism was that Harte's style (especially in dialogue passages) rather than his pathos was borrowed from Dickens. What he objected to most was that Harte's Californians all talked like Dickens's Englishmen. The attack in 1906 may reflect a growing dislike of sentimentality; it may also show that Clemens had found an easier and more vulnerable target. In any case, all other considerations aside, Harte, to the degree that he became associated in Mark Twain's mind with Victorian idolatry of Boz, was sure to draw fire.

Another of Mark Twain's comments on Dickens has puzzled commentators ever since Albert Paine included it in the collection of snippets from the notebooks he published as the "full" text in 1935. "I have," reads Paine's text, "no sense of humor. In illustration of this fact I will say this--by way of confession--that if there is a humorous passage in the Pickwick Papers I have never been able to find it."[44] Actually, when the remark is restored to its place in the 1885 notebooks the only problem it presents is that of discovering why Paine chose to distort Mark Twain's opinions by quoting them out of context. Paine published his highly edited version of the notebooks in an attempt to squelch Van Wyck Brooks and his followers by allowing Mark Twain to "have his say." Perhaps he thought this remark, standing in isolation, would sound iconoclastic enough to serve his purposes. Restored to the text the comment is hardly shocking at all--as the following paragraphs will show.

In June, 1885, Courtland Palmer, secretary of the Nineteenth Century Club in New York, wrote to Clemens asking him to appear before the club with an hour's lecture on "American Humor or some cognate theme." The letter arrived at an opportune moment; Clemens was at work preparing the Library of Humor, and the notebooks show that he was planning a preface which would explore the very subject Palmer had suggested. He began work on the lecture at once, even though he noted that he had "nearly 9 months" to prepare it.[45] After several unsuccessful attempts to formulate a distinction between wit and humor in general and British and American humor in particular, Clemens in mid-September decided that he could not make the lecture "go" and wrote to Palmer to renege. In January, 1886, Palmer was still begging him to change his mind, but Clemens persisted, writing on the envelope of Palmer's last letter, "Distinctly <u>no</u> Sir!"

Mark Twain's difficulty with the lecture reflects his curious attitude toward humor itself. Although as has been said, he carefully fostered his "image" as "the humorist who is really funny," he also resented being considered a mere funny-man and tried, at times almost desperately, to dissociate himself from humor. When Susy wrote in her biography of her father, "he is more interested in earnest books and earnest subjects to talk upon than humorous ones," he commented, "She has said it well and correctly. Humor is a subject which has never had much interest for me."[46] In the "Autobiographical Dictation" of January 29, 1907, he recalls having mailed his palm prints anonymously to several palmists. When one says he has no sense of humor he is intrigued. When another says he shows a penchant for philosophy he is pleased, but when a third finds in him the makings of a great theologian, he expresses his delight with a solemnity that reminds us that although he did write Huckleberry Finn, he too ate pork and cabbage.

That he did not care for Pickwick is clear enough. There is a tradition in Mark Twain criticism that says the "so-called funny-book" Clemens was reading in 1856 when he told Ed Brownell that he "could do better" was The Pickwick Papers. It makes a nice story, with definite symbolic value, but it is best left as a nice story. Less questionable is the frequent assertion that Clemens's choice of the pseudonym, Thomas Jefferson Snodgrass, represents both an homage to Dickens and a desire to assert a personal and nationalistic independence. Unimpeachable is the fact that in 1863 he states that he had always looked upon Pickwick's most celebrated episode "as the tamest of Mr. Dickens's performances."[47] In 1885 he did not think the book funny at all.

Why he did not is explained in a notebook entry Paine chose not to print. "No humor in Pickewick Papers [sic] except the kind the clown makes in the circus--I mean the humorist is a million times funnier to himself than ever he can be to any reader. Every line in the book says 'Look at me--ain't I funny!'" The entry then goes on to declare that English humor is "conscious" while American humor is "ostensibly unconscious" and to attack English practices of explaining the joke away with italics, parentheses, and other pointers.[48] Another entry a few pages later shows Clemens still at work on his lecture, clarifying and augmenting his ideas about Dickens's humor:

> Sidney Smith
> Major Dalgetty (good on stage, no doubt)
> Capt. Cuttle is good anywhere, & so also of all Dickens's humorous characters except those in Pickwick Papers, & the body-snatcher in Tale of 2 Cities.[49]

Thus the comment in Paine's edition should be seen as a specific (and ironic) remark about a specific book, not, as it has been seen before, a blanket condemnation of Dickens.

In the late eighties and early nineties, Mark Twain again reviewed his opinion of Dickens. In the published version of _Life on the Mississippi_ he had defended Dickens's (and other English travellers') depiction of the American scene while softening it by pointing out the changes for the better which had taken place in the Mississippi valley since 1842.[50] In a chapter which at Howells's suggestion he withheld from publication, he is even more outspoken in his defense of America's English critics. The suppressed chapter is concerned primarily with Mrs. Trollope, but _Martin Chuzzlewit_ and _American Notes_ find their fair share of support.[51] Matthew Arnold's attack on Grant's prose style in 1887 put a quick stop to Mark Twain's defense of English commentary on the States, and Dickens became one with Arnold, Griffen, and all the others who needed to be told a thing or two themselves. His change in attitude toward _Chuzzlewit_ and _American Notes_ seems to have affected his outlook toward the whole Dickens canon. In a letter to Howells he remarks on "the changes which age makes in a man while he sleeps" and attacks those who "pretend that the Bible means the same to them at 50 that it did at all the former milestones in their journey," adding, "they would not say that of Dickens's or Scott's books."[52]

To an Australian interviewer in 1895 Clemens grants Dickens a "niche in the gallery of immortals" and praises his ability to blend humor and pathos, comparing his technique with Shakespeare's handling of the Fool in _Lear_. Later in the interview he is less laudatory, echoing some of his earlier notebook entries on _Pickwick_ and, curiously, repeating the "machinery" metaphor he had employed in the _Alta California_ dispatch twenty-six years earlier:

> I must fain confess that with the years I have lost much of my youthful admiration for Dickens. In saying so, it seems a little as if one were wilfully heretic; but the truth must prevail. I seem to see all the machinery of the business too clearly, the effort is too patent. The true and lasting genius

> of humour does not drag you thus to boxes labelled 'pathos,' 'humour,' and show you all the mechanism of the inimitable puppets that are going to perform. How I used to laugh at Simon Tapperwit [sic] and the Wellers, and a host more! But I can't do it now somehow; and time, it seems to me, is the true test of humour.[53]

Howells's influence was undoubtedly at work to direct the energy generated by Arnold in this reassessment of Dickens's work. Clemens's own critical insecurity barred him from making any literary judgment without breaking into violent extremes of censure or praise; he was therefore all the more willing to accept Howells's seemingly calm and precise pronouncements. An out-of-the-way source provides this revealing statement:

> Howells...is one of the very best literary men America has produced; there is no bludgeoning with him. His is the rapier method. You English don't like him because he once adversely criticized Dickens, and I believe even Thackeray! But we honor him as a man who delivers his verdicts after weighing the evidence most carefully; a man who despatches this aspirant or that not hurriedly or with passion, but slowly, deliberately, almost lovingly.[54]

Mark Twain, the self-taught bludgeoner, is full of admiration for the delicate rapier work of the Cambridge Sage, even when Dickens is at issue.

Clemens returned to Dickens in the last decade of his life. Although the last reference to Dickens to come directly from his hand is a post-1905 reminder of the Henry

Robinson anecdote, the penultimate reference is more arresting. In the 1903 notebook he jots the telegraphic entry "Toodles--Capt. Cuttle," which is followed, without any indication of a break in thought, by the single line, "Lost at sea."[55] Anyone who has waded through the morass of heartbreaking, abortive manuscripts Bernard DeVoto labelled "The Great Dark" can feel something ominous in that one cryptic notation.[56] One wonders if, in Mark Twain's last years, his memory of "Wal'r, my lad" (who spends a third of the novel "lost at sea" and whom Dickens had originally intended to go to ruin) did not, perhaps, take on a coloring quite different from the boisterous enthusiasm of 1862, and if this lonely and embittered old man might not have preferred that John Forster had never tampered with the ending of Dombey.

The nature of its subject requires that this investigation remain somewhat inconclusive. Some things do, however, emerge clearly. For over fifty years Clemens was a constant and careful reader of Dickens, and we must not exclude Dickens's influence from the many forces that combined to shape Mark Twain's imagination. His distrust of his own critical abilities and his desire to divorce himself both from his 'rival' as humorist and, paradoxically, from the genre of humor itself in a century which read Dickens primarily as a great comic writer led Clemens to make several contradictory statements about the novels themselves; but his distaste for anything that suggested Dickens idolatry remained constant and unambiguous. As Clemens matured, so did his reading of Dickens, although his rage over *Chuzzlewit* and *American Notes* in the late eighties reflects a certain childishness he never completely outgrew. However, erupt though he might, he never abandoned the works of his great older contemporary.

Notes to Chapter II

[1]"Mark Twain," Yale Review, XXV (1935), 294.

[2]"Two Humorists: Charles Dickens and Mark Twain," Yale Review, XXIV (1934), 122.

[3]"The French Revolution and Huckleberry Finn," MP, LV (1957), 21-35; Mark Twain and Huck Finn, (Berkeley and Los Angeles, 1960).

[4]Miss Nisbet in Victorian Fiction, pp. 111-12; Miss Moers in "The 'Truth' of Mark Twain," New York Review of Books, V (January 20, 1966), 10-15.

[5]Harold Aspiz, "Mark Twain's Reading: A Critical Study," unpubl. diss. (U.C.L.A., 1944), 209.

[6]Albert E. Stone, The Innocent Eye: Childhood in Mark Twain's Imagination (New Haven, 1961), pp. 15-16.

[7]Bryant Morey French, Mark Twain and the Gilded Age (Dallas, 1965), p. 165 and note.

[8]Albert B. Paine, Mark Twain: A Biography, 4 vols. (New York, 1912), 1500-01; Henry W. Fisher, Abroad with Mark Twain and Eugene Field (New York, 1922), p. 60.

[9]This material will appear in an essay entitled "Mark Twain and Dickens," to be published in PMLA, January, 1969.

[10]Paine, Biography, 106.

[11]S. L. Clemens to Frank E. Burrough, December, 1900, TS MTP. See also Paine, Biography, 103. Paine confuses father with son.

[12]A TS of the letter to Clagget is in the MTP; the relevant passage is quoted in full in the following chapter. For the comment on Bardell vs. Pickwick see Mark Twain of the "Enterprise", ed. Henry Nash Smith and Frederick Anderson (Berkeley and Los Angeles, 1957), p. 92.

[13]Notebook 3, TS MTP, p. 2.

[14]The correct date is established by Howard G. Baetzhold, "Mark Twain's 'First Date' with Olivia Langdon," _Bulletin of the Missouri Historical Society_, XI (1955), 155-57.

[15]Adrian Stoutenburg and Laura Nelson Baker, _Dear, Dear Livy_ (New York, 1963), pp. 33-34, 38-39.

[16]Mary Lawton, _A Lifetime with Mark Twain_ (New York, 1925), pp. 8, 56.

[17]S. L. Clemens to Olivia Clemens, November 24 and December 22, 1873, Samassoud Collection, MTP.

[18]_The Mark Twain--Howells Letters_, ed. Henry Nash Smith and William Gibson, 2 vols. (Cambridge, 1960), I, 224, 225, 424.

[19]S. L. Clemens to Clara Clemens, November 5, 1892, Samassoud Collection, MTP.

[20]Olivia Clemens to S. L. Clemens, January 21, 1885, Samassoud Collection, MTP.

[21]Lawton, pp. 39-40.

[22]S. L. Clemens to Mrs. Foote, December 2, 1887, MTP.

[23]Phelps, 307.

[24]These last notebook entries are discussed more fully below.

[25]Paine, _Biography_, 1500-01.

[26]Much of Clemens's peculiar and revealing attitude toward Moffett can be seen in the memorial included in the volume _Europe and Elsewhere_, _The Writings of Mark Twain_, "Definitive Edition," ed. A. B. Paine, 37 vols. (New York, 1922-25), XXIX, 351-54. Unless otherwise noted all subsequent references to Mark Twain's published works are to this edition, cited by volume number, chapter (where applicable), and page. Significantly, Clemens never says whether or not Moffett could use or interpret his knowledge of history; for him it was enough that he could remember so many facts.

[27]XXI, xxvi, 288-89.

[28]Mark Twain to Mrs. Fairbanks, ed. Dixon Wecter (San Merino, 1949), pp. 206-09. It is noteworthy that the letter is to young Mollie. He would never take such risks with a "celebrity" and only rarely with even so close a friend as Howells.

[29]Alta California, February 5, 1868. Reprinted in The Twainian, VII (1948), 4.

[30]Edgar Johnson, Charles Dickens: His Tragedy and Triumph, 2 vols. (New York, 1952), II, 1082-83.

[31]Paul Fatout, Mark Twain on the Lecture Circuit (Bloomington, 1960), pp. 85-216.

[32]Eruption, p. 214. Clemens's memory may, of course, have been influenced by what he had read and heard of Dickens's readings during those thirty-nine years.

[33]P. 294.

[34]For example in a letter to Clara, October 9, (1906?), he writes: "I have just finished 'Henry Esmond.' There are very fine passages in it. On the whole I liked it. Its close is dramatically great. But I had a surprise: from the beginning to the end I found nothing that was familiar to me. It turns out--per the Lyon [Isabel Lyon, Clemens's secretary]--that I've not read this book before, but was mistaking 'The Virginians' for this one." Samassoud Collection, MTP.

[35]Contributions to The Galaxy, 1868-1871, ed. Bruce R. McElderry, Jr. (Gainesville, 1961), p. 74.

[36]Fatout, pp. 145-46.

[37]Mark Twain's Autobiography, ed. Albert B. Paine, 2 vols. (New York, 1924), I, 157.

[38]London, 1890, pp. 157-58.

[39]Mark Twain's Letters to Will Bowen, ed. Theodore Hornberger (Austin, 1941), p. 24.

[40] The letter is included in the "Autobiographical Dictation" of August 29, 1906, MTP.

[41] *Howells Letters*, I, 112.

[42] Undated (1877-78?), Moffett Collection, MTP.

[43] *Eruption*, pp. 265-67.

[44] *Mark Twain's Notebook*, ed. Albert B. Paine (New York, 1935), p. 184.

[45] Notebook 20, TS MTP, p. 7. Palmer's letters to Clemens are also in the MTP.

[46] "Autobiographical Dictation," March 28, 1907, MTP.

[47] *Mark Twain of the "Enterprise"*, p. 92.

[48] Notebook 19, TS MTP, p. 28.

[49] P. 36. Dugald Dalgetty figures in Scott's *Legend of Montrose*. Clemens had mixed feelings toward Scott but consistently detested Smith.

[50] For example in his comments on Cairo, XII, 214.

[51] MS DV 141, MTP.

[52] *Howells Letters*, II, 595.

[53] Sydney *Morning Herald*, September 17, 1895, MTP. One notes in the interview Clemens's self-consciousness as critic and his curiously ambiguous attitude toward pathos, both discussed above.

[54] Interview in the Johannesburg, South Africa, *Star*, May 18, 1896, MTP. The exclamation pointed "and even Thackeray" does show Clemens's awareness of the so-called "Dickens-Thackeray Controversy."

[55] Notebook 36, TS MTP, p. 6.

[56] These manuscripts have now been published under the title *Which Was the Dream?*, ed. John S. Tuckey (Berkeley and Los Angeles, 1967).

CHAPTER III

MARK TWAIN: DICKENS COMES TO DAWSON'S LANDING

In his address before the Boston Mercantile Library Association in 1844, Whipple had called for a class of novels that would illustrate American life and character by, paradoxically, imitating Dickens. The call did not go unanswered. Although Emerson, like Mark Twain's celebrated drifter who could "see no p'ints about that frog," might scratch his head in bewilderment, unable to understand what all the fuss over *The Pickwick Papers* was about, other Americans were quick to see in Dickens a master to be followed. Walt Whitman, attempting to describe a New Orleans boarding-house, had merely surrounded Todger's with Spanish moss, and Melville had sent his scrivener not to work in an office staffed by comic types borrowed from Boz. Even so "pure" a New England type as Hawthorne had found in the writing of *The Blithedale Romance* that *Martin Chuzzlewit* was right: "Self" is the key to the American character.[1] And a tidal wave of lesser imitations flooded the bookstalls. Now-forgotten novelists like George Lippard, Maria Cummins, T. S. Arthur, and Mrs. E.D.E.N. Southworth found in Dickens's sentimentality and melodrama modes eminently congenial to their purposes. Others, like Harriet Beecher Stowe and Rebecca Harding Davis, who explored that underside of American life that Whipple had optimistically omitted from his catalog of national characteristics, discovered in what Louis Cazamian called Dickens's "*Philosophie de Noel*" a convenient answer to those problems, at once private and social, that made Whipple's belief in the ultimate triumph of our "great virtues and noble aims" over our "avarice, cruelty, pride, folly and ignorance" seem laughably naive.[2]

Few writers of the century were felt to be more "illustrative of American life and character" than Mark Twain. To this "phenomenon of nature" who began his career billed as "The Wild Humorist of the Pacific Slopes" and who considered imitation a disgrace to the family name, Dickensian melodrama was but cheap effectism and Dickensian sentimentality "mental and moral masturbation." As for the "*Philosophie de Noel*," he said more in four words than William Dean Howells could ever say in page after page of elephantine irony in *Criticism and Fiction*: "I hate Xmas stories."[3] If ever there were a purely indigenous writer, so opinion went, this was he. So carefully did Mark Twain create and manipulate his own history that to this day there are authors of scholarly books who piously declare that any and all attempts to see him in contexts other than the strictly chauvinistic "smack of a desire to do him discredit."[4] Yet, as was asserted at the end of the preceding chapter, Dickens cannot be dismissed from the list of forces that helped to shape Mark Twain's imagination. It seems worthwhile, therefore, to determine what forms that influence took.

I.

The most obvious of these forms are direct imitation, burlesques, and what Mark Twain himself would call "unconscious plagiarism." The number of passages in his works that exhibit these kinds of influence is so great that it would perhaps be best to discuss the most significant and characteristic of them in catalog form. Predictably, the heaviest concentration of these passages occurs in his early, apprentice writings.

From its very beginning Clemens's career displays effects of his curiously ambiguous relationship to Dickens. His first writings of even minor consequence, a series of sketches, appeared under the name "Thomas Jefferson Snodgrass" in the Keokuk Post in 1856 and 1857. That Clemens would appropriate the poetical Pickwickian's name for his pseydonym seems an appropriate homage to an acknowledged master of humor; to couple it with the name of a great American president has been taken to be not only a comic juxtaposition of the high and low but also an attempt to assert a personal, nationalistic independence.[5] But the name's implied patriotism is, at least, ironic. The unconscious humor in the American practice of coupling lofty given names with the most plebeian of surnames provided Europeans with unending delight. Dickens's own inventions, LaFayette Kettle, Hannibal Chollop, and Jefferson Brick, echo this traditional anti-Jonathan joke, of which Clemens, even at eighteen, had read widely enough to be aware. Thus if "Thomas Jefferson" qualifies "Snodgrass," the yoking of the two creates an effect that is at least ambiguous, and one is left wondering just what Clemens's assumed stance is meant to be.

If the name does indicate a desire for independence, that desire is frail and easily denied. When the first Snodgrass letter appeared _Little Dorrit_ was still running its course of monthly numbers; Clemens turns to its most famous episode for an easy joke in Snodgrass's burlesque of a performance of _Julius Caesar_: "After that, Missis Brutus come when the other fellars was gone, and like Mr. Clennam at the Circumlocution Office, she 'wanted to know'."[6] In the third letter the episode is imitated directly. Snodgrass describes the blizzard that struck Cincinnati in the winter of 1856-57 and the difficulties of an impoverished widow in acquiring her share of the coal the municipal authorities had obtained for the relief of the poor:

> A indigent Irish woman--a widow with nineteen children and several at the breast, accordin to custom, went to the Mayor to get some of that public coal. The Mayor he gin her an order on the Marshal; the Marshal gin her an order on the Recorder; Recorder sent her to the Constable; Constable sent her to the Postmaster; Postmaster sent her to the County Clerk, and so on, tell she run herself half to death, and friz the balance, while she still had sixteen places to go yet...[7]

Like other journalists of his day Clemens got good mileage out of the Circumlocution Office. He refers to it, for example, in an expose of a young man named Macy who, in 1865, had embezzled $39,000 from the San Francisco Mint. Macy, says Mark Twain, "was the Sub-Treasurer's brother-in-law--he was a Barnacle, and had to be provided with a place in the Circumlocution Office, whether he knew enough to come in out of the rain or not."[8] Later in his life Clemens tried vigorously to deny his authorship of the Snodgrass sketches and allowed most of his newspaper pieces to pass into oblivion, being motivated in part, perhaps, by his awareness of their derivative nature. "To imitate an author, even in a sketch," he opined, "is not an elevated thing to do."[9] Yet one of the few pieces he chose to preserve in the volume Sketches New and Old, "The Facts in the Case of the Great Beef Contract," which tells of the extraordinary difficulties experienced by an Army contractor in attempting to extract payment from an insolent bureaucracy, is nothing but another, more elaborate imitation of chapter x of Little Dorrit; Mark Twain finally acknowledges the debt in his last paragraph (VII, 106-15). The same volume also contains a long sketch entitled "A Curious Dream," which echoes the graveyard satire of Bleak House and a longer "Learned Fable" in which animal characters mimic the scientific exploits of the Pickwickians (VII, 227-39, 137-67).

Other traces of a Dickens influence are to be found in Mark Twain's apprentice work. Miss Gladys Bellamy has pointed out, for example, the Dickensian flavor of such newspaper pieces as "Daniel in the Lion's Den," and Bernard Poli has shown the similarity of the relationship between the "genteel" Mark Twain and the rough "Mr. Brown" of the early travel sketches to that between Martin and Mark during their travels in Martin Chuzzlewit. Like Mark, Brown functions as the exponent of a "realistic" view of experience that is contrasted with his companion's more "ideal"--and less accurate--vision. Significantly, the good-hearted Brown is, like Mark, a frequent victim of his own benevolence, and his adventures with a poverty-stricken fellow traveller and her numberless children seem modelled directly on Tapley's relationship to the unfortunate immigrants to Eden.[10]

If some of Mark Twain's apprentice sketches directly imitate Dickens, others use him as a target for literary burlesque. One such piece is the curious--and not very successful--"Mark Twain Overpowered," which appeared in the Alta California, 2 December 1865. In it Mark Twain, out for a stroll, encounters two strangers sitting on a bank by the side of the road, gazing at the tombstones that bedeck the summit of Lone Mountain. One is a "fair-haired, sweet-faced child of about eight years of age" and the other her elderly uncle to whom she is obviously devoted and who is holding her spellbound by one of his marvelous stories, which the narrator assumes to be prompted by the funereal landscape. His description of the two carefully places them in the attitudes assumed by Little Nell and her grandfather in Phiz's illustration accompanying chapter xv of The Old Curiosity Shop. Overpowered by the seeming innocence of the girl, her devotion to the helpless old man and the pathos of their fixed gaze at the tombstones, the sentimental Mark Twain bursts into tears. Unfortunately the girl, "lill Addie," is covered with warts, the "bank" turns out to be a discarded piece of gambling equipment, and the uncle is blind drunk.[11] The sketch is unsuccessful not only because its satire is too obvious but also because it seems to involve somewhere in its motives an undecipherable private joke that detracts from its effectiveness as burlesque. The sketch appeared at the same time that Our Mutual Friend was running serially in the Golden Era, a journal that also included Mark Twain among its contributors. In that novel the termagant child Jenny Wren bears a perverted relationship to her alcoholic father that is clearly Dickens's own satire on Nellie and her grandfather. Mark Twain's sketch, therefore, puts him in the curious position of having imitated Dickens in order to burlesque him.

When Mark Twain's career led him from newspaper sketches to full-length books, he took Dickens along with him. In *The Innocents Abroad*, his first, the Mr. Brown of the travel dispatches disappears, but is replaced in the early chapters by a Mr. Blucher, who differs from him only in name. Blucher finds other ways to display his benevolence than befriending indigents, but the Martin-Mark, "genteel-realistic" axis is maintained in his relationship to the narrator. This relationship is not, however, the only sign of a Dickens influence in the book. Faced with the enormous difficulties of transforming a set of hastily written dispatches into a six-hundred page subscription volume, Mark Twain turned to other travel books for help. His borrowings from Murray's guide-books, J. Ross Browne's *Yusef*, and W. C. Grimes's *Tent Life in the Holy Land* are well known; curiously, the possibility that he did some homework in Dickens's travel writings as well has never been explored. Yet there can, I think, be little doubt that he did.

Consider, for example, the chapters on Venice in *Innocents Abroad* and *Pictures from Italy*. Venice presented a peculiar problem for Mark Twain. In his preface he had promised to write "honestly," to see Europe with his own eyes and to record faithfully what those eyes had seen. The Venice he saw was "decayed, forlorn, poverty-stricken, and commerceless--forgotten and utterly insignificant," its stagnant canals making it look like "an overflowed Arkansas town" and its famed gondolas resembling nothing so much as ocean-going hearses (I, xxii, 223). But the official culture of his day demanded an idealized Venice sugared o'er with a mist of historical and literary associations. Moreover, Mark Twain was an American and a democrat; Venice, "the Mother of Republics," seemed for reasons of political ideology particularly deserving of idealizing charity. To solve the problems of tone and attitude the city raised, he turned to Dickens, who had faced the same problems twenty years before. He too had pledged himself to record his experiences and reflections honestly, to avoid writing yet another book on Italy merely "studying the history of that interesting country, and the innumerable associations entwined about it" (XXVIII, i, 309). Yet he too realized that his attempts to be "fanciful" would in turn arouse in his readers a desire for idealizations of places, like Venice, "to which the imaginations of most people are attracted in a greater or less degree" (XXVIII, i, 310). And as an English republican he too was aware of the ideological veneration due the Mother of Republics.

Dickens's solution was simple: never describe the present-day Venice of empirical "reality" at all; rather, put the whole chapter in the form of a dream-vision so that all the poverty, insignificance, and decay can be blotted out and the Venice of historical, political, and literary association can remain a pristine ideality. He approaches the city exhausted after a whirlwind tour of northern Italy. His brain an "incoherent but delightful jumble" of impressions, he is lulled by the motions of his coach into an uneasy sleep during which he dreams his entire stay in Venice, awaking only after he has been safely deposited in the market square at Verona. For Mark Twain to have cast his chapter as a formal dream-vision would have been too obvious a plagiarism. His strategy, therefore, is to make his experience of Venice seem as much like a dream as he can without actually calling it one, to follow Dickens's path without actually stepping in his footprints. He too approaches the city exhausted by tourism, his head a gallimaufry of random impressions. He too half slumbers in his coach, silent, subdued, hardly conscious of where he is when

Venice suddenly appears as a kind of miraculous vision: "And sure enough, afloat on the placid sea a league away, lay a great city, with its towers and domes and steeples drowsing in a golden mist" (I, xxi, 217). Justin Kaplan has perceptively noted the "talismanic" quality the word "drowsing" had for Mark Twain. It occurs repeatedly in his writings and always it "conjures up an image of childhood purified by the years, a state of idyllic innocence which could be recaptured only in the imagination." It was, in other words, the term Mark Twain habitually used "to evoke the landscape of dream."[12] The dream-like atmosphere established by the initial vision of the city is maintained throughout the chapter. "It seems a sort of sacrilege," Mark Twain writes, "to disturb the glamour of old romance that pictures [Venice] to us softly from afar off as through a tinted mist, and curtains her ruin and her desolation from our view" (I, xxii, 219). Hence while just enough waking experience is scattered through the chapter to prevent implications of plagiarism, most of the descriptions are set at night when daylight "reality" fades away and a charitable moon restores the city to the realm of ideality. Then the narrator's "fancy" can picture Venice in a kind of semi-conscious revery that approximates the effects of Dickens's dream-vision.[13]

Although the Mother of Republics demands the veneration of English republicans and American democrats, her past could also evoke other, far different, emotions. At the time of writing The Innocents Abroad Mark Twain's attitudes toward the past were deeply colored by the positivist, quasi-evolutionary assumptions of the great Whig historians who tended to divide all of European history into two epochs, the nineteenth century and the Middle Ages, the one all progress and light, the other a dark chamber of horrors.[14] In other words Mark Twain was heir to the same set of assumptions that led Dickens to install in his study a set of false book-backs entitled "The Wisdom of Our Ancestors" of which the seven individual volumes were labelled Ignorance, Superstition, The Block, The Stake, The Rack, Dirt, and Disease.[15] Hence as both authors approach the Ducal Palace the dream becomes a nightmare. That Mark Twain's description is based directly upon Dickens can be seen by the closeness of the verbal parallels in the two following passages. First Dickens:

> But first I passed two jagged slits in a stone wall; the lions' mouths--now toothless--where, in the distempered horror of my sleep, I thought denunciations of innocent men to the old wicked

> Council, had been dropped through, many a time, when the night was dark. So, when I saw the council-room to which such prisoners were taken for examination, and the door by which they passed out, when they were condemned--a door that never closed upon a man with life and hope before him--my heart appeared to die within me.
>
> (XXVIII, viii, 396-97)

Then Mark Twain:

> ...two small slits in the stone wall were pointed out...these were the terrible Lions' Mouths! The heads were gone (knocked off by the French during their occupation of Venice), but these were the throats down which went the anonymous accusation, thrust in secretly at dead of night by an enemy, that doomed many an innocent man to walk the Bridge of Sighs and descend into the dungeon which none entered and hoped to see the sun again.
>
> (I, xxii, 225)

Later in the chapter Mark Twain remarks that visitors used to be shown a grizzly display of instruments of torture, which he then proceeds to catalog. That he is borrowing his information from Dickens is again indicated by the shared vocabulary and syntactical parallels. Dickens tells of seeing iron helmets "made to close up tight and smooth upon the heads of living sufferess; and fastened on to each, was a small knob or anvil, where the directing devil could repose his elbow at his ease, and listen, near the walled up ear, to the lamentations and confessions of the wretch within" (XXVIII, viii, 399). Mark Twain mentions an identical list of implements and singles out "a devilish contrivance of steel, which inclosed a prisoner's head like a shell, and crushed it slowly... On one side it had a projection whereon the torturer rested his elbow comfortably and bent down his ear to catch the moanings of the sufferer perishing within."[16]

Other parallels can be found that indicate, if not direct influence, a community of spirit between the two men. For example, Mrs. Browning might find Dickens "vulgar" because he called Michelangelo a "humbug," but Mark Twain would not.[17] Indeed, in a letter to Emeline Beach, 31 January 1868, he himself uses the term to describe "the whole gang of Old Masters."[18] Clemens did not derive his opinions on art solely from <u>Pictures from Italy</u>; however, as his letters to Miss Beach show, he was desperately uneasy about stating them in print. Dickens's precedent in seeing The Old Masters with his own instead of other men's eyes, his refusal to accept the canting art criticism of his day, and his amusement at venerated St. Sebastians "stuck full of arrows as animated pincushions" must have been reassuring if nothing else.[19]

Like his first sketches and his first full-length book, Mark Twain's first novel also shows signs of Dickens's influence working on his imagination. Contemporary reviewers saw at once that Col. Sellers of The Gilded Age was an American version of Mr. Micawber. More recent critics have noted that Senator Dilworthy's oratory is based upon Mr. Chadband's homiletics, that Mark Twain's use of "speculating fever" as an organizing principle follows Dickens's use of Chancery in Bleak House, and that the history of the Gate City settlement follows closely upon that of Eden in Martin Chuzzlewit, although the tradition that both are based upon William Muldrow's ill-fated experiment at Marion City, Missouri, has been questioned.[20] Additionally, the characterization of Washington Hawkins as well as Mark Twain's frequent moralizing on the danger of setting one's hopes on the expectation of potential, but not yet realized wealth are highly reminiscent of Dickens's handling of Richard Carstone.

Other such traces of Dickens influence can be found throughout Mark Twain's work. They are especially frequent in the "boy books," and many have been noted by the scholars. Dickens hardly invented the child as the focus of fiction, but few would deny Peter Coveney's assertion that any novel written after 1838 in which the child functions as the basis of feeling and is at the center of the author's criticism of life bears the stamp of Dickens.[22] Thus Albert Stone suggests that Mark Twain found in Dickens a potent use of the "childhood-at-bay" situation he was himself to use as a means of getting at social and historical problems in his own novels. Moreover, in Dickens's rebellious Cockney street-urchins, the Artful Dodger, Rob the Grinder, Jerry Cruncher, Jr., Clemens may have found a model for his own American Bad-Boys.[23] Bernard Poli carries the speculation one step farther. Commenting that Clemens experienced during his apprenticeship to Joseph Ament a misery similar to that suffered by Dickens at Warren's Blacking, Poli continues to make the interesting observation that "pour l'un comme l'autre, malgré tout, l'enfance s'achève brutalement et avec la nouvelle période qui s'ouvre commence à se developper un sentiment de nostalgie du bonheur passé dont on trouve le réflect dans leur oeuvres."[24] One needs, I think, to balance against this statement Clemens's tendency to recast his memory of his own experiences in dramatic, sometimes even melodramatic, form and to recognize the possibility that the fragment of autobiography upon which Poli's observation is based may itself reflect Clemens's memory not of the Hannibal <u>Gazette</u> but of <u>David Copperfield</u>.[25] Either case, however, would help explain Dickens's presence in Mark Twain's boy books.

For example, even if David Copperfield did not necessarily color Clemens's memory of his own apprenticeship, it is very likely that it motivated the creation of The Adventures of Tom Sawyer, for Franklin Rogers has made the highly plausible suggestion that the "Boy's MS," the germ from which Tom Sawyer grew, began as a burlesque of David's courtship of Dora.[26] Other signs of Dickens influence appear in the finished novel, one well known instance being the graveyard episode in which Huck and Tom are involuntary witnesses to the murder of Dr. Robinson, an episode that Mark Twain modelled on the body-snatching scene in A Tale of Two Cities.[27] The incident provides a revealing example of Mark Twain's methods and of the nature of many of his borrowings from Dickens. Grave-robbing was hardly an activity that flourished in Clemens's Hannibal, and it cannot be said to be a "realistic" occurrence in Tom's St. Petersburg. Mark Twain needed some device to get his dramatis personae assembled in the cemetery, so he simply "smouched" from Dickens with blithe disregard for probability. But if the scene is untrue when considered by the canons of verisimilitude, it nevertheless--as Robert Tracy has observed--rings with truth when the novel is considered not as a representation of "reality" but as "myth."[28]

Even Mark Twain's masterpiece has been shown to bear marks of Dickens. J. M. Ridland has pointed out similarities in situation and plot between *Huckleberry Finn* and *Great Expectations*,[29] and Walter Blair has demonstrated both that much of Tom's prison lore, exploited during the "Evasion," comes from *A Tale of Two Cities* and that Jim's hostility to the French language may echo that of Miss Pross.[30] Ridland and Blair have far from exhausted the topic. While all boys of all ages have delighted in forming secret societies, the similarities between Tom's various gangs, both in *Tom Sawyer* and in *Huckleberry Finn* and Simon Tappertit's "'Prentice Knights" in *Barnaby Rudge* are close enough to seem more than accidental, especially since we know that Clemens found Tappertit's antics particularly amusing. Additionally, the outcast Dodger's aggressive attack on the attitudes and practices of his society, his defiant inversion of popularly accepted values during his celebrated day in court in *Oliver Twist* perhaps provided Mark Twain with a precedent--if he needed one--for Huck's decision to call his man white and go to Hell anyway. But certainly another of *Huckleberry Finn*'s scenes comes straight out of Dickens.

In "The French Revolution and Huckleberry Finn," Blair pointed out that Pap's attack on Huck for learning to read and write is "highly reminiscent" of the scene in A Tale of Two Cities in which Jerry Cruncher denounces his wife for saying her prayers. The assertion is repeated in Blair's encyclopedic Mark Twain and Huck Finn, and the relevant pages of A Tale of Two Cities are reprinted in the section of "possible sources" in at least one critical edition of Huck.[31] The parallels Blair draws between the two works are certainly significant, and there is no reason to doubt that Cruncher Sr. was somewhere in the back of Mark Twain's mind when he wrote Pap's speech. However, the more immediate model for the scene in question is not A Tale of Two Cities, but rather another of Dickens's works, his last completed novel, Our Mutual Friend.

All his adult life Mark Twain was fascinated by what he called "unconscious plagiarism." "Nothing is ours," he wrote to Robert Burdette in the early eighties, "but our language, our phrasing."

> If a man takes that from me (knowingly, purposely) he is a thief. If he takes it unconsciously--snaking it out of some secluded corner of his memory, and mistaking it for a new birth instead of a mummy--he is no thief, and no man has a case against him.
>
> Unconscious appropriation is utterly common; it is...no crime; but conscious appropriation, i.e., plagiarism, is as rare as parricide. ...These

> notions of mine are not guesses; they are the outcome of twenty years of thought and observation upon this subject.[32]

He knew himself to be a frequent victim of unconscious plagiarism and liked to laugh over his "smouching" a dedication from Oliver Wendell Holmes,[33] but he seems never to have realized that he borrowed one of his most powerful passages from Dickens. In Book one, chapter six of Our Mutual Friend old Gaffer Hexam, a character similar to Pap in his viciousness, ignorance, and general unsavoriness, learns that his son Charley can read and write. In a burst of physical and verbal violence he shouts out a tirade that must have come snaking out of some secluded corner of Mark Twain's memory when he recorded the lambasting Pap gives Huck. Says Hexam in part:

> Let him never come within sight of my eyes, nor yet within reach of my arm. His own father ain't good enough for him. He disowns his own father. His own father, therefore, disowns him for ever and ever, as a unnat'ral young beggar. ...
>
> Now I see why them men yonder held aloof from me. They says to one another, "Here comes the man as ain't good enough for his own son!"
>
> (XXIII, 93)

Says Pap:

> You've put on considerable many frills since I been away. I'll take you down a peg before I get done with you. You're educated, too, they say--can read and write. You think you're better'n your father, now, don't you, because he can't? I'll take it out of you. ...

> I'll learn people to bring up a boy to put on airs over his own father and let on to be better'n what _he_ is. ...Your mother couldn't read, and she couldn't write, nuther, before she died. None of the family couldn't before _they_ died. _I_ can't; and here you're a-swelling yourself up like this. I ain't the man to stand it--you hear?
> (XIII, v, 27)

Mark Twain's scene does contain the important similarities to the scene in _A Tale of Two Cities_ that Blair notes, but its resemblance to the parallel scene in _Our Mutual Friend_ is even closer. Dickens's own repetitiousness may have served to strengthen Mark Twain's memory. Like Charley's, Huck's education has been sponsored by a "foster-parent" (in Charley's case his sister, in Huck's the Widow Douglas) behind the back of the real sire. Both Hexam and Pap seem as much concerned for their standing in the eyes of others as for their private loss of dignity, and both see their children's otherwise laudable efforts as unfilial and unnatural. Moreover, although Pap vows "he hadn't a drink all day," both are clearly drunk when they erupt, Hexam ending his scene with an outburst of violence verging towards _delirium tremens_ that foreshadows Pap's later struggles in the cabin on the Illinois shore. Although much more in control of himself than Pap, like Pap he gestures with a knife to the terror of his off-spring and even hints that he senses the presence of the Death Angel.[34] This drunken violence may have formed the link between Hexam and Pap in Mark Twain's unconscious mind.

Another variation on the same father and son theme occurs in chapter thirty-four of W. G. Simms's Woodcraft, a novel that antedates both A Tale of Two Cities and Our Mutual Friend and which Clemens and Dickens may or may not have known. There may be yet others. Although one tires of the yeast theory of the perpetually rising middle and lower classes, the accelerated mobility of nineteenth-century Englishmen and Americans may have made such scenes particularly popular on both sides of the Atlantic. But there can, I think, be little doubt that Mark Twain's immediate source is Our Mutual Friend.

II.

Dickens's influence on Mark Twain cannot always of course be reduced to the relatively simple matters of literary borrowings and unconscious plagiarism. A more typical example of the way in which Dickens worked upon his imagination is the curious and complex relationship between Capt. Cuttle of Dombey and Son and the central figure of "Captain Stormfield's Visit," a relationship which evokes something of that undersea world of hooks and eyes, unconscious cerebration, and architectonic powers which J. L. Lowes describes in his great psychological detective story, The Road to Xanadu. Capt. Stormfield haunted Mark Twain's imagination for over forty years. He began to sketch the character in 1867 when a "Capt. Waxman" appeared in the travel sketches published in the Alta California. A year later he began work on a manuscript which further developed the Stormfield character and took it on a trip to heaven; the story wouldn't "go" and was shelved. But not forgotten; Clemens's notebooks show him tinkering with the manuscript all through the seventies, eighties, and nineties. Versions of the Stormfield characters did, however, see print during these decades as "Ned Blakely" in Roughing It and as "Hurricane Jones" in "Some Rambling Notes of an Idle Excursion."[35] In the last decade of his life, Clemens returned to the Stormfield manuscript to work at it in earnest; he wrestled with it almost to the day of his death. It has been long since recognized--on Clemens's own testimony--that the Stormfield character was based upon Clemens's friend Edward Wakeman. But, as Henry Nash Smith has observed, the Stormfield character, especially in his early forms, also derived from certain stereotypes of popular drama and fiction of the order of Douglas Jerrold's melodramatic warhorse, Black-Ey'd Susan.[36] Smith's point can be made more precise if we trace the process by which Wakeman, in his transformation into Stormfield, became fused with elements and impressions coming not from Jerrold but from Dickens, both directly and by way of a now-forgotten stage personality.

When, in 1903, Clemens was working on the Stormfield manuscript, he took time out to record in his notebook a recollection of:

> The time in St. Louis in '53, aged 17½, that I took the shy pretty girl from up country to Ben de Bar's theatre to see ~~Toodles~~ [lined out] and had on 6s when my number was 7s & slipped them off & couldn't get them on again, & walked home with them under my arm--white socks & it was raining.[37]

Clemens was apparently uncertain about his memory of this particular occasion, but considerable evidence indicates that he indeed saw the man called "Toodles," and saw him in one of his most famous roles.

In the winter of 1842 the actor-producer, W. E. Burton, had brought out a domestic melodrama entitled The Broken Heart at the Park Theatre in New York. The play failed with its original audiences and Burton soon retired it. Five years later, in conjunction with his outstanding success as Captain Cuttle in Brougham's dramatization of Dombey and Son, Burton revived The Broken Heart under a new title as The Toodles. Burton's comic portrayal of the uxoriously abused Timothy Toodles quickly became even more famous than his Cuttle, so famous, in fact, that Burton himself became known as "the immortal Toodles." Burton was able to capitalize on his successes for twelve years, presenting his two vehicles, Dombey and The Toodles, together, both in New York and on the road, up until the eve of the Civil War.[38]

This was the twin bill Clemens saw sometime during the winter of 1852-53. The Daily Democrat, the only St. Louis newspaper extant from this period, did not begin publication until 5 April 1853. By that date Ben de Bar had sold out in St. Louis and was managing a theatre in New Orleans, although he did return north for a brief engagement in late May. Clemens's memory for dates is unreliable; in 1907 he recalled having seen the Bateman Children in St. Louis in 1858, whereas they had appeared there in the summer of 1853; their American tour ended the next year. Burton was not in St. Louis after 5 April 1853, but he was well remembered. The Daily Democrat for 27 May 1853 calls him the greatest Falstaff St. Louis has ever seen and on 3 May 1854 dismisses a production of The Toodles as being insignificant without him.

There are other indications that the young Clemens saw Burton's impersonation of Cuttle. One is another 1903 notebook entry, which links the names Toodles and Cuttle without comment.[40] A third, this one written in 1885, says that Scott's Major Dalgetty might be funny as a stage character while Captain Cuttle is funny anywhere.[41] Other evidence demonstrates that tendency we all possess to invest an added power and concreteness in fictional characters we have seen portrayed by a skillful actor. Burton brought Cuttle to life for Clemens in this immediate, almost literal way.[42] Perhaps as a result *Dombey and Son*, the novel, made a stronger impression on him than almost any other of Dickens's works, and of *Dombey*'s numerous and varied characters, Captain Cuttle stood out most distinctly in his mind.

He read *Dombey* during his off hours as cub pilot on the Mississippi,[43] and when, in the winter of 1861, he set out prospecting in Humboldt County, Nevada, he tucked it into his kit along with a varied assortment of other "luxuries": "Viz: ten pounds of killikinick, two dogs, Watt's [sic] hymns, fourteen decks of cards, 'Dombey and Son,' a cribbage board, one small keg of lager beer and the '*Carminia Sacrae*' [sic]."[44] *Dombey and Son* here becomes, of course, part of the joke, which yokes Watts's hymns with an astonishing supply of cards and the Carmina Sacrae with a keg of beer, but, as a passage in a letter to his friend William Clagett, written two months later shows, Clemens was not just fabricating foolery when he said he took the book along. The passage demands quotation in full; it is an interesting example of the impression Dombey made on this man who said he had tried to read Dickens but could not:

> A lot of my old St. Louis chums will be out in the Spring--and when we get Billy Dixon and the other Keokuk boys here, Oh no, we won't stuff ballot boxes and go to Congress no nothing. By no means. "I hope I'm not a oyster though I may not wish to live in crowds." Now I don't mean to say that Nipper's remark is at all pertinent, you know, but I just happened to think of "them old Skettleses," and the quotation followed as a matter of course. And equally of course, the whole Dombey family came trooping after: Cap'en Ed'ard Cuttle, mariner, as Uncle Sal's [sic] successor, polishing the chrometers [sic] and making calculations concerning the ebb and flow of the human tide in the street; and watching the stars with a growing interest, as if he felt that he had fallen heir to a certain amount of stock in them; and that old fool of a nurse at Brighton, who thought the house so "gashly"; and "that innocent," Toots; and the fated Biler; and Florence my darling; and "rough old Joey B., Sir"; and "Wal'r, my lad," and the Cap'en's eccentric timepiece, and his sugar tongs and other little property which he "made over j'intly"; and looming grandly in the rear, comes ponderous Jack Bunsley! Oh d--n it, I wish I had the book.[45]

Clemens is undoubtedly showing off (he carefully makes Clagett aware he is writing without benefit of text), but there is a boisterous enthusiasm about the passage which is both attractive and revealing.

Captain Cuttle is the central figure in the paragraph; he was to become a central figure in Mark Twain's imagination. On his first trip at sea, March 1866, he saw Cuttle figured in the ship's crew and even his fellow passengers; the first dispatch to the Sacramento Union uses Cuttle as the fictitious name for a whaling captain whose company Mark Twain found noteworthy.[46] These notebook references and the borrowing of the name show that Cuttle was very much in Clemens's consciousness when he first encountered Wakeman's apparently forceful personality. Wakeman himself, even without the graces of literary association, was a larger-than-life figure, by 1866 "already a California folk hero":

> He had been under piracy charges in 1850 for stealing a paddlewheel steamer from under the sheriff's nose in New York and sailing her around the Horn. In San Francisco he had served as a vigilante and hanged at least two men. For such services the citizens honored him with a silver speaking trumpet, a breastpin cluster of nine diamonds, and a gold watch, which, along with a gold anchor and a gold ring, hung from his neck on a massy chain seven feet long. Bearded and big-bellied, he was tattooed from head to foot--with the Goddess of Liberty holding the Stars and Stripes, a clipper ship under full sail, Christ on the Cross, and an assortment of Masonic devices.[47]

His effect on Clemens should not surprise us; in Mark Twain's imagination Wakeman fused with Cuttle into the figure who was to become "Captain Stormfield."

Clemens first met Wakeman when, in the winter of 1866-67, he sailed to New York on Wakeman's ship, the _America_. He responded to the veteran sailor with immediate warmth and delight. R. B. Browne, who has studied the friendship, explains Clemens's feelings by pointing out that Wakeman represented for the ex-pilot an epitome of professional mastery and magisterial command.[48] Browne's explanation seems plausible enough, but it is, I think, possible to add to it and go beyond it. In addition to--or rather in conjunction with--his craftly authority, Wakeman embodied, in Clemens's imaginative response, a version of Ed'ard Cuttle even more dramatic and more concrete than Burton's.

In a fragment of autobiography dictated August 29, 1906, too long for quotation here but conveniently published by Bernard DeVoto in _Mark Twain in Eruption_, Clemens recorded a long memorial of Wakeman, repeating in his oral reminiscence several phrases he had used to describe Wakeman both in the prefacatory note to "Captain Stormfield's Visit to Heaven" and in the sketch "Some Rambling Notes of an Idle

Excursion."[49] In all three pieces, especially the 1906 dictation, the portrait is remarkably undetailed. The generalizations ("hearty and sympathetic and loyal and loving...all sailor from head to heel...never a day's schooling...a liberal talker and inexhaustibly interesting," and so forth) all characterize Cuttle as exactly as they do Wakeman. Only the profanity and the eccentric excursions in Biblical exegesis are inappropriate, although Dickens's adherence to Victorian decorum forbade his dalliance with the former, while the latter recalls Cuttle's garbled "secondhand" knowledge of all the things he optimistically expects us "to make a note on, when found."[50] Lowes shows how the "deep well" of the creative imagination shapes disparate experiences into something new and strange. "Captain Stormfield's Visit" may lack the imaginative richness and moral power of "The Ancient Mariner" and "Kubla Khan," yet it was created by a parallel process; Clemens's unconscious mind converting William Burton into Ed'ard Cuttle, Ed'ard Cuttle first into an anonymous whaler and then into Ned Wakeman, and Ned Wakeman into Eli (or Ben) Stormfield by way of Waxman, Blakely, and Hurricane Jones. Appropriately, the more Mark Twain came to know and delight in his own creation, Stormfield, the mellower and less sharply defined became his recollection of Wakeman. Nor is it surprising that when, in the last decade of his life, he began to tinker once more with a manuscript begun thirty-five years earlier, his memory of Toodles and Captain Cuttle pushed its way back into his consciousness.

III.

From his first published sketches to the very end of his life and career Clemens's readings in Dickens provided rich material for his imagination, either in the form of episodes to be directly imitated, burlesqued, or unwittingly plagiarized, or in the form of character types to be percolated in the deep well of the unconscious. Even these categories do not cover the whole extent to which Clemens felt the influence. That influence could not only mold a few incidents in a novel, but determine its entire structure as well, as it seems highly plausible that it does in Pudd'nhead Wilson.

To trace Dickens's influence on that work one has to review the well-known history of Clemens's "war" with English critics of America and American life.[51] It needs here to be picked up at that point in 1887 when Matthew Arnold alleged that U. S. Grant wrote "an English without charm and high breeding," and Clemens took up arms not only against Arnold, but the whole English nation as well. Clemens immediately made a desperate attempt to put his anger into essay form, but found, after a few pages, that expository prose was an inadequate vehicle for his emotions. The manuscript is addressed to Arnold, but the names Dickens and Trollope are pencilled in at the top of the first page, underscored; undoubtedly they were to face the barrage as well.[52] When the essay wouldn't go, Clemens turned to fiction as a means of venting his spleen, pouring into A Connecticut Yankee all the venom the essay could not contain.[53] The anti-English satire in Connecticut Yankee worked as the essay had not; yet Clemens was still not satisfied. A Connecticut Yankee had shown that the English were hardly models of perfection themselves, but Mark Twain could not, in that work, also answer their charges against America. Moreover, the Yankee itself was hardly unambiguous on the question of national superiorities. Hence the notebooks show Clemens still fretting over English critics well after the novel was in print.[54]

In chapter x of The American Claimant (1892) he defended the American press against Arnold's assertion that it could "efface and kill in a whole nation the discipline of respect," but the allegations of American Notes and Martin Chuzzlewit still stood. Once again Clemens tried the essay form, writing "Dickens" as his target over the top of the first page of his manuscript, and once again the attempt proved abortive.[55] Fiction had proved effective in exposing English short-comings; Mark Twain turned back to fiction to present the other side of the story, working into the pattern of Pudd'nhead Wilson three passages exhibiting the "real" America that would set Dickens and the record straight for once and for all.

In Martin Chuzzlewit Martin and Mark buy land in a speculator's settlement on the banks of the Mississippi called "The Valley of Eden," a settlement which is described to them as a flourishing city with fine homes, market places, cathedrals, factories, and great public buildings. However, when they arrive at the town, they find something far different: Eden turns out to be all swamp, decay, and corruption, "the grim domain of Giant Despair" (VI, xxiii, 457). Most of the action of Pudd'nhead Wilson also takes place in a small town on the banks of the Mississippi, but Dawson's Landing is Eden transformed by a magic wand--and white-wash: "a snug little collection of modest one- and two-story frame dwellings...almost concealed from sight by climbing tangles of rose-vines, honeysuckles, and morning-glories" (XVI, i, 1). The date of the action in Chuzzlewit is unclear, but Kathleen Tillotson sets it somewhere between 1833 and 1843.[56] The requirements of the plot demand that Pudd'nhead begin at least twenty-five years before the Civil War. Mark Twain begins it in 1830, thus making Dawson's Landing roughly contemporaneous with Eden. This, he seems to be saying, is what river towns of the thirties really looked like. Dickens frames his description in images of corruption and slime, of rawness and squalor; Mark Twain's is full of white-wash and roses, tranquility and well-being. The maxim prefixed to the chapter, "There is no character, howsoever good and kind, but it can be destroyed by ridicule," is intended to refer to Wilson himself, but it might also apply to Dickens's description of Mississippi river towns as well.[57]

When on their way to Eden Martin and Mark arrive in the town of Watertoast, they are no sooner installed in their hotel than they are set upon by the entire community. The secretary of the local Young Men's Association requests that Martin address that body on the subject either of the Tower of London, the Elements of Geology, or "(if more convenient) upon the writings of your talented and witty countryman, the honorable Mr. Miller." A dry goods clerk who describes himself as "young and ardent" asks for the addresses of "any members of Congress in England, who would undertake to pay [his] expenses to that country, and for six months after [his] arrival," while his landlord tells him he must hold a "le-vee" or be lynched. Martin reluctantly agrees and soon finds himself buried under an avalanche of importunate humanity (VI, xxii, 440-45). When in Pudd'nhead Wilson the Italian twins, Luigi and Angelo, arrive in Dawson's Landing, they are hardly settled at the Coopers's before a slave announces that "de house is plum' jam full of people, en dey's jes a-spi'lin to see de gen'lemen!" The twins graciously agree to receive them, and in the townspeople pour. The "le-vee" ends with the twins performing piano duets for the company, and everyone, Angelo and Luigi included, has a wonderful time (XVI, vi, 47-48).

Dickens's scene is one of nightmarish horror, recalling Swift's episode in which Gulliver is pulled, poked, climbed over, and excreted upon by a swarm of gibbering Yahoos. The parallel scene in Pudd'nhead makes the reader almost wish he had been there. Mark Twain admits that some of the guests were importunate but describes their motives as "friendly" and insists that "nobody did or said anything of a regrettable kind." Even the reiterated questions, which to Martin are a source of misery, are to the twins a sign of open-hearted admiration. The attempts of Mark Twain's democratic society to express its recognition of nobility are actually quite moving, and the description of the handshaking very different from Dickens's grotesque cataloge of disembodied palms: the twins, in other words, are treated with a respect they experience no trouble in returning. Opposed to the boorish demands that Martin lecture on the Tower, Geology, or Miller's Works is the grateful appreciation of the twin's volunteered piano playing. Once again Mark Twain seems to be saying this is what backwoods society was actually like, and once again the chapter's maxim is significant: "Let us endeavor so to live that when we come to die even the undertaker will be sorry."

Finally, while Martin and Mark are in Watertoast they are invited to attend a meeting of the "Watertoast Association of United Sympathizers," which Martin learns "sympathizes" with an Irishman involved in some contest with the English "not by any means because they loved Ireland much," but because "they didn't love England at all." At its rally the Association is read a letter to the Irishman praising him wildly for his "noble efforts in the cause of freedom." However, no sooner is it read than the mail train arrives with a document that brings the Association to a sudden and unexpected end: the Irishman turns out to be an "advocate...of Nigger emancipation," and the self-styled "Sons of Freedom" take on all the aspects of a lynch-mob (VI, xxi, 435-39). In chapter xi of Pudd'nhead the twins are invited as guests of honor to a rally of the local Pro-Rum party, "the paradise of the free and the perdition of the slave." When they arrive they are both given a glass of whiskey; Luigi downs his, but Angelo refuses to drink. He is a teetotaler. But instead of being lynched, he is made an honorary member of the "Sons of Liberty" anyway and is treated to a full chorus of "He's a jolly good fellow" (XVI, xi, 96-97). The facts that both scenes are set in contexts of freedom and slavery and that the Watertoast and Dawson's Landings organizations have almost identical sub-names would indicate that here as in the other two passages Mark Twain had Dickens in mind. Once again he is vindicating Mississippi valley society against the unjust attacks of a snobbish Englishman.

These three passages serve to demonstrate that Dickens resided in Mark Twain's consciousness during the composition of Pudd'nhead Wilson. That two of them, the descriptions of the twins' reception and of the "Sons of Liberty" meeting, seem forced into the novel's structure should not prevent us from recognizing that that structure, one of Mark Twain's more successful, probably came from Dickens. If the three passages are intended as a defense of the American scene, ironically, the novel as a whole is a frontal attack upon the American experience modelled upon Dickens's indictment of his own society in _Great Expectations_. Therefore, to analyze the structure of _Pudd'nhead Wilson_ it is first necessary to look in some detail at its prototype.

The problem of finding a suitable structure for his fictions perplexed Dickens throughout the first decade of his career. Somehow he had to find a structure which would tie episodic pictures of a wide range of English scenes and people into a unified plot which would permit and support a social and moral purpose while at the same time satisfying the demands for suspense, frequent climaxes, and dramatic twists imposed by serial publication. The solution which he eventually evolved constitutes, as all readers of Edmund Wilson know, a unique genre, the detective story which is also a social fable in which the solution of the mystery is the "moral" of the story and makes the significant comment on the society.[58]

The pattern first begins to emerge in Dombey and Son, with its emphasis on organic unity of structure, plot and meaning, and its embryonic "mystery" concerning Alice Marwood, and comes to full form in Bleak House, where the solution to the mystery of Esther Summerson's parentage, discovered through Bucket's detective work, carries with it the implied social "message" of the novel. Great Expectations follows the same pattern. Here the "mystery" to be solved is the source of Pip's money, and as in Bleak House the solution embodies the major social and moral meaning of the book. But while the "detective story" provides a general format for Great Expectations, the actual structure of the novel is based on the creation of a situation so obviously and powerfully ironic that it is able to exert both a motivating and a controlling force on the action. This primary situation, or controlling irony--call it what you will--is of course Pip's belief that his wealth comes from Miss Havisham when, in reality, he is indebted to the convict Magwitch. Once this grand irony is established (the process begins on the first page of the first chapter when Pip tells that his "first and most vivid broad impression of the identity of things" came while he was being held heels over head by Magwitch, that is, that his first view of the world was of a world turned upside down), it acts as a natural frame within which all the characters and action are bound and to which all the parts are subjugated. The result is a unity of form and content and an economy of structure unique in the Dickens canon.

Bound within the framework of the primary situation, paralleling and reinforcing it, are the two narrative strands of the Magwitch plot and the Havisham plot. The two are held together primarily by the fact that they constitute the elements of the irony of the primary situation and secondarily because of the meticulousness with which they are made to parallel each other. Both Magwitch and Miss Havisham are criminals, one literally, the other symbolically. Magwitch is an embodiment of that recurrent, almost obsessive, character-type in Dickens, the criminal who is driven to crime by the oppressive inhumanity of society. While Magwitch is a criminal because society will not let him be anything else, Miss Havisham's crime is self-willed. It is the greatest possible crime against humanity, the denial of life itself. Like Magwitch she is an exile, although her banishment is a self-imposed one. Both Magwitch and Miss Havisham have their great expectations. Miss Havisham adopts the child, Estella, both to be a daughter to her and to be the instrument of revenge against the perfidy of men of which she feels herself to be the irretrievable victim. The irony of her situation, which parallels the grand irony of the primary situation, is that she fails to realize that in training Estella to fulfill the latter function, she makes it impossible for her to satisfy the former. Magwitch's actions follow the same pattern. He too feels himself, with much more justification, to be a victim, and, like Miss Havisham, tries to redeem his own life by filling its void with another person, built by him along his own ideals. Just as Miss Havisham steels Estella against the love from which she has suffered, so Magwitch protects Pip against the material want that has caused his misery. Miss Havisham uses Estella for revenge against the whole male sex; Magwitch uses Pip to settle accounts against society.

Finally, just as Miss Havisham wants and needs Estella to be a daughter to her, Magwitch wants and needs Pip to be a son to him. Moreover, the irony in the two situations is the same. Miss Havisham discovers that Estella can never be a daughter to her; Magwitch in making

Pip a "gentleman" makes it impossible for himself ever to be accepted as a father. Both demonstrate the tragedy of "owning" another human being, of treating living people as things.[59]

Just as the two narrative strands of the novel parallel and complement each other in such a way that structure becomes an integral part of theme, so do the various characters parallel and complement each other with similar results. For example, Wopsle's dream of a theatrical career provides a broad burlesque of Pip's expectations, and Wemmick's relationship with his "Aged P" is a telling inversion of Pip's treatment of Jo. Such relationships between characters are also utilized in a more profoundly symbolic way in the theme of guilt that recent critics have seen to be as central to the novel as Pip's social expectations. In a study entitled "The Hero's Guilt: The Case of Great Expectations," Julian Moynahan, for example, shows how Pip's share in the common guilt of fallen man is portrayed in the novel by the carefully plotted relationship between Pip and the creature Orlick.[60] Orlick, Moynahan demonstrates, functions as the double and <u>alter ego</u> of Pip, a darkened and distorted mirror-image who, by acting out Pip's suppressed hostilities and aggression, serves to explain Pip's obsessive feelings of guilt and contamination by crime. After the confrontation between the two at the lime kiln Pip, in remorseful awareness of his guilt, returns to London to suffer a symbolic death and be born again, cleansed, into the arms of the innocent Jo.

Like Dickens, Mark Twain also faced repeated difficulty in finding an adequate structure for his works. His primary ambition was to find a way in which the story could be made to tell itself. "When a tale tells itself there is no trouble about it; there are no hesitancies, no delays, no cogitations, no attempts at invention; there is nothing to do but hold the pen and let the story talk through it and say, after its own fashion, what it desires to say."[61] To tell itself a story must have the right "plan": "I have hardly ever started a story, long or short, on the right plan--the right plan being the plan which will make it tell itself without any help..."[62] The kind of "plan" which Clemens thought most promising was precisely the kind Dickens employed in Great Expectations, the creation of a situation so obvious and yet so powerful in its irony that it could act as both the motivating and controlling force in the creation of plot, character, and meaning. Sensing that cases of mistaken identities most easily provided controlling ironies, Mark Twain filled his notebooks with capsule ironies which contained within themselves embryos of plot, character, and meaning needing only the midwifery of pen and ink to bring them into being. Some are merely obscene:

> The 2 Mary Murphys. They go to the hospital, the one to have a tooth pulled, the other to illustrate "Malformation of the vagina" in a lecture before the students. Each gets into the room which the other ought to have gotten into.[63]

Others were recorded and then apparently forgotten:

> A man sent to superintend a private madhouse takes charge of a sane household by mistake. It is in England, & when they call him the "keeper" they do so because they think he is the new gamekeeper (who, by mistake is now in charge of the maniacs in the other house & vastly perplexed, too).[64]

But a few were born and flourished:

> Edward VI & a little pauper exchange places by accident a day or so before Henry VIII's death. The prince wanders in rags & hardships & the pauper suffers the (to him) horrible miseries of princedom, up to the moment of crowning, in Westminster Abbey, when proof is brought & the mistake rectified.[65]

Whether used or neglected, all these notations consist of a grossly ironic situation, which by itself sketches out characterizations--whether indignant Mary Murphys or bewildered princes--establishes plot lines, and implies meanings. When in chapter iii of Pudd'nhead Roxy is able both to construct an entire narrative out of a vaguely remembered incident of babies being switched in their cradles and to flesh out that narrative with fully conceived characters (the giddy and careless socialite queen, the sly servant), self-contained plot incidents (the queen's social calls, the settling of the king's estate), and implied meanings (the story is an allegory of Free Grace), she precisely duplicates the creative process Dickens employed when he conceived Pip's mistaken belief concerning the origin of his wealth and Mark Twain followed when he built his novel from the ironic germ of the substitution of Chambers for Tom Driscoll.

A "plan" for a story, no matter how pregnant with the elements of fiction, was not, however, sufficient alone if the story was to tell itself. Mark Twain had to have a "form" as well: "There are some books that refuse to be written. ...It is not because the book is not there and worth being written--it is only because the right form for the story does not present itself. There is only one right form for a story and if you fail to find that form the story will not tell itself."[66] Pudd'nhead Wilson was a book that refused to be written. Mark Twain himself outlined his difficulties in his preface to "Those Extraordinary Twins" (XVI, 207-12); Mrs. Ann Wigger has since reconstructed the full history, and D. M. McKeithan has made a cursory study of the manuscript evidence.[67] What has not been noted is that the "form" which Mark Twain found to be the right one for Pudd'nhead is taken directly from Dickens. The novel is, like Bleak House and Great Expectations, a detective story that is also a social fable in which Wilson's solution to the mystery of Judge Driscoll's murder is both the "moral" of the story and its comment on society.

Mark Twain's interest in the detective story as genre may, as Albert Stone suggests, have grown out of his exposure to the vogue for Sherlock Holmes that grew to fad proportions in the early 1890's.[68] If so, only in a negative way: Clemens detested Holmes, finding him "pompous" and "sentimental," and considering his so-called "extraordinary" powers only cheap and ineffectual "ingenuities."[69] Certainly when Mark Twain came to try his own hand at the genre in Pudd'nhead his model was Dickens, not Doyle. His novel follows the structure of Great Expectations in all its details: the ironic "plan," Roxy's switching the babies paralleling Pip's mistake concerning his wealth; its "form," the detective story as social novel; its use of narrative ironies that explore and reinforce the implications of the primary situation; and its series of inter-related characters that includes the same sort of mirror-images that we saw in Orlick and Pip.

Like Pip's, "Tom Driscoll's" history is that of the rise and violent fall of great expectations. He is a "made" man, the creation of his slave mother, Roxana. Roxy operates in _Pudd'nhead_ in the same fashion that Magwitch and Miss Havisham operate in _Great Expectations_. Like them she creates Tom after the pattern of her own ideals so that he may both be freed from the forces that have made her own life miserable (in this case, slavery) and function as an instrument of revenge against those who have wronged and hurt her. As she tells the real Tom, "I hates yo' pappy; he ain't got no heart--for niggers he ain't, anyways. I hates him, en I could kill him!" (XVI, iii, 18-19). Her actions throughout the novel indicate that she delights in both the irony of the situation and the knowledge of the subversive blow she has struck against an oppressive society. However, like her prototypes Magwitch and Miss Havisham, she herself finally becomes the ironic victim of her own ironic act. In making "Tom" a white gentleman she makes it impossible that he provide her with the filial love she wants and needs. "The dupe of her own deceptions," "she saw her darling gradually cease from being her son, she saw that detail perish utterly; all that was left was master--master pure and simple, and it was not a gentle mastership either. She saw herself sink from the sublime height of motherhood to the sombre depths of unmodified slavery" (XVI, iv, 29, 33). As in Great Expectations the underlying problem is that of owning people, using them as things; the only difference is that in Pudd'nhead ownership is the literal fact of slavery. In Great Expectations Magwitch's ownership of Pip is paralleled by Miss Havisham's owning Estella; so in Pudd'nhead the relationship between Roxy and "Tom" is paralleled by that between "Chambers" and "Tom." In the drowning incident of chapter iv "Chambers" becomes "Tom Driscoll's nigger-pappy"; just as Pip owes his life to Magwitch and Magwitch his to Pip, so does "Tom" owe his to "Chambers," and "Chambers" his to "Tom." Moreover, both are the creation of Roxy, who in turn attempts to live through them.

Roxy's attempt to turn "Tom" into a gentleman, like Magwitch's effort with Pip, succeeds only in producing an unbearable little snob. Pip, when he returns to his village from London, lords it over his former peers only to have his pretentions destroyed by the burlesque antics of Trabb's boy. "Tom" returns to Dawson's Landing from Yale garbed in a fancy suit that the villagers interpret as a personal affront. His pretensions are burlesqued by a "deformed negro bell-ringer straddling along in his wake tricked out in a flamboyant curtain-calico exaggeration of his finery" (XVI, v, 38). It is tempting to say that the one incident is based upon the other, but in an unpublished autobiographical sketch Clemens maintains that his episode is modelled upon an actual occurrence in Hannibal in the early 1840's.[70] However, the inclusion of the incident in the novel may have been prompted by Mark Twain's preconscious awareness of the parallels between "Tom" and Pip; certainly its function for the reader is to make those parallels all the more insistent. Pip's snobbishness leads him to a cruel rejection of his uncle-father, Jo; similarly "Tom" cruelly mistreats Roxy when she returns to Dawson's Landing and is consistently sadistic in his rejection of "Chamber's" loyalty.

In Great Expectations the primary situation controls the relationships between characters, these relationships in turn paralleling and reinforcing the primary situation on several levels of subtlety and meaning. Mark Twain adopts the same pattern. Thus, for example, just as Wopsle's theatrical career burlesques Pip's expectations, so does the reception of Roxy in Judge Driscoll's kitchen burlesque that of the twins in Aunt Patsy's parlor.[71] And as Dickens uses

Orlick as a dark and distorted alter ego for Pip, so does Mark Twain create mirror-images in his two sets of twins, Luigi and Angelo, Tom and Chambers. Luigi has dark hair and a dusky complection, Angelo is a blond; Luigi likes his drink, Angelo abstains; Luigi is gregarious, Angelo dislikes crowds, and so forth. The pattern of double identity is even stronger in Tom and Chambers. "Tom" is a snob, "Chambers" humble; "Tom" a coward, "Chambers" brave; "Tom" traitorous, "Chambers" loyal; and each, by the pattern of the action is shown to be inherent in the other. Each, in fact, is the other.

Mark Twain's fascination with double identity predates Pudd'nhead by many years and has, like Dickens's interest in the same subject, been the focus of much scholarly discussion almost all of which has been conducted in biographical and psychological terms. Fruitful though this discussion has been, it is, I think, incomplete without some considerations of possible literary sources and influences. Curiously, Clemens's first sustained investigation of dual personality, "Personal Habits of the Siamese Twins," was written at the end of that period of his life in which he was most intensely a reader of Dickens. His first examination of his own psychological and moral manicheanism,

"Facts Concerning the Recent Carnival of Crime in Connecticut," bears many resemblances to Dickens's Christmas story "The Haunted Man," with which Clemens may have been familiar since his San Francisco days (possibly through Bret Harte's celebrated burlesque). While the sketch follows the Christmas story, Mark Twain's description of his conscience, "a shriveled, shabby dwarf" whose "every feature and every inch" is a "trifle out of shape" (XIX, 303), turns out to be in antics as well as appearance a reincarnation of Daniel Quilp. Given Clemens's biography and psychological structure, Dickens's own interest in what students of myth call "decomposed" characters and in dual, mirror-image personalities fell, like other interests of his, on fertile ground in Mark Twain's imagination.

In Great Expectations the mystery is solved when Pip discovers that his fortune comes from Magwitch; the solution to the mystery in Pudd'nhead Wilson is the discovery that "Tom" is Chambers and has murdered Judge Driscoll. In both the social meaning of the detective story plot consists of the relevation that the protagonist's guilt is that of the entire society. Pip discovers that to be a London gentleman is to be coated with Newgate dust, that to possess wealth and social standing corrupts because the fact of possession implies moral participation in the social guilt of a materialistic and dehumanized society, a social guilt described in religious metaphor and presented in the patterns of religious myth in such a fashion that it takes on the theological implications of original sin. "Tom Driscoll" asks "Why were niggers and whites made? What crime did the uncreated first nigger commit that the curse of birth was decreed for him?" (XVI, x, 76). In other words "Tom's" drop of Negro blood is his mark of Cain, his punishment for original sin. And since "Tom" is "Chambers," and "Chambers" "Tom," black is white and white, black. Both are at once cause _and_ effect of the social crime. Thus like Pip's, Tom's guilt is his participation in the social sins of a dehumanized society. Cats may sleep on the white-washed window-sills, but the essential fact remains: "Dawson's Landing was a slaveholding town" (XVI, i, 3). Mark Twain's novel ends with the reverberations of Roxy's tragic cry "De Lord have mercy on me, po' miserable sinner dat I is!" blending with its thematic complement, the narrator's brutally blunt statement of Tom's fate: "the creditors sold him down the river." But its title is _The Tragedy of Pudd'nhead Wilson_. Wilson's tragedy is that he has, after twenty years as an outcast (and hence an innocent), become, ironically, the hero of the day and a full-fledged member of a society that he himself has shown to be sick at its very roots. As Tom's expectations are crushed, Wilson's begin. If Dickens ever had come to Dawson's Landing, he would have found it not so different from Eden at all.

Notes to Chapter III

[1]Emerson: The Journals and Miscellaneous Notebooks of Ralph Waldo Emerson, Vol. 5, ed. Merton M. Sealts, Jr. (Cambridge, Mass., 1965), pp. 482-83; Whitman: Gay Wilson Allen, The Solitary Singer (New York, 1955), p. 96; Hawthorne: A. N. Kaul, "Introduction," Hawthorne: A Collection of Critical Essays (Englewood Cliffs, N.J., 1966), pp. 8-9.

[2]Cazamian, Le Roman Social en Angleterre, 1830-1850 (Paris, 1903).

[3]Quoted in Elizabeth Wallace, Mark Twain and the Happy Island (Chicago, 1913), p. 133.

[4]French, Mark Twain and the Gilded Age, p. 237.

[5]Bernard Poli, Mark Twain: Ecrivain de l'ouest, regionalisme et humour (Paris, 1965), p. 63.

[6]The Adventures of Thomas Jefferson Snodgrass, ed. Charles Honce (Chicago, 1928), p. 12.

[7]P. 40.

[8]"The Mint Defalcation," Mark Twain's San Francisco, ed. Bernard Taper (New York, 1963), p. 182.

[9]SLC to Jane Clemens (c1877-78), Moffett Collection, MTP.

[10]Miss Bellamy in Mark Twain: Literary Artist (Norman, 1950), p. 142; M. Poli in Ecrivain de l'ouest, p. 132. Franklin R. Rogers compares the Mark Twain-Mr. Brown relationship to that of Pickwick and Sam Weller (Mark Twain's Burlesque Patterns [Dallas, 1960], p. 34). Poli's is, I think, the more precise parallel.

[11]Repr. in Sketches of the Sixties, ed. John Howell (San Francisco, 1927), pp. 191-93. The sketch and its relationship to Dickens were called to my attention by Prof. Howard G. Baetzhold.

[12]Mr. Clemens and Mark Twain (New York, 1966), p. 49.

[13]See esp. I, xxii, 223-24, where the contrast between the Venice of the day and Venice by moonlight is made explicit.

[14]The point is discussed at length in Robert B. Salomon's Twain and the Image of History (New Haven, 1961).

[15]Humphry House, The Dickens World (Oxford, 1960), p. 35.

[16]I, xxii, 228-29. Mark Twain makes enough changes to cover his tracks; "devilish," for example, is transfered from the torturer to his instrument, but it is clear that he is using Dickens for information about something he himself never saw. Both men found much in their travels to feed their lusts for the morbid. The same kind of verbal parallels can be found, for example, in the descriptions of the Paris morgue in chapter xix of The Uncommercial Traveller and chapter xiv of Innocents Abroad.

[17]George H. Ford, Dickens and His Readers (Princeton, 1955), p. 112.

[18]Quoted in Bradford A. Booth, "Mark Twain's Friendship with Emeline Beach," AL, XIX (1947), 225.

[19]The similarity is noted by Johnson, Triumph and Tragedy, I. 561.

[20]Edward Wagenknecht, Mark Twain: The Man and His Work, 2nd. ed. (Norman, 1961), 33n; DeLancy Ferguson, Mark Twain: Man and Legend (Indianapolis and New York, 1943), pp. 168-69; Howard G. Baetzhold, "What Place was the Model for Eden: A Last Word on the 'Cairo Legend'," Dickensian, LV (1959), 169-75.

[21]Mark Twain's characterization of Washington Hawkins and Washington's great expectations in the Tennessee land are, of course, rooted in Samuel Clemens's experience with his own family's inheritance. But here as elsewhere in Mark Twain when autobiography is turned into literature, it is shaped by literary models. Similarly Clemens maintained, no doubt accurately, that the original for Sellers was his cousin, James Lampton. Nevertheless, when Lampton was transformed into a fictional character, he took on many of the characteristics of Wilkens Micawber.

[22] Poor Monkey: The Child in Literature (London, 1957), p. 71.

[23] Innocent Eye, pp. 16-17.

[24] Ecrivain de l'ouest, p. 56.

[25] The fragment is published in Eruption, p. 303ff.

[26] Burlesque Patterns, pp. 101-03.

[27] Blair, Mark Twain and Huck Finn, p. 61.

[28] In "Myth and Reality in The Adventures of Tom Sawyer," The Southern Review, n.s. IV (April, 1968), pp. 530-41.

[29] "Huck, Pip, and Plot," NCF, XX (1965), 286-90.

[30] "The French Revolution and Huckleberry Finn," 21-35.

[31] MP, LV, 25; Mark Twain and Huck Finn, pp. 128-29; The Art of Huckleberry Finn, ed. Walter Blair and Hamlin Hill (San Francisco, 1962), pp. 418-19.

[32] Publ. in Robert J. Burdette, His Message, ed. Clara Burdette (Pasadena, 1922), p. 136.

[33] For example in his speech at Holmes's seventieth birthday dinner. XXVIII, 77-79.

[34] "Have we got a pest in the house? Is there summ'at deadly sticking to my clothes? What's let loose upon us? ..."

[35] XIX, 261-63. Dixon Wecter's introduction to his edition of "Captain Stormfield's Visit," published as Report from Paradise (New York, 1952), traces the history of Stormfield and the Stormfield manuscript in careful detail.

[36] Development of a Writer, pp. 65-67.

[37] Notebook 36, TS MTP, p. 10.

[38] George C. D. Odell, Annals of the New York Stage, 15 vols. (New York, 1927-49), IV, 813, V, 436-37.

[39]"Autobiographical Dictation," 1 October 1907, MTP. For the Bateman Children see the Daily Democrat and the Oxford Companion to the Theatre.

[40]Notebook 36, TS MTP, p. 6.

[41]Notebook 19, TS MTP, p. 36.

[42]Clemens was not the only American to be so affected by Toodles's art. In recalling the theatre of his youth Henry James found his imagination "beset with the Captain Cuttle of Dombey and Son in the form of the big Burton." Autobiography, p. 65.

[43]Samuel Webster, ed. Mark Twain Businessman (Boston, 1946), p. 31.

[44]SLC to Jane Clemens, 30 January 1862. Publ. Fred W. Lorch, "Mark Twain's Trip to Humboldt in 1861," AL, X (1938), 345.

[45]28 February 1862, TS MTP.

[46]Notebook 5, TS MTP, 2 p. 9; Mark Twain's Letters from Hawaii, ed. A. Grove Day (New York, 1966), p. 4.

[47]Kaplan, p. 16.

[48]"Mark Twain and Captain Wakeman," AL, XXXIII (1961), 320.

[49]Pp. 244-45.

[50]Stormfield's appropriation, in all his guises, of Cuttle's stocks in trade--the comic use of nautical jargon and the humorous misadventures of a duck out of water--also point to his Dickensian ancestry. Both traits, were, however, nineteenth-century clichés, stemming partly from Smollett but primarily from "Nautical" melodrama, a subgenre that flourished from the Covent Garden production of England's Glory, or the British Tars at Spithead, in 1795 to the immensely popular With Flying Colours of 1899; and of which the most famous examples are Black Ey'd Susan and Gilbert's satiric HMS Pinafore. (Michael Booth, English Melodrama [London, 1965], pp. 99-117.) Dickens, of course, was intimately familiar with Jerrold's play, being a close

friend of the author and having acted in it in various amateur and semi-professional productions; Clemens knew Jerrold's sketches, Mrs. Caudle's Curtain Lectures (1846), but I know of no evidence that he knew Black Ey'd Susan. Dickens, in creating Cuttle, drew upon Jerrold and the stage tradition; Clemens knew the tradition primarily through Cuttle and Burton. His description of Wakeman's home as a kind of ship (Eruption, p. 246) evokes both Cuttle and Peggotty. Clemens says the house in Oakland was like a ship, but I am not entirely sure that he ever saw it.

[51] A full account is given by D. M. McKeithan "More About Mark Twain's War," MLN, LXIII (April, 1948), 221-28.

[52] MS DV 16, MTP.

[53] See his letter to Andrew Chatto, 16 July 1889, TS, MTP.

[54] Notebook 23, TS MTP, p. 54; 24, TS MTP, p. 39.

[55] MS Paine 200 (DV 75), MTP.

[56] Novels of the Eighteen-Forties (Oxford, 1961), pp. 112-14.

[57] Dawson's Landing is a far cry from the towns of The Gilded Age and "Bricksville" of Huckleberry Finn, which are much closer to the Eden pattern. Villages of both types undoubtedly existed in the 1830's, and one would hesitate to suggest that the one was meant to be a refutation of the other were it not for the shift in Mark Twain's manner and for the existence of the other refutations of Chuzzlewit in Pudd'nhead, which can be identified with much more certainty. Mark Twain's desire to "answer" Dickens does not interfere with his desire to speak the "truth" about American life. The white-wash in Dawson's Landing turns out to be exactly that, the well-being only the moral somnambulism symbolized by the sleeping cat.

[58] "Dickens: The Two Scrooges," Eight Essays (Garden City, 1954), pp. 38-39.

[59]Dorothy Van Ghent has shown how the motif of treating people as objects is reinforced in the imagery of *Great Expectations* in which objects take on human traits. *The English Novel: Form and Function* (New York, 1961), pp. 129-31. Some of the parallels between the Magwitch and Miss Havisham plot lines outlined above are also noted by Arnold Drew, "Structure in *Great Expectations*," *Dickensian*, LII (June, 1956), 123-27.

[60]*Essays in Criticism*, X (Jan., 1960), 60-79.

[61]*Eruption*, p. 243.

[62]Letter to Henry Van Dyke, quoted in Aspiz, "Mark Twain's Reading," p. 177.

[63]Notebook 23(II), TS MTP, p. 43.

[64]Notebook 12, TS MTP, p. 1.

[65]*Ibid*.

[66]*Eruption*, p. 199.

[67]Mrs. Wigger: "The Composition of Mark Twain's *Pudd'nhead Wilson* and 'Those Extraordinary Twins': Chronology and Development," *MP*, LV (1957), 93-102; McKeithan: *The Morgan Manuscript of Mark Twain's Pudd'nhead Wilson* (Upsala, 1961).

[68]*Innocent Eye*, p. 189.

[69]SLC to Joseph Twitchell, 8 September 1901, MTP.

[70]MS DV 47, TS MTP, pp. 4-5.

[71]The scene is also reminiscent of the use of the parties in the servants's hall to comment on the christening, wedding, and funeral parties upstairs in *Dombey and Son*.

CHAPTER IV

DICKENS IN AMERICA: THE "FINER ART"

Motto for the American Critic:

Ho! the old school! Thackeray!
  Dickens!
Throw them out to feed the chickens.
Ho! the new school! James and ---!
Lay the flattery on with trowels.
--Sir Edmund Gosse

I. "The New Battle of the Books"

Readers of the Atlantic Monthly for April, 1862, were, with only slight surprise, introduced to a new literary "school" and a new term for their critical vocabularies. "Realism," they were told, was no longer a quality but a movement. Thus, according to the anonymous author of the Atlantic's "Foreign Literature" department, the efforts of Balzac, Flaubert, and Champfleury were henceforth to be understood as a conscious attempt to "incarnate in letters Nature as it is, without adornings, without ideal additions," and as an equally conscious rejection of "the excess of fancy" and "the paradox and overdrawn scenes" of the old schoolers, Houssage and Capefigue.[1] The definition has undergone many permutations in a hundred years, but "Nature as it is, without adornings" remains as good a formulation as any, especially since the perspective of time and a survey of attempts to refine upon the phrasing leads to the conviction that "realism" existed in the minds of its exponents only as an inchoate notion not susceptible of analysis and definition. "Realism" was, nevertheless, by faith and will, a reality to Gilded Age America. Moreover, the belief in "realism" as a consistent, definable literary mode had a perceptible, if elusive, effect on the form of American fiction and on Dickens's role in influencing that fiction. One may be uneasy with the capital "R" and boggle at the assurance with which scholars like Edwin Cady speak of such things as "The Realism War"; nevertheless, the periodicals of the seventies and eighties are filled with polemics thinly disguised as critical theories. While remaining suspicious of its ultimate existence and demurring from the attempt to add one more definition to the mass, one can discuss the effects of at least the _belief_ in "realism" on Dickens's influence in America.

The most obvious was to surround Dickens's reputation with confusion and ambiguity, much of it intentional but most of it unconscious on the part of the critics who created it. The generation of American novelists and critics who were becoming converts to "realism" had grown up on Dickens, his formative influence being of a quantity and quality only vaguely conceivable to the twentieth century. Whoever our literary passion may be we simply do not read him aloud to our assembled families. We can easily imagine young Henry Adams sneaking off of a summer afternoon to "devour" Dickens in an empty farmhouse, but the picture of young Henry James sobbing under a table while a cousin read David Copperfield can be conjured up only by a certain effort of the historical imagination.[2] The impact of Dickens simply as a household institution on the generation whose childhood and adolescence spanned the period of his greatest productivity was so immediate and intimate a part of their development that they themselves found it impossible to convey any of its quality even to their own children. Howells, whose father had introduced him to Dickens in family readings, could not speak of the psychological force of such experiences without feeling he gave the effect of "wild extravagance."[3] As Dickens's own works show, the center of emotional life--and therefore the focus of many of its moral and spiritual values--in nineteenth-century

America as well as England, was the home. Family readings lent to Dickens an intricate set of extra-literary associations that were for the generation growing up at mid-century inseparable from his purely esthetic qualities and that continued to vibrate with internalized values even when the esthetic qualities were denied or dismissed.

Moreover, Dickens's presence as an elemental part of life extended far beyond the home. He was in the air everywhere. Again the phenomenon was so particular and intimate an experience that those who had lived it felt unable to express it. Howells, who in his maturity frequently chastised Dickens for failing to reflect life, became dizzy when he recalled how closely, in his youth, life had reflected Dickens:

> It would scarcely be possible to impart a conception of his hold upon the fancy, the feeling, the parlance, the religion, the political economy, of his contemporaries. People talked and lived as well as read Dickens. The accidents of experience were verified and valued by constant comparison with the incidents of his invention. Characters of one's acquaintance in the flesh were ascertained to be real characters or not according as they resembled his characters in print.[4]

Growing up in a society so steeped in Dickens could not help but leave a mark upon Howells and his contemporaries. On the one hand Dickens was bred into their very bones. The ease with which they slipped into Dickens allusions indicates how deeply and firmly his works were anchored in their conscious and preconscious minds. Even when they felt their intentions to be most antithetical to the Dickensian mode, Howells could not resist reminding Mark Twain "I'm a mother myself, Mr. Copperfield," and James could find it useful to speak of a character's life coming out in installments like Nicholas Nickleby.[5]

On the other hand so profound an experience naturally produced its reaction. Writers in the seventies and eighties frequently sound as if they are embarrassed by having shared in the Dickens cult of the preceding decades and curiously suspicious that they had been somehow taken in. Their pronouncements often reveal impulses more properly psychological than esthetic--as if the Dickens inebriation had produced a peculiarly perplexing hang-over. Hence the almost resentful tone of many of their more virulent attacks, and hence the tendency to deny they had ever shared in the enthusiasm. Howells can write of the Dickens mania of the sixties with all the detachment of an anthropologist recording an exotic South Sea rite, never giving the slightest impression that he himself had ever done such a thing as choose his London hotel solely on the recommendation of David Copperfield.[6] Although his motives were somewhat special, Mark Twain followed a familiar pattern in repeatedly denying he had ever even read Dickens. Walt Whitman was a typical man of the day. In his youth he had been an eager reader of Dickens, had written enthusiastic reviews for the New York Aurora and Brother Jonathan, had imitated him freely in a series of sketches in the New Orleans Crescent, and had, in 1842, been practically the only New York editor to defend--and even praise--American Notes.[7] Yet by 1889 Whitman's memory had dimmed considerably. To Horace Traubel he admitted that he had "liked" Dickens, but that was as far as he was willing to go: "...but a dweller-upon, an enthuser, a makemucher of, I never was--never."[8]

Similar ambiguities are apparent in the more purely esthetic considerations of Dickens after the Civil War. American critics could not deny Dickens a certain power; they had, almost to a man, felt it themselves at one time or another. Moreover, the more generous and calmer among them could recognize an at least embryonic community of interest. After all Dickens could be said to have considered himself a "realist" and had pioneered subject matters and techniques many American novelists itched to explore. But, bolstered by their penchant for dogmatism and polemicism, they found the differences between their intentions and Dickens's productions more noteworthy than the similarities. Rightly or wrongly the proponents of "realism" felt they were advocating something distinctively new and were, therefore, particularly susceptible to the rhetorical urge to attack the old. Dickens, especially because of his immense popularity among the uncritical vulgar, stood readiest at hand. Thus Gosse's quatrain, written only half in jest, can stand as a fairly accurate summation of much American periodical criticism of the 1870's and '80's.[9] The result was an either/or obfuscation of the most crippling sort: _either_ you liked Dickens _or_ you liked Howells. Only the meagerest handful of Americans could objectively view both.

We must also keep in mind that it was almost impossible for critics of the seventies and eighties to see Dickens at first hand and not flavored by the sour taste left by hordes of imitators. To the proponents of "realism" the fact of imitation was culpable in itself; bad imitation was intolerable, and automatically reflected upon the innocent writer who was imitated. In the fifty years after the citizens of Boston had rushed down to the docks to shout "Is Little Nell dead yet?" to incoming British mail packets, the infant mortality rate in American fiction had been staggering. Even the most competent novelists, writers like Rebecca Harding Davis, whose intentions were explicitly "realistic" and anti-Dickensian and who won the respect and gratitude of Howells and James themselves, were guilty of wholesale infanticide. Mrs. Davis's first novel, for example, is presented to the reader as "a dull plain bit of prose" whose purpose is "to dig into this commonplace, this vulgar American life, and see what is in it," rigorously eschewing "some word of pathos or fun from the old friends who have endenizened themselves in everybody's home," that is, the Pickwicks and Mantalinis, Micawbers and Paul Dombeys of Dickens.[10] Yet the minor character Lois Yare is killed off in the final chapter entirely gratuitously; her fatal disease is simply her resemblance to Little Nell. After a while American critics found it hard to weep.

If competent novelists were guilty of lapses, the incompetents were consistently atrocious. Dickens provided the hack with a convenient shorthand. Howells wrote that he lived in "an age of Dickens allusion when to refer to this or that passage of his fiction served the purpose and saved the trouble of thinking and feeling at first hand."[11] He had in mind such phenomena as Horatio Alger's _Adrift in New York_ (1889) whose heroine is characterized solely by being named Flo. The name is expected to recall to the reader Florence Dombey, and enable him to understand why Alger's Flo continues to love her rich uncle even when he unjustly drives her from his home. Alger's hero, an impudent street urchin who befriends the outcast Flo, masquerades--not surprisingly--under the name Dodger. The contempt that Howells and others felt for this kind of thing naturally distorted their attitudes towards its unwitting source and led them to make statements baffling to modern readers for whom Alger and his ilk are only camp.

That Dickens might have considered himself a "realist" but was rejected by the more militant "Realists" indicates the difficulties created by the term. If realism is the presentation of "Nature as it is," then the problem becomes "what is Nature?". As Dorothy Van Ghent observes, Pilgrim's Progress is for a Christian a much more "realistic" book than Moll Flanders.[12] Unfortunately only a few American critics of the late nineteenth century were capable of such detachment. Of these the most informative is George Pellew, a New York journalist born in England and educated at Harvard, whose essay "The New Battle of the Books," published in the Forum, July, 1888, deserves more attention than it has heretofore received.[13] Pellew begins by noting the silliness of much contemporary, either/or, controversial criticism; after all, he wisely observes, "the controversy has become mainly one of words, a question of 'right naming'" and of drawing rather fine distinctions because "every work of fiction ever written has been, to some extent at least, realistic. The question becomes at once a question of the degree of realism that is permissible."[14] The larger question, "what is real," Pellew answers only by implication, paraphrasing Howells's assertion that fiction must "keep close to the facts of life" (564). That "facts" here carries the "scientific" meaning of data collected by empirical observation is indicated by the nature of the "realistic" elements Pellew finds in such obvious "romances" as Greene's Arcadia and Mlle. de Scudery's Le Grand Cyrus, although he does evidence some awareness, however shaky, that definitions of reality are as mutuable as literary modes. "It could not, indeed, have been the unreality of the romances that charmed their readers, since they are known to have been regarded as literally true" (560).

The insight hazily recorded in that observation is developed as the burden of the essay. The history of fiction has been, to Pellew, not a series of transformations in kind, but a linear crescendo in degree as writers have become more and more sophisticated in their methods of achieving the goal present from the beginning, the presentation of the "facts of life," or "Nature as it is." Richardson and Mlle. de Scudery were, he argues, one in their intentions; they differ only in that, from the point of view of nineteenth-century definitions of reality, Richardson, for all his obvious failings, was more successful in fulfilling them. Hence Pellew is able to recognize that the much maligned "romanticists" of the early nineteenth century were actually "realists" whose great achievement was to free the novel from the "unrealistic" conventions of eighteenth-century classicism. They erred only in that the force of will required to effect the liberation was so great its momentum carried them to opposite extremes. They "sacrificed one truth to save another" (569). Since for them reality lay primarily in the passions, the display of passions became the end-all, be-all of fiction. The generation that followed at mid-century were also "realists" whose efforts were directed toward supplying the necessary corrective. They "deserted the extraordinary and remote," which the romanticists had cultivated as the best arena for passionate displays, and "found in the denizens of city slums and country villages, passion and pain, hatred and jealousy, pity and love as poignant and pathetic as in any Greek corsair or Heaven-gifted musician" (570). Thus Pellew can quote to praise and not condemn Dickens's statement from the "Preface" to Bleak House "I have purposely dwelt on the romantic side of familiar things" and can see Dickens not as an enemy but as a valuable ally.

But despite his importance in the development of "realism," Dickens is not, in Pellew's estimation, a perfect model for young novelists to follow. His plots are still, like those of the generation preceding him, "unusual" and his characters "eccentric"; the young novelist is prone to imitate the "extravagances" and ignore the "truth" that lies behind them. Moreover, Dickens's conception of what is real is incomplete; he is too close to the "romanticists," who "disregard society to magnify the individual" because in their concept of reality "the influence of heredity and the dependence of individual character upon the social environment were not understood." Hence a return to the Dickensian mode is "now impossible" (569-70).

Pellew's historical understanding has, of course, broken down, his all-too-human sense of his generation's uniqueness exaggerating his sense of its newness. He ignores the fact, now obvious enough, that he considers heredity and the social environment to be the primary reality at least in part _because_ he grew up on Dickens. In other words he is following the familiar rhetoric of playing down the old in order to emphasize the new. Yet the "newness" of Pellew's knowledge was bound to be impressive, for he has here expressed the basis upon which nineteenth-century "realism," if it existed at all, rested: the conviction, which Erich Auerbach has traced back to Stendhal and which Dickens embodied, that "serious realism...cannot represent man otherwise than as embedded in a total reality, political, social, and economic, which is concrete and constantly evolving."[15]

Pellew's sense of "newness" in the discovery of the evolving nature of the total social reality leads him into another typical distortion. From George Gaylord Clark in the forties to Howells at the turn of the century a given of American criticism of Dickens was praise of his "democracy" on the assumption that his celebration of common, lower-class life was, like "realism" itself, ultimately equalitarian. Pellew implies that he was not democratic enough, not by any failing of his own, but because of the shortcomings of his age. Dickens is no longer a model because since his death:

> Human sympathy has broadened, society has become more democratic; a scientific study of history has shown the interdependence of all men, the comparative unimportance of exceptional men, and the all-importance of those commonplace individuals who form the mass of a people, who stamp the character of a nation's government, its art, and its religion, who alone make possible the achievements of its great men. (570)

Pellew has confused Dickens with Carlyle and forgotten who it was that helped effect the broadening he praises.

Pellew may be representative of his day in his failure on these two counts to realize that what seemed a unique point of view was actually the result of the efforts of his predecessors, and hence to give credit where due. But he is also representative in expressing that point of view, whether or not he can recognize (or admit) that it grew at least in part out of an earlier absorption in Dickens. Ultimately these failures are less important than his achievement; for despite them, more than any other critic of his day he was able to see the relationship between Dickens and the belief in "realism" and to put the war of words between the "romanticists" and the "realists" in its proper perspective:

> "What matter whether you call it pantheism or pottheism, if the thing be true?" asked Carlyle. What matter whether a work is called romantic or realistic if the thing be true? It makes no matter. What does matter is, that any restrictions whatever should be imposed upon the writer who thinks he has

> something to say and tries to say it, who thinks he has observed something and tries to describe it. (572-73)

A lot of ink could have been saved then and could be saved now had other critics of the day been so shrewd.

II. William Dean Howells

Despite a clear-headedness, which transcended that of many better remembered men, Pellew is not the best known or most important American critic of the late nineteenth century. For quantity--if not always for quality--the mark must go to Howells. Unlike Mark Twain's, Howells's knowledge of Dickens is not difficult to document, nor are his critical commentaries oblique or hidden away in obscure corners. His bibliographers index almost thirty separate discussions of Dickens in his periodical essays, memoirs, and critical studies.[16] Studies of Howells's criticism abound; there is no need to add another here. However, to trace the attitudes toward Dickens expressed in that criticism can provide valuable insights into his mind's workings and is essential to any study of Dickens's influence on the American novel. One major hindrance to understanding late nineteenth-century American literature has been the tendency of some literary historians to treat the period as if it were an undifferentiated whole, single-mindedly devoted to the propagation of "realism" with a capital "R."[17] Even Howells himself is often discussed as if in all his sixty years as a critic he underwent no development and never changed his mind, his criticism from beginning to end expressing, as Donald Pizer describes the five years of it spliced together in Criticism and Fiction, "a coherent, pervasive, and unified system of ideas" that from 1855, when he first began contributing literary gossip columns to his father's newspapers, to his last reflections from Harper's "Easy Chair" in 1920 "serves as an intellectual base for [his] critical attitudes."[18] Therefore, at the risk of producing a dry recital of facts and dates, I treat the subject strictly chronologically.

One of the early entries in the first diary Howells kept as a youth records his father reading Dickens to the family. The readings took place in Columbus, where his father was legislative reporter for The Ohio State Journal during the winter of 1851-52. The work read was probably Bleak House, then completing its run of monthly numbers; three years later when Howells made his first attempt at an extended fiction the result turned out to be, in his own words, filled with "bald parodies" of Dickens's novel.[19]

The passages surrounding the description of the family readings in the autobiographical Years of My Youth all tend to make the young Howells younger than he actually was.[20] The implications are that the readings began long before the winter in Columbus, but whenever they began they were only the prelude to a "passion" for Dickens that lasted, unabated, for well over ten years.

The circumstances of the beginnings of that passion are worth noting. Howells first read Dickens at the age of eighteen while recovering from a nervous breakdown that left its marks on him for the rest of his life.[21] By his own account some of the novels remained, all his life, "associated with the gloom and misery of that time," so much so that he could not reread them without bringing back something of its "dreadful shadow."[22] But only later were they associated with gloom and misery; their effect at the time was precisely the one desired. Dickens became the "mighty magician" whose "potent charm" cast the "spell" that, momentarily at least, banished adolescent neurosis. Writing of his early response to Dickens forty years later, Howells is remarkably adept at recapturing the spirit of his youth, but the chapter on Dickens in My Literary Passions is nonetheless colored by the opinions of the mature memoirist.

The comments about Dickens's roughness, blindness, clumsiness and air of contrivance probably belong to 1895--as does the description of him as a "masterful artist." Otherwise the enthusiasm is that of 1856. The peculiar tone produced by the superimposed attitudes is revealing and characteristic; almost all Howells's later pronouncements on Dickens display a similar division between total acquiescence and total rejection, resulting in a somewhat forced, if not grudging, tone in statements both of censure and of praise. The self-conscious flatness of the following sentence is typical: "I think Macaulay a little antedated Dickens in my affections, but when I came to the novels of that masterful artist (as I must call him, with a thousand reservations as to the times when he is not a master and not an artist), I did not fail to fall under his spell" (88).

Howells's self-consciousness is most pronounced when he must acknowledge the source of his adolescent enthusiasm. Dickens was a passion because he fulfilled the purpose for which he was read; he drew the reader out of himself. The young Howells responded wholeheartedly to Dickens's narrative strength, emotional power, and imaginative genius; the mature man is embarrassed for the young self who still lurks within him. The result is a curious kind of palinode:

> All the while that he held me so fast by his potent charm I was aware that it was a very rough magic, now and again, but I could not assert my sense of this against him in matters of character and structure. To these I gave in helplessly; their very grotesqueness was proof of their divine origin, and I bowed to the crudest manifestations of his genius in these kinds as if they were revelations not to be doubted without sacrilege. But in certain small matters, as it were of ritual, I suffered myself to think, and I remember boldly speaking my mind about his style, which I thought bad. (93-94)

Like most palinodes, it is not entirely convincing. The mature Howells knows that Dickens ought to be bad, but he cannot completely deny, even by leaden ironies, Dickens's effectiveness and his own response, past and present, to it. The same divided attitude returns later in the chapter when he recounts having reread the American scenes of _Martin Chuzzlewit_. They are "surcharged" and "caricatured"; yet they "caught the look of our life...our self-satisfied, intolerant and hypocritical provinciality, and this was not altogether lost in his mocking horse-play" (101). The litotes ("not altogether") serves only to reveal, not disguise, the conflict between what ought to be in theory and what is in actuality.

On one point, however, the youthful and the mature Howells agree. Dickens's greatest value, the element that "endear[s] him to the heart, and will keep him dear to it long after many a cunninger artificer...has passed into forgetfulness," is the moral and social texture of his novels. The ideals marking the "whole tendency" of Dickens's fiction are "equality and fraternity" (97-98). The young Howells perceived them only intuitively; the mature man is articulate and insistent. The following passage, for example, begins by sounding like Mark Twain, but the ending is pure Howells:

> I cannot laugh any more at Pickwick or Sam Weller, or weep for little Nell or Paul Dombey; their jokes, their griefs, seemed to me to be turned on, and to have a mechanical action. But beneath all is still the strong drift of a genuine emotion, a sympathy, deep and sincere, with the poor, the lowly, the unfortunate. In all that vast range of fiction, there is nothing that tells for the strong, because they are strong, against the weak, nothing that tells for the haughty against the humble, nothing that tells for wealth against poverty. The effect of Dickens is purely democratic, and however contemptible he found our pseudo-equality, he was more truly democratic than any American who had yet written fiction.
>
> (99-100)

Dickens's democracy, expressed as sympathy and love for one's fellow man, was for Howells a constant source of his strength. Howells's greatest literary passion was, of course, Tolstoi. Yet however much he might be aware of the esthetic differences between the Englishman and the Russian, he, like Tolstoi himself, knew that they were one in their ethical spirit.

It is significant that even in his youthful (and by his own account uncritical) enthusiasm, Howells was aware that Dickens's moral ideals received their fullest meanings when placed in their social context, that Dickens's democracy was in essence an ethical response to nineteenth-century industrialism. In his letter from England, published in The Ohio State Journal, January 30, 1862, he describes a train ride from Liverpool to London that had taken him through a countryside filled with literary associations. The rural areas belonged to Tennyson; Dickens was everywhere:

> I could read Dickens in those lazy haunts, and under that spreading oak, where doubtless little Nell and her grandfather had stopped to rest; I could read him in the calm villages, and pretty little country towns. There also could I read him in the grimy glare, the lurid squalor, the black wretchedness of the manufacturing towns, through which the iron horse seemed to struggle more fiercely, as if the atmosphere were stifling him.

Howells may have criticized Dickens's style in the pastoral security of Jefferson, Ohio; in England he found it the only one possible for evoking the industrial Midlands. "I cannot," he informed his readers, "impart the desolation and repulsion with which the towns of the iron and coal district filled me. It seemed to me as if life must be nothing there but toil, and poverty, and hopeless contention with inexorable destinies and systems; as if there neither peace, nor health, nor virtue could abide; as if Atheism would be a proper and justifiable thing for an established religion there." London also turned out to be Dickens's London, the dirty, dismal city of Bleak House, Little Dorrit, and Our Mutual Friend. Riding through the Strand in an omnibus Howells "experienced more profoundly than at any other time, the sense of London's vastness, hurry, struggle, murky splendor, skulking wretchedness and systematic gloom...[even] Saint Paul's Cathedral refused to exhibit anything but a sullen shape of grey, and had no more outline than Mr. Mantelini's duchess, who is well known to have had no outline at all." I have quoted at length from this perhaps negligible bit of youthful journalism to anticipate the point that twenty-five years later when the mature Howells was to turn his eye to industrial America the style--and the ethos underlying it--was to return.

Like James's review in The Nation, Howells's review of Our Mutual Friend for The Round Table, December 2, 1865, is its author's only extended discussion of a specific Dickens novel.[23] Unlike James, Howells was not disappointed. Beginning by drawing the distinction between the "novel" and the "romance" that he inherited from Hawthorne and made central to his critical theories, Howells flatly asserts that Dickens "is not at all a novelist but altogether a romancer."[24] Throughout his life Howells wavered on the relative values of the two types; his position in 1865 was that they are separate, but equal: "We are far from thinking the novelist's art less than the romancer's; only we do not think it more." Once the distinction is made and the merits of its parts established, Howells is free to discuss the book in its terms, thus gaining a perception and understanding that James, who ignores the distinction, lacks. (Indeed, the two reviews are fascinating read together precisely because of this curious reversal of their authors' normal roles.[25])

The romance attempts "a picture of events and human characteristics in their subtler and more ideal relations," all its elements being controlled by this purpose and subordinate to it. Standards of judgment appropriate to the novel ("a portraiture of individuals and affairs") are irrelevant. Thus Howells dismisses the kind of criticisms of Dickens that James, and others, were beginning to bring to bear, especially on matters of characterization and plot. Since the romance aims at "images of universal truth and value," its characters must be judged by moral and psychological yardsticks rather than by the criteria of empirical verisimilitude. Dickens's people are "types" not "persons"; hence while they are "improbable," they cannot be censured as "exaggerations." Howells's explanation of this point is significant not only because it clarifies an important distinction but also because it reveals the extent of his esteem for Dickens. So long as the characters of Our Mutual Friend are not "moral impossibilities," they are not exaggerations, "except in the sense that Lear and Othello are exaggerations; and we are rather surprised that critics who have observed the Shakesperian universality of Mr. Dickens's feeling, have not been struck with the Shakesperian universality of his art." Plot in the romance, especially as written by Dickens, assumes a triply subservient role, for it exists only for the sake of the characters and like them cannot be judged by novelistic standards of probability and verisimilitude: "If the plot is one in which a fitting part falls to each character, we think it successful, no matter what gross improbabilities it may involve as a scheme of action; it has to preserve in the characters consistency and harmony, and nothing more." The plot of Our Mutual Friend may be criticized, but only in terms of this "secondary excellence"; its failing is simply that it does not, to Howells's mind, offer the characters sufficient "opportunity for consistent development." Otherwise its major lapses are its forays into subject matter, the Lammles sub-plot, for example, more properly suited to the novel than to the romance.

Howells's theorizing about the "novel" and the "romance" helps explain the almost single-minded attention paid by nineteenth-century critics to Dickens's people. He himself says almost nothing about those elements of Our Mutual Friend that fascinate the twentieth century, its over-all symbolic structure and its social meanings. The bulk of the review is devoted to cataloguing characters since in Howells's system it is they who embody all the book's artistic and moral values, whether "ideal," symbolic, or social. Social meanings particularly are seen only indirectly through social "types." But Howells, like Pellew, does not indicate any awareness of the type in Dickens as a product of the society. Or at least he does not feel it necessary to demonstrate any awareness. For example, in Our Mutual Friend Dickens attacks nineteenth-century society on grounds that were to become the obsession of Matthew Arnold and many other social critics. Its gloomy industrialism, its commercial spirit with its emphasis on "self-help" and social climbing, its puritanical narrowness, its spirit-stifling repressions and lack of humane values all together led to the appearance of men like Bradley Headstone, who is at once its product and its expression. Howells is able to see Headstone for what he is, but he does not go, as a twentiety-century critic would, from Headstone to the society that engendered him. His comment is as follows: "Bradley Headstone, as a study of murderous human nature, is not so good as other studies by the author; but he is excellent as showing how barren and stony the mere culture of the mind leaves the soul; especially when this culture is not wide and deep enough to make the mental principle distrust its own infallibility."

Despite the usefulness of his distinction between the "novel" and the "romance," Howells cannot always stick by it. One of his remarks about Alfred Lammle, for example, is based more on standards of novelistic restraint rather than on the simplified, pointing techniques of the romance. Lammle is "not successful...though the author has taken pains to mark his devilishness with white dints in the nose, so it may be recognized at all times." More revealing are his problems with the ending. It is hard to tell whether his dissatisfaction with Rokesmith's and Boffin's masquerade results from its novelistic improbability, the creakiness of its machinery, or its failure to exhibit character types as befits a Dickens romance.[26] His dismissal of the final chapters as "a Christmas pantomime, with a boisterous distribution of poetical justice" is even more troublesome, reflecting a difficulty that plagued Howells in his own fiction as well as his criticism of Dickens throughout his life. Since the "romance" describes an "ideal," created world whose only sanctions are abstract moral realities, poetic justice should be an acceptable, even necessary, part of the order of things. The point is a cliche of romantic criticism.[27] In his first flush of enthusiasm for Dickens, Howells had been deeply impressed by his moral idealism and had seen it as justified on that plane on which morals and esthetics meet:

> While I read him, I was in a world where right came out best, as I believe it will yet do in this world, and where merit was crowned with the success which I believe will yet attend it in our daily life, untrammeled by social convention or economic circumstance. In that world of his, in the ideal world, to which the real world must finally conform itself, I dwelt among the shows of things, but under a Providence that governed all things to a good end, and where neither wealth or birth could avail against virtue or right. Of course it was in a way all crude enough, and was already contradicted by experience in the small sphere of my own being; but nevertheless it was true with the truth which is at the bottom of things, and I was happy in it.[28]

Yet after classifying _Our Mutual Friend_ as a romance, Howells casts slurs on its ending. The problem lies in the competing claims of the "ideal" world of the romance in which right comes out best and of the novelistic "real" world of social convention and economic circumstance. The discrepancy between the two is too great to make separate but equal judgments viable. The contradictions of experience that Howells was beginning to feel in the fifties had become insistent in the sixties and were to become even more so. Howells's struggle both in his criticism and in his fiction, was to find some means of mediating between his awareness of the real and his faith in an optimistic ideal. That the difficulty should first assert itself in connection with Dickens is worth noticing.

Such weighty considerations were, however, laid aside when he dined with Dickens during the winter of 1867-68. Then an assistant editor of the _Atlantic_, Howells had become the protege of Longfellow and Fields, both personal friends of Dickens. At their homes he met the Master. Like Mark Twain at the New Year's Eve reading, he experienced some difficulty in reconciling his ideal with the genial reality eating mutton across the table. The conversation at the Fields's hardly bears the significance one might expect from such a noteworthy confrontation. "One of the principal topics of discussion at table would have interested you," he wrote his family; "How far all the manuscript that Dickens has produced would reach if strung out line after line. Fields guessed 100,000 miles, Dickens 1200, Mrs. Fields 1000. By actual calculation it would only reach 40 miles." The readings, which he attended at least twice, were, he wrote his sister, "the perfection of acting," and he delighted to find that "abstractly, my conceptions of his characters for the most part were exactly the same as the author's."[29]

Dining with him at Longfellow's, Howells had found Dickens "everything in manner that his books would make you wish him to be."[30] Four years later, reviewing Fields's _Yesterdays with Authors_, he praises Fields for capturing the "ardor of such a friendship as Dickens [whom he once more insists is a romancer and not a novelist 'in the sense of a writer of realistic fiction'] alone seems to have been capable of inspiring and feeling."[31] Forster's biography, therefore, came as a disheartening shock. Reviewing the three volumes as they appeared, Howells indicated an immediate animosity to Forster and a growing dislike of Dickens himself. The latter seemed a "high pressure egotist" and the former a "jealous and greedy intimate."[32]

His increased knowledge of the man quickly translated itself into commentary on the works, Forster's account of the death of Mary Hogarth prompting him to his first devaluation of Dickens's art: "...however deeply Dickens felt, he must often have thought that he felt more deeply than he did feel. This trait made him the more effective with the vast multitudes he enraptured to laughter or tears; but it won him, in prodigiously greater degree, an actor's success, and must forbid him a place with Goldsmith, and Thackeray, and Hawthorne, perhaps the only perfect artists English fiction has known."[33] Howells makes allowances for the effect of serialization on the form of Dickens's works and for the way in which the storm and stress of his personal life led him toward melodrama and burlesque in his fiction. But when Forster recounts that he did not like _The Scarlet Letter_, Howells's patience ends. "This failure," he writes, "to understand the subtle perfection of art so far above his is all the more sadly amusing when one thinks, in connection with it of the shapelessness of his own plots, the unnaturalness of his situations, the crudity of his treatment of characters similar to those he created. The wonder is that earlier readers [apparently including Howells himself] were ever so much moved by him."[34]

That Howells's dislike for Forster and for the portrait of Dickens his biography presented colored his reaction to the works for some little time cannot be doubted; he himself admits as much. Reviewing E. P. Whipple's edition in 1878, he praises the introductions, five of which he had earlier carried in the *Atlantic*, and acknowledges that after Forster's "vulgar and conceited biography" the works had fallen into disrepute. "But those years were years of great injustice, and they are already past; the most disheartened of his old friends can already find a revival of delight in his wonderful books, and we think it will be long before a future generation shall neglect them."[35] He came as close as he ever did to balancing his feelings toward the man and toward the works in his review of the "Mamie-Georgie" edition of the letters. The review of Forster's last volume had ended with the remark "we can always escape from his life to his works, when we want to like him."[36] The later essay eschews escape to face the issue head-on. It is worth quoting at some length, both for its psychological perceptiveness and for its revelations of Howells's opinions in 1880. The letters, he writes:

> do not throw fresh light upon a character which we have learned to know in its energetic and egotistic hardness, upon a philosophy extraordinarily limited; upon the life so separately lived in its personal

> and literary phases that the same man may be said to have carried on a double train of being. In most lives authorship reflects experience, or takes form and color from it; but Dickens's work after the wreck of his domestic happiness did not lose the charm that it had drawn from such happiness, and did not cease to portray it. His iron nerve was equal to this tremendous <u>tour de force</u>; but the sort of consciousness in which it resulted is matter for no analysis less subtle than George Eliot's or Hawthorne's, and is not pleasant to imagine. It seems to have resulted at least in an intensification of his disposition to centralize all things in himself.
>
> ...His literary conscience was a matter of slow growth; the critical reader of his earlier books must see how willing he is to sacrifice truth to effect, and stage effect at that; but he cannot help seeing, too, that while Dickens clings, to the last, to certain conventionalities and mannerisms of his own, he grows more and more dramatic, and more and more true to life.
>
> ...Perhaps no greater proof of his genius could be demanded than this fact, that his own work seems greater than he in any light which he or his friends have been able to throw upon him. Great genius he was and remains, and his genius will shine more and more as his personality becomes remote.[37]

1880 is a useful date from which to have such a statement. If in 1865 Howells had granted the "novel" and the "romance" separate but equal status, in the seventies his sympathies had swung perceptibly toward "romance."[38] In the eighties the swing was sharply in the other direction. Howells, now residing in the "Editor's Study" of <u>Harper's Magazine</u>, became the pugnacious champion of the "realistic" novel, finding his greatest joy in, as he put it, "banging the babes of Romance about."[39] In 1872 he had written that

Dickens must be approached "in his own spirit, and without reserves or critical drawbacks: you cannot give half your heart to him."[40] As chief advocate and defender of the "realistic" mode, he was forced to do just that. The result was an on-again-off-again criticism filled with the kinds of ambiguities and contradictions discussed in the first section of this chapter, with a few peculiar to Howells thrown in.

The shift in allegiance may have grown, at least in part, out of his increasing awareness of the moral dichotomy between the "real" world of experience and the "ideal" world of romance. In his celebrated essay on James, published in The Century, November, 1882, he reluctantly admits a loss of faith in teleological ideality. Even on the moral plane it no longer seems "real" and cannot, therefore, sanction the esthetic structures of the "romance" as a mode for contemporary fiction: "...perhaps the romance is an outworn form, and would not lend itself to the representation of even the ideality of modern life."[41]

This change in the nature of reality, both moral and experiential, required sweeping changes in the presentation of those realities in fiction. Among other things fiction must reflect a growing sophistication in technique. Howells notes that James has the ability to win the reader's favor for certain of his characters without the "insinuation" or "downright petting" always found in Dickens. The remark is followed by his best-known statement about Boz. "The art of fiction has," he maintains, "become a finer art in our day than it was with Dickens and Thackeray. We could not suffer the confidential attitude of the latter now, nor the mannerisms of the former any more than we could endure the prolixity of Richardson or the coarseness of Fielding. These great men are of the past--they and their methods and interests" (28).

These three matter of fact sentences created a literary sensation whose shock-waves eventually washed Howells into greater dogmatism and pugnaciousness, but his initial response to the tempest was bafflement.[42] Travelling in Switzerland at the time the article appeared, he was not aware that he had, as Cady puts it, "committed a public nuisance in the Poets' Corner." Gosse quickly wrote to appraise him of the situation and, upon receiving his reply, hastily inserted an elucidation in the "Literary Gossip" column of The Athenaeum. Howells, he explained, "is sure that he has been misprinted or misunderstood if he seems to be disrespectful of those great writers. 'I always thought myself,' he says, 'quite unapproached in my appreciation of the great qualities of Dickens and Thackeray, and I can hardly believe that I have 'arraigned' them. I suspect that no Englishman could rate them higher than I do.'"[43] The answer is both accurate and highly disingenuous. His appreciation of Dickens's "great qualities" was unapproached, but he had also "arraigned" him. One of the primary tenets of the later essays collected in Criticism and Fiction is that the critic must serve a pseudo-scientific role; he may analyse and describe, but he must not judge.[44] Howells seems never to have realized the impossibility, in esthetic matters, of doing the one without at least implying the other. His letter suggests that he himself considered the sentences to be a frank description. His readers, with considerable justification, took them for a damning judgment.

For a little over six years Howells occupied the "Editor's Study" department of Harper's, utilizing to the utmost his publisher's invitation to write a "free and flexible" column devoted to "an analysis of literary traits and tendencies."[45] From the second page of the first column to the last page of the closing one Howells used the department to crusade for his new cause, the "realistic" novel.[46] In 1891 he reviewed five years of the "Study" and reprinted passages culled from some twenty odd columns under the omnibus title Criticism and Fiction. Most modern students of Howells have dismissed this "hastily contrived product of the scissors and the pastepot" as invalidated either by its method of composition or by its stylistic and intellectual inferiority to the original essays.[47] Their case is excellent; nevertheless, Criticism and Fiction is the source from which Howells's critical theories were best known in his day and are known now. As such it cannot be ignored. It is also one of the most confused and contradictory books in all American literature. However, some of its chaos can be clarified (not removed) if two important facts are borne in mind. First, its intentions are polemical and programmatic. It is meant as a guide to young critics and novelists and not as a studied work of retrospective criticism. Second, its major confusions result from Howells's failure to fuse, effectively, two seemingly mutually exclusive strands of thought. On the one hand much of the book is devoted to a historical relativism similar to that which distinguishes Pellew's "New Battle of the Books."[48] On the other, an equally large portion dogmatically asserts the existence of absolute and immututable, eternal verities. Both facts bear directly on the book's several discussions of Dickens.

Howells's polemical and programmatic aims lead him continually to emphasize what, from a "realistic" point of view, is bad in Dickens to the exclusion of what is good, Howells being in this regard more concerned with what the young novelist should avoid than with what he should seek. In a sense the vagueness of "realism" as a definable entity makes this negative approach inevitable. Moreover, one of Howells's major contentions is that imitation, of any sort and of any author, is to be rigorously avoided. The novelist, as scientific empiricist, must see life as it is and not as it has been depicted in books, particularly books which, like Dickens's, deal in "types" and "idealities."[49] Because of his immense popularity Dickens above all others stood in the way of a direct approach to experience; as Howells explained ten years later, young authors frequently felt that "it was not permitted them, on pain of public rejection, to write anything but Dickens."[50] One aim of _Criticism and Fiction_ is to show them--and the public--why they should not. His strategy is to ignore his earlier defense of Dickens as a romancer and to criticize him as if he were, in Howells's sense of the terms, a "realistic" novelist whose "effectism" and "exaggerations," once defended as legitimate, are now anathema.[51] Most to be avoided is the kind of imitation that captures the manner and not the matter or, worse yet, that cynically copies the manner without accepting the ontology it was originally created to express. If one is to write like a romantic, one must at least believe in romanticism.[52]

If Dickens is to be eschewed because of his failures as "realistic" novelist, he is also to be avoided simply because he is an Englishman. From the 1840's on a great cliche of American criticism had been the paradoxical notion that the way to produce the Great American Novel was by imitating Dickens. Howells attacks the theory head-on; American fiction has been impeded in its development most of all by its subservience to English models, particularly Dickens. Howells's pronounced nationalism is itself filled with contradictions, not the least of which is his implication that the novel will become more American by substituting continental for insular influences. But it is, nevertheless, worthy of attention. He approaches the subject from two directions, both of them designed to prove that "realism" is the distinctive American mode. On the one hand the familiar meal is once more in the firkin as Howells hauls out Emerson's injunction to "sit at the feet of the familiar and the low" and transforms it into a plea for "realistic" fiction. Those who still prefer English "romanticism" are the victims of an unamerican snobbishness--or simply senile.[53] On the other hand, Howells takes Matthew Arnold's charge that there is no "distinction" in America and turns it inside out so that it becomes a "source of inspiration" to American novelists. If America exhibits no "distinction" then its fiction should record and celebrate its "commonness."[54]

Both approaches lead to the same destination. "Realism" is the most appropriate American mode because it is the most democratic. English models are to be shunned not simply because the English novel has, to Howells's mind, stultified itself in atavistic "romanticism," but primarily because American democracy has given a unique quality to American life, and even language, that cannot be captured by English techniques.[55] Howells's exposition is again filled with paradox and contradictions. For one thing he seems unaware that his defense of the democratic basis of "realism" is itself founded upon assumptions inherited from the "romantic" primitivism of Wordsworth. A glance at his language will show that epistemologically there is no difference between Howells's call for a fiction "robust enough to front the every-day world and catch the charm of its work-worn, care-worn, brave, kindly face" and Dickens's assertion that he purposely dwells on "the romantic side of familiar things." Moreover, when his nationalism slips over into chauvinism, he forgets that he himself has repeatedly claimed that Dickens's greatness lies precisely in his democracy, a democracy stronger and more subtle than any ever expressed in an American novel.

One of Howells's more interesting assertions is that American fiction differs radically from English because of a fundamental difference between the two cultures:

> In most American novels, vivid and graphic as the best of them are, the people are segregated if not sequestered, and the scene is sparsely populated. The effect may be in instinctive response to the vacancy of our social life, and I shall not make haste to blame it. ...we excell in small pieces with three of four figures, or in studies of rustic communities where there is propinquity if not society.[56]

Howells here anticipates a major theme of twentiety-century criticism, the notion, best expressed by Lionel Trilling, that a rich sense of social texture, the given of English fiction, is denied American authors.[57] But unlike Trilling and others who follow him, Howells does not see that this lack has caused American fiction to swerve from the historical intention of the "novel," which is "the investigation of the problem of reality beginning in the social field," into a realm of "romance" whose reality is "only tangential to society."[58] The problem is complex. Granting Howells's use of the terms, Dickens is more properly a "romancer" than a "novelist." Yet his "romances" are thoroughly grounded in the social texture of nineteenth-century England and are devoted to the study of social "realities." Howells's review of _Our Mutual Friend_ demonstrates his awareness of the fundamental tendency of "romances" to subordinate all elements--plot, characterizations, symbolism, and so forth--to their themes, that is, to make empirical, primarily "social" reality subservient to abstract moral concerns. The paradox is that Dickens's themes are primarily social. Previously only one major American novel, _Uncle Tom's Cabin_, had attempted the fusion, on Dickensian lines, of romance technique with novelistic material with any degree of success. In works like _Annie Kilburn_, _The Quality of Mercy_, and _The Son of Royal Langbrith_ Howells himself was to be drawn, perhaps unwittingly, into the same effort.

Dual beliefs in eternal verities and in historical relativism need not be contradictory if one assumes an absolute truth toward the depiction of what fiction has historically worked, with relative success, as a teleological goal. But in _Criticism and Fiction_ Howells never clearly indicates that this is how he sees the two; the result is confusion and contradiction. His absolutism is typical of his age. Walter Houghton has shown that the nineteenth century was committed to the concept of absolute law partly as an inheritance from the theological concept of natural law and partly as the result of post-Baconian science.[59] The commitment in turn created the kind of dogmatic assurance, often slipping into arrogance, that marks much of _Criticism and Fiction_. Truth (both God's and science's) is "real" and absolute; the novelist who does not embody it in his fiction is not simply inartistic but immoral as well. Dickens, when he abandons allegiance to absolute truth, becomes as guilty a sinner as H. Rider Haggard.[60] But Howells is also a child of his age in his historicism, and if he can talk on one page of truth as absolute, he can, on the next, speak of it as highly relative. At times Dickens is bad because he distorts Truth, at others he is great because he presents the truth _as he saw it_.[61] Howells's contradictions do not end here, for if he speaks at times of truth "as it was" in Dickens's day, at others he turns his relativism around to talk of the historical impossibility of Dickens's ever seeing truth, of any sort, at all. In this line of argument Dickens, however valid his intentions, is the hapless victim of the "false" romanticism that caused the devolution of the English novel from the "truthful" realism of Jane Austen to its contemporary state of artistic and moral debasement.[62]

Howells's continual juggling of intellectual positions seems to reflect a dual motive of whose nature he is only partly conscious. He is unable and unwilling to deny Dickens's essential greatness, but is capable of using whatever argument comes to hand to insist that the novel must outgrow him. If he ever manages to bring absolutism and relativism into any kind of balance it is in the final chapters when he returns to the one theme consistent in all his criticism of Dickens. The context is holiday literature, and in one paragraph Dickens is transformed from an "erring" to a great "humanizing" force. Howells is quick to point out that the literary principles of Dickens's Christmas stories are, from a "realistic" point of view, atrocious and must be abandoned by all who write fiction. Yet the tales themselves are not beyond redemption. They at least observe a surface reality; their characters wear real clothes and often speak "the language of life." Artistic failures, however, vanish if these fictions are considered not as "novels," or even "romances," but as "parables." Moreover their shortcomings can be explained away if they are viewed in their historical context. The generation of readers whose imaginations had been fed on the "gross unrealities" of Bulwer and Scott readily responded to the "fantastic appeals" of Dickens. These qualifications set aside, a solid core of value remains in Dickens's democracy. "His ethical intentions told for manhood and fraternity and tolerance," and "It was well once a year if not oftener, to remind men by parable of the old, simple truths; to teach them that forgiveness, and charity, and the endeavor for life better and purer than each has lived, are the principles upon which alone the world holds together and gets forward."[63] It is this "ethical intention" that must continue to rule the writing of fiction. Once more Howells insists that fiction is now a "finer art than it has ever been hitherto," but now equally insists that its refinement is sounding brass and tinkling cymbal if it has not the charity that characterizes all that Dickens ever wrote. Indeed, the sole function of empirical "realism" is to better express moral "idealism." Truth in fiction is the presentation of life as experientially seen in order to convey the moral truth that "the divine can never wholly die out of the human." Truth is beauty and art, and "Art, indeed, is beginning to find out that if it does not make friends with Need it must perish."[64] Criticism and Fiction thus ends with a final impression of deep sympathy and communion with Dickens's aims, if not with his techniques. He becomes the hapless though well intentioned victim of his day, his faults explained away by historical relativism, his virtues placed among the eternal verities.

Howells's commentary on Dickens after 1891 presents little that is new beyond a general softening of tone from the feistiness of Criticism and Fiction. Writing on the topic "My Favorite Novelist and his Best Book" in Munsey's Magazine for April, 1897, he goes over much of the ground covered in My Literary Passions, adding to the discussion a third category of fiction, the "romantic novel," whose existence he had earlier implied but nowhere so clearly defined.[65] A hybrid offspring of the novel and the romance, the romantic novel lacks their purity and hence their validity. Curiously, Howells does not use his new term to clarify his attitude toward Dickens, who appears in the essay strictly as novelist and "great master." He acknowledges having recently reread Bleak House, David Copperfield, and Our Mutual Friend with pleasure, but not "with the old, or young ardor." The rereading had, however, caused one major shift in opinion: Dickens is now a "greater artist" than Thackeray. He erred, as did all the "romantic" school, in believing that character grew out of plot rather than plot from character; but despite "all that faking, that useless and false business of creating a plot and multiplying incidents," he somehow got his novels to stand upon their own legs and walk off, whereas Thackeray "is always holding his figures up from behind."

William Gibson has called Howells's lecture "Novel-Writing and Novel-Reading" (1899) the "fullest, most detailed, most penetrating analysis of the novelist's craft" he ever wrote.[66] Actually Howells's position here is fundamentally the same as that of Criticism and Fiction; the differences lie primarily in the shorter, more concentrated form, which allows for a more single-minded, less contradictory statement, and in the shift from the elephantine ironies of the earlier work to a gentle, subtle humor, the lecture exemplifying more than any other work I know that quiet sense of fun that endeared the man to all who knew him. Founding his remarks on the familiar "realistic" triad, Howells points out that the test for the beauty of any novel is its "Truth," experientially defined. Substituting the extremely awkward "romanticistic" for his previous "romantic novel," he maintains that Trollope, George Eliot, and Jane Austen are "truthful" novelists who work with an "ideal of truth," while Dickens, Thackeray and, because he follows Dickens's lead, Dostoievsky are "untruthful" in working with an "ideal of effect." Nevertheless Dickens is still a "great man," and Bleak House a "masterpiece" of the highest form of fiction.

The three chapters on Dickens in Heroines of Fiction (1901) resort to that kind of perfunctory nineteenth-century journalistic criticism that substitutes quotation for commentary. Howells's avuncular sense of decency causes him to dignify by marriage the relationship between Nancy and Sikes, but otherwise the chapters contain little of interest. The occasionally contemptuous tone of his attacks on Dickens's "effectism," melodrama, and "romanticistic" distortions comes as something of a shock after the mellowness of My Literary Passions, but Howells is also quick to observe that Dickens was of his day and bound to his own intentions. His heroines are brought to life "by dint of appealing to our consciences or our sensibilities, and he achieved a moral rather than an artistic triumph in heroines who are for our good rather than our pleasure."[67]

Sympathetic judiciousness returns the following year when he is faced with a Dickens "revival," a phenomenon that in no way surprises him. "In fact, it seems always to be not this or that author who revives, but the spirit of this or that author's age"; he has not been blind to the turn of the century rebirth of the "romance." Moreover, in Dickens's case, as in Shakespeare's, the renewed popular interest reflects more properly a "survival" than "revival." After recounting the Dickens mania of his youth, he ends the essay by returning to the one consistent <u>leit-motif</u> of all his criticism of Dickens and makes a grand peroration that was his summary statement on the "great master." As such, it is worthy of quotation at length:

> But Dickens could never have had his tremendous hold (which we are instructed from time to time he has never really lost) upon the English-reading world of his day if he had been merely a great literary mannerist, a prodigious convention as to how life was to be looked at in fiction, a sentimentalist of reach as wide as the whole surface of human nature. He was something far greater and better than anything of either kind. ...
>
> He was true to [his characters]; but, better than this, he was true to certain needs and hopes of human nature. He showed such tenderness for the poor, the common, the hapless and friendless, that one could not read his books without feeling one's heart warm to the author, and without imbibing a belief in his goodness, which survived distinct proofs of his peccability. Long after he appeared not quite the unselfish and generous fount from which such kindness as his ought logically to have flowed, he kept the respect, or the show of respect,

> which he had always cherished for those needs and hopes of human nature. His work made always for equality, for fraternity, and if he sentimentalized the world, he also in equal measure democratized it. ...
>
> We do not suppose he can ever return in all that influence, but in some measure of it the reading world might well rejoice in his return. His black was very black, his white was very white, and all his colors were primitive, but he painted an image of life which was not wholly untrue, though it was so largely unlike. In parables, often grotesque and extravagant, he taught a morality sane and simple and pure. ...He told a sort of fairy story, with people ostensibly of the actual world for the elves, the gnomes, the kobolds, and all the other impossible little folk, good and bad; but the principles, always somewhat excessive, which ruled them and prevailed at last were such as our personal acquaintance, and perhaps our veritable selves, would be the better for obeying. So if there is to be a Dickens revival, if the king is to come into his own again, the Easy Chair will not be the last to get itself wheeled to some convenient point, well out of the press, but favorable for seeing and welcoming the sovereign romancer back.[68]

If we are to look for a Dickens influence in Howells's fiction, it will probably be found in that community of spirit in which both made Art friends with Need.

Notes to Chapter IV

[1]IX, 525-26.

[2]Adams: The Education of Henry Adams (New York, 1931), p. 39; James: Autobiography, pp. 68-69.

[3]Readings: The Years of My Youth (New York, 1916), p. 72; "extravagance": "The Editor's Easy Chair," Harper's Monthly, CV (July, 1902), 312.

[4]"Editor's Easy Chair," July, 1902, 311.

[5]Howells: Mark Twain-Howells Letters, I, 224; James: The Europeans, ch. v; The Bodley Head Henry James, Vol. I (London, 1967), p. 83.

[6]Edwin H. Cady, The Road to Realism (Syracuse, 1956), p. 94.

[7]In the Evening Tatler, August 11, 1842. I wish to thank Mr. Edwin K. Tolan of the Schaffer Library, Union College, for making this editorial available to me. See also Gay Wilson Allen, The Solitary Singer (New York, 1955), pp. 53, 55, and 96.

[8]With Walt Whitman in Camden, vol. V, ed. Gertrude Traubel (Carbondale, 1964), p. 395.

[9]The lines were included in a letter to Howells following the teapot tempest brewed by the celebrated essay on James in The Century and are printed in Leonard Lutwack, "William Dean Howells and 'The Editor's Study,'" AL, XXIV (1952), 197.

[10]Margaret Howth: A Story of Today (Boston, 1862), ch. I, p. 6.

[11]"Editor's Easy Chair," July, 1902, 311.

[12]The English Novel, p. 34.

[13]See Edwin Cady, The Realist at War (Syracuse, 1958), pp. 39-40; Donald Pizer, Realism and Naturalism in Nineteenth Century American Literature (Carbondale, 1966), pp. 74-75. The essay itself is reprinted in a casebook, Realism and Romanticism in Fiction, ed. Eugene Current-Garcia and Walton R. Patrick (Chicago, 1962), pp. 120-28.

[14]V, 565.

[15]Mimesis (Garden City, 1957), p. 408. Auerbach, more at home with continental literature than with English, recognizes "the strong social feeling and suggestive density of...milieux" in Dickens but, curiously, finds "almost no trace of the fluidity of the political and historical background" (434). Few English or American scholars would agree. Indeed one mainstream of Dickens scholarship has devoted itself exclusively to following Humphry House's efforts in documenting the novels's groundings in contemporary historical & political change.

[16]William M. Gibson and George Arms, A Bibliography of William Dean Howells (New York, 1948).

[17]The tendency vitiates what, by its title, should be a very useful study, Helen McMahon's Criticism of Fiction: A Study of Trends in the Atlantic Monthly, 1857-1898 (New York, 1952).

[18]Realism and Naturalism, p. 38. Even such a detailed study as Everett Carter's Howells and the Age of Realism, 2nd. ed. (Hampden, Conn., 1966), often succumbs to the temptation to treat his criticism as a contemporaneous whole.

[19]My Literary Passions (New York, 1895), p. 86.

[20]See Cady, Road to Realism, p. 39 and note.

[21]Cady discusses the episode in detail both in "The Neuroticism of William Dean Howells," PMLA, LXI (March, 1946), 229-38; and in Road to Realism, pp. 54-60.

[22]My Literary Passions, pp. 92-93.

[23]N.S. XIII, 200-01.

[24]Carter is correct in saying Howells first spoke "clearly" of the distinction with reference to Dickens, but he cites the wrong essay. Howells and the Age of Realism, p. 47.

[25]Reviewing James's Hawthorne fifteen years later Howells criticizes James's use of "novel" and "romance" as if they were interchangeable. Atlantic Monthly, XLV (Feb., 1880), 282-85.

[26]Years later he was to dismiss it as cheap sensationalism. Criticism and Fiction (New York, 1891), p. 69.

[27]DeQuincey, for example, makes it a fundamental of his celebrated distinction between "Literature of Knowledge" and "Literature of Power." "What is meant, for instance, by poetic justice?--It does not mean a justice that differs by its object from the ordinary justice of human jurisprudence; for then it must be confessedly a very bad kind of justice; but it means a justice that differs from common forensic justice by the degree in which it attains its object, a justice that is more omnipotent over its own ends, as dealing--not with the refractory elements of earthly life--but with the elements of its own creation, and with materials flexible to its own purest preconceptions." Works (Edinburgh, 1882), VIII, p. 7.

[28]My Literary Passions, p. 98.

[29]Mildred Howells, Life in Letters of William Dean Howells, 2 vols. (Garden City, 1928), I, 123-27.

[30]Life in Letters, I, 122.

[31]Atlantic Monthly, XXIX (April, 1872), 498-99.

[32]Atlantic Monthly, XXXI (Feb., 1873), 239.

[33]Atlantic Monthly, XXIX (Feb., 1872), 240.

[34]XXXI, 238. Although Dickens had delighted in Mosses from an Old Manse and had repeatedly urged it on all his friends, he found that The Scarlet Letter "falls off sadly after that fine opening scene. The psychological part of the story is very much overdone, and not truly done I

think. Their suddenness of meeting and agreeing to go away together after all those years, is very poor. Mr. Chillingworth ditto. The child out of nature altogether. And Mr. Dimmsdale certainly never could have begotten her." Forster, The Life of Charles Dickens, 2 vols. (London and New York, 1927), II, p. 57.

[35]Atlantic Monthly, XLI (May, 1878), 669.

[36]Atlantic Monthly, XXXIII (May, 1874), 622.

[37]Atlantic Monthly, XLV (Feb., 1880), 280-82.

[38]Robert P. Falk, "The Literary Criticism of the Genteel Decades, 1870-1900," in The Development of American Literary Criticism, ed. Floyd Stovall (Chapel Hill, 1955), p. 123. See also Louis J. Budd, "William Dean Howells's Defense of the Romance," PMLA, LXVII (March, 1952), 32-42.

[39]Quoted in Cady, Realist at War, p. 12.

[40]Atlantic Monthly, XXIX (April, 1872), 498.

[41]XXV, 27.

[42]Cady gives a full account of the episode in Road to Realism, pp. 218-21. See also Lutwack, 196-97.

[43]No. 2874 (Nov. 25, 1882), 700. See also Life in Letters, I, 336.

[44]Pp. 29-31, 38, 46-47, and passim.

[45]Henry Mills Alden to WDH, Sept. 9, 1885. Quoted in Lutwack, 196.

[46]The first column, significantly enough, praises Mary Noailles Murfree's "realistic" techniques and local color, but criticizes her for occasionally falling into easy Dickensianisms. LXXII (Jan., 1886), 323.

[47]The phrase is Carter's. See Howells and the Age of Realism, pp. 185-90; Cady, Realist at War, pp. 14, 49-50; Pizer, Realism and Naturalism, pp. 37-38.

[48]Pizer's argument that Howells's relativism comes from Spencer, Taine, and other "evolutionary" theorists is undoubtedly sound. However, his assertion that evolutionary theory lends the book unity and coherence seems to me extraordinarily naive. See Realism and Naturalism, pp. 37-52.

[49]See especially chapter ii, pp. 6-17. Howells's contempt for those who see life in terms of literature and not vice-versa became a recurrent theme in his own fiction.

[50]"Editor's Easy Chair," Harper's Magazine, CV (July, 1902), 311.

[51]Pp. 68-69, 177-78.

[52]Pp. 63-64, 178-80.

[53]Pp. 78-81, 12-13. Emerson's idealism, of course, gets lost in the shuffle. Cf. Carter, p. 26; "Put away the formal, transcendental structure of Emerson's philosophy, or rather, hold it in the mind as a coloration rather than a creed, and you have left the moving power of the realist movement in America."

[54]Pp. 138-40.

[55]The point is most fully developed in chapters xxi and xxii.

[56]Pp. 130-31.

[57]"Manners, Morals, and the Novel," in The Liberal Imagination (Garden City, n.d.), pp. 199-215.

[58]The quotations are from Trilling, p. 206; the phenomenon is most fully traced by Richard Chase in The American Novel and Its Tradition (Garden City, 1957).

[59]The Victorian Frame of Mind (New Haven, 1957), pp. 144-49.

[60]One hardly need cite pages, but if a reference is wanted, 14, 127, and 186 are as good as any.

[61]See especially pp. 9 and 28.

[62] Pp. 14-15, 73-77.

[63] Pp. 180, 179.

[64] P. 184.

[65] XVII, 18-25.

[66] Howells and James: A Double Billing, ed. William M. Gibson, Leon Edel, and Lyall H. Powers (New York, 1958), p. 7. For a description of the circumstances of the essay see Harrison T. Meserole, "The Dean in Person: Howells's Lecture Tour." Western Humanities Review, X (Autumn, 1956), 337-47.

[67] 2 vols. (New York, 1901), I, 126.

[68] Harper's Monthly, CV (July, 1902), 312.

CHAPTER V

WILLIAM DEAN HOWELLS: IN THE SWEET BY AND BY

I.

> ...it was no more possible for a young novelist to escape writing Dickens than it was for a young poet to escape writing Tennyson."
> ---W. D. Howells

Alfred Kazin's remark that Howells "learned English at the fountain head of print," serves to remind us of the importance of Howells's apprenticeship in his father's printshops to his development as a writer.[1] Among other things he read pirated versions of Dickens's novels and stories as they appeared in William Cooper Howells's papers throughout the fifties, and it was in one of those papers that he published his first critical commentary on the author whom, he claimed, "we cannot know too well."[2] The same pages also contain an "Original Story," The Independent Candidate, Howells's first attempt at an extended fiction.[3]

The circumstances behind the novel's composition have been explained by Howells himself and retold by Edwin

Cady.[4] They need not be gone over again except perhaps to point out that the modern reader is less inclined to agree with Howells's retrospective judgment that the story was not "badly conceived or attempted upon lines that were false or wrong," than he is to credit the opinion of the old farmer who brought it to a close by remarking in its young author's presence that "he did not think that story amounted to much." A brief summary of what passes for the novel's plot will give some indication of its quality. At the beginning of the story George Berson, a young lawyer, has bolted the Whig party and announced for the legislature on an independent ticket. He sends Walter Larrie to canvass the town of Beauville, from which Larrie writes of his meeting with a local tavern keeper, Mr. Trooze, who also serves as the head of the local Whig organization. Love interest is introduced when Larrie falls under the spell of a Beauville beauty, Marla Cuffins. In the meantime Berson, having added Mr. Gilky, the local ne'er-do-well, to his campaign staff, returns to his office late one night to find himself threatened by the ominous presence of a stranger lurking in the shadows behind his desk.

Howells uses the suspense of Berson's predicament to carry the reader through a long digression on the aims and methods of his narrative in the next chapter; nor is the candidate removed from danger until we have been introduced to his political opposition, an unscrupulous party hack who suspects Berson of hereditary insanity but is unable to persuade the remarkably high-minded editor of the Whig paper to publish the smear. When we do get back to Berson, the stranger is discovered to be Robert, the alcoholic husband of Berson's late sister and father of Clara, the child whom Berson has undertaken to raise. Berson has bought Robert off in the past, but Robert uses the candidate's love for Clara to blackmail him into another pay-off. The action then switches back to Walter Larrie who continues his romance with Marla (whose last name has mysteriously changed to Carmin) and is roughed up by toughs for attempting a public address on behalf of the independent cause. Howells quickly abandons the chronicle of the campaign, treating us instead to a summary of political events that he must have had in mind when he remembered years later having helped himself out of difficult places with "bald parodies of Bleak House":

> Blubber, the sworn foe of Cubber, will shake the political paw of his old enemy--Rubber, who has not spoken to Dubber since that gentleman came in ahead of him for the hand of Miss McJiltem, will walk arm and arm with him throughout the canvass. The moral character of the Publican Nubber, will be so white-washed of all stain in the eyes of Deacon Flubber that he will bow to him on the way to church. It

> is easier to mingle oil and water than to make friends of Vubber and Gubber. Yet Vubber and Gubber will hob-nob, if need be, for the good of the cause, and so on.[5]

Election night finds Berson watching by the bedside of Clara, who has been brought low by a near fatal case of Little Nell-itus. In rushes a band of his followers led by a drunken Larrie who announces Berson's victory at the polls. The noise awakens the child who screams and faints. The scream is too much for the independent candidate. Struck mad on the spot, he rushes at Larrie in berserk rage and has to be dragged off to an adjacent padded room. A final paragraph wraps things up by jumping two years ahead to find Clara alive and happy, Robert dead, Larrie being married to Marla, and Berson slowly returning to his senses.

The foregoing synopsis bears ample testimony to the accuracy of Howells's later self-criticism: "It was all very well at the beginning, but I had not reckoned with the future sufficiently to have started with any clear ending in my mind. ...My material gave out; incidents failed me; the characters wavered and threatened to perish on my hands. ...Somehow I managed to bring the wretched thing to a close, and to live it slowly into the past." A reading of the novel itself reveals how freely the seventeen year old author borrowed from Dickens. Dickens's presence is established from the first paragraph of chapter one, signaled by Larrie's encounter with a street urchin ("My attention...was called to the fact that my horse's legs went up and down, and that I was a roarer") and by the comic use of incongruous detail in the description of Trooze's bar. One is reminded of Olov Fryckstedt's comment that the Dickens influence is to be seen not so much in specific instances as in the overall tone.[6] Fryckstedt cites the introduction of Mr. and Mrs. Gilky in chapter three; even more revealing is the description of "Man-with-an-Umberella-Men" in the penultimate installment. Despite the frequent incoherencies, the result of Howells's having written the novel at the type case, it is not difficult to see him fusing Dickens's techniques in the creation of comic types with specific memories of Sairey Gamp:

> There was Stub was [sic] Man-with-an-Umberella man. Nobody ever saw him without his Umberella. Of course, nobody ever remarked that he always had it with him. Nevertheless he had. At church, if you beheld in the vestibule, a blue Umberella with a narrow streak of white around the edge, you were safe in declaring that Mr. Stub was attending divine service. There was no mistaking the Umberella. It had a meek ivory-topped handle, and an imbecile tassel dangling therefrom. I have said that Mr. Stubs [sic] left his Umberella, as a general thing, in the vestibule of the church. This however was sheer reverence. It is to be doubted whether Mr. Stub would have suffered himself to part with his Umberella for any other feeling, let it be never so sacred. At a lecture, the Umberella supported the

> chin of Mr. Stub, while he took aim through his goggles at the lecturer. At public meetings the Umberella punched neighboring ribs. At market, the Umberella invaded egg-baskets, and spilled measures of apple butter over white napkins, and angered the dame who uttered them [sic]. There was a touch of malice in the nature of that Umberella. It took a fiendish delight in upsetting the cups on the stand of the Coffee-Woman, and bruising the wares of the Little-Molasses-Candy-Girl. What wonder? It was a Demon Umberella. Can I ever forget the moment when Mr. Stub appeared on the roof of the burning house, with his Umberella under his arm. The red flames leaped from the burning casements, as if to dash themselves upon the crowd, and roared and crackled with unearthly glee.--There seemed to be no escape; and a shudder ran through the mighty throng below, as Mr. Stub stepped jauntily to the edge of the roof. He must needs fling himself down. Everybody thought so. What was their astonishment to see Mr. Stub raise his Umberella, and sheltering himself beneath it, jump from the eave into the subtle air. He hovered over the house for a moment, and then drifting to the leeward, soared easily up towards the clouds. Every eye was strained to watch the flight of the devoted man. The Umberella waxes smaller and smaller, and at last, with coat-tails flapping frantically, Mr. Stub faded from sight.--He never came down; and perished, no doubt, a victim to his own Umberella!--Every Man-with-an-Umberella does not go up like a balloon. Yet there is a dreadful mystery hanging about such people, which may well excite in the boldest heart a willingness to give them the whole sidewalk.[7]

Other passages also make the debt to Dickens explicit. The novel reeks with domestic sentimentality of the Mary Pinch-Esther Summerson sort; the long discussion of old maids in the 4 January 1855 installment is a fair example. Exposure to the squabbling homelife of the Troozes gives Larrie an opportunity to "come out strong" like Mark Tapley, and the theatrical posing of print shop jour-men recalls Dick Swiveller. The dead of night appearance of a blackmailing relative echoes a melodramatic motif that Dickens had exploited consistently from *Nicholas Nickleby* to the recently published *Hard Times*, and the warfare of rival editors reminds us how useful American humorists had found *The Pickwick Papers* as a guide to the depiction of a trans-Atlantic phenomenon.

Critical commentary on any author's juvenilia generally takes the form of retrospective prognostication tailored to fit the critic's thesis. Thus Cady observes examples of incipient "realism" in *The Independent Candidate*, and Fryckstedt comments on Howells's attempts to come to grips with the American scene. What most strikes this commentator is an irony involving theory and practice embodied in the novel as a whole. In the "Rather Didactical" digression of chapter four, Howells states that he has no intention of imitating the "literary blood-puddings" of George Lippard and Emerson Bennett. Rather he will content himself with following the "less dazzling" author of *Bleak House*. The remark is echoed by his memory forty years later of having, throughout the novel, imitated "the easier art of Dickens." Yet the fiasco of *The Independent Candidate* should have indicated, above all, that while the Dickensian mode was both attractive and useful, it was by no means easy.

The embarrassment and pain Howells suffered from the failure of The Independent Candidate may help explain the sixteen-year hiatus between that work and his next attempt to write a novel. Even then what he produced was not quite a novel but only, as he called it, "a sort of narrative--half story, half travel sketch," which begins with the author disclaiming the ability to sustain an "involved narration."[8] The same letter that describes Their Wedding Journey as "a sort of narrative" goes on to outline Howells's intention of making it "a faithful study of our American life." His celebrated apostrophe in the novel itself, "Ah! poor Real Life, which I love, can I make others share the delight I find in thy foolish and insipid face?" (iii, 67), has echoed through the literary histories as the battle-cry of the "realistic" movement. Yet as the more perceptive critics have realized, the "realism" of Their Wedding Journey is at best limited and consistently self-conscious.[9] The rhetoric of the apostrophe itself--the capitalization of Real Life, the second person singular pronoun, and the string of coy adjectives--indicates that Howells is interested in the empirically observed commonplace not for its own sake but rather for what lurking intimations of "romance" might be found in it. Thus his narrative stance is little different from that habitually assumed by Dickens, who ushered in Household Words by announcing his aim of showing "that in all familiar things...there is Romance enough, if we will find it out," and who prefaced Bleak House with the remark that he had "purposely dwelt upon the romantic side of familiar things." Howells's Dickensian attitude is reflected in his handling of the narrative itself. Although he occasionally satirizes his newlyweds for their over-eager pursuit of the picturesque and for their inability to appreciate any aspect of the American scene without associating it in some way with Europe, it is, as Olov Fryckstedt observes, with clearly discernible relief that he carries them into French Canada, whose picturesqueness and wealth of romantic associations can be exploited without misgivings.[10]

Even the satire in the first half of the book denotes motives more complex than have been generally recognized. By poking fun at the Marches's tendency to embellish the American scene Howells can work into his narrative generous examples of the very responses that the satire, consistently bland and understated, does not entirely negate.

The reader is almost left with a choice of which attitude to accept. Moreover, to the degree that the satire stands, the narrative logic generally works to show that the Marches err not in the attempt to "romanticize" what they see, but in the way in which they do it. The point seems to be that American Real Life need not be associated with European scenes in order to be note-worthy but rather that it has an indigenous interest of its own that "Europeanized" Americans, blinded by their tendency to stock responses, cannot see.

A case in point occurs in chapter one in a passage that has been frequently cited as an example of Howells's "realism." The Marches are up early exploring on their first day in New York. Basil protests that "a knowledge of Europe made New York the most uninteresting town in America." Isabel, always prompt to assert her Bostonian snobbishness, agrees, and together they cannot "think of any one's loving New York as Dante loved Florence, or as Madame de Stael loved Paris, or as Johnson loved black, homely, homelike London." The string of maudlin adjectives attached to London is undoubtedly meant to parody the Marches's sentimental "romanticizing" of Europe. But when the narrator, whom for the lack of any dramatization granted the first person narration we must take for a version of Howells himself, steps in to correct their vision, we find him using the very same sort of rhetoric to assert that New York is just as exotic and therefore lovable as any continental metropolis:

> And as they twittered their little dispraises, the giant Mother of Commerce was growing more and more conscious of herself, waking from her night's sleep and becoming aware of her fleets and trains, and the myriad hands and wheels that throughout the whole sea and land move for her, and do her will even while she sleeps. All about the wedding-journeyers swelled the deep tide of life back from its night-long ebb.

This is the exact tone and style habitually adopted by any number of literary second-raters who struggled in the seventies to set themselves up as the American Boz. Certainly there is nothing that Howells would call "realistic" about the elaborate personification of the city, and to speak of the ebb and flow of humanity is to employ one of Dickens's favorite metaphors. Nor are we surprised to find Howells's description of the city's awakening throughout the chapter following almost exactly the pattern for such set-pieces established by Dickens in "The Streets--Morning" section of <u>Sketches by Boz</u>. Ultimately the narrator's vision blends with that of the newlyweds in a sentimental paean to youth and love. Although the Marches are appropriately self-conscious of their mawkishness in posing as Adam and Eve discovering the world, they are allowed to continue their "drolling" to the end of the chapter, and the reader comes away with his appetite for sentiment fully satisfied (i, 32-34).

The novelty inherent in Howells's discovery of indigenous "romance" (and not any incipient "realism") gives the work its period-piece charm and undoubtedly accounts for its initial popularity. Reviewing the first edition, Henry Adams was quick to indicate the ambiguity in Howells's presentation of his material. Adams notes an "almost photogenic truth to nature" in the book, but goes on to remark that "Our descendants will find nowhere so faithful and so pleasing a picture of our American existence, and no writer is likely to rival Mr. Howells in this idealization of the commonplace."[11] For the modern reader, the "idealization" far outweighs the "photography." The term "idealization" is itself as difficult as the term "romance"; one suspects that Howells would tend to equate them . For the modern reader that quality of Their Wedding Journey that Adams attempts to define as "the idealization of the commonplace" seems to be, above all, its markedly Dickensian tone. The twentieth-century critic might well hesitate to follow his nineteenth-century forebears in the general equation of "idealization" and "romance" with Dickens; nevertheless, in the specific case of Their Wedding Journey the equation is unavoidable. Thus there is little need to catalog those passages in Their Wedding Journey that indicate a direct Dickens influence, although there are many. The frequency with which they occur only provides statistical evidence of the work's overall Dickensian flavor. Despite his intentions of describing life "closely and realistically" and looking upon America "with the clear, natural eye" unencumbered by inherited instruments for optical illusions, Howells produced a vision of "the Romantic side of familiar things" that draws heavily upon Dickens's techniques to make the commonplace seem subtly exotic and remove even the celebrated "ordinary carful of humanity" in its "habitual moods of vacancy and tiresomeness" (iv, 86-87) far from what Cady calls the "tone and key of everyday or representative existence."[12] Later in his career, when Dickens had come to symbolize for him everything in the way of fictional techniques that American novelists should avoid, Howells did not classify Their Wedding Journey as a novel--although it is not clear whether the reason was his awareness of its essentially Dickensian quality or doubt over how to label its curious combination of fiction and travelogue.[13] But in either case it established a pattern recurrent throughout Howells's career. In novel after novel Howells sets out to attack certain elements in the mode of fictional presentation and certain conventions of characterization and action that, in his critical writings, he habitually associated with Dickens, only to fall back, in the end, on incidents, themes, or techniques drawn, precisely, from Dickens himself. The pattern is so assertive in the so-called "social novels" of the late eighties and early nineties as to require separate treatment. But as preparation for that discussion it is useful to look, briefly, at one representative novel falling outside the "social group."

In Indian Summer Theodore Colville, a middle-aged Western editor whose devotion to political principle has lost him his paper, finds himself in Florence trying to pick up the threads of an architectural career he had dropped some twenty years earlier. He encounters a friend of his youth, Mrs. Bowen, now widowed and living in Florence with her child, Effie, and Imogene Graham, the daughter of a friend, sent to Europe for finishing. As the novel grows so does Colville's involvement with Mrs. Bowen and her charge, especially the latter, with whom he rather backs into a ridiculous engagement. The center of interest in the novel lies in the characterization of Colville; both the comedy and the psychological analysis represent Howells at his very best, as he traces Colville's attempts to come to grips with the facts of his condition in life. Unable to accept middle-age, he nevertheless discovers quickly enough that Florence at forty-five is not Florence at twenty-three, and his efforts at probing the wounds of a jilting he had received on his first visit to Italy produces disconcertingly little pain. Aware of the vast gulf separating him from his fiancee, he views it with conflicting surges of amusement and despair, while his susceptibility to the flattery of her youthful attentions leads him, puffing and panting, from one fiasco to another. His attempt to blame himself for taking advantage of the girl's innocence is no more successful than his effort to sacrifice himself to that same innocence, and each struggle to break his engagement finds him only the more deeply entangled.

If Colville's predicament had been the thematic center of the novel, Indian Summer might well have been Howells's masterpiece. But it is not. Writing to Clemens in August, 1885, he explained that "it is all a variation of the one theme," the one theme being, of course, the pernicious effects of "romantic" literature.[14] Imogene Graham's love for Colville, it turns out, is only her desire to sacrifice herself to him in order to redeem his supposedly tragic past. Thematic concerns, then, require some means of revealing to Imogene the evil of her irrational sentimentality. Howells's solution is a burst of melodrama. He sends all his major characters on an expedition to Fiesole where their carriage, the ladies all inside, overturns. Colville's intuitive response is to call for Mrs. Bowen and Effie to jump before he thinks of Imogene, who stares at him with reproach and disdain in the brief second before he himself is thrown over a cliff. Thus her disillusionment comes not from her discovery of her own folly but from Colville's failure to live up to the code of popular fiction, which demands that the lover rescue the beloved from danger at all costs to himself and others. Colville meanwhile is ironically forced into acting out the role of the conventional hero. He does rescue the woman he truly loves and is treated to all the sentimental delights of a long convalescence during which he is faithfully nursed back to health by the woman who adores him. Imogene herself could not have asked for anything more "romantic."

But there is more to come. Colville awakes from his symbolic death, the scales fallen from his eyes, only to discover that Mrs. Bowen will not marry him. The humiliation she has suffered during his infatuation with Imogene has been too great for that ever to come to pass. He must leave once more in defeat. At this point little Effie bursts into the room, and Mrs. Bowen places upon Colville the burden of telling her he is leaving:

> Then, as if the whole calamitous fact had suddenly flashed upon her, she plunged her face against her mother's breast. "I can't *bear* it!" she sobbed out; and the reticence of her lamentation told more than a storm of cries and prayers.
>
> Colville wavered.
>
> "Oh, you must stay!" said Lina, in the self-conscious voice of a woman who falls below her ideal of herself.[15]

Despite Colville's later attempts to laugh away Effie's appearance as a pre-arranged *coup-de-théâtre*, it remains precisely that, a *coup-de-théâtre*. Little Nell has done her work once more. Howells has merely substituted one convention for another; the self-sacrificing heroines of the lady-books are replaced by the redemptive children of Dickens.[16]

II.

> I'm afraid the Brooklyn strike is lost. ...Henry D. Lloyd was here day before yesterday, and very despondent. But I believe the right will win in the end.
> --W. D. Howells

Literary historians are agreed that after the publication of _Indian Summer_ in 1886, Howells dramatically changed the form and subject matter of his fiction, shifting from comedy of manners and psychological analysis to the exploration of more specifically social and economic themes than he had treated before. The years 1886-1894 have been marked off as his period of "social fiction," and the far greater portion of criticism has been devoted to this era in his life. The list of possible causes that have been offered to explain the shift is long, ranging from his daughter's death to his involvement in the celebrated "Haymarket Affair" of 1887. Nor is the list of literary influences on his social writings any shorter: Tolstoi, Laurence Gronlund, William Morris, J. B. Harrison, T. B. Aldrich, Bjørstjerne Bjørnson, and even James Russell Lowell have all been mentioned as possible sources of Howells's interest in and treatment of social questions. The one name conspicuously absent from all these discussions is, of course, Dickens.

The reasons for this failure to consider Dickens as part of the background of Howells's social fiction are clear enough. For one thing there is the generous availability of other figures, particularly Tolstoi. No one can--or should--avoid exploring the implications of Howells's own statement that "As much as one merely human being can help another I believe that he has helped me."[17] Yet one influence need not rule out another. One recalls, for example, both the high esteem in which Tolstoi himself held Dickens--he considered him no less than the greatest novelist of the century--and the quickness of Howells's contemporaries to recognize the debt he owed to his English master.[18] Moreover, it is generally agreed that Tolstoi taught Howells nothing really new; rather, he reconfirmed him in those humanitarian ideals he had absorbed in his childhood and adolescence, ideals that in later life he explicitly associated with Dickens. Indeed, even at the risk of repeating points made in the preceding chapter, it is profitable to compare what, in My Literary Passions, he says he received from Tolstoi with what he establishes, in the same book, as the lasting values of Dickens. In each case they are three:

(1) Tolstoi "leads you back to the only true ideal, away from [the] false standard of the gentleman." Dickens "never appeals to the principle which sniffs in his reader."
(2) Tolstoi "gave me heart to hope that the world may yet be made over in the image of Him who died for it," while in reading Dickens "I was in a world where right came out best." Finally (3) Tolstoi "taught me to see life not as a chase for a forever impossible personal happiness, but as a field for endeavor toward the happiness of the whole human family," while "the base of [Dickens's] work is the whole breadth and depth of humanity itself." "Equality and fraternity...these ideals mark the whole tendency of his fiction." Clearly one literary passion blended into another, and neither can have been without influence.

Yet Howells was able to praise Tolstoi's aesthetics as well as his ethics, a feat he was rarely able to achieve in his discussions of Dickens. Later critics have undoubtedly been led by his frequent attacks on the "crudeness" of Dickens's art to dismiss Dickens as a possible influence on his fiction. Nonetheless it is important to remember that Howells insists that the "finer art" of his day is futile if it is not put to the service of social justice, and that what begins in the final chapters of _Criticism and Fiction_ as a blast at Dickens's artistic failures ends as a paean to his humanitarian zeal. In what follows I shall attempt to show that in his own social fictions Howells repeatedly draws on Dickens's art, crude or not.

Finally, the immediately apparent differences between Howells's and Dickens's social fictions may have caused some commentators to overlook the less dramatic similarities. Yet, ironically, the experience of reading Howells is often to wish that he had been rather more Dickensian than less, to realize frequently the inadequacies of his particular kind of "realism" as a means of gauging nineteenth-century social malaise. Since these failures serve to throw a kind of inverse light on the reasons for Howells's adopting Dickensian techniques when he did, it is worthwhile to examine two of the more representative of them.

One of Howells's strongest objections to Dickens was that while he recognized "the supreme claim of the lowest humanity," he erred in his tendency to "idealize" the victims of society, "to paint them impossibly virtuous and beautiful."[19] His own impulse was not to paint them at all but to limit his canvasses to middle and upper class worlds. In so doing he was able to satisfy his own critical belief that the novelist must describe only what he has seen and known--and Howells's was not a slumming personality--while at the same time following one aspect of Dickens who, from _Hard Times_ on, had made it his point that the economic systems of the Manchester school corrupted exploiter as much as exploited. Yet Howells's limited scope is often fatal. _Annie Kilburn_, for example, the first of Howells's novels explicitly devoted to social issues, is set in a small city that the class struggle, which Howells, like Dickens, sees as the inevitable concomitant of nineteenth-century industrialism, has divided into two worlds glaring at each other in thinly veiled antagonism across the railroad tracks that divide them. His heroine, who after eleven years in Europe returns to Hatboro to "do some good," quickly sounds the hollowness of her own part of town and realizes, somewhat to her shock, that, as Cady observes, "reality and the real issues...lie Over The Track."[20] That is, precisely in that part of town that Howells makes only a token effort to dramatize. Thus the real issues are left to exist in a void, and the novel perishes by that characteristic defect in Howells that Henry James perceptively labelled his failure "to build in the subject." James's criticism is worth quoting in full. Howells, he says,

> forgets sometimes to paint, to evoke the conditions and appearances, to build in the subject. He is

> doubtless afraid of doing these things in excess, having seen in other hands what disastrous effects that error may have: but all the same I cannot help thinking that the divinest thing in a valid novel is the compendious, descriptive, pictorial touch, à la Daudet.[21]

Or Dickens--as Howells's other contemporaries might have been quick to add.[22]

When Howells does take us across the tracks it is only to align himself with the influences he seems elsewhere to be avoiding. The same passage condemning Dickens for "idealizing" the poor continues, "but truth...paints these victims as they are, and bids the world consider them not because they are beautiful and virtuous, but because they are ugly and vicious, cruel, filthy." Yet one is hard pressed to say just what is ugly or vicious, cruel or filthy about the Savors, the sole denizens of Over The Tracks we are privileged to meet. Indeed Howells repeatedly celebrates their beauty and virtue. His heroine, like David among the Peggottys, Florence at the Toodles's, or Pip at the Forge, becomes part of the nourishing reality of life only in the few days she is allowed to share in the humane rhythms of their Dickensian home. Our other excursion Over The Tracks comes when Annie is taken to visit the mills. Here Howells may draw upon his own sight--seeing in the factories at Lowell, undertaken as part of his homework for the novel, but if so, his memory can only find expression in the familiar patterns of Dickens's style:

> The tireless machines marched back and forth across the floor, and the men who watched them with suicidal intensity ran after them barefooted when they made off with a broken thread, spliced it, and then escaped to their stations again. In other rooms, where there was a stunning whir of spindles, girls and women were at work... In the room where the stockings were knitted [Annie] tried to understand the machinery that wrought and seemed to live before her eyes. But her mind wandered to the men and women who were operating it, and who seemed no more a voluntary part of it than all the rest...[23]

In <u>A Hazard of New Fortunes</u> Over The Track becomes New York's East Side, but retains the same thematic function. In this novel Howells builds in his subject on a more compendious scale, treating us to several chapters of lower-class life, only to encounter a different kind of problem. Howells's notions of "realism" prevented him from constructing his novels around the kind of massive symbolism that the twentieth-century has come to recognize as the primary distinction of Dickens. As a result he was curiously unable to cope with the "economic chance world" his social novels set out to describe. Critics from C. H. Gratten to Henry Nash Smith have pointed out that Howells is consistently unconvincing in his presentation of nineteenth-century business.[24] The problem is, I think, more than, as Smith implies, Howells's failure to understand the true nature of business activity. Actually, his "realistic" approach deprives him of a system of metaphors and symbols by which he might even approximate an understanding. Frank Norris did not understand business either and had to construct an elaborate mechanism of pulleys and wheels, strings, feathers and rubber bands as a graphic means of illustrating the fluctuations of the Chicago Exchange in order to grasp even its most fundamental operations.[25] But Norris considered himself a "romanticist," not a "realist," allied himself with Dickens and Zola in opposition to Howells, and easily became enamoured of the "romance" of business, making Bulls and Bears the nineteenth-century equivalents of Saracens and Crusaders. Thus he has access to the _literary_ metaphor of business as chivalric warfare whereas Howells must content himself, as Smith observes, with the _moralistic_ equation of business and gambling. As a result the representation of economic activity in _The Pit_ is much more "convincing," that is, more conducive to the reader's suspension of disbelief, than it is anywhere in Howells--even if it is, empirically speaking, no more accurate.[26]

Howells's inability to use metaphor or symbol to describe economic operations and tie his novel together robs the descriptions of the poor in _A Hazard of New Fortunes_ of thematic significance.[27] The slums are presented solely from the point of view of Basil March, who leaves no doubt that he sees a relationship between their dislocations and the business affairs of Jacob Dryfoos, just as in, say, Our Mutual Friend Dickens sees a relationship between the sufferings of Betty Higden and the speculations of Hamilton Veneering. But Howells fails to dramatize the relationship and certainly never explains it in terms of cause and effect, establishing it only "by a process of inference that seems to lie below conscious analysis."[28] In a "realistic" novel such reliance on non-rational, intuitive responses is fatal. Dickens, operating in the symbolic mode of "romance," does not have to worry about maintaining strict, rational patterns of causation. Rather he has only to encourage the process of intuitive, non-rational cognition whereby the symbol of society as dust-heap stands as a kind of metaphoric bridge linking Veneering's manipulation of stocks and bonds to Betty's misery. Howells, therefore, to the degree that he expects the reader to concur in Basil's association of poverty with Dryfoos, is relying upon responses proper to the "romance" without supplying the machinery necessary to prompt such responses. Or put in different terms, Howells's failure in A Hazard of New Fortunes is his failure to imitate Dickens.

Elsewhere in the social novels, including Annie Kilburn and A Hazard of New Fortunes, Howells does draw freely upon Dickens, so freely in fact that it is more profitable to speak of Dickens's influence in categories than to catalog specific instances, novel by novel. Of the three categories to be discussed here one is a matter of technique, characterization, and two are thematic--"complicity" and "providence."

Howells's instinctive preference in fiction was for novels with only a "mere handful of characters," novels that, like Hawthorne's, were built on the "subliminal" drama of a small, carefully selected group.[29] The shift from comedy of manners to social themes required him to increase his casts of characters, and while none of his novels between The Minister's Charge and The Quality of Mercy is as densely populated as any of Dickens's, they do, of necessity, contain more personalities than he can ever explore in any detail, even though the most neglected of them must represent a certain economic point of view or stand for some representative social type. His most frequent solution to the problem of bringing these fringe characters to life without lavishing upon them the attention reserved for more central figures was to adopt Dickensian techniques of characterization in order to imbue them with passable vitality while at the same time "placing" them (to use F. R. Leavis's term) in their proper philosophical or sociological position.[30]

Howells had explored the possibilities of the technique and learned its usefulness long before his social period. In A Foregone Conclusion, for example, he had limited his characters to the merest handful possible. But of its four central figures only three--Florida, Ferris, and Don Ippolito--were of any abiding interest to him. The fourth, Mrs. Vervain, is merely a necessity of the plot, and Howells is content to characterize her by that same "parenthetical incoherence" he was later to call a "mere trick" that "quickly stales" in such Dickens ladies as Mrs. Nickleby and Flora Casby.[31] Her eccentric speech, however, not only brings her to life with an economy of characterization but also "places" her in relation to the novel's themes as the lowest common denominator of American tourists and dramatizes that narrow provinciality which prevents her from ever grasping the tragedy of Don Ippolito or even understanding anything more of Venice than that it is different from New York. Similarly, in The Rise of Silas Lapham

Lapham's former partner, Rogers, exists primarily to promote the action and symbolize the nemesis of the past. Accordingly Howells draws upon Dickensian techniques to sketch out the few essentials the reader needs to know about this shadowy and ultimately somewhat pathetic figure.[32] Many of his most Dickensian figures are also among his happiest creations. Whatever we may think of Howells's ultimate stature as a novelist, we must concur with Lionel Trilling in granting a certain respect to the man "who created the wealthy, guilty, hypersensitive Clara Kingsbury, called her 'a large blond mass of suffering,' and conceived that she might say to poor Marcia Hubbard, 'Why, my child, you're a Roman matron!' and come away in agony that Marcia would think she meant her nose."[33]

What Howells seems to have learned above all in these early novels was that characters could be conceived and placed with Dickensian economy most effectively by allowing them to create themselves out of their own talk, a process that is at the heart of the Dickens mode. When he encountered the demands for characterization imposed by his new social themes, his strategy was simply to perpetuate the technique; but in doing so he discovered, as Dickens had before him, that even such a fundamental point of method could, in a social and economic context, take on a peculiar force of meaning. Take, for example, one of the few characters to whom he granted a Dickensian symbolic name, the Hatboro merchant, Billy Gerrish, who first appears in Annie Kilburn and later figures in The Quality of Mercy. Gerrish represents the self-made man and "new style" entrepreneur of the post Civil War era; his speech reflects the gaucheness, the raw egotism, and the social brutality that Howells wishes us to recognize in the type. The following quotations are all from Annie Kilburn:

> "You've got to put your foot down, as Mr. Lincoln said; and as I say, you've got to keep it down."
> (viii, 83)

> "I came into this town a poor boy, without a penny in my pocket, and I have made my own way, every inch of it, unaided and alone. I am a thorough believer in giving every one an equal chance to rise and to--get along; I would not throw an obstacle in anybody's way; but I do not believe--I do not believe--in pampering those who have not risen, or have made no effort to rise...I don't expect to invite my clerks or Mrs. Gerrish's servants into my parlour. I will meet them at the polls, or the communion table, or on any proper occasion; but a man's home is sacred. I will not allow my wife and children to associate with those whose--whose--whose idleness, or vice, or whatever, has kept them down in a country where--where everybody stands on an equality; and what I will not do myself, I will not ask others to do it. I make it a rule to do unto others as I would have them do unto me."
> (viii, 86-87)

> "Understand me, sir, we do not object, neither I nor any of those who agree with me, to the preaching of Christ as a life. That is all very well in its place, and it is the wish of every true Christian to conform and adapt his own life as far as--as circumstances will permit of."
>
> (xxv, 273)

Gerrish's pronouncements are a high source of fun, fun not diminished by the fact that most of them are uttered in a room that, in honor of the gentle and benevolent John Jarndyce, Gerrish calls his "Growlery." But underneath the comedy is a kind of irony not unfamiliar to readers of Dickens. Gerrish is meant to be a "realistic" portrait of an American norm, yet, as these passages show, Howells's treatment of him inevitably drifts toward caricature, and his personality as revealed by his speech, soon shades off into the grotesque.[34] Gerrish seems ultimately a fitting companion to Elijah Pogram, Hannibal Chollop and Jefferson Brick. Inevitably, because what Gerrish represents is itself grotesque, a caricature of rationality and human decency. In _Their Wedding Journey_ Howells had found "poor Real Life" on the American scene filled with the kind of Dickensian "romance" embodied in _Sketches by Boz_. In the social novels the American scene is the Dickensian madhouse described in _Martin Chuzzlewit_ and _American Notes_. Criticizing the Christmas books Howells had observed that in Dickens's day "it was thought admirable for the author to take types of humanity which everybody knew, and add to them from his imagination till they were as strange as beasts and birds talking. Now we begin to feel that human nature is quite enough, and that the best an author can do is to show it as it is."[35] The creation of Billy Gerrish demonstrates that the attempt to present a well-known type of human nature, showing it as it is, results, in the context of social criticism, in the creation of talking beasts.[36] Conversely, in a world dominated by Billy Gerrishes, virtue tends, just as inevitably, to become distorted into a corresponding sentimentality. The portrait in A Hazard of New Fortunes of Margaret Vance kneeling by Lindau's deathbed is only partly a parody of the Esther Summerson motif in Dickens.[37]

One result of the larger casts of characters in the social novels is the indirect indication of subtle relationships between disparate groups of people. This sense of relatedness not only exists within individual novels but is augmented by the interlocking patterns between groups of novels in which characters from one reappear in another, so that the effect of reading the "social group" as a unit is not dissimilar to that of experiencing one of Dickens's "loose baggy monsters" with its conglomerate fusion of three or four plot lines involving scores of characters. In both cases form is a function of meaning, Howells's interlocking novels providing an organic metaphor for his much commented upon theory of "complicity." Complicity was, for Howells, a term embodying a complex cluster of assumptions, which for convenience may be broken down into three major, interrelated principles: (1) The universe is an inclusive, organic whole, whose realms--human, natural, and divine--are intimately inter-related. (2) Within the human realm individual beings are tied to each other by complex and often unrecognized bonds, including participation both in individual societies and in the universal brotherhood of man; and (3) the individual, in addition to his ties to other individuals, is also bound to society (as an organic unit) in a twofold relationship. He both contributes to making society what it is, and is what society makes him. None of these notions is, of course, original to Howells, and any of them could have come to him from a variety of sources, since all three must be seen in the larger context of the nineteenth-century humanistic response to the fragmentation of society attendant on industrialization, a response that attempted to negate that fragmentation by labelling it an artificial, man-made distortion of the natural, organic and fully integrated universe. What is, however, striking in Howells is the degree to which his novelistic treatment of "complicity" follows patterns established by Dickens. Since the first principle enumerated above hinges upon Howells's notion of "Providence," it is perhaps best to start with the second, the complicity of each individual in the lives and fortunes of every other.

The skill with which Dickens was able to fuse his conglomerate fictions into organic wholes hardly requires comment; Bleak House, generally considered Dickens's technical masterpiece, contains at least four major plot lines and almost a hundred characters, each of whom, through one link or another, is tied to every other. The novel's structure can be seen as a closed, inclusive unit consisting of a series of concentric circles radiating out from the central figure of Esther Summerson and tied together by an intricate system of spokes and cross bars. The intricacy of these arrangements indicates more than a Victorian distaste for loose ends and love of coincidence. It is meant to present a world in which no man is an island and where even the aristocratic Sir Leicester Dedlock is tied by chains of complicity to the gutter-snipe, Jo. What is embodied in the very structure of the novel is reinforced by metaphors within the narrative itself. For example, the ultimate source of the concept of personal complicity in both Dickens and Howells may be in Carlyle's story of the Irish widow who, denied help from the Charitable Establishments, contracts typhus and fatally infects seventeen others before dying herself:

> The forlorn Irish Widow applies to her fellow-creatures, as if saying, "Behold I am sinking, bare of help: ye must help me! I am your sister, bone of your bone; one God made us: ye must help me!" They answer, "No; impossible; thou art no sister of ours." But she proves her sisterhood; her typhus-fever kills _them_: they were actually her brothers, though denying it![38]

In _Bleak House_ the Irishwoman's typhus becomes Jo's small-pox, asserting the brotherhood of man by the same irony. Howells repeatedly exploits the same metaphor. In _The Minister's Charge_, for example, The Rev. Mr. Sewell makes elaborate efforts to disinfect himself, as it were, after each of Barker's infringements on his life, only to discover the impossibility of an antiseptic existence. In _The World of Chance_ Jo's small-pox becomes the Denton children's scarlet fever, but the moral remains the same, the attempts of the other characters to avoid contagion being viewed by Howells's spokesman, Hughes, as "the effort of each of us to escape the consequences that we are all responsible for" (xxxi, 254). At one high point in his off-again-on-again romance, Dan Mavering, the hero of April Hopes, goes to burden his journalist friend, Boardman, with his effusions. But Boardman barely has time to listen, having been assigned to cover the suicide of a Chinese laundryman. Instead he asks the elated Mavering if he wishes to go see the Chinaman:

> "Good heavens! no. What have I got to do with him?"
>
> "Both mortal," suggested the reporter.[39]

This may be Howells's most succinct statement of the doctrine of complicity. It is also an excellent two-word summary of one meaning of Bleak House.

If his doctrine of complicity held that all men are brothers under the skin, each somehow implicated in the affairs of the other, Howells was nevertheless aware that the main drift of social institutions in the post Civil War era was to drive men apart, to make fraternal intercourse among them virtually impossible. Indeed, even the attempt at communication leads, more often than not in his novels, to a widening of the very gulf it struggles to span. This is the first lesson the Rev. Mr. Sewell learns from his encounter with Lemuel Barker, and there is a sharp Dickensian flavor to the comedy of their initial meeting in Sewell's Boston home, the minister becoming more and more pompous and patronizing, more and more Pecksniffian, as

Barker grows more and more reticent, embarrassed, and angry at being made to feel embarrassed. What begins as tentative friendliness ends as open hostility. Sewell is quick to recognize what has gone wrong:

> "We were as unlike as if we were of two different species. I saw that everything I said bewildered him more and more; he couldn't understand me! Our education is unchristian, our civilisation is pagan. They ought to bring us in closer relations with our fellow-creatures, and they both only put us more widely apart! Every one of us dwells in an impenetrable solitude!"[40]

Sewell and Barker are not of different species; there should be commerce between them. The fault lies not in any lack of good-will on the part of the two individuals, but rather in the institutions of society that surround them. Ironically these are the very institutions that should serve to bring men together, to teach the unity of the race and make communication possible, but the effect of a competitive, class-conscious industrialized society has been to pervert and deflect them from their true purposes, to make the minister and his charge their victims rather than their beneficiaries. Man is, then, the product of his environment; if society is distorted, its components--both men and institutions--become distorted too. But this is only half the picture. Social determinism does not, for Howells, rule out individual responsibility. Sewell must learn the other truth that if society molds the individual, it is itself composed of individuals who make it what it is and thus share in its collective guilt. This is the burden of Sewell's celebrated sermon on complicity, the sermon that serves as the thematic culmination of the novel, and it is also the central theme of The Quality of Mercy, which ends with the lawyer, Putney, saying of its defaulter protagonist, "He was a mere creature of circumstances--like the rest of us! His environment made him rich, and his environment made him a rogue," and calling for a mercy that will recognize the complicity of all in determining Northwick's crime.[41] That it is also the burden of much of Dickens hardly requires demonstration. We are all, by this time, aware that Pip's "expectations" are those taught him by an acquisitive, class-conscious, materialistic society, that in being made rich he is made a rogue, and that the "Newgate dust" he never seems able to shake from his clothes is the collective guilt of the society he is complicite in.

One notices, however, a curious--if inevitable--pattern in both novelists. In each once a character realizes the complex relationship between the individual and society, once he understands that he is both cause and effect, his only recourse is to withdraw. His responsibility to order himself as a microcosm in such a way as to influence the shape of the macrocosm surrounding him can only be carried out, ironically, in isolation from the very society he attempts to reform. Sewell preaches his sermon and is last seen walking away, like Pip, alone.[42] The marriage of Nicholas Nickleby may symbolize the triumph of good over evil (Ralph dead, Squeers imprisoned, Gride arrested, and Dotheboys Hall broken up forever) and a corresponding restructuring of society, but the union of Arthur Clennam and Little Dorrit represents only a private accommodation that leaves the world at large unaffected. The marriage of Annie Kilburn stands in significance somewhere between the two, as does that of Matt Hilary and Sue Northwick in *The Quality of Mercy*. In *The World of Chance* there is no marriage at all, the heroine realizing that her social views make her integration into the economic chance world inhabited by her would-be husband impossible. This isolation is inevitable, of course, because what Dickens, in *Our Mutual Friend*, calls "the Voice of Society," the voice that banishes Wrayburn and Lizzie to social exile, is impervious to the attacks of any of its individual members. To confront it openly is to court disaster, shown by Howells in the rather cheap symbolism of the Rev. Mr. Peck's death by railroad in Annie Kilburn.

The self-conscious awareness of defeat and isolation that accompanies the withdrawal of Dickens's later heroes indicates their creator's full realization of their predicament, but one is hesitant to assert the same authorial consciousness in Howells. Even the running down of Peck is left open to a variety of interpretations. On one level it may represent some kind of atonement, some propitiation for the sins of society. In the earlier novels Howells had ridden his hobby-horse of the absurdity of self-sacrifice in affairs of the heart until, blown and bloody from the spurring, it collapsed beneath him. Elbridge Mavering of April Hopes speaks for the author when he calls Sidney Carton's death an "atrocious and abominable act." Yet when Howells attempted his broadest study of social problems in A Hazard of New Fortunes, self-sacrifice takes on a different meaning. Faced by a world where life, as Basil puts it, consists of "pushing and pulling, climbing and crawling, thrusting aside and trampling underfoot, lying, cheating, stealing," Howells can offer few alternatives.[43] One can either withdraw, as Margaret Vance retreats into a sisterhood, or one can, however reluctantly, become a part of it, as Basil himself becomes an owner of Every Other Week and only wistfully dreams of ever returning it to its original co-operative principles. The only other possibility is self-sacrifice. Basil, who fills the role everywhere else, must be taken as the author's spokesman when he says of Conrad's death that it "belonged to God" (V, viii, 380), that it was "his business to suffer there for the sins of others" (V, xi, 393), and that if Margaret sent him to his death, "she sent him to die for God's sake, for man's sake" (V, xviii, 431). Basil may be somewhat self-conscious about his recourse to the doctrine of the Atonement, but there is no sense of embarrassment in the wealth of religious imagery with which Howells himself surrounds Conrad, imagery that ironically only serves to strengthen the reader's inclination to associate him with Carton. A man who, Howells says, would in a Catholic age and country "have been one of those monks who are sainted after death" (III, ix, 241), he is first associated with various Old Testament types of Christ and then with Christ himself. His forehead bleeding as if from a crown of thorns, he dies with his arms outstretched to shelter Lindau, who, we recall, has earlier posed for a bust of Judas. It is, one might say, a far, far nobler thing he does than any he has done before. Howells, who earlier in the novel had wished for a Phiz to help him capture the "Dickensy" quality of the novel's world (II, xi, 160), again opts away from intended "realism" for the motifs of Dickensian "romance."

There are, however, passages in the social novels that imply that society may be redeemed without such drastic measures if one could only exploit those qualities of innate human goodness which even the most adverse environment cannot completely eradicate. Commenting on the fact that while the economic system "implies that the weak must always go to the wall, but in actual operation it isn't so," Hughes, Howells's spokesman in _The World of Chance_, observes that:

> It shows what glorious beings men and women would be if they were rightly conditioned. There is a whole heaven of mercy and loving-kindness in human nature waiting to open itself: we know a little of what it may be when a man or woman rises superior to circumstance and risks a generous word or deed in a selfish world. Then for a moment we have a glimpse of the true life of the race.
>
> (xxvii, 221)

On the surface this sounds suspiciously like yet another version of Dickens's early _philosophie de noel_. Already in the novel the hero has felt that a similar pronouncement by Hughes might easily be "worked up" into a good Christmas story for the magazines (xx, 157). But Howells, like the mature Dickens, realized the inadequacy of certain kinds of benevolence, had transformed Mrs. Pardiggle into a leather-bound American socialite named Munger, and had taken Esther Summerson's painful discovery that "between us and these people [the brickmakers] there was an iron barrier, which could not be removed by our new friend [Mrs. Pardiggle]. By whom, or how, it could be removed, we did not know; but we knew that" (XVI, viii, 131), and made it into the history of Annie Kilburn. Nevertheless, in Howells's belief in the spark of unconquerable human decency we get at the most explicitly Dickensian motif in all his novels, his notion that there is a chain of complicity linking the divine, the natural, and the human worlds and its corollary, his faith in an over-riding Providence.

Providence was Howells's way out, his strategy for avoiding the implications of his own fictional mode and the solution to the problems his novels raised. Larzer Ziff takes us close to the problem when he observes how near Howells comes in his social novels to imitating the moral structures of "romance." The romancers, Ziff points out:

> justified their Never-Never-Land tales of great feats of self-denial and superhuman love by saying that they were needed precisely because such standards were missing from society unless available in fiction. They admitted they were romancing. Howells took something which he urgently believed to be wanting, social justice, a felt harmony among men which made class differences cooperative

> expressions of the same group will rather than the signs of a basic division of interest, and attempted to show what it was. But he was a realistic novelist, not a romancer, and so Never-Never-Land was unavailable to him.[44]

Thus Howells's attempt to impose a fundamentally moralistic ideal upon empirically observed "reality" brands him as a "romanticist." This is perceptive analysis, but it is, I think, possible to go beyond it. For one thing, as indicated already, Howells is never fully able to dramatize his ideal within the worlds of his novels. Those of his characters who recognize it are either run over by trains or forced into retreat and isolation, its realization being inevitably postponed into an indefinite future. Thus the precise contours of social justice remain vague and inchoate. Even so sympathetic a reader as Hamlin Garland missed the intended point of Annie Kilburn entirely; his review left Howells feeling like the clergyman who had preached his strongest sermon against atheism only to have one of his parishioners tell him, "But parson, I do believe there *is* a God."[45] Similarly, twentieth-century commentators seem almost invariably to find that they must turn to Howells's non-fiction in order to fill in the gaps and explicate the novels.

It is true that in the utopian "romances" Howells turned precisely to Never-Never-Land in order to illustrate his ideals; but in the novels social justice is continually taken out of the hands of his characters and placed into those of Divine Providence. Of the failures of the Reverends Sewell and Peck, of Annie Kilburn and Conrad Dreyfoos, Denton and Hughes, Howells can only say as he said of the failure of the Brooklyn trolleymen's strike in 1895 "But I believe that the right will win in the end."[46] This selling out, as it were, of "hard-headed" analysis for quasi-religious faith takes many forms, ranging from implicit endorsement of Providence by the most improbable plot devices to explicit statements of a better world to come. In the early novel A Woman's Reason the heroine feels forced by circumstances to abandon her leisure class position and earn her own living by toil. Throwing herself into the economic chance world, she is nearly destroyed. But she is rescued, just at the last moment, by her naval officer lover, who it turns out, has--like Dickens's Walter Gay--not been lost at sea but only conveniently stranded on a desert island. In a later work, The Landlord at Lion's Head, the central figure, Jeff Durgin, is an amoral rascal who openly defies the doctrine of complicity on all its levels, human (his refusal to accept any responsibility in the affairs of others is symbolized by his feeding liquor to an alcoholic), social (he burns his inn in order to collect the insurance), natural (each of his successive alterations in his family home only goes farther in disrupting the natural harmony of the landscape), and divine (he openly laughs at the notion of a moral order in the universe). Yet within the framework of the novel Howells can punish his crimes only with an occasional tongue-lashing, which he easily sloughs off, and by a horsewhipping, which he does not think significant enough to require revenge. True retribution exists only in the realm of Providence. The painter, Westover, speaks for Howells when he maintains that:

> "A tree brings forth of its kind. As a man sows he reaps. It's dead sure, pitilessly sure. Jeff Durgin sowed success, in a certain way, and he's reaping it. He once said to me, when I tried to waken his conscience, that he should get where he was trying to go if he was strong enough, and being good had nothing to do with it. I believe now he was right. But he was wrong too, as such a man always is. That kind of tree bears Dead Sea apples, after all. He sowed evil and he must reap evil."

But since Westover's prediction has nothing to do with the logic of events in the narrative itself, he is forced to go on to make an extraordinary statement. Jeff, he says, will be punished, even though "He may never know it." Westover's mind may be boggling as rapidly as the reader's; at any rate, he shifts his tack slightly to pass the novel's final judgment on the issues raised by Durgin's career: "Perhaps we're all broken shafts, here. Perhaps that old hypothesis of another world where there is room enough and time enough for all the beginnings of this to complete themselves--"[47]

To solve the problems raised by the "realistic" analysis of society, then, Howells had to turn to the "ideal" world of "romance." What needs to be emphasized here, however, is how closely, outside the novels, Howells associated his providential faith in an ideal world just around the corner with Dickens's social criticism. At the time when his interest in social issues was at its peak, he wrote of Dickens a passage that is worth quoting again:

> In that world of his, in the ideal world, to which the real world must finally conform itself, I dwelt among the shows of things, but under a Providence that governed all things to a good end, and where neither wealth nor birth could avail against virtue or right. Of course it was in a way all crude enough, and was already contradicted by experience in the small realm of my own being; but nevertheless it was true with that truth which is at the bottom of things, and I was happy in it.[48]

As intimated in the previous chapter the passage embodies in miniature the very problem Howells encounters in his own fictions, the unresolved contradiction between two mutually antagonostic modes of thought: faith in "experience" and faith in "Providence." It also exhibits his characteristic resolution, the falling back on that comfortable ideality which the genteel tradition in America had milked out of the tragic vision of Romantic transcendentalism. The passage posits a dualistic universe divided into the material "real" world of empirical experience and an "ideal" world that is spiritual in nature and only intuitively perceived. Then, in direct violation of the critical and epistemological canons Howells elsewhere expounds, it asserts that the truth of experience in the "real" world is secondary to the truth "which is at the bottom of things" in the "spiritual" realm. In other words, the ideal grasshopper is, it seems, the "real," the better one after all. It is not surprising, therefore, to find that one of Howells's last attempts at social fiction reads like a Dickens Christmas story.

III.

> People always knew that character is not changed by a dream in a series of tableaux; that a ghost cannot do much towards reforming an inordinately selfish person...that want and sin and shame cannot be cured by kettles singing on the hob.
> --W. D. Howells

The Son of Royal Langbrith was not written within the years generally considered Howells's "social period," a period thought to close with the publication of the Altrurian "romances." They had been followed by such returns to the early, comedy of manners mode as The Day of Their Wedding and An Open-Eyed Conspiracy. By 1899 Howells seemed to have come full circle, publishing a novel that takes Basil and Isabel March over much the same ground they had traversed twenty-five years earlier and calling it Their Silver Wedding Journey. But retreat into the triumphs of the past was not possible; Howells found the writing of Their Silver Wedding Journey the most irksome chore of his career. Writing to his father he reflected that:

> I am an elderly man, and I ought to deal more with things of spiritual significance. This is what I have felt for some time. Outer life no longer interests me as it once did, and I cannot paint it with spirit, or give it the charm I used to find

> in it. After this I do not think I will try; and I believe I can find a new audience for my studies of the inner life. I don't know what shape they will take.[49]

Yet despite his sense of exploration and hopes for a new audience, his most interesting study of inner life was to take a familiar shape and investigate a familiar theme: the effects of one man's misdeeds on his family, their associates, and the community at large, ground he had already been over in The Quality of Mercy. Thus if The Son of Royal Langbrith is not, strictly speaking, of the "social group," it is closely allied to it. Its difference is only that it carries Howells's continuing study of the new men of the post Civil War era into their second generation.

The novel centers on the question whether it is the duty of those who know to inform James Langbrith that the father whose memory he worships was, in reality, a scoundrel. The issue comes to a head when James proposes to commission a plaque bearing his father's portrait and dedicated to his memory to be hung in public ceremony on the front of the library the elder Langbrith had given the town. Their decision, endorsed by Howells, is to remain silent, even though the concealment costs them all a considerable loss in personal happiness. Judge Garley must suffer through the ceremony in which he is called upon to eulogize a man he despises. The Rev. Mr. Enderby, who must quiet an uneasy conscience as well as a flighty and talkative wife, suffers something akin to a religious crisis, and Dr. Anther, the novel's most interesting figure, must forego his dream of marrying Langbrith's widow.

Interestingly, the decision not to disclose Langbrith's true character is based on motives more social than strictly moral. The townspeople, especially among the lower-classes, have also come to revere the dead man's memory and to see in his rise a Horatio Alger pattern that inspires them in their toil. To reveal that the success they worship was acquired by a rascal would dangerously demoralize the community, making it cynical and depraved by teaching it to place a premium on hypocrisy. There are the makings here of a telling irony, a dramatic illustration of the disintegration of the American dream of the City on a Hill in a society that must, however well-intentioned, be cynical and hypocritical in order to prevent hypocrisy and cynicism. But Howells throws it away. Apparently unsure of the efficacy of "critical realism" to expose the moral disease inherent in nineteenth-century competitive capitalism and its "acres of diamonds" philosophy, he falls back upon Dickensian melodrama. Royal Langbrith's evil, it turns out, consists primarily not in his being a ruthless robber-baron; Howells makes him a wife-beater, a drunkard, and a bigamist as well, implying that it is all right to admire economic exploitation, but dangerous to divorce the worship of success from the puritan ethic that labels wealth the reward for purity in private life--regardless of the way one conducts his public, business affairs.

The melodrama surrounding Langbrith is not the only Dickensian element in the novel. It is interesting to note as incidental information that the Wellerism was still alive in 1904, that at sixty-seven Howells's humor was still as full of Dickensian touches as it was at sixteen, and that even after the turn of the century novelists were still labelling characters. Amelia Langbrith probably owes her name to the long-suffering and weak-willed heroines of Fielding and Thackeray, while "Hope" Hawberk needs no explanation. Royal Langbrith's last name is as ironic as his first. James takes great delight in explaining that it is an Anglicization of the Norman "Longuehaleine," apparently unaware that it is all hot air. Hope's father is, like the elder Langbrith, a creature out of melodrama. Originally a partner in the mills, he had been blackmailed by Langbrith into relinquishing his rights to the invention that makes Langbrith's fortune. Embittered, he takes to opium and becomes an addict, prey to the twin hallucinations that he is being buried alive by a little green dwarf and that Royal had actually been his best friend. Anther undertakes his cure in the hope that once his memory is restored he will reveal all. The cure is successful, but Hawberk, in his new-found lucidity, also decides to remain silent and is killed in an accident a few days before James's final return to Saxmills. Thus in addition to overtones of John Jasper, Hawberk recalls a whole tradition of Dickens's characters (including Newman Noggs, Lewsome, Mr. Wickfield, and Flintwich's brother) who possess a fateful secret but are prevented by disease, dissipation, or both, usually fostered by those whom his existence threatens, from revealing it. True to form, he is surrounded by satellite characters who reinforce the Dickensian aura in which his story is placed. His mother-in-law is Howells's version of Mr. F's Aunt, a dried up old New Englander who emerges from her corner periodically to spew out hostility and prophesy disaster. Even more curious is his daughter, a remarkable combination of Lydia Blood and Agnes Wickfield, a kind of Esther Summerson dressed up as a Gibson girl.

Like her prototypes in Dickens, Hope has the function of standing as the center of all homely virtues: fresh virginal innocence, good cheer in adversity, and common sense in moments of crisis. Her devotion to her father parallels that of Agnes or Little Nell; frequently she is Jenny Wren to Hawberk's Mr. Dolls. Like Nell she is capable of laying aside her burdens occasionally and tripping through the forest, all innocence and coyness, sweetness and light. Her strength and high spirits are an inspiration for all Saxmills, but particularly, for reasons to be explained later, for the Rev. Enderby's wife. To love her is to undergo a sort of moral redemption. When James returns home after sealing his engagement to her, he finds his mother in the arms of Dr. Anther. It is the moment the middle-aged lovers have dreaded most, but James's anger is curiously impotent; "the cruelest blows he dealt them had seemed to fall like blows dealt in nightmare, as if they were dealt with balls of cotton or of down." The restraining force is, of course, his "thought of Hope."[50] Similarly at the end of the novel, when James has learned the truth about his father, his initial impulse is to throw himself into an ecstasy of self-sacrifice. He will renounce his engagement and, in an ironic re-enactment of the unveiling ceremony, expose his inherited guilt before the town. But again he is saved by Hope, who will stand for neither renunciation nor melodramatic disclosures. Rather she succors him with the wisdom of the Rev. Enderby, who teaches him that the greater sacrifice and expiation is to learn to live with his secret shame. They are married, and on Christmas Day take up residence in the ancestral home to live happily ever after.

To stress the Dickensian pattern in The Son of Royal Langbrith in the manner of the preceding paragraph is, of course, to distort the novel's tone and make it appear ridiculous. Yet the fact remains that the pattern is there. In its externals the novel recalls any number of Dickens's novels and Christmas stories in which the past continually impinges upon the present and the dead absorb the lives of the living until the ghosts are exorcised and the angel-figures enthroned. James Langbrith's history is curiously like that of Mr. Redlaw, the central figure of The Haunted Man, whose loss of memory distorts his own nature and blasts the happiness of all who meet him until he is brought, through the aid of the angelic Milly, to the ability to live with and use the "sorrow, wrong, and trouble" of the past. Howells removes the machinery of ghosts and holly boughs, but the moral remains the same.

Like most villains in Dickens's Christmas tales young Langbrith's ruling passion is his selfish egotism. Writing to H. B. Fuller, Howells explained that "Langbrith won't be the outright brute that Jeff Durgin was," but actually he is much less attractive.[51] Lacking Durgin's somewhat savage charm, he comes across as a pompous, patronizing ass, a sort of young Martin Chuzzlewit, whose purpose in life is to set himself up as some kind of hereditary lord and rule over Saxmills as if it were a collection of thatched huts. Nor are we long in realizing that the "religion" he builds around his father is only the expression of an intense self-love and a weapon for bending others--particularly his mother--to his own selfish will. He is transparent even to the briefest acquaintances; Howells says of the young sculptor commissioned to execute the medallion for the library that "He had conceived so aptly of his patron, if not of his subject, that he flattered the effigy of the elder Langbrith into a likeness of the son, who stood before it in content little short of ecstasy" (xx, 177).

Appropriately it is James's high-handed exploitation of his father's memory as a means of avoiding personal inconvenience that sets in motion the chain of events leading to his downfall. After unveiling the memorial, he leaves for Paris and a dilettante's career, placing the family business solely in the hands of his uncle. When the uncle's dyspepsia becomes acute, he writes to his nephew, requesting that he return to take over the mills so that he may placate his ulcers with an ocean voyage. James writes back that it is not convenient for him to leave Paris at the moment:

> but that, if John Langbrith wished to relinquish his charge of the mills, it would be entirely acceptable to have them left in the hands of his business lieutenant and of Mr. Hawberk, who, as the old and devoted friend of his father, would doubtless feel, as his father's brother seemed not to have felt, the importance and sacred character of the charge. (xxxiii, 316-17)

When he does return, it is to encounter his uncle on the Saxmills train. Suffering from a severe gastric attack, brought on by frolicking with baked beans and black coffee at a railroad restaurant, John Langbrith finds his nephew's pomposity and "Europeanized" airs the last straw; in a fit of dyspeptic rage, he tells him all.

The Son of Royal Langbrith, then, contains all the material for a tragedy even more stark and classical in its outlines than its author's earlier reworking of the Medea legend in *A Modern Instance*. We have a hero whose princely role in the community (both real and assumed) could elevate him to tragic stature. Like Oedipus or Agamemnon he belongs to a house blighted by the curse of ancestral wrong and displays a *hybris* equal to that of either hero. We have a Peripety and a Discovery of what Aristotle would call the "finest form" in that one attends the other and both grow directly out of the hero's pride, happening unexpectedly but clearly consequentially. Everything is there but the Suffering. When forced to make a decision about the form of his novel, Howells opts not for tragedy but for the Christmas story. His hero is redeemed, not destroyed.

Abundant evidence demonstrates that Howells was fully aware of the implications of his choice. To Fuller he observed that "The tale is tragical enough, but I have purposely refused several effects of tragedy that offered themselves to my hand," and to Clemens he expressed his pride in having "hopped over" and "sidestepped" the tragic implications of his materials.[52] But his fullest statement of intention is in the "Bibliographical" note he wrote for the never published "Library Edition":

> At times there was question whether there ought not to be a supremely tragical outcome, a ruin spreading wide and sinking deep from the sin committed and concealed; but tragedy seemed finally too easy, and I shrank from it. Now it appears to me that the father's secret came to the son in a natural and a right way, and that it ceased with him and his in a just and reasonable sort. There might have been greater theatre in the more explicit tragedy, but I doubt if there would have been greater drama; and besides, I have always loved the sweet face of Nature, the divine look of Probability.[53]

When we examine the novel itself, Probability turns out to be Providence after all. In both letters cited above

Howells defines Probability as being, in this case, the elasticity of youth, which, mastering sorrow and loss, always reverts to the joy and love natural to it. Unhappiness is not held over from one generation to the next, and a good woman's love can "master" even a James Langbrith. These notions, based on a series of Victorian assumptions continually exploited by Dickens, are sentimental enough in themselves; in the actual working out of the novel they are even more so. Youth and love turn out to be the agents of a divine Providence by which right wins out in the end on Christmas Day.

The power of the past to tyrannize the present haunts each of the novel's major characters. Anther, finding himself blocked and taunted at every turn by the ghost of Royal Langbrith, almost comes to believe, despite his faith in science and natural causation, that Langbrith has some sort of "Satanic" power to extend his evil beyond his grave. Indeed, the conflict between his scientific frame of reference and his experiences continually baffles him in his attempts to philosophize his situation. Since the material world is ruled by order and law, effect following naturally from cause, so should be the moral world. But it does not seem so; Langbrith's evil not only goes unpunished but also prevents good, Anther's own included, from being rewarded. Even his efforts to cure Hawberk turn out to be without moral meaning, for he realizes that his desire to see "justice" done is only a mask for his own selfish interests, that he wishes to restore the addict's memory not for the sake of an abstract truth but as the means of making his own engagement possible. (Ironically, even when the truth is revealed, it comes too late to do Anther any good; the doctor is dead when James returns.) Whichever way he turns, he remains in the same trap: experience is either meaningless or means evil. "If the situation had been contrived by the sardonic spirit of Royal Langbrith himself," Anther finally concludes, "it could not have had a more diabolical perfection" (xxix, 281).

Anther's philosophical difficulties are so extreme that he himself--even though he represents the "realistic" point of view in the novel--cannot find his way out of them and can only passively submit to circumstances with world-weary Stoicism. It is Howells himself who must step in to resolve the problem <u>in propia persona</u>:

> Life is never the logical and consequent thing we argue from the moral and intellectual premises. There ought always to be evident reason in it; but such reason as it has is often crossed and obscured by perverse events, which, in our brief perspective, give it the aspect of a helpless craze. Obvious

> effect does not follow obvious cause; there is sometimes no perceptible cause for the effects we see. The law we find at work in the material world is, apparently, absent from the moral world; not, imaginably, because it is without law, but because the law is of such cosmic vastness in its operation that it is only once or twice sensible to any man's experience.
>
> (xxx, 282)

We seem to be right back where we started from. Howells's desire to break new ground with "spiritual" studies of the "inner life" has brought him to the same conclusion he had reached at the end of The World of Chance eleven years earlier:

> We must own that we often saw the good unhappy, and the wicked enjoying themselves. This was not just; yet somehow we felt, we knew, that justice ruled the universe. Nothing then, that seemed chance was really chance. It was the operation of a law so large that we caught a glimpse of its vast orbit once or twice in a lifetime. It was Providence.
>
> (xlv, 375)

Again the contradictions of the "real" world of experience have been resolved by recourse to an "ideal" world governed by a benign Providence. Again Howells has set out to depict "the sweet face of Nature" (and the capital "N" may not be without meaning), to "realistically" explore the probabilities and meanings of a human situation only to fall back on the teleological optimism that, while he may have acquired it from any number of sources, he repeatedly and almost exclusively associated with Dickens.

Enderby faces essentially the same problem as that which confronts Anther, only it is in some ways more acute since he is, both philosophically and professionally, more committed to the existence of a moral government in the universe. He easily reaches his decision not to inform James of his father's true character. Besides being socially dangerous, exposure would imply a human encroachment on Divine prerogatives:

> ...we must leave it all to God now, as it has been left hitherto. ...The circumstances will arrange themselves; the atoms will fall into the order of the divine scheme. We must keep our hands off. ...Everything shall be made known, but perhaps not on earth. Whoever wished to hasten the knowledge of hidden evil, here and now, might well beware of forcing God's purposes...
>
> (xxiii, 212-13)

Providence proves him right in both cases. The threat to public morals takes care of itself; Saxmills's love-affair with the memory of Royal Langbrith is short-lived: "from the moment of the dedication of the votive tablet by the son, the myth of the father suffered a kind of discoloration, not to say obscuration" (xxxvii, 360). John Langbrith's dyspepsia fills him with delight: "The rector thought how it was written, 'Surely the wrath of man shall praise Thee.' It seemed to him that the Divine Providence had not acted inopportunely; and he was contented with the mode in which the young man had learned the worst" (xxxvi, 351). But he is still left with the fact that Royal Langbrith's sins seem to go unpunished. He accounts for it in two ways. In the first he hypothesizes that in the instant consciousness of death that accompanied Langbrith's heart attack, he may have seen his whole life passing in review and suffered accordingly in his awareness that he could never undo its evil. The second is even more remarkable. Perhaps there is a sort of Divine statute of limitations by which Langbrith's overdue moral debts are forgiven; besides, "It may be the complicity of all mortal being is such that the pain he inflicted was endured to his behoof, and that it has helped him atone for his sins" (xxxvii, 369). But in both cases the trust is still in the hands of Providence.

Ultimately neither Anther nor Enderby is Howells's spokesman in the novel. That role is reserved for the minister's wife. As full of good-will as she is short on perception, Mrs. Enderby is continually satirized for her flightiness and her tendency to "romanticize" everything--including her husband's High Church Anglicanism. But her essential goodness is not questioned, and Howells, despite the irony in his treatment of her, can never sever his point of view from hers. While he pokes fun at her busy-body eagerness to hear her husband and the doctor discuss Langbrith's case ("I should so much like to hear you discussing the civic and social significance of such a man...and getting at the psychology of him" [xxii, 203]), it is, for example, he himself who says of their interview, "Science and Religion met in the study of the life laid bare between them" (xxiii, 211). To her Enderby's second explanation of Langbrith's unpunished sins is as abstruse as the first is unlikely. But like Howells himself she accepts his belief that the whole affair should be left in the hands of Providence to await the Supreme Will as nothing less than divinely inspired. She has great hopes of James's and Hope's marriage; she looks to it "as the panacea of whatever ills life had in store for them" (xxxii, 310). Providence--and Howells--prove her hopes justified. And it is through her delight in the fact that Howells allows us to know that the marriage takes place at "the sacred time, when peace on earth and good-will was prophesied in every sort" (xxxvii, 358). Again, the point to be stressed is that, although Howells's faith in Providence could have had any number of sources, his novelistic working out of that faith within the framework of _The Son of Royal Langbrith_ follows, with extraordinary consistency, the pattern that he himself had publicly observed in Dickens's Christmas books. Indeed, the parallels can even be worked out with schematic precision.

In Criticism and Fiction Howells had cataloged the "devices and appliances" that, he said, delight the "puerilized fancy" in Dickens's Christmas stories. "People always knew," he wrote, "that character is not changed by a dream in a series of tableaux," but this is precisely what Enderby conjectures happened at Royal Langbrith's death. People always knew "that a ghost cannot do much toward reforming an inordinately selfish person," but this is precisely the effect of the ghost of the real Royal Langbrith on his son. People always knew "that want and sin and shame cannot be cured by kettles singing on the hob," but what other meaning is there in Hope Hawberk's effect on James Langbrith? In Dickens, Howells continued, the crudeness was dignified and justified by the ethical intention: "It was well once a year, if not oftener, to remind men by parable of the old simple truths, to teach them that forgiveness and charity, and the endeavor for life better and purer than each has lived, are the principles upon which alone the world holds together."[54] We must have patience and await the Divine Will, says the Rev. Mr. Enderby; we are not allowed vengeance, but we may show mercy.

The teleological optimism that Howells stresses in his criticism of Dickens and exploits in his own novels actually ends in Dickens with the wish-fulfillment conclusion of _David Copperfield_. In _Bleak House_ the view is mixed. On the one hand there is the bitter, "providential" intimation that evil will destroy itself by internal spontaneous combustion, and on the other the sense of frustration and helplessness symbolized by the "iron barrier" that separates Esther from the brickmakers. The latter view prevails in _Hard Times_, summed up by Stephan Blackpool's celebrated assessment of the social situation, "Aw--a muddle!" and dominates the major novels that followed, _Little Dorrit_, _Great Expectations_, and _Our Mutual Friend_. After _Bleak House_ the writing of Christmas stories was turned over almost entirely to Wilkie Collins and G. A. Sala. Howells's social fiction followsthe pattern of the early Dickens of _Nicholas Nickleby_ and _The Chimes_. Only _The Quality of Mercy_, with its emphasis on the frustrated will and its portrayal of society as a prison that traps Eben Hilary in Boston just as it surrounds J. Milton Northwick in the mock freedom of the Canadian wastes, comes close to the pattern typified by _Little Dorrit_. _The Son of Royal Langbrith_, with its Christmas book form, can stand for all the rest. It differs from Howells's earlier novels only in the greater explicitness of its statement and the increased sophistication of its devices. Instead of waiting for a wealthy lover to be rescued off a desert island, one waits for a dyspeptic industrialist to eat beans and pie. But Providence triumphs all the same.

Notes to Chapter V

[1]Quoted by Harry T. Moore in his "Preface" to William McMurray, The Literary Realism of William Dean Howells (Carbondale, Ill., 1967), p. vi.

[2]Ashtabula Sentinel, XXIII (28 December 1854), p. 4. I wish to thank the research staff of the Ohio Historical Society Museum, Columbus, Ohio, for granting me access to and guidance through their files of Howells's newspaper contributions and unpublished letters.

[3]Installments were serialized weekly on the first page of the Sentinel, beginning on 23 November 1854 (Vol. XXIII, No. 46) and continuing through 18 January 1855 (Vol. XXIV, No. 2) skipping one issue (XXIII, No. 49, 14 December 1854).

[4]My Literary Passions, pp. 85-87; Cady both in Road to Realism, pp. 49-51, and in "William Dean Howells and the Ashtabula Sentinel," The Ohio State Archeological and Historical Quarterly, LIII (Jan.-Mar., 1944), 43-50.

[5]Ashtabula Sentinel, Vol. XXIII, No. 51 (28 December 1854), p. 1.

[6]In Quest of America: A Study of Howells's Early Development as a Novelist (Upsala, 1958), p. 20.

[7]Ashtabula Sentinel, XXIV, No. 1 (11 January 1855), p. 1. The passage also serves to remind us of the truth of Walter Blair's assertion that without Dickens Western humor would never have been possible. "Dashiell Hammett: Themes and Techniques," in Essays on American Literature in Honor of Jay B. Hubbell, ed. Clarence Gohdes (Durham, 1967), p. 295.

[8]"Sort of narrative": WDH to J. M. Comley, 31 March 1871. MS in the Ohio Historical Society Museum. "Involved narration": Their Wedding Journey (Boston, 1872), ch. i, p. 1. Editions of Howells's novels being quoted will be identified in the notes at the first reference to each; thereafter citations will be made in the text by book (if any), chapter, and page in the cited text (thus: i, 1).

[9] See, e.g., John K. Reeves's detailed study of the manuscripts, "The Limited Realism of Howells's Their Wedding Journey," PMLA, LXXVII (December, 1962), 617-28. In the pages that follow the reader should bear in mind that, as I indicated in the previous chapter, I do not believe that the terms "realism" and "romanticism" (and their derivatives) have any great critical usefulness because they lack semantic integrity and validity. They were--and are--used to mean too much to mean anything. As I will attempt to demonstrate, Howells's major limitation as a novelist is his tendency to write novels that set out to be one thing and end up being another. The point can, I think, be best made if one avoids becoming entangled in Howells's own vocabulary. Indeed, one wonders if the vagueness and inadequacy of his critical terminology did not contribute to his difficulties as a novelist. When the terms are used, they are meant to represent Howells's mode of thought, not the present writer's.

[10] In Quest of America, pp. 108-09.

[11] NAR, CXIV (April, 1872), 444-45.

[12] "Closely and realistically," "clear natural eye": Letters to Annie Howells and Ralph Keeler quoted in Cady, Road to Realism, p. 160; "tone and key": Road to Realism, p. 161.

[13] Cady, who accepts and adopts Howells's critical vocabulary, cites the fact that Howells wrote "My first novel" on the flyleaf of a presentation copy of A Foregone Conclusion as evidence of his awareness of the "romantic" nature of Their Wedding Journey and A Chance Acquaintance. (Road to Realism, pp. 187-89.) But in the lecture "Novels and Novel Writing" cited in the previous chapter Howells describes A Chance Acquaintance as his first novel, implying that it merits that distinction simply because its descriptions of travel are more systematically subordinated to narrative concerns than those in Their Wedding Journey.

[14] Life in Letters, I, 371.

[15] Boston, 1886, ch. xxiii, p. 392.

[16] The quality of the ending of Indian Summer can be further measured if Effie is compared to James's Maisie. Like Effie, Maisie owes much to Dickens's children. But

James never falls into the kind of sentiment that Howells seems prey to. Maisie's attempts to bring people together are always surrounded by irony, and it is part of her predicament that her efforts to "square" people always come to naught. It is inconceivable that Maisie could ever function quite like Effie. James takes the Dickensian motif and molds it to his own purposes; Howells simply takes it, regardless of what it does to the thematic structure of his novel.

[17]My Literary Passions, p. 250.

[18]See Aylmer Maude, The Life of Tolstoy (Oxford, 1929), I, 177; and Ford, Dickens and His Readers, pp. 192-93.

[19]Criticism and Fiction, p. 185.

[20]Realist at War, p. 85.

[21]"William Dean Howells," Harper's Weekly, XXX (19 June 1886), 396.

[22]E.g., the anonymous reviewer who observed that Howells in saying that the "finer art" of James had been influenced by Daudet was actually paying tribute to Dickens since Dickens had so obviously and largely influenced Daudet, making it evident that "all this brave talk about that mannerism which cannot now be suffered, means only that the American likes a literary influence better when he gets it diluted by way of France." "American Literature in England," Blackwood's Magazine, CXXXIII (January, 1883), 138.

[23](New York, 1889, ch. xii, pp. 149-50. Besides the intimations of mad, mindless, jerking motions and such patent quirks of style as the workmen watching the machines "with suicidal intensity," one notices the overall Dickens strategy of humanizing the machines and dehumanizing the people. The passage may be compared with the descriptions of mills in ch. xliv of The Old Curiosity Shop or throughout Hard Times. On Howells's visit to Lowell, see Cady, Realist at War, p. 64.

[24]Grattan: "Howells: Ten Years After," American Mercury, XX (May, 1930), 42-50; Smith: Mark Twain's Fable of Progress: Political and Social Ideas in A Connecticut Yankee (New Brunswick, N.J., 1964), pp. 20-35.

[25]Franklyn Walker, Frank Norris: A Biography (New York, 1963), pp. 275, 278.

[26]Michael Millgate has also noticed the preponderance of chivalric metaphors in The Pit, although he turns it to slightly different account. American Social Fiction: James to Cozzens (New York, 1964), pp. 41-42. The metaphor is easily reversed. Thus what Crane learned by depicting economic battle in Maggie and "The Bowery Tales" needed only to be turned around to produce The Red Badge of Courage.

[27]It is clear from the several passages describing it that the elevated railroad is meant to have some sort of symbolic content. But even after several readings one is still hard pressed to say just what that content is.

[28]Smith, Mark Twain's Fable, p. 29.

[29]Budd, "William Dean Howells's Defense of the Romance," 40.

[30]"Henry James's First Novel," Scrutiny, XIV (September, 1947), 299. Leavis cites Mr. Leavenworth in Roderick Hudson as a character "placed" in his thematic role by Dickensian techniques of characterization.

[31]Heroines of Fiction, I, 129.

[32]Howells's debt has been somewhat over-enthusiastically described before: "Rogers, a being of small initial promise, develops into a specimen of grotesque admirable enough to suggest a profane comparison with Dickens." Oscar W. Firkins, William Dean Howells: A Study (Cambridge, Mass., 1922), p. 116.

[33]"William Dean Howells and the Roots of Modern Taste," in The Opposing Self (New York, 1959), p. 84.

[34]Of course Dickens was not the only caricaturist to whose methods Howells had been exposed. But, nevertheless, characters like Gerrish can clearly be labelled "Dickensian." Cf. Ford, Dickens and His Readers, p. 211: "In general, the kind of 'Dickensisms,' as James calls them, which are most readily identified in post-Dickens novels are characters whose eccentricities are strongly marked.... All novels...of course contain them, and in many novels before Pickwick

Papers there were strongly marked eccentrics. Dickens has nevertheless usually been given credit for inspiring those which have followed.... Thus in Loving, by Henry Green, a novelist who disapproves of Dickens...has yet created a talkative, gin-drinking cook, Mrs. Welch, who was described by reviewers as 'Dickensian.' And everyone knows what is meant."

[35]Criticism and Fiction, p. 177

[36]The same tendency of a certain type to slip over into caricature, especially if the characterization is achieved primarily through speech, can be seen in the character of Lorenzo Pinney in The Quality of Mercy and even in the "advertising essence," Fulkerson, in A Hazard of New Fortunes, one of Howells's finest--and most Dickensian--creations.

[37]If pure young girls presented a problem, social critics and reformers were even more difficult to handle. In a rather self-conscious passage in The World of Chance one of the characters remarks of another, "I don't know why a reformer should be so grotesque; but he is, and he is always the easy prey of caricature. I couldn't help feeling to-day how very like the burlesque reformers the real reformers are." (New York, 1893), ch. xvii, p. 129.

[38]Past and Present, "World's Classics," (London, 1957), p. 154.

[39](New York, 1888), ch. xxvi, p. 238.

[40](Boston, 1887), ch. iii, p. 37.

[41](New York, 1892), Bk. III, ch. xi, p. 474.

[42]In, of course, the first ending. Sewell says, "If I thought I could never do anything more for Barker, I should be very unhappy," but he never does (xxxv, 460).

[43]Signet Classics (New York, 1965), Bk. V, ch. viii, p. 380.

[44]The American 1890s (New York, 1966), p. 37.

[45]Life in Letters, I, 419.

[46] *Life in Letters*, II, 59.

[47] Signet Classics (New York, 1964), ch. liv, pp. 303-04. The "broken shafts" are more than just an oblique reference to Browning, who may be the immediate source for this particular passage. In the context of the novel they serve, ironically, to link Westover's ultimate position with that of a group of characters whose fondness for the Ouija board Howells had employed to symbolize and satirize the disintegration of New England Puritanism.

[48] *My Literary Passions*, p. 98.

[49] Publ. in G. Ferris Cronkhite, "Howells Turns to the Inner Life," *NEQ*, XXX (December, 1957), 475-76.

[50] (New York, 1904), ch. xxvii, p. 254.

[51] *Life in Letters*, II, 181.

[52] *Life in Letters*, II, 181, 186.

[53] George Arms, "Howells's Unpublished Prefaces," *NEQ*, XVII (December, 1944), 585.

[54] Pp. 178-79.

CHAPTER VI

HENRY JAMES: THE ILLUSTRATOR'S POINT OF VIEW

> *Le Petit Chose*, his first long story, reads today like the attempt of a beginner, and of a beginner who had read and enjoyed Dickens. I risk this allusion to the author of *Copperfield* in spite of a conviction that Alphonse Daudet must be tired of hearing that he imitates him. It is not imitation; there is nothing so gross as imitation in the length and breadth of Daudet's work; but it is conscious sympathy, for there is plenty of that. There are pages in his tales which seem to say to us that at one moment of his life Dickens had been a revelation to him...
>
> --Henry James

I.

There is no need to lavish upon James the kind of minute attention to his readings in and responses to Dickens that is elsewhere devoted to Mark Twain, Howells, and Norris.

That James read Dickens and read him well is common knowledge; moreover, the nature and quality of his response has been admirably delineated by others.[1] Nor is it necessary to attempt to argue with the kind of either/or criticism, stemming from a celebrated remark that The Bostonians is "Martin Chuzzlewit redone by an enormously more intelligent and better educated mind," that flourished in the late forties and the fifties. One may profit from Mr. Leavis's admirable and useful insights without necessarily accepting the critical eccentricity and a priori dogmatism that prompted them. The house of criticism also has its many rooms.[2]

Therefore, in lieu of a systematic study of James's readings in and comments upon Dickens, there need only be reasserted the facts that James did read Dickens, that he commented upon him repeatedly in his critical writings, and that he was deeply influenced by him. If not all his comments are laudatory, neither do they--as he himself best knew--deny the fecundity of Dickens's impression upon his imagination. Dickens had, for James, that quality of greatness that transcends criticism. In a remarkable passage in A Small Boy and Others James analyses, in a way rich in lessons for students of literary indebtedness, both the Dickens phenomenon and his own relationship to it:

> Such at least was to be the force of the Dickens imprint, however applied, in the soft clay of our generation; it was to resist so serenely the wash of the waves of time. To be brought up thus against the author of it, or to speak at all of the dawn of one's early consciousness of it and of his presence and power, is to begin to tread ground at once sacred and boundless, the associations of which, looming large, warn us off even while they hold. He did too much for us surely ever to leave us free--free of judgment, free of reaction, even should we care to be, which heaven forbid: he laid his hand on us in a way to undermine as in no other case the power of detached appraisement. We react against other productions of the general kind without "liking" them the less, but we somehow liked Dickens the more for having forfeited half the claim to appreciation. That process belongs to the fact that criticism, roundabout him, is somehow futile and tasteless. His own taste is easily impugned, but he entered so early into the blood and bone of our intelligence that it always remained better than the taste of overhauling him. When I take him up to-day and find myself holding off, I simply stop: not holding off, that is, but holding on, and from the very fear to do so; which sounds, I recognise, like perusal, like renewal, of the scantest. I don't renew, I wouldn't renew for the world; wouldn't, that is, with one's treasure so hoarded in the dusty chamber of youth, let in the intellectual air. Happy the house of life in which such chambers still hold out, even with the draught of the intellect whistling through the passages. We were practically contemporary, contemporary with the issues, the fluttering monthly numbers--that was the point; it made for us a good fortune, constituted for us in itself romance, on which nothing, to the end, succeeds in laying its hands.[3]

Few authors have ever received such moving tribute from a fellow master of the craft. James is James and Dickens is

Dickens; but one may learn by differing as well as concurring; in both cases the organic relation of child to parent asserts and maintains itself. We grow to be our own men, but our "blood and bone" is that of our forefathers. The James writing above is nearly seventy, but he is the same James who at twenty-two had written a review of Our Mutual Friend that is, as George Ford observes, "both a declaration of independence and a manifesto of his own aims as a future novelist."[4] The review is a systematic listing of what, to a "yearning dabbler in the mystery," are "the limitations of Dickens"--indeed, the essay was, years later, reprinted under that title. But if it tells us more about Henry James than it illuminates its subject, it also pays consistent homage to Dickens as "an honest, an admirable artist."[5]

James's remarks on Daudet that stand at the head of this chapter go far in explaining his own relationship to Dickens. Although, unlike Daudet, James was capable of writing pages that do suggest something "so gross as imitation," his most interesting--to our purposes--writing is that which shows him to be in "conscious sympathy" with Dickens, which bear out his statements in the autobiographical writings that at more than just one moment of his life "Dickens had been a revelation to him."[6] The task of this chapter, then, will be to examine some of the forms in which James embodied his conscious sympathy with Dickens and some of the uses he put it to.

II.

It is both amusing and a little disconcerting to discover that contemporary reviewers objected to The Princess Casamassima because it was not enough like Dickens.[7] Today the consensus is that the novel is the one in which James most clearly displays a conscious sympathy with the Master. That such would be the case seems, given James's own account of its birth, inevitable: "...this fiction proceeded quite directly, during the first year of a long residence in London," says James in the "Preface," "from the habit and the interest of walking the streets." A page later he records the celebrated origin of the novel's central figure: Hyacinth Robinson "sprang up for me out of the London pavement."[8] At least part of the interest for James of walking the London streets resided, he implies, in the possibilities of casting himself as a kind of Hyacinth in reverse. Hyacinth's predicament is to be that while one side of London speaks to him "of freedom and ease, knowledge and power, money, opportunity and satiety" he finds "every door of approach shut in his face," doors that are, to James, "all conveniently...opened into light and warmth and cheer, into good and charming relations." But Hyacinth intimately knows the other London, its "dense categories of dark arcana...the lower manners and types, the general sordid struggle, the weight of the burden of labour, the ignorance, the misery and the vice," a London from which James feels his own exclusion to be "a state of weakness" (V, vi-viii). Hyacinth's _entrée_ into the world of light--light that, ironically, fails--comes, of course, through the agencies of the Princess's boredom and Pinnie's bequest. James's guide to the dark arcana is Dickens. In a revelatory passage in _The Middle Years_ James recalls how much in his walks he found the underside of London

> reeked, to my fond fancy, with associations born of the particular ancient piety embodied in one's private altar to Dickens; and that this upstart little truth alone would revel in explanations that I should for the time have feverishly to forego. The exquisite matter was not the identification with the scene of special shades or names; it was just that the whole Dickens procession marched up and down, the whole Dickens world looked out of its queer, quite sinister windows--for it was the socially sinister Dickens, I am afraid, rather than the socially encouraging or confoundingly comic who still at that moment was most apt to meet me with his reasons. Such a reason was just that look of the inscrutable riverward street, packed to blackness with accumulations of suffered experience, these, indescribably, disavowed and confessed at one and the same time, and with the fact of its

> blocked old Thames-side termination, a mere fact of more oppressive enclosure now, telling all sorts of vague loose stories about it.[9]

To the degree, then, that the novel sprang from the London streets, it derived from Dickens--as is evident from its first pages, which record the interview between the little dressmaker and the formidable Mrs. Bowerbank. One notices first the Dickensian names, the appropriateness of Pynsent, the irony of Bowerbank; then the triumphantly Dickensian quality of the humor. Scores of nineteenth-century American novelists struggled painfully to be funny in the Dickensian mode; James shows himself here to be one who could succeed. Mrs. Bowerbank attempts to turn the conversation to her sister, Mrs. Chipperfield (the echo of "Copperfield" is the reader's clue how to take the scene), in order to unfold "the whole history of the dropsical tendencies of [her] husband, an undertaker with a business that had been a blessing because you could always count on it," but Pinnie's curiosity has been aroused by her visitor's profession, and she wants all the morbid details:

> "And aren't you frightened of them--ever?" she enquired, looking up at her visitor with her little heated face.
>
> Mrs. Bowerbank, who was very slow, considered her so long before replying that she felt herself to be, to an alarming degree, in the eye of the law; for who could be more closely connected with the administration of justice than a female turnkey,

> especially so big and majestic a one? "I expect they're more frightened of me," she declared at last; and it was an idea into which Miss Pynsent could easily enter.
>
> "And at night I suppose they rave quite awful," the little dressmaker suggested, feeling vaguely that prisons and madhouses came very much to the same.
>
> "Well, if they do we hush 'em up."
>
> (V, I, i, 6-8)

The elements of the comedy are not hard to discern: Pinnie's timid curiosity and her deference to her supposed social superior--both are ironic foreshadowings of her "romantic" attitude toward titled aristocracy; Mrs. Bowerbank's portentous capitalizing upon that deference; her matter-of-fact acceptance of her grotesque job, echoed in her remark upon her brother-in-law's employment; Pinnie's association of her new friend with the institutions she represents and her sudden reversal of sympathies as she empathizes first with the lady turnkey then with her wards whom she suddenly sees as sharing her own terror; her ironic association of the prison with the madhouse. But while any number of American imitators could read Martin Chuzzlewit and borrow Mr. Mould's joke about his profession, only James could catch just the right Dickensian combination of comedy and brutality represented in Mrs. Bowerbank's last remarks and then sum up all its sinister implications in a name. For if Mrs. Bowerbank represents "the majesty of the law," then the law consists solely of its prison-houses, which are in turn associated with asylums. Pinnie will later learn that although the prison is located beside the river it is hardly, as the matron's name might suggest, a slope of flowers:

> They knew it in fact soon enough when they saw it lift its dusky mass from the bank of the Thames, lying there and sprawling over the whole neighbourhood with brown, bare, windowless walls, ugly, truncated pinnacles and a character unspeakably sad and stern. It looked very sinister and wicked, to Miss Pynsent's eyes, and she wondered why a prison should have such an evil air if it was erected in the interest of justice and order--a builded protest, precisely, against vice and villainy. This particular penitentiary struck her as about as bad and wrong as those who were in it; it threw a blight on the face of day, making the river seem foul and poisonous and the opposite bank, with a profusion of long-necked chimneys, unsightly gasometers and deposits of rubbish, wear the aspect of a region at whose expense the jail had been populated. She looked up at the dull, closed gates, tightening her grasp of Hyacinth's small hand; and if it was hard to believe anything so barred and blind and deaf would relax itself to let her in, there was a dreadful premonitory sinking of the heart attached to the idea of its taking the same trouble to let her out. ...The child suddenly jerked away his hand and, placing it behind him in the clutch of the other, said to her respectfully but resolutely, while he planted himself at a considerable distance:
>
> "I don't like this place."
>
> (V, I, iii, 42-43)

It is this passage and the scene that follows it that more than anything else sets the seal of Dickens on the novel. The best known sign of a Dickens influence on the <u>Princess</u> is the similarity between Rose Muniment and Jenny

Wren;[10] one could point to others: the possibility that Mr. Vetch owes his profession to Frederick Dorrit; the relationship between Pinnie and Peggotty as warm and good, though limited, mother substitutes; the gross imitation in the scene in which Hyacinth attends a musicale at the home of his employer, who "was the occupant of a villa all but detached, at Putney" (V, I, vii, 107); the stylistic borrowings in those passages which evoke "accumulations of suffered experience" (these passages are, appropriately, especially concentrated in II, xxi, the chapter in which Hyacinth takes the vow to assassinate the Duke), and even the remarkable number of parallels between Hyacinth's story and that of Hugh-of-the-Maypole in Barnaby Rudge.[11] But all these evidences are subordinate to and subsumed under the prison episode's massive display of sympathy--and the style is too clearly Dickensian for it to be other than conscious--with the author of Great Expectations, Little Dorrit, and Our Mutual Friend, the "socially sinister Dickens" who met James "with his reasons" as he wandered through the streets of London. It is not simply that the description of the outside and inside of Millbank appropriates Dickens's style; it is the use of that style to establish the moral tone that dominates the novel's evocation of a society: the shadow of the prison-house, blighting the face of day, hangs over the

Princess as pervasively as it casts its gloom over *Little Dorrit*. Pinnie's adult consciousness establishes the prison as symbol, but, in the manner of Dickens, it is the child, Hyacinth, who provides the telling evaluation of the symbol's meaning: "I don't like this place."[12] And with the artistry that we expect of him, James skillfully maintains Pinnie's point of view as the "register" of the scene while at the same time allowing us to sense the full moral impact of the child's terror in reacting to images of almost surrealistic horror that are themselves modelled directly on Dickens. Florentine Vivier looms up before her son as Miss Havisham appears before Pip, a grotesque waxworks figure made all the more hideous by the fixed brightness of her sunken eyes, and her repeated cry, "Il a honte de moi--il a honte," is as incomprehensible and terrifying to Hyacinth as is the wierd "guru-guru" of the pawn-broker to David Copperfield. Both Oscar Bargill and Edwin Bowden have commented on James's use of Dickens in evoking the terrors of childhood; no better example could be wanted than this scene.[13] But again the point to be made is that this, perhaps the most Dickensian scene in all of Henry James, is not only crucial to the development of the plot in that it will motivate both Hyacinth's initial commitment to anarchism and his later inability to murder the Duke but also determines the grey tonality of the novel's portrait of a society and fixes the author's judgment of that society. Like those of Little Dorrit, the characters of The Princess Casamassima are all, each in his own way, caged in a prison that baffles the will and erodes the ability to act. The meanings of Hyacinth's inevitable suicide are, ultimately, all embodied in the Dickensian representation of Millbank. Conscious sympathy with Dickens has created and controlled an entire novel.

If the Princess is an extreme case, it is not the only novel in which James displays conscious sympathy with Dickens. Indeed Richard Poirier has provided the necessary reminder for critics for whom "significance is all" that James, in his fundamental attitude toward fiction and his motivations in writing it, is closer to Dickens than he is to any other novelist: both are totally absorbed by the "fun" of fiction, the excitement of creation and the entertainment provided by it for both author and reader. Hence the "theatricality," the sense of the novelist as performer who delights the audience by the "achieve of," the mastery of the exhibition, that underlines the comic vision of both and creates, among other things, the "verbal flamboyance" of characters like Urbain de Bellegarde and Seth Pecksniff (the one, I am convinced, drawing directly upon the other) that delights us when they themselves most appall and the comic extravagance of the authors's most imaginative metaphors.[14] Thus in a sense any attempt to discuss the peculiarly Dickensian quality of James's humor would, ultimately, prove to be only a series of footnotes to and accumulated demonstrations of Poirier's argument, except, perhaps, for one observation.

Nineteenth-century taste is dominated by the fundamental assumption that the highest, most pleasing form of literature is that which blends humor and pathos. The difficulty of deciphering whether Dickens created the taste or the taste created Dickens does not obscure the fact that the two are, in the critical mind of the century, inextricably fused. James in his own fiction shows that he went one step beyond popular conceptions to recognize that the true power of Dickensian comedy is its fusion not of humor and pathos, but of humor and terror. The dialogue between Pinnie and Mrs. Bowerbank cited above is a good example of what James learned from his predecessor. Much of the edge to the passage comes from Pinnie's essential childishness, her innocence and *naiveté*, her automatic assumption of an inferior role _vis-a-vis_ her rather imposing guest. (One notes the extraordinary number of diminutives James applies to her in the scene.) When the fusion of comedy and terror becomes the predominant mode in the presentation of a literal child who stands at the center of the author's criticism of life, the elements are assembled that make _What Maisie Knew_ a distinctively Dickensian novel.

Maisie's Dickensian innocence is the novel's _raison d'être_; amusing proof comes from the classroom, where on two separate occasions students unversed in the Dickens tradition have rejected James's fundamental assumption, and hence the novel, _in toto_. Absurd to maintain, they say, as James does, that Maisie is capable of "sowing on barren strands, through the mere fact of presence, the seed of the moral life" (XI, viii), when, by all rights, given her situation, she should become nothing more--or to their point of view, less--than a screaming neurotic.[15] But that she does not is, of course, evidence of her kinship with the redemptive children of Dickens. Moreover, if Mrs. Beale has chosen the wrong character in remarking that Mrs. Wix rather resembles Mrs. Micawber (XI, xiv, 126), the remark is useful in reminding us that Maisie inhabits a Dickensian world of whose creation her innocence is the novelist's sole justification. We are all inclined to agree with James himself that the lavishing of so much attention on such dingy people would be but a tawdry and singularly unedifying exercise were it not for the "stray fragrance" of the ideal provided by her presence. (Similarly, the Lammles provide limited interest except for their effect on Georgiana Podsnap as she, like Maisie, takes "occasional frosty peeps out of childhood into womanhood" [XXIII, I, xi, 160].) Hence the novel's Dickensian characterizations, frequently noted in the case of Mrs. Wix, but even more striking in those of Moodle, Susan Ash, and Mr. Perriam. Hence the repeated echoes of Dickens, as in, for example, "Mr. Farange's remedy for every inconvenience was that the child should be put at school--there were such lots of splendid schools, as everybody knew, at Brighton..." (XI, vi, 36), or Maisie's being pulled to her mother's breast, "where, amid a wilderness of trinkets, she felt as if she had been suddenly thrust, with a smash of glass, into a jeweller's shop-front" (XI, xv, 144), recalling Pip's torture by the pins protruding from Mrs. Jo's leather-clad bosom; hence the use of Dickensian irony in both caricature ("It was comfortably established between them that Mrs. Wix's heart was broken" XI, vi, 36) and grotesque comedy (Maisie, feigning stupidity, achieves "a hollowness beyond her years" XI, ix, 69) to insulate Maisie's situation from the sentimental and to make it all the more horribly telling; hence the supremely Dickensian fusion of humor and pathos, humor and terror in the two scenes of which James was most proud, Maisie's interviews with the Captain in the park and with Beale at the Countess's. Maisie is a far cry from Little Nell, or even Oliver, David or Pip, but without them it is hard to conceive of her knowing what she knows.

Other elements in other novels similarly bespeak a James for whom Dickens had been a revelation, one such being his well-known fondness for melodrama. Both of the two most rewarding discussions of melodrama in James acknowledge his debt to Dickens while employing the term in its broadest sense as the tendency to depict moral conflict in terms of pure evil and unspotted good.[16] Few would deny that James and Dickens share a black and white moral vision. James may write in the Preface to What Maisie Knew of the "terribly mixed" nature of human existence (XI, viii), but it is none-theless true that his villains tend to be as dastardly as Ralph Nickleby and his heroes as high-minded as Nicholas. Even such seemingly "mixed" characters as Mrs. Wix and Sir Claude are actually limited white and limited black rather than humanly grey. The term melodrama, however, also describes patterns of action as well as moral vision, the one, of course, more often than not depending upon the other. Thus we speak of Nicholas's rescuing Madeline Brey from Arthur Gride, Basil Ransom's performing the same service for Verena Tarrant, the conflagration at Satis House and the burning of Poynton all as "melodramatic." What is remarkable, however, is not that both authors are given to melodramatic incidents, but that both tend to use them in similar ways.

That James's melodrama derives largely from Dickens is evident from the opening pages of his first novel. The hero of that work, pausing in the lobby of his hotel to check his appearance before setting out to offer once more marriage to a woman who has twice rejected him, finds himself distracted by the singular conduct of an entering stranger. The ensuing passage is so blatant and so awkward an attempt to imitate Dickens's manner and style that it constitutes a kind of grotesque parody, demanding quotation:

> This was a man of less than middle age, good-looking, pale with a pretentious, pointed moustache and various shabby remnants of finery. His face was haggard, his whole aspect was that of grim and hopeless misery. He walked straight to the table in the centre of the room, and poured out and drank without stopping three full glasses of ice-water, as if he were striving to quench some fever in his

> vitals. He then went to the window, leaned his forehead against the cold pane, and drummed a nervous tattoo with his long stiff finger-nails. Finally he strode over to the fireplace, flung himself into a chair, leaned forward with his head in his hands, and groaned audibly. Lawrence, as he smoothed down his lavender gloves, watched him and reflected. "What an image of fallen prosperity, of degradation and despair!"[17]

One notes how proud the young James must have been of the touch provided by the lavender gloves. When Lawrence returns after his third denial his uneasy sleep is broken by the stranger's failure at murdering his daughter and success at suicide. Thus Nora Lambert becomes Lawrence's ward under the most melodramatic of circumstances.[18]

James's second novel is hardly free of melodramatic episodes--witness the storm with which its action concludes--but James begins to put melodrama to a new and more sophisticated use, a use for which he could have found ample precedent in Dickens. For example, when Rowland Mallet learns that Christina has broken her engagement with the Prince, he goes, bearing commissions from both the Cavaliere and old Mrs. Hudson, to see Roderick:

> He found him in his sitting-room, which had been closely darkened to keep out the heat. The carpets and rugs had been removed, the floor of speckled concrete was bare and lightly sprinkled with water. Here and there, over it, certain strongly-odorous flowers had been scattered. Roderick was lying on his divan in a white dressing-gown, staring at the frescoed ceiling. The room was deliciously cool

> and filled with the moist sweet fragrance of the circumjacent roses and violets. ...Roderick lay motionless except that he slightly turned his head toward his friend. He was smelling a large white rose, which he continued to present to his nose. In the darkness of the room he looked exceedingly pale, but his beautiful eyes quite shed a light. He let them rest for some time on Rowland, lying there like a Buddhist in an intellectual swoon, a deep dreamer whose perception should be slowly ebbing back to temporal matters. "Oh, I'm not ill," he said at last. "I've never been better in my life."
>
> (I, xx, 393-94)

The melodramatic action here is not the creation of James, but of Roderick, who has conceived the _tableau vivant_ as a means of literally acting out his emotions and in so doing reveals his character as we both laugh and wince at the absurdity of the pose. The scene, like so many others in which young Hudson is a figure, reads like an episode in a cheap production of a hack dramatization of _Scènes de la vie de bohème_, or as if Roderick had cast himself as Bunthorne. In other words, he is behaving like Dickens's characters, who are habitually delineated by their own tendency to conceive of themselves as performers in a melodrama:

> Some men in his blighted position would have taken to drinking, but as Mr. Swiveller had taken to that before, he only took, on receiving the news that Sophy Wackles was lost to him forever, to playing the flute; thinking after mature consideration that it was a good, sound, dismal occupation, not only in unison with his own sad thoughts, but calculated to awaken a fellow-feeling in the bosoms of his neighbours.
>
> (XI, lviii, 199)

From the beginning of the novel to its end James characterizes Roderick by insisting on his propensity toward melodramatic action and rhetoric; his probable suicide in chapter xxvi is as much in keeping with his character as is his smashing of Striker's bust in chapter ii; first and last his speeches echo the theatre. And like Dickens, James uses self-dramatization not only for the sake of characterization and comedy but also for thematic and moral ends. Like _Martin Chuzzlewit_, the Dickens novel it draws upon most, _Roderick Hudson_ is a study in the evils of Self. Roderick's inevitable disaster is predicated not simply upon his predilection for melodramatic posing but also upon the raw egotism his theatrics represent. If, as we are told, Rowland carries his volume of Wordsworth into the Alps, Roderick, surely, must have brought along his _Childe Harold_. Indeed, the word "egotism" recurs as insistently in the final chapters as Dickens's finger-shaking "Self! Self! Self!" pops up in _Chuzzlewit_.[19] Like Dickens's, James's mind, in conceiving characters, seems to work in parallel columns labelled "good" and "bad," "selfless" and "selfish"; the distinguishing characteristic is whether or not a person conceives himself to be perpetually on stage. The theatricality of Christina is noted in the novel even by the other characters, as is, on the other side of the line, Mary Garland's quiet naturalness.[20] But even the minor characters are placed in the same categories by the same criterion. Over against Mme. Grandoni's unassuming rhetoric, for example, we are asked to place Mrs. Light's outbursts of Dickensian stage speechifying (see especially I, xx, 397-98). In *Roderick Hudson* James takes the giant step beyond *Watch and Ward* from the conception of his action in terms of Dickensian melodrama to the Dickensian use of melodrama for purposes of characterization, theme, and, of course, high comedy.

In his next novel, *The American*, James moves one step farther. Here again, as in *Watch and Ward*, we have action conceived in highly melodramatic patterns and, as in *Roderick Hudson*, the theatrical posing--it is this above all that links Urbain de Bellegarde with Pecksniff. But a new use of melodrama is added, and again one notes its Dickensian flavor. In *The American* melodrama is used for something more than just characterization in the traditional sense; it is also used to portray a quality of consciousness, a state of mind, a pattern of mental processes. The point is best made clear, perhaps, by looking at Dickens first. In chapter xxxviii of *Oliver Twist* Mr. and Mrs. Bumble meet with Monks in a deserted mill to inform him of Oliver's true identity and to allow him to destroy the evidence that proves Oliver to be his half-brother. The scene is melodrama in its purest form: the night is dark and stormy, the setting is an area inhabited by "low and desperate ruffians," the mill itself is rotten and ruined, filled with rats and damp, and the entire action is predicated upon the melodramatic plot machinery of destroyed wills, death-bed secrets, and purloined lockets. Even Monks's own actions, his threats, his omnious incoherencies, his devilish hallucinations in response to the thunder, are true to the conventions governing half-crazed, demonic stage villains. But what stands out in the scene is that it is not purely the creation of Dickens's own melodramatic imagination, but rather that it is entirely conceived and engineered by Monks. *He* creates it in order to engender in his interlocutors a sense of melodramatic foreboding, to force their minds to work in melodramatic patterns in order to place himself in a position to manipulate their responses, which, he accurately predicts, will, given the setting, follow the conventions of melodramatic action. Bumble's comic terror is the measure of Monks's success. One notes that in the manuscript the passage in which Bumble swears secrecy "on everybody's account, young man; on my own, you know, Mr. Monks," is followed by:

> "You may as well teach yourself to drop that name, do you mind?" said the person whom he had addressed.
>
> "Certainly"--answered Mr. Bumble, still retreating.
>
> "And if we meet again anywhere there's no call for us to know each other--you understand?" said Monks frowning.
>
> "You may depend upon my not saying a word to you, young man, or about you, on no account."
>
> (xxxviii, 256n)

The demands on space created by serialization may have caused Dickens to cut this interchange. But it is easily sacrificed, for Monks has so thoroughly placed Bumble in a melodramatic frame of mind that such assurances are superfluous. But, paradoxically, in so ordering the scene Monks chooses a setting and a pattern of incident that serves, for the reader, as a kind of objective correlative of Monks's own gothic consciousness. His self-assumed role as a performer in a melodrama is something more than Dickens's habitual means of characterization; it is a reflection of Monks's distorted mental processes, Dickens thus achieving a depth of character analysis far beyond that usually associated with Newgate drama.

In chapters xxi and xxii of _The American_ James employs the same technique for the same ends. Again the scene in question is conceived in terms of classic melodrama. Newman, following up the clues provided him by Valentin's death-bed confession, arranges a secret interview with Mrs. Bread, who tells him a gothic tale of murder and deception and provides him with the evidence (in the form of yet another death-bed message) that will allow him to expose the villains. But once again the immediate author of the scene is not James but Newman. It is he who picks the site for the rendezvous, he who is playing detective in a Newgate drama, and he who engineers the more lurid aspects of the episode--all precisely because he is in a melodramatic frame of mind. Baffled in his attempt to penetrate, both socially and intellectually, the world of the Bellegardes and outraged by the moral ugliness of Valentin's death, he comes to Fleurieres with mind primed to see the unfolding of the melodrama his last interview with his friend has prefaced. It is in this mood that he first confronts the seat of the Bellegardes:

> He stood there a while, looking through the bars at the large time-stained face beyond and wondering to what special misdeed it was that the dark old dwelling with the flowery name had given convenient occasion. It had given occasion, first and last, to tyrannies and sufferings enough, Newman said to himself; it was an evil-looking place to live in. Then suddenly came the reflection: what a horrible rubbish-heap of iniquity to fumble through!
>
> (II, xxi, 424-25)

This is the American looking upon the European past, Mark Twain in the Ducal Palace in Venice: excluded from history (Newman looks through bars) and conceiving of it solely as a chamber of horrors straight out of gothic melodrama. To Christopher Columbus Newman Fleurieres could well be the stage setting for a production of The Castle Spectre. Because his mental processes are dominated by the conventions of melodrama, he experiences no difficulty in picking a time and place for the interview: "Try this evening at dusk. Come to me in the old ruin there on the hill, in the court before the church" (II, xxi, 428). Like Monks in his manipulation of the Bumbles, Newman may be counting upon the theatrical back-drops to loosen Mrs. Bread's tongue; she, at any rate, seems aware that she has been cast in a specific kind of role. She wears her very best dress and, when she falters in her determination to tell all, is motivated to go on by a review, accompanied by the appropriate stage gestures, of the melodrama in her own history: like all the old serving-women who come forth in the last act to expose the villain, Mrs. Bread has her grudge. Newman, who at each pause in Mrs. Bread's narrative "makes almost the motion of turning the page of a 'detective story'" (II, xxii, 452), finds, like Monks (who at the end of his scene is afraid to be left alone in the dark), that the tableau he has arranged only serves to reinforce the melodramatic cast already controlling his consciousness. Even his rhetoric, here more than any other place in the novel, rings with the passion of the stage:

> "I want to bring them down--down, down! I want to turn the tables on them--I want to mortify them as they mortified me. They took me up into a high place and made me stand there for all the world to see me, and then they stole behind me and pushed me into this bottomless pit where I lie howling and gnashing my teeth! I made a fool of myself before all their friends; but I shall make something worse of them."
>
> (II, xxii, 442)

These are the accents of Varney the Vampire, precisely the kind of speechifying that Hyacinth Robinson and Millicent Henning must have applauded in _The Pearl of Paraguay_, that brought cheers for Vincent Crummles and his theatrical troop, or that distracted Strether and Maria Gostrey from their contemplation of Chad at the _Francais_. James is certainly aware of its absurdity. Indeed, with the possible exception of Pip's account of Wopsle's performance as Hamlet, there is no more delightful burlesque of the nineteenth-century theatre than that in the _Princess_. Millicent follows "with attention, though not always success, the complicated adventures of the Pearl of Paraguay through scenes luxuriantly tropical, in which the male characters wore sombreros and stilettos and the ladies either danced the cachucha or fled from licentious pursuit." Later she is moved to tears when in the third act the Pearl "dishevelled and distracted, dragging herself on her knees, [implores] the stern hidalgo her father to believe in her innocence in spite of circumstances appearing to condemn her--a midnight meeting with the wicked hero in the grove of cocoanuts" (V, II, xxii, 188-90). Yet, like Dickens, James could see that melodrama could be used as a means of representing a state or quality of mind without destroying, but rather enhancing, its comic potentialities. Newman's theatrics and their stagey setting are, like Monks's, a correlative of his consciousness. After the rendezvous in the ruined chapel, we are prepared for both the comic irony of his histrionic reaction to the wailing of the nuns (Claire is not, as he assumes, among them) and the heroics of his rejection of revenge.

The three patterns of Dickensian melodrama that James worked out in his first three novels were to remain stock in trade for the rest of his career. Washington Square, for example, is based almost entirely upon melodramatic incident, and Mrs. Penniman, one of James's most Dickensian creations, is a prime example of a consciousness finely tuned to the patterns of melodrama. Melodramatic action provides rousing endings for, most notably, The Portrait of a Lady, The Bostonians, The Princess Casamassima, and The Spoils of Poynton. The Other House conforms so closely to the conventions of the lurid stage that the Hearst newspapers greeted it with banner headlines proclaiming: "HENRY JAMES' NEW NOVEL OF IMMORALITY AND CRIME; THE SURPRIZING PLUNGE OF THE NOVELIST..."[21] A highly selective list of James's people who are characterized by their tendency to adopt theatrical poses, to conceive of themselves as performers in a melodrama, would include Gilbert Osmond, Selah Tarrant, Mrs. Gereth, Julia Dallow, Mrs. Brook, and even Kate Croy. And if in The American Newman's melodramatic frame of mind leads to heroic action, James was to show in other novels that such a consciousness could also narrow and distort. Significantly, the tendency to view the world in patterns of thought derived from stage stereotypes is, in James, most frequently associated with Americans and more often than not serves to explain their failure to understand experience, their inability to "live" in the sense Strether urges upon Little Bilham. Like that of the hidalgo in The Pearl of Paraguay their sternness reflects the emotional and moral atrophy resulting from their placing too much credence in melodramatic circumstance. A midnight meeting in the grove of cocoanuts can, for them, mean only one thing. In an early novel, The Europeans, Roger Acton rejects the Baroness Munster because he discovers Clifford Wentworth hiding in her cottage after midnight. Eugenia is, of course, innocent--ironically, Clifford is there because she has undertaken to civilize him. But Acton cannot understand because he, like the rest of the marvelously comic--and, one notes, Dickensian--New Englanders in the novel, can comprehend this exotic victim of a morganatic marriage only if he squeezes her into the role of Wicked Seductress or Fatal Woman of melodrama. Twenty-five years later James was still reaping comic rewards from the same tendency of the American mentality, having Sarah Pocock of The Ambassadors descend on Paris like Carrie Nation with her axe, armed to smash the chains of lurid melodrama that, she believes, have trapped her brother. But whatever the novel and whatever the form, James's melodrama remains, first to last, a sign of sympathy with Dickens.

As do certain other elements in his fiction, especially in the area of characterization. The discussion so far has indicated that James's use of Dickensian melodrama (or rather Dickensian use of melodrama) often overlaps Dickensian patterns of characterization. Nevertheless, bearing the overlapping in mind, it is fruitful to talk of characterization as a separate category of James's indebtedness, a category that, like the use of melodrama, contains several subheads. The most obvious is the importing of Dickensian figures to serve as extras in the crowd scenes. For examples one need look no farther than James's first novel. Nora's father has already been mentioned as a "gross imitation" of Dickens; a more successful use of Dickensian techniques can be seen in the portrait of Fenton's business partner:

> Mr. Franks was a small meagre man, with a whitish colouring, weak blue eyes and thin yellow whiskers, suffering apparently from some nervous malady. He nodded, he stumbled, he jerked his arms and legs about with pitiful comicality. He had a huge protuberant forehead, such a forehead as would have done honour to a Goethe or a Newton; but poor Mr. Franks must have been at best a man of latent genius. ...[Nora's] presence seemed to redouble his agitation; she remained for an hour gazing in painful fascination at his unnatural shrugs and spasms, as he busied himself at his desk. The Muse of accounts, for poor Mr. Franks, was, in fact, not habitually a young woman, thrice beautiful with trouble, sitting so sensibly at his elbow. Nora wondered how George had come to choose so foolish an associate; then she guessed that it was his want of capital that had discovered a secret affinity with Mr. Franks's want of brains.
>
> (ix, 197-98)

The most striking thing about this passage and others like it in the later novels is, however, its sheer conventionality. Any number of nineteenth-century Americans, from

Rose Terry Cooke to William Dean Howells, could have written it. Much more interesting is James's habit of using Dickensian techniques of characterization as a means of "placing" his people, critically, in proper relation to the novels's themes. Howells's use of the technique has been discussed earlier; James's is very similar. The method has been noted by F. R. Leavis, who points to Mr. Leavenworth in Roderick Hudson as a prime example of its use.[22] That Leavenworth is a Dickens character there can be little doubt; if Mrs. Hominy of Martin Chuzzlewit is "The Mother of the Modern Gracchi," Leavenworth, surely, is The Father. But he is more than a marvelous demonstration that James can be truly and validly funny in the Dickens manner; the Dickensian comedy that surrounds him is James's method of fixing, with consummate economy, the reader's attention on certain thematically important, distinctly American, attitudes toward art. (Like Mrs. Hominy and her friends, the Two Literary Ladies, Leavenworth is, above all, Ideal and Transcendental.) Similarly, Dickensian techniques are used, with greater complexity, to "place" another prominent American attitude in the characterization of Barnaby Striker, the Northhampton lawyer. As his name implies, Striker is another character straight out of Martin Chuzzlewit; he must be "one of the most _re_-markable men in the country." When Rowland explains that Roderick should be allowed the opportunity Europe affords for the study of the antique, Striker is quick to provide a definition: "An antique, as I understand it...is an image of a pagan deity, with considerable dirt sticking to it, and no arms, no nose and no clothing" (I, iii, 58-59). Later when he tries to play upon old Mrs. Hudson's fear of nudity, Rowland parries with an attempt at sophisticated straightforwardness only to be met with the same supreme disregard for logical consequence as that which so often dumbfounds Martin and Mark:

> "Now this study of the living model," Mr. Striker pursued. "Give Mrs. Hudson a sketch of that."
> "Oh dear, no!" cried Mrs. Hudson shrinkingly.
> "That too," said Rowland, "is one of the reasons for studying in Rome. It's a handsome race, you know, and you find very well-made people."
> "I suppose they're no better made than a good tough Yankee," objected Mr. Striker, transposing his interminable legs. "The same God made us!"
> (I, iii, 59)

But a page or so further on we see Striker from a slightly different angle:

> "I suppose you're a very brilliant young man...very enlightened, very cultivated, quite up to the mark in the fine arts and all that sort of thing. I'm a plain practical old boy, content to follow an honourable profession in a free country. I didn't go to any part of Europe to learn my business; no one took me by the hand; I had to grease my wheels myself, and such as I am, I'm a self-made man, every inch of me! Well, if our young friend's booked for fame and

> fortune I don't suppose his going to Rome will stop him. But, mind you, it won't help him such a long way neither. If you've undertaken to put him through there's a thing or two you had better remember. The crop we gather depends upon the seed we sow. He may be the biggest genius of the age: his potatoes won't come up without his hoeing them. If he takes things so almighty easy as--well, as one or two young fellows of genius I've had under my eye--his produce will never gain the prize. Take the word for it of a man who has made his way inch by inch and doesn't believe that we wake up to find our work done because we have lain all night a-dreaming of it: anything worth doing is plaguy hard to do!"
>
> (I, iii, 62-63)

Again we are asked to laugh at the pomposity and chauvinistic Philistinism, at all the things in the speech that recall LaFayette Kettle and Elijah Pogram. But there are also elements here about which we can honestly reply with Rowland "that this seemed pregnant sense." Subsequent events are to prove that Roderick should have been listening; the crop he will reap does depend on the seed he sows. That one of the novel's themes would be embodied in the words of Barnaby Striker is but proof of the imaginativeness and subtletly with which James could use Dickens.

James's use of Dickensian techniques to "place" characters in their proper thematic roles does not end with the early novels. Such a "placed" character in a great work of the major phrase is Waymarsh, the "Sitting Bull" of _The Ambassadors_. The identification has been made before:

"Whenever Waymarsh appears, it is like a Dickensian ballet-sequence."[23] Few readers would disagree, and we laugh at Waymarsh's "sacred rage" much in the same manner that we laugh at Leavenworth's "Ideal of Intellectual Refinement"; it can no more be separated from him than Mrs. Gamp's umbrella can be removed from her grasp. Like the also Dickensian Miss Barrace we are repeatedly moved to gasp, "He's wonderful!" "He's like the Indian chief one reads about, who, when he comes up to Washington to see the Great Father, stands wrapt in his blanket and gives no sign" (XXI, V, i, 206). The "Project" of the novel James submitted to Harpers's makes Waymarsh's role explicit: his "office in the subject is...that of a contrast and foil to Strether."[24] As such it is appropriate that he be described in terms of that Bergsonian "rigidity" that characterizes so many of Dickens's great comic creations. Like Strether, Waymarsh, despite superior opportunities, has never "lived," but unlike Strether he is incapable of recognizing what he has missed and can only look at his friend's elasticity and sense of adventure with uncomprehending and unyielding dismay. His repeated admonition to Strether, "Quit this!," becomes as much a Dickensian tag-line as "Barkis is willin'" or "which her name is Harris." Like the Dickensian characters in Roderick Hudson Waymarsh's thematic function is to be the comic embodiment of certain American essences in this novel of international contrasts. If Mrs. Newsome is "The Voice of Woollett," Waymarsh is "The Spirit of Milrose," from which Strether, from the opening page, desires a vacation. Waymarsh's representativeness developes with the progression of events, continually picking up new complexities of overtone. His stubborn contrariness in the early chapters, for example, evokes a relatively simple response; we laugh easily and openly both when he pierces "with his sombre detachment the plate glass of ironmongers and saddlers, while Strether [flaunts] an affinity with dealers in stamped letter-paper and in smart neckties" and when Strether explains to Maria his friend's Milrosian melodramatic assumptions: "He thinks us sophisticated, he thinks us worldly, he thinks us wicked, he thinks us all sort of queer things" (XXI, I, iii, 40, 42). The "ballet" climaxes with Waymarsh plunging into the jeweller's shop under the compulsions of the "sacred rage" to buy, we assume, the most garish thing he can find, thus clinching the sequence in the manner of Dickens's black-outs. But later when "the ordeal of Europe" has led Waymarsh to cultivate his suspicions and dissent into feelings of exclusion and even resentment, the comedy takes on a somewhat sinister coloring. We still laugh at Strether's embarrassing predicament when Waymarsh begins direct communication with Woollett and even more when he parodies Strether's behavior by becoming Sarah Pocock's squire, but our laughter is not quite so open. Yet it is still Dickensian.

One could continue indefinitely cataloguing characters in James who seem to emerge from a conscious sympathy with Dickens. But one recurrent, almost obsessive, type appears so often that it perhaps requires special mention. Surely not every American journalist of the late nineteenth century modelled himself on Colonel Diver or Jefferson Brick, but every one in James does. Like de Tocqueville--and above all like Dickens--James realized that the ultimate horror of American newspapers was not simply what in The Question of Our Speech he called "the mere noisy vision of their ubiquitous page...the grimaces, the shouts, shrieks and yells, ranging over the whole gamut of ugliness, irrelevance, dissonance, of a mighty maniac who has broken loose and who is running amuck through the spheres alike of sense and sound."[25] Rather, American journalism horrifies because it reflects a fundamental tendency in democratic life inimical to the maintenance of any "cultured"--in the Arnoldian sense--decency and hence to the possibility of individual fulfillment. As it was for Dickens, the issue is crucial to James:

> One sketches one's age but imperfectly if one doesn't touch on that particular matter: the invasion, the impudence and shamelessness, of the newspaper and the interviewer, the devouring <u>publicity</u> of life, the extinction of all sense between public and private. It is the highest expression of the note of "familiarity," the sinking of <u>manners</u>, in so many ways, which the democratization of the world brings with it.[26]

His method of expressing his outrage at "the intrinsic scoundrelism of the aggression" of the newspapers against all he valued was to portray journalists as Dickensian grotesques.[27] Like Dickens, James recognized the usefulness of reductive caricature, which by presenting a character as something less than human exposes him for what he is. Thus Dickens's Jefferson Brick becomes reincarnated in James's Matthias Pardon; the one is even made to look like the other. Pardon is, of course, the extreme example, but even Henrietta Stackpole has, at times, difficulty in disguising her Dickensian ancestry. Ralph Touchett, for example, seems to sense it almost at once and, accordingly, lards his conversations with her with echoes of Dickens (e.g., III, xiii, 169). Indeed, with the possible exception of old Mr. Luce she is the closest to a pure Dickens character of anyone in the *Portrait*. One notes, parenthetically, the extraordinary tribute to Dickens's genius in capturing particular essences of the national scene embodied in the fact that James could no more than any other American novelist of the nineteenth-century represent certain types of his own countrymen without drawing upon *Martin Chuzzlewit*.

George Flack, the "villain" of *The Reverberator* reveals James's debt in his very name. Like *The Europeans* a minor classic of Jamesian comedy at its lightest and happiest, *The Reverberator* derives much of its strength from the introduction of the figure of the American journalist into the context of an "international" theme, a device carried over from the *Portrait* and looking back, ultimately, to *Martin Chuzzlewit*, in which the force of the satire upon the American press depends upon its examination from a European point of view. The comedy is at once most uproarious, most Jamesian, and most Dickensian in chapter x when Mme. de Cliché is scandalized to find Francie alone in Flack's company and Francie unwittingly reveals to her escort the assorted skeletons lurking in the Probert closets. On the surface the elements of the humor may seem far removed from *Martin Chuzzlewit*. Mme. de Cliché's shock at the violation of propriety, Flack's awareness of the "baseness" on which

European standards rest, the rich intimations that violations have been frequent among the Proberts themselves; Francie's innocent lack of decorum, Flack's not so innocent vulgarity; the racing of Flack's melodramatic imagination which turns out to be as lurid as he accuses the European mind of being; our awareness that he is out to stir up trouble but is incapable of conceiving precisely the nature of the trouble he makes; our sense that Francie, who understands so little, understands most; and the play upon the juxtaposition of the horrors of newspaper publicity with the fact that the Proberts do, indeed, have much to hide: all these elements at work in the scene surround each sentence, each phrase, each word even with a complexity of ironies that seems far beyond the comparatively simple, straightforward manner of Dickens. But when the correspondent for *The Reverberator* later puts the clincher on the joke by being totally incapable of understanding why he has not made everyone happy--after all, has he not served his own and Francie's best interests by breaking up her engagement to Gaston and making it possible for her to align herself with him? Has he not fulfilled the highest function of his profession, which is to give the public what it wants, personalities and scandal? And, to top it all off, has he not given the Proberts the rich pleasure of seeing their names in print? When the farce ends on this note we realize that the progression from Brick to Pardon to Flack is a direct line. And when the reverberations of the "anecdote" end in Gaston Probert's gaining his manhood, when he grasps the American wisdom of Waterlow's assertion that his family is doing their best to kill him morally by rendering him "incapable of individual life" (XIII, xiv, 205), we are brought up face to face with the realization that James has built his novel upon the same fundamental and over-powering irony that lies at the heart of the American chapters of *Martin Chuzzlewit*. After all, Martin *is* redeemed in Eden.

III.

> He saw everything he related. It passed before him as he spoke, so vividly, that, in the intensity of his earnestness, he presented what he described to me with greater distinctness than I can express. I can hardly believe, writing now long afterwards, but I was actually present in these scenes; they are impressed upon me with an astonishing air of fidelity.
>
> --Charles Dickens

> The essence of any representational work is of course to bristle with immediate images...Anything that relieves responsible prose of the duty of being, while placed before us, good enough, pictorial enough, above all *in itself*, does it the worst of services.
> --Henry James

With the possible exception of the question of "point of view," no aspect of James's art has received more critical comment than the "pictorial" quality of his work. If as he himself says in the "Preface" to *The Golden Bowl* the highest function of narrative prose is to produce "an effect of illustration," to so "bristle with immediate images" that it will "reduce one's reader, 'artistically' inclined, to such a state of hallucination by the images one has evoked as doesn't permit him to rest till he has noted or recorded them, set up some semblance of them in his own other medium, by his own other art" (XXIII, ix-x), then on these grounds alone James could qualify as one of our greatest novelists. In the pages that follow I would like to make the perhaps radical suggestion that this intensely visual quality is yet another sign of James's conscious sympathy with Dickens, especially to the degree that James tends to write passages shaped in the manner of formal illustrations and to use these passages as a device not only for the psychological exploration of character but also for purposes of social commentary. To trace the use of what might be called Dickensian "internal illustrations" throughout the James canon would provide the material for a monograph, not one section of one chapter; therefore the discussion here is restricted, primarily, to one representative novel. But first Dickens.

That Dickens is also one of our most visual, specifically pictorial novelists is critical cliché. Like his own Mr. Pegotty, "he saw everything he related" (XV, li, 348). James himself once remarked that in "the power of evoking visible objects and figures" Dickens has no rival in English but Shakespeare.[28] The tendency to perceive and record experience in images whose primary appeal is visual seems to have been built into the deepest recesses of his being. To read his letters is to realize that the pictorial quality of the novels reflects an extraordinary fusion of <u>persona</u> and personality. Moreover, from its very beginnings his career as a novelist was closely tied in almost symbiotic relation to the work of his illustrators; perhaps as a result he shows an ever increasing tendency not merely to write <u>for</u> illustration but <u>in terms of</u>

illustration, to write his own pictures. A letter to Seymour, 14 April 1836, indicates both his concern for the close relation between text and illustration as mutual contributions to effect and his habit of insisting that his illustrators follow his verbal pictures faithfully and closely:

> I am extremely anxious about "The Stroller's Tale," the more especially as many literary friends on whose judgment I place great reliance, think it will create considerable sensation. I have seen your design for an etching to accompany it. I think it extremely good, but still, it is not quite my idea; and as I feel so very solicitous to have it as complete as possible, I shall feel personally obliged to you if you will make another drawing. ...I think the woman should be younger, the "dismal man" decidedly should, and he should be less miserable in appearance. To communicate an interest to the plate, his whole appearance should express more sympathy and solicitude: and while I represented the sick man as emaciated and dying, I would not make him too repulsive. The furniture of the room, you have depicted _admirably_.[29]

His letters to Cruickshank show that by _Oliver Twist_ he was writing scenes with the qualities necessary for successful illustration specifically in mind; during the composition of _Our Mutual Friend_ he was still touring the London suburbs to point out buildings and shops to his illustrator to be used for models.[30] Since Browne could not accompany him on his first American trip he had his publishers buy a series of American _vignettes_ for Browne to use as guides for the illustrations of Martin Chuzzlewit.[31] Chuzzlewit also provides a revealing example of Dickens's tendency to prescribe illustrations that not only recreate his verbal pictures in graphic form but also complement the text by underscoring its thematic symbolism. In the illustration accompanying chapter lii, Pecksniff falls to the floor under the force of Old Martin's cane; the two books which he knocks from Tom Pinch's hands in his descent are, appropriately, Le Tartuffe and Paradise Lost.[32]

The combination of the inherently visual quality of his imagination and the acquired stylistic habits developed through close association with his illustrators led Dickens to evolve a pictorial method that allowed him to build his novels around intensely visual images and scenes described in terms of formal drawings, which, to use James's phrases, produce "an effect of illustration," and are pictorial above all in themselves. The point may seem so obvious that even the summary argument developed here belabors the readily apparent. That risk is taken in order to emphasize a larger point: that as much as the eccentric or grotesque character and the use of the child as the center of the author's criticism of life, his pictorial method is one of Dickens's major contributions to and influences on the nineteenth-century novel. Therefore, while there is no incontrovertible proof--nor, ultimately, can there be--that James or any other nineteenth-century novelist was directly and solely influenced by Dickens in the use of a method primarily pictorial, such use can, nevertheless, be said to be "Dickensian."

To observe, as it were, the method in action, one need only look again at Great Expectations, the one Dickens novel in which the illustrations are of necessity internal and verbal for the simple reason that it is the only one that was not originally accompanied by graphic plates. In an earlier chapter I commented at some length on its structure, its "form"--the detective novel as social commentary--and its "plan"--the use of a primary situation so obvious and powerful in its irony that it operates as both the motivating and the controlling force on the creation of plot and character--and implied its union of structure and theme. In a sense it is because the plot tells the theme that Dickens is enabled to use a pictorial method; the fusion gives his vision its greatest freedom and impact. But looked at from a different perspective, the relationship is reversed; the use of a pictorial method allows Dickens to rely more on visual impressions and symbols than on complexity of plot or depth of character analysis in order to make his points.

Ultimately, however, method, structure, and theme are so totally fused that relationship cannot be described in terms of cause and effect. Consider Miss Havisham. In the working out of the thematic implications of the plot, Miss Havisham is made to bear a heavy burden. She must represent both the decay of the old order in society and the evil capacities of wealth: the denial of the heart's humanity, the rejection of life, the use of others as things for the gratification of the perverted will. She must be what Dickens makes of her, a figure of extraordinary power. But her power derives not from any psychological depth shown in her characterization (which merely appropriates cliches from stage melodrama--the jilted lover fleeing from reality, living off pain and for revenge), nor from her actions (indeed, she hardly acts at all), but rather from the intense visual image we have of her:

> She was dressed in rich materials--satins, and lace, and silks--all of white. Her shoes were white. And she had a long white veil dependent from her hair, and she had some bridal flowers in her hair, but her hair was white. Some bright jewels lay sparkling on her neck and on her hands, and some other jewels lay sparkling on the table. Dresses less splendid than the dress she wore, and half-packed trunks, were scattered about. She had not quite finished dressing, for she had but one shoe on--the other was on the table near her hand--her veil was but half arranged, her watch and chain were not put on, and some lace for her bosom lay with those trinkets. ...I saw that everything within my

> view which ought to be white, had been white long ago, and had lost its lustre, and was faded and yellow. I saw that the bride within the bridal dress had withered like the dress, and like the flowers, and had no brightness left but the brightness of her sunken eyes. I saw that the dress had been put upon the rounded figure of a young woman, and that the figure upon which it now hung loose, had shrunk to skin and bone. Once, I had been taken to see some ghastly waxwork at the Fair, representing I know not what impossible personage lying in state. Once, I had been taken to one of our old marsh churches to see a skeleton in the ashes of a rich dress, that had been dug out of a vault under the church pavement. Now, waxwork and skeleton seemed to have dark eyes that moved and looked at me.
> (XXII, viii, 64-65)

The novel is full of such powerful visual images: the opening scene on the moors, Magwitch hugging his shoulders and limping off into the fog; Jaggers in London, washing his hands, the grease stains on the wall of his office, the surrounding buildings seeming to lean over to peer through his sky-light; comic images like Jo pouring gravy on Pip's plate until it floods the table; Wopsle in his Hamlet costume; the list is endless.

Even Pip's progress itself is portrayed in a visual way. We do not follow him through an elaborate psychological development in which one frame of mind shades off gradually into another like colors on a spectrum. Rather we <u>see</u> him at isolated points on a continuum, the intervening points having been erased away and left for us to replace by inference, see him in a series of attitudes, attitudes fostered by the plot and illustrating the theme. In other words, we see him in a series of pictures which "tell" his psychological narrative in the manner of the eighteenth-century "progress prints."[33] Thus the easily seen ironies and big telling moments are, again, presented in a highly dramatic, specifically visual way. Indeed, the whole meaning of the novel might be said to reside in one picture: Magwitch climbing the stairs to Pip's quarters, coming continually upward as he moves in and out of the little circle of light thrown by Pip's upheld reading lamp, Orlick crouching in the shadows below.

Most discussions of James's pictorialism attempt to relate it to his well-known interest in and knowledge of painting and sculpture. In one of the best essays written on James, Miss Viola Hopkins attempts to compare his fictional style with the painterly techniques of the Impressionists and the Mannerists.[34] But as Miss Hopkins herself observes, there must always be severe limitations on the comparative study of literature and art. Safer, perhaps, to compare James's visual method--and especially his tendency to present the big telling moments as "framed" pictures not with Renoir or Tintoretto, but with the use of internal illustrations in Dickens.

From earliest childhood text and illustrations in Dickens were, for James, inextricably fused. Indeed, if Howells as a youth had ordered his sense of experience according to the dictates of Boz, James, at a comparable age, seems to have seen the world with the eyes of Phiz. A certain dentist lived in his memory as the embodiment of Joey Bagstock in the plates to Dombey and Son; his childhood drawing master "was to remain with [him] a picture of somebody in Dickens, one of the Phiz if not the Cruikshank pictures." Oliver Twist "perhaps even seemed to [him] more Cruikshank's than Dickens's; it was a thing of such vividly terrible images."[35] When he himself was to agree to allow illustrations in the New York Edition he was to provide his photographer with instructions as detailed and demanding as any Dickens ever sent Seymour, Browne, Leech or Stone. Like Dickens he could give not only the neighborhood but the street and number of buildings to be consulted for models, be they in London or Paris.[36] James was well aware that text and illustration fused so completely in his childhood memories of Dickens precisely because Dickens wrote pictorially, wrote his own illustrations rather than relying upon the plates to do the work of the prose. In comparing him with Balzac and Shakespeare, he speaks of his "intensity of imaginative power, the power of evoking visible objects and figures" as the result of his seeing them himself "with the force of hallucination and making others see them all but just as vividly."[37] His major objection to Our Mutual Friend in the review mentioned above is that it disappoints the expectations Dickens has created in his audiences: it is too much "told," too little "seen." But of course the more telling evidence is James's habitual use of internal illustrations in his own fictions.

Miss Hopkins has provided us with a useful catalog of such "framed" scenes in James. The opening scenes in Confidence; Rowland's vision of the three artists standing before Roderick's statue of Eve in Roderick Hudson, Isabel standing before young Rosier "framed in the gilded doorway" and dressed in black in The Portrait of a Lady; Hyacinth's vision of Sholto standing before Millicent in The Princess Casamassima; Strether's vision of Chad and Mme. de Vionnet floating down the river in The Ambassadors; Milly Teale seeing Kate Croy standing in a window and sensing that Densher has returned in The Wings of the Dove; all these and others are presented in the manner of Dickens almost as memoranda to an illustrator. And one notices that like the internal illustrations in Dickens they all present a powerful visual image that itself, rather than action or even characterization, bears the burden of theme. It is, for example, our almost hallucinatory vision of Hyacinth's betrayal that makes it so horrible. Sight is insight: Millicent's symbolic prostitution, Sholto's lust. James has carefully prepared us for the picture; as Sholto's eye travels up and down the front of Millicent's dress we recall--as Hyacinth must too--his earlier off-hand remark about the bar-maid: "That was rather a nice little girl in there; did you twig her good bust? It's a pity they always have such beastly hands."[38] And that Millicent might openly exploit her sexuality to escape from Lomax Place comes as a disappointment, not a great surprise. But the point is that to recount the scene's meanings--for Millicent's future as well as Hyacinth's--is simply to redraw the picture. The visual image _is_ the meaning.

In _Great Expectations_ all the novel's social themes converge upon and are contained in the picture of Magwitch climbing the stairs to Pip's quarters; in the _Portrait of a Lady_, James similarly defines and extends social meanings by means of a telling internal illustration. In its analysis of social themes _The Portrait_ is more subtle than its critical reputation implies, in that the work as a whole recreates a total society and what it recreates it mostly avoids discussing. Henrietta Stackpole's accusations; Madame Merle's empty "intellectual" talk: "What do we call the self"; old Mr. Touchett's vague speculations about "social and political changes"; Osmond's patronizing comments on the vulgar modern; all are part of the pattern of the society represented. They do not define that society any more than the discussions held on contemporary television symposia define ours. They merely--or powerfully--suggest the quality of the society that Isabel Archer, the lady whose portrait the novel paints, confronts.

These reflections are prompted by a question raised by R. P. Blackmur: that after building an individual psychology in The Portrait the wonder is that James should turn to novels about society: The Bostonians, The Princess Casamassima.[39] The answer seems to be that James imaginatively conceived his artistic issue to be a social one, that for him as for Dickens the key to personal fulfillment lay somehow in the nature of the society to which the individual is exposed. Isabel's condition, surely, is seen thus, and the novel records her search for a milieu in which to fulfill herself.

In his earlier novels, most notably *The American* and *The Europeans*, James had drawn portraits of society in the tints of classic comedy. As he felt himself mature as a novelist he seems to have wanted to do something more ambitious, to make a "realistic" analysis of his society in the manner of Dickens through highly imaginative caricature. This is his achievement in *The Portrait*, with its peculiar collection of eccentric and unreconciled characters who together compose a sort of fun-house mirror's image of the world.

One of the novel's themes is that of the natural in society *vs*. the unnatural, and we can easily see how the novel moves from the natural Gardencourt world to the unnatural world of Osmond as Isabel tries to put herself into a nourishing relationship with life. The Gardencourt world is clearly fated; it has barely worked for old Mr. Touchett, as Mrs. Touchett's breakaway shows. Lord Warburton and the doomed Ralph are well-mannered oddities in a world that is at least natural, a world in which good manners symbolize good morals, and the old order, with its beauties, holds good. Everywhere else, however, excesses and vulgarities reign. One of the most appealing aspects of the *Portrait* is the way in which James builds a beautiful burlesque of society by composing the world of the novel almost entirely of expatriated "Dickensian" Americans with rude, vulgar, or eccentric mannerisms. Henrietta Stackpole is continually raging (although at heart she is good); Isabel and Casper have horrible scenes; Isabel and her aunt meet with an exchange of rudenesses; Mme. Merle carefully hones the cutting edge of almost everything she says. These bad manners are emblematic not, as is the good behaviour at Gardencourt, of the natural, but of the uprooted, unsettled, bravely--but at base hopelessly--independent state. Henrietta and Mrs. Touchett may glory in their independence, but they must also admit to being displaced and very lonely, as we observe through the ironic humor of the lady journalist's insisting that anyone and everyone get married. Both women illuminate and highlight Isabel's situation: Mrs. Touchett is socially independent, Henrietta anti-socially independent. Isabel's course lies between.

This parody of the flux that was society in James's day exposes a world that echoes the Veneering's dinner parties in *Our Mutual Friend*. Bad manners and bad scenes belie the seemed security of upper class life and reflect its inability to sustain variety and vitality, to allow peaceful co-existence (much less harmony and mutuality) between people of different sorts and classes. For James, as for Dickens, the surest condemnation of a society is its inability to support generosity. Old Touchett's real legacy, like Old Trent's efforts at building one, destroys because society itself is corrupt. Isabel must suffer as surely as Little Nell must die; indeed, the two have more in common than obviously meets the eye.

We see Isabel's predicament and James's burlesque of society most clearly in the high comedy of the novel's most explicitly Dickensian episode, Isabel's encounter with Mr. Luce and friends in Paris and her condemnation of the sad, vapid, expatriated life that leads nowhere. Society seems, as the novel progresses, less and less able to support her. She takes a trip around the world, and the world bores her. She then turns to the private life and accepts Osmond's proposals.

Osmond and Mme. Merle represent, of course, the unnatural life where good manners are too good; their mannered behaviour both hides and signifies bad morals: the sins of hypocrisy, the lack of generosity, the evil of using people symbolized by sexual immorality. But in the celebrated fireside scene Isabel, in coming to realize the contradiction in Osmond's character--he pretends to hate society yet knows he is tied to it and serves it--really states the contradiction in which all the characters are caught, even she herself:

> But this base, ignoble world, it appeared, was after all what one was to live for; one was to keep it forever in one's eye, in order not to enlighten or convert or redeem it, but to extract from it some recognition of one's own superiority. On the one hand it was despicable, but on the other it afforded a standard. Osmond had talked to Isabel about his renunciation, his indifference, the ease with which he dispensed with the usual aids to success; and all of this had seemed to her admirable. She had thought it a grand indifference, an exquisite independence. But indifference was really the last of his qualities; she had never seen anyone who thought so much of others. ...He was unable to live without [society], and she saw that he had never really done so; he had looked at it out of his window even when he appeared most detached from it.
>
> (IV, xlii, 197-98)

Society, all agree, _is_ vulgar, although they all have different ideas about what constitutes society. They all yearn for a private life; yet they must live a social one. Even the independent Mrs. Touchett cannot leave Isabel and Warburton together in the drawing room after ten o'clock. All are bound to society by money, by shame, by the sense of what is "proper," and by ties of feeling. (As so often in Dickens love ensnares in this novel, as underscored by the repeated net and cage imagery: Isabel is "caught" in her marriage, "trapped," and "in a cage.") Isabel cannot accept Casper at the end because his argument that society cannot hold them back does not, for her, stand up. The defeated heroes of Dickens's last great social novels achieve fulfillment (limited at that) only by retreat and escape; Eugene Wrayburn, for example, marries Lizzie in full knowledge that "The Voice of Society" will banish them to exile and ineffectual isolation. Isabel's decision is, perhaps, more noble. She cannot submit in the end to the strength of Casper's passion, a passion indicative of a vitality seen nowhere else in the novel, because her own character is too deep not to live the contradiction she has come to understand. Society does not nourish her feelings, her sensibilities, her generosity, but she must obey its values for the only honor available to her. She must maintain her largeness even in the face of the world's smallness. In living in line with the world Isabel is not granted a natural life; but she need not be like Osmond, for her resignation to society is without illusions about herself and, above all, is generous, not small. Isabel returns at the end to Italy because she must live the contradiction through her ties to Pansy. In the society in which she lives, motherly love for her step-daughter is the only thing that Isabel can give.

Pansy is perhaps more Dickensian symbol--the child at the center of the author's criticism of life--than personality; she never has the chance to be natural even though (and because) she is a "natural" child. Her manners are perfect, but she is too cloistered for them to register anything save her basic goodness and her slavery to her father. She is shy, but underneath her mannerly surface her real feelings are smothered. She has to obey Osmond; she wants to, but at the same time she knows she is being trapped. While Pansy forms the outlet for Isabel's generosity, even this relationship is blighted by the unnatural society that surrounds it: Isabel's affection for the girl is made the object of cruel scorn by Mme. Merle and her friends. And Isabel can act only in a negative way for her step-daughter; she cannot help her marry Rosier, she can only send Warburton away. Indeed, the almost inert image of their static relationship is one of the novel's most poignant features. Caught in a world she never made but which she has come to understand, Isabel lives by standards that suit a world in which feeling might be rewarded and in which a natural life might be possible because the worldly alternative (the Countess Gemini) implies total decay. Isabel Osmond would rather cling to her values and the hope of an unfound social orientation their presence implies.

Practically all the characters in the Portrait are conceived in poetic relation to Isabel. Like the minor figures who surround the protagonists of Dickens's Hogarthian progresses, their function is to mirror and define, by graphic relation, her predicament. Some are in clear opposition, as Osmond and the Countess Gemini; Pansy's slavery to Osmond counterpoints Isabel's independence. Henrietta, surprisingly enough, humorously embodies the novel's social themes. Her career parallels Isabel's, and her outbursts give the key to what Isabel may, in deeper ways, feel about the stages of society to which she is introduced. It is revealing that when Isabel makes her only direct open judgment on the world, Mrs. Touchett immediately accuses her of talking like the lady journalist.

As one might expect in a novel by James, social meanings are embodied in a series of carefully chosen metaphors and symbols. Throughout the book Isabel's dream of the natural life is symbolized by flowers--as even the name "Gardencourt" implies. Osmond's world, on the other hand, is suggested by works of art. One of Mme. Merle's first remarks is "I'm afraid there are moments in life when even Schubert has nothing to say to us. We must, however, admit that they are our worst" (III, xviii, 245), and in

Rome the number of masterpieces that are thrown at us is stupendous. The old order, the world of old Mr. Touchett and his son, is represented in an image, one of the most beautiful in all James, in which art and nature are combined: "His [Ralph's] serenity was but the array of wild flowers niched in his ruin" (III, v, 54).

The discussion so far may seem to have wandered far from Dickens and the pictorial method. But such is the richness of James's Dickensian art that all that has been said is necessary prelude to even a summary explication of the way in which symbol, characterization, plot and theme all converge, ultimately, upon one "picture" framed as an internal illustration by a convenient doorway in the one scene in which Isabel stops short while the whole novel turns. Isabel returns from a walk with Pansy carrying a bouquet of flowers she has picked far from the walls of Rome. She finds Osmond and Mme. Merle in silent conversation, she standing, he sitting, and the reader becomes immediately aware of what is wrong in her household. Nothing is said, nor does the narrator make any comment. As in the "picture" of Magwitch climbing Pip's stairs, moving in and out of the little circle of light, the visual image conveyed by the internal illustration makes comment superfluous. It is the comment.

In external situations the manners of Osmond and his ex-mistress are perfect, so over perfect indeed that contrasted to the natural good manners of Gardencourt they symbolize the cunning and evil hypocrisy of the novel's portrayed society. Isabel comes upon them in a relaxed, private moment with their veneer of perfect deportment removed. Osmond's indecorous composure is all the more striking because not only does it contrast greatly with his usual behavior but it also reveals, to the reader as to his wife, his true nature. A much lesser author would have had the flowers Isabel carries seem to fade on the spot. James does not, but their presence in the picture is as necessary for its meaning as the falling books in the penultimate plate in Martin Chuzzlewit. And if we recall their association with Ralph, who, off-stage, is dying, they add new depths to Isabel's domestic tragedy. The ruins from which Isabel has returned suggest the decline of society. Wedded as a symbol to Ralph's health, they denote the decline of grace and sensibility to the beautifully artificial. The flowers "niched" among them represent in an extremely poignant way Isabel's hope for a natural life. Indeed, one of the most touching aspects of The Portrait is the persistence of feeling arising even in the most hopeless circumstances. But the ruins are also the ruins of Isabel's marriage, and it is the contrast between the two realities symbolized by the flowers and Osmond's ease that gives the tableau its tremendous dramatic power. All the meanings outlined above merge into a sense of the poignant contradiction that it is the novel's purpose to show. Isabel's subsequent rejection of Goodwood is just her determination to live that contradiction, which is her completed sense of her destiny. Her cynicism after her marriage is only seeming, but the feeling--not despair, but resignation--it reveals runs deep. She is aware that her society cannot support feeling and that feeling cannot survive an unhealthy relationship to the world which has produced it. Her determination to be generous at all costs and to nourish--through her relationship to Pansy--the world that has not nourished her is the novel's last implied note.

This is hardly the first time that the importance of Isabel's vision of Osmond and Mme. Merle has been observed. But to consider the scene in the light of the Dickensian use of internal illustration as a means of analyzing social themes is to realize that Blackmur's assertion requires a certain rephrasing. After developing an individual psychology in The Portrait of a Lady James was precisely enabled to develop the social themes already embodied in that novel, enabled to move on to the achievements in both psychological and social analysis of The Bostonians and the Princess. Nor should we be surprised that those novels are even more explicitly Dickensian than their predecessor. Leavis remarks that James's debt to Dickens "involves more than a mere manner; he was helped by him to see from the outside, and critically place, the life around him."[40] To which we add that the writing of the Portrait proved that one way to analyse, critically, the structure and nature of society was to adopt, like Dickens, the illustrator's point of view.

Notes to Chapter VI

[1]Most particularly by George H. Ford, Dickens and His Readers, pp. 203-12 and passim. See also William T. Stafford, "Literary Allusions in James Prefaces," AL, XXXV (March, 1963), 60-70; and Laurence Barrett, "Young Henry James, Critic," AL, XX (1949), 385-400.

[2]Indeed, one may even be somewhat amused at the silent-on-a-peak-in-Darien sense of discovery with which Mr. Leavis has more recently pointed to strengths in Dickens that Dickensians have recognized for years. See his essay on Dombey and Son in The Sewanee Review, LXX (Spring, 1962), 177-201. One wonders even if the essay would ever have found a publisher had it been submitted under any other name.

[3]Autobiography, p. 68.

[4]Dickens and His Readers, p. 205.

[5]The Nation, I (1865), 786-87; reprinted in Views and Reviews (Boston, 1908).

[6]Partial Portraits, p. 222. In "A Note on Literary Indebtedness" Q. D. Leavis presents a convincing case study in the difference between gross imitation and conscious sympathy. Mrs. Leavis cites three passages describing the reaction of a desperately unhappy young woman to the ruined grandeur of Rome. The passages are taken from (1) Little Dorrit, (2) Middlemarch, and (3) The Portrait of a Lady. The relationship between (2) and (1) shows one writer constructively using, "by extending and deepening," the invention of another artist, while (3) is "in its relation to both the others, an example...of the parasitic." Thus, she argues, we must recognize two radically different kinds of indebtedness, "as distinct from influence"; the one indicated by the relation of (2) to (1) and the other by that of (3) to (1) and (2). (Hudson Review, VIII [Autumn, 1955], pp. 423-28.) The distinction is extremely useful, especially if one removes the connotations of value judgment Mrs. Leavis attaches to the word "deepening" by referring to George Eliot as "great" and Dickens as "less profound," and recognizes instead that the greater "depth" of George Eliot's passage is not necessarily a mark of greater "profundity"

but rather a sign that she is working in a different mode for different ends. James, of course, would label the relations (3):(1) and (2) gross imitation and (2):(1) conscious sympathy.

[7] Richard N. Foley, Criticism in American Periodicals of the Works of Henry James from 1866 to 1916 (Washington, D.C., 1944), p. 42.

[8] The Novels and Tales of Henry James, Reissue of the "New York Edition," 26 vols. (New York, n.d.), V, v-vi. Unless otherwise noted, all subsequent references to James's fiction are to this edition, purposely chosen as reflecting James's final intentions toward the Dickensian elements in his work. Citations will supply volume number, book, chapter, and page references. (Thus Hyacinth will be found reading Dickens to Pinnie V, I, x, 153.)

[9] Autobiography, p. 572.

[10] Noted by Lionel Trilling, The Liberal Imagination, pp. 84-85.

[11] The characterizations are, of course, entirely different, but both men are bastards, the off-spring of a sexually exploitative genteel father and a lower-class foreign, "criminal" mother; both are excluded from society and exploited by emotionally hollow grasping aristocrats, and both turn upon society with intended or enacted violence, violence that is, in both cases, clearly depicted as patricidal. Moreover, one notes that Hyacinth is torn apart by the conflict between his sense of social injustice and his appreciation of the value of socially acquired, aesthetic "culture," which, he believes, will be destroyed by those who desire to strike back at the society that has injured them. In other words he faces the same dilemma that confronted Dickens in the writing of Barnaby Rudge. The dilemma destroys Hyacinth; it also destroyed Dickens's novel, which is fatally divided between deep sympathy with its social victims and horror at their culturally destructive rage. These parallels should, of course, be seen as supplementing rather than contradicting or competing with the well-known parallels between the Princess and Turgenev's Virgin Soil. See Daniel J. Lerner, "The Influence of Turgenev on Henry James," Slavonic and East European Review, XX (December, 1941), 46-51.

[12]For James as for Dickens the child's intuition is an infallible moral guide. For example, we know, essentially, all we need to know about the characters involved when in the second chapter of Roderick Hudson little Bessie snuggles up to Rowland and says she does not like Roderick. (I, ii, 21).

[13]Cargill, The Novels of Henry James (New York, 1961), p. 260; Bowden, The Themes of Henry James (New Haven, 1956), p. 85.

[14]The Comic Sense of Henry James, 2nd ed. (London, 1967), pp. 5, 58-68, and passim. As he himself acknowledges, Poirier's reading of James is very similar to Robert Garis's reading of Dickens in The Dickens Theatre (Oxford, 1965), although, fortunately, much less dogmatic and monomaniacal.

[15]The same sort of twentieth-century assumptions, it seems to me, lie, on a more sophisticated plane, behind the reading of the novel given by those critics who posit Maisie's systematic corruption and maintain that her ultimatum to Sir Claude--"I'll give up Mrs. Wix if you'll give up Mrs. Beale"--carries with it the conscious lure of her virginity. See Harris W. Wilson, "What Did Maisie Know?," CE, XVII (1956), 279-82; Edward Wasiolek, "Maisie: Pure or Corrupt?," CE, XXII (1960); and John C. McCloskey, "What Maisie Knows: A Study in Childhood and Adolescence," AL, XXXVI (1965), 485-513. The opposing argument is set forth by James W. Gargano, "What Maisie Knew: The Evolution of a 'Moral Sense'," NCF, XVI (1961), 33-46; Tony Tanner, "The Literary Children of James and Clemens," NCF, XVI (1961), 205-18; and Joseph A. Hynes, "The Middle Way of Miss Farange: A Study of James's Maisie," ELH, XXXII (1965), 528-53.

[16]Jacques Barzun, "Henry James: Melodramatist," in The Question of Henry James, ed. F. W. Dupee (New York, 1945), pp. 254-72; Leo B. Levy, Versions of Melodrama: A Study of the Fiction and Drama of Henry James, 1865-1897 (Berkeley and Los Angeles, 1957).

[17]Watch and Ward, ed. Leon Edel (London, 1960), ch. i, pp. 21-22.

[18]One must in all fairness admit that there are moments in these opening scenes in which James' is

eminently successful in the Dickens manner: the wife of the hotel's proprietor, for example, "was a kindly woman enough, but so thoroughly the mistress of a public house that she seemed to deal out her very pity over a bar" (i, 30).

[19] One also notices James's appropriation throughout the novel of Dickens's ironic Edenic imagery.

[20] Like Dickens, James delights in symbolic settings. When Christina reappears in _The Princess Casamassima_ we see her first at the theatre, where the surroundings reflect both her fondness for self-dramatization and her tendency to treat others as if they were merely performers in a play being staged for her own private amusement, to mitigate her boredom and disillusionment.

[21] Quoted in Abigail Ann Hamblen, "Henry James and the Press: A Study of Protest," _Western Humanities Review_, XI (1957), 172.

[22] "Henry James's First Novel," 299; _The Great Tradition_, p. 162.

[23] Ford, _Dickens and His Readers_, p. 211.

[24] _The Notebooks of Henry James_, ed. F. O. Matthiessen and Kenneth B. Murdock (New York, 1961), p. 377. The "Project" gives Waymarsh's name as "Waymark"; one wonders if James changed it because the original version was too much of a Dickensian pointer.

[25] (Boston, 1905), p. 43.

[26] _Notebooks_, p. 82.

[27] The phrase occurs in a letter to James Russell Lowell, written 16 November 1886, in regard to Julian Hawthorne's making public certain of Lowell's private remarks about British politics, an incident that provided one of the "germs" for _The Reverberator_. First publ. in George Knox, "Reverberations and _The Reverberator_," _Essex Institute Historical Collections_, XCV (1959), 353.

[28] _French Poets and Novelists_ (New York, 1884), p. 147.

[29] *Letters*, I, p. 69.

[30] *Letters*, I, pp. 102, 106, and 125; III, p. 380.

[31] See the letter to Browne publ. in John Butt, "Dickens's Instructions for *Martin Chuzzlewit*, Plate XVIII," *REL*, II (1961), 49-50.

[32] The connection between *Le Tartuffe* and Pecksniff's hypocrisy is obvious enough; the presence of *Paradise Lost* is more subtle. It represents, ironically, Pecksniff's exposure and fall from grace in addition to picking up the Edenic symbolism of the American chapters. But references to Adam and Eve occur elsewhere throughout the novel: the Chuzzlewit family is introduced as their direct descendents; Sarah Gamp ministers unto the curse pronounced upon them; Pecksniff's Wiltshire is repeatedly described as a withered, post-lapsarian garden; Pecksniff himself, spade in hand, explains that he "does a little bit of Adam still"; and so forth. In an essay tentatively entitled "Moliere, Milton, and *Martin Chuzzlewit*" I hope to explore the significance of these and other allusions to *Paradise Lost* in the novel.

[33] Edward B. Benjamin comments that "*Martin Chuzzlewit* falls naturally into three parts, showing the rise, triumph, and fall of hypocrisy, like the old prints showing a drunkard's progress." ("The Structure of *Martin Chuzzlewit*," *PQ*, XXXIV [1955], 45.) One could, I think, build a strong argument that the "progress print" was, early and late, Dickens's favorite structural model.

[34] "Visual Art Devices and Parallels in the Fiction of Henry James," *PMLA*, LXXXVI (1961), 561-74. See also F. O. Matthiessen, "James and the Plastic Arts," *Kenyon Review*, V (1943), 533-50; and Adeline Tintner, "The Spoils of Henry James," *PMLA*, LXI (1946), 239-51. Bowden, *The Themes of Henry James*, continues the line of investigation initiated by Matthiessen and Miss Tintner, which, ultimately, is more concerned with thematic allusions to art than with James's use of the pictorial method.

[35] *Autobiography*, pp. 39, 69, 117.

[36]Alvin L. Coburn, "Illustrating Henry James," transcript of the British Broadcasting Corporation Third Programme, 17 July 1953. See also Joseph J. Firebaugh, "Coburn: Henry James's Photographer," _AQ_, VII (1955), 230-33.

[37]_French Poets and Novelists_, p. 147. James's use of the word "hallucination" may be an echo of George Henry Lewes's celebrated study of Dickens, the first to explore Dickens's visual quality in any detail. One notes that James also uses the word in the "Preface" to _The Golden Bowl_ to describe the effect of prose that does the work of illustration in itself.

[38]IV, II, xx, 331. In _The Other Victorians_ Steven Marcus cites a retired Major who appears in _My Secret Life_ as a kind of touchstone by which we can realize the aggressive and exploitative sexual vulgarity that Dickens has euphemistically concealed in his characterization of Joey Bagstock. (New York, 1966, p. 110.) Actually there is little need to consult such exotic sources; one can learn as much from recognizing the connection between Bagstock and Sholto. When Sholto "twigs" the bar-maid's bosom or remarks to Hyacinth: "My dear fellow, I've seen many women, and the women of many countries...and I've seen them as intimately as you like, and I know what I'm talking about..." (V, II, xv, 266), James is making explicit what his model only implied.

[39]_Literary History of the United States_, ed. Spiller, _et al_. (New York, 1960), pp. 1058-60.

[40]_The Great Tradition_, p. 162.

CHAPTER VII

DICKENS IN AMERICA: THE RETURN TO ROMANCE

I. The "American Dickens"--Once More

> This characterization has been applied to so many feeble witted persons during the past quarter of a century, and frequently with such disastrous results... that it has come to be regarded rather as a term of obloquy or ridicule, and one that no self-respecting or intelligent literary man coveted.
>
> --James L. Ford

Twelve years after William Dean Howells had dogmatically asserted that the art of fiction had become a "finer art" than it was at mid-century, David Copperfield was still, by one index at least, the most popular novel in America and Dickens the most popular novelist.[1] In 1893 the Philadelphia house of J. Selwin Tait & Sons, concerned no doubt with sounding the market, had requested from each of the larger public libraries in the country, numbering at that time well over a thousand, a list of the hundred and fifty novels most in demand at their call-desks. The lists were tabulated, and the most frequently named novels ranked according to the number of lists on which they appeared. David Copperfield came first, being named on a phenomenal 92 per cent of the lists.[2] Eight other Dickens novels made the honor-roll; the least popular of these, Little Dorrit, appeared on only 29 per cent of the lists, but placed well ahead of the only two Howells works to appear, The Lady of the Aroostook and The Rise of Silas Lapham, both ranked at 22 per cent. James did not appear at all.[3] On the list of authors most frequently appearing, Dickens again ranks first; Mark Twain is thirteenth, and Howells trails at twenty-sixth.[4]

Almost as interesting as the lists themselves are the remarks on their significance made by Hamilton Wright Mabie in The Forum, December, 1893. Eight years earlier, in a review of Silas Lapham, Mabie had taken decided exception to Howells's contention that the "realistic" novel displayed a "finer art" than that of Dickens and Thackeray. Significantly, his criteria were moral and philosophical rather than esthetic. Equating art with idealism, he maintained that in Dickens's day art was "based on the conception that life is at bottom a revelation; that human relations of all kinds have spiritual types behind them; and that the discovery of these universal facts, and the clear, noble embodiment of them...is the office of genius and the end of art." "Realism," in its devotion to the empirical surface of life and implied rejection of the "romantic," transcendental equation of natural facts with spiritual facts, is in essence immoral. "It is," he said, "...practical atheism applied to art."[5] Hence in '93 he views the overwhelming popular preference for Dickens as justifying considerable patriotic pride. Reassured by the cool reception granted "atheism applied to art," Mabie is freed to direct his attention to the esthetic rather than philosophical characteristics of popular tastes. Metaphysical concerns are subsumed under the larger (and vaguer) category of "human interest." Since, for example, The Scarlet Letter is to Mabie's mind more tightly constructed and greater in "depth and intensity of human interest" than The Marble Faun, the popular preference for the former over the latter demonstrates that "the finest art does not fail to charm when it allies itself with the deepest life." By "deepest life" we must assume that Mabie means the emotionally effective presentation of the spiritual facts and types lying behind primary human relationships. He is even willing to rank emotional effect over idealistic refinement. Noting the high rating given

Vanity Fair, he remarks that "less perfect in form, less delicate in insight into the finer qualities and in feeling for the subtle differences of personal and social ideals than 'Henry Esmond,' it is more powerful, direct and compelling in its narrative force and its human interest." It is, therefore, "the greatest novel in our language." Throughout the essay Mabie insists that moral idealism must be accompanied by emotional intensity and narrative drive if it is to constitute great art. Thus he is unwilling to fault out and out "romantic" melodrama if it shows a "masterly dealing with the old-time and all-time elements of adventure and incident." Better yet is melodrama combined with moral allegory. The public rightly prefers Stevenson's Dr. Jekyl and Mr. Hyde to his Prince Otto; the latter may be written in a subtler style, but the former "deals with a moral problem of universal personal significance." "It is clear," he observes

> that the American reading public recognizes literary quality and prefers it when it is vitalized by deep and real human interests. It is clear also that this same public retains its old-time liking for a strong story-element; in other words, for dramatic quality and power.

All of Mabie's standards converge in his statement that the "popular instinct is not astray" in granting the highest honors to David Copperfield. Although it may, in

Mabie's opinion, lack the close construction and some of the drama of A Tale of Two Cities, which appears further down the list, it is nonetheless, more characteristic of Dickens's virtues as a whole. A "beautiful tale," its "personal note" lends sweetness and freshness to its sentiment and insures its deep human interest. However, sentiment and human interest are no excuse for sentimentality or for disregard for form. Mabie notes that "it is significant of a sound taste also, that 'The Old Curiosity Shop' and 'Dombey and Son,' in which, to recall [Andrew] Lang's phrase, Dickens wallowed in a sea of sentimentalism, appear well down the list, and that 'Barnaby Rudge' does not appear [at all]."

Mabie ends the essay with a stern warning:

> The reading public, so far as it uses the public libraries, is like some other publics; it has sound instincts, it knows good work; it is likely, in the long run, to remember what is sound and to forget what is bad; but it is somewhat capricious; it often fails to know its own mind; and it makes great blunders by the way. It is a public, however, with which no writer can safely trifle.

The *caveat* was in many ways unnecessary, for the most interesting group of young novelists and critics coming to maturity in 1893 were in essential agreement with popular esthetics. Although perhaps ambiguous in their attitudes toward the philosophical idealism inherent in Mabie's views, they shared his--and the public's--respect for story-telling, for narrative drive and dramatic, even melodramatic, power, and his preference for Stevensonian moral allegory over Jamesian psychological analysis. Restive under what were to them the stultifying restrictions of Howells's brand of "realism," they longed for a return to the greater freedoms of the Dickensian mode. They dreamed, once more, of "The Great American Novel," and, like their grandfathers, saw that elusive work as somehow associated with imitations of Boz.

One of the most emphatic statements of their intentions is an essay by James L. Ford, which appeared in _Munsey's Magazine_ for April, 1900, entitled precisely, "The Chance for an American Dickens."[6] Despite its late date and its assertion that the American Dickens has yet to come forward, Ford's article may be read as a retrospective view of the efforts of many of the most significant novelists to emerge in the nineties. As such the essay helps to make many things clear that are otherwise obscure. It can, for example, clarify the implications for Dickens's reputation of, say, Garland's attempt to substitute his term, "veritism," for Howells's "realism," and help us to see what is specifically Dickensian in Crane's Bowery tales.

Like most programmatic critics Ford is more forceful in stating what he is against than what he is for. "Realism," or as he prefers to call it, the "analytical novel," has run its course. Brought into vogue only by the fact that the supply of superior sensation fiction (Ford specifically mentions Oliver Twist and The Woman in White) was inadequate to the demand, it produced a few works (unnamed) of genuine merit and then wore itself out in tedium and inanities. Restricted to the mere surface of life, it had "nothing to feed upon" and has begun simply "running emptyings." Moreover, it has become economically as well as esthetically dead. For two decades the reading public had been fed nothing but works by men who are "masters of no craft save that of describing everything that is not worth a second thought." When, almost by accident, publishers brought out two or three American "novels of incident" (Ford may have in mind anything from Crawford's Don Orsino to Crane's The Red Badge of Courage) their success was phenomenal, indicating beyond doubt that "the public literally hungered after long novels of dramatic action rather than of torpid and sentimental thoughts."

The "realistic" novelist, Ford maintains, not only tends to "work from the surface" and to take himself "too seriously," but also to become increasingly cut off from the sources of artistic life. Alienated from the reading public, he withdraws with others of his own tastes into "mutual admiration societies," limiting his range to upper middle-class social life, enlivened only by occasional slumming forays into the lower depths, depths that are seen from a tourist's point of view. It is this that above all makes "realistic" novels torpid and sentimental. In other words Ford is positing yet another shift in the definition of reality. Howells, James, and Pellew, as spokesmen for the "analytical school," had moved the position of the "real" on the philosophical plane from moral, essentially teleological idealism to empirical materialism--or so, at least, critics like Mabie had thought. Ford moves it on the social and economic plane; the "real" is no longer upper middle-class. "I cannot," he insists, "conceive of a really great New York story springing from the brain of a man who does not know what a bung starter is." Significantly--and predictably--Ford associates the depiction of lower-class life with sensation, lurid incident, and melodrama. Turning briefly to the theatre he notices that the vogue for "society plays" was contemporaneous with the flourishing of the "analytical" novel, but that now "the taste for strong melodrama is growing every day." In a sense Ford is merely importing the main thrust of the "experimental school" of French "naturalism," the tendency, which Erich Auerbach traces back to the brothers Goncourt, to introduce the fourth estate into literature and present it seriously as the material for tragedy rather than mere low comedy and farce. There is even in Ford's emphasis on the lurid and sensational a hint of what Auerbach calls in the Goncourts and their followers "the aesthetic attraction of the ugly and pathological."[7] The important thing to note, however, is that Ford builds his entire argument not on the example of Zola, but on that of Dickens.

Hence Ford's equation of the Great American Novelist and the American Dickens is inevitable. He is to be to New York what Dickens was to London: "He will give us stories dealing with metropolitan life in its entirety, and studied from the inside, and will not be content to show us merely one or two highly polished facets of its exterior." The operative phrases here are, of course, "in its entirety" and "from the inside." The leaders of the "analytical school," Ford admits, sneer at Dickens as "a master of bathos, a caricaturist, a man whose pen had the newspaper taint," but, he claims, the writer who is to produce the Great American

Novel must study the "magic art" of Bleak House and master it. The "realists" may be able to depict "certain corners" of New York and "certain phases" of its social life; Dickens's greatness was his ability to present all of society from Chesney Wold to Tom-All-Alone's. Moreover, he was "inside" his world. The "realist" had only "the local color that he secures by riding up and down in a cable car"; Dickens, the "great master of story-telling," was "as thoroughly at home...in the squalid court where the poor law writer died as Blondin was on a tight rope stretched over-Niagara Falls." Ford continues, "that is the best simile I can think of when I think on the difficulties that beset the path of a writer who really wishes to obtain a mastery over the conditions of life that prevail in a city that offers to him now fully as much as London did when Dickens was a law reporter."

The reference to Dickens's journalistic experience is also inevitable. Obviously Ford's American Dickens cannot come from the effete mutual admiration societies of Fifth Avenue. To depict New York life from the inside he must have had a more intimate glimpse of it than any afforded by the car routes. And who is more inside New York than the newspaper man? The American Dickens

> will come from Park Row in the person of some reporter who shall unite with a thorough apprecia-tion and knowledge of various conditions of New York life, the Dickens ability to knit them together by plausible links and [by] those qualities of humor and imagination which are the essentials of good fiction.

Interestingly enough, Ford's remarks are, historically, more accurate than he himself could ever have known. The univer-sally acknowledged leader of the "analytical school," Howells himself, had cut short his own career as a reporter when he discovered that he was psychologically incapable of facing up to the "realities" of a metropolitan police court, retreating instead to the writing of literary gossip columns.[8] But the young writers coming to maturity in the nineties, Crane, Frederic, Harding-Davis, Ade, and Dreiser, for example, were more at ease around the city desk than at literary teas. Their Dean of Letters was not Howells, but Charles A. Dana, the archetype of the hard-boiled editor whose literary masters were Dickens and Balzac and who thought all other writers fools.[9]

Ford continually predicts that the American Dickens must set his Great American Novel in New York City. Not all of the young journalist-novelists for whom he spoke would have agreed. One of them in particular vigorously main-tained that there were story cities on the West Coast as well. Equally disillusioned with the limited range of Howellsian "realism" and equally eager to get "inside" Life with a capital "L," Frank Norris had, three years before Ford's essay, pointed out that "London had her Dickens...but San Francisco still waits for her novelist."

II. The Responsibility of the Novelist

> Le vrai peut quelquefois n'être pas vraisemblable... Les romanciers devront souvent corriger les événements au profit de la vraisemblance et au detriment de la vérité...Le réaliste, s'il est un artiste, cherchera, non pas à nous montrer la photographie banale de la vie, mais à nous en donner la vision plus complete, plus saissante, plus probante que la realité même.
>
> --Balzac

Dickens does not appear in the catalog of Norris's library that his widow prepared for a Swedish researcher, but his close knowledge of Dickens's novels cannot be questioned.[10] It began early with a series of after-dinner readings in which the Norris family, like thousands of others across the nation, made their way through the family set of Works. Norris's mother did the reading, bringing to it both her considerable natural talent and the training she had acquired during her career as a professional actress. The novels thus took on a special kind of life and a peculiarly intimate set of associations for her over-protected son. Franklin Walker's assertion that "Dick Swiveller and the Marchioness, Barkus and Uriah Heep, Quilp, Sairey Gamp, and Bill Sykes [sic] were to him more real than his own playmates" can be written off as the projection of a somewhat sentimental biographer with few hard facts to work with, but that these readings left their mark on Norris is clear both from the scattered references to Dickens in his critical writings and from the impressive admixture of Dickensian elements in his fiction itself.[11]

Norris the critic refers to Dickens only four times; and one of these allusions, the inclusion of Dickens in a list of great English novelists, hardly illuminates his assessment of Dickens's value.[12] The other three references are more revelatory. The first occurs in an early essay entitled "An Opening for Novelists: Great Opportunities for Fiction Writers in San Francisco," published in the Wave, May 22, 1897.[13] Norris here expresses his abiding belief that San Francisco is a place where "things can happen" to provide materials for those with "the instinct for fiction" and deplores the absence of a literature adequately exploring its fruitful field. "London had her Dickens," he says, "...but San Francisco still waits for her novelist." The statement has a decidedly programmatic ring. Norris had at this time already completed Vandover and the Brute, subtitling it "A Study in the Life and Manners of an American City [i.e., San Francisco]," and was at work on McTeague, which he originally called "The People of Polk Street" and later subtitled "A Story of San Francisco."[14] The article itself was followed by a procession of stories with a San Francisco setting. In other words Norris, at least in part, saw himself as being to San Francisco what Dickens was to London. That these works, especially McTeague and such sketches as the "Little Dramas of the Curbstone" series, would have a distinct Dickensian flavor is, therefore, not surprising; we have merely encountered another version of the old paradox that to be distinctly American one imitates Dickens, here embodied in Norris's intuitive awareness that the way to capture the "indefinable air" of a Western city is to employ Dickensian techniques.

Norris's explanation of San Francisco's fitness as a locale for fiction does much to explain why he found Dickens peculiarly appropriate as a guide in evoking its atmosphere.

It is a place where things can happen primarily because of its isolation:

> Isolation produces individuality, originality. The place has grown up independently. Other cities grow by an accretion from without. San Francisco must grow by an expansion from within; and so we have had time and opportunity to develop certain unhampered types and characters and habits unbiased by outside influences, types that are admirably adapted to fictitious treatment.

"Unhampered types and characters": judging from Norris's own fiction, one suspects this means Dickensian eccentrics and grotesques. Howells's followers might scoff at Dickens's "exaggerations," but Norris seems to feel that they are precisely what makes fiction possible. His own "unhampered" characters, Grannis and Miss Baker in McTeague, Hooven in The Octopus, Aunt Wess', Grossman, and Landry Court in The Pit, have all been labelled Dickensian by one critic or another. His tendency to characterize in terms of types, worked out explicitly in the series of apprentice pieces entitled "Western Types" and carried over into the novels themselves, reflects partly a kind of inchoate determinism and partly an over-reliance on novelistic shorthand. It also suggests an inclination to see the world in Dickensian terms.

"Type" was for Norris a recurrent problem, both in his criticism and in his fiction. His so-called "naturalistic" tendency to see man as the product of deterministic forces, particularly heredity and environment, implies that individual characteristics are minimal and unimportant since a given environment coupled with a given set of racial genes will automatically produce a certain "type"; thus all men are types and any one may stand for the group to which he belongs, as Hoang in _Moran of the Lady Letty_ stands for the whole debased breed of Chinamen and Moran the entire race of Vikings. Yet as a novelist with a strong leaning toward what he called "romance," Norris realized that individuality is the stuff of fiction. "Romance," he explains in an often cited passage, "is the kind of fiction that takes cognizance of variations from the type of normal life."[15] The example of Dickens provided a way out of the dilemma by proving the paradox that the more eccentric and individual a character, the better he may stand for a type. Seen from this angle, Simon Tappertit is the type of the apprentice, Mr. Guppy the clerk, Micawber the shabby-genteel, Fagin the wicked Jew, Riah the good Jew, and so on. Yet it is only to the degree that they come alive as "unhampered" eccentrics that they can bear their archetypical roles. Riah, for example, fails not because he is required to be The Good Jew but because he does not exist as a person. Norris absorbed the principle even if he was not always successful in reproducing the technique.

Norris's third reference to Dickens also concerns technique; this time the context is structure. In his "Weekly Letter" to the Chicago American for June 8, 1901, he remarks on the opening of novel-writing schools in New York and San Francisco, using the occasion as an excuse for climbing on one of his favorite hobby-horses, the "mechanics" of fiction.[16] Rebelling against the sentimental concept of the novelist as dreamy-eyed idealist, the untutored genius who merely looks into his heart and writes, Norris insists that fiction is a craft whose rules and principles must be learned. Particularly important are architectonics: "The construction of a novel is as much of an exact science as the construction of a temple or a sonnet. The laws and rules of this construction have never been adequately formulated, but they exist." Dickens, included in a curious melange with Kipling, Zola, and Lew Wallace, "knew them and built [his] novels upon them"; as a result his works are "interesting" and "powerful." This is high praise and significant praise. Norris goes on in his tautological way to attack novels that are "sprawling, loose-jointed...overbalanced, unsymmetrical, [and] out of proportion," all terms that reproduce or approximate serious objections made to Dickens by Howells and his followers. Norris stands apart in anticipating the later view that the novels are organic wholes. The letter goes on to state the necessity for a rising action, implying that Norris has found that Aristotelian virtue in Dickens, but says nothing of what has come to be called "symbolic unity." Norris's own novels, however, bear ample proof that he was at least intuitively aware of Dickens's use of symbolism as a unifying principle.[17]

Norris's final direct reference to Dickens is at once the most laudatory and the most dubious. In his column "Salt and Sincerity," in The Critic for July, 1902, he replies to a charge made by Sir Donald Mackenzie Wallace that contemporary literature contains nothing to compare with the productions of the mid-Victorian giants.[18] Sir Donald had explained this deplorable fact by suggesting that the ever increasing demands of a growing reading public has led to a watering down of the supply of literature. Norris's beliefs compel him to answer the charge on several grounds. Turning Howells's famous remark inside out, he refuses to admit that the art of fiction has deteriorated since the days of Dickens and Thackeray. "True," he admits, "we have no men to equal them as yet, but they are surely coming." The problem is that the very greatness of the mid-Victorians stands in the way of the developing writer, eroding his self-confidence and diverting his energies into feeble imitations. What is needed, says Norris in a characteristic passage, is some "Man of Iron" who will break through the ice-jam imposed by the great reputations and open the way for "the wind of Life" to blow over a new fiction, leaving the fourth-rate imitators behind to perish in the cold.

The notion that public demands for reading matter would corrupt literature is, for Norris, unthinkable because it implies the sentimental idealization of the artist as dreamer, always pushing at doors marked "Pull," who, secure in his study, draws his airy notions from a delicate "genius" not to be taxed. Norris had already attacked this figment of genteel aestheticism a year earlier in characterizing the Muse of American fiction as "a robust, red-armed *bonne-femme*, who rough-shoulders her way among men and affairs, who finds a healthy pleasure in the jostlings of the mob and a hearty delight in the honest, rough-and-tumble, Anglo-Saxon give-and-take knockabout that for us means life."[19] The writer's brain, he informs Sir Donald, is not a "storehouse" that may be depleted and does not supply the material for fiction. That material is "life itself, inexhaustible and renewed from day to day." The public may have made great demands on

Dickens, Norris admits; yet because Dickens immersed himself in the knockabout of London, he was able to be "unusually prolific" without suffering any diminution in the "quality" of his work--as the public was well aware. Sir Donald's remark becomes, ultimately, the occasion for Norris to haul out one of his pet theories, his belief that "in the last analysis the People are always right." David Copperfield, the work of a "real Master," has sold over the years close to two hundred million copies, Norris wildly asserts, and is still selling. What better proof of his somewhat rosy-hued, democratic faith in popular taste could there be? The People (always with a capital "P") may be occasionally misled, but not for long; Trilbys come and go, but David Copperfield remains.[20]

If Franklin Walker's assertions that Norris's critical essays are "immature in reflective power" and "filled with contradictions and excesses" seem somewhat hasty, and Donald Pizer's attempts to prove that they reflect a "unified and coherent system of ideas" a little too pat, one may, nevertheless, deduce from them a loosely related series of beliefs propping up Norris's critical platform.[21] To try to juggle them into a hypothetical assessment of Dickens is a much more perilous venture. Indeed, it seems almost sophomoric, reminding one of students who come away from the "Essay on Criticism" with a burning curiosity to know what Pope would have thought of Joyce and Henry Miller. But by proceeding cautiously and remembering that he is answering what is essentially a non-question, one may make tentative observations.

Norris's fundamental conviction is in the novelist's "responsibility." Since prose fiction has become the dominant literary form, read by a vast audience covering the entire economic, social, and intellectual spectrum of society, the novelist incurs the moral duty to present the "Truth" about life.[22] But to require the novelist to give _the_ People _the_ Truth is, as Norris knows, to raise Pilate's question. It is all very well to attack falsity--if one can say what constitutes veracity. Norris alternates between two answers, both of which convey important implications concerning his attitude toward Dickens. First, that is true which has a "purpose," and secondly, that is true which is "vital." To consider these propositions in order, we begin with Norris's assertion that those novels which fulfill the novelist's responsibility to tell the People the Truth have a purpose, or, as he puts it, "prove something" about life.

Norris divides all fiction into three categories: (1) novels like The Three Musketeers that merely tell a story, (2) novels like Romola that by close analysis of character "show something" about the workings of the human mind, and, finally, (3) novels like Les Miserables that by drawing "conclusions from whole congeries of forces, social tendencies, [and] race impulses, devote [themselves] not to a study of men but of man" and therefore "prove something" necessary to know. This third class is best for artistic as well as moral reasons, since in order to prove a novel must tell and show as well. From his emphasis on drawing conclusions from the investigation of forces, tendencies and impulses and from his statement later in the same essay that this third class of novels sets out "to find the value of X," Norris would seem to have most in mind the "scientific" case studies of Zola, but the actual novelists he mentions, Hugo, Mrs. Stowe, and Hardy, illustrate that one may apparently prove something without necessarily following the formulas of Le Roman expérimental. The novel with a purpose must be a preaching novel, "fearlessly" proving, among other things, "that power is abused, that the strong grind the faces of the weak, that an evil tree is still growing in the midst of the garden, that undoing follows hard upon unrighteousness," all themes traditionally associated by American critics with Dickens, so that while Norris does not mention Dickens by name, it is clear that he would pass the test.[23]

While maintaining that the best novels preach, Norris declares that the novelist himself must never mount the pulpit lest he degenerate from artist to pamphleteer. He must, to use the currently fashionable terms, show not tell, carefully preserving his artistic detachment. This might suggest that Norris would join the attack on Dickens for lacking objectivity and for sermonizing common among even sympathetic critics of the day, but actually his position is more complex and less clear. After positing that were Hardy to write a novel exposing the injustices suffered by Welsh coal-miners he would, whatever his personal feelings of indignation, remain as an artist absolutely indifferent to the British labor system, Norris goes on to ask:

> Do you think that Mrs. Stowe was more interested in the slave question than she was in the writing of Uncle Tom's Cabin? Her book, her manuscript, the page to page progress of the narrative, were more absorbing to her than all the Negroes that were ever whipped or sold. Had it not been so that great purpose-novel never would have succeeded.

Yet Uncle Tom's Cabin, the most explicitly Dickensian American novel of any stature written in the nineteenth century, propagandizes in all the polemical spirit of The Chimes. Mrs. Stowe wept over Uncle Tom sold and beaten as copiously as Dickens ever sobbed for Trotty Veck. Just exactly what Norris has in mind here seems unfathomable; one even wonders if he has ever read Uncle Tom's Cabin. But whatever his point, it certainly does not imply censure of Dickens.

In order to prove something about life the novelist, according to Norris, must put down his books, come out of his study, and immerse himself in the hurly-burly of the streets, grounding his fictions in the concrete reality of people and places actually observed.[24] Again Norris's theories resolve into paradox. On the one hand he seems to be calling for the kind of meticulous "documentation" demanded by Zola; yet on the other he repeatedly asserts that the "impression" of life is more important than its minute reproduction and that the extraordinary and never-seen may be more telling than the ordinary and seen. On the basis of Norris's own works, one suspects that he would settle the seeming contradiction by pointing to the practice of Dickens, who continually placed sensational actions in a concrete setting evoked by impressionistic sketches of well-known landmarks and who, after conceiving the extraordinary character of Sampson Brass, set out for Brevis Marks to find a house to serve as his home.

Norris's second definition of truth in fiction holds that to be true which has "*vital*" as opposed to "*aesthetic*" interest. (The italics are his own.)

> Say what you will, Maggie Tulliver--for instance--is far more a living being for Mrs. Jones across the street than she is for your sensitive, fastidious, keenly critical artist, litterateur, or critic. The People--Mrs. Jones and her neighbors [i.e., the highest Critical Court of Appeal]--take the life history of the fictitious characters, these novels, to heart with a seriousness that the aesthetic cult have no conception of. The cult consider them almost solely from their artistic sides. The People take them into their innermost lives.[25]

Thus Norris would ask of Dickens characters not if they are, "artistically" considered, exaggerations (as Howells and even Garland had found them), but rather if they come alive for Mrs. Jones and her neighbors.[26] His rather wild-eyed assertion that *David Copperfield* had sold a phenomenal 200,000,000 copies strongly suggests that he thought they did. By the circularity of Norris's argument, Dickens offers The People The Truth; therefore Dickens is a proper novelist.

Moreover, Norris would argue that a novelist may exaggerate and still remain true; for he realizes, as had--on different grounds--Balzac and James before him, that in the realm of art veracity and verisimilitude are not necessarily equatable terms. What is unreal in life may seem real in literature and vice-versa. Fiction attains truth through vitality, and vitality can be achieved by creating an "impression" of reality as well as, if not better than, the "accurate" reproduction of life itself. In "A Problem in Fiction: Truth vs. Accuracy" Norris cites two examples, a painting in which the artist uses blue paint to achieve the impression of a brown horse and the scene in Ivanhoe in which Rebecca describes a battle in impossibly high-blown language. Both painting and description, while patently inaccurate and unreal, are nevertheless true:

> Paint the horse pea-green if it suits your purpose; fill the mouth of Rebecca with gasconades and rodomontades interminable: these things do not matter. It is truth that matters and the point is whether the daubs of pea-green will look like horse-flesh and the mouth-filling words create the impression of actual battle.

Thus Norris would presumably have dismissed the recurrent attacks on Dickens for distorting "real" life as misleading and irrelevant.[27]

Howells's contention in Criticism and Fiction that Dickens falsified nature, modified psychology to his own ends, and turned recognizable human types into rarae aves in terris would be particularly distasteful to Norris, who, like Ford, Garland, Crane and others, equated Howellsian "realism" with the photographic reproduction of the mere surface of life and therefore dismissed it as inadequate. He complains that the "realist" presents only clothes and declares that what is needed is a novel that can "see the man beneath the clothes, and the heart beneath both."[28] The technique required is not "realism" but "romanticism," which Norris elsewhere defines as "an instrument with which one may go straight through the clothes and tissues and wrappings of flesh down deep into the red, living heart of things." "The reason why one claims so much for Romance and quarrels so pointedly with Realism," he continues in a celebrated passage,

> is that Realism stultifies itself. It notes only the surface of things. For it Beauty is not even skin-deep, but only a geometrical plane, without dimensions of depth, a mere outside. Realism is very excellent so far as it goes, but it goes no farther than the Realist himself can actually see, or actually hear. Realism is minute, it is the drama of a broken teacup, the tragedy of a walk down the block, the excitement of an afternoon call, the adventure of an invitation to dinner. It is the visit to my neighbor's house, a formal visit, from which I may draw no conclusions.

"But to Romance," on the other hand, "belongs the wide world for range, and the unplumbed depths of the human heart, and the mystery of sex, and the problems of life, and the black, unsearched penetralia of the soul of man."[29] For over fifty years, American critics, both hostile and appreciative, had held Dickens's works up as The Exemplars of "romance"; Norris himself knew Dickens to be no slouch at exploring the "unplumbed depths of the human heart" and such portraits as Jonas Chuzzlewit would have proved him, to Norris, an admirable prober of "the black, unsearched penetralia of the soul," especially in the sense that Norris understood his own terms. Moreover, Dickens was also at the time acquiring a certain notoriety as a depictor of the "mystery of sex." For the Young Turks who pleaded for greater latitude in the treatment of post-pubescent relations in fiction, Dickens, who had presented a prostitute as a sympathetic character, filled his novels with illegitimate children, and made a central episode of a seduction, could be wheeled out for argumentative artillery at the drop of a row of asterisks.[30] Norris was undoubtedly aware of the controversy and of Dickens's role in it; as the next chapter will show, he himself absorbed from Dickens a knowledge of the mystery of sex extending much deeper than anything taught by the off-stage hanky-panky of Steerforth and Littly Em'ly. At any rate Dickens, as "romanticist" and <u>bête-noire</u> of the "realists," fulfilled the primary responsibility of the novelist: Is it permissible to say that Accuracy is realism and Truth romanticism? I am not so sure, but I feel we come close to a solution here."[31]

In other words, the nature of Norris's response to Dickens can be reduced to a fairly simple syllogism. Norris valued the kind of fiction he labelled "romance." Since Dickens's works conform to Norris's definition of "romance," Dickens was, for Norris, a proper novelist. Hence Norris's frequent discussions of "romance" constitute a kind of oblique commentary on Dickens, and his extended criticism of Zola not only sheds light on his conceptions of "romance," "truth," and "vital interest," but also serves as an index to his assessment of Dickens. In an early essay, "Zola as a Romantic Writer," for example, he establishes the realism-romance, Howells-Zola polarities that are the basis of his esthetic.[32] Realism is, as usual, equated with the meticulous presentation of the surface of ordinary life. "Naturalism," far from being the "inner circle of realism" many contemporary critics thought it to be, is actually a form of "romance," dedicated to the presentation of the extraordinary: "Terrible things must happen to the characters of the naturalistic tale. They must be twisted from the ordinary, wrenched out from the quiet, uneventful round of everyday life, and flung into the throes of a vast and terrible drama that works itself out in unleashed passions, in blood, and in sudden death." "Romance," and by implication "truth," are, in other words, to be found in the same time-proven formulas of sensationalism and melodrama that Dickens had found so congenial to his purposes. Norris, in his penchant for making the same point two or three times over, goes on to elaborate that in Zola, as in an obvious romanticist like Hugo, "we have the same huge dramas, the same enormous scenic effects, the same love of the extra-ordinary, the vast, the monstrous, the tragic." These may be the qualities of Hugo and Zola; they are also qualities that for fifty years American critics had found in Dickens.

While Norris shows a nonchalant indifference to the transcendental idealism traditionally forming the philosophical basis of romanticism, he frequently echoes romantic theories of psychology and epistemology, especially in his discussions of the development of the novelist and of the art of story-telling. Again, both discussions have important implications concerning his attitudes toward Dickens. The best novelists, he maintains, are story-tellers, and story-tellers are simply people who have grown up without losing the powers of imagination and fancy (both terms used in their Wordsworthian senses) incident to childhood.[33] In industrialized American society, which values money-making over literature, the fancy is normally snuffed out early and the embryonic novelist is molded into a financier. But should the child grow up maintaining his fancy, he can with proper training in the mechanics of fiction, either acquired by his own efforts or taught to him in schools, become an instinctive writer with an intuitive "sense of fiction."[34]

On the one hand this seems nothing but Wordsworth and Coleridge as they percolated down to the popular consciousness of the nineteenth century, especially since Norris makes the imaginative vision of the child an explicit locus of value. On the other hand it is, at least in part, a projection of Norris's own experience. He had, in his teens, composed an elaborate epic concerning the chivalric adventures of one "Gaston le Fox" as the outgrowth of his younger brother's having been given a set of lead soldiers. Throughout his life he was convinced that these "lamentable tales of the Round (dining-room) Table," as he called them, were the beginnings of his career as a novelist.[35] Yet, curiously, his theories of the development of a novelist may have come to him straight out of Dickens, for _David Copperfield_, the one Dickens novel he ever mentions by name, is among other things a dramatization of the romantic theories that Norris expounded and wove into his conception of himself. _David Copperfield_ is, in this sense, Dickens's _Prelude_, outlining 'the growth of a novelist's mind.'[36]

The two qualities, says Norris, that make the child a natural story-teller are his fancy, his ability to project a sentient life on the external world so that an "easy chair is a comfortable old gentleman holding out his arms," and his peculiar powers of vision.[37] Both qualities are repeatedly attributed to young David as incipient novelist; indeed, if one were to make a word count of the novel's vocabulary, versions of the verb "to see" and the word "fancy," both as noun and verb, would probably dominate the list. One example of David's fancy may stand for hundreds:

> The carrier's horse was the laziest horse in the world, I should hope, and shuffled along with his head down, as if he liked to keep people waiting to whom the packages were directed. I fancied, indeed, that he sometimes chuckled audibly over this reflection, but the carrier said he was only troubled with a cough.[38]

As for David's extraordinary visual powers, they form the backbone of the novel's narrative and moral structures. In a rather self-conscious, but revealing, passage David, the middle-aged narrator, accounts for his detailed descriptions of events that took place in his extreme youth:

> This may be fancy, though I think the memory of most of us can go back farther into such times than many of us suppose; just as I believe the power of observation in numbers of very young children to be quite wonderful for its closeness and accuracy. Indeed, I think that most grown men who are remarkable in this respect, may with greater propriety be said not to have lost the faculty, than to have

> acquired it; the rather, as I generally observe such men to retain a certain freshness, and gentleness, and a capacity of being pleased, which are also an inheritance they have preserved from their childhood.[39]

The passage strongly implies that for Dickens, as for Norris, "vision" in a child means not only sense impression but moral cognition as well, an implication worked out explicitly in the novel itself. David, for example, feels "a child's instinctive dislike" at his first sight of Mr. Murdstone (XIV, ii, 25) and his "fancy" leads him to "see" Uriah Heep's face in the ugliest gargolyes protruding from Mr. Wickfield's house (XIV, xv, 269).

But the child's fancy and vision are precarious attributes, especially in a business-oriented society. Norris explains that we could have all the novelists we want if children were encouraged to develop their imaginative powers rather than "being crammed with commercial arithmetic...How many marbles did _A_ have? If a man buys a piece of goods at 12½ cents and sell it for 15 cents, etc., etc."[40] The direct paraphrase of Dickens seems unmistakable; Murdstone attempts to crush David's fancy with just such a commercial connundrum: "If I go into a cheesemonger's shop and buy five thousand double-Gloucester cheeses at fourpence-halfpenny each, present payment..." (XIV, iv, 65). Norris goes on to warn that "when you have choked the powers of imagination and observation, and killed off the creative ability, and deadened the interest in life, don't call it lack of genius."[41] David's worst fear in the bottling warehouse is that he, "a child of excellent abilities, and with strong powers of observation," has been "thrown away. ...The deep remembrance...of the misery it was to my young heart to believe that day by day what I had learned, and thought, and delighted in, and raised my fancy and emulation up by, would pass away from me, little by little, never to be brought back any more; cannot be written" (XIV, xi, 184, 186. Italics supplied).

"Sometimes," says Norris, "the little story-teller does not die, but lives on and grows with the man, increasing in favor with God, till at last he dominates the man himself."[42] David is saved from being made, in his words, "sullen, dull, and dogged" by running from the double-Gloucester cheeses to the novels of Smollett, Fielding, and LeSage. These serve a twofold function. First, as David succinctly puts it, "They kept alive my fancy." In other words books function for the future novelist in David Copperfield as they do for the future poet in The Prelude; they mitigate the stultifying influences of the "real" world, and they encourage the child to project his fancies on externalities:

> Every barn in the neighborhood, every stone in the church, and every foot of the churchyard, had some association of its own, in my mind, connected with these books, and stood for some locality made famous in them. I have seen Tom Pipes go climbing up the church steeple; I have watched Strap, with the knapsack on his back, stopping to rest himself upon the wicket-gate; and I _know_ that Commodore Trunnion held that club with Mr. Pickle, in the parlour of our little village ale-house.
>
> (XIV, iv, 67)

Secondly, they give David that schooling in the mechanics of fiction that Norris sees to be both the requisite of the novelist and an outstanding quality in Dickens. David discovers that by drawing upon his reading he can spin out his own fictions and please audiences ranging from the aristocratic Steerforth to the bedraggled inmates of King's Bench Prison. Moreover, David, like Dickens himself, owes his success to his retention of the vision, both physical and moral, of the child. Dickens captures the physical and emotional point of view of the child so completely that generations of readers have shared George Orwell's youthful impression that the early chapters had been written by a child.[43] As for moral vision, one notes that time after time David will record a moral judgment in terms of something he "saw" as a child and then add "and still do to this very day." In other words, even in his adulthood the basis of David's ethical understanding resides in the maintenance of a child-like point of view:

> A little child stands in the midst of the wise men and the learned, and their wisdom and their learning are set aside and they are taught that unless they become as one of these they shall in no wise enter into the Kingdom of Heaven.

But the hand upon the vox humana in the passage just quoted is not Dickens's but Frank Norris's.[44]

Norris realized that writers exist who have lost the story-telling ability but who, nevertheless, become successful novelists. Calling them "novelists of composition," he explains that they compensate for the loss of child-like beatitude by dint of intense efforts of analysis and intellection. To illustrate the differences between composers and story-tellers he hauls out George Eliot as an example of the one and Dumas as an example of the other. But he might as well have used Dickens as Dumas, for as George Ford has shown, the contrasting of George Eliot's powers of analysis with Dickens's powers of narration was a cliche of late nineteenth-century criticism.[45] And while Norris grants the effectiveness of some "composed" novels, his loyalties are clearly with the story-tellers.[46] His own penchant for story-telling and his critical emphasis on "vital" narration achieved through Dickensian techniques of caricature, sensation, and melodrama lead, both in his criticism and in his novels, to a dangerous glorification of "effect." In "The Mechanics of Fiction" he goes so far as to reduce the whole art of the novel to a single phrase, "preparation of effect."[47] Effect is prepared by following those "rules of construction" he had observed in Dickens: dramatic rising action and symbolic unity. Paradoxically it is these Dickensian structural elements that most derogate from his own fictions. Pizer's comment on Old Baker and Miss Grannis in McTeague could be applied to Norris's work as a whole: "They fail not because they are Dickensian but because they are weakly Dickensian."[48] Dramatic rising action becomes the kettledrum crescendo of the penny-dreadful. "The movement of the whole business is very slow at first," he wrote of The Octopus in a celebrated letter

> [and] don't really get under weigh till after the first 15,000 words...then with the first pivotal incident it quickens a bit, and from there on I've tried to accelerate it steadily till at the last you are--I hope--just whirling and galloping and tearing along until you come bang! all of a sudden to a great big crushing END, something that will slam you right between your eyes and knock you off your feet--all this I hope for. Sabe?

Symbolic unity becomes a kind of game at "I Spy" as he hides gold through-out McTeague and sprinkles wheat over The

Octopus. It is noteworthy that his letters describing his novels are, like the one quoted above, heavily larded with phrases like "savvy?," "get it?," and "catch on?," and that he calls "naturalism" "the game I play best."[50]

But despite their shortcomings Norris's critical theories and his working out of them in his novels were of vital importance to the role of Dickens as an influence on American fiction. By attacking Howellsian "realism" as a stultifying restriction of fiction to the ordinary, empirical surface of life and by affirming that a vital impression of life is often more effective than the photographic reproduction of "reality," he explicitly as well as implicitly removed from Dickens much of the critical opprobrium into which he had fallen. In his call for a "responsible" novel that would embody the qualities of "truth" and "romance" as he defined them: purpose, (melo)drama, sensation, vastness, sincerity, love of the extraordinary--he opened the way for a body of fiction that could admit Dickensian elements by program as well as by actual performance. Norris's peculiar brand of unphilosophical naturalism may have had Zola for its ostensible model, but its roots were sunk deep in Dickens. Nonetheless, interesting and important though it is, Norris's criticism is actually only a kind of appendix to his novels, and for a full sense of Dickens as incorporated into the literature of the American 1890's, it is to the novels themselves that we must now turn.

Notes to Chapter VII

[1]Hamilton W. Mabie, "The Most Popular Novels in America," The Forum, XVI (Dec., 1893), 508-16. See also Hart, The Popular Book, p. 183; and Adrian, "David Copperfield: A Century of Critical and Popular Acclaim," 330.

[2]Others in the top ten were, in order, Ivanhoe (88%), The Scarlet Letter (87%), Uncle Tom's Cabin (86%), Ben Hur (83%), Adam Bede (80%), Vanity Fair (80%), Jane Eyre (78%), The Last Days of Pompeii (78%), and John Halifax, Gentleman (77%).

[3]The other Dickens novels named are Pickwick Papers (49%), Nicholas Nickleby (45%), Oliver Twist (45%), The Old Curiosity Shop (45%), Dombey and Son (43%), Bleak House (35%), and A Tale of Two Cities (34%). One notes that very few of the novels on the master list had been published within the preceding ten years. The implication is that the reading public tended to purchase current fiction rather than call for it at libraries. Moreover, it would naturally take some time for a book to become known to all those who might prize it highly. See Hart, pp. 183-84.

[4]The top ten are, in order, Dickens, Miss Alcott, Scott, Roe, Cooper, George Eliot, Hawthorne, Holmes, Bulwer and Thackeray. The advantage, of course, goes to prolific authors with the most books in the ratings.

[5]"A Typical Novel," Andover Review, IV (Nov., 1885), 417-429. See also Cady, Road to Realism, pp. 241-43.

[6]XXIII, 281-85.

[7]Mimesis, pp. 437-40, 445, 449-52.

[8]Cady, Road to Realism, pp. 65-67.

[9]Ziff, The American 1890's, p. 147.

[10]Lars Ahnebrink, The Beginnings of Naturalism in American Fiction (Upsala, 1950), Appendix F. The list is incomplete.

[11]Frank Norris: A Biography, pp. 11 and 13.

[12]The Literary Criticism of Frank Norris, ed. Donald Pizer (Austin, 1964), p. 123. Hereafter Lit. Crit.

[13]Reprinted in Lit. Crit., pp. 28-30.

[14]"People of Polk Street": The Letters of Frank Norris, ed. Franklin Walker (San Francisco, 1956), p. 23.

[15]"A Plea for Romantic Fiction," Lit. Crit., p. 76. "Type" here, of course, refers primarily to action, but its implications for characterization are clear, since for Norris character determines plot. One notes that the shift in the meaning of "romance" from a work based on transcendental idealism to a work exploiting the exotic and melodramatic carried with it a corresponding shift in the meaning of "type." As implied above, the shift in the use of "romance" may be seen by comparing Mabie's review of Lapham with Ford's recipe for the American Dickens. The redefinition of type becomes evident when one observes that Howells, in reviewing Our Mutual Friend, saw its characters as primarily moral abstractions while Norris would see them primarily as "unhampered" eccentrics.

[16]Lit. Crit., pp. 9-10.

[17]The search for the source of Norris's symbolic technique is complicated by a kind of cross-fertilization of influences. His avowed master was, of course, Zola, who frequently exploits massive symbols as structural devices--as Norris was well aware. Thus Norris uses the wheat in The Octopus as Zola had used the soil in La Terre; The Pit opens and closes in the shadow of the enigmatic facade of the Board of Trade just as Germinal opens and closes in the shadow of the Mining Offices. But Zola himself was heavily influenced by Dickens, his use of the Mining Offices in Germinal, for example, following Dickens's use of Chancery in Bleak House, the smoke stacks in Hard Times, and so forth. It would be naive to say that Norris acquired his symbolic techniques directly from either Dickens or Zola; obviously he got them from both, the one reinforcing the influence of the other.

[18]Lit. Crit., pp. 209-11.

[19]"Novelists of the Future: The Training They Need," Lit. Crit., p. 13.

[20]Scholarly cliché has it that Norris's belief in "the Plain People" as the final arbiters of literature comes directly from Tolstoy. (See, e.g., Ernest Marchand, Frank Norris: A Study, Standford, 1942, pp. 11-13; Ahnebrink, p. 164; Pizer, Lit. Crit., pp. xviii, 82.) Actually the notion was something of a commonplace of the day. Mabie implies it in his remarks on Tait & Sons' poll, and Garland had set it forth explicitly eight years before What is Art? was published. ("The West in Literature," The Arena, VI [Nov., 1892], 669.) It is, however, noteworthy that Tolstoy also singles out David Copperfield's universal appeal as proof of his contention that majority opinion will always seek out the very best art. (What is Art?, trans. Aylmer Maude [Oxford, 1950], pp. 243-44.)

[21]Walker, Biography, p. 288; Pizer, Lit. Crit., p. xiii. Other discussions of Norris's criticism that I have found useful are the chapters on The Responsibilities of the Novelist in Marchand and Ahnebrink and the following articles: Charles G. Hoffman, "Norris and the Responsibility of the Novelist," SAQ, LIV (October, 1955), 508-15; H. Willard Reninger, "Norris Explains The Octopus: A Correlation of His Theory and Practice," AL, XII (May, 1940), 218-27; and George W. Johnson, "Frank Norris and Romance," AL, XXXIII (March, 1961), 52-63.

[22]"The Responsibilities of the Novelist," Lit. Crit., p. 97.

[23]The circularity of Norris's argument is again reminiscent of Tolstoy. The greatest art, says Tolstoy, has as its purpose proving something about life, i.e., demonstrating the love of God and the brotherhood of man. Like Norris he specifically mentions Les Miserables and Uncle Tom's Cabin, but adds to the list A Christmas Carol, The Chimes, and A Tale of Two Cities. (What is Art?, p. 242.) But great art must also be universal when judged at the bar of public opinion. Thus purpose requires universality, and universality implies purpose. Elsewhere Tolstoy specifically equates purpose with "sincerity"; Norris echoes the equation again and again. (What is Art?, pp. 229-30; Lit. Crit., pp. 86-87, 98, 141, and so forth.)

[24]"Novelists of the Future: The Training They Need," Lit. Crit., pp. 10-14.

[25] Lit. Crit., p. 96.

[26] In a letter dated February 25, 1934, Garland recalled that "as a student of fiction in Boston, I ridiculed his [Dickens's] exaggerations and deplored his characters--for that was the fashion among the younger critics." Quoted in Ahnebrink, p. 68n.

[27] Lit. Crit., pp. 57-58. Despite the obvious similarities between Norris's position and those of Balzac and James, it is important to note the differences. Norris's emphasis on the impression rather than the reproduction of reality is heavily colored by his emotionalism and somewhat immature love of effect. What generally seems to move him most is not the subtle, Balzacian and Jamesian trompe-d'oeil by which pea-green creates the impression of brown but rather the kind of overt play upon the emotions that Scott called "the big Bow-Wow."

[28] "The True Reward of the Novelist," Lit. Crit., pp. 85-87.

[29] "A Plea for Romantic Fiction," Lit. Crit., pp. 75-78. As Pizer observes, Norris equates "romance" with "naturalism" and defines both simply in terms of subject matter and technique, showing little interest in--or even awareness of--the philosophical underpinnings they rested upon abroad: the transcendental idealism of English romanticism and the deterministic materialism of French naturalism. See Realism and Naturalism, pp. 35-36; Lit. Crit., p. 69.

[30] See, e.g., two articles in The Arena: Albert Ross, "What is Immoral in Literature," III (March, 1891), 440; and (the Rev.) Howard MacQueary, "Moral and Immoral Literature," VIII (Sept., 1893), 450.

[31] "Weekly Letter," August 3, 1901, Lit. Crit., p. 75.

[32] Lit. Crit., pp. 71-72.

[33] "Story-tellers vs. Novelists," Lit. Crit., pp. 65-66.

[34] "Novelists to Order--While You Wait," Lit. Crit., p. 15.

[35]See, for example, the Dedication to The Pit, and Walker, Biography, pp. 22-23, 34-35.

[36]In an essay entitled "Thoughts on David Copperfield," REL, II (July, 1961), 65-74, Arnold Kettle quotes from Sylvère Monod's Dickens romancier as follows: "Dickens aurait presque pu donner pour sous-titre à son roman (comme Wordsworth appelait son Prelude the growth of a poet's mind) the growth of a novelist's mind." However neither Monod or Kettle follows up the suggestion in any detail.

[37]Lit. Crit., p. 66.

[38]XIV, iii, 33. I choose this passage because it reminds us once more how deeply indebted Mark Twain was to Dickens's use of child-like fancy for comic effect.

[39]XIV, ii, 15. Again we are reminded that the use of a visual technique, imbued with moral value and frequently coupled with a child's point-of-view (as in, say, What Maisie Knew) was Dickens's most pervasive point of influence on nineteenth-century fiction.

[40]Lit. Crit., p. 16.

[41]Lit. Crit., pp. 16-17.

[42]Lit. Crit., pp. 66-67.

[43]Collected Essays (London, 1961), p. 43. Significantly Orwell sees Dickens's "visualizing tendency" as his primary means of recording the mechanisms of the child's mind.

[44]Lit. Crit., p. 68.

[45]Dickens and His Readers, pp. 181-85.

[46]Cf. his remarks on Anna Karenina, Lit. Crit., p. 68.

[47]Lit. Crit., p. 60.

[48] The Novels of Frank Norris (Bloomington, 1966), p. 74.

[49] Letters, pp. 67-68.

[50] Letters, p. 48.

CHAPTER VIII

FRANK NORRIS: THE NATURALIST AS DICKENSIAN

I.

> London had her Dickens
> ...but San Francisco still
> waits for her novelist.
> --Frank Norris

Two of Frank Norris's seven novels may be dismissed from this study fairly quickly. _Moran of the Lady Letty_, his first published, is a delightful romp and woefully neglected camp, but while Norris draws freely on Stevenson, Kipling, and general insanity for its sources, he overlooks Dickens altogether. His fourth, _A Man's Woman_ is without doubt the worst ever written by any American novelist of any stature. Even such perennial candidates as Mark Twain's _A Horse's Tale_ and James's _The Outcry_ pale by comparison. Fortunately there is only a remote possibility of even an oblique Dickens influence on it.

Nevertheless, for what it is worth, I shall summarize the evidence. In 1856 Dickens collaborated with Wilkie

Collins on a melodrama called The Frozen Deep, later managing and starring in its production. Ten years later Collins revised the script for a second production, and in 1874 reworked it into a novelette, which he read extensively on his last American tour and which he subsequently published both in England and America as the title work of a two volume collection of short pieces. Collins's novelette was, until 1966, the only published and readily accessible version of the work Dickens had originally co-authored.[1] I know of no evidence that Norris read it, but there is an uncanny similarity in the plots of The Frozen Deep and A Man's Woman. Both involve Artic expeditions stranded in polar regions; in both two of the explorers are rivals for a lady's hand, and in both the unsuccessful lover, doubting his chances of returning alive, makes a generous gesture of self-denial towards the successful. Moreover, both employ a crude symbolism in which the uncharted wastes of the Artic north represent what Norris would have called "the unplumbed depths of the human heart." However, lacking concrete proof of Norris's familiarity with Collins's work, one is reluctant to push the connection.

Blix, Norris's most extensive foray into fictionalized autobiography, deserves more attention. It is, in many respects, his most programmatic novel, a systematic attempt to prove his favorite contention that there is as much "romance" in the modern world as there was in the middle ages. And, for all Norris's insistence on the importance of environment in his more openly "naturalistic" works, _Blix_ is his one novel in which the milieu is absolutely essential to the action and meanings. He himself was aware of the paradox; writing to Isaac Marcossen shortly before its publication he points out that:

> I'm not so sure but what "McTeague" could have happened in any big city anywhere. But it would be absolutely impossible for "Blix" to have occurred anywhere else but San Francisco. It is more intimately _Californian_ than anything I have ever done.[2]

When we remember that in an earlier critical essay Norris had associated San Francisco's availability as a "story city" with a specifically Dickensian treatment of its possibilities, another of his programmatic aims becomes clear. In making _Blix_ "intimately Californian" Norris, undoubtedly ignorant of the claims of Mrs. Louise Clappe, who under the pseudonym of "Dame Shirley" had set herself up in the early fifties as "The Lady Dickens of the West," and disdainful of the efforts of Bret Harte, asserts himself as the San Francisco Dickens.[3]

Norris's manner of presenting San Francisco as the citadel of romance--if only one turns the right corners, meets the right people, and maintains the proper openness of spirit--comes, *mutatis mutandis*, straight out of *Sketches by Boz* and its successors in Dickens's epic romance of London. For the most part the Dickensian flavor in *Blix* is somewhat vague and elusive, being more a matter of atmosphere and tone than of specific borrowing, but occasionally it becomes distinct and unmistakable. The evocation of the "delicious charm" of a sporting-goods store by means of a Dickensian catalog of gear, tackle, and trim is an example; or the description of a woman who can speak for hours about the Alps, the history of Denmark, and the science of fortification but cannot tell Gibraltar from Kosciusko because she is still purchasing her encyclopedia on the installment plan. Lifted from the yet unpublished *Vandover and the Brute* is a long piece of comic business concerning the ineptitudes of a kitchen-maid pressed into dining-room service that seems, in turn, borrowed directly from the antics of David's and Dora's "Incompetents" in *Copperfield*, and so forth. "London had her Dickens"; *Blix* is Norris's attempt to be San Francisco's novelist. Yet while his lovers continually snigger at the insipidities of Marie Corelli and The Duchess, their story is not, in its telling, far removed from the sentimentalities of popular feminine novels of the day, and *Blix* is rightly known today only to the specialists. More general interest focusses on Norris's four so-called "naturalistic" works.

The first written but last published of these, Vandover and the Brute, is a novel more interesting read about than read. It does unquestionably fulfill Norris's requirement that the characters of a romance be "wrenched out from the quiet, uneventful round of every-day life, and flung into the throes of a vast and terrible drama," as it follows its protagonist down the not unprecedented slide from Harvard Yard to Skid Row.[4] Fundamentally a study (in the Zolaesque sense) of atavism and devolution, its central character regresses from a sensitive young artist to a flophouse derelict with the unsettling habit of ripping off his clothes and padding around on all fours, howling like a wolf. It may be romance, but it is not romance that readily admits of Dickensian treatment. However, a few of the *dramatis personae*, Old Vandover and Bancroft Ellis, for example, are granted Dickensian quirks of character, and several scenes are vaguely reminiscent of pages in "The Master," the drinking scene in chapter four being but one. Incipient in *Vandover* is Norris's habit, absorbed from Dickens and Zola, of using reiterated symbols to establish thematic and structural unities. The railroad engine that had steamed out of Dombey and Son into La Bête humaine pulls up in the first chapter of Vandover just as the hero's mother draws her last breath on the depot platform. It later becomes, as it had been in Dombey, an explicit symbol of the inexorability of nature, time, and fate.[5] An ornately tiled stove is made to stand for the hollowness of Vandover's flirtation with "decadent" aestheticism just as Jip's pagoda stands for the emptiness of David's marriage with Dora. Vandover's literal and metaphorical transformation into a wolf follows the pattern of imagery by which Jonas Chuzzlewit regresses from the level of humanity to that of the more distasteful orders of rodent, and Vandover's decline is documented by a succession of symbolic houses and rooms ranging from his father's mansion on Sacramento Street to the Reno Hotel in the South-of-Market slums. Pizer says of these dwellings:

> Both Norris and Dreiser could capture with excellent detail the external reality--of rooms, clothing, of food, and of money, as though these were the fundamental realities of life. Yet both used this detail to symbolize the social positions and social longings which in a middle-class world are equivalent to moral and emotional states.[6]

What Pizer does not say is that this particular brand of symbolism comes to Norris and Dreiser as a direct legacy from Dickens, with capital gains accrued during the years it had been held in trust by Howells and James.

Less obtrusive than these Dickensian elements of incident, characterization and symbolism, but ultimately more important, is the curious role played by one aspect of the Dickensian ethos in the novel's moral structure. Norris's failure to establish a consistent ethical position in *Vandover and the Brute* (as well as in *The Octopus*, *The Pit*, and, to a lesser degree, *McTeague*) is notorious to modern criticism. The points to be stressed here are (1) that the novel's moral structure *is* helplessly muddled in a confusion of materialistic determinism with notions of free will and moral responsibility; and (2) that Norris, in those passages which express a belief in free will, draws upon a decidedly Dickensian set of assumptions. Indeed, Norris's very contradictions can be traced back to Dickens, who could, in one and the same novel, posit a Charley Bates as the hapless victim of what a "naturalist" would label heredity, environment, and sexual impulse (Dickens is surely aware of the *double entendre* in his repeated references to "Master Charley Bates") and an Oliver Twist who despite his illegitimate birth, association with thieves, and prepubescent stirrings always makes a free choice for the good. In at least half of Norris's novel Vandover is presented not as the pawn of birth, milieu, or genitality but, like a long procession of Dickens characters that includes Frederick Verisopht, Steerforth, Richard Carstone, Henry Gowan, and Eugene Wrayburn, as the victim of his own pliable and indolent nature, his own lack of good Victorian earnestness and backbone, of which his dissipation and disease are the symptoms and not the cause. Moreover, following the Wordsworthian pattern that pervades Dickens, Norris specifically attributes Vandover's decline to his loss of those "associations" that in Dickens serve to shore up the ethical will: the home, the good woman, and art.

The ethical system that proscribes moral earnestness bolstered by association with the "finer" influences of home, woman, and art is not the exclusive property of Charles Dickens. He hardly invented it, and later novelists could have absorbed it from any number of sources.[7] Yet in _Vandover_, as in _The Octopus_ and _The Pit_, Norris's reliance on the "Victorian" ethos follows Dickensian patterns so closely that one is reluctant to describe the relationship simply in terms of coincidence or _Zeitgeist_--as I hope the following scrutiny of one of these novels will show.[8]

"I am going back _definitely_ now to the style of McTeague," Norris wrote in November, 1899, "and stay with it right along...I think I know where I am at and what game I play the best. The Wheat series will be straight naturalism with all the guts I can get into it."[9] "Naturalism" meant to Norris primarily "romance," and "romance" implied Dickens, whose influence on The Octopus, the first of the Wheat series, has never been doubted. V. L. Parrington, one of the first commentators on Norris and still one of the best, finds the novel's Dickensian flavor attributable to its host of supernumeraries, its symbolism, its melodrama, and its moralism.[10] To take up these elements in order we may begin by noting that the use of Dickensian supernumeraries--Hooven is the character in The Octopus most frequently pointed out as such--is hardly new either to the American novel or to Norris. Nor is the use of a massive cluster of closely related symbols for structural and thematic unity, although the impulse behind Norris's recourse to this Dickensian technique in The Octopus has a historical significance worth examining.

Norris's exposure to Spencerian evolutionary theory and Zolaesque "naturalism" taught him to think habitually of "nature" in terms of broad, irresistible forces--race, sex, environment and so forth. The predominant fact of the *social* life of the period was the constantly accelerating movement of industrialism toward vast, consolidated and standardized corporations that existed almost as independent organisms exercising their built-in powers and following their inherent directions above and beyond the nominal control of the bureaucracies that administered and supposedly ran them. This phenomenon, which affected almost every element of American life, may have inclined Norris to consider society in terms of equally vast and impersonal forces of economic law. From Dickens's practice, confirmed perhaps by Zola, he could well have learned that the most effective way to present forces of these proportions in fiction was by means of monolithic symbols. Thus on one of The Octopus's many levels of meaning the clash at the irrigation ditch is not between Delaney, Genslinger, and Behrman on one side and Hooven, Broderson, and Annixter on the other, but rather between the forces of nature symbolized by the wheat and the forces of society symbolized by the League and the Railroad, of which the human actors are but pawns whose insignificance is apparent when their pismire proportions are measured against the vastnesses of the San Joaquin.[11]

One of the most commented upon patterns in Dickens's development is his progression from the early presentation of social evil resulting from the machinations of a few wicked men to his more mature vision of that evil springing from broad social phenomena that control the actions of individuals and not vice-versa. The development may be traced in the growing impersonality of the representation of evil in his novels. He begins by offering a Ralph Nickleby to torment Nicholas and Kate, then presents a Gashford who almost single-handedly engineers the Gordon Riots. Later we are given a Montague Tigg who stands behind an institution but obviously controls it, but by the time of Little Dorrit (originally entitled "Nobody's Fault") institutions have come to control individuals. In Our Mutual Friend human villainy, in the traditional sense, has disappeared almost altogether to be replaced by the dust heaps and what Twemlow calls simply "the voice of Society." What Dickens achieved in a single career American fiction labored at, painfully, for over half a century. The historian Samuel P. Hays has pointed out that the most difficult adjustment for Americans to make to industrialism was to realize that its dislocations were attributable not to the evil deeds of a few designing men but rather to broad, impersonal economic change.[12] George Lippard, a pioneer American social novelist, had in The Quaker City (1844-45) followed the early Dickens in attempting to tie social corruption to the orgiastic activities of a handful of libertines. Norris, taking his cue from the later works, presents an ultimately sympathetic portrait of a robber-baron and a symbolic representation of social malaise in the massacre of a herd of sheep by a high-balling freight.

Yet Norris is not consistent in his response to social suffering. In the passages tracing Mrs. Hooven's *via dolorosa* he implies, granted somewhat obliquely, the kind of individual villainy presented in Dickens's early sentimental melodrama. The guests at the dinner party hold no personal animosity toward the widow, but they are clearly held accountable for her suffering. Norris drew the details for the scene from two newspaper articles he clipped and pasted in his notebook, one describing a dinner party at the home of a railroad executive, the other recounting the death of a woman who, accompanied by her young daughter, starved to death on a New York street. But his novelistic treatment of these accounts and the impulse behind it are clearly inspired by Dickens.[13] Mrs. Hooven is, for example, irresistibly drawn in her wanderings toward Nob Hill, her death occurring in a little park right in front of the railroad baron's mansion, just as in, say, *Bleak House*, Jo is drawn, as if by magnet, to the doorstep of The Society for the Propogation of the Gospel in Foreign Parts.

Symbolism, melodrama, and a moralizing attitude combine in another of the novel's incidents frequently identified as influenced by Dickens, S. Behrman's celebrated death in an avalanche of wheat. Unfortunately critics have been too willing simply to dismiss the scene as "Dickensian," using the term as a pejorative equivalent of "cheaply melodramatic" and ignoring its crucial implications for the novel as a whole. Like the conflict between free will and determinism in *Vandover*, the tension between vitalistic evolutionary optimism and muckraking social pessimism in *The Octopus* has led to interpretations that are as drastically opposed as political left and right. If one accepts Presley as the novel's *raisonneur* and his conclusion, drawn from his conversations with Shelgrim and Vanamee, that all things in the large view work toward good as its explicit meaning, then *The Octopus* becomes an elaborate defense of *laissez-faire* economics and the Utilitarian Greater-Happiness Theory.[14] But if one reads Presley as an unreliable commentator whose interpretation is distorted both by his inability to come to grips with "real life" and by his too eager acceptance of the partial views of the Nabob and the Shepherd, views unsupported by events in the novel itself; then it becomes a plea for social justice at the expense of <u>laissez-faire</u>.[15]

The confusion, which one is finally forced to admit is simply inherent in the novel, seems to have existed in Norris's mind even before he began writing. In an often quoted letter to Howells he states his intention to present the more smiling aspects of life (i.e., cosmic optimism) while in a lesser known letter to a Mrs. Parks he puts himself implicitly on the side of the trust-busters (i.e., social protest).[16] As might be expected he ultimately turns to a formula used again and again by American novelists in the nineteenth century, and extricates himself from a thematic dilemma by hauling in Dickensian melodrama. Behrman's death, whose most obvious parallels are Ralph Nickleby's suicide, Carker's annihilation by the railroad and Steerforth's drowning, functions to sharpen the points on both horns of the dilemma. On one side it illustrates the wheat as cosmic force, literally burying evil in its remorseless flow toward good; while on the other it draws on the affective irony of a social villain hoist, as it were, by his own petard. Yet cheaply melodramatic though it may be, Behrman's death also serves to soften the very contradiction it dramatizes. It qualifies each of the novel's meanings in a crucial way because of the simple fact that Behrman's body is never found.[17]

Norris's chronology is not explicit, but he implies that Behrman dies on the same day that the _Swanhilda_'s hold is sealed and her prow pointed westward. His death is not mentioned in the conversation between Presley and Cedarquist, nor is it included in Presley's final catalog of the novel's fatalities. The clear implication is that no one has discovered it. Thus on the one hand the social villain meets his just desserts, but his evil lives after him. Living he has spoiled the lives of the ranchers; dead he spoils the wheat intended for the starving Eastern masses. And thus while the Wheat may be inherently a force for good, the _Swanhilda_'s bill of lading includes death as well as life. It is indeed a curious cargo, composed of a defeated poet, wheat, and a rotting carcass. The Anglo-Saxon spirit, optimistically envoked by Cedarquist, carries, it seems, grisly _impedimenta_ on its long voyage around the globe, and Cedarquist's pointed parting words take on a disturbingly morbid irony: "Man does not live by bread alone."

Another feature of the novel that has escaped critical commentary is Annixter's peculiar fondness for _David Copperfield_. Norris habitually uses a character's reading as a clue both to his personality and to his thematic significance: Annie Derrick's predilection for such (to Norris) effete authors as Ruskin, Dobson, and Pater, for example, underscores both her constitutional unsuitability for life in the San Joaquin and Norris's own contempt for literary aestheticism as an approach to life. Norris's notes for the novel suggest that Annixter's well-thumbed copy of *Copperfield* is meant to serve a similar dual function, but its significance is more complex and more difficult to assess. One suspects at first that Norris is merely echoing contemporary critical hostility to Dickens's longwindedness by implying that, in support of the dried prunes that always accompany it, the reading of *David Copperfield* works by sympathetic magic to unlock Annixter's chronically constricted bowels. But Norris's own high estimation of the novel and his assertion elsewhere that The People are Right in loving it undercut the scatology and force us to look for other explanations.

From the standpoint of characterization, Annixter's single-minded devotion to *David Copperfield* reflects his eccentricity, his intolerance and stubbornness and their concomitant, his tendency toward *ex cathedra* judgments.[18] His pride, strong-headedness, carelessness, and lack of a real guiding purpose in life are all reminiscent of Steerforth--as is his attempt, albeit clumsy, to lure Hilma Tree into an unsanctified liaison. Moreover, his attachment to Copperfield prepares us for his later development, hinting from the start that a buried stream of sentimentality flows under his gruff exterior. Mr. Peggotty frequently refers to himself as "a babby in the form of a great sea porkypine." Annixter's outside is as testy as Mr. Peggotty's is rough; underneath they are both soft--and vulnerable. The absence of purpose in Annixter's character not only links him to Steerforth, but also indicates the significance of his reading Copperfield in the thematic structure of The Octopus. Annixter is, of course, the man redeemed by love, the character whose existence is fructified by his human passion for Hilma just at the moment that the cosmic passion of Father Sun for Mother Earth brings forth the new-born Wheat. His fondness for David Copperfield not only testifies to his essential softness, but also points the way by which his salvation is to be achieved. In Annixter Norris returns to the Dickensian theme of the moral influence of a good woman's love, a theme nowhere more strongly asserted than in the rancher's favorite book.

The resting places of all moral values are throughout that novel in the innocent eye of childhood and the gentle bosom of Agnes, David's "Good Angel." The mellowing and steadying "influence" of Agnes permeates the book like honey in Turkish pastry; the "spirit of Agnes" is invoked so many times that the reader somes to think of it as some sort of airplane or yacht. Even Jip, we are asked to believe, cannot resist the benign spell of her presence. Like Annixter, David struggles to find a purpose in life and to remain firm in pursuit of it. The Murdstones's malignant firmness only repells him; his aunt's admonitions, while they are met with agreement, generate no discernible psychic energy. The sole source of what strength he finally achieves is, he asserts again and again, Agnes. Like a character in a Morality play he is granted a Good Angel and a Bad: Steerforth who lures him into reckless aimlessness and Agnes who holds him to the Carlylean gospel of work.

David, exercising his Wordsworthian propensities, "associates" two separate but converging clusters of value-laden imagery with Agnes's moral presence. The first, religious, is introduced when he first enters Wickfield's house:

> I cannot call to mind where or when, in my childhood, I had seen a stained glass window in a church.

> Nor do I recollect its subject. But I know that when I saw her turn round, in the grave light of the old staircase, and wait for us, above, I thought of that window; and I associated something of its tranquil brightness with Agnes Wickfield ever afterwards.
>
> (XIV, xv, 267)

The second, pastoral, is developed more gradually and largely by implication, becoming explicit in occasional passages like that in chapter xxxix describing David's return to Kent after his installation in Doctors Commons. Both strands of imagery unite and are fused with what I have earlier called the novel's <u>Prelude</u> theme in the somewhat maudlin but revealing chapter "Absence," which strongly suggests that Dickens had spent the months preceding his writing the last double number reading Wordsworth's great autobiographical epic.[19] David, attempting to recover from the deaths of Dora, Steerforth, and Ham, wanders across the continent sorely afflicted with the chronic romantic malaise, described in a phrase that in a quiet way curiously anticipates Matthew Arnold's celebrated description of Byron: "I see myself passing on among the novelties of foreign towns, palaces, cathedrals, temples, pictures, castles, tombs, fantastic streets--the old abiding places of History and Fancy--as a dreamer might; bearing my painful load through all." David goes on to make the nature of his ailment specific. In addition to an "undisciplined heart," he has "no purpose, no sustaining soul within [him] anywhere."

In such a state he crosses the Alps and arrives one sunset at a Swiss village in an Alpine valley whose description draws not only on Dickens's memory of his own earlier stay at Lausanne but also, one strongly suspects, on Book VI of The Prelude. There he receives a letter from Agnes. Memories of stained glass windows fuse with the pastoral landscape; the great "Presences" of Nature exert their force; the imagination is restored; purpose is reborn, and work commences:

> I resorted humbly whither Agnes had commended me: I sought out Nature, never sought in vain; and I admitted to my breast the human interest I had lately shrunk from...I worked early and late, patiently and hard. I wrote a Story, with a purpose growing, not remotely, out of my experience...After some rest and change, I fell to work [again], in my old ardent way, on a new fancy, which took strong possession of me.[20]

David's rebirth is accompanied by no bursting forth of sprouting wheat, but Agnes's letter is nonetheless a gentle shower to his dried-up soul.

Hilma Tree is never explicitly associated with stained glass, but she is always portrayed bathed in a stream of light coming straight from Heaven, and her hair glows in its rays like the nimbus of a saint. Her association with the moral values of pastoralism is so patent as hardly to require documentation. In the passage in which Annixter puts down his copy of David Copperfield and goes to watch her at work in the dairy, she is not only Aphrodite but also Flora and Perdita, "the queen of curds and whey." In Annixter's Moralitas she is the good angel; the bad angel is part of Annixter himself, residing in that restless, prickly, purposelessness that is the Steerforth side of his personality. Dickens parodies and qualifies the Agnes theme in the sub-plots of his novel, the relationship between the Micawbers, for example, reducing feminine moral influence to the level of burlesque, and Mr. Wickfield, in a variation on the Little Nell-Old Grandfather motif, demonstrating that even love of Agnes can become warped and distorted, crippling rather than sustaining the moral will. But Norris presents the spirit of Hilma unalloyed.

In keeping with his Wordsworthian assumptions, Dickens specifically rejects the mind, rationality and intellection, as the source of moral perception and action, endorsing instead the feelings and emotions, or what David, in a revealing phrase, calls "the mind of the heart."[21] Norris, who believed that "to feel" is better than "to think," echoes the same assumptions. When Annixter suffers his dark night of the soul, his coming redemption is signalled by a shift in his psyche: "Slowly...the imagination, unused, unwilling machine, began to work. The brain's activity lapsed proportionally. He began to think less and feel more." Although the metaphor of the imagination as machine would be anathema to Wordsworth and Dickens, Annixter is thus prepared for his salvation by the influence of Hilma, which takes place "by a supreme effort, not of the will, but of the emotion" (II, ii, 80-81).

Although his "romantic" imagination is set into motion by his love for Hilma, Annixter does not, like David responding to Agnes, sit right down and write a story. But later, when Presley comes under Hilma's spell, Norris implies that this good angel nourishes the imagination not only in its function as synthesisor of the soul and moral perceptor but also in its role as the agency for creative, specifically literary, activity (II, ix, 338-39). One wonders, almost, whether Presley too has been reading _David Copperfield_.

The preceding hardly exhausts the catalog of the signs of Dickens's presence in _The Octopus_. It ignores, for example, the fact that the disintegration of Magnus Derrick is handled in a faintly Dickensian way, and it overlooks the sub-plot involving Dyke, the railroad engineer and hop-farmer, Norris's variation on that recurrent Dickens character, the social victim turned outlaw. It does, however, serve to show how much to one early practitioner "straight naturalism" consciously or unconsciously suggested Dickens and the Dickensian ethos.

Norris's last novel, The Pit, is also intended for "straight naturalism," and like The Octopus its most obvious sources are in historical fact and Zola, in this case Joseph Leiter's 1898 corner on the wheat market and L'Argent.[22] But again the Dickens influence is marked. There are the usual Dickensian eccentrics: Aunt Wess', Grossman, and Landry Court (a Mr. Guppy with an unlikely flair for business); the usual symbolic evocation of milieu; and the usual tendency toward melodrama--both financial and domestic. Moreover, the novel once more displays Norris's confusion between the depiction of amoral force and the moralizing exploration of free will and ethical responsibility. True to form, the latter exploration draws heavily on the Dickensian ethos.

The problem comes most clearly into focus in the character of Curtis Jadwin, the heroic financier who momentarily achieves an almost superhuman corner on the wheat market only to be crushed by the very forces he thought he controlled. In approximately half the novel Jadwin is considered the pawn of irresistible forces, both his instinctive mania for speculation and the cosmic presence of the Wheat. As pawn he is not responsible for his actions. In the other half he is an ethical being possessed of free will and held accountable for his moral decisions. In one passage he expresses, with Norris's endorsement, an olympian scorn for the allegation that he is personally responsible for famines in southern Europe, while in another he is praised for the prosperity his bullish tactics have brought to farmers in the American middle-west. He blithely, amorally destroys competitors with one hand while with the other he runs a Sunday-school and orphanage--on "business principles," no less. In the pivotal scene he is punished for trying to tamper with the cosmic machinery of supply and demand, being metaphorically buried, like S. Behrman, under an avalanche of wheat; but he is subsequently dug out, reunited with his estranged wife, and, redeemed by his previous good deeds, sent West to begin anew.

As one might expect, Jadwin's moralistic redemption is cast in the Dickensian mold. In the first place he is a "benevolent" man, a kind of Cheeryble of the Chicago Exchange, as his devotion to his Sunday-school and his paternal affection for its inmates attest. Secondly, in a re-enactment of the Agnes theme, he is a man redeemed by the moral influence of a woman. In the morality-play structure of *The Pit* home and office are, as in *Dombey and Son*, the platforms on which the good and bad angels (in this case Speculation and Wife) stand in their hazard for Businessman's soul. But unlike *The Octopus* and like *A Man's Woman*, *The Pit* presents erotic fantasies that are tinged with unsettling morbidity. The rather alarming scene, for example, in which Laura, who has perhaps been reading *A Doll's House*, dresses up as Carmen and dances a frenzied fandango for a husband who only wants his brow soothed, having no desire at all for fun and games. Despite the bizarre nature of her marriage, Laura, terrified at her near-miss with adultery, eventually represses her itch and becomes an antiseptic Agnes, gathering up her emasculated husband and inspiring him to start a new life. Norris in other words runs headlong into the difficulties inherent in the use of "Agnes figures" that had plagued American novelists for fifty years. Laura is first attracted to Jadwin by the sexual stir his masculine force and energy arouse in her femininity. But they can achieve a viable relationship only after his masculinity has been crushed in the Wheat Pit.

Finally Jadwin's salvation is prepared for by his act of poetic justice in restoring Old Hargus's fortune.[23] Here Norris's Dickensianism becomes most clear and his moral structure most murky. Hargus is a definite Dickensian type, the broken old man whose brains have been scrambled in the frying-pan of villainy, hanging around the Exchange that has destroyed him like the addled Miss Flite hangs around Chancery. True to type he even has a Little-Nell--Jenny Wren of a niece who, sharing his poverty and degradation, watches after him and tries to tend his broken spirit. Years ago this "naturalistic" Newman Noggs had, like Jadwin, attempted to corner the market, only to be sold out by his partner, Scannel--even the name is Dickensian. Jadwin, an Old Martin Chuzzlewit come to judgment, anonymously manipulates the market to get Scannel under his control in order to force him into repaying Hargus's original loss plus twenty year's interest at six per cent, or two-thirds of a million dollars. In a tear-jerking little melodrama Jadwin confronts Scannel with Hargus and turns the money over to the latter with all the smugness of a Brownlow (IX, ix, 328). But while Jadwin is playing _deus ex machina_ with Hargus, he is also, unwittingly, ruining his best friend who, at the end of the very same chapter commits suicide. Yet Jadwin is ultimately saved. Apparently a little girl's riches outweigh a financier's corpse on Norris's moral scales.

Norris's failure to arrive at a consistent moral structure in The Pit, as well as his confusions in The Octopus and Vandover, provides an excellent lesson in the liabilities he incurred when he attempts to assume a Dickensian stance. The Dickensian ethos on which he draws is, after all, in most respects a viable approach to experience and certainly capable of sustaining an impressive literature. It is hardly necessary at this date to argue the greatness of Dickens himself. Nor is it necessary to consider any sign of a Dickens influence in an American novel as an automatic mark of shame. But the American world of the nineties with which Norris struggles to come to grips is not Dickens's world of mid-century England. The "spirit of Agnes," for example, seems grotesquely out of place in Norris's universe of Newtonian and Darwinian forces. His most explicitly Dickensian elements in characterization, incident, melodrama, morality, and even symbolism all seem curiously facile and flaccid, like the easy formulas and cheap banalities of a literary second-rater. In this respect The Pit, for example, is closer to a novel like In His Steps than to its "naturalistic" counterparts in England

and on the continent. Ironically--but appropriately--the novel had a subsequent career first as a stage melodrama and later as a card game.[24] This does not mean that Dickens had nothing to offer the nineties, but in order to find his real value for them novelists had to probe deeper than eccentric characters, good angels, and poetic justice. Norris in McTeague does just that; if some of his other novels are instructive in illuminating the liabilities of the Dickensian mode, McTeague in characterization and theme shows triumphantly the servicability of Dickens to the "new" American novel in achieving its worthwhile goals--no matter how melodramatically those goals were (over)stated: not what Norris called Howells's afternoon stroll and teacup surface of life, but "the unplumbed depths of the human heart, and the mystery of sex, and the problems of life, and the black, unsearched penetralia of the soul of man."[25]

II.

> The American experimenters in naturalism... dealt with new topics, thus broadening the scope of American fiction. If they dealt with old themes, they treated them in a new way. Poor people were, for instance, no longer described in the manner of Dickens.
> --Lars Ahnebrink

No one would deny that parts of McTeague are, in Pizer's phrase, "weakly Dickensian." The scattered references to Dickens's influence in earlier studies of the novel have focussed almost exclusively on its melodramatic conclusion and on the sub-plot involving Old Grannis and Miss Baker. Parrington adds Norris's "patent effort" to achieve dramatic unity through the use of gold as symbol, labelling it "an exaggeration that is almost Dickens-like with its warped singleness."[26] These signs of a facile Dickensianism in the novel are worth noting, but they are hardly the whole story.[27] Also noteworthy, for example, is Norris's reliance on a direct, specifically visual narrative technique. Indeed the visual quality in McTeague is so strong that when Erich von Stroheim prepared his classic film of the novel he found, like David Lean after him in the filming of Oliver Twist and Great Expectations, that he had only to let the camera follow the narrating eye to achieve his most powerful effects.

More significant, however, is the curious shift in Norris's attitude and tone in his depiction of lower-class people. Originally attracted to Polk Street for somewhat olympian, if not downright snobbish, reasons, Norris thought the poor suitable subjects for fiction because they were "simpler," somehow more pure in their conditioned responses, than the more "complex" members of his own social class.[28] Thus a certain amount of aristocratic scorn vitiates the "objective" presentation of McTeague and his world in the early chapters. However, as Norris lives with and comes to know the dentist, his wife, and their associates, his objectivity is threatened from the other direction, the tone and attitude shifting to a sympathy, understanding, and even tenderness that is decidedly Dickensian. McTeague, "crop-full, stupid and warm," comes to demonstrate complexities that surprise his very creator. Norris may occasionally give way to an upper-class sneer at the dentist's taste in pictures, but the Sieppe's picnic and the theatre scene, even down to Owguste's celebrated mishap, for example, are treated with an empathetic understanding recalling such scenes in Dickens as the Nubles's trip to Astley's and Kit's determination to show little Jacob "what oysters meant" in _The Old Curiosity Shop_. Norris, like Dickens, realized that there is something touching in the amusements of the poor.

But Norris's shift in tone indicates more than an awareness of the pathos of lower-class life. To be touched by the poor is in itself a kind of bourgeois condescension. His perhaps unexpected discovery of human complexity beneath the dentist's animalistic surface, his awareness as the novel progresses of the inadequacies in his original "naturalistic" formula of McTeague as draft-horse, "immensely strong, stupid, docile, obedient," living only by habit and seeking only animal comforts, bears significance not only for the history of Dickens's fortunes in America but also for the whole course of modern fiction. For it dramatically demonstrates that Norris has both instinctively fixed upon the fundamental technique in the creation of character that aligns Dickens with Shakespeare in literary greatness and, perhaps by accident but nonetheless effectively, exploited it as a way out of the _cul-de-sac_ of "scientific" fiction that traps him in such novels as _A Man's Woman_. The technique is so central to Dickens's art and so crucial to Norris's success in _McTeague_ that the reader will, I hope, bear with me if I take some time to explain.[29]

Cyril Connolly's famous aphorism maintains that inside every fat man there is a thin man struggling to be free; inside every so-called "flat" character of Dickens is a living human being either struggling to find his way out or, more often, happily acquiescing in his own eccentricities. Almost all Dickens's types, stock characters, eccentrics, grotesques, call them what you will, nurture underneath the dazzling array of peculiarities that forms their two-dimensional surface a spark of life and vitality that is all their own, and not, as the mainstream of Dickens criticism would have it, simply a conjured imputation from the author.[30] They may be ninety per cent mechanical, but they are also ten per cent human; this is, I think, what Spilka means when he observes that Dickens's characters, like Kafka's, "attempt to show the human spirit, alive and responsive, in the cage of its own making."[31] It is precisely the reader's shock at discovering individual humanity underneath the machinery that is the source of their power. Indeed, Dickens's most habitual practice is to play the one off against the other. Thus his characters haunt our imagination because they afford us with a glimpse of life where we would least expect to find it.

The technique is not peculiar to Dickens. Ralph Baldwin observes that Chaucer brings the stock types of *The General Prologue* to life by catching the reader off-guard with a "quick glimpse of the interior man," an "unexpected percipient thrust which throws the character into momentary bold-relief."[32] Shakespeare is the great master of the technique. Like Chaucer's, like Dickens's, his characters are almost all stock types; they come to life when we discover a human spirit stirring under their typicality. Without it they are cardboard. Parolles, the hanger-on of *All's Well That Ends Well*, is an instructive case. Parolles is clearly a stock type. As befits a hanger-on, he is the Imposter or *Poseur*. In E. M. Forster's terms he is a "flat" character in that we always recognize him when he re-enters and can always predict more or less what he is going to say and do. Above all we know that the plot is going to lead through one stratagem or another to his exposure. Yet when the stratagem is complete, when Parolles has been exposed, and we are prepared to see him disappear, he astounds us with a remarkable statement: "Who cannot be crushed with a plot?" Suddenly we are confronted not with a mechanical figure, but with a living human spirit. Having thus thrown us off balance, Parolles capitalizes on our amazement by bouncing back into his role, carrying all his new-found humanity with him and demonstrating beyond question that his cage is of his own creation. As he himself says, "Simply the thing I am shall make me live." Thus humanity flourishes where we least expect it, and Parolles redeems an otherwise rather left-handed play.

Dickens's importance is that he applied the technique to the stock characters of prose fiction so consistently and so skillfully that in the nineteenth and twentieth centuries the paradoxically flat, mechanical, yet vital character has been seen as his most distinctive creation. (Hence any such character in any novel written after 1836 can properly be called Dickensian.) To take but one example, Pecksniff, like Parolles, is a stock type. Archibald Coolidge puts him in the category of "wicked and avaricious businessmen,"[33] but he also, like Parolles, belongs to the larger literary type of the _Poseur_ and Hypocrite. And like Parolles, he is flat; we always recognize him and can always more or less predict what he is going to say and do, although we never fail to enjoy it. Our interest is maintained by seeing Pecksniff act out himself as hypocrite and by the suspense of not knowing how or when he will receive his inevitable come-uppance. But as we watch him, we begin, under Dickens's guidance, to see that Pecksniff is human as well as Hypocrite. In the drinking scene of chapter nine, for example, when punch and the charms of Mrs. Todger arouse his amorous propensities, we see him behaving not merely as a hypocrite but also as a very human spirit. The high comedy of the scene depends, no less, on our awareness of the juxtaposition of the mechanical and the human. Hence our deep disappointment when he is finally locked in his room, never to emerge and shock us again--until the next chapter.

When Pecksniff is finally unmasked by Old Martin, he does not point out that anyone can be crushed by a plot, but he does observe an equivalent: "'I have been struck this day,' said Mr. Pecksniff, 'with a walking stick (which I have every reason to believe has knobs upon it)...'" (VII, lii, 474). And like Parolles, he asserts and preserves his humanity by audaciously bouncing back into the stock role he has chosen for himself, demonstrating that a cage protects as well as imprisons. The _thing_ he is makes him _live_. Our dissatisfaction with the ending (in which Pecksniff becomes a begging, whining alcoholic) stems not from his having abandoned his role, but from his having rejected his humanity.

The importance of this analysis of Dickens's fundamental technique to a discussion of Frank Norris should be fairly clear. Norris was committed, at least in part, to a "scientific" theory that fostered an essentially mechanistic view of human existence and tended to reduce all men to certain rigidly fixed types. Yet types ruled by external and internal forces are recalcitrant, if not impossible, materials for fiction. Malcolm Cowley gets at part of the problem faced by American "naturalists" when he attacks their tendency always to explain the complex in terms of the simple: "To say that man is a beast of prey or a collection of chemical compounds omits most of man's special nature; it is a metaphor, not a scientific statement."[34] One may argue, of course, that to speak in terms of "special natures" is also to employ metaphor. Nevertheless it is a metaphor embodying a set of assumptions absolutely essential to the production of literature. Norris's shift from a "naturalistic" to a Dickensian treatment of his lower-class characters--and Ahnebrink not-withstanding the shift does occur--is a shift from explaining phenomena in terms of the simple to an honest attempt to grapple with the complex.

The shift redeems the novel, preserving it from the "niggling analysis" that makes A Man's Woman, say, with its purely mechanical characters such a dreary affair, and providing most of its impact. What comes to fascinate us in McTeague is a sense of humanity struggling to survive under machinery that threatens to crush it. Norris's elaborate attempts to place the dentist in a world of force and rigid types only prepare us for the Dickensian shock of discovering life where we least expect it. "What is important," says Spilka of the Dickensian nature of Gregor Samsa, the "ungeheueres Ungeziefer" of Kafka's Die Verwandlung, "is the rich and careful portrayal of a way of life, an existence which continues under the most adverse conditions. For the principle at stake is Gregor's humanity, not his vileness."[35] The same may be said of McTeague; the principle at stake is Norris's discovery that the dentist is a human being and not a draft-horse. Paradoxically his draft-horse qualities become a part of his humanity. Like Gregor's shell and, say, Wemmick's castle in Great Expectations or Pancks's steamboat motions in Little Dorrit, they are the mechanical means by which the dentist strives to reach an accommodation with a hostile universe dominated by destructive forces. That McTeague is ultimately defeated does not deny his humanity; rather it merely pushes his story toward the realm of tragedy, that final affirmation of man's special nature.

Hence, among other things, Norris's insistence on taking the canary into Death Valley. Like Miss Flite's finches, from whom it perhaps descends, the canary is a symbol of life, alive and responsive, chittering (albeit feebly) in a cage constructed of vast, vague social and psychological forces.

In his discovery of the ten per cent human lurking under the ninety per cent mechanical in McTeague, Norris uncovers a "romantic" element in the Dickensian mode capable of leading him out, in an effective and meaningful way, from what he thought the "stultifications" of "realism." And by juxtaposing the two, Norris, like Dickens, achieves his peculiar modernity. The twentieth-century reader may chafe at characters made whole by the stained-glass aura of angelic Agnesses, but he will certainly credit a portrayal of life struggling to maintain and even assert itself in the face of a universe governed by impersonal, hostile force.

Norris penetrates beneath the Dickensian surface of melodrama, overdrawn symbolism, visual techniques, and plot parallelisms again when, consciously or intuitively, he discovers in Dickens a reiterated pattern and theme useful to his programmatic purposes of re-opening the American novel to the concerns and techniques of "romance." Early commentators on McTeague described it as a study of economic force and personal greed.[36] More recently critics have read it as primarily concerned with sexuality.[37] Actually the novel is about both, the two being combined in a manner that, I hope to demonstrate, Norris absorbed from Dickens. Once again to understand the pattern in Norris we must look in some detail at Dickens himself.

Throughout his career Dickens associates distorted attitudes toward money with grotesque or perverse sexuality. The most powerful presentation of the association is, of course, in The Old Curiosity Shop, where all the novel's sources of horror, from Old Trent gambling away his money to the satanic mills of the Black Country chapters, converge upon and are summed up by the single image of Quilp sprawled obscenely in Little Nell's bed. But it is elsewhere as well: in Nicholas Nickleby, Martin Chuzzlewit, Little Dorrit, Our Mutual Friend. In David Copperfield, the Dickens novel Norris seems most to have admired, Uriah Heep's ugliness is most effectively conveyed not though his greed but through his designs on Agnes. Indeed, the one functions as a euphemism for the other. The horror of the novel resides in the repeated references to his smacking his bloodless lips at the mention of Agnes and in David's mental vision of his repulsive form sharing a marriage bed with her ethereal purity. It is this nightmare, and not the monetary misfortunes of Old Wickfield to which it is allied, that haunts the book. At least four-fifths of the imagery surrounding Heep is either animalistic, slimy, or phallic; often it is all three. In one paragraph alone he is associated with an eel, a corkscrew, and a snake (XV, xxxv, 97). When he announces, "Oh...with what a pure affection do I love the ground my Agnes walks on!," David's reaction itself is almost pathological in its violence, vertigo, and sense of archetypical horror:

> I believe I had a delirious idea of seizing the red-hot poker out of the fire, and running him through with it, It went from me with a shock, like a ball fired from a rifle: but the image of Agnes, outraged by so much as a thought of this red-headed animal's, remained in my mind (when I looked at him, sitting all awry as if his mean soul gripped his body), and made me giddy. He seemed to swell and grow before my eyes; the room seemed full of the echoes of his voice; and the strange feeling (to which, perhaps, no one is quite a stranger) that all this had occurred before, at some indefinite time, and that I knew what he was going to say next, took possession of me.
>
> (XIV, xxv, 455)

The morbid extremes of David's reaction stem not only from the image of Agnes outraged by a red-headed animal but also from the very notion of sex itself; in David's world normal, healthy sexuality is virtually non-existent. Male-female relationships are shown only in two lights. In the one they are horrible and destructive. Betsy Trotwood's love for her husband becomes distorted by his cruelity and rapaciousness into a hatred of the institution of marriage itself: when she is not sending the maid out to chase donkeys, she is giving her lectures on the necessity of abjuring men. Annie Strong's normal desires, frustrated by her marriage to a man old enough to be her grandfather, bring disaster to all involved. Steerforth preys upon Emily's womanly aspirations, and two whole families are brought to ruin. Moreover, when these three plot lines are cataloged together, we notice that in all three sex acts as a disruptive force primarily through the agency of its association with money. In the other half of the novel male-female relationships are shown to be so completely antiseptic that Freudian commentators like Lindsay and Marcus have described them as abortive sublimations of Dickens's own oedipal fanatasies.[38] The only possible exceptions to this either/or pattern in David Copperfield are the Micawbers's fertile union and the somewhat alarming horse-play that goes on in the harem Tommy Traddles assembles of his wife's flock of nubile sisters--and one hardly knows what to make of that except to hazard that Traddles's license is totally innocent because he is repeatedly shown to be a financial incompetent.

Dickens's asexual male-female relationships are so notorious to modern criticism that they hardly require mention were it not for the importance one has in the working out of the greed-sex association in Copperfield. No physical consummation crowns the Indian summer union of Barkis and Peggotty. Peggotty's attraction to the carrier is motivated only by her desire for economic stability, for a place to go after the Murdstones drive her out, and Barkis's desires do not extend beyond apple-pastries. David himself insists on the post-climacteric "innocence" of their marriage.[39] Precisely because Barkis is without sex, his avarice is as innocent as his marriage. He is possessed by miserly greed, his love for the box containing his wealth exceeding even his love for sweetmeats. He is attached to it as if to a sexual fetish. He carries it with him everywhere he goes in his cart; when he retires he keeps it under his marriage bed. In his illness he banishes Peggotty from the bed and takes the box into it, finally dying with it clasped in his arms as if it, and not Peggotty, were the wife of his bosom. Yet one immediately feels a strain the moment he begins to speak of Barkis in terms of greed and sexual distortion; no one would ever classify him with Quilp, Ralph Nickleby, or Uriah Heep. But the only thing that seems to separate them is the simple fact that Barkis is impotent.

It is this pattern linking impotence with innocence as polar to sexuality and greed, quite distinctive in Dickens, that Norris, intuitively perhaps, absorbed. That the pattern *is* distinctly Dickensian can be seen by comparing his depiction of the union of sex and avarice with that of stage melodrama in which the villain demands the rent while leering at the heroine. Dickens may have inherited the association from the melodrama, but he deepened it and made it his own; his villains demand the heroine and leer at the rent. Closer to the stage tradition are such novels as Thackeray's *The Newcomes* in which Barnes's villainy is exposed when it is discovered that he has seduced a mill-worker's daughter and abandoned his illegitimate children to starve. But unlike Dickens, Thackeray makes no attempt to link Barnes's greed with his sexuality. The two are presented merely as separate compartments of his multiform evil.[40]

Explaining the reasons why--or even the process by which--Norris was attracted to this recurrent theme in Dickens may be more properly the province of clinical psychology than literary history, but whatever the explanation, the greed-sex association is the controlling theme of *McTeague*. Norris, who liked to call himself "The Boy Zola," may have set out to write a "naturalistic" study of heredity and environment; what he actually produced is a Dickensian exploration of the relationship between attitudes toward sex and attitudes toward money. When we first meet Trina she is neither miserly nor even frugal. She gives Maria a dollar for the lottery ticket simply to avoid embarrassment, an action that would be unthinkable to her later in the novel when she refuses to give her husband even a nickel for car-fare on a rainy day. The problem, then, becomes to define what has happened to her in the interim.

Trina can afford to be free with her dollars in chapter two precisely because she is yet a sexual neuter. Norris, in his fondness for tautology, makes the point three times over. McTeague is disturbed by Trina's feminine presence in his parlors, but she is "perfectly at ease; doubtless the woman in her was not yet awakened; she was yet...without sex. She was almost like a boy..." (VIII, ii, 20). But if her womanhood is unawakened, it is shown to be there dormant; McTeague might well be troubled by her sexual allure.

As Trina and McTeague are forced into the grotesque physical intimacy imposed upon them by the processes of dental repairs, McTeague grows more and more troubled by the stirrings of that Old Adam which Lawrence's gamekeeper was later to rename John Thomas. The dentist is plunged into confusion as he can neither understand nor accept the forces which grip him. Norris focuses almost entirely on McTeague in these passages, but the aura of sensuality he describes as filling the Parlors is so intense that Trina cannot escape it either. The first crisis comes when McTeague succumbs to his "lower nature" and kisses Trina "grossly, full on the mouth" as she lies helplessly etherized in his operating chair. Trina awakes--in more ways than one--to express a coyness that triumphs even over the sordid accoutrements of oral hygiene. "'I never felt a thing' [she said], then she smiled at him very prettily beneath the rubber dam" (VIII, ii, 28). At this point McTeague blurts out his first offer of marriage.

Trina's reaction is worth noting. She is immediately filled with terror, terror that Norris labels "the intuitive feminine fear of the male." The point of view suddenly shifts to her, and McTeague looms before us as a grotesque monster as her eyes focus on his huge hands and immense shoulders. McTeague stalks closer and closer. Trina vomits. Trina's nausea is more psychosomatic than physiological.[41] Like David Copperfield's vertigo (in which Heep also swells to gigantic proportions) it is a violent reaction to the very notion of sexuality, in this case both McTeague's as he towers over Trina and her own as it is jolted into life and recoils from the dentist's suffocating bulk.

That Trina fears her own sexuality as much, if not more, than she fears McTeague's brute masculinity is shown repeatedly in the chapters describing their courtship. The long and curiously convincing analysis of her response to her engagement at the beginning of chapter six illustrates the turmoil into which her awakened womanhood has thrown her. Well aware that McTeague's only appeal is sexual, she is incapable of accepting her own response. On the one hand McTeague's embrace and her yielding to it had "suddenly thrilled her from head to foot with a quick, terrifying gust of passion, the like of which she had never known," while on the other she clings, baffled, to her knowledge that she is a "pure girl," that "this sudden commotion within her carried with it no suggestion of vice." Somehow the two will never come into balance; her only recourse is the fatalistic acceptance of her engagement, whether "blessing" or "curse," as a *fait accompli*. But even fatalism proves inadequate. Her fear of herself, continually growing more and more exacerbated, begins to hint of the psychic distortion that will eventually destroy her. She comes to require stronger and stronger assertions of masculine force from McTeague, her demands to be over-powered by his brute strength representing, in Freudian terms, the need of the super-ego (her concept of herself as a "pure girl") to be violently crushed before the libido (her "gust of passion") can express itself openly. Only then can she and McTeague, who understands nothing of her turmoil, find release.

The crisis in Trina's development--or more properly, degeneration--comes with the wedding itself. In the atmosphere of crude sensuality established by the wedding dinner, Trina is suddenly left alone with her husband. Despite her mother's reassurances, she is again overcome by terror. Norris's writing rises to his very best as he presents Trina's fear in a way we have come to see as highly Dickensian, objectifying it in a powerful visual image of the dentist's enormous back, framed by a door-sill as if for illustration (VIII, ix, 154). It is here that Norris begins to plant the seeds of the money-sex association that is to control the rest of the novel. Seen from Trina's point of view, the light streams from the door like "a gold bar."

Trina's wedding night fears are primarily of McTeague, but that they are also of herself is indicated by Norris's reference to her "strange desire of being conquered and subdued," her inability to accept the consummation of her marriage unless it is turned into symbolic rape. In the weeks following the wedding, even though she finds delight and fulfillment in having yielded, she is still unable to accept her sexuality. In one revelatory scene she steals to the door of the parlors to find McTeague spending Sunday in his old fashion:

> The little stove was crammed with coke, the room was overheated, the air thick and foul with the odors of ether, of coke gas, of stale beer and cheap tobacco. The dentist sprawled his gigantic limbs over the worn velvet of the operating chair; his coat and vest and shoes were off, and his huge feet, in their thick grey socks, dangled over the foot-rest; his pipe, fallen from his half-opened mouth, had spilled the ashes into his lap; while on the floor, at his side, stood the half-empty pitcher of steam beer. His head had rolled limply upon one shoulder, his face was red with sleep, and from his open mouth came a terrific sound of snoring.
>
> (VIII, x, 159)

She responds with horror and revulsion. What repulses her is not so much McTeague, although the picture is certainly unattractive enough, but McTeague as he here symbolizes her own sexuality. As the object of her sexual desires, he becomes the projection of them; that she is drawn to this obscene giant can, to her mind, only mean that the drives that compel her are themselves grotesque and obscene. In this somewhat clinical climate the Dickensian pattern asserts itself. Trina for a while oscillates between revulsion and sudden bursts of passionate affection, but gradually settles into what Norris calls "an equilibrium of calmness and placid quietude." The balm soothing her ruffled nerves is none other than money, for in the same paragraph we are told that she begins to regulate "the expenditure with an economy that often bordered on positive niggardliness" (VIII, x, 161).

McTeague in the meanwhile has followed a different course of development. Immediately following the wedding he is blissfully happy in the consummation of his sexual desires, but once his somewhat limited needs are fulfilled, he slips into indifferent satiety. Moreover, he is both baffled and repulsed by the sexual response he has released in his wife. Whereas earlier he had been delighted by her sudden bursts of passion and had roared with pleasure to have her perch on his lap and tousle his hair, he is now only made uncomfortable by such antics. Eventually he loses his interest in her altogether, his previous love turning to bitter hatred.

Hence Trina's peculiar dilemma. The dentist has both awakened in her drives that she is incapable of accepting and ceased to satisfy those drives when they become most insistent. Her responses are two, both of them following the Dickensian mold. On the one hand she channels her sexual frustrations into a fetishistic attachment to her money, whereby greed becomes an expression of sexuality; while on the other she experiences a masochistic enjoyment of McTeague's sadistic brutality whereby his acts of hatred are inverted to the caresses of love and her physical pain assuages the guilt she feels both for her sexualitv and for the avarice that has come to symbolize it.

As Trina's sex life degenerates, her greed grows, each stage of the one marking out a step in the other. The farther apart the McTeagues move, the closer she clutches her treasure trove, which, with appropriate Dickensian symbolism, she keeps hidden beneath her wedding dress. After justifying her miserliness on the same fatalistic grounds on which she had earlier rationalized her sexuality, she comes to decide that avarice is "a good fault." (VIII, x, 180). The stratagem is transparent: avarice is a "good" fault as sexuality is a "bad" one. The petting session that Schouler interrupts when he comes to say good-bye, having already reported McTeague to the licensing authorities, is the last physical expression of affection that passes between them. Correspondingly, Trina's niggardliness begins to show signs of pathology as she mimics the antics of Dickens's Noddy Boffin, but with the difference that Trina is in earnest. The earlier scene in which she had been repulsed by the sight of the dentist sprawling in his operating chair is repeated when McTeague, filled with whiskey, passes out on the bed, "stupefied, inert, his legs wide apart" (VIII, xv, 257). But far from feeling revulsion, Trina merely begins to search his pockets for coins.

Norris sums up her regression in a sentence. Her emotions, he says, "reduced themselves at last to but two, her passion for her money and her perverted love for her husband when he was brutal" (VIII, xvi, 263). She comes to reproduce on the clinical plane the comic antics of such Dickens characters as old Mrs. Smallweed, who cackles about coins and per cents until her husband knocks her out of her chair. After McTeague has deserted her, taking her savings along with him, she weeps over the bag in which she had kept them "as other women weep over a dead baby's shoe" (VIII, xix, 301). In other words her money has become the symbol of her ultimate fulfillment as a woman. The nadir is soon reached; having retrieved all her lottery winnings from Oelbermann, she makes them the specific means of sexual release:

> One evening she had even spread all the gold pieces between the sheets, and had then gone to bed, stripping herself, and had slept all night upon the money, taking a strange and ecstatic pleasure in the touch of the smooth flat pieces the length of her entire body.
>
> (VIII, xix, 306)

The two sub-plots reinforce the Dickensian pattern of the central action. Maria Macapa's sexual frustrations (she envies the soda-fountain girls and feebly attempts to imitate their dress because "they had their young men") express themselves in demented fantasies of golden table-ware. In the trauma of childbirth the fulfillment of her womanhood purges her of her autism, even though the child, a reincarnation of Caddy Jellyby's ink-stained baby, dies. Zerkow is from the beginning a fetishist, the object of whose desires is gold, which he revealingly calls "the pure virgin metal." He marries Maria simply to hear her describe the gold dishes as fetishists of a different sort have been known to marry overweight women simply to get near their corsets.

Miss Baker and Old Grannis represent the other, the Barkis and Peggotty side of the coin. Although they are irresistibly drawn to each other, they are clearly past the age of sexual activity. Thus they run no risk of being destroyed by money. Like Trina, Grannis comes into a small fortune quite by chance. But far from having sold his happiness for "some miserable banknotes" as he originally thinks he has, he has precisely found it. Miss Baker, sensing his desolation, is emboldened to enter his room; the two declare their love; they "walked hand in hand in a delicious garden where it was always autumn" (VIII, xvii, 280). Even the sentimental rhetoric is reminiscent of Barkis "drifting out with the tide," blissfully, but innocently, embracing his beloved box.

While the sub-plots of McTeague are either lurid or saccharine, the psychological penetration displayed in the depiction of Trina contributes toward making the novel the minor classic that it is. Above all, the affirmation of elementary humanity struggling for existence in a world of dehumanizing force in the story of McTeague and the description of the human damage wrought by confusing money with the vital processes of life in the story of Trina demonstrate that as the nineteenth century became the twentieth, Dickens had lost none of his value as a presence in American fiction.

Notes to Chapter VIII

[1]Robert L. Brannan, ed., Under the Management of Charles Dickens: His Production of "The Frozen Deep" (Ithaca, 1966), pp. 1-2.

[2]Letters, p. 30.

[3]For Dame Shirley see California in 1851 and 1852: The Letters of Dame Shirley, ed. Carl I. Wheat (San Francisco, 1933). In 1898 Norris explained to Marcossen that, regarding Harte, "the country has long since outgrown the 'red shirt' period." Letters, p. 23.

[4]Lit. Crit., p. 72.

[5]Pizer, Novels, pp. 39-41, 49.

[6]Novels, p. 48.

[7]Pizer, for example, argues that Norris's formula for Vandover's "higher" and "lower" natures comes from Herbert Spencer by way of Joseph LeConte. ("Evolutionary Ethical Dualism in Frank Norris' Vandover and the Brute and McTeague," PMLA, LXXVI [December, 1961], 552-560.) But LeConte, like Spencer, kept a well-thumbed set of Dickens in his study. His autobiography attests his close familiarity with Dickens and continually speaks for the moral power of love for a good woman. (The Autobiography of Joseph LeConte, ed. William Armes [New York, 1903], pp. 46-47, 100, 108-09, 112-13, 120-21.) In his one published essay on the novel, in the Overland Monthly (2nd ser. V, [1885], 337-47), LeConte specifically comments on Dickens's morality. For the ethics of earnestness and ennobling associations, to the degree that it formed the material of fiction, was throughout the nineteenth century almost invariably associated with Dickens.

[8]I use the phrase "Victorian ethos" purposely to echo the title of Robert W. Schneider's shrewd essay "Frank Norris: The Naturalist as Victorian," Mid-continent American Studies Journal, III (Spring, 1962), 13-27. My position differs from Schneider's primarily in my belief that the more specific term "Dickensian" can and should be substituted for the more general term "Victorian."

[9]Letters, p. 48.

[10]The Beginnings of Critical Realism in America: 1860-1920 (New York, n.d.), pp. 333-34.

[11]Pizer points out that the railroad operates as a symbol in a two-fold way. In the first it represents the social displacements and sufferings brought on by industrialism (it is, in other words, "the machine in the garden"), while in the second it stands for one element in the "natural" law of supply and demand. Novels, pp. 147-51. This doubling-up itself comes as part of Norris's legacy from Dickens, who in Dombey and Son, for example, uses the railroad both as a correlative of Dombey's turbulent mind as it carries him to Leamington and as a symbol of beneficent social change as it knocks its way through Camden Town.

[12]The Response to Industrialism, 1885-1914 (Chicago, 1957), p. 24.

[13]The notebook is in the Frank Norris Collection of the Bancroft Library. Norris's scene is often paralleled to that in Germinal juxtaposing the miners' hunger with the feasting of the managers; one could also point out the scene in L'Assomoir in which Gervaise, hungry and degraded, walks the streets surrounded by signs of leisure and wealth. Both scenes in Zola, however, are highly Dickensian.

[14]This view, a favorite with hostile, Marxist critics of the thirties, is best stated by Charles Child Walcutt, "Frank Norris and the Search for Form," University of Kansas City Review, XIV (Winter, 1947), 126-36.

[15]Most recent readings tend toward this conclusion, admirably set forth by James K. Folsom, "Social Darwinism or Social Protest?: The 'Philosophy' of The Octopus," MFS, VIII (Winter, 1962-63), 393-400.

[16]Letters, pp. 34 and 44.

[17]Curiously, the broad meanings of this fact have never been explored. Only Kenneth Lynn has even noted it, but he fails to comment on its implications. The Dream of Success (Boston, 1955), pp. 199-200.

[18]"No doubt, there was not much use in poetry, and as for novels, to his mind, there were only Dickens's works. Everything else was a lot of lies." The Complete Edition of Frank Norris, 10 vols. (Garden City, 1927), Vol. I, ch. i, p. 24. (All subsequent references to Norris's novels are to this edition and will be indicated in the text by volume number in Roman capitals, chapter number in lower-case Roman, and page number in Arabic; thus: I, i, 24.) The contradiction involved in using a preference for a novel that he elsewhere claims has had two hundred million readers to illustrate a character's eccentricity seems never to have occurred to Norris.

[19]The posthumous edition of The Prelude appeared in July 1850; the final number of Copperfield the following November. There is no published evidence that Dickens read the poem. In a private letter Mr. Graham Storey, co-editor of the "Pilgrim Edition" of Dickens's letters, reports that none of the unpublished material he has uncovered reveals Dickens's knowledge of it. However, I am still reluctant to reject the possibility.

[20]XV, lviii, 460. Surprisingly enough, the perfect pentameter line, "I sought out Nature, never sought in vain," is a paraphrase rather than a direct quotation from Wordsworth.

[21]XV, xlii, 226. One notes that when young David, ragged, dirty, and heartsick, arrives at Dover after fleeing the bottling warehouse, his aunt, for all her racking her brain, cannot think out a course of action. It is Mr. Dick, whose intellectual powers are non-existent, who arrives at the thing to do: "Have him measured for a suit of clothes directly" (XIV, xiv, 253). Later, when the Strongs's marriage reaches its impasse, the rational characters again are powerless; only the simpleton Dick can effect their reconciliation and mutual understanding.

[22]The Leiter corner is discussed by Charles Kaplan, "Norris's Use of Sources in The Pit," AL, XXV (March, 1953), 75-84; the influence of L'Argent in Ahnebrink, pp. 301ff.

[23]The point is made by Hoffman, p. 513. However, Hoffman does not explore the episode's debt to Dickens.

[24]Walker, Biography, p. 296. Another case in point is Norris's handling of minor characters in Vandover and the Brute. Bancroft Ellis's Dickensian eccentricity evokes a fictional world at odds with the novel's dominant tone of lurid horror. More at home in its milieu is the true grotesque, Dummy, a mute who bursts into erratic speech when drunk. Norris handles the formulaic Ellis with off-hand facility; Dummy's intense possibilities are never achieved.

[25]Lit. Crit., p. 78.

[26]P. 331.

[27]One wonders, incidently, why the other sub-plot (Zerkow and Maria Macapa) has not also been called Dickensian, especially since it seems even more so than the Grannis-Baker action.

The Death Valley chapters might also require some comment. The Dickensian label was first attached to them by William Dean Howells, and it has stuck ever since. Howells's remark is an obvious slur; what is surprising is that it has never been challenged. While no one would deny Dickens's fondness for melodramatic irony, it is difficult to think of anything quite so blatant in his novels. Yet even accepting the label, one can see something instructive in Norris's chapters, for they illustrate once more the tendency of American novelists to fall back on "Dickensian" techniques when faced by difficult structural problems.

Norris's theory of "effect" stated that the "pivotal scene" should take place a little over three-fourths of the way through the narrative, leaving the remaining chapters for wrapping-up. This placement, of course, follows the pattern most often employed by Dickens, whose architectonics Norris praises in his critical writings. But Dickens's pattern was governed and made possible by serialization, the last two numbers of his novels being published together as a single unit to ensure the sale of the concluding installment. Thus the penultimate number usually includes the pivotal scene while the final number trails away in marriages and funerals. Norris lacked the built-in aid of serialization to ensure his readers' interest to the very end after the novel has been "solved" by the pivotal scene, in this case Trina's murder. Something has to happen, and that something must be commensurate in interest and impact ("effect") to what has gone before. So just as Howells had given Squire Gaylord apoplexy in an Indiana courtroom and James had sent

Roderick Hudson out in an Alpine storm, so Norris turns to "Dickensian" formulas of melodrama. In ten of his fifteen novels Dickens had shown that the best way to revive the reader's interest was by means of a good rousing chase. Norris follows suit. Once McTeague has been caught by Schouler, there is nothing to be done with either except kill them both off, which Norris, who loved a "WHAM-BANG" end, does as sensationally as possible.

[28] Malcolm Cowley, "'Not Men': A Natural History of American Naturalism," Kenyon Review, IX (Summer, 1947), 425-26.

[29] In what follows I have profited greatly by several suggestions contained in Wolfgang Keyser's impressive study The Grotesque in Art and Literature, trans. Ulrich Weisstein (Bloomington, 1963). Many of Keyser's insights are picked up by Spilka in Dickens and Kafka. See especially chapter III. My argument builds on both works.

[30] This tradition, which grows in part out of George Henry Lewes's pioneer study of Dickens's methods, is best stated by E. M. Forster, who attributes the paradoxical liveliness of Dickens's "flat" characters to a "conjuring trick" by which Dickens's own vitality is projected onto his otherwise dead creations who, vicariously, "borrow his life and appear to lead one of their own." Aspects of the Novel, Pocket Edition (London, 1949), pp. 68-69. Unsatisfactory as it is, the theory is still very much alive.

[31] P. 69.

[32] "The Unity of the Canterbury Tales," in Chaucer Criticism, ed. Richard J. Schoeck and Jerome Taylor (Notre Dame, 1960), p. 25.

[33] Charles Dickens as Serial Novelist (Ames, 1967), p. 189.

[34] "'Not Men,'" 432.

[35] P. 77. A similar point is made by Edward Sackville-West in a comparison of Dickens, Kafka, and Dostoievsky. "Books in General," The New Statesman (December 11, 1948), 527.

[36]E.g., V. L. Parrington.

[37]E.g., Donald Pizer.

[38]Long before he had worked out his theories of the oedipal relationship, Freud himself had been disturbed by Dickens's "colorless" (i.e., asexual) heroines. See Ernest Jones, The Life and Work of Sigmund Freud, 2 vols. (New York, 1953), I, 174.

[39]E.g., XIV, x, 175.

[40]Dickens's use of the sex-greed association reflects not only his insight into abnormal psychology but also certain unconscious attitudes inherent in the climate of his age. In his study of My Secret Life, the anonymous sexual autobiography of a mid-Victorian gentleman, Steven Marcus comments at length on the way in which the memoirist unconsciously associates money and sex, pointing out that the episode in which he fills a prostitute's vagina with coins hardly needs or deserves comment. The Other Victorians pp. 155-60.

One of the most obvious facts about nineteenth-century sexuality is that enormous numbers of prostitutes were to be found in the cities and towns of both England and America. Prostitution explicitly exploits the power of money to turn people into objects, thus dehumanizing both harlot and client. In this, as Ruskin and others often pointed out, it reproduces microcosmically the macrocosmic tendency of laissex-faire Utilitarianism, which looked on people and their services as things to be bought and sold on the labor "market." In such novels as Great Expectations Dickens's primary concern was to show the power of money and the desire for wealth and status to dehumanize people, turning them into things, while in such works as Martin Chuzzlewit he teaches that the power of money to make people into objects can be exploited to achieve sexual gratifications of a clearly distorted, sadistic nature.

[41]Norris gleaned his expertise on fillings, bridges, and the use of ether in oral surgery from Thomas F. Fillebrown's A Textbook of Operative Dentistry, frequently transcribing passages almost verbatim, as in his description of McTeague's preparation of gold mats. (The relevant passages of Fillebrown are reprinted by Charles Kaplan in "Fact into Fiction in McTeague," Harvard Library Bulletin,

VIII [Autumn, 1954], 381-85.) Interestingly, Fillebrown advocates the liberal use of ether on the grounds that it is practically the only anesthesizing agent that does _not_ induce nausea.

CONCLUSION

DICKENS IN AMERICA

> "...and so there ain't nothing more to write about, and I am rotten glad of it, because if I'd a knowed what a trouble it was to make a book I wouldn't a tackled it and ain't agoing to no more."
> --Huck Finn

In September, 1841, Dickens announced to his readers that publication of Master Humphrey's Clock would cease the following November. Coupled with the announcement was another notice: "Taking advantage of the respite which the close of this work will afford me, I have decided, in January next, to pay a visit to America. The pleasure I anticipate from this realization of a wish I have long entertained, and long hoped to gratify, is subdued by the reflection that it must separate us for a longer time than other circumstances would have rendered necessary." Pleasure was anticipated on both sides of the Atlantic. A New York scribbler, Charles Frederick Briggs, who--for reasons that largely escape the modern reader--enjoyed a certain popularity for writings published under the pseudonym "Harry Franco," recorded the mood of the country in painfully jocular doggerel:

> Last year about this time...the whole country from one end to the other
> Left off talking of Nicholas Biddle and began to talk of Nicholas Nickleby's mother;
> And every district school, academy and college
> Renounced Greek and Latin and began to acquire a knowledge
> Of choice Pickwickean phrases and Samivel Wellerisms;
> And cultivators of domestic Greek forget all the oyster-cellarisms,
> And hard-hearted Wall-street brokers no longer spoke of dollars,
> But talked about "the rosy" like "glorious Apollers;"
> And lawyers and judges quoted "Bardell *vs.* Pickwick" but happily they were fewer
> Who treated Boz to profound legal jokes, like old Mr. Duer.
> And nobody knew anybody but Kate Nickleby; and there was nothing like
> Cheeryble Brothers, Miss La Creevy, Tim Linkinwater and poor Smike.
> And there was nothing little but Little Nell, and nothing big but big Jo Brodie;
> And every embryo Esculapius drank nothing but brandy-and-water and soda,
> Like Bob Sawyer and his friend; and everything must be Pickwickious,
> And all over the country BOZ! BOZ! BOZ! was conspicuous.[1]

American Notes and *Martin Chuzzlewit* temporarily scotched but could not kill the Dickens mania in America. How could one remain angry at the creator of Elijah Pogram when he was also the author of Pecksniff and Sairey Gamp?

When, some twenty-five years later, the news flashed that Dickens was to return, the country threw itself, according to Mark Twain, into a "frenzy of enthusiasm." American publishers offered the reading public no fewer than thirty-one different editions of his collected works in honor of the event.[2] The morning tickets went on sale for the New York readings five thousand people were lined up outside the box office of Steinway Hall. On the day of his arrival all but two of the nineteen hundred volumes of his works in the Mercantile Library were in circulation.[3] His death in 1870 brought on national mourning, and some Americans refused to believe that they had heard the last word from "Boz." In 1873 a publisher in Brattleboro, Vermont, offered an octavo volume entitled _Edwin Drood Complete_. Its first two hundred pages reproduce the text originally carried as a serial in _Harper's Weekly_ three years earlier; its final three hundred are "by the spirit-pen of Charles Dickens, through a medium." And it promised more to come: "I am happy to announce," said the medium in his preface, "that the first chapter of the next work, 'The Life and Adventures of Bockley Wickleheap,' is finished; and opening with all the peculiar characteristics of its author, bids fair to equal anything from his pen on earth."[4]

Dickens dominated not only popular taste but also the American novel for sixty years; without him it could not have been what it was. It is not simply that New England cultists could believe themselves the recipients of words from beyond the grave or that unknowns could ride his coat-tails into momentary fame, that Bret Hartes could brag that they were the best imitators of Dickens in the country or George Rockwoods could try to sell their photographs by parasitic sales-pitches:

> The art which it has been my pride to properly represent in America for the last thirty years, Charles Dickens in another way has made illustrious throughout the English speaking world. While he, with an artist's touch, has conveyed to paper the charms of Nature, and the characteristics of Humanity, so that they hang like pictures on the walls of memory, it has been my aim to produce similar beauties in a form more tangible, yet equally lovely, true and exact.[5]

Rather, as it has been the purpose of this study to show, even the most important, the most significantly original American novelists of the second half of the century revealed themselves, again and again, to be in what James called "conscious sympathy" with Dickens, wrote page after page indicating that at one moment or other in their lives "Dickens had been a revelation" to them. In 1854 the seventeen year old son of an Ohio newspaper editor makes his first attempt at writing a novel and fills it with "bald parodies" of Bleak House. Two years later a rambunctious journey-man printer sells a sketch to an Iowa paper that echoes of Little Dorrit. In 1871 a promising young critic publishes his first novel; it opens on a scene of pure Dickens melodrama. Twenty-seven years later a Californian who signs his letters "The Boy Zola" writes a fictionalized account of his own courtship and marriage that will, he hopes, establish him forever as San Francisco's Dickens. In his last major novel Howells returned to the frontier Ohio of his youth to find it a region inhabited by Dickensian grotesques. Mark Twain died while still working on a manu-script whose original impulse stemmed from a youthful enthusiasm for Dombey and Son. James, in the last, great "major phase" found Dickensian techniques still eminently useful in the art of the novel. Norris's tragically short career ended with a novel crammed full of Dickens.

No four more disparate artists could be found than these. Mark Twain would have rather been "damned to John Bunyan's heaven" than read a novel by James; Norris thought Howells the writer of tragedies of broken teacups; Howells somehow managed to be the friend of each of the other three, but was very careful never to bring any of them together, and so forth. Each was his own man, his own artist with his own goals and ideals for the novel. In one of the most celebrated passages in all literary criticism James observes that:

> The house of fiction has in short not one window, but a million--a number of possible windows not to be reckoned, rather; every one of which has been pierced, or is still pierceable, in its vast front, by the need of the individual will. ...But they have this mark of their own that at each of them stands a figure with a pair of eyes, or at least with a field-glass, which forms, again and again, for observation, a unique instrument, insuring to the person making use of it an impression distinct from every other. ...The spreading field, the human scene, is the "choice of subject"; the pierced aperture, either broad or balconied or slit-like and low-browed, is the "literary form"; but they are, singly or together, as nothing without the posted presence of the watcher--without, in other words, the consciousness of the artist.

Each of the four authors studied here stood at his own window, pierced by the need of his individual vision and by the pressure of his individual will. Yet in the shadows behind each of them stood Charles Dickens, making suggestions as to the contours of sill and frame and pointing out scenes of interest in the field below. What emerges most from these pages is a sense of the extraordinary tribute embodied in the demonstration that one man could offer so much to so many. Nothing speaks so movingly or impressively of the vitality and variety of Dickens's art than that

Henry James and Frank Norris, Mark Twain and William Dean Howells, could all call him Master.

In the sixty-eight years since the turn of the century American novelists have pierced many new windows in the house of fiction, but the ghost of Dickens still haunts its rooms. Miss Havisham is now Miss Emily; Harmon's Dust Heaps are presently presided over by the watchful eyes of Dr. T. J. Eckleburg; the guiding principle of the Circumlocution Office is currently known as Catch-22. And in book stores and bus stations, drug stores and card shops Dickens is still a best-seller.

Notes to Conclusion

[1]"A Long-metre Letter to the Editor," The Knickerbocher, XXI (January, 1843), 91.

[2]Hart, Popular Book, p. 103.

[3]Johnson, Triumph and Tragedy, II, 1081. On the same day, the steamship Quaker City landed in New York, back from the Holy Land; its passengers, including one Samuel Langhorne Clemens, were lost in the shuffle. But Clemens was undaunted; writing his family from his room at the Westminster Hotel, he observed: "You bet you when Charles Dickens sleeps in this room next week it will be a gratification to him to know that I have slept in it also." Mark Twain, Businessman, p. 95.

[4]Unfortunately, Bockley Wickleheap never appeared in print. See Wilkens, First and Early American Editions, pp. 50-51.

[5]"Preface" to The Humor and Pathos of Charles Dickens (New York, 1885), p. iv.

A SELECTED BIBLIOGRAPHY

Anon. "Foreign Literature," Atlantic Monthly, IX (1862), 525-526.

________. Edwin Drood Complete. Brattleboro, Vt., 1873.

________. "American Literature in England," Blackwood's Magazine, CXXXIII (1883), 136-161.

Adams, Henry. "Their Wedding Journey: A Review," NAR, CXIV (1872), 444-445.

________. The Education of Henry Adams. New York, 1931.

Adams, Percy G. "Young Henry James and the Lesson of His Master Balzac," Révue de Littérature Comparée, XXXV (1961), 458-467.

Adrian, Arthur A. "David Copperfield: A Century of Critical and Popular Acclaim," MLQ, XI (1950), 325-331.

Ahnebrink, Lars. The Beginnings of Naturalism in American Fiction. Upsala, 1950.

Allen, Gay Wilson. The Solitary Singer. New York, 1955.

Arms, George. "The Literary Background of Howells's Social Criticism," AL, XIV (1942), 260-276.

________. "Howells's New York Novel: Comedy and Belief," NEQ, XXI (1948), 313-325.

Aspiz, Harold. "Mark Twain's Reading: A Critical Study." Unpubl. diss., University of California, Los Angeles, 1949.

Auden, W. H. "Huck and Oliver," The Listener, L (1953), 540-541.

Auerbach, Erich. Mimesis, trans. Willard Trask. Garden City, 1957.

Baetzhold, Howard G. "Mark Twain's 'First Date' with Olivia Langdon," Bulletin of the Missouri Historical Society, XI (1955), 155-157.

________. "What Place was the Model for Eden: A Last Word on the 'Cairo Legend'," Dickensian, LV (1959), 169-175.

Barrett, Laurence. "Young Henry James, Critic," AL, XX (1949), 385-400.

Beach, Joseph Warren. The Method of Henry James. 2nd ed. Philadelphia, 1954.

Bellamy, Gladys. Mark Twain as Literary Artist. Norman, 1950.

Benjamin, Edward B. "The Structure of Martin Chuzzlewit," PQ, XXXIV (1955), 39-47.

Bennett, George N. William Dean Howells: The Development of a Novelist. Norman, 1959.

Bergler, Edmund. "Little Dorrit and Dickens's Intuitive Knowledge of Psychic Masochism," American Imago, XVI (1957), 371-388.

Blair, Walter. "The French Revolution and Huckleberry Finn," MP, LV (1957), 21-35.

________. Mark Twain and Huck Finn. Berkeley and Los Angeles, 1960.

Blues, Thomas. "The Strategy of Compromise in Mark Twain's 'Boy Books'," MFS, XIV (1968), 21-31.

Bodelson, Carl A. "Some Notes on Dickens's Symbolism," English Studies, XL (1959), 420-431.

Boege, Fred W. "Point of View in Dickens," PMLA, LXV (1950), 90-105.

Booth, Bradford. "Mark Twain's Friendship with Emeline Beach," AL, XIX (1947), 219-230.

Booth, Michael. English Melodrama. London, 1965.

Bowden, Edwin T. The Themes of Henry James. New Haven, 1956.

Bracher, Peter. "Dickens and His American Readers, 1834-1870." Unpubl. diss., University of Pennsylvania, 1966.

Brashear, Minnie. Mark Twain, Son of Missouri. Chapel Hill, 1934.

Briggs, Charles Frederick ["Harry Franco"]. "A Long Metre Letter to the Editor," The Knickerbocher, XXI (1843), 91-92.

Brooks, Van Wyck. The Ordeal of Mark Twain. Rev. ed. New York, 1955.

Brown, E. K. "David Copperfield," YR, XXXVII (1948), 651-666.

Browne, Ray B. "Mark Twain and Captain Wakeman," AL, XXXIII (1961), 320-329.

Budd, Louis J. "William Dean Howells's Debt to Tolstoi," American Slavic and East European Review, IX (1950), 292-301.

________. "William Dean Howells's Defense of the Romance," PMLA, LXVII (1952), 32-42.

Burdette, Robert J. Robert J. Burdette, His Message, ed. Clara Burdette. Pasadena, 1922.

Butt, John and Kathleen Tillotson. Dickens at Work. London, 1957.

Butt, John. "Dickens's Instructions for Martin Chuzzlewit, Plate XVIII," REL, II (1961), 49-53.

Cady, Edwin. "William Dean Howells and the Ashtabula Sentinel," Ohio Archeological and Historical Quarterly, LIII (1944), 39-51.

________. "The Neuroticism of William Dean Howells," PMLA, LXI (1946), 229-239.

________. The Road to Realism. Syracuse, 1956.

________. The Realist at War. Syracuse, 1958.

Cargill, Oscar. The Novels of Henry James. New York, 1961.

Carlyle, Thomas. Past and Present. World's Classics. London, 1957.

Carter, Everett. Howells and the Age of Realism. Hampden, Conn., 1966.

Cazamian, Louis. Le roman social en Angleterre. Paris, 1903.

Chase, Richard. The American Novel and Its Tradition. Garden City, 1957.

Chesterton, G. K. Charles Dickens. London, 1906.

Clappe, Louise ["Dame Shirley"]. California in 1851 and 1852: The Letters of Dame Shirley, ed. Carl I. Wheat. San Francisco, 1933.

Clemens, Samuel L. ["Mark Twain"]. "Dickens's Readings," San Francisco Alta California, 5 February 1868.

________. The Writings of Mark Twain. Definitive Edition, ed. A. B. Paine, 37 vols. New York, 1922-25.

________. Mark Twain's Autobiography, ed. A. B. Paine, 2 vols. New York, 1924.

________ Sketches of the Sixties, ed. John Howell. San Francisco, 1927.

________. The Adventures of Thomas Jefferson Snodgrass, ed. Charles Honce. Chicago, 1928.

Clemens, Samuel L. ["Mark Twain"]. Mark Twain's Notebook, ed. A. B. Paine. New York, 1935.

________. Mark Twain in Eruption, ed. Bernard DeVoto. New York, 1940.

________. Mark Twain's Letters to Will Bowen, ed. Theodore Hornberger. Austin, 1941.

________. Mark Twain, Businessman, ed. Samuel C. Webster. Boston, 1946.

________. Mark Twain to Mrs. Fairbanks, ed. Dixon Wecter. San Marino, Calif., 1949.

________. Report from Paradise, ed. Dixon Wecter. New York, 1952.

________. Mark Twain of the "Enterprise", ed. Henry Nash Smith and Frederick Anderson. Berkeley and Los Angeles, 1957.

________. Mark Twain--Howells Letters, ed. Henry Nash Smith and William Gibson. 2 vols. Cambridge, Mass., 1960.

________. Contributions to The Galaxy, 1868-1871, ed. Bruce R. McElderry, Jr. Gainesville, Fla., 1961.

________. Mark Twain's San Francisco, ed. Bernard Taper. New York, 1963.

________. Mark Twain's Letters from Hawaii, ed. A. Grove Day. New York, 1966.

________. Which Was the Dream?, ed. John S. Tuckey. Berkeley and Los Angeles, 1967.

________. The Mark Twain Papers. General Library, University of California, Berkeley.

Coburn, Alvin L. "Illustrating Henry James." Transcript of the British Broadcasting Corporation Third Programme, 17 July 1953.

Collins, Philip. Dickens and Crime. 2nd ed. London, 1964.

Connolly, Thomas E. "Technique in Great Expectations," PQ, XXXIV (1955), 48-55.

Coolidge, Archibald. Charles Dickens as Serial Novelist. Ames, Ia., 1967.

Coveney, Peter. Poor Monkey: The Child in Literature. London, 1957.

Cowley, Malcolm. "'Not Men': A Natural History of American Naturalism," Kenyon Review, IX (1947), 414-435.

Cox, James M. Mark Twain: The Fate of Humor. Princeton, 1966.

Cronkhite, G. Ferris. "Howells Turns to the Inner Life," NEQ, XXX (1957), 474-485.

Cummings, Sherwood. "Science and Mark Twain's Theory of Fiction," PQ, XXXVII (1958), 26-33.

Denny, Margeret and William H. Gilman, eds. The American Writer and the European Tradition. Minneapolis, 1950.

Dickens, Charles. The Works of Charles Dickens. Gadshill Edition, ed. Andrew Lang [and B. W. Matz]. 38 vols. London, 1897-1908.

________. The Letters of Charles Dickens. Nonesuch Edition, ed. Walter Dexter. 3 vols. Bloomsbury, 1938.

________. The Heart of Charles Dickens, ed. Edgar Johnson. New York, 1952.

________. Oliver Twist. Clarendon Edition, ed. Kathleen Tillotson. Oxford, 1966.

________. Under the Management of Mr. Charles Dickens: His Production of "The Frozen Deep", ed. Robert Louis Brannan. Ithaca, 1966.

Drew, Arnold P. "Structure in Great Expectations," Dickensian, LII (1956), 123-127.

Dubler, Walter. "The Princess Casamassima: Its Place in the James Canon," MFS, XII (1966), 44-60.

Dupee, F. W., ed. The Question of Henry James. New York, 1945.

Dupee, F. W. *Henry James*. 2nd ed. New York, 1965.

Eble, Kenneth E., ed. *Howells: A Century of Criticism*. Dallas, 1962.

Edel, Leon. *The Life of Henry James*. 3 vols. London, 1953-1962.

Emerson, Ralph Waldo. *The Journals and Miscellaneous Notebooks of Ralph Waldo Emerson*, vol. V, ed. Merton M. Sealts, Jr. Cambridge, Mass., 1965.

Engel, Monroe. *The Maturity of Dickens*. Cambridge, Mass., 1959.

Falk, Robert P. *The Victorian Mode in American Fiction, 1865-1885*. East Lansing, 1965.

Fatout, Paul. *Mark Twain on the Lecture Circuit*. Bloomington, 1960.

Ferguson, DeLancey. *Mark Twain: Man and Legend*. Indianapolis and New York, 1943.

Fiedler, Leslie A. *Love and Death in the American Novel*. Rev. ed. New York, 1966.

Fielding, K. J. *Charles Dickens: A Critical Introduction*. 2nd ed. Boston, 1965.

Firebaugh, Joseph J. "Coburn: Henry James's Photographer," *AQ*, VII (1955), 215-233.

Firkins, Oscar W. *William Dean Howells: A Study*. Cambridge, Mass., 1922.

Fisher, Henry W. *Abroad with Mark Twain and Eugene Field*. New York, 1922.

Foley, Richard N. *Criticism in American Periodicals of the Works of Henry James from 1866 to 1916*. Washington, D.C., 1944.

Folsom, James K. "Social Darwinism or Social Protest? The 'Philosophy' of *The Octopus*," *MFS*, VIII (1962-63), 393-400.

Ford, George. *Dickens and His Readers*. Princeton, 1955.

________, and Lauriat Lane, Jr., eds. *The Dickens Critics*. Ithaca, 1961.

Ford, James L. "The Chance for an American Dickens," *Munsey's Magazine*, XXIII (1900), 281-285.

Forster, E. M. *Aspects of the Novel*. London, 1949.

Forster, John. *The Life of Charles Dickens*. Everyman Edition. 2 vols. London and New York, 1948.

Foster, Richard. "The Contemporaneity of Howells," *NEQ*, XXXII (1959), 54-78.

Fox, Arnold B. "Howells's Doctrine of Complicity," *MLQ*, XIII (1952), 56-60.

French, Bryant Morley. *Mark Twain and the Gilded Age*. Dallas, 1965.

Fryckstedt, Olov W. *In Quest of America: A Study of Howells's Early Development as a Novelist*. Upsala, 1959.

Gard, Roger. "*David Copperfield*," *Essays in Criticism*, XV (1965), 313-325.

Gardner, Joseph H. "Mark Twain and Dickens," *PMLA*, LXXXIV (1969), 90-101.

Gargano, James W. "*What Maisie Knew*: The Evolution of a moral Sense'," *NCF*, XVI (1961), 33-46.

Garis, Robert. *The Dickens Theatre*. Oxford, 1965.

Garland, Hamlin. "The West in Literature," *The Arena*, VI (1892), 669-676.

Gerber, John C. "Mark Twain's Use of the Comic Pose," *PMLA*, LXXVII (1962), 297-304.

Gibson, William M. "Materials and Form in Howells's First Novels," *AL*, XIX (1947), 158-166.

Gibson, William M. and George Arms. A Bibliography of William Dean Howells. New York, 1948.

Gohdes, Clarence, ed. Essays in American Literature in Honor of Jay B. Hubbell. Durham, 1967.

Gordon, George S. Anglo-American Literary Relations. London, 1942.

[Gosse, Edmund]. "Literary Gossip," The Athenaeum, No. 2874 (25 November 1882), 700.

Grattan, C. H. "Howells: Ten Years After," American Mercury, XX (1930), 42-50.

Hagan, John H., Jr. "Structural Patterns in Dickens's Great Expectations," ELH, XXI (1954), 54-66.

Hamblen, Abigail Ann. "Henry James and the Press: A Study in Protest," Western Humanities Review, XI (1957), 169-175.

Harding-Davis, Rebecca. Margaret Howth: A Story of Today. Boston, 1862.

Hart, James M. The Popular Book. Berkeley and Los Angeles, 1961.

Hays, Samuel P. The Response to Industrialism, 1885-1914. Chicago, 1957.

Heilman, Robert B. "The New World in Charles Dickens's Writings," NCF, I (1946), 25-43.

Hoffman, Charles G. "Norris and the Responsibility of the Novelist," SAQ, LIV (1955), 508-515.

Holland, Laurence B. The Expense of Vision: Essays on the Craft of Henry James. Princeton, 1964.

Hopkins, Viola. "Visual Art Devices and Parallels in the Fiction of Henry James," PMLA, LXXVI (1961), 561-574.

Hough, Robert L. The Quiet Rebel: William Dean Howells as Social Commentator. Lincoln, Neb., 1959.

Houghton, Walter E. The Victorian Frame of Mind. New Haven, 1957.

House, Humphry. The Dickens World. Oxford, 1960.

Howe, Irving. Politics and the Novel. New York, 1957.

Howells, William Dean. "The Independent Candidate," Ashtabula Sentinel, XXIII, No. 46 (23 November 1854); XXIII, No. 47 (30 November 1854); XXIII, No. 48 (7 December 1854); XXIII, No. 50 (21 December 1854); XXIII, No. 51 (28 December 1854); XXIII, No. 52 (4 January 1855); XXIV, No. 1 (11 January 1855); XXIV, No. 2 (18 January 1855).

________. "Literary Notes," Ashtabula Sentinel, XXIII, No. 51 (28 December 1854), 4.

________. "A Letter From England," Columbus Ohio State Journal, 30 January 1862.

________. "Our Mutual Friend: A Review," The Round Table, n.s. XIII (1865), 200-201.

________. "The Life of Charles Dickens: A Review," Atlantic Monthly, XXIX (1872), 239-241; XXXI (1873), 237-239; XXXIII (1874), 621-622.

________. "Yesterdays with Authors: A Review," Atlantic Monthly, XXIX (1872), 498-499.

________. Their Wedding Journey. Boston, 1872.

________. A Chance Acquaintance. Boston, 1873.

________. A Foregone Conclusion. Boston, 1875.

________. "Dickens's Works: A Review," Atlantic Monthly, XLI (1878), 669.

________. The Lady of the Aroostook. Boston, 1879.

________. "Dickens's Letters: A Review," Atlantic Monthly, XLV (1880), 280-282.

Howells, William Dean. "Hawthorne: A Review," Atlantic Monthly, XLV (1880), 282-285.

________. "Henry James, Jr.," The Century, XXV (1882), 25-29.

________. "The Editor's Study," Harper's Monthly, LXXII (1886), 323-324.

________. Indian Summer. Boston, 1886.

________. The Minister's Charge. Boston, 1887.

________. April Hopes. New York, 1888.

________. Annie Kilburn. New York, 1889.

________. Criticism and Fiction. New York, 1891.

________. The Quality of Mercy. New York, 1892.

________. The World of Chance. New York, 1893.

________. My Literary Passions. New York, 1895.

________. "My Favorite Novelist and His Best Book," Munsey's Magazine, XVII (1897), 18-25.

________. Heroines of Fiction. 2 vols. New York, 1901.

________. "The Editor's Easy Chair," Harper's Monthly, CV (1902), 308-312.

________. The Son of Royal Langbrith. New York, 1904.

________. The Years of My Youth. New York, 1916.

________. The Leatherwood God. New York, 1916.

________. Life in Letters, ed. Mildred Howells. 2 vols. Garden City, 1928.

________. "Howells's Unpublished Prefaces," ed. George Arms, NEQ, XVII (1944), 580-591.

Howells, William Dean. Howells and James: A Double Billing, ed. William M. Gibson, Leon Edel, and Lyall H. Powers. New York, 1958.

________. The Shadow of a Dream and An Imperative Duty, ed. Edwin Cady. New Haven, 1962.

________. The Landlord at Lion's Head. Signet Classics. New York, 1964.

________. A Modern Instance. Signet Classics. New York, 1964.

________. The Rise of Silas Lapham. Dolphin Books. New York, n.d.

Hynes, Joseph A. "The Middle Way of Miss Farange: A Study of James's Maisie," ELH, XXXII (1965), 528-553.

James, Henry. "Our Mutual Friend: A Review," The Nation, I (1865), 786-787. Reprinted Views and Reviews. Boston, 1908.

________. French Poets and Novelists. New York, 1884.

________. "William Dean Howells," Harper's Weekly, XXX (1886), 394-395.

________. Partial Portraits. London and New York, 1888.

________. The Question of Our Speech. Boston, 1905.

________. The Other House, ed. Leon Edel. Norfolk, Conn., 1947.

________. The Autobiography of Henry James, ed. F. W. Dupee. New York, 1956.

________. Watch and Ward, ed. Leon Edel. London, 1960.

________. The Notebooks of Henry James, ed. F. O. Matthiessen and Kenneth B. Murdock. New York, 1961.

________. Confidence, ed. Herbert Ruhm. New York, 1962.

James, Henry. The Bodley Head Henry James. 5 vols. 1967-.

________. The Novels and Tales of Henry James. New York Edition (Reissue). 26 vols. New York, n.d.

Johnson, Edgar. Charles Dickens: His Triumph and Tragedy. 2 vols. New York, 1952.

Johnson, George W. "Frank Norris and Romance," AL, XXXIII (1961), 52-63.

Jones, Ernest. The Life and Work of Sigmund Freud. 2 vols. New York, 1953.

Kaplan, Charles. "Norris's Use of Sources in The Pit," AL, XXV (1953), 75-84.

________. "Fact into Fiction in McTeague," Harvard Library Bulletin, VIII (1954), 381-385.

Kaplan, Justin. Mr. Clemens and Mark Twain. New York, 1966.

Kaul, A. N., ed. Hawthorne: A Collection of Critical Essays. Englewood Cliffs, N.J., 1966.

Kelley, Cornelia P. The Early Development of Henry James. Rev. ed. Urbana, 1965.

Kettle, Arnold. Introduction to the English Novel. 2 vols. London, 1951.

________. "Thoughts on David Copperfield," REL, II (1961), 65-74.

Keyser, Wolfgang. The Grotesque in Art and Literature, trans. Ulrich Weisstein. Bloomington, 1963.

Kitton, Frederic G. Charles Dickens by Pen and Pencil. London, 1890.

Knox, George. "Reverberations and The Reverberator," Essex Institute Historical Collections, XCV (1959), 348-354.

Lane, Lauriat. "Dickens and the Double," Dickensian, LV (1959), 47-55.

Lawton, Mary. A Lifetime with Mark Twain. New York, 1925.

Leacock, Stephen. "Two Humorists: Charles Dickens and Mark Twain," YR, XXIV (1934), 118-129.

Leavis, F. R. "Henry James's First Novel," Scrutiny, XIV (1947), 295-301.

________. The Great Tradition. Garden City, 1954.

________. "Dombey and Son," Sewanee Review, LXX (1962) 177-201.

Leavis, Q. D. "A Note on Literary Indebtedness: Dickens, George Eliot, Henry James," Hudson Review, VIII (1955), 423-428.

Le Conte, Joseph. "The General Principles of Art and Their Application to the 'Novel'," Overland Monthly, 2nd. ser. V (1885), 337-347.

________. The Autobiography of Joseph Le Conte, ed. William Armes. New York, 1903.

Lerner, Daniel J. "The Influence of Turgenev on Henry James," Slavonic and East European Review, XX (1941), 28-54.

Lettis, Richard and William E. Morris, eds. Assessing Great Expectations. San Francisco, 1963.

Levy, Leo B. Versions of Melodrama: A Study of the Fiction and Drama of Henry James, 1865-1897. Berkeley and Los Angeles, 1957.

Lewes, George Henry. "Dickens in Relation to Criticism," Fortnightly Review (1872), 141-154.

Lewis, R. W. B. Trials of the Word. New Haven, 1965.

Lindsay, Jack. Charles Dickens. New York, 1950.

Lorch, Fred W. "Mark Twain's Trip to Humboldt in 1861," AL, X (1938), 343-349.

Lutwack, Leonard. "William Dean Howells and the 'Editor's Study'," AL, XXIV (1952), 195-207.

Lynn, Kenneth. The Dream of Success. Boston, 1955.

MacKenzie, Manfred. "Ironic Melodrama in The Portrait of a Lady," MFS, XII (1966), 7-23.

MacQueary, Howard. "Moral and Immoral Literature," The Arena, VIII (1893), 446-455.

McCloskey, John C. "What Maisie Knows: A Study in Childhood and Adolescence," AL, XXXVI (1965), 485-513.

McKeithan, D. M. "More about Mark Twain's War with English Critics of America," MLN, LXIII (1948), 221-228.

________. The Morgan Manuscript of Mark Twain's Pudd'nhead Wilson. Upsala, 1961.

McMahon, Helen. Criticism of Fiction: A Study of Trends in the Atlantic Monthly, 1857-1898. New York, 1952.

McMaster, R. D. "Man into Beast in Dickensian Caricature," UTQ, XXXI (1962), 354-361.

McMurray, William. The Literary Realism of William Dean Howells. Carbondale, Ill., 1967.

Mabie, Hamilton W. "A Typical Novel," Andover Review, IV (1885), 417-429.

________. "The Most Popular Novels in America," The Forum, XVI (1893), 508-516.

Marchand, Ernest. Frank Norris: A Study. Stanford, 1942.

Marcus, Steven. Dickens: From Pickwick to Dombey. New York, 1965.

________. The Other Victorians. New York, 1966.

Martin, Jay B. Harvest of Change: American Literature, 1865-1914. Englewood Cliffs, N.J., 1967.

Matthews, Cornelius. The Career of Puffer Hopkins. New York, 1842.

Matthiessen, F. O. "James and the Plastic Arts," Kenyon Review, V (1943), 533-550.

________. Henry James: The Major Phase. New York, 1944.

Maude, Aylmer. The Life of Tolstoi. 2 vols. Oxford, 1929.

Meisel, Martin. "The Ending of Great Expectations," Essays in Criticism, XV (1965), 326-331.

Meserole, Harrison T. "The Dean in Person: Howells's Lecture Tour," Western Humanities Review, X (1956), 337-347.

Miller, Perry. The Raven and the Whale. New York, 1956.

Millgate, Michael. American Social Fiction: James to Cozzens. New York, 1964.

Moers, Ellen. "The 'Truth' of Mark Twain," New York Review of Books, V (20 January 1966), 10-15.

Monod, Sylvère. Dickens romancier. Paris, 1953.

Norris, Frank. The Complete Edition of Frank Norris. 10 vols. Garden City, 1928.

________. The Letters of Frank Norris, ed. Franklin Walker. San Francisco, 1956.

________. The Literary Criticism of Frank Norris, ed. Donald Pizer. Austin, 1964.

________. The Frank Norris Collection. Bancroft Library, University of California, Berkeley.

Odell, George C. D. Annals of the New York Stage. 15 vols. New York, 1927-1949.

Orwell, George. Collected Essays. London, 1961.

Paine, Albert B. Mark Twain: A Biography. 4 vols. New York, 1912.

Parrington, V. L. The Beginnings of Critical Realism in America: 1860-1920. New York, n.d.

Pellew, George. "The New Battle of the Books," The Forum, V (1888), 564-573.

Phelps, William Lyon. "Mark Twain," YR, XXV (1935), 291-310.

Pizer, Donald. Realism and Naturalism in Nineteenth-Century American Literature. Carbondale, Ill., 1966.

________. The Novels of Frank Norris. Bloomington, 1966.

Poirier, Richard. The Comic Sense of Henry James. 2nd. ed. London, 1967.

Poli, Bernard. Mark Twain: Ecrivain de l'Ouest, regionalisme et humour. Paris, 1965.

Reeves, John K. "The Limited Realism of Howells's Their Wedding Journey," PMLA, LXXVII, (1962), 617-628.

Reninger, H. Willard. "Norris Explains The Octopus: A Correlation of His Theory and Practice," AL, XII (1940), 218-227.

Ridland, J. M. "Huck, Pip, and Plot," NCF, XX (1965), 286-290.

Rockwood, George. The Humor and Pathos of Charles Dickens. New York, 1885.

Rogers, Franklin R. Mark Twain's Burlesque Patterns. Dallas, 1960.

Ross, Albert. "What is Immoral in Literature," The Arena, III (1891), 438-448.

Rouse, H. Blair. "Charles Dickens and Henry James: Two Approaches to the Art of Fiction," NCF, V (1950), 151-157.

Sackville-West, Edward. "Books in General," The New Statesman, 11 December 1948, 527.

Salomon, Roger B. Twain and the Image of History. New Haven, 1961.

Schneider, Robert W. "Frank Norris: The Naturalist as Victorian," Midcontinent American Studies Journal, III (1962), 13-27.

Schoeck, Richard and Jerome Taylor, eds. Chaucer Criticism. Notre Dame, Ind., 1960.

Smith, Henry Nash. Mark Twain: The Development of a Writer. Cambridge, Mass., 1962.

________. Mark Twain's Fable of Progress. New Brunswick, N.J., 1964.

Spilka, Mark. Dickens and Kafka. Bloomington, 1963.

Spiller, Robert E., et al. Literary History of the United States. 3 vols. New York, 1948.

Stafford, William T. "Literary Allusions in James's Prefaces," AL, XXXV (1963), 60-70.

Stevenson, Lionel, ed. Victorian Fiction: A Guide to Research. Cambridge, Mass., 1964.

Stone, Albert E. The Innocent Eye: Childhood in Mark Twain's Imagination. New Haven, 1961.

Stone, Harry. "Dickens's Use of His American Experiences in Martin Chuzzlewit," PMLA, LXXII (1957), 464-478.

Stoutenberg, Adrian and Laura Nelson Baker. Dear, Dear Livy. New York, 1963.

Stovall, Floyd, ed. The Development of American Literary Criticism. Chapel Hill, 1955.

Stowe, Harriet Beecher. Uncle Tom's Cabin. Dolphin Books, New York, n.d.

Tanner, Tony. "The Literary Children of James and Twain," NCF, XVI (1961), 205-218.

Taylor, Walter Fuller. The Economic Novel in America. Chapel Hill, 1942.

Tilley, W. H. The Backgrounds of The Princess Casamassima. Gainesville, Fla., 1960.

Tillotson, Kathleen. Novels of the Eighteen Forties. Oxford, 1961.

Tintner, Adeline, "The Spoils of Henry James," PMLA, LXI (1946), 239-251.

Tolstoi, Leo. What is Art?, trans. Aylmer Maude. Oxford, 1950.

Tracy, Robert. "Myth and Reality in The Adventures of Tom Sawyer," The Southern Review, n.s. IV (1968), 530-541.

Traubel, Horace. With Walt Whitman in Camden. Vol. 5, ed. Gertrude Traubel. Carbondale, Ill., 1964.

Trilling, Lionel. The Liberal Imagination. Garden City, n.d.

________. The Opposing Self. New York, 1959.

Van Ghent, Dorothy. The English Novel: Form and Function. New York, 1961.

Wagenknecht, Edward. Mark Twain: The Man and His Work. 2nd. ed. Norman, 1961.

Walcutt, Charles C. "Frank Norris and the Search for Form," University of Kansas City Review, XIV (1947), 126-136.

Walker, Franklin. Frank Norris: A Biography. New York, 1963.

Wallace, Elizabeth. Mark Twain and the Happy Island. Chicago, 1913.

Ward, J. A. The Search for Form: Studies in the Structure of James's Fiction. Chapel Hill, 1967.

Wasiolek, Edward. "Maisie: Pure or Corrupt?," CE, XXII (1960), 167-172.

Weitenkampf, Frank. "American Illustrators of Dickens," *Boston Public Library Quarterly*, V (1953), 189-194.

Westbrook, Max. "The Critical Implications of Howells's Realism," *University of Texas Studies in English*, XXXVI (1957), 71-79.

Whipple, E. P. *Lectures on Subjects Connected with Literature and Life*. Boston, 1866.

Whitman, Walt. "Dickens's *American Notes*," Brooklyn *Evening Tatler*, 11 August 1842.

Wigger, Ann P. "The Composition of Mark Twain's *Pudd'nhead Wilson* and 'Those Extraordinary Twins': Chronology and Development," *MP*, LV (1957), 93-102.

Wilkens, W. G. *First and Early American Editions of Dickens*. Cedar Rapids, Ia., 1910.

Wilson, Edmund. *Eight Essays*. Garden City, 1954.

Wilson, Harris W. "What *Did* Maisie Know?," *CE*, XVII (1956), 279-282.

Ziff, Larzer. *The American 1890's*. New York, 1966.